The New York Times
CULTURED TRAVELER

**100 TRIPS FOR CURIOUS MINDS
FROM AGADIR TO YOGYAKARTA**

The New York Times
CULTURED TRAVELER

100 TRIPS FOR CURIOUS MINDS FROM AGADIR TO YOGYAKARTA

EDITED BY
BARBARA IRELAND

TASCHEN

FOREWORD

By Amy Virshup **6**

UNITED STATES & CANADA

Chicago, United States **14**	Pigeon Forge, Tennessee, United States **62**
Detroit, United States **20**	Rigaud, Quebec, Canada **68**
Inside Passage, Alaska, United States **28**	San Francisco, United States **74**
Los Angeles, United States **36**	Taos, New Mexico, United States **80**
Maui, Hawaii, United States **42**	Vancouver Island, British Columbia, Canada **88**
Miami, United States **50**	Walloon Lake, Michigan, United States **96**
New York City, United States **56**	

LATIN AMERICA & THE CARIBBEAN

Cartagena, Colombia **104**	Mexico City, Mexico **132**
Havana & Pinar del Río, Cuba **110**	Oaxaca, Mexico **138**
Jardín, Colombia **118**	Salvador da Bahia, Brazil **144**
Managua & León, Nicaragua **126**	

EUROPE

The Alentejo, Portugal **152**	Cognac, France **206**
Amsterdam, Netherlands **158**	Cornwall, England **212**
Andalusia, Spain **164**	Corsier-sur-Vevey, Switzerland **218**
Astigarraga, Spain **170**	Cremona, Italy **224**
Asturias & Basque Country, Spain **176**	Delft, Netherlands **230**
Attersee, Austria **182**	Delphi, Greece **238**
Barcelona, Spain **188**	Den Bosch, Netherlands **244**
Bratislava, Slovakia **194**	Dordogne, France **250**
Brussels, Belgium **200**	East Frisia, Germany **256**

Elsinore, Denmark	262	Paris & Périgord, France	404
Florence, Italy	268	Provence-Alpes-Côte d'Azur, France	410
Fontainebleau, France	274	Rome, Italy	416
Georgia & Turkey	280	Shetland Islands, Scotland	422
Grasse, France	286	Sicily, Italy	428
Istanbul, Turkey	294	Siena, Italy	436
Italian Libraries, Italy	300	Sintra, Portugal	444
London, England	308 & 314	Soria, Spain	450
Madrid, Spain	322	The Spreewald, Germany	456
Majorca, Spain	330	Stockholm & Adelso, Sweden	462
Northern Ireland	338	Trollstigen to Kristiansund, Norway	470
Nuremberg, Germany	346	Urbino, Italy	476
Ostend, Belgium	352	Usedom, Germany	482
Outer Hebrides, Scotland	360	Venice, Italy	488
Oxford, England	366	Vienna, Austria	496
Oxfordshire & Wiltshire, England	372	Warsaw, Poland	502
Paris, France	378, 384, 390 & 396	Weimar & Dessau, Germany	508

AFRICA & THE MIDDLE EAST

Agadir to the Sahara Desert, Morocco	518	Maji Moto, Kenya	544
Cape Coast & Elmina, Ghana	526	Nazareth, Israel	550
Dar es Salaam, Tanzania	532	Nile River, Egypt	556
Jerusalem to Jericho, Israel & the West Bank	538	Osun-Osogbo, Nigeria	564

ASIA & OCEANIA

Amritsar, India	572	Naoshima, Japan	624
Bangkok, Thailand	578	Shanghai, China	630
Cambodia	584	Singapore	636
Chandigarh, India	590	Sydney, Australia	642
Dunhuang, China	596	Tamil Nadu, India	648
Kerala, India	604	Tokyo & Osaka, Japan	654
Kyoto, Japan	610	Ubon to Khong Chiam, Thailand	660
Mekong River, Laos	618	Yogyakarta, Indonesia	666

FOREWORD

What does it mean to be a cultured traveler?

Is it enough to be the kind of person whose first stop in Copenhagen is the Glyptotek, who travels every summer to Bayreuth for "The Ring," or who has been to Art Basel in Basel, Miami, and Hong Kong?

Perhaps. But there's a good argument to be made that filling your cup at a sagardotegi, or traditional cider house, in the Basque Country, taking a drive along Thailand's "gong highway," or just knowing that in Germany there is something called the Gurkenradweg (literally: pickle bike path) should count.

The 100 articles and accompanying photographs in this volume, all drawn from The New York Times's *Travel pages by the longtime* Times *editor Barbara Ireland, take the latter, more expansive view of culture. Culture is not just something that hangs on a wall or is performed on a stage. It is the products of a land and of its people, and it offers travelers the truest expression of a place. The intrepid reporters collected here — writing from 43 countries and all the continents except Antarctica — explore culture as a way of understanding where they are, whether it's British Columbia, Dar es Salaam, or India's Cardamom Hills. And, happily, they are willing to take us along for the ride.*

In some cases, they follow an artist who has left behind a clear breadcrumb trail. In wintry Venice, the writer Rachel Donadio traces the Russian-born poet Joseph Brodsky's footsteps. When he writes in his celebrated prose poem "Watermark" that the Sunday morning air "is part damp oxygen, part coffee and prayers," she knows exactly what he means. Larry Rohter, a former foreign correspondent for The Times, *explores the Brazilian city of Salvador da Bahia in the wake of the acclaimed writer Jorge Amado. Rohter notes that Amado wanted tourists to see not just his beloved city's "'beaches, our churches embroidered with gold, the blue Portuguese ceramic tiles, the Baroque, the picturesque popular festivals and the fetishist ceremonies,' but also 'the putridity of the slum houses on stilts and the whorehouses.'" Using Amado's novels as his Baedeker, Rohter shares Amado's city with us, and also discovers it again for himself.*

Stalking Mozart in Vienna, Vermeer in Delft, Josephine Baker in the Périgord, or Paul Bowles in Morocco gives us a new appreciation for both the place and the artist. How did they shape each other? What imprint of the terroir can be found in their work, and how did their artistry imprint itself on the place?

In these pages you can discover the essence of chocolate in Brussels, catch the lingering scent of perfume in Grasse, France, the perfume capital's perfume capital, and drink coffee with butter in one of Singapore's kopitiam, or old-school coffee shops. Each entry is accompanied by suggestions of how to explore further on your own — books to read, movies to watch. Partaking of these creations offers a window into the places where they are made, one that runs through the senses of taste, touch, and smell.

Sometimes, the trail is faint. Martha S. Jones searches Paris for evidence of Abigail, a woman enslaved to the American founding

FOREWORD

father John Jay in the 1780s. She remains elusive, but Jones gives us new understanding of French and American history. Andrew Ferren combs Stockholm for "any traces" of a "secretive artist who destroyed all her correspondence" before she died, and whose work was created "with virtually no record of anyone seeing or discussing" it. The artist: Hilma af Klint, whose record-breaking show at New York's Guggenheim Museum made her an art world phenomenon more than 75 years after her death. With the help of museum curators, biographers, and af Klint descendants, Ferren found "that it is possible to move around Stockholm…and connect with her life—almost from cradle to grave—and its artistic context."

Connecting culture and travel—that's the puzzle these writers are often trying to complete. At times, what they find undermines the carefully presented narrative of a place. In the Indian city of Chandigarh, famously laid out on a grid by the modernist Swiss architect Le Corbusier, Jada Yuan delights in the counterpoint of Nek Chand's Rock Garden, a piece of outsider art rich in delight: "Think Antoni Gaudí's similarly sized Park Güell in Barcelona, but homespun, distinctly Indian, and made entirely of industrial waste and found rocks."

And some of it is just plain fun, like the choreographed madness of a baseball game between the Yomiuri Giants and the Hanshin Tigers taken in from a seat in the upper deck of the Tokyo Dome. Or the fact that a writer going in search of Jimi Hendrix in London came upon a residence-turned-museum called Handel Hendrix House: The two musical giants lived in two adjoining buildings 200 years apart and are now both celebrated there.

Following in the path of these assembled writers and photographers, whether to Sydney's Opera House or on a visit to the Maasai in Kenya or in search of the perfect cigar in Havana, is an adventure for the mind. These cultures endure, and they're waiting for you.

—Amy Virshup
Travel Editor, *The New York Times*

Page 2 Capitol Complex designed by Le Corbusier, Chandigarh, India.
Page 6 The Duomo, Florence, Italy.
Opposite Pumpkin sculpture by Yayoi Kusama, Naoshima, Japan.
Following Lighthouse, Mahabalipuram, India.

THE TEEN STREETS OF JOHN HUGHES'S CHICAGO

If you look for them, glimmers of Ferris Bueller, the Breakfast Club kids, and their pals light up their creator's hometown. — BY FREDA MOON

It was a luminous late-summer day, but I was stuck in a police station in the northern Chicago suburb of Des Plaines, a 1970s-era concrete behemoth that had the cool sterility of a hospital. Speed walking ahead of me were two officers, middle-aged men with buzz cuts, Smokey Bear hats, and shiny black patent-leather belts. They were on the hunt, and I was racing to keep up. I had never been in this maze of hallways, linoleum floors, and dreary courtyards before, yet the building was as familiar to me as any deeply embossed memory from childhood. Which, in a way, it was. I was raised on John Hughes movies, and this was the setting of one of his most beloved films, *The Breakfast Club*, from 1985.

Hughes, the writer, director, and producer who helped define '80s pop culture, died of a heart attack in 2009, at age 59. Best known for his high school trilogy (*Sixteen Candles*, *The Breakfast Club*, and *Ferris Bueller's Day Off*), Hughes was responsible for creating a new kind of teenage movie. His work included more than two dozen movies during his 15 years as one of Hollywood's go-to filmmakers, including *Pretty in Pink*, *Some Kind of Wonderful*, and three holiday classics, *Home Alone*, *National Lampoon's Christmas Vacation*, and *Planes, Trains and Automobiles*. And though style and tone varied from slapstick to sentimental, one character turned up again and again: his adopted hometown, Chicago.

Like many Chicagoans, Hughes — who moved from the Detroit area to the northern suburb of Northbrook, Illinois, when he was in junior high school — was deeply loyal to his city. As a rising star, he insisted that Universal Pictures let him shoot his movies there. In an early interview with Roger Ebert, Hughes complained about the local news media referring to him as a former Chicagoan. "As if, to do anything, I

CHICAGO United States

Previous The water tower in Northbrook, Illinois, where "Save Ferris" was painted for John Hughes's film *Ferris Bueller's Day Off.*

Left *Flamingo,* an Alexander Calder sculpture in Federal Plaza, figured in Ferris Bueller's peripatetic tour of Chicago.

Opposite In *She's Having a Baby,* Kevin Bacon's character waited for his train at this Metra station in Glencoe.

had to leave Chicago," he told Ebert. "I never left. I worked until I was 29 at the Leo Burnett advertising agency, and then I quit to do this." For him, it seemed, the city's main appeal was its lack of pretension. "This is a working city," he said, "where people go to their jobs and raise their kids and live their lives."

It seems counterintuitive, then, that his films are set on the North Shore, a collection of suburbs along Lake Michigan — places like Evanston, Glencoe, Highland Park, and Winnetka, where the *Home Alone* house is located — that are often dismissed as affluent and culturally homogeneous. But Hughes, whose father was a roofing salesman, was exploring issues of class, status, and consumerism, as well as the tension and attraction between suburb and city.

I had come to the North Shore looking for Hughes, for traces of what fed his filmmaking, and for hints of how his hometown had changed since he painted it as an American Every Town. Online, I had found fan sites listing his many Chicago-area shooting locations: Glenbrook North High School, where Judd Nelson triumphantly raises his fist on the football field at the end of *The Breakfast Club* (and from which Hughes graduated); the college town of Evanston, where Anthony Michael Hall cruises in a Rolls-Royce down Central Street in *Sixteen Candles*; the glass house in *Ferris Bueller's Day Off* from which Cameron's father's 1961 Ferrari explodes. I could have wandered aimlessly around these touchstones, but on a whim, I reached out to Hughes's oldest son, John Hughes III, hoping he might also point me to some of his father's off-camera hangouts. The Hughes family is known to be private, but to my surprise, he offered to give me a tour.

And that is how I ended up in the basement of a police station with John Hughes III and two state police officers. The building's facade, imposing in a Soviet sort of way, looked exactly as I remember it from *The Breakfast Club,* when it played the role of Shermer High (it actually had been a high school, Maine North High, which closed in 1981). Hughes parked, and we walked around the back, curious if its football field was still there. A squad car slowed beside us. "Can we help you?" one officer asked, in the way that officers do when they mean "What are you doing here?"

It might have been all the John Hughes movies I had been watching, movies that I had seen over and over growing up, but I was suddenly struck by the impulse to run, like one of the filmmaker's teenage characters up to no good. Instead, I froze. So Hughes's son took over, bending his long frame to talk through the window. His dad had filmed a movie here years ago, he explained. Maybe they had heard of it? Immediately, everything changed.

"Do you want to see the inside?" one officer asked, clearly excited. "I'm obsessed with that movie."

As we sped through the empty corridors, no longer lined with lockers, I didn't know what we were looking for. The officers wanted to show us something, but even in their own station, they were lost. I flashed to the Brain, the Athlete, the Basket Case, the Princess, and the Criminal, racing through these halls, sliding on the linoleum, nearly getting caught by Principal Vernon.

"You didn't get the smartest, but we're definitely the nicest," one of the officers said. "And the most handsome," the other added. Finally, they found it, a modest shrine to the building's previous life as one of the most famous high schools in American film: a handful of artifacts in an old trophy case.

I had met John Hughes III — a tall, thoughtful music producer — at a Starbucks near his studio, and we drove past the Skokie Lagoons, where kayaks traced lines in the placid water. It was the first week of school, and he had just dropped off his children. The leaves were still thick on the trees, and the air was warm and clean, with barely a hint of fall. This is the same season in which *Ferris* would have been filmed; it was a flawless late-summer day.

As we toured, Hughes repeatedly tracked down film locations, and then remembered a place nearby tied to his family's history. In Glencoe, we drove past the Metra station where Kevin Bacon's character in *She's Having a Baby* waits for the commuter train to a soul-sucking office job; Hughes pointed to his parents' first apartment, just across the road. The scene in *Sixteen Candles* in which Anthony Michael Hall knocks on a friend's window in the middle of the night was a half block from the house that his parents lived in when the younger Hughes was born. The street was almost within eyeshot of the "Save Ferris" water tower — still there, but sadly no longer tagged with its

Above "I never left," Hughes said. This football field, which appears in *The Breakfast Club,* was at his own high school.

Opposite Memorabilia from *The Breakfast Club* in the Northbrook building where many of its scenes were filmed.

pro-Ferris slogan—which itself is just a few blocks from the modest midcentury home where the director lived as a teenager. And his high school, Glenbrook North, wasn't far away, on Shermer Road—the inspiration for the fictional Chicago suburb where so many of his movies took place: Shermer, Illinois.

We parked in front of Glencoe's stately brick church, which appeared in the final scene of *Sixteen Candles*. "We can sneak in, right?" Hughes said, opening the old wooden door with a reverberating clang. Inside, it smelled like cats and, incongruously, there was a sign for a morning yoga class. Leaving, I flashed to a classic Hughes film moment: Jake Ryan, leaning against his red Porsche, waiting for Samantha (Molly Ringwald) as she leaves her sister's wedding. Of course, as we crossed the street, a red Porsche cruised by.

I had seen a nearly identical sports car the day before, in downtown Chicago, while on the trail of Ferris. My husband and I had driven south along Lake Michigan's shore, where the water was turquoise and the beaches were crowded with end-of-summer sunshine revelers, to seek out Chez Quis, the fine French restaurant where Ferris took Sloan on their big downtown date and where, to secure a table, he impersonated Abe Froman, "the Sausage King of Chicago." But the Gold Coast restaurant was fictional, so we went for white tablecloth French-Vietnamese at Le Colonial, where a table of women were speaking French and celebrating a birthday with copious amounts of Champagne. Close enough.

Ferris's trail also took me to Wrigley Field, home of the Chicago Cubs (though the Cubs were away that week), and north to Highland Park, where Cameron's house was recently sold after several years on the market. At the Willis Tower (formerly the Sears Tower), another stop on Ferris's day-off itinerary, the line for the observation deck was hours long, a wait

Photographs by Kevin Miyazaki

that wily Ferris would surely have found a way to circumvent.

On Hughes's suggestion, my husband and I went to Coalfire Pizza on Grand Avenue, a family favorite in the years just before his father died, when they would drop by en route to a baseball game or hockey match. The pizza was Neapolitan, and wonderful. Hughes said his father loved it so much he had a pizza oven built in his house. After we ate, I asked for the owner, Dave Bonomi, who remembered the filmmaker and his culinary questions.

"Before we knew who he was, he would sneak one in—a question about flour or San Marzano tomatoes," Bonomi said. "As a restaurant, you're paranoid about industry secrets." Then, he recalled, he learned who the patron was, and "we'd tell him anything."

WHAT TO READ AND WATCH

Sixteen Candles and **The Breakfast Club**, directed by John Hughes. Films about teenagers, set in Chicago, that were 1980s hits. Their subtle insights about the experience of growing up are timeless.

John Hughes: A Life in Film: The Genius Behind Ferris Bueller, The Breakfast Club, Home Alone, and More, by Kirk Honeycutt. An illustrated tribute to Hughes. Includes interviews with the stars who acted in his movies.

Life Moves Pretty Fast: The Lessons We Learned from Eighties Movies, by Hadley Freeman. A *Guardian* columnist makes a case for the relevance of films by Hughes and others of his era.

John Hughes's Commentary on Ferris Bueller's Day Off. From the 1999 DVD of the film; missing in later releases. A clip focused on a museum scene has been posted several times on the Internet and is worth searching for.

UNITED STATES   DETROIT

THE ARCHITECT OF DETROIT

Self-promotion wasn't Albert Kahn's style. Innovative design was, and he gave his city hundreds of memorable buildings. — BY JOHN L. DORMAN

In America's industrial Golden Age, the automotive industry transformed Detroit. Cars and trucks rolled off the city's assembly lines by the millions, and money flowed. The population grew from about 285,000 in 1900 to more than 1.6 million by 1940. During those decades, ornate office buildings, regal academic buildings, and grand manors sprouted across the city and the region, largely because of the ingenuity of Albert Kahn.

Kahn, frequently referred to as "the architect of Detroit," designed between 400 and 900 buildings in the city. A few have been demolished, victims of redevelopment or urban decay. But scores of his most important works, including the Art Deco Fisher Building and Belle Isle Aquarium, continue to be captivating.

Albert Kahn was born into a Jewish family in 1869 in Germany. He immigrated to the United States in 1880, settling in Detroit. He worked a string of odd jobs to help support his parents and seven siblings before landing a position as a draftsman in the office of the architect George D. Mason, despite having only a seventh-grade education.

"Kahn is one of the last generation of apprentice architects who just came up by working in an office," said Michael H. Hodges, a fine arts writer at *The Detroit News* and the author of *Building the Modern World: Albert Kahn in Detroit*. "Mason really took a shine to him and saw his intelligence, ambition, and hard work."

In 1891 Kahn won a scholarship to study abroad. He traveled across Europe, sketching architectural details alongside Henry Bacon, who would go on to design the Lincoln Memorial in Washington. The experience was a defining event, and in 1895, back in Detroit,

DETROIT   UNITED STATES

Previous Burton Memorial Tower, one of the Albert Kahn–designed structures at the University of Michigan in Ann Arbor.

Left Carillon bells in the Burton Memorial Tower.

Opposite The lobby of the Detroit Athletic Club, which Kahn modeled in part on the Villa Borghese in Rome.

he founded his own firm, Albert Kahn Associates. He was 26 years old. From then until his death in 1942, he designed nearly 2,000 buildings around the world.

Now, after decades of sinking toward obscurity, his outsize influence is again being recognized.

Claire Zimmerman, an associate professor of architecture and art history at the University of Michigan, sees a connection between his work and his personal style, which made him markedly different from high-profile contemporaries like Frank Lloyd Wright. "Kahn is striking for the fact that he's so low-key and his immense talents were hidden behind a quite conventional persona," she said. "I think that's true of the buildings as well. The buildings are conventional-looking, and that tends to throw you off the scent in terms of their innovation and modernity."

I wanted to see Kahn's architecture and understand more about his enduring impact on design, so I devised my own tour of some of his most significant works. It proved to be eye-opening and rewarding.

Mack Avenue is a major thoroughfare that runs northeast from Midtown Detroit and gradually approaches the tony suburb of Grosse Pointe. It is an area of deep contrasts. On one side of Mack are neighborhoods of Detroit's East Side, many of which have fared slightly better than large swaths of the city but still show the effects of economic decline. On the other side is Grosse Pointe, which is surrounded by four cities: Grosse Pointe Farms, Grosse Pointe Park, Grosse Pointe Shores, and Grosse Pointe Woods.

When it was first developed, the Grosse Pointe area was the epitome of upper-crust Detroit society, with Tudor Revival and classic American Colonial houses, some of them mansions. It is still decidedly affluent, abundant in quiet, leafy streets with English names like Kensington and Yorkshire. Posh estates dot the shoreline of Lake St. Clair, part of the natural water corridor connecting Lakes Erie and Huron.

At the northern end of Grosse Pointe Shores is the Edsel and Eleanor Ford House, designed by Kahn and completed in 1929. Edsel Ford, Henry Ford's only child, was the president of Ford Motor Company from 1919 to 1943. He was fond of the architecture of the Cotswolds in England and wanted his home to resemble it. It was natural that he turn to Kahn to design it; they were friends, and Kahn had designed buildings over many years for Henry Ford, beginning with the Highland Park Ford Plant.

Edsel's house is fronted by sandstone and has a slate roof, stone shingles, and prominent chimneys. It is open for tours, and when I stepped inside the foyer, I was taken by the beautiful wide oak staircase. The décor in many of the rooms is traditional, but the Art Deco rooms on the second floor are filled with curvy furniture and leather wall panels. The Ford House is the kind of grand property that could have fallen into the trap of being too big for its own good, but it radiates class.

Fine paintings, including Paul Cézanne's *Bouilloire et Fruits*, line the walls. Edsel Ford was an art collector and patron. As a trustee of the Detroit Institute of Arts, he financed the renowned Detroit Industry murals by Diego Rivera, created from 1932 to 1933, that show factory laborers at work.

I wandered through a courtyard and onto a small path that overlooked Lake St. Clair. In the distance was a Great Lakes cargo ship. On the property were a pool house, a powerhouse, a lodge, and a playhouse with miniature furniture. The grounds, designed by the famed Danish-American landscape architect Jens Jensen, feature a picturesque island bird sanctuary, a lagoon, and gardens.

For a look at one of Kahn's most beloved public buildings, I headed to Belle Isle, a 982-acre island park in the Detroit River, to see the Belle Isle Aquarium. It opened in 1904, when industry dominated most of Detroit's waterfront. The aquarium's Beaux-Arts-style front entrance, featuring dolphins and the seal of Detroit carved in stone, is alluring, but it's the interior that reveals Kahn's vision and creativity. The fish tanks at eye level are no surprise, but above them is a high vaulted ceiling made of green opaline glass, suggesting that the entire space is in an underwater world.

Some of Kahn's most famous buildings are clustered in downtown Detroit, on or near Woodward Avenue, the city's spine. The First National Building, a 26-story skyscraper built between 1921 and 1930, was designed in a striking Z shape to give most offices natural light and ventilation. Next door, the neoclassical-style Vinton Building, opened in 1917 as an office building and designed with a prominent parapet, has been converted to apartments. The long-shuttered

Above An organist and her teacher at the University of Michigan Hill Auditorium, one of many prized Kahn designs.

Opposite A Kahn tour de force, the Fisher Building in central Detroit offers scheduled public tours.

National Theater has terra-cotta latticework towers. The former Detroit Free Press Building and the former Detroit News Building both blend smooth limestone facades with Art Deco detailing.

A few blocks away is Kahn's Detroit Athletic Club, an upscale neo-Renaissance clubhouse that opened in 1915. It was inspired by the Palazzo Borghese in Rome, known for its majestic facade and stunning courtyard arcades. The lobby of the club, with its chandeliers and finely crafted wood paneling, was once a grand gateway for Detroit's elite. But for much of the club's existence Jews, as well as African Americans and women, were barred from holding memberships. The club resolved to make an exception for Kahn, but he refused.

Roughly four miles north of downtown, the New Center neighborhood was an upscale retail district at midcentury and home to the world headquarters of General Motors from 1923 to 2000. New Center fell on hard times but is now buzzing with energy, a part of Detroit's revitalization. Its gem is Kahn's Art Deco Fisher Building, which opened in 1928 and which a placard in the lobby describes as the city's "largest art object."

With a virtually unlimited budget, Kahn installed more than 600 bronze elevator doors, both interior and exterior, and 1,800 bronze windows, along with a gilt-tile roof, giving the building a golden glow. The barrel-vaulted arcade that welcomes a visitor inside is unquestionably beautiful, with enormous chandeliers and colorful frescoes and mosaics.

My guide, Ryan Patrick Hooper, a radio journalist in Detroit, had been giving tours of the building for several years through the company Pure Detroit. "I still genuinely enjoy giving tours," he said. "A big part of the experience is surprising people or changing their minds about architecture that's in Detroit."

Across the street, the Albert Kahn Building, a limestone 1931 Art Deco structure, housed the

Above The conservatory in Belle Isle Park. Kahn's buildings there also include the beloved Belle Isle Aquarium.

Opposite Kahn's designs for the Fords ranged from this opulent house for Henry's son, Edsel, to the Model T plant.

offices of Albert Kahn Associates. The firm is still in business but moved to renovated space in the Fisher Building, allowing the Kahn Building to be repurposed for apartments.

On the tour of the Fisher Building, visitors can see the rooftop of Cadillac Place, the former General Motors headquarters, a Kahn project with almost 1.4 million square feet of space. Kahn's design of a wide two-story base with four separate 15-story buildings avoided the fortress-like quality such a huge building might have projected and allows for sunlight from different angles. The first floor, richly decorated with marble and an elaborate globe chandelier, is open to the public.

There's much more of Kahn downtown, but I moved on to the Brush Park neighborhood to see the house he built for himself and occupied from 1906 to 1942. Now the headquarters of the Detroit Urban League, it's stately and turreted, suggesting the fortune Kahn's success allowed him to amass. Kahn was, among other things, a pianist, so it's not difficult to imagine his furnishings would have included a grand piano.

Much of Kahn's fortune originated in his designs for the auto industry. The Highland Park Ford Plant, where the Model T was produced, became the first automobile facility in the world with a continuously moving assembly line and was also where Ford implemented the eight-hour workday and paid livable wages to unskilled workers, creating an instant market for his cars and disrupting the American class system. Most of the plant is gone, as are Kahn's buildings at the massive Ford River Rouge complex, but they were integral to the heyday of Detroit.

"Kahn truly influenced the Modern movement with his industrial work," said Alan Cobb, the president and chief executive of Albert Kahn Associates. "Gropius and Mies van der Rohe looked to Kahn for their philosophies. Basically, while they were creating

Photographs by Kevin Miyazaki

the philosophy behind modern architecture, Albert Kahn was quietly building it."

That was clear when I entered the Hill Auditorium at the University of Michigan in Ann Arbor, about 40 miles from downtown Detroit, and heard beautiful crisp notes coming from the stage, a tribute to Kahn's understanding of acoustics. The Burton Memorial Tower, which has a student-operated carillon, is another of the university's numerous Kahn-designed buildings.

"In the 1920s, Kahn worked with other members of the University of Michigan community to modernize the campus plan," Zimmerman, the University of Michigan professor, said. "They really turned the campus from a 19th-century campus to a much more modern 20th-century campus."

In Ann Arbor and in Detroit, Kahn's architecture seems not just modern, but timeless.

WHAT TO READ AND WATCH

Building the Modern World: Albert Kahn in Detroit, by Michael H. Hodges. Tells the story of Kahn's rise from poverty to success as a versatile, prolific, and groundbreaking architect.

A History Lover's Guide to Detroit, by Karin Risko. The auto industry is only part of the story in this overview of the city, which looks ahead as well as backward.

Once in a Great City: A Detroit Story, by David Maraniss. The great city that Kahn helped to build and the reasons for its subsequent decline. "Elegiac and richly detailed." — Michiko Kakutani in *The New York Times*.

American Experience: Henry Ford, a PBS documentary. An intriguing portrait of Kahn's most powerful client.

UNITED STATES   INSIDE PASSAGE, ALASKA

ALASKA, IN JOHN MUIR'S ICY WAKE

It isn't easy now to explore the Inside Passage in a dugout canoe. But to catch the spirit, skip the cruise ships and ride the ferries. — BY MARK ADAMS

Long before his extravagantly bearded profile appeared on postage stamps and commemorative coins, John Muir was a struggling travel writer. Muir, revered today as the founder of the Sierra Club and an early advocate for American national parks, was largely unknown to the reading public in 1879, when he first left San Francisco bound for Alaska's mysterious Inside Passage, a seafaring route through clusters of islands on the Pacific coast.

His primary goal was to study Alaska's glaciers, but he also wrote newspaper travelogues to pay the bills. His adventures, guided hundreds of miles by Tlingit natives paddling a dugout cedar canoe, became rhapsodic dispatches that found an enthusiastic audience. Within a few years, West Coast steamships were hawking Alaska sightseeing trips to the "frozen Niagara" of the Muir Glacier, a spectacular river of ice—today located in Glacier Bay National Park and Preserve—discharging massive bergs from its 300-foot-high face.

Newspaper editors might have hired Muir solely on the basis of his expense reports; he endorsed sleeping on the ground and often carried little more than bread, a notebook, and a change of underwear on his long rambles. Today's prototypical Alaska visitor, a passenger on a weeklong Inside Passage cruise, expects a significantly higher level of comfort. The cruise ships, many of them carrying thousands of passengers, usually follow the aquatic path Muir popularized, departing from Seattle or Vancouver with stops in Ketchikan, Juneau, and Skagway, but with rigidly structured itineraries. Only two per day are permitted to enter Glacier Bay National Park and witness the icy glories immortalized in Muir's classic book *Travels in Alaska*.

INSIDE PASSAGE, ALASKA   UNITED STATES

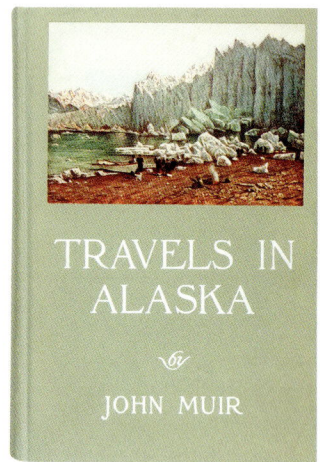

Previous The gateway road to Glacier Bay National Park and Preserve. Muir introduced this part of Alaska to the wider world.

Left Muir's *Travels in Alaska*, published in 1915, became a classic.

Below Pumps from the 1930s sit outside the only gas station for the 450 year-round residents of Gustavus, Alaska.

Opposite The Lynn Canal, a 90-mile-long fjord. Ferries pass through on the way between Juneau and Haines.

Muir, who returned to Alaska again and again, would almost certainly not approve the proliferation of tourists in huge ships. He was a spiritual rover, in awe of natural grandeur waiting to be discovered.

Thumbing through an old copy of *Travels in Alaska*, I began to wonder if it was still possible to wander the Inside Passage serendipitously, as Muir had, "borne smoothly over calm blue waters, through the midst of countless forest-clad islands." Fortunately, there's a seagoing option that allows for flexibility and discovery: the Alaska Marine Highway System, a flotilla of utilitarian ferries sometimes known as the Blue Canoes because of their signature color scheme.

Alaskans are a seafaring people. Most of the state's 740,000 residents live in towns and cities near the coast. Alaska's huge size and crazy topography make road construction impractical; even Juneau, the capital, can be reached only by sea or air. The marine ferries are used primarily by Alaskans, who find them an inexpensive way to move themselves and their vehicles from place to place as they read, work, or watch the miles go by. I bought a couple of waterproof notebooks and flew off to join them.

Late on a May evening, I boarded the MV *Kennicott* in Bellingham, Washington, along with 300 other passengers and a few dozen cars, pickups, and recreational vehicles. At the purser's desk I picked up the keys to a tiny roomette with a folding narrow bed. I fell asleep almost instantly to the low hum of the engines.

The cafeteria opened at 4 a.m. and had a menu that reminded me of my high school lunchroom—cold cereal and scrambled eggs; burgers for lunch. I snagged a spot next to Beau Bailey, a retired hydrologist and inveterate global traveler. He knew all about Muir's visits north and had traveled up the Inside Passage multiple times. "This journey on the ferries is probably my favorite in the whole world," he told me.

The trip from Bellingham to Ketchikan takes about 38 hours. As the green shoreline of British Columbia scrolled slowly past behind a blue-gray screen of mist, I thought of Muir's last trip to Alaska, as a member of the Harriman Expedition in 1899. He and two dozen other leading American naturalists had been invited as guests of the railroad magnate Edward Harriman. When this all-star team of scientists disembarked to stretch their legs amid the temperate rain forest, they encountered knee-deep mosses and nail-sized thorns, a land as impassable as the Amazon jungle.

In Ketchikan, I landed in a scene far different from what Muir saw. When he sailed through in 1899, this spot held a salmon cannery and a few shacks. Today it is a metropolis by Alaska standards: home to 8,000 residents and, on most summer days, several 10-story cruise ships. The waterfront was thick with shops pushing souvenir T-shirts and knickknacks.

I boarded another ferry to Wrangell, a former timber town. The boats' schedules left me with several days to stay there, and I checked into the Wrangell Extended Stay and Trading Post, run by Mike and Lydia Matney, who also sew hats and mittens out of beaver, mink, and otter furs.

Muir described the Wrangell of his day as "a rough place," and with good reason. Upon returning in 1880 for his second glacier-seeking expedition, he learned that the Tlingit chief who had guided him the year before had been shot dead.

Today much of the town looks unchanged since 1899: false-front buildings and clapboard churches, including the one where Muir slept on the floor on his very first night on Alaska soil.

"I sometimes feel bad for kids who grow up on Wrangell Island," Mike Matney shouted aboard his boat one afternoon. He and Lydia had invited me out to check their very full Dungeness crab pots. "But then I think about kids like that." He pointed at two boys, probably 10 and 12, out on the water unchaperoned and fishing from what looked like a motorized rowboat; they had recently hauled in a prize king salmon.

After a few days I caught a ferry to Juneau, where I splurged on a stay at the Westmark Baranof Hotel. In 1899, when Muir stopped in Juneau with the Harriman Expedition, the gold rush was in full swing. Nowadays Alaska's economy runs on oil. A 2008 spike in gas prices paid for the gorgeous new $140 million State Libraries, Archives, and Museum, where I browsed through the 12 beautiful bound volumes of *The Harriman Alaska Series*, chronicles compiled by Muir and his fellow naturalists. The series had a

Opposite You might have to brave a chilly wind, but the view from the Gustavus shoreline is worth it.

Right A totem pole carved by the Tlingit people stands near the Huna Tribal House and the Glacier Bay park lodge.

huge influence on President Theodore Roosevelt's decision to preserve what is now the 17-million-acre Tongass National Forest, the scenic wilderness that encompasses most of Alaska's Inside Passage.

Downtown Juneau is small and hilly, like a pocket-size San Francisco, and easy to navigate. I had a day to spare before my next ferry, so I caught a city bus that dropped me off about a mile from the Mendenhall Glacier Visitor Center. I arrived an hour before the daily cruise-ship shuttles started unloading, and so had the place almost to myself. The glacier, a frozen river that winds back 13 miles, is spectacular. Muir described the color inside its ice caves as "the most startling, chilling, almost shrieking vitriol blue." (Sadly, there are no longer ice caves reachable by foot. The ones that remain require special expertise and equipment.)

The next leg on my Passage voyage was from Juneau to Haines via Lynn Canal, a 90-mile-long fjord lined with glaciers and snow-capped mountains. Occasionally a passenger on the ferry would spot some wildlife — a black bear, a pod of dolphins, the splash of a whale's tail. The captain announced it over the PA system, and everyone rushed to one side of the boat.

David Nanney, the founder of the Haines John Muir Association and operator of the Chilkat Eagle B and B, collected me at the Haines ferry terminal. He wore a visor adorned with flames, fingerless gloves, and a timepiece on each wrist. The back of his SUV was littered with kites. "You never know when you'll get the sudden urge to fly a kite," he said as we drove toward town.

Nanney related the story of Muir's first visit to the area, which was a stronghold of the feared Chilkat Tlingit tribe. The Chilkats loved Muir, whose famous dictum, "When we try to pick out anything by itself, we find it hitched to everything else in the universe," emphasized the interconnectedness of all things, an attitude that echoed their animist worldview.

To me, Haines's chief attractions were a pedestrian-friendly layout; an excellent coffee shop; a superb library and bookstore; and perhaps the prettiest setting in Southeast Alaska, snow-capped mountains that rise almost straight out of Lynn Canal.

I knew exactly where I was going to finish my Inside Passage trip even before I finished reading the transcendent chapter "The Discovery of Glacier Bay" in *Travels in Alaska*. For it was in this bay that Muir unexpectedly encountered "a picture of icy wilderness unspeakably pure and sublime."

Gustavus, the tiny town that serves as the gateway to Glacier Bay National Park, is one of the fastest-

Above Ferries, yachts, and wilderness seekers all stop off in the old timber town of Wrangell.

Opposite The Andrew P. Kashevaroff State Library, Archives, and Museum, also known as the SLAM, in Juneau.

growing municipalities in Alaska—by acreage, anyway. Over recent decades, average air temperatures near Glacier Bay have increased, and billions of tons of ice have melted. One family has unexpectedly reclaimed enough solid ground from the surrounding waters to open a nine-hole golf course.

Kim Heacox, a former park ranger who has written extensively on Muir's time in Alaska, drove me down to the tidal flats to see where his adopted hometown was expanding. "This is land being born, man," he said. "That still amazes me."

Gustavus is hemmed in on all sides by snowy mountains and has a dock too small for cruise ships. It feels a million miles from anywhere.

I passed two gorgeous days riding one of Heacox's old mountain bikes up and down the main road, past moose and fields of purple lupine. At the historic Gustavus Inn, I was seated for a family-style meal with some congenial Colorado farmers who had come up for salmon season and insisted climate change was a hoax.

In 1899, the Harriman Expedition's luxury steamship spent several days anchored in front of Muir's namesake glacier, bobbing in a slurry of newly birthed icebergs a safe distance from what Muir once called "the tremendous threatening cliffs of the discharging wall."

Eager to see some calving glaciers, I booked the final leg of my marine journey on a Glacier Bay tour boat out of Bartlett Cove. The full-day, 130-mile round-trip circuit of the bay provides an excellent narration by a National Park Service naturalist as well as food and drink.

We motored slowly past a chunk of rock swarming with bald eagles on top and sea lions below, and approached the spot that, in the 1890s, had marked the terminus of Muir Glacier. The inlet was now open water. The onboard ranger explained that the onetime

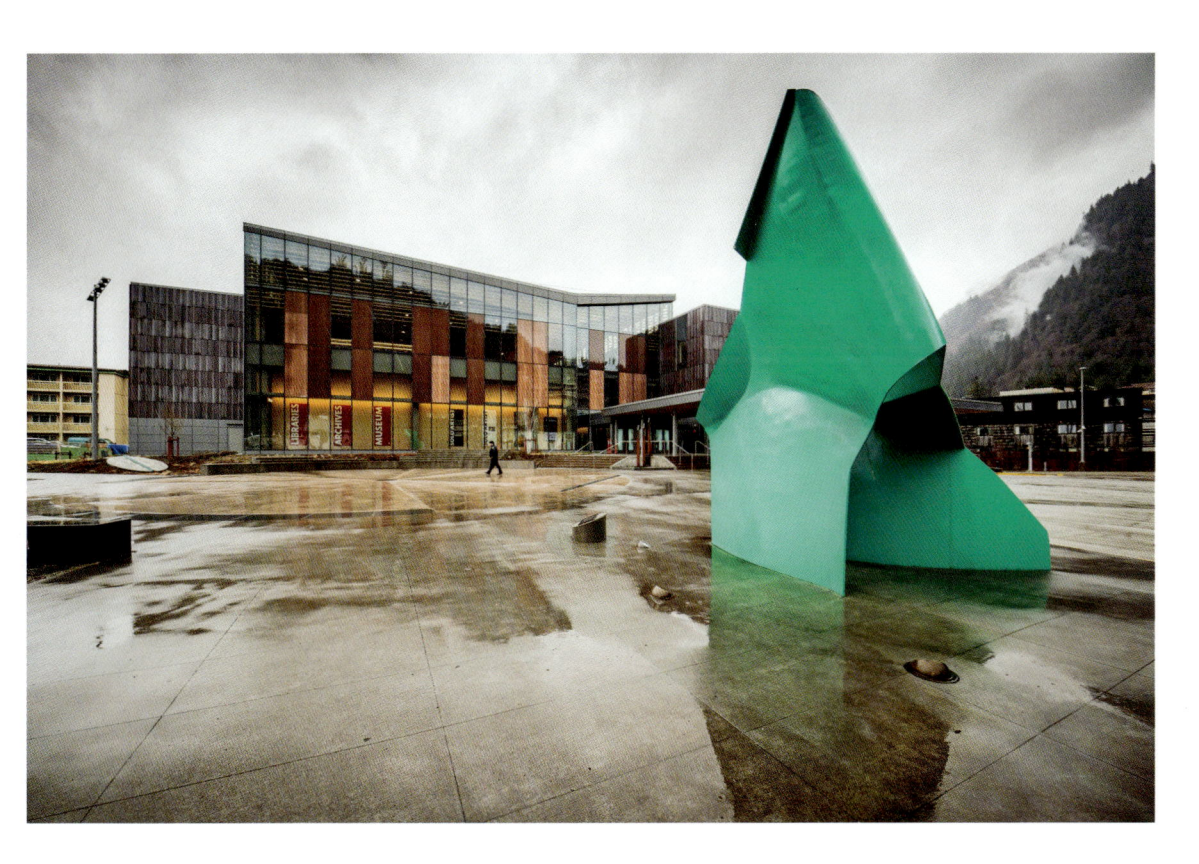

*Photographs by
Christopher Miller*

showpiece of Glacier Bay has receded out of sight, a retreat of more than 30 miles since Muir first saw it.

Continuing north, we eventually stopped in front of the Margerie Glacier and parked next to a gigantic cruise ship. Every 10 minutes or so, a thunderclap rang out and a chunk of ice plummeted from the Margerie's mile-wide blue face, creating an epic splash. The effect was spellbinding.

Glaciers advance and retreat; that's their natural cycle. But the tidewater glaciers of Alaska—those that extend to the water's edge—are almost entirely in retreat these days. The causes are complicated, and Glacier Bay's ice has been receding since the mid-1700s, but human-caused climate change is accelerating the process. Even the most remote corners of the Last Frontier are hitched to everything else in the universe. It seems likely that the Alaska writings of John Muir will outlast the ice that inspired them.

WHAT TO READ AND WATCH

Tip of the Iceberg: My 3,000-Mile Journey Around Wild Alaska, the Last Great American Frontier, by Mark Adams. From the author of this article, a book-length chronicle of his travels in today's Alaska.

John Muir and the Ice That Started a Fire: How a Visionary and the Glaciers of Alaska Changed America, by Kim Heacox. The story of John Muir in Alaska and the effect its glaciers had on his worldview.

Brave New Arctic: The Untold Story of the Melting North, by Mark C. Serreze. A firsthand account of how scientists realized that climate change was occurring and came together to research how and why.

Between Earth and Sky: Climate Change on the Last Frontier, directed by Paul Hunton. A film documentary examining climate change through the lens of its impacts on native Alaskans and their environment.

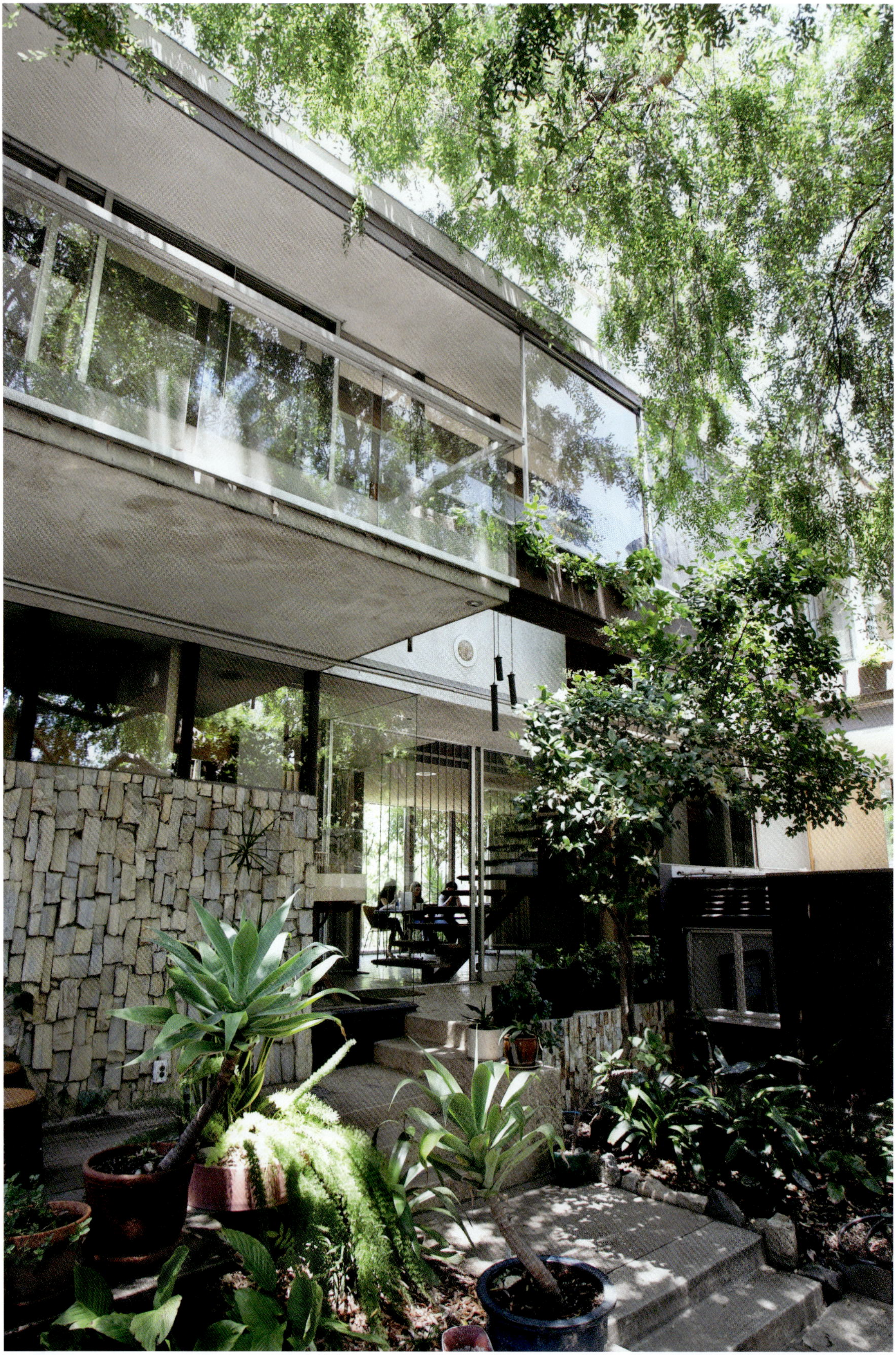

UNITED STATES   LOS ANGELES

DREAMIN' IN A CALIFORNIA HOUSE

Celebrities in Los Angeles aren't all human. Some of them are 20th-century houses by star architects.
— BY ANDREW FERREN

Perhaps the most clichéd Los Angeles tourist activity is the curbside ogling of celebrity homes. But take away the famous residents, and Los Angeles is still the ultimate showplace of American dream houses. With legions of architects and Hollywood set designers equally adept at building a Southern plantation or a medieval Transylvanian castle, it's no wonder that some streets are lined with English Tudors and Mexican haciendas that somehow look more authentic than anything you'd find in Chichester or Chihuahua.

But for a handful of early and mid-20th-century American and European émigré architects, the city offered an opportunity to create distinctly "California" houses that would suit (and perhaps even mold) the families who lived in them.

Rather than faking the grandeur of faux chateaux or other historical models, they took humble materials like clinker bricks, poured concrete, and redwood shingles, and combined them with then-novel materials like Formica, linoleum, and acres of plate-glass windows that brought the outdoors inside and inspired a fresh, informal approach to living that eventually spread around the globe.

Some of the most adventurous houses, like those designed by the visionary John Lautner, are still private homes and can only be viewed from the street. His 1960 Chemosphere, which hovers against the Hollywood Hills like a spaceship and has even made an appearance (in cartoon form) on *The Simpsons*, is an example of Lautner's style of integrating bold architecture into its setting.

But several innovative properties, including houses that architects built for themselves, are open for tours on schedules easily accessible on the Internet.

Previous The Richard Neutra VDL II house, the quintessence of "California modern."

Left The Gamble House in Pasadena was designed for a member of the family behind Procter & Gamble.

Opposite John Lautner turned a steep uphill site into an asset when he designed the Chemosphere house, built in 1960.

When I sought out five of them to visit, I found both exciting architecture and glimpses of some of the area's most charming neighborhoods — from Pasadena to Pacific Palisades.

The oldest and grandest property I saw was the Gamble House in Pasadena. Built between 1907 and 1909, it is an icon of the American Arts and Crafts movement, with its emphasis on the complete interior in which the furniture, lighting, and carpets were designed by the architects.

Before Florida's beaches beckoned, wealthy Midwesterners wintered in the West, building beefed-up English manors and Italian villas in the California sun. But George and Mary Gamble (of the Procter & Gamble Gambles) went native, hiring the California architects Charles and Henry Greene to design their winter retreat.

The home's wow factor is the gorgeous woodwork seen throughout its paneled rooms, with artfully exposed mortise and tenon joinery. Luminous stained-glass windows tint the interiors by day; at night iridescent art-glass lanterns, hanging from leather straps looped through the teak and mahogany beams, glow softly.

My guide had a head for figures. The interiors, I was told, were made using 17 exotic woods in the hands of 10 master carpenters. The house took six months to design, nine to construct, and was finished one month early.

It cost $50,500 even before the Gambles spent another $10,000 on custom furniture, like Mrs. Gamble's dresser with carved dogwood motifs to complement a Rookwood art pottery vase the architects knew would be sitting on top of it.

Today such detail feels almost Old World, but it was incredibly bold in its day — especially on Millionaires' Row where the Gambles' neighbors' houses had reception halls and ballrooms lined in marble and gilt bronze.

If you want to spend the day in this part of the Los Angeles area, the Huntington Library and Gardens in nearby San Marino displays furniture and decorative arts by the Greenes, Gustav Stickley, and many other Arts and Crafts artists.

But I wanted to get to Hollywood, where Frank Lloyd Wright's Hollyhock House crowns a hill just below Griffith Observatory. Built between 1919 and 1923, this was the first of five houses Wright built in Los Angeles in the 1920s. The hollyhock was the favorite flower of Aline Barnsdall, a free-spirited heiress and arts patroness. She bought an undeveloped city block known as Olive Hill with plans to build a theater and arts complex as well as her own home. She hired Wright to build it all, but their relationship soured during the construction of the house and the rest of the project was abandoned.

In Tinseltown parlance, Wright's career was in turnaround. His success with Prairie houses built in the Chicago area was a memory, and he had yet to find his new architectural idiom. In California he looked to pre-Columbian models for inspiration, and with its slightly stepped, temple-like appearance, Hollyhock House evokes both Mayan temples and Southwestern adobes.

Inside, the house is a stunning example of Wright's ability to manipulate space, modulating ceiling heights and window placement to draw people through the building.

An early adopter of reinforced concrete, Wright employed it here for the exterior's hollyhock motifs and even for the front door, which was the only concrete door I had ever seen. His furniture designs for the house were also among his most innovative, especially the tall, elegant chair backs — abstract designs based on hollyhocks.

Just minutes away, on the edge of Silver Lake reservoir, sits Richard Neutra's VDL II house, developed in 1932 as Neutra's studio and family home. It is named for the Dutch industrialist Cornelius Van der Leeuw, a champion of Modernism who was so impressed by the architect's work that he gave him $3,000 to build it.

The original house, a white box wrapped with narrow bands of windows, burned down in 1963, and an updated version, built three years later, is what awaits visitors today. With its open plan and exposed staircase rising through the center of the house, it is the quintessential "California modern" house. The roof terrace, with its views of the reservoir, is a hip urban oasis.

Above An outdoor fireplace and a windowed wing of the Schindler House, by the architect Rudolph Schindler.

Opposite Familiar Frank Lloyd Wright themes play out in his Hollyhock House, designed for the heiress to an oil fortune.

Visitors are encouraged to linger — to lounge on the sofas or watch the light shimmer off the reservoir. The house is run by the architecture and landscape design schools of California State Polytechnic University, Pomona. Students lead the tours and work on restoration projects.

Neutra came to Los Angeles at the behest of Rudolph Schindler, the Viennese architect whose own house is also open to the public. (Both architects worked for Wright in the city.)

The one-story Schindler House, in West Hollywood, was built in 1921–22 and feels remarkably modern with its lack of decorative fuss. The unpainted concrete walls feature narrow strips of glass set at regular intervals. Other walls are made of redwood frames and stretched canvas; some open onto the gardens.

Schindler described the house as fulfilling "the basic requirements for a campers' shelter: a protected back, an open front, a fireplace, and a roof." It integrates the interior and exterior with several protected outdoor "rooms" — some with fireplaces on the exterior walls.

The last stop on my self-designed tour was the Eames House, also known as Case Study House No. 8. Like the Gamble House, the Eames House offers a bit of time travel. Built by the husband-and-wife team of Charles and Ray Eames in 1949, it was a phenomenon of the postwar years, when home building for the middle and working classes was exploding across the United States. Case Study Houses were products of a program sponsored by *Art and Architecture* magazine, which commissioned major architects to design intelligent, affordable housing.

The Eames House interior is rarely opened to the public, but the grounds are open by appointment. And since the house is mostly clad in glass and is just one room deep, viewing it from the outside allows peering inside. It's like looking into a diorama of the Eameses'

*Photographs by
Ann Johansson*

casual California lifestyle, complete with examples of their iconic furniture designs and artwork amid overgrown houseplants and Ray's collections of ceramics and colored glass still on display in the kitchen.

Sheltered in a eucalyptus-shaded meadow that seems to float above the ocean in Pacific Palisades, the house is built entirely from prefabricated parts ordered out of catalogs. The property includes two aligned rectangular structures separated by a small patio. One of these structures is the studio where the Eameses once worked; today it houses the offices of the Eames Foundation. Here you'll be greeted and given information about the house and the legacy of Charles and Ray Eames before being sent off into the meadow to explore on your own.

WHAT TO READ

Case Study Houses, from the TASCHEN Basic Art series, by Elizabeth A. T. Smith, edited by Peter Gössel. A survey, with photos and text, of model homes built from 1945 to 1966, designed by major architects including Neutra, the Eameses, and Eero Saarinen.

L. A. Modern, photography by Tim Street-Porter. Documents Los Angeles's role as a center of American Modernism with photos of both residential structures and iconic public and commercial buildings.

Schindler House, by Kathryn Smith. Offers an analysis and portrait of a house that was a radical departure when it was built in 1921–22 and is now a Modernist icon.

Neutra, by Barbara Lamprecht and ***Lautner***, by Barbara-Ann Campbell-Lange, both edited by Peter Gössel. Comprehensive but concise summaries of each architects' work, from the TASCHEN Basic Art series.

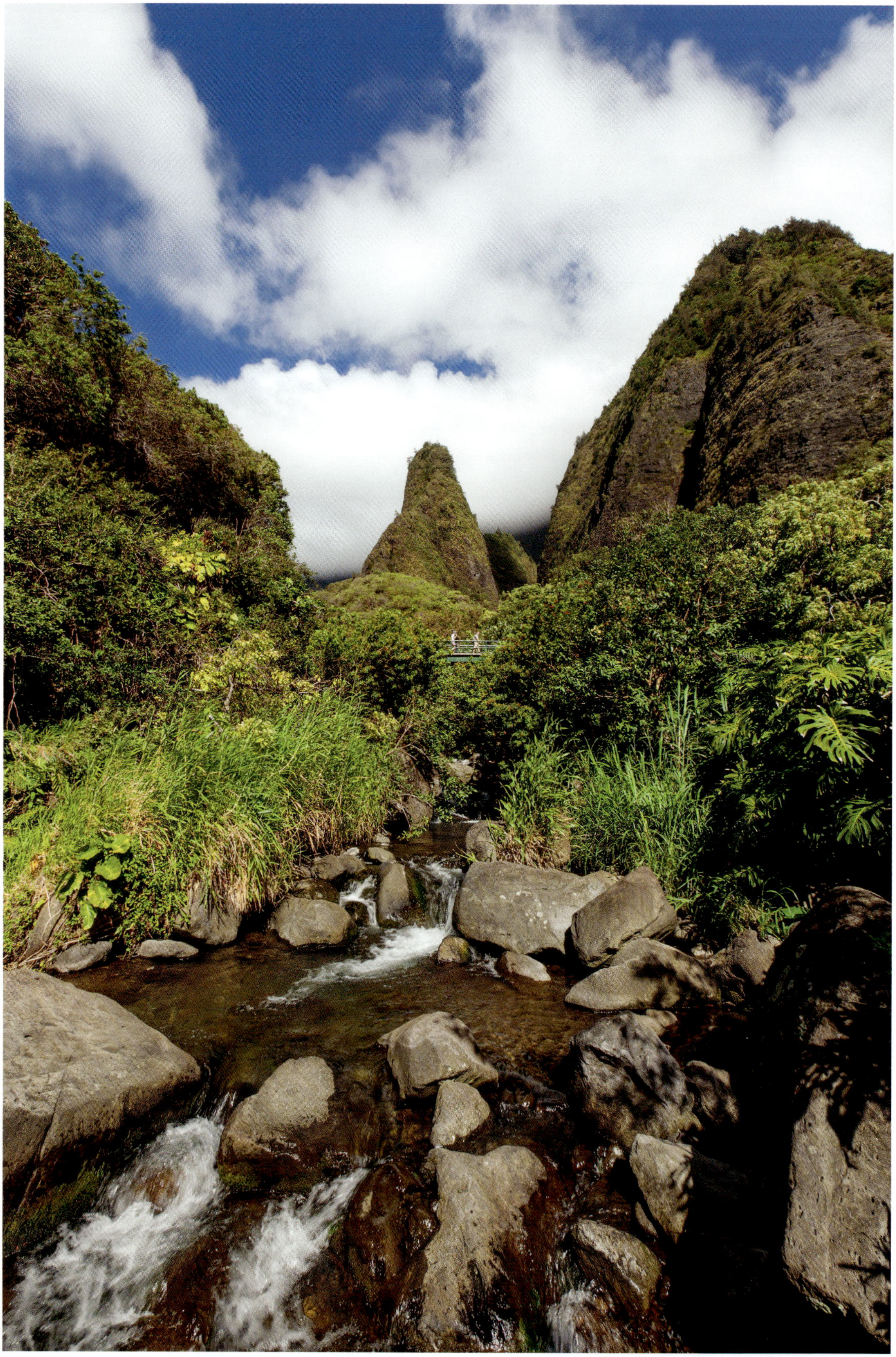

THE TROPICAL PALETTE OF GEORGIA O'KEEFFE

On the path of O'Keeffe in Maui, there's nary a cow skull in sight. — BY TONY PERROTTET

Early in 1939, Georgia O'Keeffe, the artist most famous for depicting the arid American Southwest, was recruited to paint America's diametrically opposite landscape—the lush tropical valleys of Hawaii. In an era when advertisers often hired fine artists to add a touch of class to their campaigns, the "least commercial artist in the US." (as *Time* described her) was persuaded by the Dole pineapple company to visit the Hawaiian Islands and produce two canvases.

The offer came at a critical time in O'Keeffe's life. She was 51, her career seemed to be stalling (critics were calling her focus on New Mexico limited and branding her desert images "a kind of mass production"), and her marriage to Alfred Stieglitz was under serious strain.

Despite initial reservations about the project, her many letters back home show that her experience of the then little-known Territory of Hawaii was a revelation. O'Keeffe ended up spending nine weeks on different islands, of which by far the most productive and vivid period was on Maui, where she was given complete freedom to explore and paint.

Back on Oahu, where she had first arrived, she had been incensed that Dole officials refused to let her stay on a working pineapple plantation because it was unseemly for a woman. When they delivered to her hotel a pineapple already peeled and sliced, she tossed it out in disgust. But on Maui she was able to seek out an unfiltered view not only of pineapple fields, but of nature. She went directly to the most remote, wild, and verdant corner of the island: the port of Hana.

She reported back to Stieglitz about Hana's dark rain forests, exuberant flora, black sand beaches, and lava washed into "sharp and fantastic shapes." Staying on the Kaeleku sugar plantation, the notoriously prickly O'Keeffe was given Patricia Jennings,

MAUI, HAWAII   UNITED STATES

Previous The Iao Valley in Maui. The Dole company invited O'Keeffe to Hawaii, but once there she didn't paint pineapples.

Left Tending to a clay oven at Hana Farms, a community farm with a produce stand, bakery, and deli.

Opposite Torch ginger in a garden near Hana. O'Keeffe, always drawn to flowers, found a lush tropical setting in Maui.

the 12-year-old daughter of the plantation manager, as her private guide, and they became unlikely friends. For 10 days they visited sea caves, ruins, and beaches, and later, with Patricia's father, made excursions to the dramatic Iao Valley and Haleakala Crater.

I first stumbled across this exotic biographical interlude in the New York Public Library, where I found a 1990 catalog for an exhibition of O'Keeffe's Hawaii paintings at the Honolulu Academy of Arts. The images of emerald chasms, gleaming waterfalls, and brilliantly tinged bird of paradise flowers were the very essence of the tropics.

Today Hana is one of the most famous destinations in Hawaii, but few people spend the night there. Most travelers base themselves in the big beach resorts on the other side of Maui, rush along the 68-mile road to Hana (as much as they can rush, considering there are more than 50 bridges, most of them one-lane, and some 600 hairpin bends), and then, pressed for time, are forced to return too soon. But it's quite possible to stay overnight in the eccentric township of Hana and explore every bit of the coastline that so bewitched O'Keeffe.

When I arrived in Hana, its half-dozen streets above the bay were eerily quiet and the manicured lawns of my hotel, the Travaasa (later renamed the Hana-Maui Resort), seemed detached from the rest of the world. When O'Keeffe arrived, Hana was a thriving community of 3,500 people. Its six sugar plantations attracted a cosmopolitan mix of workers: Japanese, Chinese, Filipinos, Portuguese, Pacific islanders, and native Hawaiians. Hana had two cinemas, three barbershops, several restaurants, and a pool hall. Although the last plantation closed in 1946, memories of those days linger. On the volcanic sand beach, a crumbling jetty still extends into the surf, with railway tracks for loading the sugar boats still visible. The Hasegawa General Store is still run by the same family who were the proprietors when O'Keeffe bought a broad-rimmed straw hat there—the same hat she's seen wearing in photographs, grinning like a carefree teenager. (Ansel Adams once said, "When O'Keeffe smiles, the earth cracks open.")

Patricia Jennings, O'Keeffe's young Maui guide, died in 2014, at age 87. But she left behind *Georgia O'Keeffe's Hawaii*, a 2012 book in which she recounted her memories of her time with the artist. Her recollections are charming, combining the innocence of a little girl with the wisdom of an adult looking back on her own childish observations. And they are revealing of O'Keeffe's personality.

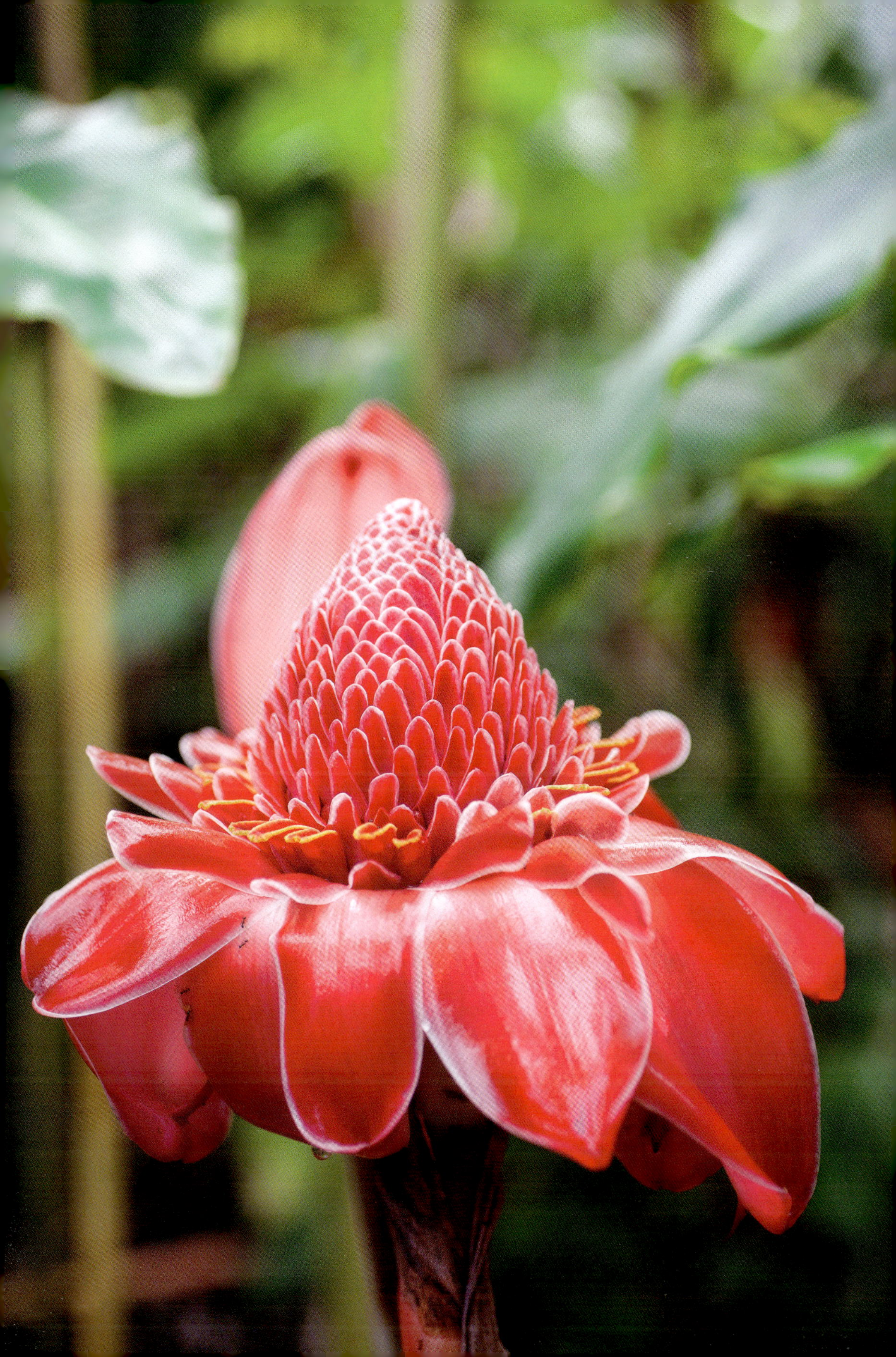

MAUI, HAWAII UNITED STATES

With her mother away on the mainland, Patricia was terrified of meeting the notorious artist, who had caused a sensation by posing nude for Stieglitz; a heavily cropped image had made it to Hana in the pages of *Time*. And when she arrived, tired from a long car ride, O'Keeffe seemed cold at first. When shown her cottage, she said only, "Yes, it's very nice." But at dinner in the plantation house with four male officials, she suddenly transformed herself, glowing as she told a story of her life in New York. The men all appeared fascinated.

Patricia also distinctly recalled her handsome father, Willis, and Georgia exchanging glances. A couple of nights later, she saw them walking hand in hand in the moonlight. And the next day, she writes, "Dad and Georgia looked rested and content."

I found the plantation house still tucked away in a corner of the Travaasa resort, which was using it for group events. An elegant timber home, it is recognizable from photographs. Behind it, one of three original cottages had survived as a caretaker's shed, although the one in which Georgia stayed was gone.

"You would laugh to see where I am now," O'Keeffe wrote in one of her daily letters to Stieglitz, describing the dazzling glimpses of the blue Pacific through the sugarcane and the ever-present smell of molasses from a nearby refinery. She explored the tropical grounds, with its mango, litchi, tamarind, star fruit, and avocado plants. She even ate "raw fish" — either sushi or poke, the Hawaiian ceviche.

It was from this idyllic base that Patricia and Georgia departed every morning on excursions in a company car. Despite O'Keeffe's stern nature and her aversion to Patricia's beloved pet dog, O'Keeffe became intrigued by this barefoot tomboy growing up at the end of the world. Once, when it was raining and O'Keeffe had retreated to the car to paint, she even allowed Patricia to watch her as she worked, a sight strictly forbidden to other mortals.

Some of the places O'Keeffe visited are now major tourist attractions, but staying in Hana meant that I could visit before all the day-trippers arrived. A stunning cascade of natural swimming holes at Oheo Gulch — dubbed the Seven Sacred Pools — is now part of Haleakala National Park, and by noon the pools are crowded with frantic visitors. At 9 a.m., however, I could dive into the most inviting pool with just a few campers for company, protected from the crashing ocean by a ring of lava rocks, and picture O'Keeffe standing on the banks with her easel.

On occasion, following the O'Keeffe itinerary led to minor adventures. She had written to Stieglitz about swimming in a cave near Waianapanapa Beach, but I had difficulty finding the place. After scrambling through foliage above the black sands, I ran into two locals named Gina and Terry, who pointed me in the right direction. "You can swim under a ledge and find two carved Hawaiian thrones," Gina said. "It's pretty trippy."

The cave was filled with crystalline water that reflected the overhanging ferns. I eased myself into the icy pool and breast-stroked toward a dark recess on the left, trying not to jump whenever a palm frond brushed across my legs. Soon I was in total darkness, as complete as in a sensory deprivation tank. I had already learned that in Maui one should always carry a swimsuit and water shoes to prepare for any eventuality. Now I realized I should also carry a flashlight.

I dashed up to the car and dug out my headlamp. As I swam back into the void, the light revealed two rocky outcrops poised above the waterline that did indeed resemble thrones. According to the grisly Hawaiian legend, this was where a beautiful princess and her maid hid from a jealous king until he found them and killed them both in a rage.

Despite O'Keeffe's claims in her letter, Patricia's book makes clear that Georgia did not swim at the cave, although she did listen intently to Patricia's

Previous The artist herself posing at the vista of her painting *Black Lava Bridge, Hana Coast, No. 2*.

Above Coastline along the road to Hana. O'Keeffe wrote home to Alfred Stieglitz about rain forests and black sand.

Opposite Kaupo, a tiny blip in the road featuring the Kaupo Store, a relic from the past.

stories about it, and she admired the shiny black stones, called Pele's tears, that Patricia picked up in the water. In fact, O'Keeffe seems to have routinely sat on dry land while other people went swimming.

Coastal hikes were different: O'Keeffe liked them and memorialized what she found in her work. She painted two lava bridges, natural arches formed over the crashing waves of the ocean below. Finding the first was not hard; it's visible from the parking lot on the cliffs of Waianapanapa Beach. But to find the second, I set off on the Coastal Trail south of Hana township, where I was whipped by sea spray as I traversed several farms where cows stared at me and dogs yapped at my heels. After about 45 minutes, I spotted the lava bridge.

One of the last places on my O'Keeffe itinerary was an ancient temple just north of town, inside what is now Kahanu Garden, part of the National Tropical Botanical Garden. When I saw the temple, Pi'ilanihale Heiau, it stopped me in my tracks. An enormous terraced platform, some 300 by 300 feet, loomed as tall as a five-story building, crowned by a cluster of palm trees. Built in the 14th century and expanded in the 16th, the site had been excavated since O'Keeffe's visit. But as the tropical twilight filtered down and birds screeched overhead, the impact could not have been more powerful. The structure seemed to project all the mystery of the ancient Hawaiian religion, with a spiritual aura as intense as that of Machu Picchu or the Egyptian Pyramids.

Back in Manhattan, O'Keeffe completed a series of 20 sensual, verdant paintings. Dole executives were exasperated to learn that she had painted almost everything except pineapples, including papaya trees, heliconia plants, and even fishhooks. They had a whole fresh pineapple couriered to her by seaplane, which she graciously did paint. ("It's beautiful," she conceded disingenuously to a reviewer at *Time*. "It is made

Photographs by Susan Seubert

up of long green blades and the pineapples grow on top of it. I never knew that.")

Artistically, the trip was a success, and Stieglitz's Madison Avenue gallery, An American Place, was turned into a "madhouse" by fans eager to see the new collection—a "health-giving" dose of Pacific color and sunshine—when it was displayed in the freezing February of 1940. A critic for The New York Sun wrote that the works "testify to Miss O'Keeffe's ability to make herself at home anywhere."

Patricia never saw Georgia again, but they did correspond for a time. "I will always remember you as a little girl," O'Keeffe wrote in a fond letter that is reproduced in Patricia's book, "a very lovely little girl—in a sort of dream world."

WHAT TO READ AND WATCH

Georgia O'Keeffe's Hawai'i, by Patricia Jennings, with Maria Ausherman. Includes Patricia's recollections and O'Keeffe's letters to Alfred Stieglitz.

Georgia O'Keeffe: Visions of Hawai'i, by Theresa Papanikolas and Joanna L. Groarke. A companion book to a 2018 exhibition of O'Keeffe's Hawaii paintings at the New York Botanical Garden.

O'Keeffe, by Britta Benke. A survey of O'Keeffe's career with reproductions of her work. Part of TASCHEN's Basic Art series.

Maui Trailblazer: Where to Hike, Snorkel, Surf, Drive, by Jerry and Janine Sprout. Provides detailed descriptions of trails and remote natural sites.

Georgia O'Keeffe, directed by Bob Balaban. A made-for-television movie focusing on the relationship between O'Keeffe (Joan Allen) and Stieglitz (Jeremy Irons).

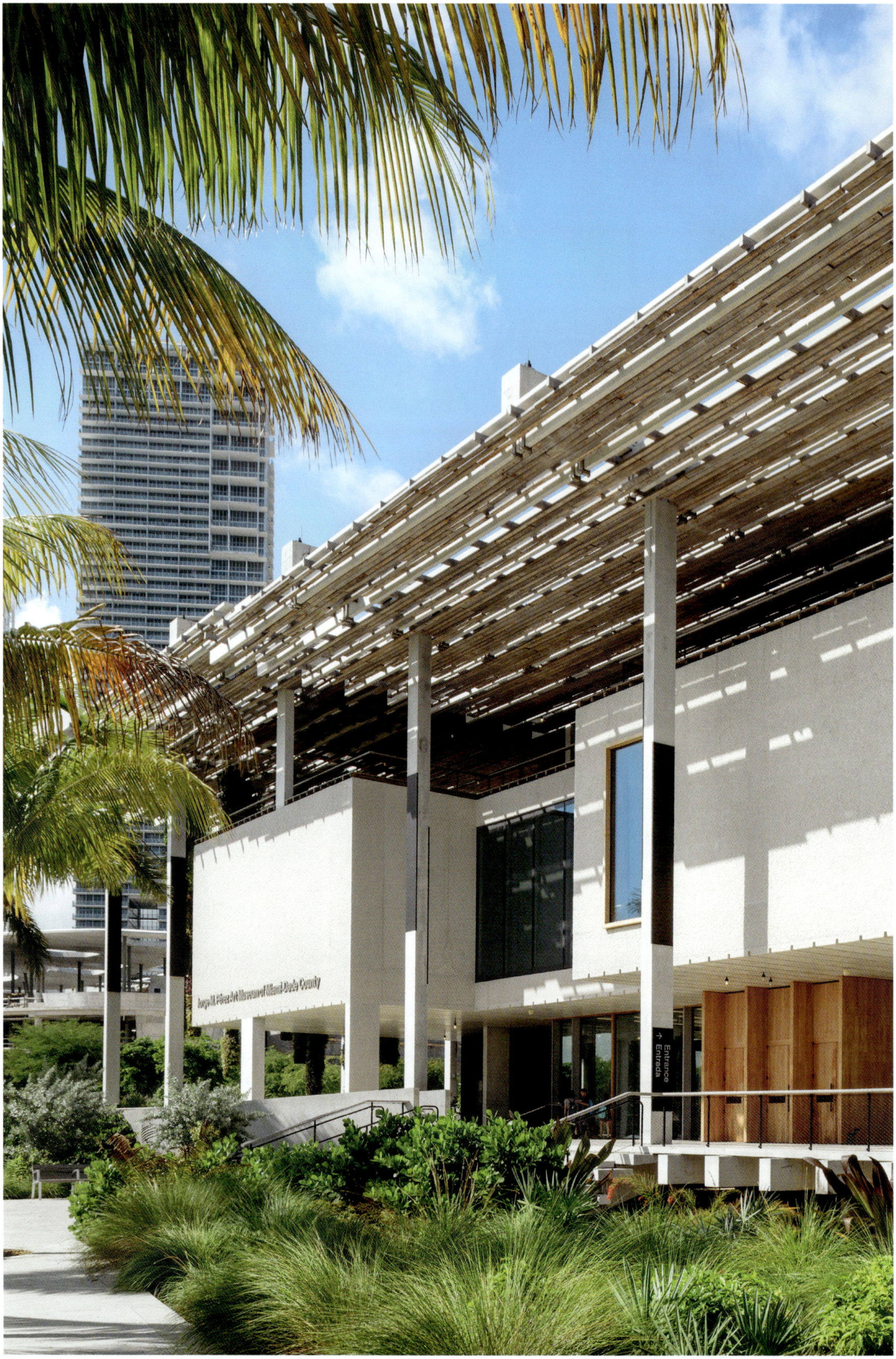

→ Entrance
Entrada

THE BRAINY SIDE OF THE BEACH

When baking the body in a swimsuit gets boring, Miami offers a growing menu of options to stimulate the mind. — BY ELAINE GLUSAC

On the kind of balmy February evening that draws snowbirds by the flocks to South Florida, I split from the flip-flop crowd clogging Lincoln Road Mall in Miami Beach and veered one block north to the New World Center, a Frank Gehry–designed, glass-and-steel symphony hall. When it opened in 2011, the New World Center at once established South Beach, the toniest part of Miami once known mainly for sunny excess, as a cultural destination.

A cluster of patrons formed a white-haired clot in front of the box office, and I soon learned that the evening's program, a recital by a third-year horn fellow with the center's New World Symphony, was sold out. True, it was a free event, but it required reservations, and Dominic Rotella, the musician, was apparently the hottest ticket in town.

"Get in line," a reedy patron said, indicating the informal queue of unfortunates hoping for a ticket miracle. "You're number seven."

If a sellout at a musical fellow's concert is any indication, Miami craves culture. And thanks in part to the influence of the city's immensely popular annual Art Basel, the city has accrued a critical mass of cultural attractions. From the Pérez Art Museum Miami to the thriving muralist district of Wynwood, Miami has developed a brainy complement to its long-established beach allure.

The attractions have just kept coming. Faena Forum, a 50,000-square-foot exhibit space that opened in 2015, occupies an arresting, curvaceously embellished white cylinder designed by Rem Koolhaas. The Bass Museum of Art added 50 percent more display space behind its Art Deco facade, a gift to lovers of contemporary art. And the Phillip and Patricia Frost Museum of Science, in a 250,000-square-foot space including a dramatic vertical aquarium, now shares

Previous The Pérez Art Museum Miami, an ingredient in the city's identity as part beach town, part cultural hub.

Left The collection of the Wolfsonian–FIU explores change in the modern era.

Opposite Frank Gehry's New World Center, a symphony hall, draws crowds to its performances.

the waterfront Museum Park with the Pérez. Older standbys are still part of the mix, too, like touring through the city's famous collection of Art Deco buildings, viewing the decorative arts collection at the Wolfsonian Museum, and exploring the private galleries. That's enough rich cultural fodder to keep a visitor busy outside the Art Basel season.

The Pérez, which is ringed with a generous veranda, is a 200,000-square-foot museum in a fluid building by the Swiss architectural firm Herzog and de Meuron that seems to invite visitors outdoors as well as in. It was inspired by Stiltsville, a group of houses in Biscayne Bay built over the water, a docent explained on an architectural tour. Chiseled concrete panels and floor-to-ceiling windows largely wrap the building. Inside, partly shaded windows flood second-story galleries with light and views of the giant hanging planters that ring the porch.

"This is a very porous space," said the guide. "You're meant to move in and out of the building. It's playful. You want to run around the veranda."

Designed to reflect the immigrant complexion of Miami, the Pérez focuses on modern and contemporary art from Atlantic Rim cultures, including Latin America, Africa, and Europe. Inside, a group of schoolchildren sat on the floor, drawing, in front of *Western Sun*, an orange sunrise rendered in light tubes by the artist Mark Handforth. A few individual artists such as Gary Simmons, whose commissioned mural *Frozen in Time* filled an entire wall, had their own spotlight galleries. In the larger rooms I enjoyed making the acquaintance of the collagist William Cordova via 100 small works mounted together in homage to the jumpy editing of the late Afro-Cuban filmmaker Nicolás Guillén Landrián.

As demonstrated by the outdoor-friendly Pérez, the weather helps shape the art scene. In the Wynwood neighborhood, north of downtown, Miami's sultry climate and tropical palette merge in Wynwood Walls, a constantly changing street art exhibit splashed across 80,000 square feet of exterior walls by more than 40 artists. The developer Tony Goldman, who is credited with reviving South Beach as well as SoHo in New York before his death, began the mural project in 2009, inviting street artists to use the area's squat industrial warehouses as canvases. The murals have made the neighborhood a destination, attracting locally owned shops, restaurants, and microbreweries. The mix of entertainment and culture has married the party to the paintings, especially during Saturday night art walks, which draw food trucks, musicians, and thousands of gallery crawlers.

Martha and Bruce Clinton
The Clinton Family Fund Ensemble Room

Above What better place for outdoor art than sultry South Florida? Wynwood Walls invites artists to join in.

Below The artist Tim Buwalda at work at Wynwood Walls.

Opposite Rem Koolhaas's firm designed Faena Forum, a 50,000-square-foot exhibit space.

I perused Wynwood's murals with Ryan Ferrell, known as Ryan the Wheelbarrow, a local artist and guide, who pointed out graffiti tags that mark the neighborhood but steer clear of defacing the murals. "Wynwood's cool news in Miami," he said, "but among the graffiti world, it's a mecca."

Back in South Beach, the New World Center offers its own night-life spectacle via a giant video wall that screens outdoor movies and concert simulcasts. It also programs late-night symphonic concerts with DJs and club lighting. Short and sometimes free concerts take aim at younger patrons who may be wary of an extended classical commitment, leaving them time to dash over to the nearby Bodega Taqueria y Tequila.

From in-the-round seating in the main concert hall to its glassed-in lobby and practice rooms, the center seems designed to rejuvenate classical conventions, beginning with its chief tenant, the New World Symphony, led by the conductor Michael Tilson Thomas as a virtual finishing school for graduates of music programs around the country. The New World Center also offers a variety of programming outside of symphony season. When I visited during the O, Miami Poetry Festival, an annual event, I saw both a quintet of French Baroque singers performing indoors

*Photographs by
Moris Moreno*

and a Bill Murray movie entertaining the folding-chair-and-cooler crowd on the expansive lawn.

When I managed to beg a ticket to the winter recital by the symphony's horn player, I joined a rapt crowd in listening to everything from Bach to the "Interstellar Call" from Olivier Messiaen's *From the Canyons to the Stars*, performed to a celestial slideshow. Seated beside me at the concert, Hilary Glen, then a first-year cellist with the symphony and a newcomer to town, confessed her initial skepticism of the city's cultural hospitality.

"I wasn't sure I would like Miami when I got here, but I have found it very interesting," she said. "And I never go to the beach."

WHAT TO READ AND WATCH

Lonely Planet Pocket Miami, by Regis St. Louis. A travel guide focusing on what to see and do.

South Beach Deco: Step by Step, by Iris Chase with photos by Susan Russell. A guidebook with walking tours, vignettes, and attractive photographs.

The Corpse Had a Familiar Face, by Edna Buchanan. Narrative of Miami's dark side as seen by the Pulitzer Prize–winning crime reporter for *The Miami Herald*.

The Last Resort, directed by Dennis Scholl and Kareem Tabsch. An evocative documentary of a paradise lost: the era when Miami Beach was a glorious haven for retirees, especially the Jewish community.

The Man Who Built Miami Beach, produced by WLRN, a PBS television station. Documents the transformation of a swampy peninsula into a luxury island resort with the help of Carl G. Fisher, who also built the Indianapolis Speedway.

"MVSIC HALL" · FOVNDED BY · ANDREW CARNEGIE

UNITED STATES　　　　　　　　　　　　　　　　　　　　　　　　　　　　NEW YORK CITY

WHERE DESTINY SEIZED BOB DYLAN

Before worldwide fame and long before the Nobel Prize, the singer and his music found kindred spirits in Greenwich Village. — BY JUSTIN SABLICH

One October night in Greenwich Village, the famous bohemian neighborhood of New York, a few friends showed up at Gerde's Folk City to celebrate Mike Porco's birthday. Gerde's was a restaurant turned music venue, and Porco was its owner. The poet Allen Ginsberg was there, as were the familiar folkies Phil Ochs and Bob Neuwirth. But no one in the group was better known than Bob Dylan and Joan Baez, the two biggest stars of the folk music era of the 1960s. They had first met at the original Gerde's, and that night they performed there again.

But this wasn't the early 1960s folk scene. The year was 1975, and Dylan, not yet a Nobel Prize winner but long since a songwriting legend, was in the middle of his third stint living in the Village. That night, he and his artist friends weren't just celebrating Porco, a man who Dylan said "became like father to me." They were also rehearsing for his coming Rolling Thunder Revue tour, deliberately planned to take their music to small venues where they could be close to the people in their audiences.

Dylan would soon move on from the Village scene for good. The neighborhood was far from what it had been when he first lived there. Fame had made his life different, too. He could no longer expect to walk down a city street without being recognized.

In the early '60s, the Village had been a place of artistic discovery for him. "I'd come from a long ways off and had started a long ways down," he wrote his 2004 memoir *Chronicles*, describing his feeling in those early days. "But now destiny was about to manifest itself. I felt like it was looking right at me and nobody else."

Greenwich Village today is drastically different even from the place Dylan left behind in 1975. Gentrification

Previous Carnegie Hall in Manhattan. Bob Dylan got here, but not before finding his start in Greenwich Village.

Left Dylan and his girlfriend Suze Rotolo on the cover of the 1963 album *The Freewheelin' Bob Dylan*.

Opposite The scene in 1967 at Cafe Wha?, where Dylan performed. It is still a venue for live music.

has settled in, and businesses have turned over. The original location of Gerde's is now the Hebrew Union College–Jewish Institute of Religion. But there are still remnants to be found from Dylan's days of leading a generation-defining music scene. And for anyone interested in imagining the Village as he saw it then, there are landmarks to explore.

Bob Dylan was still Robert Zimmerman when he arrived in January 1961, at age 19, from his home state of Minnesota. He had already been performing and had become interested in American folk music. "I was there to find singers, the ones I'd heard on record," he wrote in *Chronicles*, but "mostly to find Woody Guthrie," the folk hero he would model himself after in his early performing days.

He soon found Guthrie at a hospital in New Jersey, being treated for Huntington's disease. But even before that, on his first day in New York, Dylan persuaded Fred Neil, who ran the daytime show at the Greenwich Village coffeehouse Manny Roth's Cafe Wha?, to let him perform there. He described the cafe as "a subterranean cavern, liquorless, ill lit, low ceiling, like a wide dining hall with chairs and tables," but "that's where I started playing regular in New York."

Cafe Wha? is still a fixture of MacDougal Street, and one of the few Dylan haunts operating under the same name in the same location. But like the Village itself, it has been evolving. The original Cafe Wha? closed in 1968. Then the location had a long run as a Middle Eastern restaurant. It opened again as Cafe Wha?, under new management, in 1987. Music is still the main draw, with the talented Cafe Wha? Band headlining most nights. They'll play at your wedding, too.

Dylan was fired by Roth after being late for three gigs, and he soon made his way to Caffe Reggio, the Commons, Caffe Dante, and several other coffeehouses in the Village. "They were small and ranged in shape, loud and noisy and catered to the confection of tourists who swarmed through the streets at night," he wrote.

Caffe Reggio, which claims to have served the first cappuccino in the United States, remains open and is much as it was, minus the music, on MacDougal Street. At Caffe Dante, now called Dante NYC, small plates have replaced protest songs.

The Commons, also on MacDougal, near Minetta Lane, was where Dylan wrote "Blowin' in the Wind," and was later renamed Fat Black Pussycat. It has since become Panchito's Mexican Restaurant and Cantina, which in 2011 erased the last tie to its musical past when it painted over the faded lettering reading "Fat Black Pussycat Theatre" above its entrance.

In Dylan's mind, none of these smaller coffeehouses compared with the Gaslight Cafe at 116 MacDougal, a "cryptic club" that "an unknown couldn't break into," he wrote, though he managed to eventually. The Gaslight "had a dominant presence on the street, more prestige than anyplace else."

The Gaslight closed in 1971, and the location is now an apartment building. But the Kettle of Fish bar, which Dylan and his contemporaries frequented next door, is still in business. It moved and is now at its third location, at 59 Christopher Street, where it attracts far more Packers fans than folkies.

As for the Fat Black Pussycat, it's now a night spot featuring a lounge, pub, and downstairs dance club at 130 West Third Street. Its front room was once Kettle of Fish's second home, and photographs and paintings still pay tribute to that bar's history.

When Dylan found time to sleep, he crashed on a lot of couches before finding his first apartment at 161 West Fourth Street. He moved there in December 1961 with Suze Rotolo, who was his girlfriend for a few years. They paid $60 a month rent. The structure, built in 1910, sold for $6 million in 2015.

Next door at 169 West Fourth Street is the Music Inn, where he sometimes borrowed instruments to play. Rotolo described it in her memoir as "an impossibly cluttered store that sold every kind of instrument ever made in the entire world." It's still cluttered, still sells all kinds of instruments, and has an open-mic night on Thursdays.

A short walk from the West Fourth Street apartment is the site of what Anthony DeCurtis, writing in *The New York Times*, called "one of the most evocative images of Greenwich Village in the 1960s." It was a photo of Dylan and Rotolo strolling down a snow-covered Jones Street in February 1963, and it was the cover of the album *The Freewheelin' Bob Dylan*.

"It was freezing out," Rotolo told DeCurtis. "He wore a very thin jacket, because image was all."

The album, which featured some of Dylan's best-known songs, including "Blowin' in the Wind," "A Hard Rain's Gonna Fall," and "Girl from the North Country," propelled him to larger New York venues like Town Hall, Carnegie Hall, and Lincoln Center's Philharmonic Hall, now called David Geffen Hall.

Above The Music Inn, where Bob Dylan sometimes borrowed instruments to play. He lived next door.

Opposite Caffe Reggio, a coffeehouse where Dylan played and sang, now concentrates on cappuccino, not live music.

Immense fame ensued, and it chased Dylan and the woman he eventually married, Sara, from Greenwich Village to upstate New York.

The house they purchased was in the Byrdcliffe artist colony, near Woodstock in the Hudson Valley — the same Woodstock that gave its name to the famous 1969 music festival, although that event was actually held in Bethel, another Hudson Valley town. (Dylan did not perform at the festival.) The Woodstock home was a disappointment. It didn't provide the kind of privacy he craved for his family.

They returned to the Village in 1969 and purchased a 19th-century townhouse at 94 MacDougal Street. Despite his celebrity, he remembered, he was relatively unbothered by people who lived and worked in the neighborhood. But there was no respite at his new home from the obsessive fans who tracked him down and "paraded up and down in front of it chanting and shouting, demanding for me to come out and lead them somewhere," he wrote in *Chronicles*. His family was forced to seek peace elsewhere when they could. There was another problem with this new Village. "The stimulation had vanished," he told *Playboy* in 1978. "Everybody was in a pretty down mood. It was over." He would later call his return to the Village with his family "a stupid thing to do."

Yet, years later, after making his first major tour since the mid-'60s and enduring a bitter divorce from Sara, he found himself back in the Village, this time living alone. He started hanging out at some of his old favorite spots, like Gerde's, which had moved from its original location at 11 West Fourth Street to 130 West Third Street, and the Kettle of Fish, and found some peace at the Bitter End on Bleecker Street, where he played pool, watched bands, and sometimes went onstage to perform. "I made sure no one bothered him," the owner, Paul Colby, said in *The Greenwich Village Reader*, a book published in 2001.

Photographs by
Robert Wright

Kris Kristofferson told *The Times* that the Bitter End was the place where "people like me and Bob Dylan didn't just perform, we came to hang out."

The Bitter End now considers itself to be New York's oldest rock club. It opened in 1961 and built a legendary reputation by hiring young performers like Joni Mitchell and James Taylor and comedians like Woody Allen and Billy Crystal.

Of all the surviving Dylan hangouts, the Bitter End may retain the look and feel of his day more than any other. But while the distinctive brick walls and intimate setting are intact, bar bands now dominate the bill, and the musicians you see there are no longer likely to be famous.

Or at least they're not famous yet.

WHAT TO READ, WATCH, AND LISTEN TO

100 Songs, by Bob Dylan. Lyrics of the writer's most memorable songs. "Dylan remains the rare singer whose work is worth reading on the page," Jason Zinoman wrote in *The New York Times*.

Chronicles: Volume One, by Bob Dylan. In this autobiography, written in the 21st century, Dylan looks back at landmarks in his life, including the Greenwich Village music scene of the 1960s.

A Freewheelin' Time: A Memoir of Greenwich Village in the Sixties, by Suze Rotolo. The girl on *The Freewheelin' Bob Dylan* album cover tells her own story of that time and place.

No Direction Home and ***Rolling Thunder Revue***. Two films by Martin Scorsese about Bob Dylan.

The Nobel Lecture, by Bob Dylan, audio accessible at nobelprize.org. Dylan speaks for himself on "how my songs related to literature."

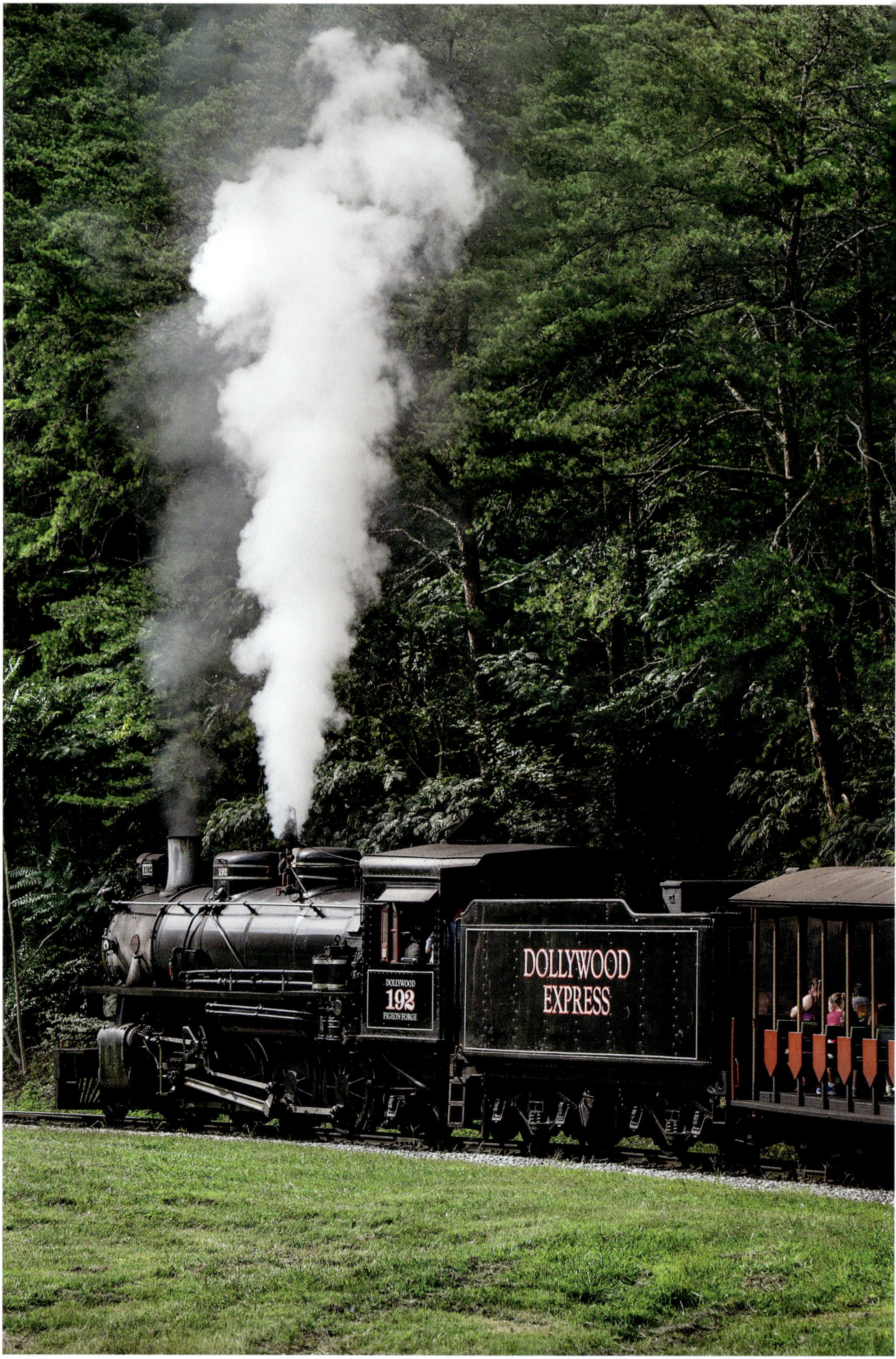
DOLLYWOOD
EXPRESS
DOLLYWOOD
192
PIGEON FORGE

UNITED STATES PIGEON FORGE, TENNESSEE

A LITTLE BIT COUNTRY, A LITTLE BIT GAY

Dollywood, the theme park celebrating Dolly Parton, attracts very different groups of fans, but all are united in their love for the cinnamon rolls. — BY KIM SEVERSON

At Dollywood, the place on a Venn diagram where gay camp and Southern camp overlap, cinnamon rolls might be the great equalizer. They're more loaf than roll, really. You find them at the Grist Mill, a working water-powered replica of an old country mill inside the wildly popular theme park. Workers cut deep slashes into small loaves of bread dough and toss them into pans of cinnamon and sugar, then bake them; the crusty top gives way to soft, sugary canyons inside.

On a sunny Saturday, the women behind the counter sold about 1,200 of them—including one to me. A little plastic cup of white frosting was a dollar extra, which I gladly paid.

The hot loaves of sin are not for the gluten-free, nor for those who might select their food based on where it came from. But there didn't seem to be many of those people moving through the Grist Mill, one of the park's most popular food venues, that day.

There were, however, large groups of Southern Baptists who showed up in matching T-shirts that proclaimed their church affiliations. There were exhausted families from North Carolina trying to get Grandma out of the wilting heat. There were rowdy college students from Ohio on a summer road trip, and a single mom from Georgia looking to entertain her young son.

And then there was us, a middle-aged lesbian couple in expensive yet practical footwear who traveled from Atlanta to see if we could find the campy gay undercurrent that runs through Dollywood, arguably the most culturally conservative amusement park in the country. (It is hard to imagine Disney, for example, selling a purse with a pocket for a concealed weapon, or leather Bible covers.)

PIGEON FORGE, TENNESSEE · UNITED STATES

Previous A locomotive named Klondike Katie winds through hills above Dollywood, Dolly Parton's homespun theme park.

Left Memorabilia at Dollywood celebrates Dolly Parton's life.

Opposite The poster for *Nine to Five,* the hit 1980 movie that starred Parton, Jane Fonda, and Lily Tomlin.

In a lot of ways, we were just like the rest of the nearly three million people each year who make their way to the foothills of the Smoky Mountains, about 30 miles east of Knoxville, to enter Dollywood. We wanted to dip into the unapologetic mix of corn pone, roller coasters, and celebrity that is Dolly Parton's very lucrative Appalachian Southern fantasy.

It is hard to dislike Parton, who grew up in a family of 12 children a few miles from here in conditions so poor her father paid for her birth with a bag of grain. She left for Nashville the day after she graduated from high school and has been in the music business ever since. She is a smart and driven businesswoman and has dedicated herself to helping the poor region where she grew up. Opening the lucrative Dollywood (with business partners who already had a more limited park on the property) was part of that mission; it became the largest employer in Sevier County.

That Dolly Parton is also a gay icon would probably be news to many of the guests in cargo shorts and tennis shoes who wait patiently in line each day until "The Star-Spangled Banner" is sung and the park opens. But for the rest of us, it is not.

First of all, it's no secret that she is a patron saint of drag queens. Her look, she has said, is patterned after the bleached hair and red lipstick of the town tramp, whom she admired. It both embraces and mocks the best and worst of country glamour and feminine features.

She likes to joke that if she hadn't been born female, she would have ended up a drag queen. She even entered a drag contest (in which several Dolly Parton lookalikes were also competitors) once in Santa Monica—and lost badly.

More broadly, Dolly Parton is nothing if not a survivor, which feeds her status among her gay fans. She has defied critics, stayed true to herself, and turned stereotype into power.

Nearly every corner of Dollywood reflects that. One can see both a replica of her childhood cabin and the inside of her tour bus, her ragged childhood clothes and her glittery gowns. She embraces her roots in a way that never seems manipulated but only serves to make her entire narrative stronger.

This, in turn, has drawn gay travelers for years. Over dinner recently, a friend of mine who grew up as a gay teenager in North Carolina talked about how she and her friend, who identified themselves back then as "queer punks," would drive to Dollywood just to party in the parking lot.

Parton remains a supporter of the gay community, now broadened as LGBTQ+ "I've always been a freak and different, oddball even in my childhood and my own family," she once said in an interview. "So I can relate to people who are struggling and trying to find their true identity."

Still, neither she nor the park has fully embraced the LGBTQ+ fans who make their way there. An informal Dollywood "gay day" organized by fans in the mid-2000s (participants showed up at the park in red shirts) lasted five years. Eventually lawyers for park officials sent a letter to organizers asking them to stop using the Dollywood name. After that and threats from the Ku Klux Klan, organizers disbanded.

Dollywood has also become a magnet for gays and lesbians who work in the entertainment field or simply love the culture that surrounds Dolly Parton. But it's an odd existence in which one's personal life is sometimes lived in the shadows — a reflection of life for many LGBTQ+ residents in the rural South, where a don't-ask-don't-tell survival strategy is sometimes necessary. Raymie Wolfe, a songwriter and performer working in New York, was thrust into that culture when he came home to East Tennessee in 2003 to nurse his dying father. He and his partner, a writer, took over the 185-acre family ranch near White Pine, a small town in the shadow of the Smoky Mountains.

Wolfe took a job performing at Dollywood. He became one of the Gem Tones, a popular roving a cappella group. He and other gay Dollywood performers have formed a loose-knit alliance, he told me, and many feel that Dollywood is a safe haven in the rural South. But the mission statement of Herschend Family Entertainment, the corporation that owns the park with Parton, ends with the phrase "All in a manner consistent with Christian values and ethics." For some Christians, that means rejecting homosexuality. So, some employees told me, they fear their jobs might be at risk if they didn't keep a low profile.

"Frankly, if Dolly ever heard that, it would break her heart," said Fatima Mehdikarimi, a spokeswoman for the company. "We are technically a Christian company, but at the same time the biggest thing we have is that everybody's on the same level playing field."

Indeed, Dollywood can seem either super gay or super country, depending on one's lens. Consider the Chasing Rainbows museum, which we spent a couple of hours wandering through. The rainbow gay pride flag was created in San Francisco in the 1970s. Parton is fond of saying, "If you want the rainbow, you gotta put up with the rain." The link is only in the eye of the beholder, but still.

The museum was an interactive story of triumph over adversity, filled with elaborate displays that wound through artifacts from her childhood (love letters from former schoolmates, for example), handwritten lyrics, and shoes and glittery costumes, including her famous patchwork coat of many colors.

Walls were covered with photos of Parton and a cascade of stars, and there was a personal love note from Lily Tomlin (a lesbian icon who co-starred with Parton and Jane Fonda in the film *9 to 5*). There were several chatty references to Judy Ogle, Parton's lifelong friend. The two had been rumored to be romantically involved, but Parton said in interviews that they are just best friends. (Parton and her husband, Carl Dean, celebrated their 50th wedding anniversary in 2016.)

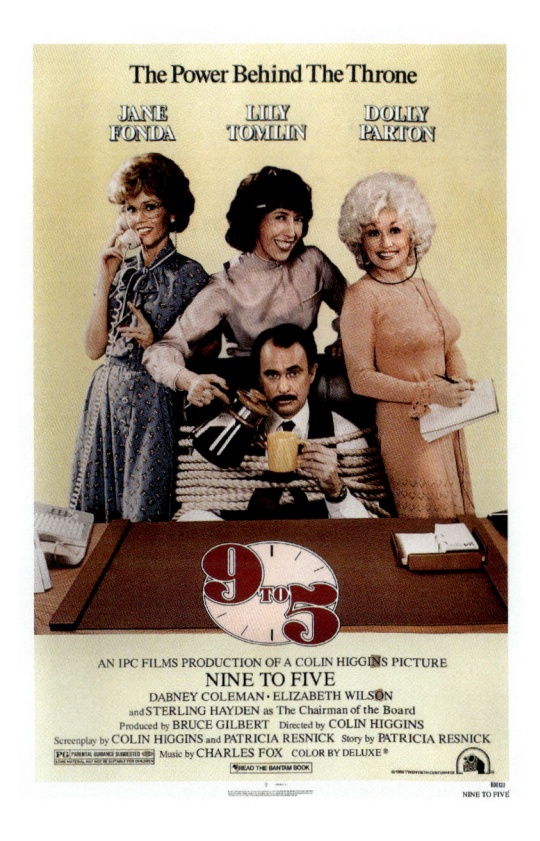

Above Fans at Dollywood. "We're in the business for all families," Parton said. "A family is a family whether you're a gay family or a straight family."

Opposite The Gem Tones, a roving group of singers, in a section of Dollywood called Jukebox Junction.

We filed into a large, mostly empty auditorium to watch "My People," Parton's personal 50-minute show featuring a five-piece band, as well as an assortment of Parton siblings and nieces. She appeared on a giant screen over the stage and interacted with the live performers in a well-timed but odd combination of video magic, singing, banjo playing, and storytelling. Lines in the song "Family," a study in familial dedication, caught my ear: "Some are preachers, some are gay. Some are addicts, drunks and strays. But not a one is turned away when it's family."

After we filed back out into the Tennessee sun, I caught up with Jada Star Andersen, a niece of Parton who performs in the show. She considers herself "a flaming liberal" in the family. Parton has close family members and staff members who are gay, she said, adding that her aunt loves that Dollywood is a mecca for gays—though that's not a sentiment shared by everyone in the family. "It's that thing where she is as loving as she can be about it, but there's also a lot of people in our family who don't like it," she said. "It's a line she walks."

I asked Parton herself about the Dollywood mix when she was promoting her DreamMore Resort, a 300-room hotel, spa, and pool complex near Dollywood. The resort's rooms were designed for traveling families, so parents could have private space but children could sleep close by. Floors have rows of adjoining rooms perfect for family reunions. But what kind of families?

"We're in the business for all families," she said. "A family is a family whether you're a gay family or a straight family. If that's your family, you should be treated with the utmost respect, and we do that no matter what. I say a good Christian wouldn't be judging anyway. We're supposed to love and accept each other."

Still, as we stood in line in Dollywood for the FireChaser Express, a backward-traveling roller

Photographs by
William Widmer

coaster that is a tribute to Appalachian firefighters, I got the distinct feeling that holding hands might not be the best idea. Parton, though, has always found a way to appeal to the better angels of the South's nature, one in which gentleness, civility, and faith shine.

That notion struck me as we climbed the stairs and prepared to strap ourselves into the Wild Eagle, a 21-story winged roller coaster that screams down the track at 60 miles per hour.

As we shuffled toward our turn, I locked eyes with a man in a goatee and a red shirt that said "My Lifeguard Walks on Water." He was holding a pan filled with a cinnamon loaf. We smiled at each other, climbed in, and took off.

Everyone, after all, loves a roller coaster.

WHAT TO READ AND WATCH

Gone Dollywood: Dolly Parton's Mountain Dream, by Graham Hoppe, part of the *New Approaches to Appalachian Studies* series. An exhaustive but readable look at Dollywood and its links to Appalachian culture.

Smart Blonde: Dolly Parton, by Stephen Miller. A biography of Parton and her brand.

Hollywood to Dollywood, directed by John Lavin. A documentary following identical twins Larry and Gary Lane, both gay Dolly Parton fans, as they cross the country hoping to meet her in Dollywood. The soundtrack includes several of Parton's songs.

9 to 5, directed by Colin Higgins. An iconic Hollywood comedy starring Jane Fonda, Lily Tomlin, and Dolly Parton. Parton's title song was an Oscar nominee.

The Dollywood cinnamon roll recipe can be found on the websites of *Travel + Leisure* magazine and the Hallmark Channel.

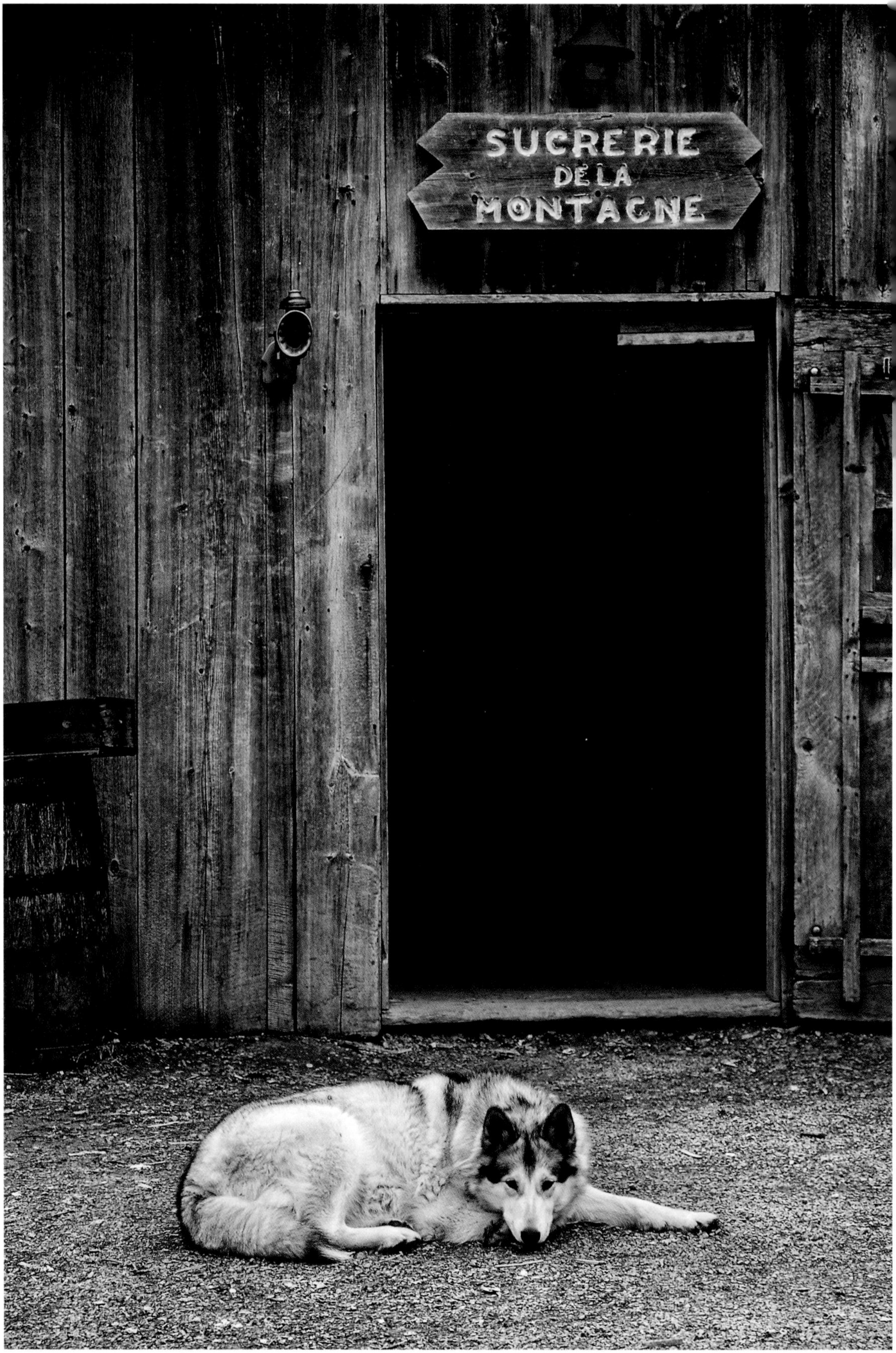
SUCRERIE
DE LA
MONTAGNE

CANADA   RIGAUD, QUEBEC

MAPLE SYRUP IS GOOD WITH EVERYTHING

In rural Quebec, urbanites congregate for a ritual of snow, folkloric music, and sweet indulgence.
— BY OLIVER STRAND

I never thought much about maple syrup until I watched it being made. I knew that tapping sugar maples and boiling the sap is one of winter's most enduring images. But it's one thing to glance at the tiny illustration that decorates almost every bottle of maple syrup (trees and snow, buckets and a cabin) and quite another to spend a frigid day visiting a Quebecois cabane à sucre, or sugar shack, and discover that it's all true: the snowy hills and horse-drawn sleigh, the buckets hanging from trees emptied by burly men with beards.

Or at least that's what I found at Sucrerie de la Montagne, a rustic compound of split-log cabins that's just a 45-minute drive from downtown Montreal, in Rigaud, but looks as though it could be from the 18th century. With just 1,500 tapped trees spread over 120 acres, it's a tiny syrup operation for Quebec, where 75 percent of the world's maple syrup supply is produced.

There are hundreds of cabanes à sucre in Quebec. Usually, a visit is just a day trip, but I was planning to spend the night, and Sucrerie de la Montagne is one of the few that offers accommodations. The rate for my two-story maisonette included dinner, traditional Quebecois foods served in a cavernous hall while a fiddle-driven rigodon band played bouncy folkloric music. Because the real reason why you go to a cabane à sucre is to eat and dance.

Originally, the feast was the daily reward for the workers who trudged waist-high in snow to collect sap. At its most traditional, it is made up of the sort of food you'd find in a larder at the end of winter: beans and salted pork, potatoes and eggs. Eventually, some cabanes à sucre started serving the public, and over

RIGAUD, QUEBEC   CANADA

Previous Downtown Montreal is only 45 minutes away, but Sucrerie de la Montagne exists in a world of rustic tradition.

Left Stirring the pot at a sugar shack in Sorel, Quebec, around 1890.

Opposite Horses, sleighs, cabins, and snow combine to give urbanites a taste of authenticity before they down their pancakes.

time the dinner was embellished. Now it's not unheard of for a cabane à sucre to serve egg rolls or hot dogs, and a few have taken the haute road, offering oysters on the half shell or grilled wild salmon.

Sucrerie de la Montagne hews to custom. So it was with understandable anticipation that a stream of wholesome-looking families poured out of their cars on a sunny Saturday in March when the parking lot was as icy as a hockey rink. A crew of teenagers in puffy jackets directed traffic as my wife and I watched the arrival of a horse-drawn sleigh the size of a small school bus. I grabbed our suitcases, and we climbed on.

We didn't go far. It was only a three-minute ride to the dining hall, where the bar doubled as the front desk. It would have been a five-minute walk on foot, though an awkward one on the icy paths with our luggage, but this was the first sleigh ride of my life, and I was nearly as giddy as the five-year-olds clambering down onto the snow.

We stepped into the entrance of the dining hall to find Pierre Faucher, the owner, chatting with some guests by a cast-iron wood-burning stove the size of a bank safe. There was no mistaking Faucher: the Père Noël beard, the bearlike build, the traditional garb complete with a ceinture fléchée — a brightly-colored sash wrapped tightly around his waist.

Mitsy, his sister-in-law, ran my credit card and gave me my key and two dining tickets. Though weekend dinners are served all day, most guests schedule their meal according to when the musicians take the stage. The next show was two hours away, at 6 p.m., so we walked to our cabin.

I was told that it had once been a pigsty, but now that the cabin was given over to humans, it was comfortable and simple, if a little rough. Upstairs was a queen-sized bed and not much else. Downstairs was a double bed with a cast-iron frame, a kitchenette, and some rocking chairs by the deep fireplace. Most important, there was an ample supply of wood. The walls, for all their handmade appeal, had a fair share of gaps, and with temperatures dipping below 10 degrees Fahrenheit at night, I was a little concerned about the chill.

But a crackling fire lulled us to sleep, and after a quick nap we set off to explore the grounds and to look at the sugar maples. These days most sugar shacks run plastic hoses from the trees to save workers the chore of trudging through the snow several times a day. But here they were still using galvanized aluminum buckets — some 3,000 of them — which had to be emptied by hand. The warmer it gets, the more the sap runs, and by the end of the season the taps can drip like leaky faucets and buckets have to be emptied two or three times a day. But it was a cold day, and the buckets were nearly empty.

We didn't stray far from the buildings, which were spread out along a short hill. They included the overnight cabins, a century-old sawmill, an office, and a store that sold maple syrup, maple syrup candy, and frontier-era crafts like rabbit pelts and rag-wool socks.

From there, it was a short walk to the large shed that held the évaporateur, the enormous steel trough where sugar maple sap is boiled down to syrup. This évaporateur was wood-fired (these days many use gas), and it filled the room with sweet-smelling steam. When the process is as artisanal as this, it takes all day to turn sap into syrup.

Later, I was told that all the buildings had been built by hand, many of them by Faucher himself, with ash and cedar hewn from trees cut down on the land. He bought the property in 1978 and then in 1981 started serving food year-round, a radical idea for the time. During maple syrup season, February through April, the restaurant serves an average of 1,500 people in a weekend.

It takes roughly 40 gallons of sap to make one gallon of syrup. The end product is worth money, enough so that when a gang of thieves stole 3,000 tons of it from the Federation of Quebec Maple Syrup Producers in 2012, the value of their haul was estimated at $18.7 million. The theft was soon dubbed the Great Canadian Maple Syrup Heist. Eventually the law caught up with the perpetrators, and one ringleader was sentenced to eight years in prison. In 2018 Netflix aired an hourlong documentary about the incident, *The Maple Syrup Heist*.

It was almost 6 o'clock by the time we reached the dining hall, and it was busy but not unpleasantly so. Stéfan, the owner's son, was handing out wineglasses of "caribou," a typical Quebecois cocktail of sweetened wine and whiskey. I took a sip, tasted the blueberry wine in the mixture, and ordered a blond ale.

We were led into a large hall with a cathedral ceiling and a stage at the far end. The sun was setting, but there was a glow from a giant stone fireplace that took up almost the entire back wall. This was the largest of three dining rooms and held around 400 people. Only half of the long, rough-hewn tables were full

Above Pails hanging from the tapped trees collect sap in the traditional way.

Opposite Pierre Faucher, owner of Sucrerie de la Montagne, checks on maple sap boiling down into syrup.

that night, but we sandwiched ourselves between a small group from Valencia, Spain, who were visiting friends in Montreal, and a couple of Quebecers who now lived in Ottawa.

For the Quebecers, this was an annual event. One of them estimated that he had eaten at 40 different cabanes à sucre in his life. "This one is the best," he said, "because it's the most traditional."

As we got acquainted, the waiters set down one-liter bottles of maple syrup with a theatrical flourish, along with loaves of white bread baked in the wood oven next door and mason jars filled with pickled beets, carrots, and tomatoes. The waiters were mostly teenagers and mostly female, and they were dressed in a vaguely traditional costume of white blouses and printed apron smocks. It was camera-ready pageantry.

The first course was hearty split-pea soup. And just as the soup bowls appeared, a fiddler and a pianist started playing rigodon music, a style that originated in the south of France and has the same rollicking exuberance you hear in Cajun music. If it's played well, you find yourself dancing before you know it.

But not before eating. A parade of waiters streamed by with platters of thick-cut ham, sausage links, piles of crisp bacon, golf-ball-size meatballs, meat pie (which the Quebecers meticulously doused with ketchup), omelets, mashed potatoes, and baked beans. The diners passed around the platters, family-style.

The table held a constant bounty. As soon as a platter was empty, it was replaced without any of us asking. The food might not have been particularly refined, but it was enormously satisfying, especially when doused with maple syrup. It turns out maple syrup goes with everything.

I should say, real maple syrup. Much of what's sold in the United States isn't pure (be wary of "pancake syrup," which is often made with corn syrup).

*Photographs by
Yannick Grandmont*

And not all pure maple syrups are the same. Large commercial operations use reverse osmosis to speed up the process, losing layers of flavor.

At its best, maple syrup is more than just sweet. It has gradations of caramel, wood, and sometimes smoke, nuances that come from the fire, the evaporation, and the open buckets. A good maple syrup is delicious on its own: at some point in the evening, everybody at the table poured a little syrup on a spoon and ate it straight.

I was stuffed by the time dessert was brought around, but I still had a few pancakes and a slice of tarte au sucre, which is custardy maple syrup baked in a crust. (Imagine pecan pie without the pecans.) By 8 p.m. the crowd started to disperse, and an hour later we were back in our cabin.

WHAT TO READ AND WATCH

The Maple Syrup Cookbook: Over 100 Recipes for Breakfast, Lunch & Dinner, by Ken Haedrich and Marion Cunningham. One of the most popular of the many maple syrup cookbooks on the market.

The Sugar Season: A Year in the Life of Maple Syrup, and One Family's Quest for the Sweetest Harvest, by Douglas Whynott. A comprehensive look at the maple syrup business from a well-regarded writer of nonfiction.

Sweet Maple: Backyard Sugarmaking from Tap to Table, by Michelle Visser. Instructions on making syrup from backyard trees, with recipes, family stories, and nutritional information.

Sugaring Time, by Kathryn Lasky, with photographs by Christopher G. Knight. A Newbery Honor book for children.

The Maple Syrup Heist, directed by Brian McGinn. A documentary in the Netflix *Dirty Money* series.

Southwest
Chinese New Year Festival & Parade
快樂之旅
就是以你為本
A blissful journey begins with our service to you.
END
JACK KEROUAC
PSYCHIC
PALM &
AROT CARD
READINGS
986.9320
TOW-AWAY NO STOPPING
TAXI ZONE
SUSIE HOT
ATM MACHINE AVAILABLE
255
GUINNESS
ST. JAMES'S GATE DUBLIN IRELAND
Vesuvio cafe
3333

LITQUAKES AND BEATS

The world's most enthusiastic book town might just be San Francisco, and not only at festival time.
— BY GREGORY DICUM

On a balmy fall evening in the Mission District of San Francisco, hundreds of people spilled onto Valencia Street, where they chatted happily for a few minutes before pouring back into bookstores, cafes, and theaters. It was a giddy, animated crowd, but most of all bookish — a collection of fans and believers, together to listen to the written word.

The occasion was an annual event called Litquake, which, over 10 days, draws thousands of residents and visitors to readings by scores of authors, many of them — like Amy Tan and Daniel Handler (a.k.a. Lemony Snicket) — local celebrities. The "Lit Crawl" finale alone has featured hundreds of readings at bars, laundromats, and even the police station, in a single evening.

Litquake, which has been around since 1999, happens once a year, but on almost any day or night in San Francisco, there is likely to be something for the literary-inclined — a poetry reading at a bar, a book swap in a cafe, a reading in the book-lined lobby of the Rex Hotel. This is the city, after all, with landmarks like Mark Twain Plaza, Alice B. Toklas Place, Frank Norris Street, Robert Frost Plaza, and the Robert Louis Stevenson Memorial.

Independent bookstores have survived, though their numbers have dwindled as rents have risen with relentless gentrification, and as Amazon has taken over much of the country's book business. The survivors rely in part on a corps of local readers who seem to view books not only as a pleasure, but as a cause.

Books, we have been told, are a half-millennium-old technology in danger of being swept away forever. So a journey to San Francisco to immerse oneself in them might seem the cultural equivalent of going

Previous Vesuvio Cafe in North Beach, where reading at the table is routine. City Lights Books is just across Jack Kerouac Alley.

Left The Beat writers who gravitated to San Francisco in the 1950s live on in the Beat Museum, home to original manuscripts, letters, and other memorabilia.

Opposite Dog Eared Books, part of San Francisco's concentration of one-of-a-kind bookstores.

to visit the glaciers before they melt. But in San Francisco, the home of many of the very technologies that have drawn a bead on the book — in its printed form, at least — visitors will find a living, historically rooted literary scene that, while battered, isn't giving up.

The same quality that gave rise to the city's proliferation of small bookstores — compact, walkable neighborhoods with a militant objection to chain stores — makes it easy for visitors to explore the city's literary terrain. Though the center of gravity has moved around over the years — from the old Barbary Coast in the days of Mark Twain and Ambrose Bierce to North Beach during the Beat era to the Haight a decade later — today the scene is most visible in and near the Mission District.

Valencia Street around 20th Street is a good place for a visitor to begin. Borderlands, a science fiction and fantasy bookstore, and Dog Eared Books, a used-book store, are surrounded by cafes and bars that host regular literary events. Not far away is Meyer Boswell, a shop that specializes in antiquarian law books.

Bolerium, on Mission Street a few blocks away, specializes in 20th-century leftist politics, including political movements that began with limited support and have since gone mainstream, like feminism and gay rights. When I visited, I found groaning shelves of books producing the wonderful side effects of deadening all sound and scenting the air with the drowsy, musty perfume of old wood pulp — intangible features of the book world we are losing.

John Durham, the owner, sat at a desk surrounded by piles of books, seeming to be at one with his cluttered environment. An expert in his field, Durham is the archetype of the bookstore obsessive. In response to a research need for a book I was working on, he drew my attention to *The Masses*, an early 20th-century radical monthly. He then pointed out a collection of lyric sheets that featured songs with titles like "Albania, Our Beacon" and "Eternal Glory to JV Stalin."

"If you sing that one," he said, "you have to make sure everyone knows you're kidding."

More one-of-a-kind bookstores are scattered around the city. If, for instance, you're exploring Noe Valley, seek out Omnivore, a tiny, carefully curated shop that fulfills the food-mad city's appetite for gastronomic literature. On Haight Street, Bound Together is a longstanding anarchist collective, a closet of a shop crammed floor to ceiling with the heavy, serious literature of a parallel universe (among the shelves, near "Magic and Spirituality," I found one marked "Against Religion"). The Green Arcade, on Market Street at the edge of Hayes Valley, focuses on sustainability and eco-living.

Even the sprawling used-book store Green Apple, on Clement Street in the Richmond, maintains a distinctive feel thanks to staff members who know their way around its shelves and around the world of books itself. "It's not the kind of thing people could create from scratch these days," said Pete Mulvihill, one of the owners.

The essential stop on a literary tour is City Lights, in the heart of North Beach, the neighborhood associated with the Beat writers of the 1950s. City Lights is the grande dame of the city's independent bookstores. Founded in 1953 by Lawrence Ferlinghetti, the poet and artist, as the first all-paperback bookstore in the country, it made its name when it published Allen Ginsberg's incendiary *Howl and Other Poems* in 1956. The matchless publicity of an enduringly influential obscenity trial made *Howl* a bestseller and—improbably—part of the American literary canon. In the process, it turned City Lights into a tourist destination.

I went down to City Lights one gloriously sunny Saturday, strolling past strip joints and seedy bars. The bookstore was comfortably bustling as I walked between the tall shelves of political philosophy and gender studies and made my way up a narrow staircase leading to the Poetry Room. There, next to a window open to the Pacific breeze, I found a chair with a hand-lettered sign tacked to the wall behind it: "Have a Seat + Read a Book." I made for the Ginsberg shelf and, bypassing the 50th-anniversary annotated edition of *Howl*, selected the slim original, still published in the same disarmingly bland cover.

I bought the book and went across the lane (Jack Kerouac Alley, where Beat verse is inlaid in the sidewalk) to the Vesuvio Cafe, a bar that was once a Beat hangout. Vesuvio is a cozy space of dark wood, tiled floors, and stained glass, with framed photos of the neighborhood greats—Kerouac, Ginsberg, Ferlinghetti—covering the walls. I ordered a shot and a beer, which seemed an apt Beat lunch, went upstairs to the narrow mezzanine, and began reading: "Visions! omens! hallucinations! miracles! ecstasies! gone down the American river!"

A couple at a table behind me were discussing Neal Cassady's role as connective tissue between the Beats and the Merry Pranksters. At a small table in the corner, light streaming in the open window next to him, a bearded, bespectacled man sat hunched over a book with the intensity of a monk, an empty glass and a stack of new books beside him. Looking up, he announced that he was reading Henry Miller's *Tropic of Cancer* in a single sitting. "I'm reading my way out of a breakup," he explained. "I read books in cafes, then leave them behind when I'm done."

This is literature as sustenance. And it is commonplace in San Francisco, where the average annual per capita expenditure on books is perennially among the highest in the United States. The same goes for alcohol. Hence all the readings in bars.

"There isn't an enormous publishing and entertainment industry in San Francisco," said Jack Boulware, a journalist and author who is one of Litquake's founders. "If you're a writer here, you

Above The heart of the book scene: City Lights, founded in 1953 by the poet Lawrence Ferlinghetti.

Opposite A scene at Vesuvio. Writers find freedom in this city, an observer said. "And everyone is stoned and sitting in cafes in the middle of the day."

aren't bound by restrictions you might find in other cities; you can express yourself and innovate and experiment."

"And," he deadpanned, "everyone is stoned and sitting in cafes in the middle of the day."

The flourishing of the literary scene in San Francisco is not accidental. Much of it stems from work by local authors who wanted to carry on a legacy that includes Jack London's smoking ruins, Dashiell Hammett's dark alleys, Jack Kerouac's dawn railroad yards, and Amy Tan's Chinatown.

"Litquake came from a group of writers sitting in a bar realizing that we needed to do something," Boulware said. "We launched at the height of dot-com fever in San Francisco. If we were less inclined to be attached to literature, we would have started websites."

Literary and artistic events proliferated, growing so numerous that Charles Kruger, a blogger, spent a summer attending 90 of them in 90 days and writing about it. Evan Karp dived into the scene by recording hundreds of author readings and posting them on YouTube. Then he founded Litseen, a website with a daily calendar of the city's literary events.

Each reading series around town has a distinctive flavor. Some regularly pack bars even on Monday nights. I attended one where a panel of judges put a group of readers through an Iron Chef–like competition. Bookswap, an event hosted by Booksmith, a beloved neighborhood store in Haight-Ashbury, is more studiously literary. Participants bring favorite books and discuss them in small groups. I took *Howl* on an evening when the novelist K. M. Soehnlein helped lead the discussion.

"The longer you are in San Francisco, the more you realize it is just one big scene with a lot of different ways of making itself known," said Soehnlein, whose own novels, including *You Can Say You Knew Me When*

Photographs by
Thor Swift and Jason Henry

and *Robin and Ruby*, live on the gay-lit shelf. "In San Francisco people ask more questions. In New York or Los Angeles it's like crickets out there, even if they are very attentive. Do they think they're too cool to ask questions?"

At that point, crickets sounded appealing to me — I needed to find somewhere to put the finishing touches on a piece I was planning to read at Litquake. I headed for the Mechanics Institute Library.

Founded in 1854, this little-known gem is the oldest library on the West Coast. Its nine-story building houses reading rooms, a top-floor chess room, and 160,000 books. I bought a day pass to gain entry, then I walked inside into Gilded Age splendor.

Amid its marble, oak, and cast iron, the library had a cozy feeling. I settled into a desk by a window, pulled out my project, and fell into another world.

That's what readers and writers do.

WHAT TO READ AND WATCH

The Place That Inhabits Us: Poems of the San Francisco Bay Watershed, edited by Sixteen Rivers Press. An anthology of poetry about the area, by writers famous and not.

San Francisco Stories: Great Writers on the City, edited by John Miller. A collection by writers ranging from Jack London to Jack Kerouac to Anne Lamott.

The Beat Generation in San Francisco: A Literary Tour, by Bill Morgan, edited by Lawrence Ferlinghetti. A guidebook to the haunts of the Beat writers, with accompanying stories.

Cool Gray City of Love: 49 Views of San Francisco, by Gary Kamiya. A portrait of the city focusing on 49 sites. "Kamiya's relish is contagious." — *The San Francisco Chronicle*.

Ferlinghetti: A Rebirth of Wonder, directed by Christopher Felver. Released in 2009, the year Lawrence Ferlinghetti turned 90.

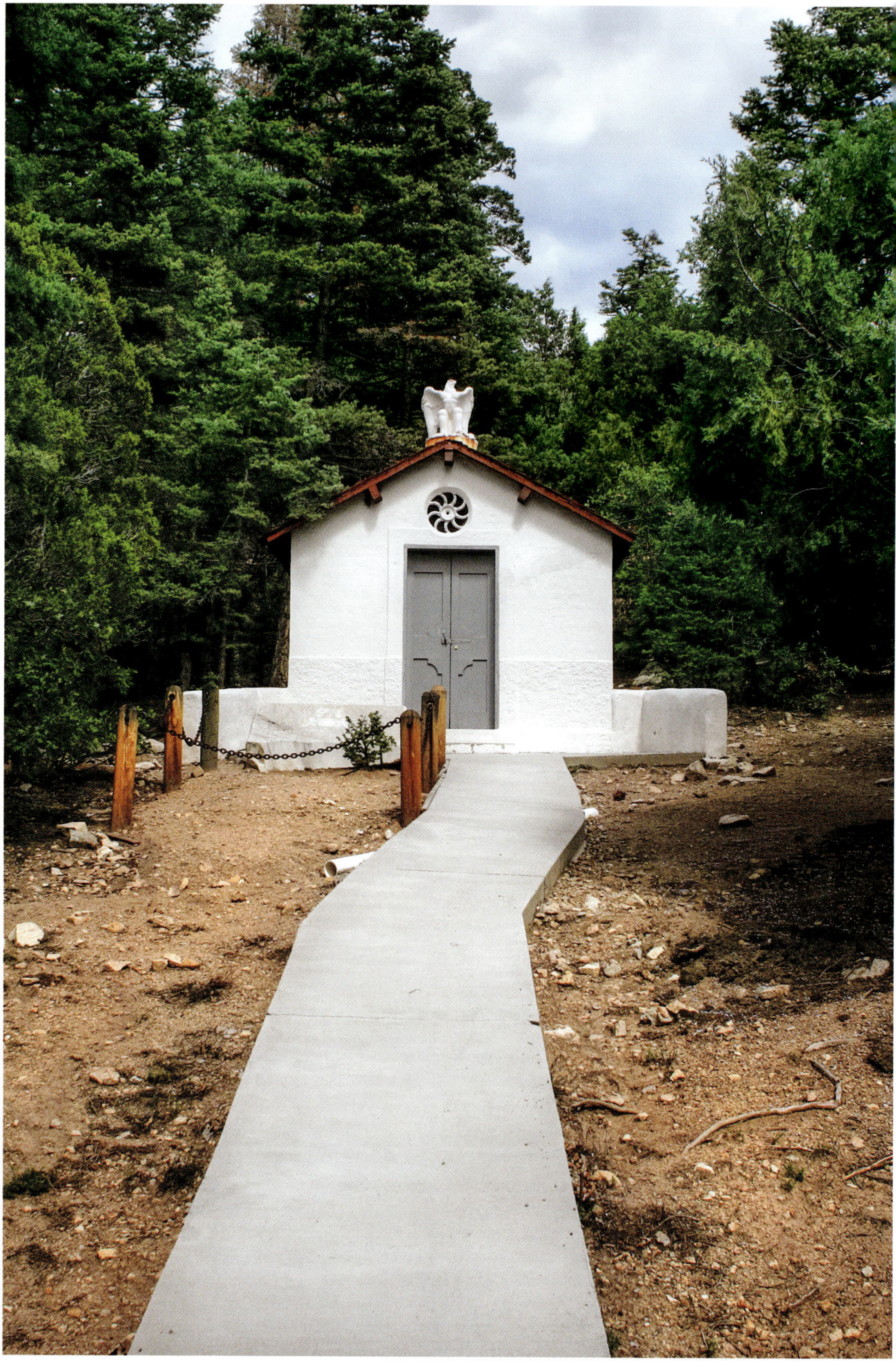

THE NEW MEXICO THAT SPOKE TO D. H. LAWRENCE

He felt the grip of Taos, where his ranch is now his memorial, and knew the powerful presence of its mountains. — BY HENRY SHUKMAN

There's something about the first glimpse of the Taos Mesa as you travel north from Santa Fe, up the narrow canyon of the Rio Grande past Embudo. A series of long, sweeping bends brings you over a brow, and suddenly the view ahead opens out onto empty, bare land, with a smoky gorge cut into it like the Great Rift Valley of Africa. Ten miles off stands a bulk of dark, brooding mountains. One of the biggest, bald Taos Mountain, sits bolted to the plain like a remonstrance. At its foot the town of Taos spreads like litter glinting in the sun.

It would be impossible to live at the foot of that mountain for a thousand years, as the people of the Taos Pueblo have done, and not come to think of it as sentient — the Kong of northern New Mexico. This was, in a sense, why the painters who "colonized" the area in the early 1900s came. As one of them, Maynard Dixon, put it: "You can't argue with those desert mountains — and if you live among them enough — like the Indian does — you don't want to. They have something for us much more real than some imported art style."

D. H. Lawrence, who came to Taos partly in search of a welcoming place to write and partly to ease the symptoms of tuberculosis, felt the power of those mountains, the sense of something present. He wrote of the desert winter:

"In a cold like this, the stars snap like distant coyotes, beyond the moon. And you'll see the shadows of actual coyotes, going across the alfalfa field. And the pine trees make little noises, sudden and stealthy, as if they were walking about. And the place heaves with ghosts. But when one has got used to one's own home-ghosts, be they never so many, they are like

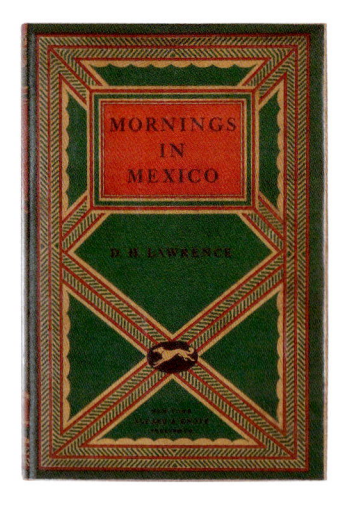

Previous The D.H. Lawrence Memorial is on Lawrence's ranch, the only home he ever owned.

Left A first edition of *Mornings in Mexico*. In some of its essays, D.H. Lawrence wrote poetically about his New Mexico ranch.

Below Taos Gorge, a part of the landscape where Lawrence came with his wife, Frieda, for clear air and literary inspiration.

one's own family, but nearer than the blood. It is the ghosts one misses most, the ghosts there, of the Rocky Mountains."

That's Lawrence's prose at full throttle: Lawrence the poet as much as the novelist. The book was *Mornings in Mexico*, and he was writing about his ranch in Taos.

The American modernists who clustered in this part of New Mexico in the early decades of the last century had a creed: Taos would be a fount of a new Americanism in art, an ever-flowing alternative to Europe. But Taos also had its appeal for Europeans. Lawrence, Aldous Huxley, Carl Jung, and Leopold Stokowski were only a few of the European artists and thinkers who found their way there. The reason they went was one pioneering American woman.

It was from the foot of Taos mountain that Mabel Dodge Luhan—heiress, patroness, columnist, early proponent (and victim) of psychoanalysis, memoirist, and hostess—planned the rebirth of Western civilization. She moved to Taos from the East Coast in 1917 and fell in love not only with the place but also with Tony Lujan (later anglicized to Luhan), a chief in the nearby pueblo. She promptly left her third husband, married Tony, and expanded a house on the edge of town, turning it into an adobe fantasy castle (what Dennis Hopper, who owned it in the 1970s, would later call the Mud Palace), and began to invite scores of cultural luminaries. The idea was to expose them to the Indian culture she believed held the cure for anomic, dissociated modern humanity. After dinner, drummers and dancers from the pueblo would entertain the household.

Today her house is a museum, guesthouse, and literary shrine all in one. For anyone on the trail of Lawrence in New Mexico, it's an essential port of call. As I made my way up the groaning narrow stairs, the sense not just of history but of peace hit me: no TVs, no jangling telephones. Instead, the deep quiet of an old, applianceless home. The house has a bathroom with windows that Lawrence painted in colorful geometric and animal designs in 1922 to protect Mabel Luhan's modesty. The floorboards are the same ones that Ansel Adams, Alfred Stieglitz, Georgia O'Keeffe, and Thomas Wolfe creaked across. (Wolfe stayed only one night. He arrived late and drunk, decided he didn't like it, and fled the next morning.)

With its kiva fireplaces and gleaming cabinets of books, the Mabel Dodge Luhan House is a strange mix of adobe curvaceousness and a country house fit for an Agatha Christie mystery. Behind it, sage scrub sweeps up to the hills. Before it, a rough-hewed colonnade gives onto a courtyard of uneven flagstones. At each corner of the main building giant adobe buttresses keep the walls up, as if they might otherwise slump like wet sand.

It's a fascinating place to stay, with all the rooms eccentrically different. The best is Luhan's solarium at the top of the house, a glassed-in room where in spring you can watch blizzards of fluffy seeds float among cottonwoods and birches gauzy with new leaf. Through the trees to the north, the blue massif of Taos Mountain looms.

Luhan particularly set her sights on Lawrence, seeing in him her ideal spokesman. She pleaded with famous friends to intercede and even sent Lawrence's wife, Frieda, a necklace steeped in irresistible Indian magic. Her schemes worked, and Lawrence arrived in 1922. But relations between Luhan and the Lawrences soon soured, and she packed them off to a ranch she owned in the mountains 17 miles north of Taos.

Today the University of New Mexico administers the ranch, running limited opening hours for visitors and occasional lectures and events. It's the second essential place to follow Lawrence in New Mexico.

On one of my trips to the D. H. Lawrence ranch, snow lay on the ground, the roofs were crisp with a frozen bed of it, and long gray icicles hung from the gutters like beards on old-time Russian mystics. The bottoms of the clouds drifted through the big ponderosas. My mother was with me, visiting from England, and was overawed to be standing in the home of her early-adulthood hero. "Why did he ever leave?" she kept musing aloud, as we peered through the windows into the locked cabin.

Lawrence was here three times from 1922 to 1925. He spent only 11 months in total in New Mexico. But the ranch was the only home he ever owned. With her undaunted generosity, Luhan gave it to him. The Lawrences didn't like feeling indebted, and in return they gave her the manuscript of his novel *Sons and*

Previous Mabel Dodge Luhan lured Lawrence to her house in the shadow of Taos Mountain and hoped he would stay.

Above Trinidad Archuleta from the Taos Pueblo painted this mural on the Lawrences' cabin.

Opposite The house where Luhan hosted literary and artistic celebrities. Dennis Hopper called it the Mud Palace.

Lovers. It was a move they would regret when they discovered that as much as they loved the ranch, it was worth $1,000, whereas the manuscript might have fetched $50,000.

The ranch seems to have less to do with the Southwest of the Indian that Lawrence was looking for than with that of the cowboy. Three old log cabins with dark planks, low roofs, and rough board doors have the look of the haven of one of those cantankerous old mountain men in a Western. Inside, the cabin originally had a "blood floor," I was told by a local man who knew the place well. Apparently cow's blood was mixed with adobe to make a smooth, slick surface. Wood was too expensive.

The blood is gone now, replaced by boards. But outside a painting of a buffalo is fading on the cracked adobe wall. It was painted by Trinidad Archuleta, a man from the Taos Pueblo, who signed his name "TRNRDOD."

Next door to the Lawrences' house is a cabin maybe eight feet square, with a small stove. This was where Dorothy Brett, an English aristocrat and painter who doggedly followed Lawrence around the world, sometimes stayed. Hard of hearing and permanently armed with a long ear-trumpet, she had probably fallen in love with Lawrence and followed him to New Mexico after a disastrous affair with the writer and editor John Middleton Murry, whose wife, the writer Katherine Mansfield, had died only three months before. (The gossip of one time becomes the literary history of the next.) She lingered on in Taos after Lawrence had gone, living in a nearby house until her death in 1977.

Lawrence had his own reasons for coming to New Mexico. It had the high, dry, clean air that eased the symptoms of his tuberculosis. But he also hoped to pursue a dream he'd had for years of founding a utopian community, to be called Rananim. With Lady

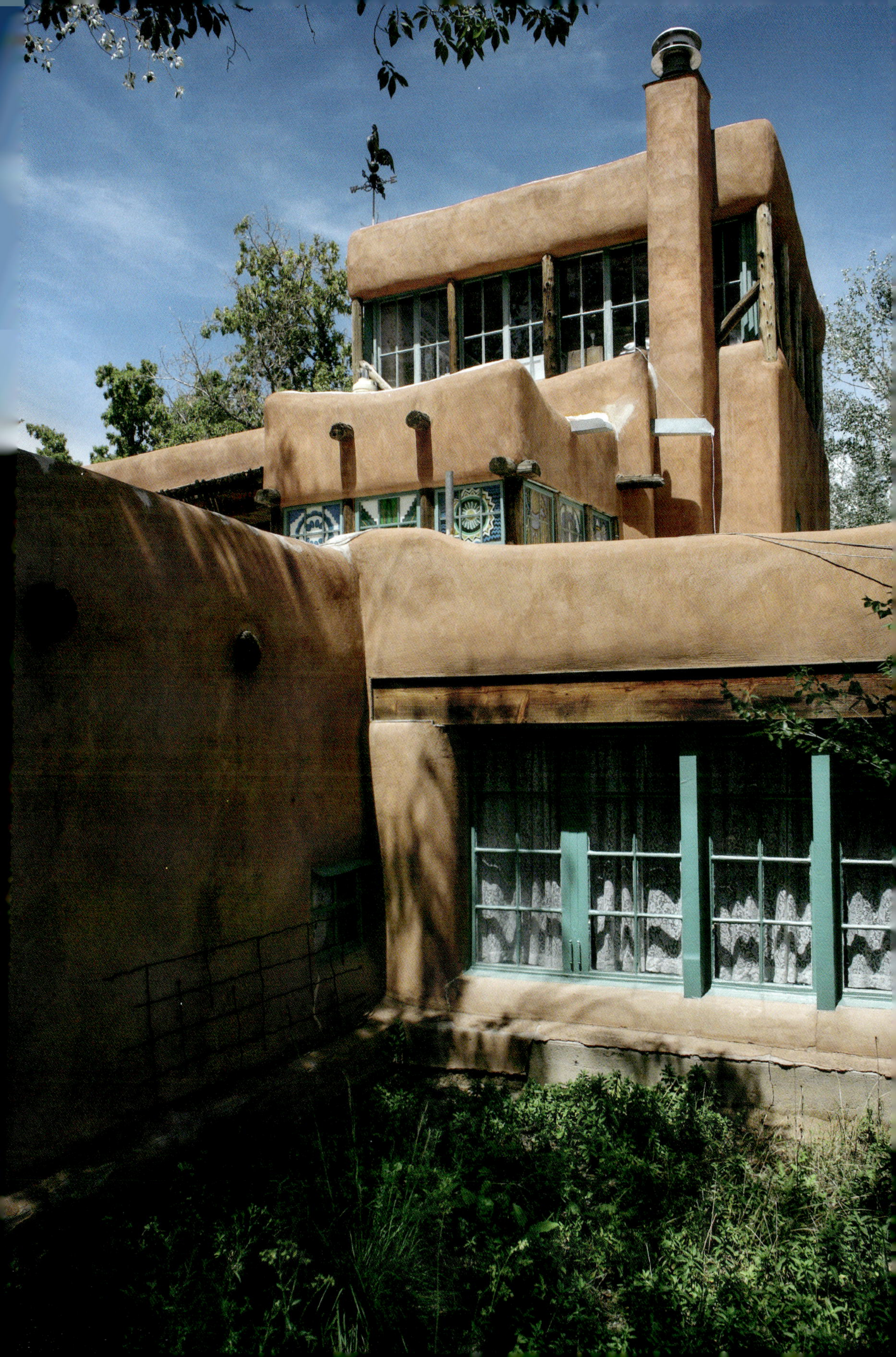

Above Proving that he was an artist as well as a novelist, Lawrence painted these designs on Luhan's windows in 1922.

Opposite Frieda is said to have embedded Lawrence's ashes in the concrete of his memorial to keep them from Luhan.

Brett next door, and Lawrence and Frieda in the main cabin, this was as close as Rananim ever came to reality: three Europeans flung up a mountain north of Taos.

Here Lawrence not only wrote under a lofty pine later immortalized by O'Keeffe in her 1929 painting *The Lawrence Tree*; he also began to dabble in painting himself, signing his canvases "Lorenzo." Today nine Lawrence oils hang in La Fonda Hotel on Taos plaza. They were exhibited in London in 1929, but the show was closed at once on grounds of obscenity, a move prompted more by Lawrence's notoriety as the author of *Lady Chatterley's Lover* than by the paintings, which are tame. After Lawrence died, Frieda Lawrence continued to live in New Mexico, and the paintings wound up in La Fonda. Their leering faces, awkward postures, and swaths of muddily painted human flesh — something like Gauguin on a very bad day — now make up the hotel's small Lawrence gallery.

Lawrence died in Provence in 1930, and five years later Frieda arranged for his ashes to be shipped to Taos, where she was building a mausoleum at the ranch. It seems she and Mabel Dodge Luhan had divergent plans for his ashes. Luhan thought Lawrence would have wanted them scattered, while his wife, who died in Taos in 1956, intended them for the shrine. To end the debate, she is said to have tipped the urn into a batch of fresh cement, ensuring that the remains wound up in her memorial. According to some locals, Frieda Lawrence, ever mindful of Lady Brett and Luhan, then declared: "Now let's see them steal him."

In many ways Luhan's message to the world worked. She put Taos, where she died in 1962, on the map as one of the preeminent centers of American modernism. And under Hopper's stewardship in the 1970s, the old house continued to be host to a glowing countercultural guest list, including Bob Dylan and Leonard Cohen.

*Photographs by
Rick Scibelli Jr.*

Lawrence may have been incurably restless, but I can understand my mother's bewilderment at why he ever left his ranch. Northern New Mexico is one of those places that exert a power over the imagination that is a kind of love. As Lawrence put it: "It is the ghosts one misses most, the ghosts there, of the Rocky Mountains, that never go beyond the timber. I know them, they know me: We go well together."

WHAT TO READ AND WATCH

Mornings in Mexico, by D. H. Lawrence. Lawrence's observations, in short essays, of places and people he saw while living in New Mexico and Mexico in the 1920s.

Utopian Vistas: The Mabel Dodge Luhan House and the American Counterculture, by Lois Palken Rudnick. Scholarly but readable.

Edge of Taos Desert: An Escape to Reality, by Mabel Dodge Luhan. An adventurous thinker's account of her discovery of the American Southwest and its transformative effect on her life.

D. H. Lawrence: The Life of an Outsider, by John Worthen. Insightfully and readably explores the interplay of Lawrence's life experiences and his novels.

Priest of Love, directed by Christopher Miles. A film portrayal of Lawrence's last 18 years, beginning with his arrival in Taos. Ian McKellen plays Lawrence, and Ava Gardner is Mabel Dodge Luhan.

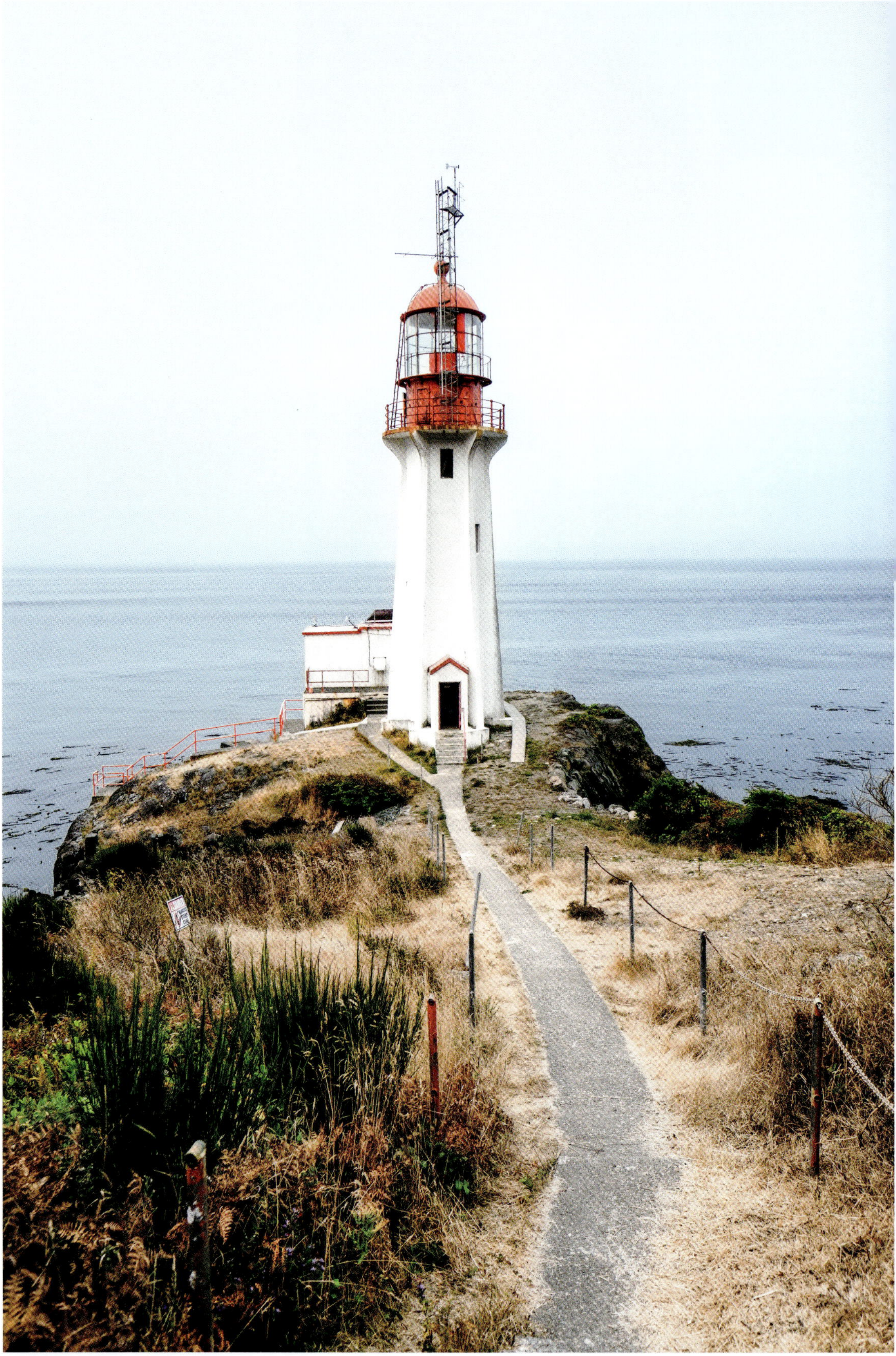

THE ARTIST OF VANCOUVER ISLAND

Emily Carr, the iconic Canadian painter, brought a unique, mystic vision to the deep forests and brooding clouds of British Columbia. — BY SUZANNE MACNEILLE

A light rain was falling in Victoria, but it wasn't keeping anyone inside on a Saturday afternoon. The horse-drawn carriages and pedicabs were out in force, a ska band was tuning up by the harbor, and all along Wharf Street, people strolled, most of them without umbrellas. This was British Columbia, after all, and no one was going to let a little rain get in the way.

Fresh off the ferry from the mainland, a friend and I joined the other sodden tourists heading to the splendid buildings of the Inner Harbour: the British Columbia Parliament complex, with its arched doorways, domes, and oceanic lawn, and the Fairmont Empress, a grande dame of a hotel where the ritual of afternoon tea is alive and well for those who want to immerse themselves in what Emily Carr once called "the most English-tasting bit of all Canada."

Carr is the unexpected element in this scene: an aging woman from another era, with a monkey on her shoulder, a dog at her feet, and a pad of paper on her lap. She sits — or rather a bronze sculpture of her sits — in the center of everything: on the grounds of the Empress, a place where she experienced both intense joy (in its conservatory) and acute boredom (in the tearoom).

Painter, writer, admirer of forests and totem poles, skeptical observer of human nature, environmentalist before the word was popular, Carr was an ardently independent woman at a time when women weren't necessarily applauded for striking out on their own. Born here in 1871, she is an unlikely symbol of not just Victoria and Vancouver Island, but, some would say,

VANCOUVER ISLAND, BRITISH COLUMBIA   CANADA

Previous Sheringham Point Lighthouse signals treacherous waters in the Juan de Fuca Strait.

Left Emily Carr, born on Vancouver Island in 1871, painted its landscapes and indigenous culture with an intense reverence.

Opposite A Carr painting of local woodland. "Down deep we all hug something," she wrote. "The great forest hugs its silence."

the whole of British Columbia. How she attained that status is a tale of devotion — her own devotion — to her art, certainly, but also to the nature and culture of Pacific Canada.

Her paintings of the landscapes of British Columbia are rich and intensely colorful, some light-filled seascapes, others brooding forest interiors and portraits — there is no other word for them — of trees, whether towering red cedar or fledgling pine. The best of her work is animated with an almost palpable energy — "the singing movement of the whole," as she called it. Her vision resonates in a time when environmental threats are of great concern.

Traveling in southern Vancouver Island, my ultimate goal was to get a sense of the land through her eyes.

On a gray but dry morning, we paid a visit to James Bay, a pretty neighborhood of old houses and tidy gardens. In 1863, Emily's father, Richard Carr, purchased a sizable property, erected an Italianate-style house, and turned his land into English gardens, cow pastures, and fields. It was a magical place for Emily. In a memoir of her childhood, she writes about the flowers ("our wild Canadian lilies…white with bent necks and brown eyes looking back into the earth"); her older sisters; and her gentle, unwell mother. On visits to her father's import business on Wharf Street, she could observe with great interest the Songhees First Nations reserve across the harbor.

Carr would eventually travel in Canada, the United States, and Europe. But most of her life was spent in James Bay, where she lived; worked; and in a priory that is now an inn, died, in 1945.

She worked for many years before her art found recognition. Painting didn't pay the bills, and so she ran a boardinghouse on Simcoe Street where her tenants ranged from "inanimate, mincing ninnies" to "door slammers." Around the corner is the Emily Carr House, her family home, now a National Historic Site. Its small rooms are crammed with books, prints, old china, furniture, and, in high season, Emily Carr fans.

We explored Beacon Hill Park, the subject of many Carr paintings. Western red cedars, Douglas firs, ponds, peacocks, frothy fountains, stone bridges (one is now named for Carr) — it is an enchanting park, and, occasionally, a place of high drama. As we strolled, a terrible screeching arose. It was nesting season, and dozens of great blue herons burst from the mid-reaches of some tall trees. The reason for their frenzy: a bald eagle circling overhead patiently, menacingly. It was a drama that showed no signs of abating by the time we left.

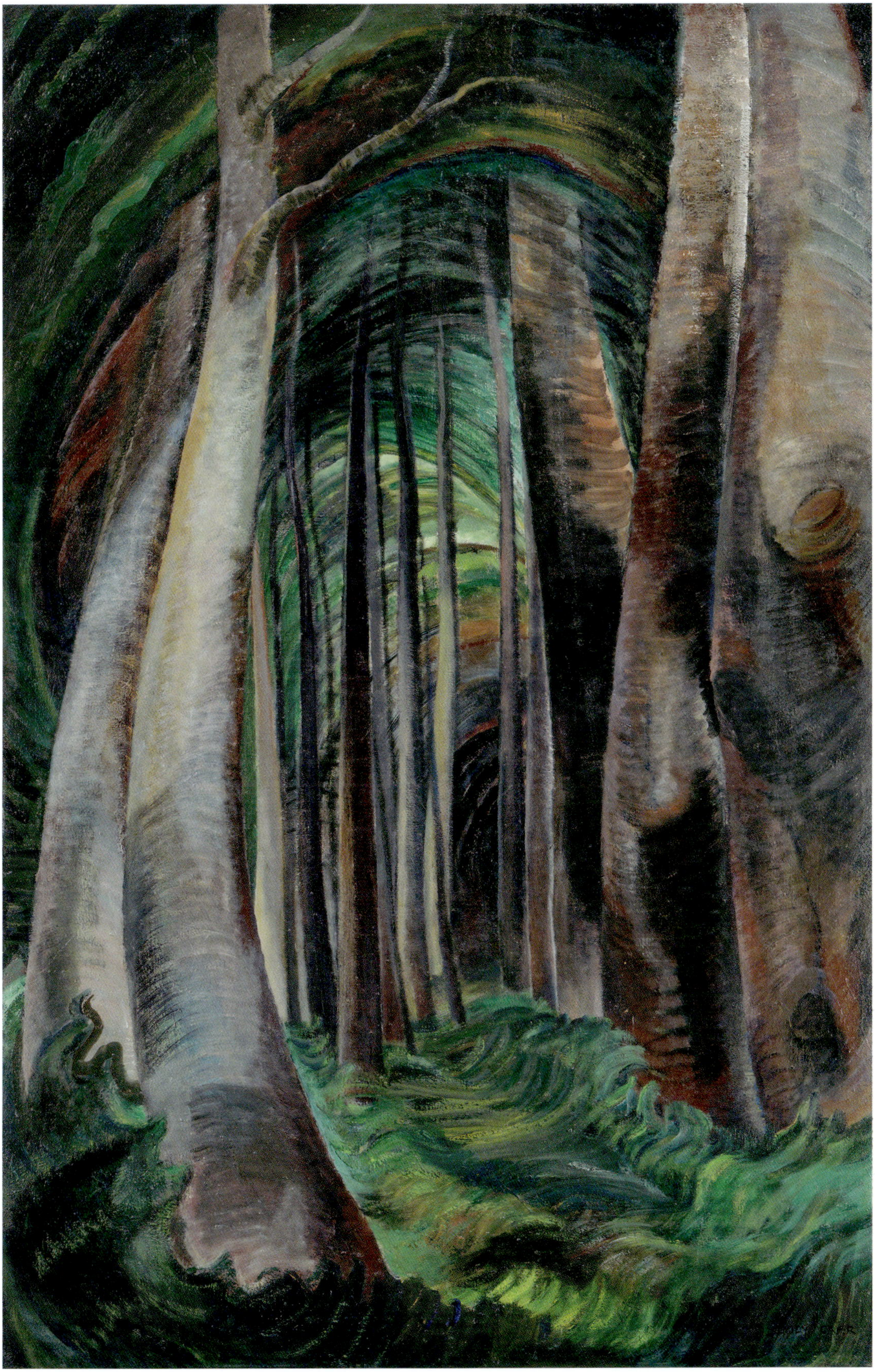

When Emily was a teenager, her mother died, and she became mysteriously distant from her father. Though she would remain close to her older sisters and had a few friends, loneliness remained a constant theme in her journals. She once compared herself to "a lone old tree." But she also took pleasure in solitude, writing stories deep into the night and sketching during the day. Success for her was a complex, spiritual matter; the business of melding art and godliness was an unending quest. And she had her animals for company: a Javanese monkey that got into all sorts of trouble, multiple dogs, and a white rat.

And then there was the forest. "I sought my companionship out in the woods and trees rather than persons," she wrote. "It was as if they had hit and hurt me...so that I went howling back like a smacked child to Mother Nature."

And so, with the aid of a trailer-like caravan she called the Elephant, she began producing some of her best work as she entered her 60s. "Nothing ever, ever stands still," she wrote, "and we never, never catch up."

It doesn't take long to find wilderness on Vancouver Island. Ten miles out of Victoria, we walked down a wide trail in Goldstream Provincial Park, more than 900 acres of Douglas fir, cedar, hemlock, and other trees. Through it all runs a river where salmon spawn each fall.

Emily Carr loved to anthropomorphize; after reading about her brown-eyed lilies and screaming trees, it was easy to imagine that the giant fern fronds on the trail weren't just brushing against our legs, but reaching out beseechingly, or at least curiously.

In 1933, Emily had the Elephant towed to the Goldstream River flats, and there she settled down for a lengthy visit. It wasn't her first. A few years earlier she had been there, producing sketches in which, say, a cedar branch was not a static thing, but a moving wave of foliage. (One of her most famous works, *Red Cedar*, illustrates this effect.) No doubt she expected to experience the same productivity this time, but a parade of parkgoers wasn't helping. "They started early this morning — the Public," she wrote. "The air is riled up with motor snorts, dog parks, and children's screechings." Add to that the antics of Woo, her monkey — who consumed her green paint and had to be treated with Epsom salts — and the rain

Opposite The Emily Carr House in Victoria, where the artist was born in 1871, is a museum and interpretive center.

Above Hiking in Goldstream Provincial Park, a wilderness enclave about 10 miles from Victoria.

and the darkness. "I am not afraid, but it's creepy," she wrote, before leaving.

Moving on, we stopped in the Royal Roads Forest, a hauntingly beautiful woodland where some of the largest Douglas firs on the island are found, and then drove to Esquimalt Lagoon, a fragile bird sanctuary protected by a wisp of land. Carr, seduced by the "wide sweeps of sea and sky," arrived there on a beautiful spring day in 1934. Her caravan was deposited on a field of daisies. "Woo rolls among the daisies with her four hands in the air," she wrote happily. But that night, an epic storm rolled in: "Everything inside blew out and outside things blew in till in and out were all mixed up."

A few years later she would return to this area off the coast and find inspiration in something that was basically ugly: gravel pits. Paintings called *Above the Gravel Pit* show scenes of denuded land and tree stumps, all beneath a brilliant, rippled sky. There would be more paintings of bare landscapes, some with spindly second- or third-growth trees struggling upward beneath a blue sky.

"There's a torn and splintered ridge across the stumps I call the 'screamers,'" Carr wrote. "These are the unsawn last bits, the cry of the tree's heart, wrenching and tearing apart just before she gives that sway and the dreadful groan of falling, that dreadful pause while her executioners step back with their saws and axes resting and watch." Later on our trip, those words would resonate.

Still on the island's southern coast, we found Albert Head beach, edged with trees and strewn with driftwood, an understated arc of paradise on a developed part of the island's shore. Here and nearby, Carr found fodder for luminous sky-and-sea paintings like *Strait of Juan de Fuca* and *Lagoon at Albert Head*.

In the artsy resort town of Sooke, where we stayed one night, our waitress warned, "You will lose

Above Sombrio Beach, a desolate spot reachable by forest trails.

Opposite The British Columbia Parliament building in Victoria. A bronze statue of Carr is nearby.

coverage" when we described our planned route, northwest up the coast of the island, then circling back toward the east and south to return to Victoria. "But you will see animals, guaranteed. I saw elk and eagles and bears last time."

She told us that she had been born on the island, moved to Toronto, and returned. "Sometimes I kayak to work," she said.

Earlier, a park volunteer had expressed similar enthusiasm when we told her we were on our way to the wild western coast. "Nothing but ocean till you get to Japan!" she said.

I thought of Carr, who had generally been eager to return home from her travels.

In her journal, she recounts an exchange with a Vancouver art promoter: "'It's a shame to think of you stuck out here in this corner of the world unnoticed and unknown,' says he. 'It's exactly where I want to be,' says I."

Continuing our travels, we found trails to places where the trees closed around us and the forest floor was laced with ferns. Some led to desolate beaches like Sombrio Beach, strewn with driftwood and coffee-colored ribbons of kelp, as shiny as glass in the sun. At Botanical Beach, tide pools were filled with limpets, mussels, and sea anemones. At Avatar Grove, situated off a steep and deeply potholed road, a boardwalk and stairs led to ancient Douglas firs and red cedars. We felt immersed in what we saw in paintings like Carr's *Wood Interior* series, and in journal entries where she wrote about "the awful solemnity of age-old trees," or the forests' "helter-skelter magnificence."

Away from the coast, we circled back to our starting point — past valleys, sunlit meadows, streams, grazing elk. And then, abruptly, the landscape changed. Felled trees, like matchsticks, tumbled messily down steep slopes. It looked like a massacre,

Photographs by
Robert Leon

limbs strewn carelessly, gnawed bones after a meal. Shadows of clouds rippled across the bare hills in the late afternoon. So this was what clear-cutting looks like. We were speechless.

"They are their own tombstones and their own mourners," Carr wrote of the remnants of trees that had been cut down.

We remained silent as we drove through the more populated wine-growing country of the Cowichan Valley. And then, all at once, we were on the last stretch, lined with gas stations and motels, back to Victoria. Once there, we still needed to find Emily's grave, walk along her beloved Dallas Road, and, if time allowed, return to Beacon Hill to check on the herons.

To the south, clouds were rolling in off the water, but we weren't going to let a little rain stop us.

WHAT TO READ AND WATCH

Hundreds and Thousands: The Journals of Emily Carr. Carr's journal entries are a delight to read and include many anecdotes about her camping trips and the places where she found inspiration.

Emily Carr: A Biography, by Maria Tippett. First published in 1979, Tippett's detailed biography goes deep into the artist's personal life and career.

The Forest Lover, by Susan Vreeland. A fictionalized account of the life of Emily Carr.

Emily Carr's B.C.: Book One, Vancouver Island, by Laurie Carter. An exhaustive and entertaining guide by an Emily Carr aficionado, part of a series of Emily Carr guides.

Winds of Heaven, directed by Michael Ostroff. This documentary on Carr pairs her paintings with contemporary photos of the scenes they depicted. Narration in Carr's own words is read by the actress Diane D'Aquila.

SMOKED
FISH

UNITED STATES   WALLOON LAKE, MICHIGAN

HEMINGWAY'S 'LAST GOOD COUNTRY'

Finding his way as a writer, Ernest Hemingway returned again and again to his memories of the woods and streams of northern Michigan.
— BY JOHN O'CONNOR

In 1898, the year before Ernest Hemingway was born, his parents bought 200 feet of frontage on Walloon Lake in northern Michigan, out in the backlands of Petoskey, a Lake Michigan resort town. The Hemingways were fresh off a luxury Great Lakes steamship from Oak Park, Illinois, looking to chuck the suburban grind for the seasonal joys of lake country. For $400 they soon had a 20-by-40-foot clapboard cottage built in Ojibwe country that was short on nearly every amenity except peace and quiet. It wasn't pioneer life — they had brought along a maid — but the surrounding woods were populated by black bears, lumberjacks, and bootleggers. Most crucially for "Ernie," who would eventually pack all this stuff into his fiction, the fishing was extraordinary.

"Absolutely the best trout fishing in the country. No exaggeration," he later wrote to a friend about the Petoskey area, perhaps exaggerating a tad but hitting on an essential truth of summer in the Michigan boonies: "It's a great place to laze around and swim and fish when you want to. And the best place in the world to do nothing. It is beautiful country...And nobody knows about it but us."

By all accounts, northern Michigan had a seismic effect on Ernest Hemingway and his future work. He spent his first 21 summers there, fishing, hunting, drinking, and chasing girls — with the notable exception of 1918, when he was in Europe driving an ambulance in World War I.

Hemingway's Michigan was a place where men lived hard and lean, ran trotlines to catch the fish, and considered bilge water a beverage. "Good stuff for essays," he wrote in a 1916 journal entry, recording fishing-trip details he would later channel into his Nick Adams short stories. "Old Couple on Boardman,"

WALLOON LAKE, MICHIGAN UNITED STATES

Previous Fishing is still the lifeblood of the region in Michigan, where Ernest Hemingway learned to love the outdoors.

Left A clutch of Hemingways and friends in the area around Petoskey in 1920. Ernest is second from right.

Opposite Generations of enthusiasts have come here to fish. This memorial is near the Sturgeon River.

he wrote, referring to a river. "Mancelona-Indian girl, Bear Creek…tough talking lumberjack, young Indian girl, kills self and girl."

It's an odd juxtaposition to think of Hemingway, years later, sipping espresso in Paris cafes while writing about Nick Adams — a semi-autobiographical stand-in for his own manly wanderings in the Michigan wilds. Take the famous Adams story "Big Two-Hearted River": "Holding the rod far out toward the uprooted tree and sloshing backward in the current," he wrote, "Nick worked the trout, plunging, the rod bending alive, out of the danger of the weeds into the open river."

Many of those 25-odd Adams stories — including extraordinary nuggets like "The End of Something" and "The Last Good Country" — as well as his first published novel, *The Torrents of Spring*, are set in and around Petoskey. And Michigan pops up again and again in later such works as *The Snows of Kilimanjaro* and *A Moveable Feast*.

Yet even Hemingway fans might draw a blank on his Michigan connection. Havana, Key West, Idaho, Paris, Pamplona — these locales tend to conjure vintage Papa: a kerchiefed, bloated, rum-drunk Nobel laureate. Petoskey? Not so much. The gatekeepers of Hemingway's legend have largely ignored the place.

As a native Michigander, I feel I can pose the question: Perhaps northern Michigan, despite its inexhaustible beauty, isn't that sexy?

But if you want to understand the writer, you have to start here. Michigan-era Hemingway is threshold Hemingway — young and raw, before the fame and subcutaneous padding and 16-daiquiri lunches. It's where he experimented in delinquency, learned to cast a fly rod, stepped unmoored into the wilderness, and experimented with a prose style that would one day make him famous.

Despite having grown up three hours south of Petoskey and having fished many of the local waters that Hemingway did, I couldn't recall ever setting foot in the town. Nowadays I live out East and rarely find my way back home. And so, one June, I finally made it to Michigan, intent on tracing Hemingway's boyhood orbit and seeing the country where Nick Adams came of age.

Driving up the east coast of Lake Michigan to Glen Arbor, I cut across the pinkie of Michigan's mitten-shaped Lower Peninsula to Traverse City, known for its cherry crop, and then bent north. I chugged through terraced farmland dusted with pollen and yacht-filled beach towns jammed with fudge shops and lighthouses and broad, sugary dunes sliding into the water. In Petoskey, which sits on a bluff overlooking Little Traverse Bay, a warm breeze swept off the lake and wheeled and skidded through the streets.

Petoskey is the kind of place where, at least in summer, everyone seems to be wearing tank tops and eating ice cream. The year-round population count, 6,000, is the same as it was in Hemingway's day, and in some ways, little has changed. My hotel, Stafford's Perry, even hosted the great man for a night in 1919. There is a photo from that time of a teenage Hemingway, corncob pipe in his mouth, holding three good-size trout. Taken right after he returned from Italy, where he had been wounded in the war, it captures a cataclysmic moment in American literature. Hemingway was gathering himself, nurturing a different kind of wound, one that would soon find expression in his fiction.

In the morning I drove out to Walloon Lake, 10 miles south of town. The water, a pure cerulean, seemed to have been piped in from Bermuda. I took off my shoes and waded in.

Walloon ranked low among Hemingway's hallowed fishing spots, as it fell within his mother's jurisdiction; the two maintained testy relations for much of their lives. He preferred Horton Bay on nearby Lake Charlevoix and trout streams like the Black, Pigeon, and Sturgeon Rivers. (He was late for his first wedding, in Horton Bay, because the fishing on the Sturgeon was so good.)

Probably the river most people associate with Hemingway is the Two-Hearted in the Upper Peninsula, thanks to "Big Two-Hearted River." An archetype of minimalism, the story depicts Adams as a veteran wrestling with the trauma of war while trout fishing in deepest Michigan. It's tough to fathom it today, but in 1925, these staccato lines were the literary equivalent of a knife fight: "It had been a hard trip. He was very tired. That was done. He had made his camp. He was settled. Nothing could touch him."

Of course, no true fisherman would give up his spot so easily. Except for a spring steelhead run, the fishing on the Two-Hearted has never been great. Hemingway liked the name for its metaphorical resonance. A section of the Fox River, near the town of Seney, was his actual model for the story.

I kept my distance from the Hemingway cottage, called Windemere, which is still in the family and not open to the public. Over the years this has produced some confusion. Ernie Mainland, Hemingway's nephew, occasionally emerged from his bathroom to find strangers — convinced they had discovered an unlisted Hemingway museum — riffling through his belongings. Mainland died in 2021, but the cottage is still owned by his family.

"People have taken divots out of the lawn," said Michael R. Federspiel, a professor of history at Central Michigan University and the author of the coffee-table book *Picturing Hemingway's Michigan*. "It's literally sacred ground."

Federspiel and I were drinking iced teas at the City Park Grill, a former Hemingway haunt in Petoskey. "Many people wouldn't recognize the Hemingway from up here," he said, pointing above the bar to a reproduction of Yousuf Karsh's iconic 1957 photo of Papa in which the author, wearing a turtleneck sweater, very much resembles a longshoreman about to take a swing at you. "Exhibit A. It's the drunken Hemingway, the four-times married, loutish guy he was at the end of his life," Federspiel lamented. "The Hemingway we had here was a thoughtful, observant young man."

A few blocks away, at 602 State Street, was the old Eva Potter's boardinghouse — today a private home — where Hemingway rented a room in the fall of 1919 and where, Federspiel said, the budding writer was tinkering with a fresh approach.

"Nick Adams wasn't born there," he said, adding that it wasn't until Paris in the 1920s that Hemingway tacked a Michigan map to his wall and mined his early life for fiction. "But it was the genesis of that tight, concise, impressionistic style. Northern Michigan

Above The Horton Bay General Store is still a center of local business and social life.

Opposite The Red Fox bookstore in Horton Bay specializes in Hemingway books and memorabilia.

was his first Eden, and it got seared into his emotions. From that came great stories."

The village of Horton Bay, which zips by in a flash on County Road 56, was a major fixture of Hemingway's adolescence. At pains to escape his mother, he often walked the four miles from Walloon to fish and swim there. Horton Bay makes cameos in several stories, including "Summer People," "Up in Michigan," and "Wedding Day."

Hemingway was a regular at the Horton Bay General Store, still in operation (it opened in 1876), and at the Pinehurst and Shangri-La cottages, where his 1921 wedding reception was held (Shangri-La is now a vacation rental).

Halfway down Lake Street, before I reached the bay, I found the spring from "Summer People" in which Nick Adams imagines soaking his war wounds. It was just as Hemingway describes it: "The water came up in a tile sunk beside the road, lipping over the cracked edge of the tile and flowing away through the close-growing mint into the swamp," he wrote. "Nick thought, I wish I could put all of myself in there. I bet that would fix me."

Lots of people dislike Hemingway for some pretty good reasons, like his machine-gunning mako sharks from his boat or the ugly vein of misogyny, homophobia, and anti-Semitism that litters his fiction and personal correspondence. But the man burned relentlessly from one end of his life to the other, trying to tap into something we all feel in danger of losing, whether it's the vitality of youth, the security of a childhood home, or simply our memories of a vanished world.

So much of his early work has a special poetry to it — a song of summer, you might say — that is in every way alive to youth's inevitable, sad decline.

Except for a single night in 1947, when Hemingway passed through Michigan on his way out West, he never saw Petoskey again after his Horton Bay wedding.

Photographs by
Jenn Ackerman

The thinking from scholars is that he didn't want to ruin his memory of a place he loved so much.

"The Last Good Country," another Nick Adams ramble through Petoskey's outback, was a story Hemingway worked on right up until his death in 1961.

"This is about the last good country there is left," Nick tells his younger sister in the story as they flee into the woods, dodging a pair of surly game wardens.

The quiet dark of the trees puts them in mind of religion. "That's why they build cathedrals to be like this," Nick says, echoing a sentiment that saturates the author's writing on the region.

It's a perfect example of how, in an important way, Hemingway spent his whole life returning to northern Michigan.

WHAT TO READ AND WATCH

The Nick Adams Stories, by Ernest Hemingway. The short stories that Hemingway based on his own experiences as a boy and young man, and on his memories of northern Michigan.

Ernest Hemingway: A Biography, by Mary Dearborn. One of the most recent of the biographies of Hemingway; attempts to uncover the man behind the legend. (The classic biography, published in 1969, is by Carlos Baker.)

Picturing Hemingway's Michigan, by Michael R. Federspiel. A coffee-table book with more than 250 images of Hemingway and northern Michigan.

Ernest Hemingway — Wrestling with Life, directed by Stephen Crisman and narrated by Hemingway's granddaughter Mariel Hemingway. A documentary in A&E's Biography series.

Ernest Hemingway, directed by Ken Burns and Lynn Novick. A later, more complete television biography.

Mexico City 132

Oaxaca 138

Managua & León 126

Havana & Pinar del Río 110

Cartagena 104

Jardín 118

LATIN AMERICA & THE CARIBBEAN

Salvador da Bahia
144

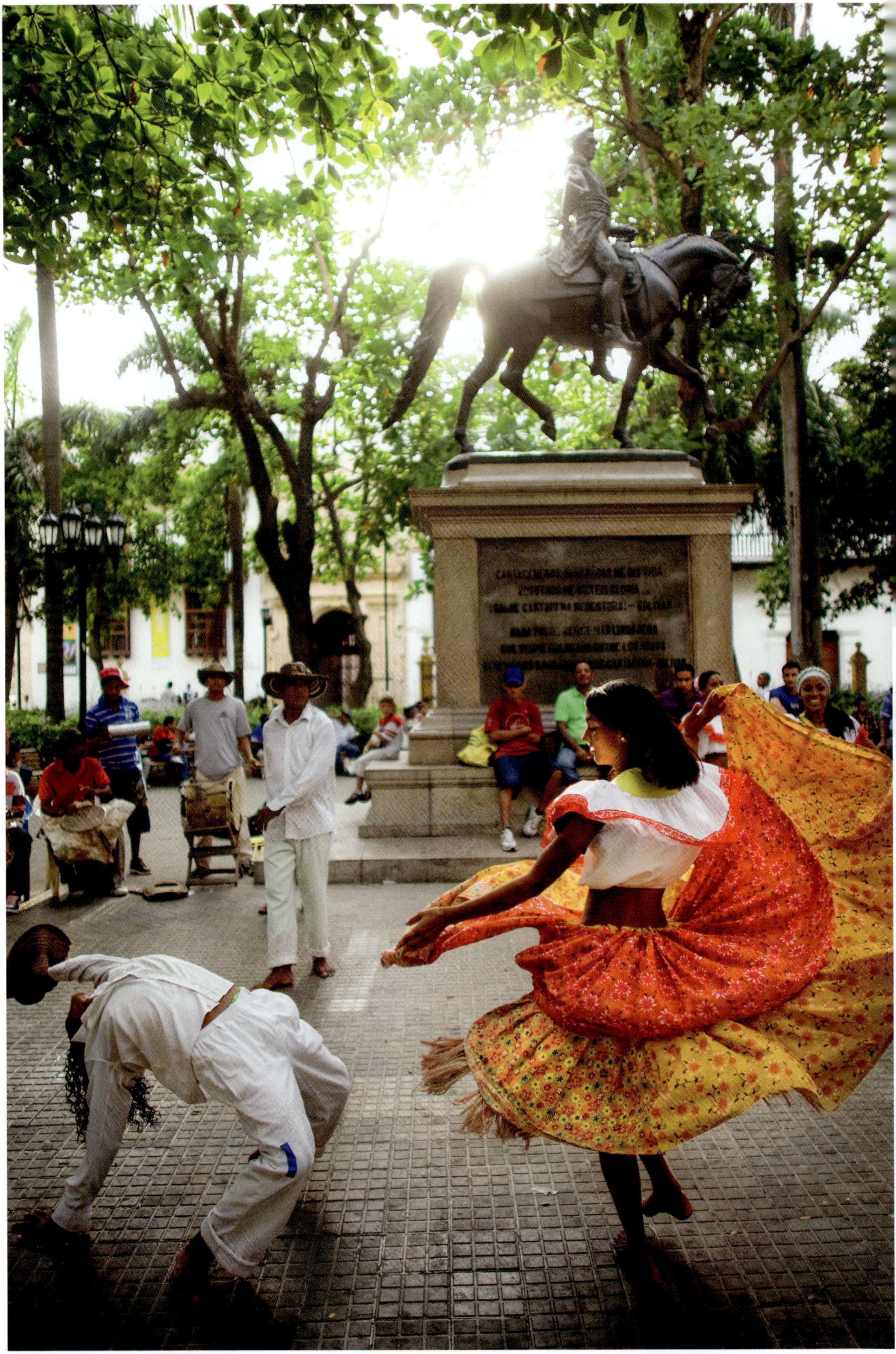

LOVE AND CARTAGENA

In all of his books, Gabriel García Márquez said, there were threads of Cartagena. A traveler's challenge is finding them. — BY ANAND GIRIDHARADAS

In the deep recesses of the Bazurto Market, a man is shaving the face of a pig. A razor in his hand, he glides across its face to remove the fuzz. The pig will soon be dinner. Not far away, cow hearts are on sale, and beside them cow eyes, staring out ominously, bound for a hearty potage. A shopping cart full of limes whizzes past. Alcatraz birds loom on the corrugated-tin roofs. "My Sweet Lord" is playing in one corner; in another, Caribbean songs pour from a bar lined with drinkers. It is not yet noon.

Truth can be stranger than fiction in Cartagena, the Colombian city whose real-life blend of seediness and charm was an important inspiration for one of the most imaginative writers of the modern era, Gabriel García Márquez. It is a city so pregnant with the near magical that, when García Márquez took a visiting Spaniard on a tour one day that included a Creole lunch and a stroll through the old city, it lowered his opinion of García Márquez's talents. The Spaniard told García Márquez, as he would later record in an essay, "You're just a notary without imagination."

Imagine a city that could make Gabriel García Márquez, the Nobel Prize–winning giant of magical realism, seem like a notary.

The world speaks of Dickens's London, Balzac's Paris, and Rushdie's Bombay, but the association between García Márquez and Cartagena is less known. And yet Cartagena was an important if brief chapter in his own story. It is the city — throbbing with the varied cultures whose mixing he chronicled — that propelled his writing career; the city of the surreal, where toucans land on a table at its finest hotel; the city where García Márquez arrived with nothing and learned to spin local tales into literature; the city

Previous A swirl of color at Plaza de Bolívar, disguised as Plaza of the Cathedral in *Love in the Time of Cholera*.

Left Feeding pigeons in the Plaza de San Pedro Claver. The color and variety of everyday Cartagena found their way into García Márquez's fiction even after he left the city.

Opposite Gabriel García Márquez in 1976. "I would say that I completed my education as a writer in Cartagena," he once told an interviewer.

awash in myths; the city that, in furnishing the reality for his magic, made him a writer.

"I would say that I completed my education as a writer in Cartagena," he once told an interviewer for a local documentary about Cartagena by the actor and filmmaker Salvatore Basile.

But for all of García Márquez's popularity, Cartagena was slow to claim him, at least in the assertive way other cities promote their connections to great writers. He cut his teeth in Cartagena but was a sporadic presence later, despite maintaining a home here.

García Márquez arrived in Cartagena in 1948 as a penniless student from Bogotá and left the next year, never to live in the city full-time again. But his parents and siblings moved to Cartagena two years after he left, so he continued to visit after settling down in Mexico City (where he died in 2014), and even in his 80s, often stayed in Cartagena in the winter.

A group of historians and scholars became determined to make García Márquez's connection to the city clearer to the world. To identify the places and people behind his works, they interviewed his friends and relatives, examined his public statements, and cross-referenced passages in his books with real estate records and other documents. Now García Márquez–themed tours guide visitors to the places in Cartagena that were important to him and his fiction.

Situated on Colombia's northern coast, Cartagena was among the most important trading ports in the colonized Americas. Late in the 20th century, its walled old city fell into shambles as the wealthy old families that García Márquez wrote about began to move out to the Miami-like suburb of Bocagrande, while the poor moved in. Many of the centuries-old colonial houses that define the old city were reduced to empty shells, with proud doors and high, pastel-hued walls masking the ruins and tall grass within. Then came a national reawakening as civil conflict and drug-tinged violence were curbed. Cartagena resurfaced with boutique hotels, fusion-seeking restaurants, and new fashion labels. Tourists now cycle past shops and galleries, stroll idly down byways, and revel with locals at New Year's Eve parties in public plazas.

One place to begin a García Márquez tour is Plaza Fernández de Madrid. Cartagena, dangling into the Caribbean, its lanes lined with flower-filled balconies, is a city for lovers; and it was the setting for García Márquez's novel *Love in the Time of Cholera*, regarded by critics as one of the 20th century's great literary love stories.

It is the story of a young man of humble means, Florentino Ariza, who falls instantly in love with a girl named Fermina Daza, the daughter of a merchant. He courts her by letter, only to be rejected. Aspiring to move up in society, she marries and enters the elite Cartagena of her husband, Dr. Juvenal Urbino. For 50 years, Florentino pines for her, consoling himself with meaningless, frantic copulation — until, upon Dr. Urbino's death, he gets a chance to assert his undying love once again.

What may come as a surprise even to the novel's most ardent fans is that García Márquez, famous for his wild imagination, drew heavily on the reality of Cartagena for *Cholera* and other works.

In the Plaza Fernández de Madrid, which he recast in his love story as the Park of the Evangels, a traveler can sit precisely where the hopeless young man would have sat, "on the most hidden bench in the little park, pretending to read a book of verse in the shade of the almond trees." A horse-drawn carriage, carrying tourists, might clip-clop past, allowing you to imagine Fermina passing by. Even the house where Fermina grew up was not wholly fictional. According to scholars, you can see it on the plaza today — the white house with a second-floor balcony on the eastern side of the square.

Another spot where García Márquez found inspiration was the Plaza Bolívar, within the old city. On one side of the square is a colonnaded arcade, known in *Cholera* as the Arcade of Scribes: "an arcaded gallery across from a little plaza where carriages and freight carts drawn by donkeys were for hire, where popular commerce became noisier and more dense."

Under the arcade, Florentino, rejected by Fermina and tormented within, found a way to redeploy the surplus love that he could not use: "He offered it to unlettered lovers free of charge, writing their love missives for them in the Arcade of Scribes." On one occasion he realized that he was writing letters for both parties in a budding courtship, his words slowly coaxing them together.

For hints of the real-life García Márquez, one might start with his home. It is not open to the public, but even the view from the outside gives a sense of who the man was. The house stands on the edge of the old city, in the San Diego quarter, facing the sea.

Above An intimate moment under Cartagena's fortress wall. The city's oldest walls and buildings date to the 1500s.

Opposite The narrow streets of old Cartagena. Visitors to the city can take García Márquez–themed tours.

It is a rare product of architectural subversion in a city of architectural conformity: not a colonial house in the Spanish style, but a modernist dwelling that García Márquez ordered built. It looks like a straight-edged castle, with orange-red walls, a ring of holes running around the property, a swimming pool, and a sprawling lawn.

Opposite the García Márquez house is the venerable Sofitel Santa Clara hotel, where the writer sometimes stopped for a drink. The hotel was a hospital before it was a hotel, and a convent before it was a hospital, and it shares the city's mildly haunted air.

Working as a reporter in the late 1940s, before he owned a home nearby, García Márquez was reputedly sent to that hospital to investigate a tip that a skeleton had been found, belonging to a girl with 22 meters, or 72 feet, of hair. Whether or not he ever actually saw such a relic, the story appears in altered form in his novel *Of Love and Other Demons* — another illustration of the strange dance of myth and reality, fiction and truth, in Cartagena. Today, what remains of that era is a small crypt below El Coro, the hotel bar, that any guest can enter. But the atmosphere is incongruous: craft cocktails are on order, and Colombian couples may be shuffling gracefully on the dance floor, the men in untucked short-sleeved shirts and white shoes, the women in elegant dresses.

It is in Getsemaní, a neighborhood just beyond the walls of the walled city, where the gritty, rum-soaked Cartagena that García Márquez first fell in love with can still be found. Getsemaní is on the rise, but it is still possible there to imagine the roadside restaurants and bars where the young García Márquez made friends, chased rumors, and began to find his voice.

He arrived in the city in 1948 from Bogotá, after political riots there started a fire that burned down his hostel. It took with it all of his possessions, including his typewriter. He went to Cartagena and began

Photographs by
Robert Caplin

again, finding work within days at *El Universal*, a newspaper that became a kind of journalism school for him. He wrote of submitting articles and then watching as the editor crossed out virtually every word, writing a new article between the lines of the old. It was the journalism of an earlier age, when writers and editors sat along the pier relishing steak with onion rings and green banana at dives, mingling with poets and prostitutes, telling tales, and, in turn, converting anecdotes heard into articles for the next day's paper.

"All of my books have loose threads of Cartagena in them," García Márquez said in the documentary by Salvatore Basile. "And, with time, when I have to call up memories, I always bring back an incident from Cartagena, a place in Cartagena, a character in Cartagena."

WHAT TO READ AND WATCH

Love in the Time of Cholera, by Gabriel García Márquez. One of the author's greatest novels, with settings modeled after the Cartagena of his experience.

Of Love and Other Demons, by Gabriel García Márquez. A sad love story involving hair that grows magically.

Gabriel García Márquez: A Life, by Gerald Martin. The standard English-language biography of García Márquez, exhaustive and analytical.

Solitude & Company: The Life of Gabriel García Márquez Told with Help from [Others], by Silvana Paternostro. "A book that gathers his old friends together, as if around a table, and lets them talk." — Dwight Garner in *The New York Times*.

Gabo: The Creation of Gabriel García Márquez, directed by Justin Webster. A 2016 documentary looking back over the author's entire life and career.

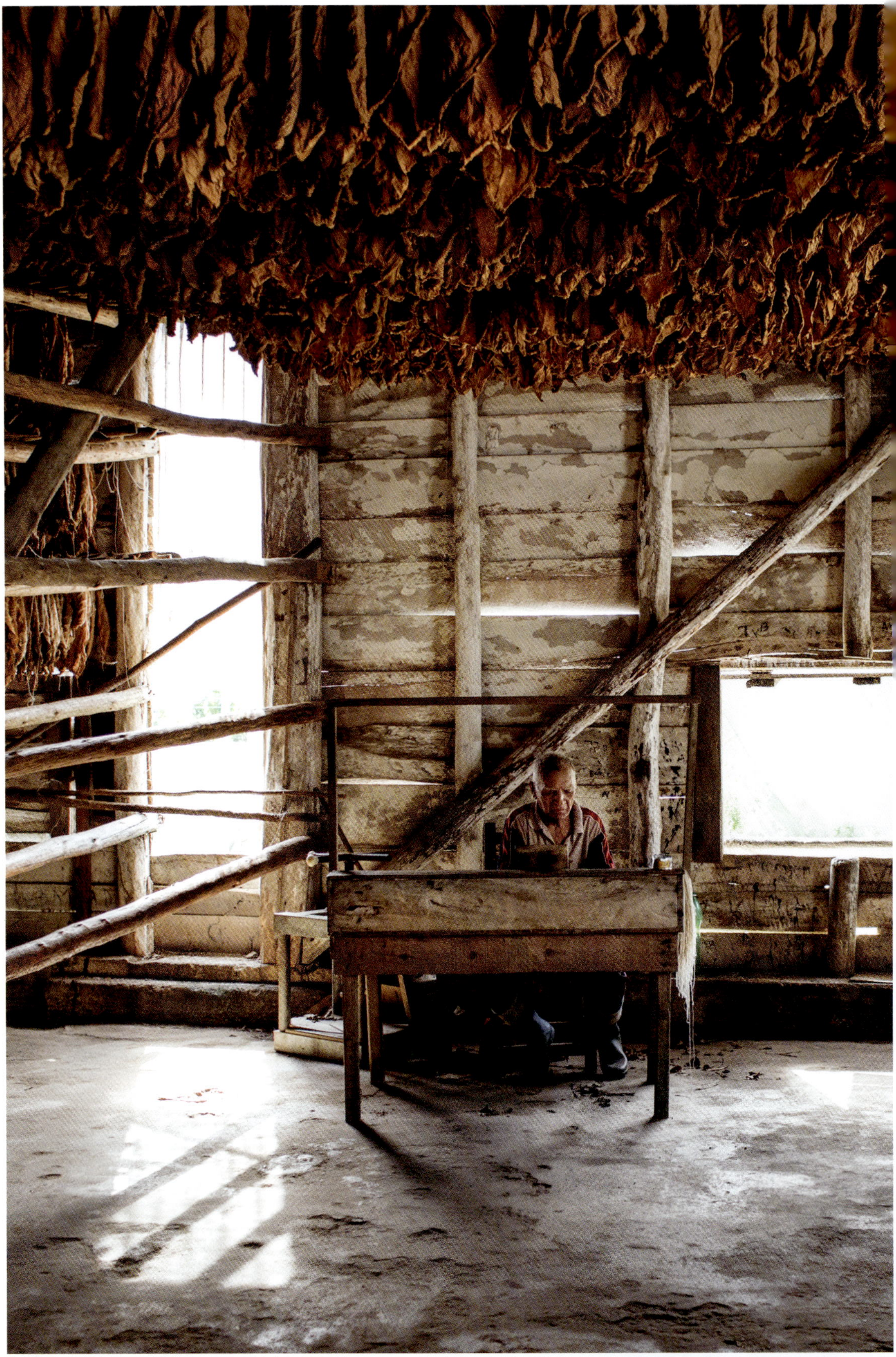

A CIGAR LOVER'S TOUR OF CUBA

To learn what turns tobacco leaves into a prized extravagance, go to the island where it's done best.
— BY RON STODGHILL

Walking along the gritty, darkening streets of Havana, I felt a sense of foreboding wash over me. A few paces ahead was a stranger. Jorge, he called himself, a young street hustler I had just met at a taxi stand outside the Hotel Capri. Jorge's style of dress was decidedly urban: an oversize San Diego Padres jersey, baggy denim shorts, and Adidas sneakers. Jorge was also charming, and through broken English he had enticed me from the touristy environs of downtown into what was eerily morphing into a barren, crumbling neighborhood of sagging rowhouses. The object of seduction: a box of Habanos, or hand-rolled cigars.

My sense of vulnerability was heightened by the clop-clop of my sandals on the cobblestone streets. It seemed too late to start chastising myself for being a naïve tourist dumb enough to be coaxed into the night for a few stogies. Ahead of me, Jorge, looking more sinister by the second, waved me on. Moving deeper into the Havana 'hood, I was, it seemed, at God's mercy now — in a country noted, incidentally, for its dearth of churches and religion (despite the island's warm reception of Pope Francis in 2015).

Soon we reached a dilapidated brick building in the central neighborhood of Vedado. "Here, my friend!" Jorge said. "Good price here on Montecristo, and Cohiba, too!"

Jorge rang a doorbell. A window two flights up opened, and keys dropped to the ground. He led me up a dim stairwell to an open apartment door, where we were greeted by a shirtless man and an elderly woman who spirited me into a back room. And there it was on a wooden table, its lid majestically open: a box of Cuban Montecristo No. 2s.

Previous Cuba is known for exceptional tobacco, which is skillfully rolled into the country's prized cigars.

Left The finished product. The finest cigars are mostly for export. Few Cubans can afford them.

Opposite Fidel Castro in 1964 with his trademark cigar. In a 1994 interview with a cigar magazine, he declared his preference for Cohibas.

For the uninitiated, let me shed light on this treasure trove. Celebrated for its complex blend of creamy and spicy aromas, the Montecristo No. 2 is arguably the Cadillac of Cuban cigars.

I stepped over to admire the 25 torpedo-shaped beauties, light brown in hue and just over six inches long, each adorned with a chocolate-brown band emblazoned with a white sword insignia. Montecristo No. 2, the name inspired by the Alexandre Dumas novel, had long been among my favorites, although I couldn't remember the last time I smoked one.

"Gracias," I told the woman, who shot me a weary smile as she wrapped my bounty in newspaper. The low price I paid would have sparked envy among cigar smokers anywhere. "You happy, my friend?" Jorge asked. I shook his hand and then hugged him as if he were family.

I had come to Cuba to explore its famous cigar culture. Cigar enthusiasts are a discriminating bunch, yet most agree that Cuba is blessed with a unique combination of sun, soil, and moisture — coupled with a rich history of careful curing and hand-rolling — that makes for the world's most flavorful cigars. While Cuba can't claim to be the birthplace of cigars (historians give those bragging rights to farms in Guatemala), the island reigns as producer of the world's best.

For lodging in Havana, I chose the Hotel Capri, a favorite haunt of the notorious mobster Meyer Lansky, near famous cigar shops and rolling factories as well as nightclubs flowing with Havana Club rum and Afro-Cuban music.

Cigar smokers, actually smokers in general, enjoy rare freedom in Cuba, despite official bans on smoking in enclosed public places. On my first evening, after a delicious seafood risotto on the balcony at the Café Laurent, a penthouse *paladar* (or privately owned restaurant) overlooking the seaside esplanade called the Malecón, my waiter glanced at my newly acquired Montecristo No. 2 resting on the table. I had planned to smoke it during a stroll after dinner, but moments later, my cigar was cut and its tip was aglow. I savored its creamy aroma, marveling at the perfection of the moment: the city lights and the rumba music wafting up from the streets.

Even the non-cigar smoker must concede that a kind of Habanos romance swirls across this island. Cubans cherish cigars, literally. The works of the late Cuban poet Heberto Padilla have been compared to a great cigar: balanced, full-flavored, and serene. In the late 1960s, before Castro's regime imprisoned and tortured him for criticizing the government, and before such intellectuals as Susan Sontag and

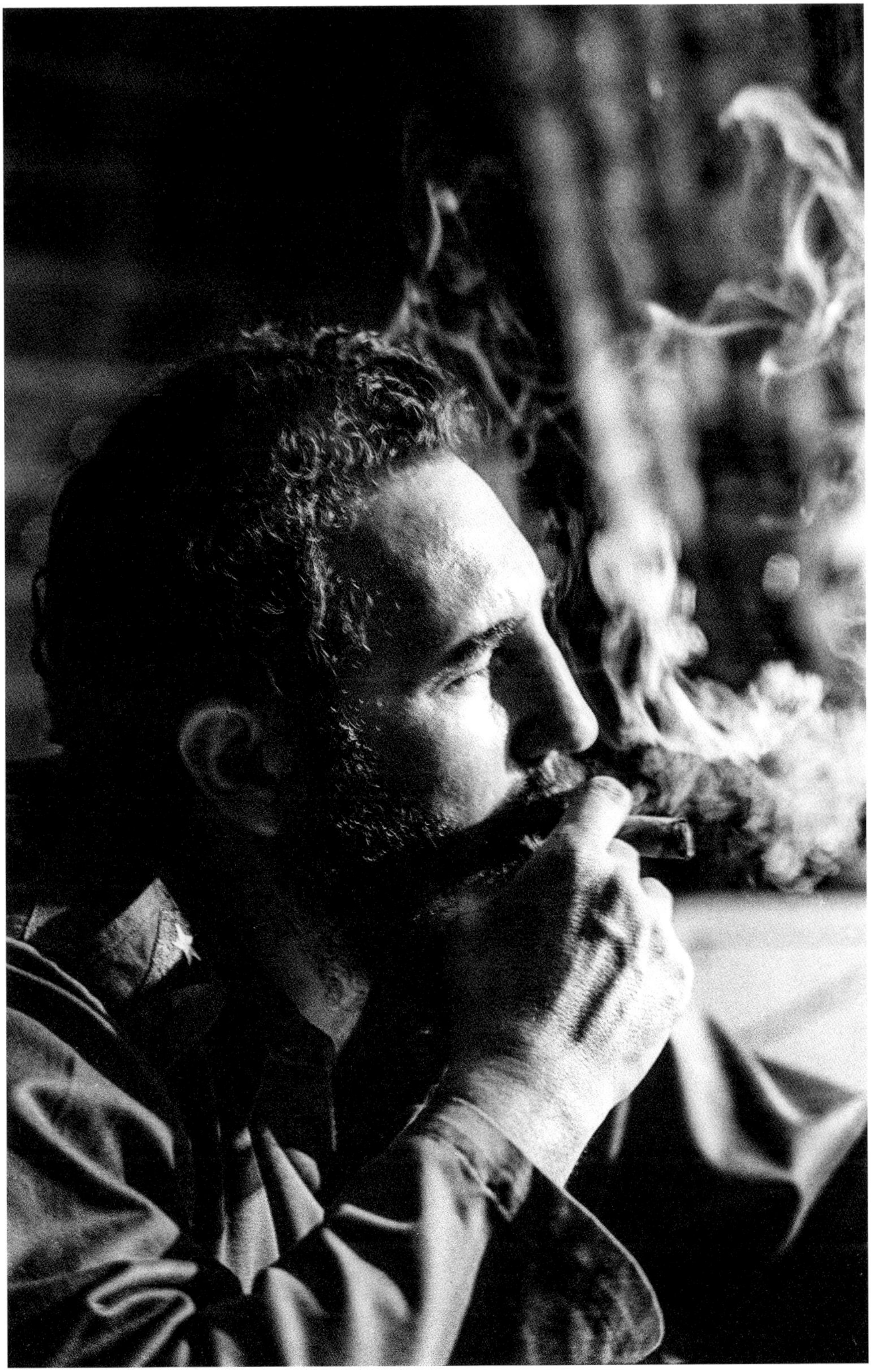

Jean-Paul Sartre successfully campaigned for his release, Padilla had written, rather presciently: "General, I can't destroy your fleets or your tanks / and I don't know how long this war will last / but every night one of your orders dies without being followed / and, undefeated, one of my songs survives."

Such lyricism inspired the Padilla 1968 Golden Bear cigar, an earthy-flavored tribute to the poet. It's called the 1968 Series because that's the year Padilla published the anthology *Fuera del Juego* (*Out of the Game*), which ultimately got him locked up for "having plotted against the powers of the state." Cigar novices might mistake this hard-to-find cigar band's red and gold illustration for a crown, but aficionados know it's actually the nib of the poet's fountain pen.

Cigar nostalgia abounds in Cuba, and I encountered few more eager to share it than Michael Phillips, a Briton who moved to Havana many years ago to teach English. He was a devoted member of the city's Cigar Aficionado Club, he told me, whose members — foreign diplomats and businessmen — met monthly for dinner, cigars, and conversation. Sitting in the spacious living room of his apartment in the upscale Miramar neighborhood, he poured Cognac and held out a tray of unbanded cigars, from short coronas to lengthier Churchills, tan Habanos to darker Maduros. He grinned at my selection, pyramid-shaped and walnut in color.

"Don't ask me where it came from," he said mischievously, "because I cannot tell you."

After some prodding, he explained his suspiciously bandless cigar menu: "The rollers in the factory have a quota, but many of the women find a way to sneak a few extras out. So they roll for eight hours in the factory, and then come home and roll for another two hours."

He lit up, drew from his cigar, and watched the plume rise. "There was one girl who worked at the Romeo y Julieta factory; she was pregnant for three years!" He chuckled at such clever smuggling. "But yes, these are as good as the ones from the factory."

In Cuba, those smoking the finest cigars tend to be visitors, expats, senior government officials, and international businesspeople. Most Cubans can't afford hand-rolled cigars of export quality. Cubans do smoke local cigars, but they cost about a nickel in

Opposite A cigar-rolling demonstration for visitors at the Robaina Tobacco Plantation in Pinar del Río, west of Havana.

Above The road from the Robaina Tobacco Plantation. The Cuban countryside is lush and green but mostly poor.

American currency and can be fodder for swindling undiscerning tourists.

To learn more about where all Cuba's cigar refinement starts, I visited the Alejandro Robaina Tobacco Plantation, arguably the most famous tobacco farm in the world. The home of the late farmer Alejandro Robaina, known as the face of the Cuban cigar, Robaina is tucked away in the town of San Luis in the Pinar del Río province, the westernmost section of Cuba. Founded in 1845, the farm is known for its robust yields of high-quality wrapper leaves; so impressive, in fact, that in the early 1980s Fidel Castro—a cigar-smoking Cohiba man himself—branded these cigars with the Robaina family name, the only Habanos to boast such a distinction.

For the two-hour trip from Havana, my guides wisely traded in the hulking 1950s Chevrolet taxi we'd used in the city for a late-model Pontiac rental. As dense, boisterous Havana receded and the urban landscape turned into rolling green countryside, I saw another side of Cuba: rural and scattered with clapboard shanties and mules, donkeys, and chickens. One is reminded of the island's poverty, even if it is offset by a tight-knit culture where the sound of laughter and chatter envelops fruit stands displaying bananas and papayas. At one roadside stop, I treated myself to a 10-cent cigar and a cookie stuffed with guava jam.

When we turned down a dirt lane to the Robaina farm, the landscape turned into a bright green panorama of tobacco plants rustling in the breeze.

Yanelis Delgado, a longtime neighbor and family friend in her early 40s, greeted me and began spinning yarns about Alejandro Robaina. He smoked his first cigar at age 10, she said, and took the reins of the operation after his father died in 1950. On a terrace adorned with flags representing the home countries of visitors to the farm over the years was a life-size carving of him sitting in a rocker gazing across the

Above Drinks on the balcony at the Café Laurent, a penthouse *paladar* (a privately owned restaurant), in Havana.

Opposite Moody skies over Havana, Cuba's historic, lively metropolis.

field. The memorabilia on display included photos of world leaders and celebrity guests at the farm, and a handwritten note of encouragement from Alejandro to his grandson, Hirochi Robaina, who later became the farm's owner.

The Robaina plantation is known for Alejandro Robaina's growing techniques, which became synonymous with such premium brands as Cohiba and Hoyo de Monterrey. His tight relations with senior government officials—including Cuban presidents Fidel Castro and his brother Raúl—led to the government's creating one of the island's 27 brands in his honor.

It takes nearly two years for a cigar to move from germination of tobacco seeds to the rolling factory, Delgado explained, with much of that time devoted to curing and drying the leaves according to a carefully controlled process. In the curing barn I watched a farm veteran lay out leaves and, within minutes, construct a flawless cigar, which he handed to me.

Serious cigar smokers wax poetic with the language of wine aficionados, referring to a cigar's flavor as "spicy" or "creamy" with hints of "honey," "cocoa," and "cinnamon." Cuba's tobacco farmers take fierce pride in producing the most flavorful cigars in the world. Their nemesis is the expanding market not only for Cuban knockoffs but also for iconic Cuban brands whose leaves and labor are actually from other parts of the world.

For instance, the premium brand Cohiba was embroiled in litigation as the Cuban state-run cigar company contested the right of an American firm, the General Cigar Company, which manufactures in the Dominican Republic, to sell under the Cohiba brand.

Cuban cigar culture, of course, can't be exported. On my final day in Havana I came across the Hotel Conde de Villanueva, billed as the world's only hostel dedicated to cigars. In the atrium, peacocks strutted as a *torcedor* rolled cigars for guests. Each of the

Photographs by
Todd Heisler

nine guest rooms was named after a tobacco farm. A gorgeously restored 18th-century mansion adorned with stained-glass windows, the hotel also had an excellent cigar shop, plus an intimate smokers' lounge. Gracing one wall were photographs of celebrities smoking cigars (among them, Demi Moore, Denzel Washington, Groucho Marx, Ernest Hemingway, Winston Churchill, and Sigmund Freud). The hotel was surrounded by shops selling everything from chocolate to perfume.

    The atmosphere didn't feel exactly authentic, so I walked a couple of blocks away, deeper into Old Havana, and found a quiet seat beneath a canopied outdoor bar. It was a perfect spot to relax, to enjoy the distant sound of rumba and the view of vintage cars moving along the streets. I ordered a mojito. And then I lit my last cigar in Cuba.

WHAT TO READ AND WATCH

The Ultimate Cigar Book, by Richard Carleton Hacker. All about cigars: history, growing, manufacturing, and how to enjoy them with sophistication.

Cigar Smoking, by Winston Carter. The subtitle says it all: "The Fast & Easy Way to Go from Novice Cigar Smoker to Know-It-All Cigar Aficionado!"

Self-Portrait of the Other, by Heberto Padilla. A memoir by the Cuban poet whose condemnation by the Castro regime was criticized by intellectuals and famous cultural figures around the world.

Legacies: Selected Poems, by Heberto Padilla. Padilla's own selection from his work, translated into English by Alastair Reid.

Cuba Loves Lovers, directed by Claudio del Punta. A cinematic love story set in Cuba, featuring exuberant professional dancing. Many views of contemporary Havana.

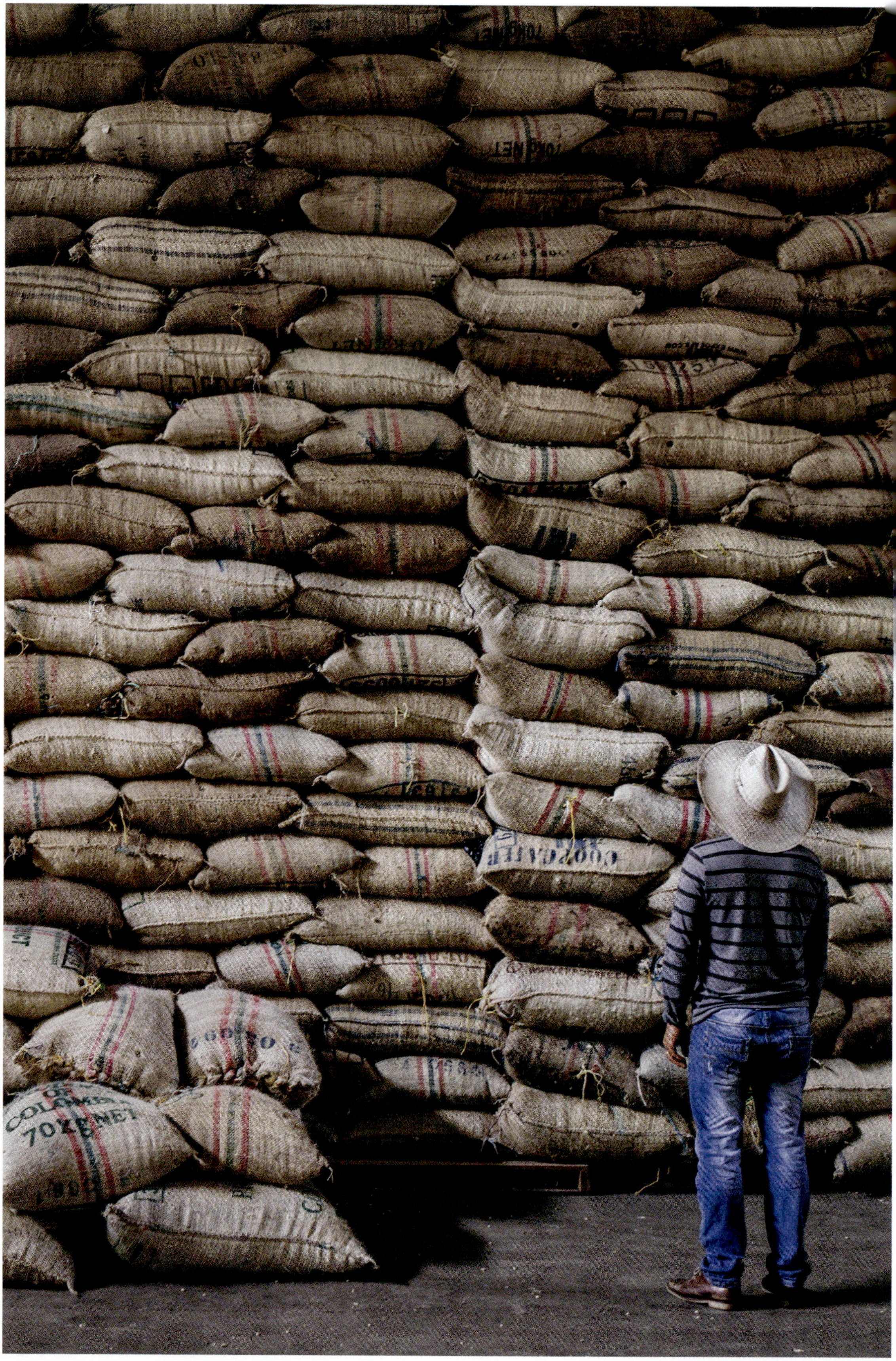

COLOMBIAN COFFEE AT THE SOURCE

On a tour of Andean coffee farms, the people are warm, the scenery is inspiring, and the tasting is a revelation.
— BY GUSTAVE AXELSON

There were more than 20 restaurants and cafes selling coffee by the cup in the lively pastel-splashed plaza of Jardín, a quaint Colombian pueblo, or village, nestled in the northern reaches of the Andes Mountains. I chose one, settled in at a streetside table painted bright blue like an Easter egg, and ordered a *café tinto* — straight black — for 800 pesos, about 25 cents.

It was a Monday morning, and the Paisas, as the folks in this region south of Medellín are called, were socializing. Some looked to be friends and family chatting and laughing in the shadow of the double-spired basilica. Some, I was told, were shopkeepers who took the day off after a busy weekend catering to tourists. At the table next to me, a campesino relaxed with his cowboy hat pulled over his face and his chair tilted back against the wall.

Had I been here on a certain day during the harvest season, I might have seen farm owners standing outside the Bancolombia branch with bags of paper cash, surrounded by police officers for security and workers who came to be paid. On Saturday nights, this plaza is a raucous cacophony of pounding discoteca beats and campesinos parading into town astride show horses, but there are still tintos among the cervezas on the trays waitresses carry between tables.

Coffee is at the heart of Jardín, as corn is to small-town Iowa, underpinning a local economy that forms a cultural identity. When my tinto arrived, it was easy to see why. The flavor, strong and bold, flowed directly from the beans, not a burned layer from roasting. I took another sip from my teacup-size demitasse and noticed that amid all the people drinking coffee around

Previous Surveying sacks of coffee in a warehouse of the Delos Andes cooperative in Jardín, Colombia.

Left An Andean cock-of-the-rock. Birders make up a major part of the tourist trade in the Andean coffee country.

Opposite In the Andes Mountains near Jardín, the hillsides abound with coffee bushes.

me, a travel mug or paper cup was nowhere to be found. No one was taking coffee to go. Everyone was sitting, sipping, enjoying.

This was why I had come: to indulge my love of coffee. And Jardín is a perfect place, in the heart of a coffee belt in southwestern Antioquia, the largest-volume coffee producer of Colombia's 32 departments.

In the 1990s, a collapse in commodity coffee prices hit Colombia hard. Half of its coffee market value vanished, and thousands of families in coffee-growing regions were pushed into poverty. As a strategy for the future, the Colombian government began encouraging and supporting farms to grow higher-quality beans that qualify for specialty coffee markets, where prices are higher and more stable.

Jardín embraced the specialty trend with gusto. Most of the beans sold at the town's coffee cooperative warehouse go straight to Nespresso, the high-end Swiss company known for selling coffeemakers through George Clooney on TV ads. The hills here are bustling with family fincas, or farms, competing with one another to grow the best coffee. With the help of a hired guide—José Castaño Hernández, himself the son of coffee farmers—I was ready to see where the rich brew in my cup came from, to explore the coffee terroir of the northern Andes.

Tell your relatives that you're going to Colombia, and you may still provoke a shudder and a warning to be careful in a country where there were once rampant drug violence and kidnappings by a rebel group, the Revolutionary Armed Forces of Colombia, or FARC. In 2016 the government signed a peace deal with FARC to end more than a half century of bloody conflict. Jardín is in a relatively safe area where the unrest was never as bad, because the many coffee farms grounded the local economy in legitimate commerce.

Hernández picked me up in his car and we drove through a military checkpoint just outside of town. After the soldiers waved us through, he told me we would be taking the scenic route to visit a coffee finca above 6,000 feet in elevation. By scenic, he meant a route for equestrians.

At the mountain foothills, he parked at the roadside and we met up with another guide who had horses saddled and ready to go. The ride up a cobble-strewn path was a series of pinch-me moments—glorious vistas of the northern Andes, rays of morning sun shooting through fluffy clouds, the occasional ridiculous-beaked toucan flying by.

After a few hours we stopped and tied up the horses, and Hernández unlocked a gate at a barbed-wire fence. This was the back door to the Cueva del Esplendor. The public entrance to this tourist attraction is a parking lot on the other side of the ravine. From this side, we rappelled down wire cables into jungle. At the bottom we entered a small cave with a sunlit waterfall shooting through the rock ceiling — another pinch-me moment.

We had lunch at the finca, a simple farmhouse near the mountaintop with white stucco walls and blue trim. There was a view of more than a dozen Andean peaks rolling out to the horizon, with bushy coffee plants climbing up every mountainside.

Three women hustled out to lay the lunch spread on a table on the covered porch: fried eggs with runny yolks, fried plantains two ways — one ripe and sweet and the other not-quite ripe and starchy; red beans; and chicharrón, strips of fried pork rind crunchy on the outside and chewy inside, all to be topped with a chunky picante paste. The whole mix was simple and satisfying. Around the corner, the farmworkers and their families sat at another table, a mix of men, women, and children all eating beans and eggs and chicharrón.

"Colombians eat a big lunch; it's their main meal," Hernández said. "It takes a lot of food to work this farm."

After the empty plates were collected, one woman poured me a cup of the house coffee, served tinto. I smiled and sighed at the pure flavor: so earthy and saturating on my palate, yet exiting cleanly without a trace of aftertaste.

Then the farm's manager, Juan Crisóstomo Osorio Marín, beckoned me to follow a dirt path up into the coffee bushes. Marín runs the farm's field operations for his father, who is the owner.

We arrived at a spot where bundles of green and bright red coffee berries weighted down seemingly every branch. These are prodigious plants, each one growing the equivalent of a pound of finished, ground coffee.

The red coffee berries, resembling cranberries, were ripe and ready to pick. I challenged Marín to a quick coffee-picking contest, and in 30 seconds I had 50 berries in a basket. Marín had more than 200.

During harvest season, Marín will haul down several baskets of coffee berries that add up to 500 pounds

Above Picking coffee beans. An experienced picker can pull down 500 pounds in a day.

Below The ripe beans, before drying and roasting, remind outsiders of cranberries.

Opposite Jardín farmers' lives are up close and intimate with their coffee crops.

by the end of the day—this off a ridge so steep I found it somewhat difficult to stand up straight. Other relatives do the same.

Still, the production here pales next to the output on corporate coffee plantations. The Marín family emphasizes quality over quantity. Nespresso grades these beans as Triple A, its highest rating for quality and sustainability. Marín said three factors favored his coffee: the elevation high enough to keep pestiferous coffee borer bugs at bay; the humidity from passing clouds that provide a steady stream of moisture; and the red soil laced with volcanic ash.

Back at the farmhouse, I got a tour of the depulping grinder that expunges beans from the fruit (like extracting pits out of cherries), and the drying rack for beans. I bought a bag of Marín's Triple A coffee.

On the ride back to Jardín, Hernández told me I was only his second coffee tourist in seven years of guiding. All of his other clients were birders, but he hoped to do more trips like this. He dropped me off at the inn where I was staying and told me he would take an afternoon siesta and be back in a few hours. I did likewise and stretched out in the rainbow-colored hammock strung up on the balcony of my second-floor room overlooking Jardín. At 6 p.m. Hernández

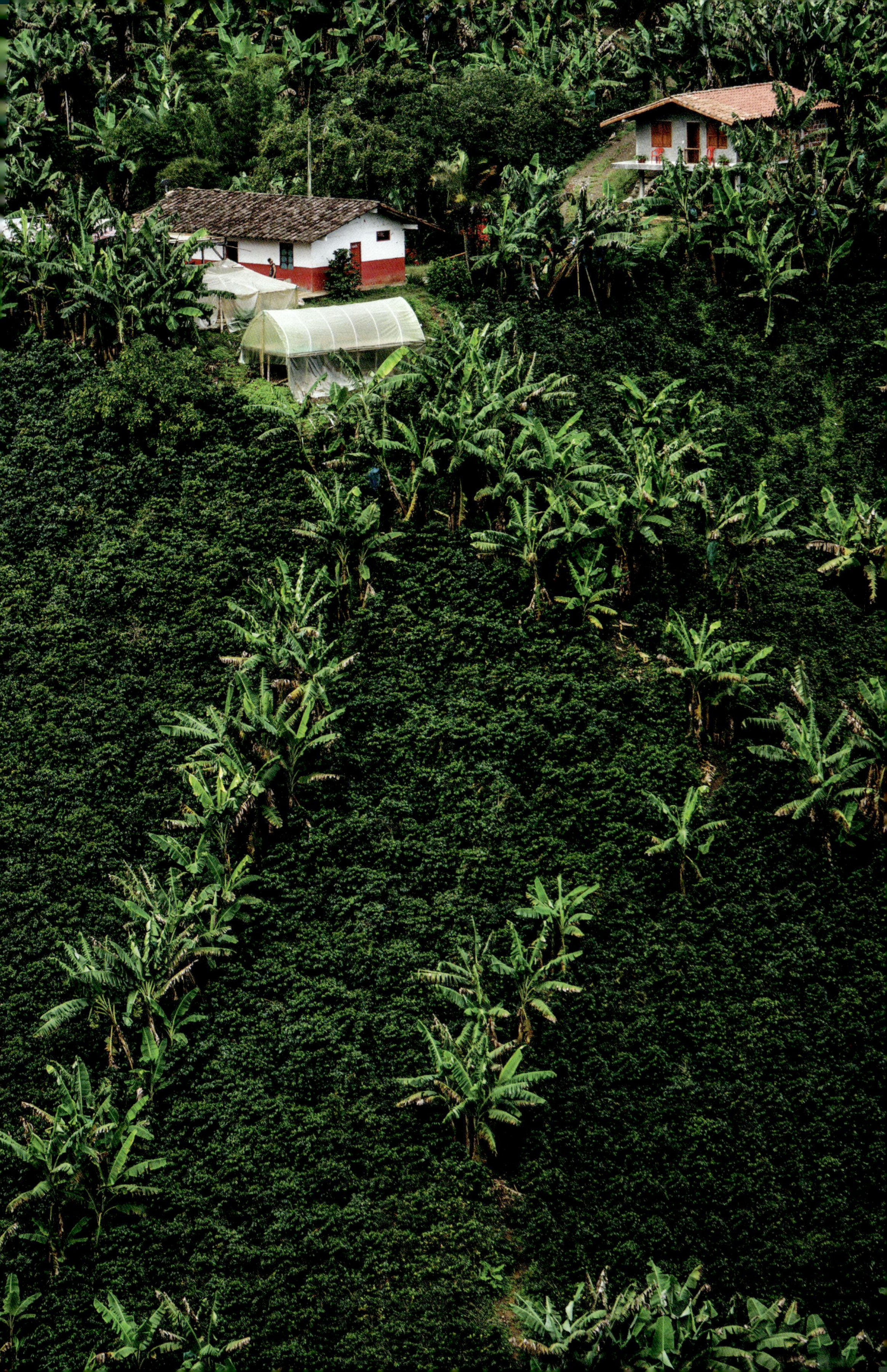

Above Drying coffee beans outside a home in Jardín. The beans may seem to dominate local life, but the brewed coffee is everywhere too.

Opposite This rider in Jardín introduced his horse as a Paso Fino, a breed prized for its gait and traceable back to the earliest Spanish imports.

retrieved me for dinner at another finca, also up in the hills but shrouded in a forest canopy.

At the farmhouse, a family bustled out of the door — father and mother, flanked by a little boy and a toddler girl — to greet me warmly, the first North American to visit their home. (Swiss men from Nespresso had been there.) The farm owner, Francisco Javier Ángel, grinned and waved us to the dining room table on the open-air porch.

At 37, Ángel seemed young to own a farm, but he was enterprising. He had worked this farm when a local priest owned it, and the priest, impressed by his work ethic, sold him the land. His farm is certified by the Rainforest Alliance, and his beans earn specialty grades.

His wife, Mónica, disappeared into the kitchen and came back bearing glasses of fresh-squeezed lemonade sweetened with panela, a form of unrefined sugar. Through Hernández, Ángel explained that panela can also be used as a sweetener for *chaqueta café*, "jacket coffee," served when days turn cold or to give coffee pickers a boost of energy for the fields.

Dinner soon followed — beans, plantains and chicharrón accompanied by strips of beef, avocado slices, and cornmeal cakes called arepas. It was better than any of the meals I ate at restaurants in town (where the chicharrón can be a chewing marathon).

I followed Mónica into the kitchen to watch her make the after-dinner coffee. She heated a liter of water to just near boiling, stirred five spoonfuls of ground coffee into the pot, turned off the heat, and let it sit for five minutes. "Silencio," she said. Finally, she poured coffee through a tiny sieve into cups preheated under hot water. Back at the dinner table, I took a sip and was astounded by a simple cup of coffee for the third time that day.

Ángel's coffee-farming lineage goes back three generations, and he had the idea to grow the same

Photographs by
Federico Rios Escobar

variety of beans his grandfather grew 100 years ago — a heritage coffee, of sorts. Those seeds were nowhere to be found, so he went treasure hunting in abandoned farms and eventually, scavenging in fallow fields, he found the old variety of beans.

Everyone in town thought he was insane for planting them, he said. But slowly his heritage coffee is winning converts. He sells it under the name Pajarito, or little bird, because he sees lots of birds among the bushes where this coffee grows.

Hernández and I said goodbye and walked out into the night. The air buzzed with insects whirring a fervent nocturnal chorus. A sea spray of white lights, like twinkling stars, glittered in the dark forest beyond us — the lights of families' houses on their fincas on the next mountain ridge.

It was a reminder that coffee here is a family affair. And if you slow down, sip, really savor, you can taste lifetimes of devotion.

WHAT TO READ AND WATCH

Uncommon Grounds: The History of Coffee and How It Transformed Our World, by Mark Pendergrast. "With wit and humor, Pendergrast has served up a rich blend of anecdote, character study, market analysis, and social history." — Betty Fussell in *The New York Times*.

The World Atlas of Coffee: From Beans to Brewing, Coffees Explored, Explained, and Enjoyed, by James Hoffmann. An encyclopedic tour of the world of coffee, including photographs.

In the Americas with David Yetman, Season 3, Episode 3: *Colombia: Capital and Coffee*, directed by Daniel Duncan. Getting to know Colombia through coffee.

Coffee with Ana, directed by Sean King and Taylor King. Boy meets girl and viewer meets Colombia in this romantic comedy. The Ana of the title plays both leading lady and travel guide.

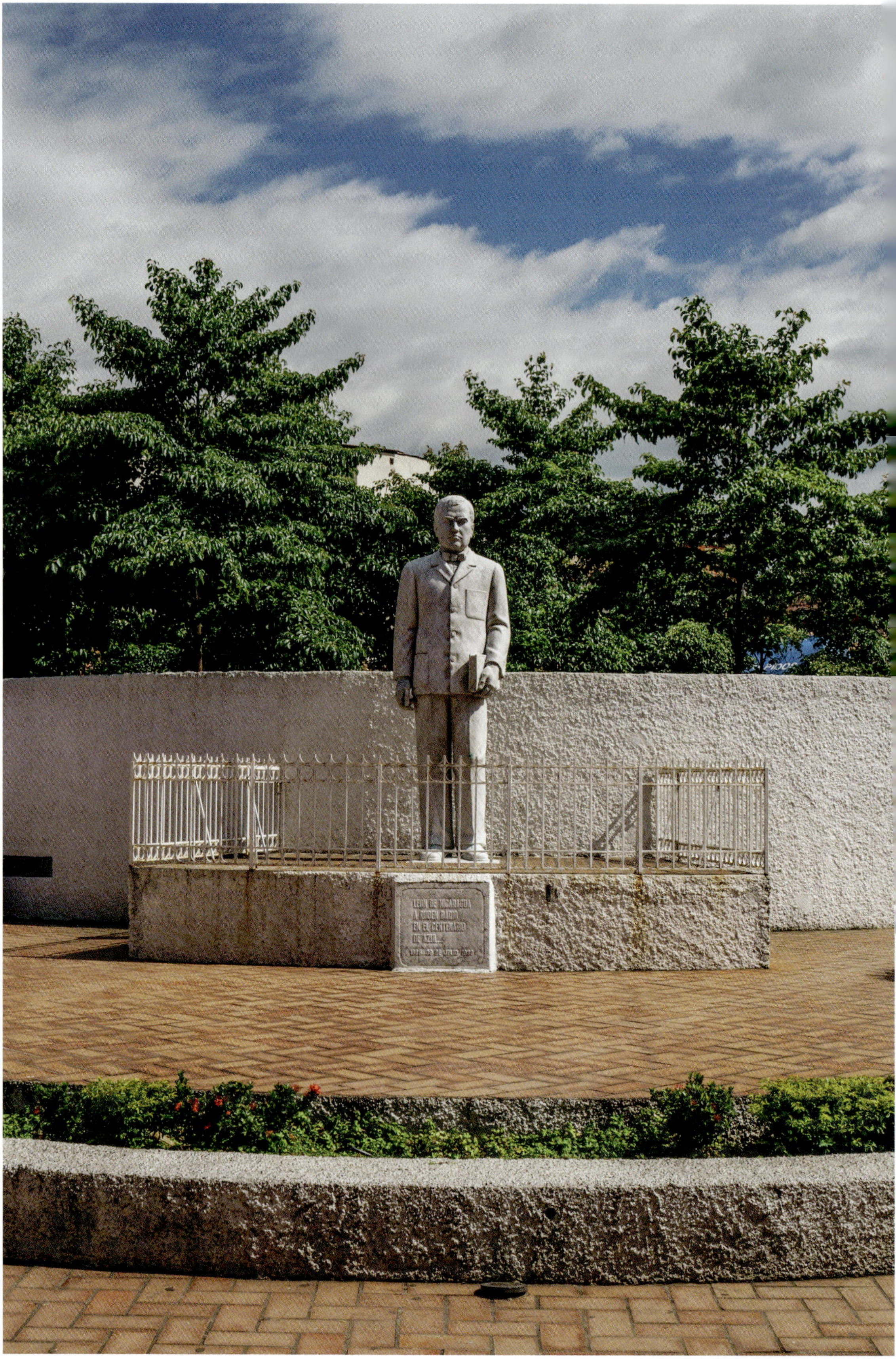
LEON DE NICARAGUA
A RUBEN DARIO
EN EL CENTENARIO
DE AZUL...

THE INESCAPABLE POET OF NICARAGUA

Rubén Darío, who breathed new life into the Spanish language, is a national hero, remembered everywhere.
— BY TIM NEVILLE

Once you know him, you see him everywhere. He's in the airport and in the park. He's by the hotel entrance and inside the theater. I even caught a glimpse of him on the side of an armored bank truck in Managua.

Almost any Spanish speaker will know the name Rubén Darío. He wasn't just a writer. He was the father of Modernismo, a man who gave them their language back. Madrid has a Rubén Darío metro station. You'll find Calle Rubén Darío in Mexico City, Panama City, San Salvador, and Tegucigalpa, Honduras. Rubén Darío Middle School sits next to Rubén Darío Park in Miami.

But Darío was born in Nicaragua in 1867 and died there in 1916, and although he spent most of his life in other countries, to the Nicaraguans he's 100 percent theirs.

"He's everything to us!" said a night clerk in Granada.

"He's the identity of our culture!" said a musician in Managua.

"Want to hear a joke about Darío?" asked a waitress. "It's naughty."

I had come to Nicaragua not to surf or hike or do yoga on the beach, but to explore the profound love that Nicaraguans hold for Darío, the tremendous national pride that he inspires. In Managua, I met up with Immanuel Zerger, a German immigrant whom I had hired in advance to be my guide. Immanuel, who runs his own tour company, looked something like a 19th-century writer himself, with graying hair and lugubrious eyes.

He fetched me from the Los Robles hotel, a relaxed posada with a tropical courtyard in the heart of

Previous A statue of Rubén Darío in León. Nicaragua remembers him with intense pride.

Left A Darío mural. His lines translate to: "The book is strength, it is courage, it is power, it is food; torch of thought and spring of love."

Opposite A Darío book from 1910. "Darío sent Columbus's caravan back and freed Spanish literature from Spain," said Francisco Arellano Oviedo, a Nicaraguan academic.

Managua. Immediately the legacy of the United States' involvement in Nicaragua stood out. A statue of Augusto César Sandino, a rebel against American military occupation of the country who was murdered in 1934, loomed in the distance. Sandino is perhaps the only figure more revered here than Darío.

Darío himself was weary of the United States' role in Nicaraguan affairs, particularly during the banana wars of the early 20th century. In 1905 he wrote a poem called "To Roosevelt." "You think that life is fire, / that progress is an eruption; / that the future is wherever / your bullet strikes," Darío wrote. "No."

Low-slung buildings painted in pinks, yellows, and greens slid past the windows of Immanuel's truck as we drove toward the Rubén Darío National Theater. Greater Managua, with a population of about 2.6 million people, feels less like a metropolis than a loose bag of a suburb. In 1972, an earthquake reduced all but 10 percent of the city to rubble and left Managua with an ill-defined city center and a strange vernacular for navigating. North becomes *al lago*, meaning toward Lake Managua, which borders the city; east is *arriba*, as in up. The address on a postcard sent to Managua will read like clues to pirate treasure: "Arriba from the little tree, last house al lago."

The theater has bold Bauhaus-style lines and sits near the lake, across from a plaza where Pope John Paul II delivered a fiery sermon in 1983 when the country was deep in a civil war. The theater survived the earthquake with only cosmetic damage and escaped the war unharmed. "Every side claims Darío as their own," Immanuel said. "He is untouchable."

Ramón Rodríguez Sobalvarro, the general director of the theater and an accomplished oboe player, welcomed me in his office. He had been rehearsing for a coming performance that would put Darío's poetry to music. Above his desk hung a picture of Darío with broad shoulders and a thinker's stare. "For me Darío is a Nicaraguan artist in the maximum sense," Rodríguez said as we walked around the theater. "He gave us our cultural identity, something that was ours that we could then project out into the world instead of copying what had already been done."

In the theater's early days — it was built in 1969 — nearly all of the shows were foreign productions: Duke Ellington, Mexican folk ballets, Marcel Marceau. Now 90 percent are Nicaraguan. Today some 40,000 children come for workshops; subsidies help keep ticket prices low.

Darío may be the only Nicaraguan to have earned worldwide acclaim as a poet, but others, like Azarías

Pallais, Salomón de la Selva, and Alfonso Cortés (who lived, wrote, and went insane in Darío's childhood home) come close. All of these men hailed from León, where Darío also grew up.

I got to León thanks to a budding architect and translator named Gabriel Galeano, whom Immanuel asked to accompany me. Gabe, as he told me to call him, had a love for banter, and when he picked me up for the 60-mile journey from Managua, I knew he'd be good company. Soon we were whipping down a highway lined with jicaro trees. Old American school buses trundled by sporting new green bumpers, chrome horns, blue piping, and loud checker wraps. It was if they were finally free to ditch the school uniform and become their fabulous selves.

León immediately felt more manageable than Managua, with sidewalks and plazas and people wandering about. Long the left-leaning fulcrum of the country, it is the country's second largest city, with about 210,000 people, and was among the first to rebel against the dictator Anastasio "Tachito" Somoza DeBayle, whose similarly dictatorial father, Anastasio "Tacho" Somoza, had been gunned down here in 1956 by Rigoberto López Pérez. López, a national hero with his own statue in Managua, was another poet from León.

Gabe led me to the José de la Cruz Mena Theater in the southwest side of the city. The lobby buzzed with TV crews. Girls dressed in Greco-style costumes with winged hats and fanfare trumpets lined up nervously along the wall. A Rubén Darío Symposium was underway, and the who's who of the Nicaraguan literary scene had come to see performances, recite poetry, and hear lectures.

Darío taught himself to read at age 3 and wrote poetry not long after. He left Nicaragua for El Salvador at 15. At 19 he moved to Chile where, at age 21, he published *Azul*, a collection of poems and prose that came to define the Spanish Modernist movement and catapulted him into literary stardom. The book, which built on the work of other poets like José Martí, shattered the stodgy literary norms of the day and breathed new life into the language.

"Everything written in Spanish afterward has been affected in one way or another by that great renascence," wrote the Mexican poet and Nobel laureate Octavio Paz in the prologue to *Selected Poems of Rubén Darío*, translated by Lysander Kemp. As Francisco Arellano Oviedo, the director of the Nicaraguan Language Academy, told me: "After so many centuries, Darío sent Columbus's caravan back and freed Spanish literature from Spain."

After a restaurant lunch of fried plantains, chicken, and *repollo* salad (a kind of cabbage slaw), we headed to the house where Darío moved in with his aunt when he was just 40 days old. Rosa Sarmiento, his mother, fleeing an abusive marriage, would later end up in Honduras and have no relationship with her son. The aunt's house now contains a museum. A sofa given to Darío by Manuel Estrada Cabrera, the Guatemalan dictator, sat in a main room, along with Darío's formal suits from his time as a Nicaraguan envoy to Argentina and Spain. Two large doors opened to the city outside.

Darío's tomb is in the Cathedral of the Assumption of Mary on a large main square. It lies near the altar under a life-size sculpture of a lion with a face frozen in anguish. The seal of Nicaragua with its volcanoes and two oceans is nearby. I sat in a pew,

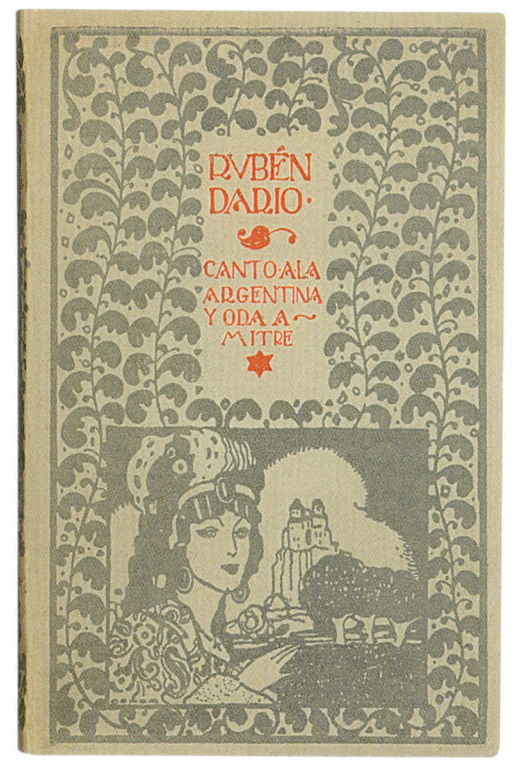

Above Salvador Allende Port, a tourist stop on Lake Managua. The Rubén Darío National Theater is a short walk away.

Opposite Darío described Momotombo volcano, a dominating Nicaraguan landmark, as "lyrical and sovereign."

alone, noticing that no one seemed to be coming inside for the saints.

Darío returned to Nicaragua only five times over the course of his career. He spent much of his life traveling as a journalist. He edited some of the day's most esteemed literary journals while in Europe and wrote for newspapers in Spain and South America and for *The New York Times*. All in all, he crossed the Atlantic 12 times and explored some 30 countries on three continents.

Perhaps Darío's most important trip was in Nicaragua itself. On November 23, 1907, by now a famous writer, he landed at the Pacific port of Corinto. A crowd greeted him, and tens of thousands more people lined the railroad tracks across the countryside to see him as he toured. Darío's return remains in the Nicaraguan consciousness today—there are books and plays about it—though I got the feeling the moment carries some wistfulness. "If one's homeland is small, you dream it big," Darío wrote in a poem about his trip, "Retorno."

Immanuel fetched me in León, and we drove northward to Corinto. On the way we saw the 4,255-foot Momotombo volcano, "lyrical and sovereign," as Darío described it. "The return to the native land has been so / sentimental, and so mental, and so divine / that even the crystalline dawn drops are / in the jasmine of dream, of fragrance and song," he wrote.

Corinto felt like what it is: a port town with container yards and cranes and a gray beach lined with tin-roofed shacks. The United States landed marines here numerous times, and in 1983 President Ronald Reagan, fearing Nicaragua's Communist rise, had the port mined. After that Reagan turned to more clandestine counterrevolutionary measures, eventually leading to the Iran–contra affair.

I drove with Gabe from Managua to Ciudad Darío, formerly San Pedro de Metapa, where Darío

**Photographs by
Federico Rios Escobar**

was born. The village sits in the mountains, just across the Darío Bridge. At a park across from a mobile phone shop off Poets Boulevard, we found sculptures of Darío and the house where he spent the first month of his life: a 200-year-old structure with earthen walls.

Darío died in León. Gravely ill, he had returned to Nicaragua for his fifth and final time. When the "ruler of kings" came for him, he was lying on his left shoulder, mouth agape, his body hollowed out by a failing liver. A photographer took a picture of him. A doctor removed his brain. Forty-nine years old, and that was that.

"I am an agèd tree that, when I was growing, / uttered a vague, sweet sound when the / breeze caressed me," Darío wrote in his 1907 poem "In Autumn." "The time for youthful smiles has now / passed by: / now, let the hurricane swirl my heart to / song!"

WHAT TO READ AND WATCH

Selected Poems of Rubén Darío, translated by Lysander Kemp. An introductory essay by Octavio Paz explains Darío's pivotal role in the late 19th-century revival of literature in the Spanish language.

Selected Writings, by Rubén Darío, translated by Andrew Hurley. Poems, prose, and letters.

The Oxford Book of Latin American Poetry, edited by Cecilia Vicuña and Ernesto Livon Grosman. An anthology covering 500 years of poetry.

Walker, directed by Alex Cox. Ed Harris plays William Walker, a 19th-century American adventurer, now little remembered in the United States, who organized military interventions into Nicaragua and briefly usurped its presidency.

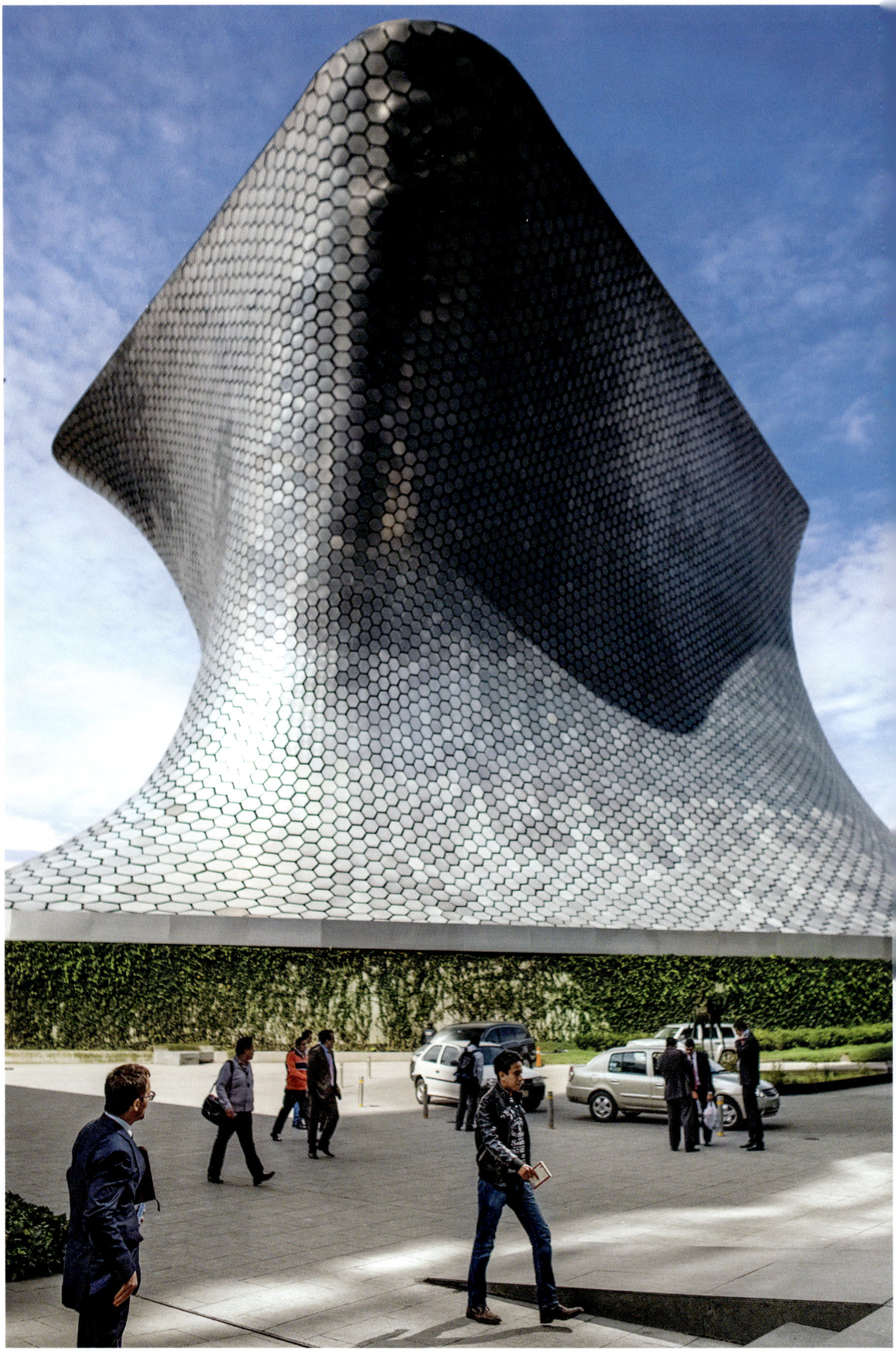

THE NEW ARCHITECTURE OF MEXICO CITY

Who better to design a tour for a traveler than the architects themselves? — BY SAM LUBELL

When you first arrive in Mexico City, your senses are overwhelmed by the sheer size and the never-ending hum of activity. Choosing a focal point can be exhausting. Every facet of the city seems as important as the next.

If you're an architecture enthusiast, this feeling is multiplied twofold. Every building, no matter how undistinguished its lineage, tries to show itself off. The cityscape is a wonderland of blazing colors, mismatched windows, projecting planes, bold facade graphics, wacky patterning, stray ornaments, and unexpected textures.

Amid such size and variety, it's easiest to concentrate on the usual buildings—the historic center, the big churches, the plazas. But those are as on the beaten path as you can get. To experience Mexico City's new and vivacious architecture, a little more is required.

One solution is to take a guided tour. In my case, it was a somewhat privileged one. My itinerary was shaped by two talented, middle-aged stars of the new guard of architects in Mexico: Fernando Romero and Michel Rojkind. They led me through a collection of new and old galleries, museums, neighborhoods, institutions, and restaurants, as well as buildings of their own designs. Not every traveler can have these guides. But the itinerary they created for me is one that travelers on their own can replicate.

I first set off with Romero, a baby-faced, Prada-clad designer whose firm, FR-EE / Fernando Romero Enterprise, created the famous swooping and vaguely mushroom-shaped Museo Soumaya, about six miles west of the city center. The building contains the art collection of his father-in-law, Carlos Slim Helú, one of the world's richest men.

Previous Museo Soumaya, designed by the architect Fernando Romero to hold the extensive art collection of his father-in-law, the multi-billionaire Carlos Slim.

Left The Cineteca Nacional contains a theater and the national film archives of Mexico. Architect Michel Rojkind designed its redevelopment in 2012.

Opposite A mural of the National Autonomous University of Mexico depicts the country's history.

I found Romero to be an unabashed Mexico City booster. I had chosen to visit at a time people call MeMo, or Mexico's Moment, he exclaimed from the rooftop of a gallery he designed, overlooking the city. The country, he said, was emerging from the economic and cultural shadows. "It's extremely exciting. I've never seen anything like it in my life," he said.

I met him at that gallery and design institution, Archivo, which sits in the San Miguel Chapultepec neighborhood near the gigantic Chapultepec Park, home of several museums and the president's austere residence, Los Pinos. Romero's gallery, the city's first dedicated space for contemporary design objects, is inside a minimalist 1952 house by the modernist architect Arturo Chávez Paz. Romero built a snaking path tunneling from the street and creating a mesmerizing transition from dark to light; inside he opened up the space and assembled a collection of more than design and architecture objects. The collection has grown, and there are rotating exhibitions. The large, glazed rooms, surrounded by a jungle-like yard (designed by the legendary Mexican architect Luis Barragán) that seemed to make its way inside, created an enchanting environment.

We stopped over next door at Casa Estudio Luis Barragán, the house that Barragán, who died in 1988, designed and lived in. It's now a Unesco World Heritage Site. Romero was a docent there when he was younger. For me it was a jaw-dropping sight. Walking into the entry hall felt like staring up the stairs at a three-dimensional painting: Every angle, every dimension, every shadow, every color, and every light beam seemed composed to alter and enhance the viewer's senses.

From there, we toured some nearby galleries. First was the Galería Labor, a tall, open space that was showing off *The Fractal Zoo*, a collection of large, angled steel poles joined by plastic heads by the French artist Étienne Chambaud. Then came Kurimanzutto, a shed-like building infused with light from a long skylight, designed by another leading Mexican architect, Alberto Kalach.

We took a break at the delightful Café Zena, a hole in the wall whose designers, a collaborative of architects called ELHC, outfitted a long alley with tables and chairs. At the end of this tunnel — just past the overhang of a sinuous staircase — was a large light well made of patterned cinder blocks.

Over coffee (excellent), Romero spoke again about the country's upward trajectory, noting the outlay of billions on security and infrastructure. But he was making the wrong pitch. He was leaving out that instead of being a sprawling, impenetrable city, this one is full of charm, with a bit of sophistication amid beautiful, lush, walkable neighborhoods.

We finally made our way to Romero's Museo Soumaya. The museum, in an emerging, formerly industrial area called Nuevo Polanco, was designed to reflect organic forms growing out of the earth, Romero said. It is a shock at first that a building can look like this one does. The torquing, windowless facade is clad with 16,000 hexagon-shaped aluminum panels, few of them alike and none of them touching. It's one of those buildings that, love or hate it, you can't stop looking at. There are so many variations of color, light, and form that the viewer's eye never gets enough.

Inside, the highlight is the top floor, a circular space dominated by a giant skylight, from which projects an explosion of radiating structural beams. For a museum that's emphatically contemporary, the art inside is surprisingly not so. The bulk is made up of European works from the 15th to 19th centuries. The sculptures of one of the artists represented, Rodin, also helped inspire the contorted form of the building.

Our last stop was the Museum of Anthropology, designed in 1963 by the Mexican architect Pedro Ramírez Vázquez, just off the Paseo de la Reforma in the stately Polanco District. The building itself is hard to fathom — particularly its giant concrete canopy, which hovers above the main courtyard atop a single column. The collection inside is, simply, the finest record of Maya, Aztec, Oaxacan, and other Mesoamerican civilizations.

The next day my guide was Michel Rojkind, whose pierced eyebrow and seriously scruffy hair suggested that he would be a very different guide from Romero. He is a literal rock star — the former drummer for the popular Mexican band Aleks Syntek y la Gente Normal; he still gets stopped on the street by fans.

And unlike my first tour guide, whose elite connections somewhat remove him from the local architecture scene, Rojkind lives to be part of it, eagerly teaming up with other designers and constantly promoting the city's large collection of emerging architectural talent.

"When you see your parents fighting all the time, you don't want to repeat that pattern," he said, explaining his generation's propensity to work together.

Above At the Museum of Anthropology, a giant concrete canopy hovers atop a single column.

Opposite Boxes and angles are characteristic of Cineteca Nacional's design.

Rojkind's architecture strives not just to show off but also to transform the space around it, as we saw at our first stop, the Cineteca Nacional. Originally an aloof series of rough black plaster boxes in the scruffy Xoco neighborhood, it was transformed by Rojkind into a thriving campus. He removed a parking lot in front, making it the theaters' main green space. An aluminum canopy cut with triangular perforations shelters it and knits his new buildings together with the original ones. On the far side of his new construction he built yet another park, this one designed for outdoor movies projected onto a wall that's meant to be a giant screen.

He directed me next to one of the city's great unknown architectural gems: the main campus of Mexico's National Autonomous University, or UNAM, about 11 miles south of the historic center. The expansive campus, built in the 1950s, looks a bit worse for wear, but it is about as close as you can come to a museum of modernist architecture, warts and all. You stroll past examples of early Modernism, Streamline Moderne, Structural Expressionism, the International Style and much more, taking in sleek glass curtain walls, monumental facades, colorful building-size murals, gigantic arched roofs, and zigzag-shaped structures. There were no tourists, just students and families, kicking soccer balls and eating street food.

And after a brief nearby sojourn into some more conventional tourism (a visit to Trotsky's house — yes, he was assassinated in Mexico City; a walk through Coyoacán's beautiful square and its many food stalls), I met Rojkind for drinks at a sushi restaurant he designed, Tori Tori, back in Polanco. The place looked like nothing from the street; there was not even a sign. But inside, I saw that Rojkind had covered the facade of an old house with two layers of diamond-patterned white steel. A patio was walled in by a rain forest's worth of vegetation. The highlight

*Photographs by
Alexandre Meneghini*

was a small, Zen-like wood-clad room with another lush green wall at its far end.

The last architecture stop, on the third day of my tour, was the Chopo Museum, designed by Enrique Norten, in Cuauhtémoc, near the historic center. Norten installed a shimmering glass bar-shaped structure for exhibits in the upper reaches of a turn-of-the-20th-century wrought-iron building that was once moved here, piece by piece, from Germany.

It could have been a metaphor for the city, marrying new with old, European culture with Mexico's own original vision and creativity.

After a goodbye meal at a taco joint, Rojkind and I went our separate ways. My tour was over, but Mexico City's adventure with contemporary architecture certainly was not.

WHAT TO READ AND WATCH

Fernando Romero: FR-EE Architecture. Romero's designs and design philosophy, presented through text, photos, and architectural drawings.

The Life and Work of Luis Barragán, by José Maria Buendía Júlbez and Juan Palomar. "Strikes just the right balance between the factual and poetic sides of the architect." — Martin Filler in *The New York Times*.

Mexico City: Architectural Guide, by Sarah Zahradnik. A tour of 100 buildings and monuments, from many eras, with photographs, drawings, and maps.

In the Americas with David Yetman, Season 6, Episode 3: *Mexico City*. Architecture is not the focus, but this video is an intelligent introduction to the city's history and character.

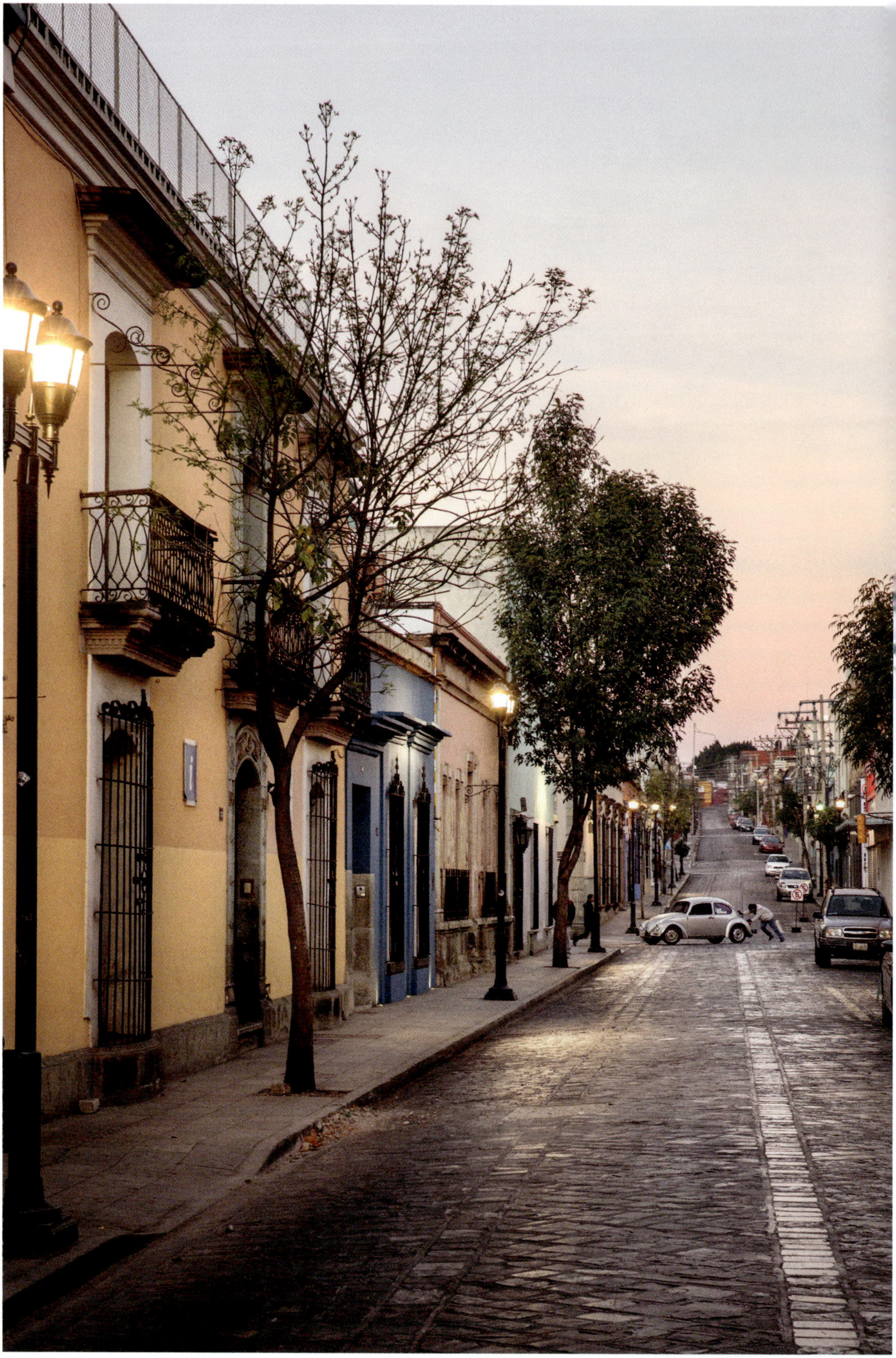

THE HEART AND SOUL OF MEXICO

Oaxaca, in arid highlands, distills the country's greatest charms and offers variations of its own.
— BY FRANCINE PROSE

When friends visiting Mexico for the first time ask me where to begin, I tell them: Go to Oaxaca, one of the most scenically beautiful, historically interesting, and simply enjoyable cities south of the border. The climate is pleasant, temperate all year round, and it's an easy trip of less than an hour, by air, from Mexico City. Above all, it offers a concentrated education in Mexico's culture and complex heritage, an immersion course sweetened by a succession of pleasures and delights — brightly colored houses, pleasant public squares, and stately churches, all set in the midst of a gorgeous desert landscape in the highlands of the Sierra Madre del Sur.

A lovely colonial city that has been designated by Unesco as a World Heritage Site, Oaxaca has a history that goes back to far before the era of the Spanish colonizers. In the city and its environs are several of Mexico's most important archaeological sites. Half an hour away by car (most hotels can put guests in contact with safe, reliable drivers) is the ancient city of Mitla. It functioned as a religious center for the Zapotec civilization, which predated Christ by centuries, and later for the Mixtec people, who ruled the area until they were conquered by the Spanish conquistadors in the 16th century.

Though the exact date of its initial construction is uncertain, we know that Mitla thrived from the eighth century until the Spanish conquest. Yet what's most striking about Mitla is not so much its age as its beauty. Decorating its walls, its pillars, lintels, and archways are fragments of brightly painted frescoes, as well as remarkably well-preserved and stunningly elaborate geometric designs made of mosaics of small stones set into the stucco around them — an

Previous Early morning in the city center. Oaxaca offers insight into every era of Mexico's culture and history.

Left Stirring up some Oaxacan-style hot chocolate in the 20th of November Market.

Opposite The cathedral, in the center of the city, is a popular place to stroll during the winter holiday season.

architectural feature unique in all of Mesoamerica (the area encompassing much of Mexico and Central America). On a trip I took there with my family, even the grandchildren were excited by Mitla, by the sensation of being able to move from one enclosed space to another, almost like going from outdoor room to outdoor room in a magnificent ruined house.

On the outskirts of Oaxaca, and easily accessible by road atop a mountain overlooking sprawling suburbs, is Monte Albán, also built by the Zapotecs, and dating from 500 B.C. Its ruins spread out in a vast complex of pyramids, a palace, a shrine, a ball court, and a variety of carved bas reliefs. Standing in the central plaza, it's impossible not to feel awestruck and even slightly overwhelmed by its sheer monumentality, its grandeur, and its scope. A museum near the entrance contains a small selection of artifacts and documents the history of this archaeological marvel.

In Oaxaca itself, most notably in the city's hilly, cobblestone-paved historic centro, are dozens of churches that exemplify the ways in which the Spanish conquistadors imported their religion and culture while employing the talents (and in some cases the imagery) of the indigenous population. The Cathedral of Our Lady of the Assumption, on the edge of the city's pleasant, shaded zócalo — which is itself a terrific place for watching local families and groups of teenagers — is by far the largest, the grandest, and the most exuberant of these structures.

But my favorite is the Templo de Santo Domingo de Guzmán, which was built by the Dominican friars in the 16th and 17th centuries. The ornately gilded interior features a ceiling decorated with bright polychrome figures, including a lively representation of Santo Domingo's family tree that evokes pre-Columbian images of the Tree of Life. The bas reliefs on the western facade were done by local sculptors, descendants of the artisans responsible for the carving at Mitla, and in one chapel is the statue of a saint dressed in an indigenous costume.

A few blocks away, the Rufino Tamayo Museum showcases an extensive and exquisitely curated collection of pre-Columbian art.

There's a lot to see in Oaxaca, but above all, it is a wonderful place to be: to stroll, to shop, to spend time in the food, flower, and handicrafts markets, and — not insignificantly — to eat. And it's a great walking town. Around nearly every corner in the historical center, you may come upon a bright blue, yellow, or orange wall, stenciled with the inventive advertising posters for which Oaxaca is known.

I have found the most crowded (and to me, the most colorful, vibrant, and thrilling) section of the city to be the covered 20th of November Market, a few blocks from the zócalo. On a shopping trip there, amid a circus-like atmosphere of smells and sights and sounds, one can buy spices, chocolate, vegetables, tropical fruits, and even roasted and ground crickets, a local delicacy.

On our family trip, I bought several woven bags decorated with Mexican folk motifs — perfect for carrying books, papers, and (small amounts of) groceries. I also found a mask made from straw that, as the vendor helpfully showed us, could be rolled into a sort of tubelike parcel and easily stowed in a suitcase without damage. At one end of the market, farthest from the zócalo, is the section where — as in all the greatest Mexican markets — one can eat at counters and small stalls. Here, the adventurous can sample tropical fruit juices and an enormous range of delicious foods.

In the market, too, are glittering displays of mezcal bottles, many with gorgeous labels advertising their origin in small local distilleries.

Agave, from which mezcal is made, is grown throughout the Oaxaca Valley and is one of its most important crops. Driving along the well-marked roads surrounding Oaxaca, one passes agave farms, lined with attractive orderly rows of plants that resemble a cross between an aloe and a pineapple top. Travelers with an interest in sampling the local product (served straight up or in elaborate cocktails) can do so at one of the many stylish mezcal bars that have sprung up throughout the centro.

Several smaller and more low-key markets selling crafts — beaded purses, embroidered shirts, woven belts, filigree earrings, as well as the painted, whimsical wooden animals made in the nearby village of Arrazola — are on the other side of the zócalo. And throughout the centro are dozens of small, inviting boutiques selling clothes, accessories, and household goods that combine traditional craft with high design.

Some nearby villages are known for their particular specialties. San Bartolo de Coyotepec is celebrated for its unique black glazed pottery. In Teotitlán del Valle, nearly every household appears to be involved in weaving gorgeous woolen rugs.

Above It's an easy road trip just outside the city to Monte Albán. The ruins date to the Zapotec civilization of more than 2,000 years ago.

Below Traditional costumes make an appearance for a parade at Templo de Santo Domingo de Guzmán.

Opposite The ancient city of Mitla, close to modern Oaxaca, thrived from the eighth century until the Spanish conquest.

Oaxaca is justly famous for its mole, a piquant sauce with a complex blend of spices and flavors including (in one of its more familiar iterations) chocolate. There are many variations. Large numbers of talented chefs, inspired by the region's culinary heritage, have dedicated themselves to reinventing traditional dishes and to preparing elegant yet unpretentious food served in surroundings ranging from funky and cool to luxurious, stylish, and ultramodern.

At one of the most popular and elegant of the high-end restaurants, Los Danzantes, our group of four adults, two children, and a baby in a stroller were made to feel completely at home. Among the dishes we tried were subtle little tostadas of tuna tartare, chiles stuffed with corn fungus, a green leaf — *herba santa*, which tastes a bit like shiso leaves — rolled around locally made white cheese, candied pork ribs, and coconut shrimp.

The first time I went to Oaxaca, more than 30 years ago, I returned home with a heavy suitcase packed full of figurines, masks, woven shawls, rugs, and dozens of those little boxes in which skeletons, traditionally connected with the Day of the Dead holiday, enact little dramas. Over many visits, I have collected more. But by far my favorite souvenir, which I bought

*Photographs by
Brett Gundlock*

in the central market, was a generous amount of the Mexican chocolate for which Oaxaca is famous. Cups of the steaming hot chocolate are among the most reliable ways I know to keep spirits up during a cold winter and in unsettling times.

Sipping the chocolate, I think about Oaxaca and feel ever so slightly warmer as I imagine walking its cobbled streets, past its painted houses, its shaded plazas, and Baroque churches. And I watch the video we took on New Year's Eve in the courtyard of the Templo de Santo Domingo. Behind those bright swirls of light inscribed on the dusky twilight are two granddaughters with twirling sparklers, celebrating the joy of being in this magical place, with their family, on a perfect holiday evening.

WHAT TO READ AND WATCH

Oaxaca Journal, by Oliver Sacks. An exploration of the Oaxaca region by a writer whose "boundless curiosity is always a reward," as a reviewer in *The New York Times* put it.

On the Plain of Snakes: A Mexican Journey, by Paul Theroux. The legendary travel writer drives first along the United States border and then explores Chiapas and Oaxaca.

Mexican Street Food with Mark Wiens, Season 1, Episode 5: *Oaxaca*. Mexico's great variety of indigenous foods lends itself to delicious variations.

Woven Lives: Contemporary Textiles from Ancient Oaxacan Traditions, directed by Carolyn Kallenborn. Traditional Zapotec art and design go into the weaving of Oaxaca, and this film examines the techniques and the life of the people.

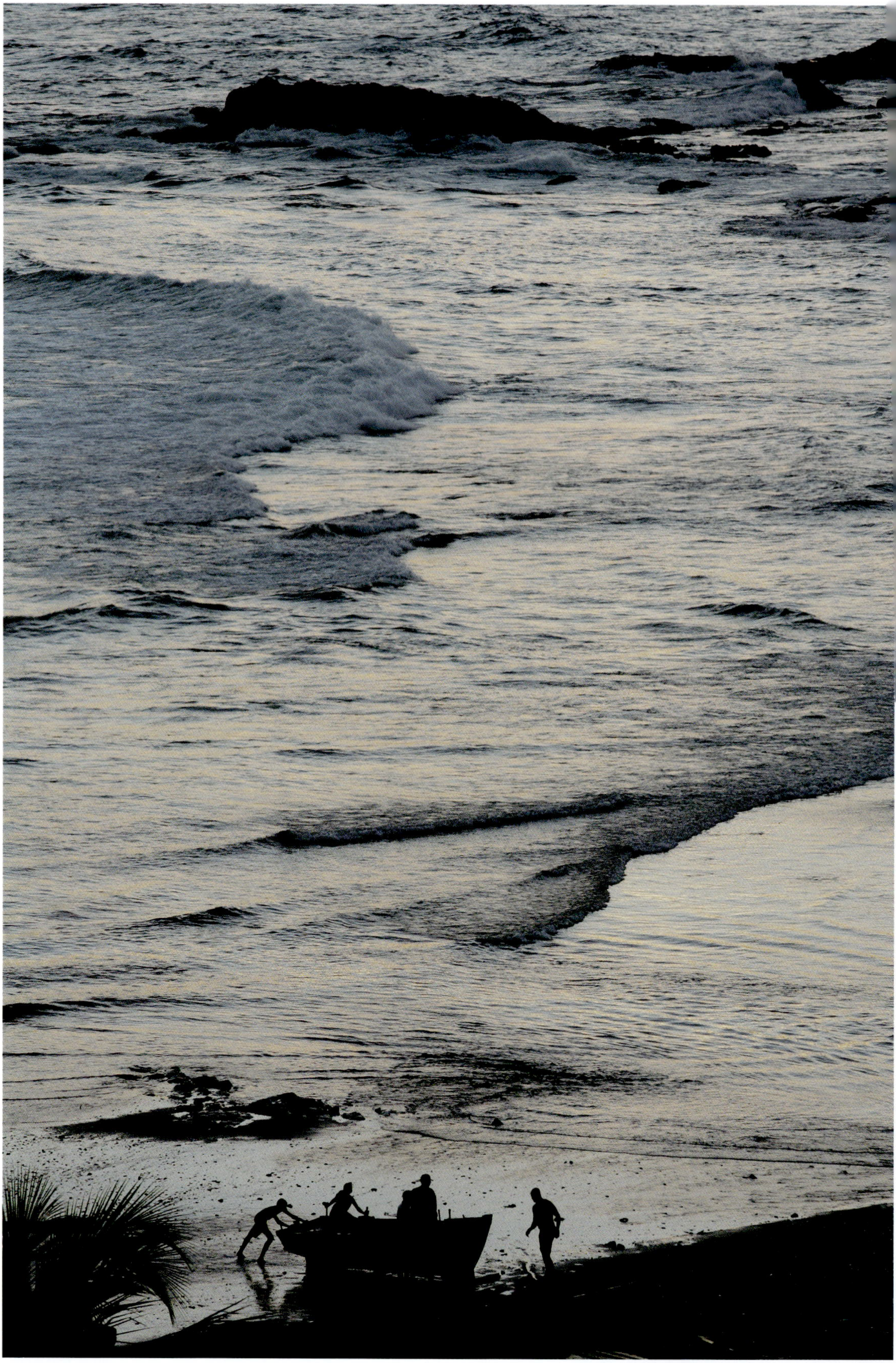

JORGE AMADO'S BELOVED CITY

Dark and light, rich and poor — Brazil's renowned novelist saw life's everyday extremes in Salvador da Bahia. — BY LARRY ROHTER

In Portuguese, "amado" means "beloved," and in more than a score of novels, the Brazilian writer Jorge Amado made clear his eternal passion for Salvador da Bahia, the city that took him in as a teenage boarding student and became his home. Salvador, in turn, loved him back, and even now, many years after his death in 2001, Amado's exuberant spirit, aesthetic, and characters seem to permeate the streets of the place he described both as "the most mysterious and beautiful of the world's cities" and "the most languid of women."

For visitors keen to experience those tropical mysteries, Amado went so far as to suggest an itinerary in his novel *Tereza Batista: Home from the Wars.* He wanted tourists to see not just "our beaches, our churches embroidered with gold, the blue Portuguese ceramic tiles, the Baroque, the picturesque popular festivals, and the fetishist ceremonies," but also "the putridity of the slum houses on stilts and the whorehouses."

That kind of dichotomy was typical of Amado, who, especially in his early years, tended to see everything as pairs of opposites: good and evil, black and white, sacred and profane, rich and poor. He even managed to impose that Manichean vision on the geography of Salvador, scorning Rua Chile, then the main commercial street of the upper city, and its well-to-do clientele in favor of the lower city and the port, where sailors, longshoremen, beggars, prostitutes, and grifters saturated him in "the greasy black mystery of the city of Salvador da Bahia."

Nowadays, the heart of the lower city has been restored and gentrified. The beach where the homeless street urchins of his 1937 novel *Captains of the*

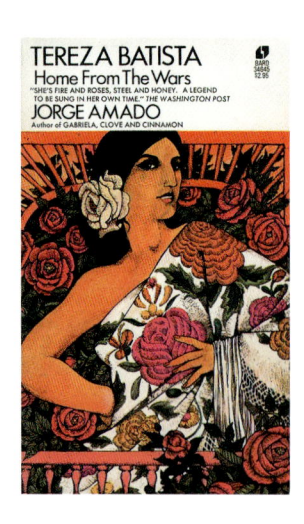

Previous Fishermen at Rio Vermelho beach. The workaday, sometimes gritty side of Salvador inspired Jorge Amado.

Left *Tereza Batista: Home from the Wars*, an Amado novel from 1972.

Opposite Eighteenth-century Portuguese tiles at the São Francisco monastery in Salvador.

Sands struggled to survive has disappeared, replaced by modern buildings and a yacht harbor. The Mercado Modelo just down the road caters to tourists with small shops selling souvenirs, but there's a lingering flavor of the old days a bit farther away on the waterfront at the Feira São Joaquim. Its stalls sell fruit and meats, including various animal organs, and also herbs, magic potions, aphrodisiacs, and amulets.

The link between the scruffy lower city and the imposing "black mass on the green mountain above the sea," as Amado referred to the upper city in *Pastors of the Night*, is the 191-foot Lacerda Elevator, which was itself featured in *Sea of Death*, published in 1936. At its upper terminus, the elevator opens onto a square that provides a sweeping view of the city and the bay.

As much as its people, Salvador's streets and landmarks are characters in Amado's novels. Salvador overwhelmed the author with its sights, sounds, and smells. "In Bahia, popular culture enters through the eyes, the ears, the mouth (so rich, colorful, and tasty the culinary arts) and penetrates all the senses," he wrote in *Bay of All Saints*, a guidebook published in 1945.

Amado's own presence is felt at the museum on Pelourinho Square that bears his name. One part of the permanent exhibition is a display of first-edition covers, in Portuguese and in translation into more than 40 languages, of each of his novels.

As you sit on the museum steps, the most famous scene from Amado's best-known novel, *Dona Flor and Her Two Husbands*, also made into a movie in the 1970s, comes readily to mind. Even with the cobblestoned plaza cluttered by touts trying to sell trinkets to sunburned tourists in Bermuda shorts, the image of Flor walking with Teodoro on one side and the naked ghost of Vadinho on the other seems an indelible part of the landscape.

Just across the square, Largo do Pelourinho 68 is the address of the boardinghouse where Amado lived when he came to Salvador from the provincial town of Ilhéus in 1928, at the age of 16, to study. Not coincidentally, an early novel written in Socialist Realist style, *Sweat*, is set in that building.

Legend says that Salvador has 365 churches, one for each day of the year, and each meant to be more spectacular than the last. The most dazzling of the lot is probably São Francisco, a frothy Baroque confection a couple of blocks from Pelourinho that is awash in gold arabesques and is connected to a monastery whose walls are decorated with gorgeous 18th-century Portuguese tiles.

But Amado always felt a special affection for the more austere Igreja de Nossa Senhora do Rosário dos Pretos because of its links to the historical suffering of the Black people who make up the majority of the city's population. The church is at the foot of Pelourinho Square, where in colonial days slaves were flogged, and Amado, sometimes unjustly accused by his critics of favoring exoticism and sentimentality over substance, never forgot that.

"The church was all blue in the late afternoon, the church of the slaves in the square where the whipping post and pillories had been erected," he wrote in *Tent of Miracles*, published in 1969. "Is that the reflection of the sun or a smear of blood on the cobblestones? So much blood has run over these stones, so many cries of pain rose to heaven, so many supplications and curses resonated on the walls of that blue church."

Food was also essential to Amado's world, as the title of *Gabriela, Clove and Cinnamon* clearly conveys. Amado's humble heroines are frequently of the belief that the surest way to a man's heart is through his stomach, and more often than not they are proven right. "If after confronting all the dangers and obstacles that life offers, you don't eat well, then what's the point?" one character observes in *The Violent Land*.

Walking down the slanted sidewalk of Pelourinho Square, I caught the unmistakable fragrance of *dende*, or palm oil, and peanut sauce wafting from a doorway. It turned out to be the entrance to the Museu da Gastronomia Bahiana, which offers a solid introduction to the culinary delights of Amado's novels. Just downstairs from a restaurant operated by Senac, a government training school for hotel workers, waiters, and chefs, the museum displays the ingredients of typical Bahian dishes along with the utensils required to make them. A shop sells cookbooks and comestibles, and the restaurant has choices like *vatapá*, a savory paste made from shrimp, coconut milk, palm oil, and nuts, or *quindim*, an intensely yellow custard that combines egg yolks, sugar, and ground coconut.

Like Pedro Archanjo, the hero of his novel *Tent of Miracles*, Amado was a lapsed Communist and atheist who eventually became so involved in Candomblé, the African-derived religion that is Brazil's equivalent to voodoo, that he became an *obá*, or honorary high

Above Fita ribbons, thought to bring good luck. "In this land of Bahia, saints and enchanted beings perform miracles and sorcery," Amado wrote.

Opposite Salvador is said to have a church for every day of the year. The Baroque São Francisco dazzles with the gold of the Portuguese conquistadors.

priest, in the cult of Xangô, the deity of lightning and justice. Candomblé beliefs and practices pervade Amado's novels and motivate many of his characters, especially in *The War of the Saints*, the last of his great novels, published in 1988.

"In this land of Bahia, saints and enchanted beings perform miracles and sorcery," Amado wrote, "and not even Marxist ethnologists are surprised to see a carving from a Catholic altar turn into a bewitching mulatto woman at the hour of dusk."

The terreiros, or open-air Candomblé sanctuaries, which Amado frequented back when they were illegal and subject to police raids, now flourish and are open to visitors. Some hotels organize trips to what they advertise as Candomblé ceremonies. But these tend either to be bogus or at the very least watered down. A better option is to make arrangements with one of the established terreiros to attend a worship service and, since most of the tabernacles are in poor, outlying neighborhoods, hire a taxi. Amado was fond of both the Casa Branca group in the Vasco da Gama neighborhood and Ilê Axé Opô Afonjá, in the Cabula area, which the Brazilian government designated a national treasure in 2001.

Ilê Axé Opô Afonjá was "my house," Amado wrote, where "I have my chair at the side of the high priestess and at times am her spokesman." He also urged visitors to be sure to ask their own *orixá*, or divinity, for protection just as soon as they arrived in Salvador.

"The pathways of Salvador are guarded by Exu, one of the most important orixás in the liturgy of Candomblé," he wrote in *Bay of All Saints*. But Exu is often confused with the devil, so "woe be unto those who disembark with malevolent intentions, with a heart of hatred or envy, or stop here tinged by violence or acrimony."

For most of the last decades of his life, Amado lived at Rua Alagoinhas 33 in the Rio Vermelho

Photographs by
Lalo de Almeida

neighborhood, far from both the lower and upper city. At one point in *Dona Flor*, a character complains that "the worst address can only be Rio Vermelho, with its isolation and impostors, an end-of-the-world, almost suburban kind of place, and so ordinary."

But in fact the area is charming, and Amado's house, the Casa do Rio Vermelho, is decorated with blue-and-white tiles with images of birds and fruit. It has been converted into a museum.

"The years of freedom I spent on the streets of Salvador da Bahia, mixing with the people of the docks, of the markets and fairs" and other somewhat disreputable and picaresque locations were "my best university," Amado said when he was inducted into the Brazilian Academy of Letters in 1961. Or as one of the characters in *Captains of the Sands* muses, "There is nothing better in the world than to walk like this, at random, through the streets of Bahia."

WHAT TO READ AND WATCH

The Violent Land, by Jorge Amado. The novelist's favorite of his books. Written in 1942 while he was in exile in Uruguay and Argentina, it is a powerful novel of the bloody struggle in that area's cocoa plantations.

Gabriela, Clove and Cinnamon and ***Dona Flor and Her Two Husbands***, by Jorge Amado. The most popular of the author's novels, both deeply sympathetic to their female protagonists.

Dona Flor and Her Two Husbands, directed by Bruno Barreto. In this 1976 film version, Sônia Braga plays the title character, who has one living husband and one who left her widowed and reappears as a ghost.

Captains of the Sands, by Jorge Amado. A story of a gang of boys in the slums of Salvador da Bahia illuminates social injustice.

Trollstigen to Kristiansund 470

Shetland Islands 422

Outer Hebrides 360

Northern Ireland 338

Elsinore 262

Oxford 366

Oxfordshire & Wiltshire 372

Cornwall 212

London 308, 314

Ostend 352

East Frisia 256
Amsterdam 158
Delft 230
Den Bosch 244

Weimar & Dessau 508

Brussels 200

Nuremberg 346

Paris 378, 384, 390, 396

Fontainebleau 274

Corsier-sur-Vevey 218

Cognac 206

Paris & Périgord 404

Dordogne 250

Italian Libraries 300

Venice 488

Cremona 224

Asturias & Basque Country 176

Provence-Alpes-Côte d'Azur 410

Urbino 476

Astigarraga 170

Florence 268

Sier 436

Grasse 286

Soria 450

Barcelona 188

Rome 416

Madrid 322

Sintra 444

Majorca 330

The Alentejo 152

Andalusia 164

EUROPE

- Stockholm & Adelso 462
- sedom 482
- The Spreewald 456
- Vienna 496
- Bratislava 194
- Attersee 182
- Warsaw 502
- Istanbul 294
- Georgia & Turkey 280
- Delphi 238
- Sicily 428

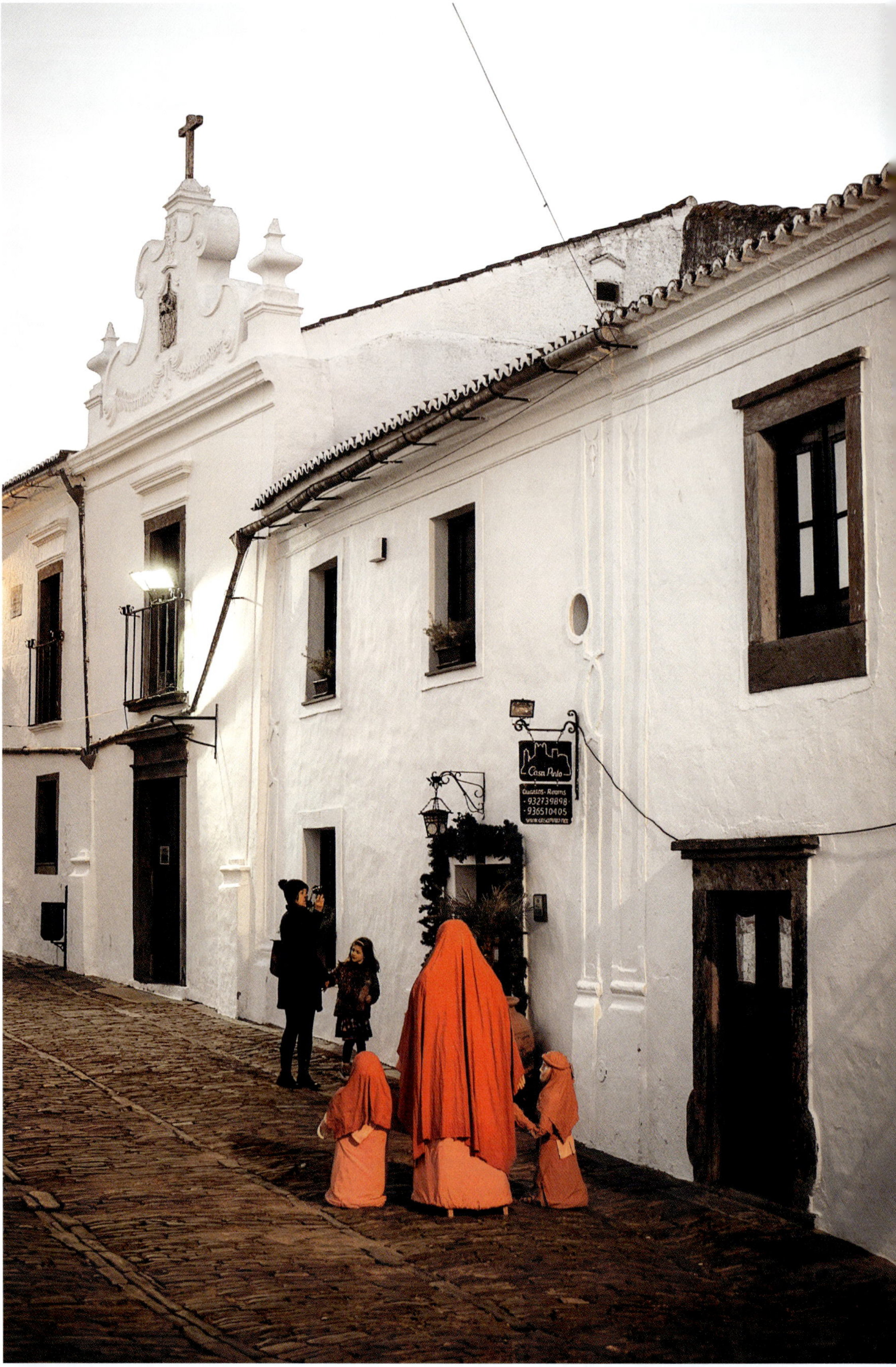
Casa Pinto
Quartos - Rooms
932739898
936510405

THE ALENTEJO, A LAND FINELY AGED LIKE WINE

Southeast of Lisbon, country roads lead to mountain towns, sun-baked fields, and vineyards.
— BY ELI GOTTLIEB

The surprising thing about touching down at Lisbon Airport is how fast, heading south in a car, you find yourself transported into deep countryside. I arrived on a mild October morning, was met there by my old friend Martin Earl, and within a few minutes was crossing the Vasco da Gama Bridge, one of the longest in Europe, an affair of towers and cables that stretches like a single bolt of flung steel across the Tagus River estuary. Immediately thereafter we swerved off the highway and decelerated into the dreaming, older world of the Alentejo (the word literally means "beyond the Tejo" or Tagus).

For the next five days we would be traveling among medieval whitewashed villages, rolling hills, mountain forts, and a constellation of sparklingly modern vineyards. Martin and I had been friends since college, where we were part of a group of five guys all starstruck by the dream of literature. Now, somewhat inexplicably, we were middle-aged, and Martin, a poet, had a Portuguese wife and lived for decades in Portugal. On this trip, he would be my guide.

Forty minutes from the airport, we were passing through sun-dappled alleys of plane trees with, beyond them, irregular row upon row of cork oaks. The beautiful cork oak somewhat resembles a stouter, leafier olive tree, and is hand-harvested of its bark once every 10 years. The forests themselves are both a giant cash cow for the national economy — 60 percent of the global cork trade originates in Portugal — and one of the most concentrated examples of biodiversity on earth.

Meanwhile, the whitewashed villages kept coming, one after the other. We stopped for a coffee in a

Previous On a car trip through the Alentejo, whitewashed villages pop out one after another. This one is Monsaraz.

Left Black pigs feast on acorns from the Alentejo's cork oak trees. They reappear as flavorful ham and sausage.

Opposite Cork oaks can live 200 years, plenty of time for multiple harvests of their bark to make corks for wine bottles.

particularly sleepy, sun-blasted one called Montemor-o-Novo. Amid the mostly deserted low buildings there seemed to be a single cafe. But was it a cafe? The sign above it read, "Grupo de Pesca Desportiva à Linha de Montemor-o-Novo." This was a local hand-line fishing club, Martin explained, devoted to the old, pure form of the sport in which the line is held in the hands, dropped to the bottom and jiggled in emulation of live bait. These clubs are usually members-only, but the cheerful potbellied locals seated outside immediately waved us in.

An excited barista explained that they were about to celebrate something extraordinary. The traditional cante Alentejano, a kind of polyphonic choral singing unique to the region, had been designated by Unesco to be listed as an Intangible Cultural Heritage of Humanity. One of the singers was right there and about to be feted. We watched as a waiter presented the singer — a middle-aged man distinguishable from the other patrons only by his dyed blond hair — with a tray bearing a white cube, roughly the size of a small brick. When I asked what this was, one of the old boys, to the merriment of the others, grunted at me like a pig.

"Lard," Martin said simply. I had lived in Italy for years, and in Rome had often seen ribbons of the stuff draped on plates and consumed like a kind of bacon sushi, but this was a block of pure porky fat, unadorned, and I watched amazed as the singer tucked a napkin into his collar and began hacking off pieces and then forking them into his mouth with a great smacking of the lips.

We drank some of the deliciously bitter coffee and continued on our way. The route lay southeast, in the direction of Spain, and we took secondary roads to savor our surroundings. With the windows open, our little car buzzed like a blender. Roadside eucalyptus trees sent a delicious tang through the air.

We turned off for lunch in a smallish town called Redondo and found a promising-looking place called Porfírio's with Mediterranean tavern décor of white-washed walls and beamed ceilings.

A tray of the tasty pay-as-you-go appetizers, or entradas, typical in Portugal, was soon placed on our table: herbed and vinegared olives, breads, sausages, and two kinds of fresh cheese. The lunch itself opened with an exquisite dogfish soup — the dogfish is a kind of shark, white-fleshed and sweet — followed by a first course of something called *arroz de pato*, or duck rice. The lid of baked egg atop the rice was dotted with broiled bits of incredibly savory bacon and *chouriço*, a sausage similar to chorizo, both of them sourced from local pigs. Plunging your fork through the lid released a jet of flavorful steam, and below the rice, a vein of moist, darkly delicious duck. A staple of the Portuguese menu, this dish characteristically distills the simplicity of its ingredients into something that explodes on the tongue like a bomb.

The local specialty is *porco preto*, or black pig, a member of the swine family fed mostly on the acorns that fall from cork trees and presented in sausage, bacon, and chops and as an enriching agent in a variety of stews. The animal's intense depth of flavor is due partly to that acorn-heavy diet, and as a bonus, those acorns imbue the flesh with oleic acid, the same heart-friendly ingredient found in olive oil.

The next two days took on an easy natural rhythm of eating, sightseeing, and drinking the cheap, wonderfully well-structured local wines. We stayed in the beautiful mountain towns Monsaraz and Marvão. Each of them was originally built as a fortified redoubt against invasion from nearby Spain and was visible from the valleys below looking like a kind of terra-cotta headpiece set high in the hills. Each was entered through several miles of switchbacks; and inside the thickly fortified walls, each had a similar array of aerobically steep cobbled streets, a castle, a small museum, shops, restaurants, and panoramic views.

In Monsaraz we stayed at the immaculate Casa Pinto, a three-star hotel whose rooms were furnished with reminders of the once-mighty Portuguese colonial empire. My room was called Mombasa and boasted beautiful Moorish-cum-African décor, with wreathing ibex horns, dark wood ceilings, and a lovely, mood-lit stone grotto bathroom.

As we progressed, I began to feel the weight of the tourist trade wearing away some of the Alentejo's indigenous sparkle. The restaurants in the showcase mountain towns tended toward the tired, and the little ateliers and stores that honeycombed the alleyways seemed filled mainly with kitsch.

After two days of sojourning at altitude, we returned to the plains. We were not far from Évora, the region's famous capital, with its stunning combination of Roman, Gothic, and Baroque architecture. Also fairly close was the Almendres megalithic site, created 2,000 years before Stonehenge and among

Above A vineyard near Évora. One local vintner boasted of wines that are "velvety and well-balanced."

Opposite Évora's cathedral. Heavy stone walls and fortifications in Alentejo once protected against invasion from Spain.

humanity's oldest known monuments. But those were for another trip. Instead, we began following signs for "rota dos vinhos" — the wine route.

These soon brought us to the Adega Mayor winery, a hypermodern collection of cubes and cantilevers set out in the hills and designed by the famous Portuguese architect Álvaro Siza. We toured the ingeniously constructed building and sampled some of the exquisite wines.

But it would be at lunch the next day that Portugal would finally offer up a truly world-class dining and drinking experience, one worth flying seven hours for and then driving a bunch more. It took place at Herdade dos Grous, a giant vineyard and estate in a village south of Beja.

In the high-ceilinged dining room, with views over the quilted green vineyards and a man-made lake, we ordered the chef's tasting menu accompanied by paired wines. The meal opened with a luxe version of typical entradas, the flavor of each small meat, cheese, and vegetable dish as particularized as the panes of a stained-glass window. A lighter-than-air dogfish soup was followed by a veal medallion set in two Nike swooshes of mustard sauce, served with fingerling potatoes, a topping of radish sprouts, and roasted chickpeas.

With the paired wines of Herdade dos Grous, the net effect was of one of the great culinary transports of my life.

Afterward I spoke with Luís Duarte, the man responsible for the extraordinary wines I'd just drunk.

"I belong to the first class that studied winemaking in school, professionally," he said. "My particular innovation was that instead of working in the Douro" — Portugal's traditional wine region, farther north — "I decided to head south to the unsung Alentejo. It was my good luck to get in on the ground floor of the worldwide growth of wine and ride that wave."

Photographs by James Rajotte

Portuguese winemakers have 315 grape varieties to work with, he said, and have developed their own style. "You want a velvety and well-balanced wine at a good price? Think Portugal."

Martin and I strolled a bit in the nearby vineyards, watching workers industriously trim vines, and then walked back toward the winery's main building. As we came close, we saw a golden retriever ambling out to greet us, but it paused when it was approached by a barnyard cat. Instead of fighting, the two touched noses.

"Around here," Martin said with a wry smile, "everyone's so happy that even interspecies enemies kiss and make up."

We laughed and turned back toward the car. It had been five days in that peculiar suspension of real life known as the road trip, and it was time to go home.

WHAT TO READ

Alentejo (Bradt Travel Guide), by Alex Robinson. A wealth of information for Alentejo travelers from a publisher of guidebooks in areas that often get short shrift.

Lonely Planet Portugal, by Regis St. Louis, Kate Armstrong, Anja Mutic, and Andy Symington. One of several popular guidebooks for travelers to Portugal.

Alentejo Blue, by Monica Ali. A well-received novel about villagers dealing with change and displacement as expats and tourists move in.

My Portugal: Recipes and Stories, by George Mendes with Genevieve Ko. Mendes, chef and owner of Aldea in New York, introduces Portuguese cuisine and interjects stories of his Portuguese heritage.

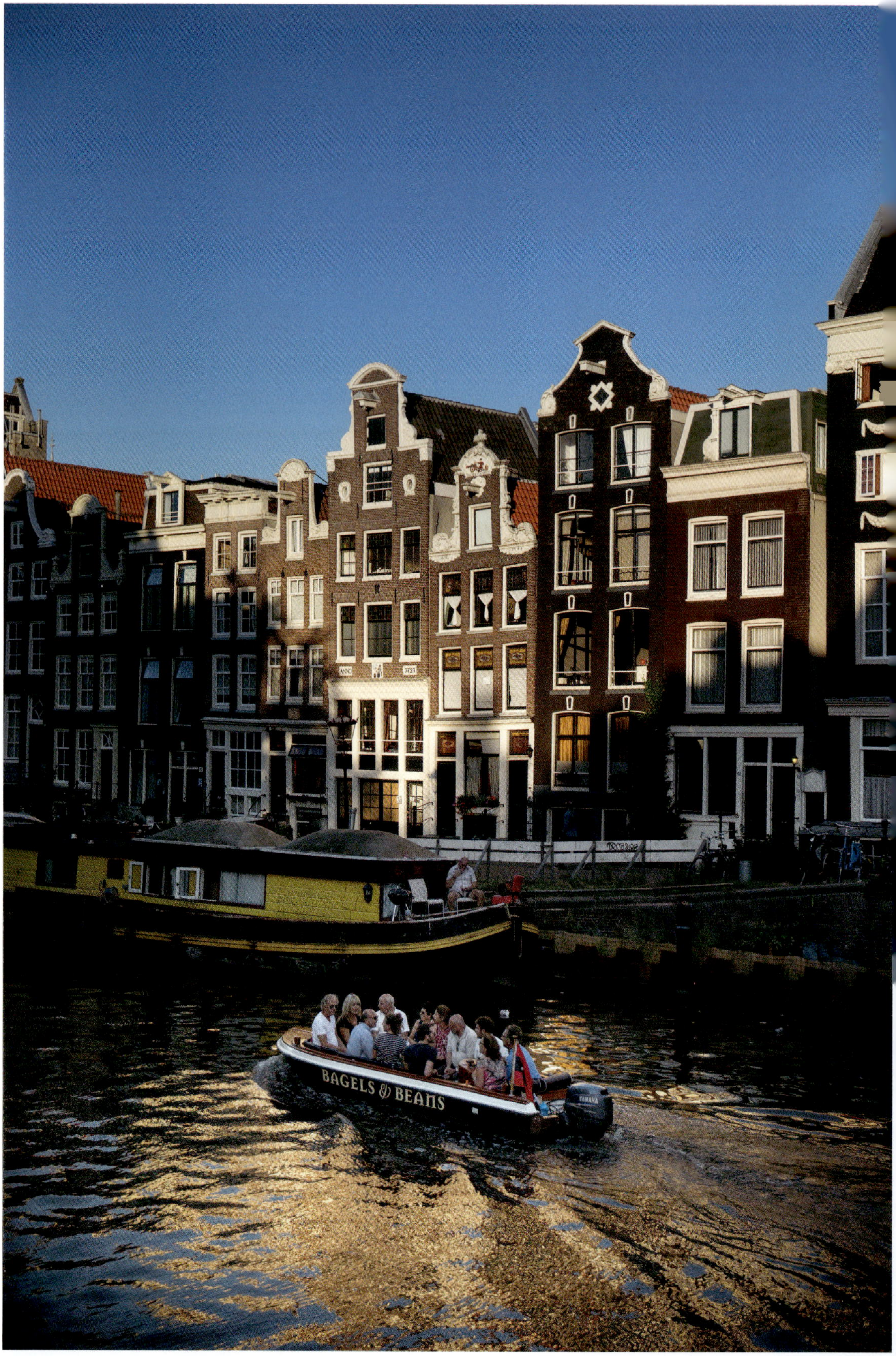
BAGELS & BEANS

NETHERLANDS　　　　　　　　　　　　　　　　　　　　　　　　　　AMSTERDAM

RETURN TO AMSTERDAM

A beloved city is changing fast, but amid the slender houses and silent canals, its familiar spirit endures.
— BY RUSSELL SHORTO

For my family, Amsterdam is not just any destination. I lived in the city for seven years and wrote a book about it. My partner, Pamela, lived there for 23 years. We met in Amsterdam. Our son was born in the city. We have friends, family, colleagues, memories, and roots there. It is, logically and in our hearts, our second home. And yet, three years after returning to the United States, we realized that it had become shockingly remote in our lives. So when we went back for a summer vacation, our real motive was to spend a couple of weeks reclaiming Amsterdam.

We had been hearing and reading that the city had changed dramatically in the short time since we moved. The population was growing, the urban landscape was being reshaped. Real estate prices were spiking, new hotels were opening, and the Airbnb phenomenon had arrived. To all of that we had to add the ineffable: that global hipsterism had deemed Amsterdam—with its orderly northern languor, its human scale, its society built around coffee and beer—a place of relevance.

On our arrival, however, it seemed that nothing had changed. Taking the train from the airport and stepping out of Central Station, we encountered the familiar detritus, the same ragged rumble of buses and traffic, ugly shops, and wayward tourists heading up the streets called Damrak and Rokin toward the city center. Also unchanged, thankfully, was the canal zone, the heart and soul of Amsterdam. Here, where gabled brick houses line the central canals, it is always the Dutch Golden Age. And this was where we would be staying, in a classic canal house, circa 1600, that belonged to our friends. Each room looked out onto the medieval and ruminative Oudezijds Achterburgwal canal.

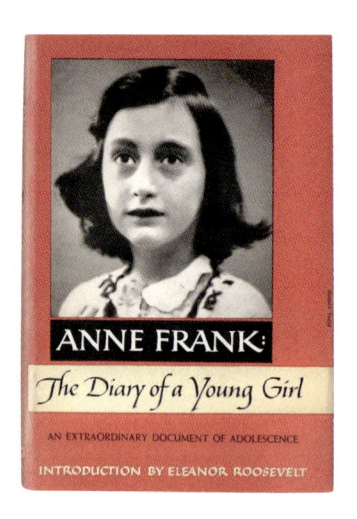

Previous The closest Amsterdam has to a defining monument is one that people live in: the canal house.

Left A first edition copy of *Anne Frank: The Diary of a Young Girl*.

Below A new generation has rediscovered the quiet district of Noord, or Amsterdam North.

Opposite Barges and handcarts served warehouses along an Amsterdam canal in this image from 1905.

Each day we ate breakfast—croissants and coffee from the bakery around the corner—in our kitchen. With low ceilings, enormous beams, and Delft tiles lining the hearth, it seemed almost unchanged from the period when the house was built. Rembrandt lived in this part of the city, and it occurred to me one morning, mid-croissant, that the artist could conceivably have known the occupant and sat in this very kitchen.

As it turned out, the antique facade of the neighborhood—the Binnenstad, or Inner City—belied vigorous change. Wealthy foreigners, especially Russians and Chinese, our friend told us, were buying up many of these tilting, toylike houses, often as rarely used pieds-à-terre, driving up the prices and eroding the sense of community.

After we rented bicycles (the only proper way to get around the city), other changes became apparent. Amsterdam's popularity as a travel destination has applied mostly to its center, and to some extent its long-gentrified southern districts. Now gentrification and tourism had reached farther.

In the Indische Buurt, or Indies Neighborhood, long the home of Turkish and Moroccan immigrants, artists and young families have moved in to escape high real estate prices elsewhere. Cruising down the Javastraat, the main thoroughfare, we passed an olive oil boutique, a frozen yogurt shop, a women's boutique with purses arranged atop distressed wood tables, and, as if to underscore the transformation, a coffee bar called Bedford-Stuyvesant.

In the western reaches of the city, the Spaarndammerbuurt is one of the neighborhoods where the Amsterdam School architects of the early 20th century developed their style, turning simple brick dwellings into artful and sometimes whimsical statements. It was always a workers' quarter. We found it alive with wine purveyors and vegetarian takeouts, and we had a great dinner there at a tapas restaurant.

Amsterdam has long had a bit of a split personality issue because the section called Amsterdam North sits across the harbor from the rest of the city. Not many tourists visited Noord until 2012, when the EYE Film Institute opened on the waterfront just opposite Central Station, looking like an intergalactic cruiser out of *Star Trek*. It soon became a cultural anchor. A few years later, the 22-story building beside it, once the headquarters of Royal Dutch Shell, opened as a hotel, performance studios, and artist lofts. We skipped those to be rocketed 300 feet up in an elevator to an observation platform called the A'Dam Lookout. There were sweeping, cleansing views, miles in every direction.

How far have the changes gone? One of the pleasures of Noord I remembered was pastoral quiet away from the waterfront. Now I saw a newspaper article saying in effect that in Noord you can't see the cows anymore for all the BMWs.

If Amsterdam's outer reaches have changed, so has the city center. The Rijksmuseum, the national repository of Dutch art and history, has been renovated and is staggeringly lovely. The redesign accomplished the tricky task of keeping the integrity of the original 19th-century structure while at the same time opening it up. What might have come across, to today's tastes, as a clunky knight's castle instead feels stately and inviting. Like the city, the museum is more popular than ever.

Taco Dibbits, the Rijksmuseum's director, sat down with me to discuss the museum and the city. When I asked why both were now so popular, he referred me to the time, circa 2000, when Bill Gates caused a stir by saying he didn't need to collect art because in a digital age you could have any painting appear on your screen. "Instead," Dibbits said, "what we're seeing is that in a virtual world, people want to experience real things."

Long-known for its Rembrandts, the Rijksmuseum added to its offerings by purchasing, jointly with the Louvre, a pair of Rembrandt wedding portraits for 160 million euros. The museums take turns displaying them, but during our trip they were at the Rijksmuseum, given pride of place next to Rembrandt's masterpiece *The Night Watch*. The paintings are the first life-size portraits Rembrandt completed and had

Above The EYE Filmmuseum, a cultural anchor in Amsterdam North.

Below A bicycle, the tried-and-true transport of Amsterdam, makes it easy to get beyond the touristy city center.

Opposite Amsterdam's tall houses and quiet canals began as practicalities and survive as symbols of the city's identity.

been in private hands since they were painted in the 17th century.

At that time, only royalty was deemed worthy of such treatment. Rembrandt was just 28, newly arrived in Amsterdam, and eager to make his mark. By giving the wealthy but untitled couple in these portraits the royal treatment, he was making a statement about them, about himself, and about the city. Amsterdam was in the midst of its rise to the status of most powerful city in the world. Its economic engine was powered by ordinary citizens who had worked their way up to the top, forging great companies whose commerce spanned the globe. The pair of paintings, so alien but so evocative, embody what Amsterdam is all about.

Yet Amsterdam has always been modest in size, and that, too, is part of its identity. It's not an accident that the city has no central, representative monument: no Big Ben or Notre Dame or Colosseum. The closest Amsterdam has to a defining monument was the one we were staying in: the canal house. An individual family dwelling is an apt symbol for the city because Amsterdam shaped itself around the power and needs of individuals. Where other European capitals were built around the might of the church or a monarch or both, here the central forces were

Photographs by
Ilvy Njiokiktjien

commerce, art, and science. All are pursuits spearheaded by individuals.

In the Golden Age, the city's traders gathered the exotic goods of the wide world and brought them here, their ships sailing right up the canals to Amsterdam's front doors. Dutch interior paintings of the 17th century celebrated the particular brand of domesticity that the Dutch traders fostered. *Gezelligheid* — an untranslatable word that means something like "the warm feeling that comes from being secure and in the embrace of friends and family" — is what animates those paintings.

Indeed, it still animates Amsterdam. We felt it on our return to this city that has meant so much to us. And we wondered how long it would endure.

WHAT TO READ AND WATCH

Amsterdam: A History of the World's Most Liberal City, by Russell Shorto. The author, who is also the writer of this article, is a historian and journalist.

Amsterdam Tales (City Tales), edited by Paul Vincent. A collection of prose fiction, memoirs, and anecdotes about the city.

Amsterdam, by Geert Mak. An insider's view from a prominent Dutch historian and journalist.

The Fault in Our Stars, directed by Josh Boone. A young couple falls in love in a cancer support group. The film is notable for its many views of Amsterdam.

Restaurante CHIKITO
Antiguo Café Alameda
Homenaje a los miembros de
la tertulia literaria de
El Rinconcillo
Federico García Lorca
Manuel de Falla
Constantino Ruiz Carnero
José Mora Guarnido
Miguel Pizarro Zambrano
Hermenegildo Lanz
Francisco García Lorca
Juan Cristóbal
Fernando de los Ríos
Ángel Barrios
Andrés Segovia

GARCÍA LORCA, SPAIN'S MURDERED POET

Andalusia, arid and beautiful, majestic and tragic, inspired him and remembers him. In 1936 its merciless politics killed him. — BY DOREEN CARVAJAL

It takes about five miles along a red dirt road in the semidesert of Andalusia to reach the 18th-century ruins of the Cortijo del Fraile. Alone in the scorching sun and dry winds, this decaying Dominican farmhouse and chapel seems to stand through some sheer force of its literary fame. It holds together with stones and mortar — a neglected national treasure that was the real-life setting for a classic tragedy of betrayal and murder in Spain's southernmost region.

The arid lands and immense nights inspired the early 20th-century Spanish poet and playwright Federico García Lorca to write his greatest drama, *Blood Wedding*, based on the true crime story in 1928 of a runaway bride who fled her arranged marriage on horseback to be with her true love. He was killed by her relatives. She died long after García Lorca did, an elderly recluse, buried in 1987 in a secret tomb.

García Lorca drew deeply on the landscapes of his native Andalusia and found inspiration in its history, colors, and rural simplicity — crushed grass, the splash of fountains, the smell of the Sierra Nevada, and the whitewashed caves carved into homes in the russet hills of the region.

"I feel linked to it in all my emotions," he remarked in a 1934 interview in Buenos Aires for the Argentine newspaper *Crítica*, describing this passion as his "agrarian complex."

"My earliest boyhood memories taste of earth," he said.

To search for García Lorca's Andalusia is to chase fragments of poetry and loss. He was silenced at age 38 — murdered in the summer of 1936 by a paramilitary death squad at the outset of the Spanish Civil War, targeted for his anti-Fascist sentiments and his

Previous García Lorca in bronze at his corner table in Chikito, which was called Cafe Alameda in the 1920s.

Left The collection of the Federico García Lorca Center in Granada includes thousands of manuscripts, books, and drawings.

Opposite García Lorca frequently drew as well as wrote, as in this letter to a friend.

homosexuality. His exact burial site, in an anonymous mass grave somewhere in fields outside Granada, remains a mystery.

But his powerful voice is still one that binds Spain as it struggles with tensions between the Catalan independence movement and the Spanish state.

In 2017, his verses offered a measure of comfort after a deadly jihadist van attack along the Ramblas, the heart of Barcelona. Over booming loudspeakers, thousands of antiterrorism protesters listened to a recital of his tribute to the Ramblas: "The street where all four seasons live together. The only street I wish would never end."

When he was 18, in 1917, he set off from Granada on the first of four expeditions by steam train, with his art history professor and other students, to tour Andalusia. It was then, he said, that "I became fully aware of myself as a Spaniard." He was seeking memories of "the ancient souls who once walked the solitary squares we now tread."

Much of García Lorca's writing explores the rural tragedies of women in Andalusia and an earthy culture where death and love are deeply intertwined. In his family home in Granada, he wrote the trilogy of his greatest plays, *Blood Wedding*, *Yerma*, and *The House of Bernarda Alba*. The house, Huerta de San Vicente, is now a museum and whitewashed sanctuary surrounded by linden trees and roses. The downstairs living room is furnished with black-and-white photos from many decades ago, along with García Lorca's baby grand piano and a pensive portrait of him, with dark wavy hair and sharp eyes, wearing a mustard robe. Upstairs, his bedroom and study had a single bed and an oak desk stained with ink.

In Granada, his vast archives are housed in the striking white Federico García Lorca Center building, by the tranquil Plaza de Romanillo. The archive includes documents from manuscripts and letters to theater programs and musical scores, and it mounts rotating exhibits and programs.

García Lorca alienated the local society by complaining that Granada was inhabited by a cold, introverted ruling class. Yet, despite the mutual loathing, he held court there in the 1920s with his young literary circle of intellectuals, called El Rinconcillo. At a restaurant known then as Cafe Alameda, he would read his works aloud from a corner table.

Today his refuge is named Chikito, and the restaurant's cuisine is typically Andalusian with a popular tapa of tiny snails with ham and almond sauce and its specialty, an oxtail stew. In 2015, the writer's favorite corner was transformed into a shrine with a life-size bronze statue of García Lorca seated at a vintage marble table and wearing a dapper bow tie.

The most touching memorial, though, is spontaneous — an annual midnight-to-dawn flamenco tribute every August 19 on the anniversary of García Lorca's death that is an open secret among performers and locals. It takes place in the hills northeast of Granada in El Barranco de Viznar, near the likely mass graves. When I saw it, trembling voices rose from the dark forest to the sound of cante jondo, or deep song — music that inspired the poetry of García Lorca, who was a musician himself. He likened its rhythms and wavering stammers to the trilling of birds and the music of forest and fountain. And he believed it had to be preserved because it represented the ancient music of the persecuted and oppressed of Andalusia — Arabs, Jews, and Gypsies — who fled into the mountains in the 15th century to escape the Spanish Inquisition.

Seville offered more openness and tolerance than Granada, something García Lorca considered a reflection of physical geography and the Guadalquivir River that flows within Seville and outward to the Atlantic Ocean, shooting through, he wrote in a poem, like "a constant arrow."

One place to look for the city's spirit is the sprawling San Fernando municipal cemetery. At its entrance is an exotic neighborhood of tombs and shrines devoted to Seville's Andalusian aristocracy of flamenco stars and fallen bullfighters like Francisco Rivera Pérez, "Paquirri," who is sculpted in a matador's suit and poised to guide a bull's final attack.

It was in Seville that García Lorca befriended Ignacio Sánchez Mejías, a bullfighter who was also a poet and a playwright. After Ignacio was gored in a post-retirement bullfight in 1934, at age 43, García Lorca wrote a classic elegy, a 1935 poem of disbelief and grief about his friend's early death. There is no more affecting place to read aloud his lament — "Oh white wall of Spain! Oh black bull of sorrow! Oh hard blood of Ignacio!" — than beside the matador's simple grave. It lies in the shadow of an enormous tomb for Ignacio's fellow bullfighter and brother-in-law, Joselito, who was killed in 1920 by a bull named Bailaor. A marble-and-bronze sculpture depicts Joselito in his draped coffin, shouldered by 18 distraught men and women. One of the figures is Ignacio, head cast to beseech the cloudless skies.

Death, honor, and frustration are themes that endlessly fascinated García Lorca. In Madrid in 1933, he staged the premier of *Blood Wedding*, which draws on the 1928 newspaper accounts of the defiant bride, Francisca Cañadas. She abandoned her fiancé — her sister's brother-in-law — hours before their pending marriage, fleeing deep into the countryside with her beloved first cousin. Francisca's sister and her husband tracked them down, fatally shooting the cousin and strangling Francisca, leaving her for dead on the road to Nijar. The bride survived, living for decades with the enmity of her village, which blamed her for provoking the tragedy.

In his drama, García Lorca transformed the key characters and heightened the bloodshed. He conceived of the set inside a spacious cave like the ancient enclaves in Purullena and Guadix, southern towns in the province of Granada known for mazes of whitewashed caves fashioned into homes, with inhabitants called trogloditas. He was struck by the rare accommodation of life and earth in the labyrinth of cave dwellings. Some date back to the 16th century.

The cave communities are still active. Some caves are thoroughly modern, with wrought-iron guard

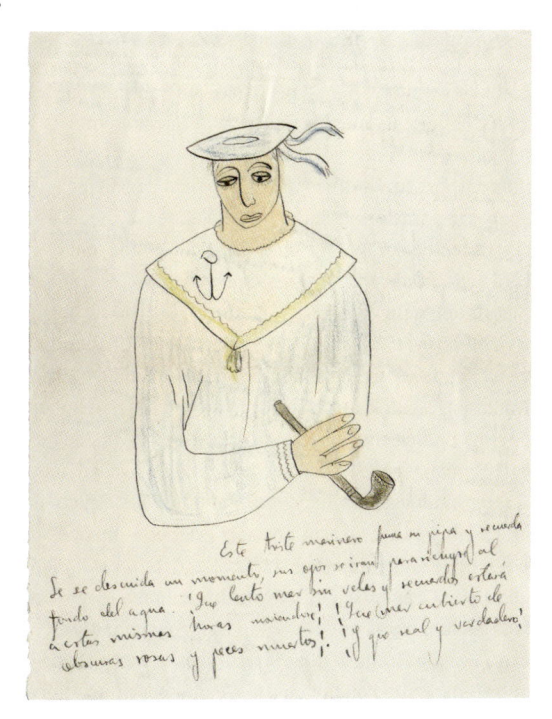

Above A flamenco statue in Granada. García Lorca valued regional traditions, and flamenco figures in tributes to him.

Opposite Dwellings carved in rock in the village of Purullena. The tragic heroine of *Blood Wedding* lives in a cave.

gates, chimneys, marble floors, Wi-Fi access, and television antennas poking out of the oatmeal-colored hills. Others are gothic ruins from past centuries, poetry in white against the blue splendor of the skies. (Purullena is known for blue: the cobalt blue of its ceramics, made with a special polychrome technique that dates to the 1500s.)

When I was touring Purullena with my husband, on a back road in a cave neighborhood a silver-haired woman in a black coat and carrying a cane noticed us photographing the homes. She beckoned us inside her cave, which had a red tiled awning and an arched door.

Her kindness reminded me of another basic element of Andalusia that García Lorca cherished — its people. On the same day that she spoke to us, we stopped nearby in Graena, a small town that is home to spring-fed thermal baths and an outdoor barbecue restaurant, Bar La Pradera, that specializes in lamb chops and steak grilled on hot coals. We had not dined there in five years, and tourists rarely stop there. But the owners welcomed us back with kisses and then invited us to their home.

No journey inspired by García Lorca could be complete without witnessing the real-life last act of *Blood Wedding*. We rumbled along a dirt road to reach the Cortijo del Fraile, the crumbling farmhouse where Francisca Cañadas lived with her father, who owned the property then. Today it is a surreal landmark of ruin and romance in Europe's only semi-desert, the Cabo de Gata Nature Preserve in Almería, Spain's southeastern corner.

The fragile farmhouse was surrounded by a wire fence to prevent entry of tourists. Its facade had been minimally restored, but there was much more work to be done. A plain marker explained its literary pedigree and also noted its role as a backdrop in various movies, among them Sergio Leone's spaghetti western *The Good, the Bad, and the Ugly*.

*Photographs by
Javier Luengo*

From the ruins, we headed toward the town of Níjar and stopped at one of its oldest municipal cemeteries. Its white walls were full with rose and blue silk flowers and tribute plaques to the village's dead, including members of the star-crossed Cañadas family.

Every time I visit Andalusia, I try to find some trace of the grave of the runaway bride. She never married and was essentially buried in life by the scorn of her village. And every year nothing changes in the essential rural tragedy imagined by García Lorca.

A lone cemetery worker offered me a vague hint that Francisca Cañadas's tomb is placed near a soaring cypress tree, a symbol of mourning and hope. But a stone plaque was nowhere to be found. According to the family's wishes, the worker said, it is marked with a false name.

WHAT TO READ AND WATCH

Blood Wedding, by Federico García Lorca and Ted Hughes. A sensitive reworking, for English-language audiences and by a longtime English poet laureate, of a play that is mysterious and poetic.

Poet in Spain, by Federico García Lorca, bilingual edition. In Spanish with English translations by Sarah Arvio, this selection includes *Gypsy Ballads*, love sonnets, and *Blood Wedding*.

Poet in New York, by Federico García Lorca. Works from the poet's 10-month stay, beginning in 1929, in New York. For him, the city was a dark revelation of urban complexity, social injustice, and the panic of the stock market crash.

The Disappearance of García Lorca, directed by Marcos Zurinaga. A thriller in which a fictional journalist attempts to unravel the mystery of García Lorca's death decades after the fact. Andy García stars as García Lorca.

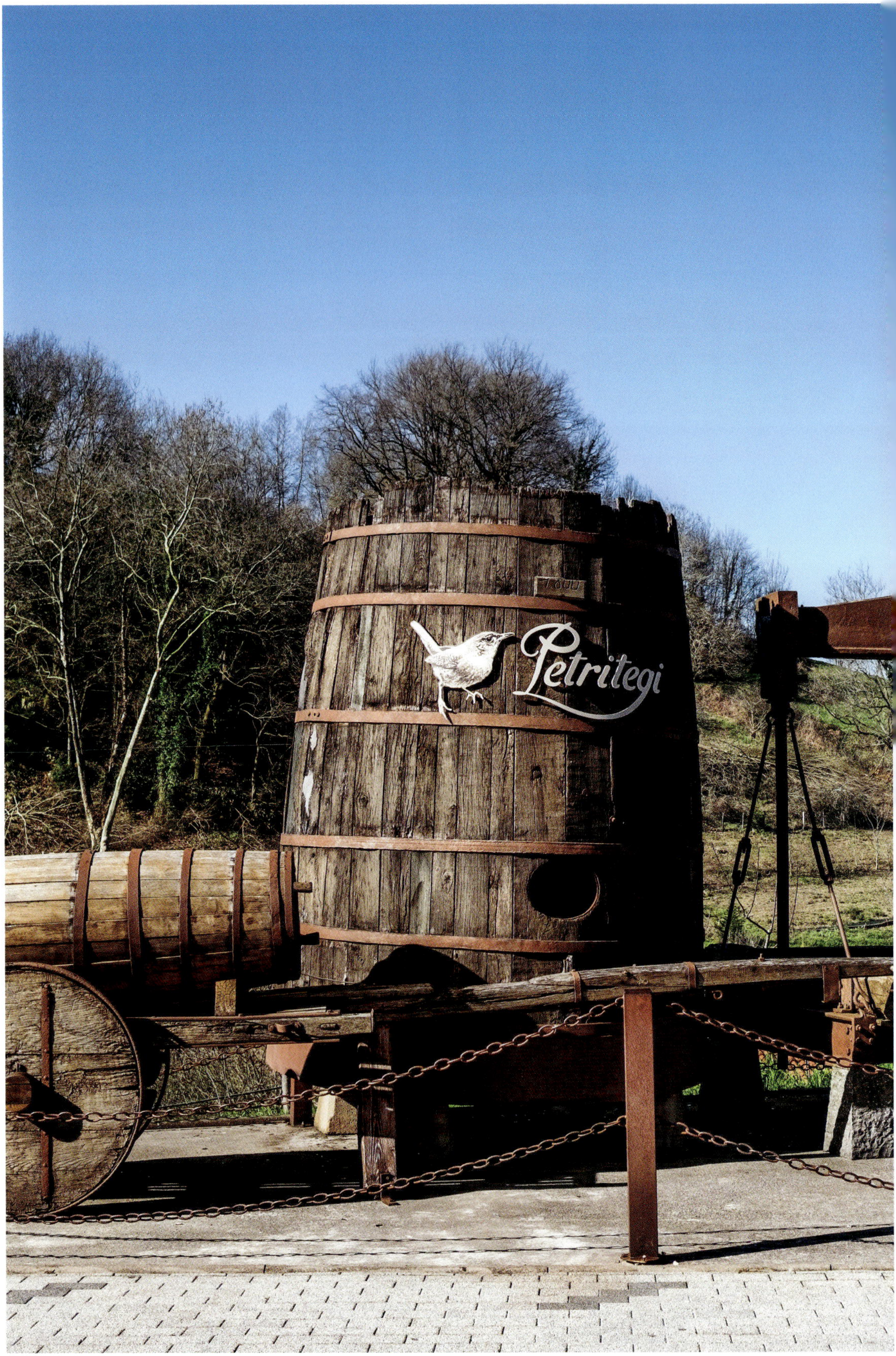
Petritegi

BASQUE COUNTRY
WHEN THE CIDER FLOWS

The barrels are tapped, a man with a bucket yells "Txotx!" and it's party time.
— BY JASON WILSON

No one really tells you what to do when you first arrive at a *sagardotegi*, or traditional Basque cider house, especially if you don't speak Basque. You're simply given a glass, led to one of the long wooden tables in a vast room, and immediately served a plate of chorizo, followed by a cod omelet. It's left up to you to figure out how to get a drink.

My brother, Tyler, and I learned this on our first night in Astigarraga, Spain, 15 minutes southeast of San Sebastián, which happens to be the cider capital of Spanish Basque Country. In this town of just under 6,000 people there are an astonishing 19 cider houses, as well as a cider museum that runs tastings and hiking tours. We had arrived in late January, at the start of the traditional cider season that runs through April. With Spanish-style ciders becoming more popular among cider enthusiasts, I wanted to see what they tasted like at the source.

At Gartziategi, a sagardotegi in a big stone barn on the outskirts of town, we learned that when a guy with a bucket yells "Txotx!" (pronounced "CHOACH") that means he's about to open the tap on one of dozens of huge 13,000-liter barrels, shooting out a thin stream of cider. You're supposed to stand up from your meal, get in line, and hold your glass at just the right angle to catch a few fingers of cider from that hissing stream. You drink the small amount in your glass and then follow the cidermaker to the next barrel.

Thinking it was a free-for-all, I committed my first faux pas by coming at the stream from the wrong side and essentially butting in line. Then, I couldn't quite figure out how to hold my glass so that the cider hit at the right angle, to "break" the liquid and create foam. Fortunately the crowd at the Basque cider house was

Previous "Here, cider is not just an alcoholic beverage," said a guide at Petritegi Cider House. "It's a way of life."

Left Even if you master the art of getting the cider to flow into the glass, drips on the floor may be inevitable.

Opposite Cider dates back centuries in the Basque Country. This cider house, Gartziategi, is one of the oldest.

very forgiving. A kind white-haired man in a sweater, whose group was eating next to us, showed me the ropes, hopping up and waving me along with him at the next shout of "Txotx!"

We eventually learned on our cider house tour that advice was forthcoming if you sought it out. At a modern cider house in the town center, called Zapiain, a hand-painted mural of "don'ts" was on the wall: Don't cut in line; don't fill your glass all the way up; don't sit on the barrels. Tyler grasped the technique much faster than I did.

"Here, take it here, at an angle," said Igór, our tour guide at Petritegi, another sagardotegi just down the road from Gartziategi (the suffix "tegi" means "place of"). I did as Igór said, allowing the stream to hit the very rim of my glass, spraying a little bit on the floor, just as the locals do. (I got the hang of it on my fourth glass.) Some older sagardotegi actually have worn grooves in the cement floors from years of streaming cider. The point, Igór told us, was to make sure the cider has good txinparta, or foam; if the cider is healthy, that foam should dissipate quickly. The cider in the glass disappears quickly too. The flavors are funky, crisp, and acidic, and usually bone dry — nothing like the cloying, over-carbonated ciders that are often on tap in the United States.

In late January, Astigarraga was still relatively mellow. But as txotx season rolls on, more than 15,000 cider enthusiasts can crowd into the town's cider houses each weekend.

Some get their orientation from the cider museum Sagardoaren Lurraldea, a great resource with tastings and hiking tours. Visitors can also book reservations for local cider houses on the museum website.

Txotx season follows the apple harvest of September and October, then fermentation of the cider in early winter. In fact, in late January, some of the barrels might not be fully finished fermenting. "The cider in the barrel is still evolving," Igór said. "If you come back in two months and taste the same barrel, it will have evolved." In Basque Country, most cider is made by spontaneous fermentation, with no added commercial yeast, in a process similar to natural winemaking. Once the season ends in April, whatever is left in the barrel is bottled.

The annual ritual harkens back to an era when cidermakers would invite clients, perhaps innkeepers, restaurateurs, or the famed gastronomic societies of San Sebastián, to taste and choose which casks they wanted to purchase. "Here, cider is not just an alcoholic beverage," Igór said. "It's a way of life." Petritegi, for instance, dates to 1526.

Over the years, a meal became part of the ritual. Every cider house serves the same basic menu: chorizo; cod omelet; roasted cod with green peppers; thick, medium-rare *chuleta* steak; Basque cheese (such as Idiazabal) served with walnuts and quince paste. And all the cider you can drink. The cider house ritual is just one of many Basque Country cultural touchstones that make this autonomous coastal region a very different place from the rest of Spain.

In Astigarraga, a sleepy but pleasant town, we took a lovely, steep, and tiring hike up to an old church that had been a stop on the ancient Camino de Santiago pilgrimage. (Religion is a familiar theme here: St. Ignatius Loyola, founder of the Jesuits, was Basque.) As we wandered past orchards overlooking the bay of San Sebastián, our guide, Ainize, told us stories of the Basque golden age. In the 16th century, Basque ships were built around the cider barrels, and each sailor drank up to three liters of cider per day to fend off scurvy. The result, according to lore, was that the Basque fishermen and whale hunters were the healthiest and most renowned on the sea, fishing far from their home waters. Their range was so famous that, only a few years ago, the remote West Fjords of Iceland repealed a 400-year-old law that ordered the murder of any Basque visitor on sight.

"The 16th century was the golden age of cider, but cidermaking is much older than that," Ainize said. "The original meaning of txotx, in our language, is 'to speak.' Now it's an invitation to drink cider."

As we descended back into the town square, Ainize pointed out the local pelota court, where the traditional Basque handball game is played. Many believe pelota, the forerunner of jai alai, originated with the ancient Greeks. We also saw huge stones with handles that are used for lifting and carrying in yet another Basque sport. The day before, we'd drunk cider with a woman named Olatz who told us, "I carry a stone of 550 kilos with eight women." She added, with a laugh: "We have our own sports here."

At Petritegi, Igór took us through the orchards where we learned about Basque varieties of apples like Goikoetxe, Moko, Txalaka, Gezamina, and Urtebi

Above Cider spurts out of the barrel, delivered from a tap. The barrel holds a flood's worth: more than 3,000 gallons.

Below Cider paired with cod at the Lizeaga cider house. Basque ciders are crisp, acidic, and dry.

Opposite "If you come back in two months and taste from the same barrel," a guide said, "it will have evolved."

—a far cry from Granny Smith and Golden Delicious. A Basque cider can be made from more than 100 varieties — some bitter, some acidic, some sweet — and 40 to 50 might be blended in a single cider. We were told that one kilo of apples will make one bottle. We were also told by a number of people that apples are sometimes trucked in from Normandy or Galicia to keep up with demand.

In the town center, Sidería Bereziartua operated a tasting room, and so we booked a tasting. "Cider is deep in our culture," said Mikel, our pourer. "We don't even know when we started making it." Ciders using the official denomination of origin, Euskal Sagardoa, created in 2016, must be made entirely from Basque apples. When he poured Bereziartua's Euskal Sagardoa, Mikel said, "If you want to take one bottle, drink this one." Then he poured a cider with a Gorenak label, one that can use foreign apples in the blend but must adhere to strict standards and be approved by official tasters. "If you want to drink three bottles, you take this one," he said.

On our last evening, we went to Lizeaga, a sagardotegi in a 16th-century farmhouse. Earlier, our stone-carrying friend Olatz had described the house as "the real txotx." Our reservation at one of the long tables

*Photographs by
Daniel Rodrigues*

was marked with a long baguette. There were no chairs. After the opening plate of chorizo, we strolled into the barrel room. Gabriel, the cidermaker, was opening the ancient taps with what looked like pliers. He went from cask to cask, and we followed along, dashing back into the dining room at intervals for the omelet, the cod, the steak.

After the eighth or ninth (or tenth?) txotx, and after some debating of technique with my brother, I thought I had finally gotten the catch down like a true Basque. But on the next txotx, when I put my glass under the stream, Gabriel gently corrected my form: "No, no," he said, "have the cider hit here." Well, no matter. Soon enough he tapped another barrel, and there was another chance to learn.

WHAT TO READ AND WATCH

The Cider Revival: Dispatches from the Orchard, by Jason Wilson. A cider travelogue, full of facts and stories, from the writer of this article.

Cider, Hard and Sweet: History, Traditions, and Making Your Own, by Ben Watson. A compendium of information on cider, cidermaking, and the apples at the start of it all.

Basque Country: A Culinary Journey through a Food Lover's Paradise, by Marti Buckley. Authentic recipes and insight into Basque customs and traditions.

The Basque History of the World: The Story of a Nation, by Mark Kurlansky. A summary of the long, rich history of the Basques from pre-Roman times, illuminating the Basque identity.

The Land of the Basques, directed by Orson Welles. A unique view into Basque life and customs, as they still existed in 1955, with the famed filmmaker as guide.

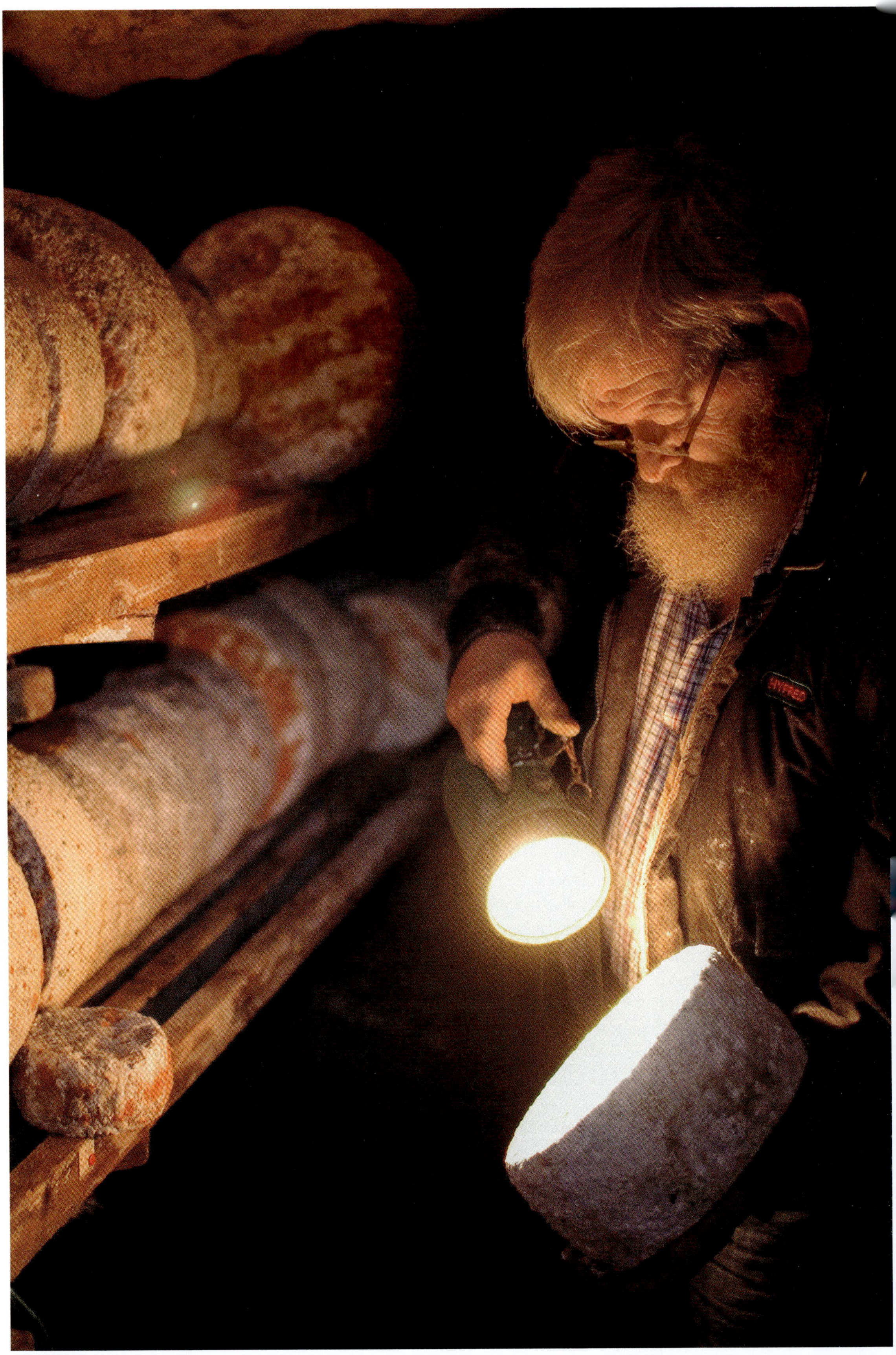

NIBBLING THROUGH CHEESE COUNTRY

How to make savory Spanish cheese: Age the wheels in Grandpa's cave, and keep the sheep happy.
— BY DANIELLE PERGAMENT

I entered a pitch-black cave, following a woman wearing tight jeans and with a small light strapped to her forehead. My eyes refused to adjust to the blackness, but soon we arrived at our goal. "These are my babies," she said, sweeping her arm toward a few hundred small wheels of hard blue cheese resting on a stack of shelves. "You would like to try?"

I was in Asturias, a sliver of northern Spain on the Bay of Biscay, drawn there by the region's tagline: "The Land of Cheese." I am, by any measure, a cheese person. While other people go to Tuscany for Brunello or the Pacific Northwest for salmon, I follow cheese. I want the stuff I can't get at home, the magic recipes that seduced the palates of the ancient Romans, the sharp ones, the stinky ones, the delicate artisanal ones that taste like little white flowers.

In the cave, I was following Raquel Viejo, whose family had lived in Asturias for generations. The specialty of the region — and what was stored on those shelves — is Cabrales, a blue cheese from cow's milk that is named after the town in Asturias where it was first made. We were in the foothills of Picos de Europa (Peaks of Europe), where everything is vertical: sheer mountain faces, steep pine trees, skinny roads dotted with tiny cars nervously hugging the shoulders. Flocks of sheep perched in rocky pastures, lone goats stood expertly on their hind legs munching from thickets of low-hanging leaves, and a cacophony of cowbells and beams of sunlight warmed it all. Cheese country.

There are thousands of caves hidden in the hills here, and for centuries people have been using them to age cheese. The specifics of each brand of cheese in various regions of Spain are regulated by a denomination of origin, or DO, and Cabrales's says it must be stored in cavelike conditions for at least two months

ASTURIAS & BASQUE COUNTRY　　　　　　　　　　　　　　　　　　　　　　　　　　　　　　SPAIN

Previous Juan Sobrecueva checks his work. Cheese has been aged in northern Spain's natural caves for centuries.

Left Raquel Viejo kneads curds for her Cabrales, a cow's milk cheese made in her cheese factory in Asturias.

Opposite Happy sheep are the key to good cheese, farmers say. What keeps the sheep happy? Green grass and peace.

so the good bacteria can kill off the bad. Several years ago, the Spanish government created new regulations. Some of the old methods, like straining the milk with horsehair sieves, were done away with in favor of more modern technology, like metal strainers and mechanical devices. But the most important requirements—the dairy breed, the aging process, the lack of pasteurization—remained.

Back in Raquel Viejo's home, amid the intoxicating smell of sour milk, I tasted a slice of her cheese, named José Antonio Bueno García after her husband. It was drier and saltier than the blues I was used to, but it didn't taste overly blue, as some softer cheeses can. Delicious, and a good start on my cheese tour.

A few villages over, I found Oliva Peláez Amieva, a small, wrinkled woman who had been making cheese for 60 years and was famous for resisting modernity in her methods. Her cheese couldn't be Cabrales because she ignored the DO guidelines; in fact, it didn't have a name. She made only about 200 wheels a year, most of it going to friends and family. For the moment, I was in the inner circle.

"The health department wants me to put in all sorts of regulations, but it wouldn't be as good," Amieva said. "I used to sell it at the market, but I got in trouble with the police."

Her cheese was a wonderfully sharp, dry, crumbly blend of goat and sheep milk that tasted slightly of salt and soil. And it was labor-intensive. Without modern equipment, all of Amieva's animals were milked by hand. Once the cheese was poured into molds, she rubbed each mound with salt and turned it over daily to ensure that it aged evenly; by the end, over 90 percent of the original milk volume was gone.

This isolated nook of the country has spawned hundreds, if not thousands, of artisanal cheese makers for generations. The cheese is cruder than French fromage and not as recognizable as Italian counterparts, but here, each wheel is as idiosyncratic as the person who makes it. The cheese of northern Spain is, like the land that produces it, rough, coarse, and sharp, and there's no way to taste it without traveling there.

I worked my way through a quarter of a wheel as we sat in Amieva's modest living room. She offered me homemade cider, the gently effervescent, lightly alcoholic beverage that always accompanies a piece of cheese in this area. It was the perfectly sweet balance to her defiantly unnamed snack.

"The reason my cheese is so delicious," Amieva said, without a trace of modesty, "is my hands." She turned her meaty, callused palms over for inspection.

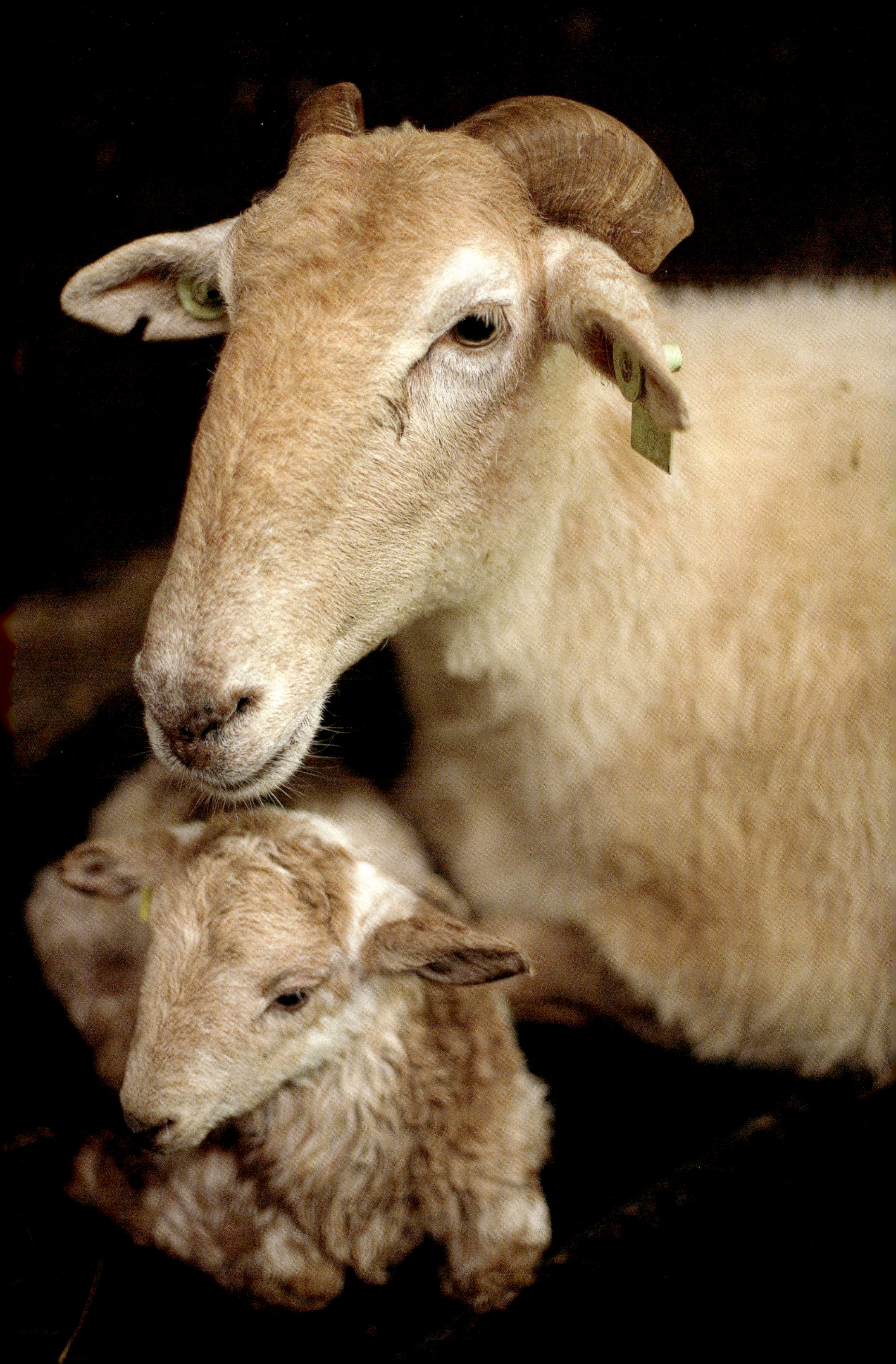

Above Cider is the traditional accompaniment, but for his cheeses, José Manuel Etxeberria also suggests wine.

Opposite Raquel Viejo with her Cabrales. Spain's regional cheeses are regulated by a denomination of origin, or DO.

"The natural bacteria in my skin makes the cheese more flavorful."

To travel from village to village in this region is to string together a perpetual cheese-and-cider festival, each farming community fiercely proud of its own, certain its concoctions are the best. Several people in Asturias asked me if I thought Cabrales was superior to Basque cheese. The correct answer, of course, is "Of course." But I had never tried Cabrales's rival, so I made my way farther west to Basque Country.

The first thing I noticed was that the cars all had the same bumper sticker: a cute, puffy sheep, the symbol of the region. A promising sign.

"You won't find anyone here who likes Cabrales," said Patxi Baskaran, a farmer in the hills not far from Guernica (Gernika to Basques), the town bombed during the Spanish Civil War in a notorious Luftwaffe raid. His disdain for the cheese of rival Asturias was, I soon discovered, common among the Basques. Baskaran's family had been making the same cheese for over a century on his farm. He learned the method from his father, but in order to stay competitive, he had to teach himself how to work with modern equipment.

Baskaran's Idiazábal was a hard sheep's cheese with a strong, earthy flavor. He was quick to tell me that he didn't deserve credit, his sheep did. So that I could meet the flock, he drove his Toyota 4Runner up a deathly steep dirt road that led us above the clouds. We stood on the summit of the mountain in the damp, white air, jagged cliffs looming like giant shark fins piercing the fog. "Big farms don't make cheese like we do in Basque country because the sheep eat grains and they're more stressed, so the milk is weak," he said. "My sheep live peaceful lives."

Farther on in Basque Country, I met the least stressed sheep in all of Spain. Just west of San Sebastián, above the small town of Zumaia,

Photographs by Matías Costa

hundreds of them were mowing a verdant field, mouthful by mouthful. They had trees for shade, a brook for water breaks, and 30 acres overlooking the dark, roiling Atlantic.

The cheese made by their owner, José Manuel Etxeberria, was a hard variety with a sharp bite and the fragrant taste of clover—strong, milky, and grassy. His secret ingredient? Keep the sheep happy eating nothing but sweet green grass, he said. They will return the favor with delicious cheese that goes perfectly, as he put it, "with a glass of red wine and a beautiful girl."

So did I ever find the world's best cheese? Mr. Etxeberria's came awfully close, but I had to stop short of calling it perfect because of something he said. "Cheese is like sheep; they all have a different personality," said Mr. Etxeberria, who has actually named most of his sheep. "And I could never choose my favorite sheep. They are all my favorites."

WHAT TO READ AND WATCH

The Oxford Companion to Cheese (Oxford Companions), by Catherine Donnelly. An encyclopedia of cheese with entries covering everything from Cheddar's triumph over Cheshire to the legend that the moon is made of cheese.

A Field Guide to Cheese: How to Select, Enjoy, and Pair the World's Best Cheeses, by Tristan Sicard. Facts, photos, maps, and graphics combine in a guide to 400 kinds of cheese.

The Telling Room: A Tale of Love, Betrayal, Revenge, and the World's Greatest Piece of Cheese, by Michael Paterniti. Part memoir, part fantastical nonfiction tale of Spanish cheesemakers and a blood feud. Good storytelling.

Made in Spain, Season 1, Episode 1: *Asturias: How They Cook Back Home*. For José Andrés, the chef who hosts this PBS television series, home is Asturias, and cheese is on the menu.

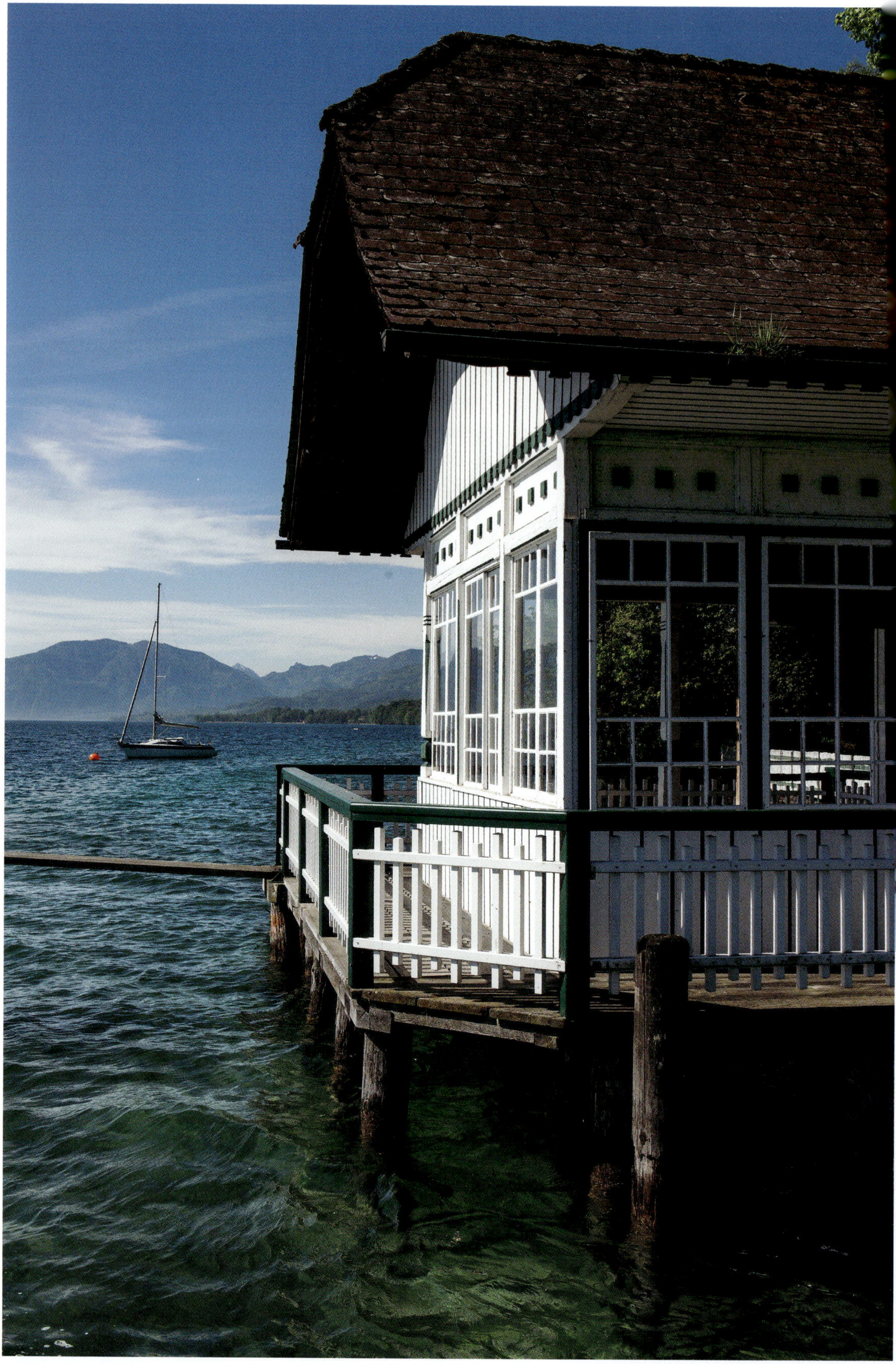

SEEING LIKE KLIMT ON A SHIMMERING LAKE

Bedeviled in Vienna by heat and prudish critics, Gustav Klimt escaped to the Attersee, where he found peace and a focus for his unique style of painting.
— BY LAURIE LICO ALBANESE

The Viennese painter Gustav Klimt first visited the stunning turquoise waters of the Attersee (Lake Atter), in northern Austria, as a young man in search of a summer refuge. "It is terrible, awful here in Vienna," Klimt wrote to a friend. "Everything parched, hot, dreadful, all this work on top of it, the 'bustle'—I long to be gone like never before."

Klimt, the leader of Austria's turn-of-the-century modern art movement and Vienna's most famous painter, was helping to support two lovers, two children, his mother, and two sisters. His need for escape should come as no surprise. Fond of sketching naked models in his studio, he was facing accusations of pornography even as wealthy matrons were lining up to have him paint their portraits.

At the age of 38, Klimt journeyed to the Salzkammergut region and made his way to a stone-and-turreted villa at the northern tip of the Attersee, at the edge of the Austrian Alps. There he shed city clothing for floor-length robes, temporarily abandoned his city mistresses, and traded stylized portrait painting for the bracing, vivid landscapes of his summer idyll.

Klimt had found his *Sommerfrische*—literally, "summer fresh"—the extended sojourn into the countryside that began as a tradition with the 19th-century Hapsburg emperors and is still beloved by Austrians. He returned to the Attersee for 15 more summers until his death in 1918, creating more than 45 of his 50 landscapes in the tiny lakefront towns of Seewalchen, Litzlberg, and Weissenbach.

"Anyone who wants to know anything about me as an artist—and this is the only thing that matters," Klimt told a journalist, "should look attentively at my pictures and try to discern from them who I am and what I want."

Previous Cool breezes and sweeping views still bring Viennese vacationers to the Attersee (Lake Atter).

Left Gustav Klimt with Emilie Flöge in 1910. Ever the non-conformist, he roamed the area wearing flowing robes.

Opposite A Klimt painting of Unterach, a village on the Attersee, in 1916.

To even attempt to know the man behind Klimt's masterpieces, one must first go to Vienna. And then one must visit the Attersee, which retains the same open-air charm that drew royalty and artists here more than a century ago.

After a steaming week in Vienna researching Klimt's life and work for a novel—and finding the city as hot and demanding as Klimt did—my husband and I followed his footsteps and drove two and a half hours west, slipping into a low-key, lush countryside where extended families vacation in simple lake houses, cyclists spin through the valley on long treks, and weekend sailors ply the lake waters.

We settled into a room with a sweeping water view at the Hotel-Restaurant Häupl and then headed out to follow some of Klimt's routine, rowing in an old-fashioned wooden boat for hours, diving from a silvered wooden dock into bracing water, dining on whole fish cooked on a long stick over open coals, and hiking on lush hillsides.

In the 21st century, the art world, admirers of Klimt's work, and collectors with money to spend have all shown a renewed interest in Klimt's pastoral paintings. For decades his iconic gold- and silver-accented works *Adele Bloch-Bauer I* and *The Kiss* eclipsed his innovative landscapes. But in 2011 his colorful *Litzlberg on Attersee* was auctioned at Sotheby's for $40.4 million, and in 2012 the Leopold Museum in Vienna mounted a retrospective that gave equal weight to his landscapes. In 2017, *Cottage Garden*, also from Klimt's years of summering at the Attersee, sold at Sotheby's for nearly $60 million.

The Gustav Klimt Theme Trail, which takes in the towns of Seewalchen, Kammer, and Schörfling, is a pathway through the painter's work at the Attersee and invites leisurely walks. Touring along it, we saw colorful kiosks along the water where we were treated to a recap of the artist's career highlights. Later, we climbed aboard a small motorized skiff with a local guide for a private tour we had arranged through the Attersee tourism office.

The lake water was a brilliant, almost unreal blue and the breeze was making a brisk headwind as we left the shore, eyes peeled for the highlights of the landscape Klimt immortalized in his work.

"Klimt painted here only for himself," our guide, Katrin Mekiska, told us as we approached the private Litzlberg Island, where the artist stayed for a time. "He mostly painted from the rooms where he lived. He opened the window and he painted."

A bulky man with a sprightly face, Klimt must have cut an unusual figure as he stomped about the area in his trademark loose-flowing robes. He often went for long walks through the foothills, sometimes carrying a sketchpad. The locals nicknamed him the Wood Goblin or Wood Gnome and apparently laughed when they saw him rowing to the middle of the lake with art supplies in tow.

Onboard our own small boat, Mekiska gave us an exact replica of the 1.75-inch-square cardboard stencil Klimt used to isolate and frame small chunks of the landscape here. The artist called this stencil his "seeker"; it is the tool that changed the way he saw and painted the lake and its surroundings.

We were invited to look across the lake as the artist did: with one eye closed, seeking a tiny square of scenery worthy of an entire painting. Peering through Klimt's "seeker" allowed us to understand exactly how this modest device led the painter to flatten perspective, raise the horizon line, and fill a large canvas with blue water and only a sliver of sky — a revolutionary vision that he immortalized in his 1900 landmark work *On Lake Attersee*.

"It was really kind of brave," Mekiska said. "He wanted something new." He created it here by fusing a modern and boundaryless view of nature with color and emotion.

Back on shore, my husband and I made our way to the stone-and-turreted Villa Paulick, where Klimt stayed on his first trips to the lake and which

Above Litzlberg Island. A $40 million sale of Klimt's painting *Litzlberg on Attersee* drew new attention to his landscapes.

Below A soufflé at the Hotel Häupl am Attersee, where views of the lake compete with the restaurant menu.

Opposite Since the days of the Hapsburgs, vacation homes on Lake Atter have been a summer tradition.

continued to be the centerpiece of his social life in the Salzkammergut region.

Klimt never married, but his younger brother wed Helene Flöge, who ran a fashionable couture shop in Vienna with her sister, Emilie. Cemented by the bond of creative arts and shared affection for Flöge's niece—Gertrude Flöge, known as Trudie—Gustav Klimt and Emilie Flöge became lifelong companions (although reportedly not lovers) and spent their summers together at the Attersee. Flöge's brother married into the Paulick family, and the Villa Paulick became the three families' meeting place.

Tucked behind a hedgerow and buttressed against the lakeshore, the villa can be elusive for first-time visitors. But after hearing from a Viennese museum curator that his wife rented a room at the villa each summer, my husband and I made a few local inquiries, procured an invitation, and entered the Villa Paulick through the old garden gate.

Inside, we saw parlor rooms in which all windows opened to the Attersee. The spaces—full of original straw chairs, wood and metal furnishings, red velvet upholstery, cozy window seats, and cool stone porches—offered the same sense of deep, eternal ease they must have held in Klimt's time. Far below us, Klimt's

*Photographs by
Josef Polleross*

refurbished rowboat bobbed in the shady lake house, awaiting a captain.

After leaving the lake in September 1913, Klimt wrote to Emilie of his trip home: "Had very mixed feelings during the journey (as if a piece of me was missing)."

For those staying at the Villa Paulick, like Romona Uhl, a professor from Linz whom we met in the garden, there are no mixed feelings. "To me this is paradise," she said. "Now I know where God lives in the summer."

WHAT TO READ AND WATCH

Gustav Klimt: Complete Paintings, text by Tobias G. Natter. Massive and complete, with high-quality reproductions. A TASCHEN coffee-table book.

Klimt, by Gilles Néret, and ***Vienna 1900***, text by Rainer Metzger. Also from TASCHEN, these two affordable volumes explain and reproduce Klimt's work.

The Lady in Gold: The Extraordinary Tale of Gustav Klimt's Masterpiece, Portrait of Adele Bloch-Bauer, by Anne-Marie O'Connor. The true story of the determined struggle of Maria Altmann to reclaim the famous stolen painting of her aunt, Adele Bloch-Bauer.

Woman in Gold, directed by Simon Curtis, starring Helen Mirren. Film version of the O'Connor book.

Stolen Beauty, by Laurie Lico Albanese (also author of this article). Told as a novel, the dramatic personal stories of Adele Bloch-Bauer, who may have had an affair with Klimt, and her niece Maria Altmann, who escaped from Nazi-ruled Vienna.

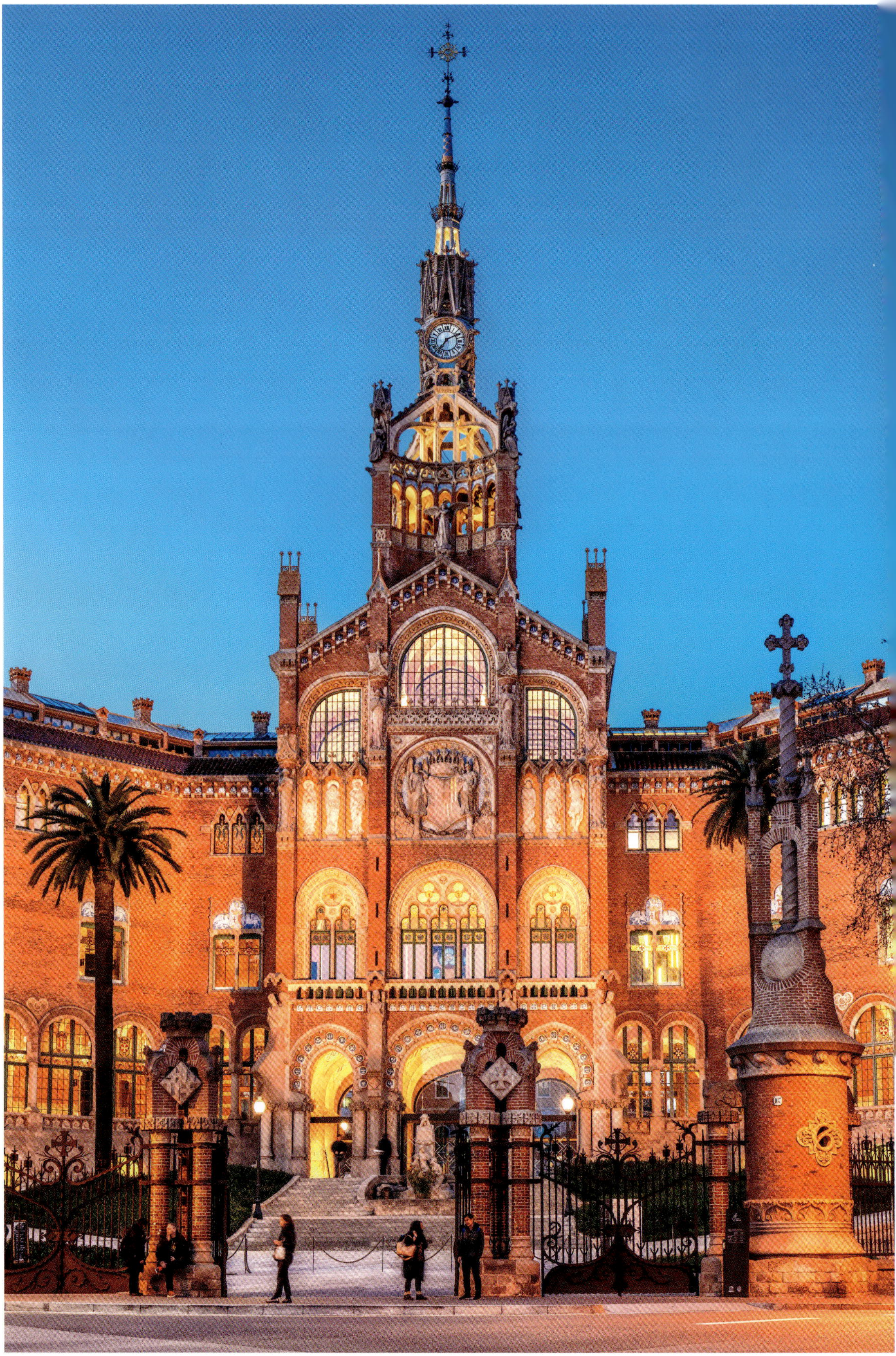

BARCELONA'S OTHER ARCHITECT

Antoni Gaudí's flamboyant buildings etch themselves in memory, but once you've seen the work of Lluís Domènech i Montaner, that can't be forgotten, either.
— BY ANDREW FERREN

It's sometimes hard to have a conversation about Barcelona that does not include the name Gaudí. The world is so gaga for Antoni Gaudí—the genius of Catalan Modernisme (the Spanish version of Art Nouveau) whose early 20th-century buildings are virtual emblems of the city—that most of his modernista contemporaries go little noticed by tourists.

But there's more to Barcelona Modernisme, and one architect whose works shouldn't be missed is Lluís Domènech i Montaner (1849–1923), an unsung hero of the movement.

Domènech is often hailed as the most modern of the modernistas, notably for his mastery of lightweight steel construction. Unesco, at least, doesn't give him short shrift, having designated his most important buildings in Barcelona a World Heritage Site—just as it has the works of Gaudí. Multifaceted and astonishingly productive, Domènech wore many hats. He is known best as an architect and professor—Gaudí was his student at Barcelona's School of Architecture. But he was also a prominent politician and Catalan nationalist and a preeminent scholar of heraldry.

For architects, Barcelona at the turn of the 20th century was the right place at the right time. Nineteenth-century industrialization had brought tremendous wealth, and between the Universal Exposition of 1888 (for which Domènech created two of the most noteworthy buildings) and the construction of the Eixample—the vast grid of streets laid out in 1859 to decongest the old city—there was a heady mix of civic pride and social ascension in the air. The rising middle class was eager to make its mark on the rapidly growing city, and the new modernista style,

BARCELONA SPAIN

Previous Lluís Domènech i Montaner intended for his Hospital de Sant Pau to have the feel of a fantastical village.

Left Strappy wood and ceramic wainscoting, part of Domènech's design for the restaurant of the Hotel España.

Opposite Twenty pavilions on 40 parklike acres make up the Sant Pau complex.

with its neo-Gothic motifs recalling Barcelona's rich medieval history, seemed perfect for that purpose.

Robert Lubar, an associate professor at New York University's Institute of Fine Arts, pointed out that, much more so than Gaudí, Domènech was influenced by the English Arts and Crafts movement of Ruskin and Morris. "He believed that 'the complete interior' served some kind of ethical purpose," Lubar said.

Domènech's most "complete interior" is the 1908 Palau de la Música Catalana (Palace of Catalan Music), a stunning concert hall miraculously shoehorned into a small lot at the junction of the old city and the new. Domènech, who has often been likened to an orchestra conductor, knew how to get the best performance from the sculptors, ceramicists, and woodworkers who executed his designs. Inside the Palau de la Música Catalana, nearly every surface is adorned with color, texture, and relief, and, because the walls and ceiling are made almost entirely of stained glass, bathed in colored light.

Atop the balcony's mosaic-clad columns, bronze chandeliers tilt like sunflowers toward the stained-glass sun that seems to float in midair from the ceiling's inverted dome. The astonishing expanses of glass were achieved with the use of structural steel—invisible beneath so much decoration.

Michael Kimmelman, *The New York Times* architecture critic, noted that the Palau was designed with a working-class audience, and a noble purpose, in mind. The hall was meant partly as a domain of local choral societies, whose usual métier was folk songs. The intent was to bring their sensibility together with serious music by composers like Wagner and Brahms, thus spreading an appreciation of international music to the Catalan masses. The building's tile and stained glass celebrated crafts with Catalan roots.

The other pillar of Domènech's World Heritage status is the Hospital de Sant Pau, formerly the Hospital de la Santa Creu i Sant Pau (Hospital of the Holy Cross and Saint Paul), set on 40 parklike acres at the northern edge of the Eixample. Heeding the latest theories of hygiene, Domènech envisioned a complex of 20 pavilions to ensure ventilation and access to sunshine. He built 12 of them, and his architect son completed the last eight.

Domènech ingeniously sank the corridors and service areas of the hospital underground so that patients and visitors in the pavilions and gardens above would feel as if they were in a village—a fantastical one with myriad domes, spires, finials, sculptures, and mosaics. The result is a temple to something like the graceful and daring eye candy often associated with Art Nouveau, but here more properly identified as Catalan Modernisme, reflecting this style's unique Catalan roots.

The complex, a hospital until 2009, now holds museums devoted to the history of medicine and to Domènech himself, as well as space for cultural events and offices occupied by humanitarian organizations.

To find more of Domènech, use the map and guidebook of the Barcelona Modernisme Route, available at kiosks around the city and posted at rutadelmodernisme.com. It will allow you to lead yourself around Domènech's residential structures in Barcelona, most of which are clustered between the Passeig de Gracia and Carrer Girona.

One of the grandest of his palatial homes, Casa Fuster, at the top of Passeig de Gracia, is now a five-star hotel. In its street-level cafe, you can sip Champagne and admire a vaulted ceiling and a forest of marble columns. The facade of the hotel, with the name clearly shown above the door, made an appearance in the film *Vicky Cristina Barcelona*.

Near the city port is the Hotel España, which, though not built by Domènech, had its restaurant, La Fonda España, renovated by him a century ago. It has been spruced up and shines anew with Domènech's strappy wood and ceramic wainscoting, murals by Ramon Casas, and a sculptural fireplace by Eusebi Arnau.

Want to see more? Eighty miles south, in the town of Reus, is Casa Navàs, another "complete interior," which surrounds you the minute you step into the stair hall—a tiny indoor garden of flowers and vines wrought in mosaic, stained glass, and carved stone. Throughout the house, the capital of each column features a different floral motif. Most of the rooms contain their original, exuberant furnishings by master craftsmen like Gaspar Homar.

On the outskirts of Reus, the Pere Mata Institute, a mental health hospital begun by Domènech in 1898, was meant to counter the tradition of keeping the mentally ill out of sight. Today you can visit one of the six pavilions, the one that housed "rich and illustrious men." As a guide explained on my 90-minute tour, arranged through the Reus tourism office, the sumptuously decorated men's pavilion has a billiard room, grand salon, and formal dining room. It could almost

Above The main pavilion at Sant Pau. The complex is now used as museum, event space, and offices.

Below Even a banister didn't escape Domènech's passion for detail at Casa Roura, a house in Canet de Mar.

Opposite Domènech's 1908 concert hall Palau de la Música Catalana is a jewel of Catalan Modernisme.

be confused with a typical men's club, but the delicate-looking leaded-glass windows were reinforced with iron to keep the patients in.

Upstairs, the rooms on the tour contained many of their original furnishings, including clever armoires with basins (and running water) built into them. There were also suites with office spaces (and secretaries) for those patients who still had empires to run.

About 50 miles northeast of Barcelona in the coastal town of Canet de Mar, one can see three charming structures in the space of about 100 yards. Domènech's mother was from the region, and he also had a home there, which is now a museum that displays his drawings and original furnishings. Across the street is the Ateneu Canetenc, once a cultural and political club and now a library.

Perhaps the most satisfying stop in Canet is Casa Roura, a little fortress of a house that is now a restaurant. The facade's bravura brickwork creates a lively play of light and is further animated by turrets, parapets, and gleaming roof tiles glazed in cobalt blue and canary yellow. The old double-height salon with its baronial fireplace is now the main dining room. On my visit, the amazing lunch menu was on par with the architectural surroundings.

Photographs by
Lourdes Segade

And then there is the place where Domènech's love of medieval architecture may have begun: at his mother's house—one of them anyway. The Castell Santa Florentina, in the hills above Canet, has been in the Montaner family for centuries. It is still a private home, but information about booking a tour can be found on its website, and it hosts an annual festival of classical music. The castle, whose exterior stone walls still powerfully recall its medieval origins, also served as a setting in *Game of Thrones*.

Around 1909, Domènech expanded the original fortified stone house and redesigned its interior rooms, deftly mixing his neo-Gothic riffs with authentic Gothic architectural elements like columns, portals, and arcades "harvested" from a defunct monastery. In the process he created a modernista masterpiece, one that quite literally spans the ages.

WHAT TO READ AND WATCH

Lluís Domènech i Montaner, Palau de la Música Catalana, Barcelona, by German architecture critic Manfred Sack with photos by Hisao Suzuki. An in-depth examination of the Catalonian architect's legacy and one of his most famous buildings.

Modernismo: Architecture and Design in Catalonia, by Borja de Riquer. Explains Domènech's impact.

Barcelona, by the Australian writer, art critic, and producer Robert Hughes. Explores the city's history, architecture, and character.

Vicky Cristina Barcelona, directed by Woody Allen. A film in which Barcelona is almost as much a character as the women in the title.

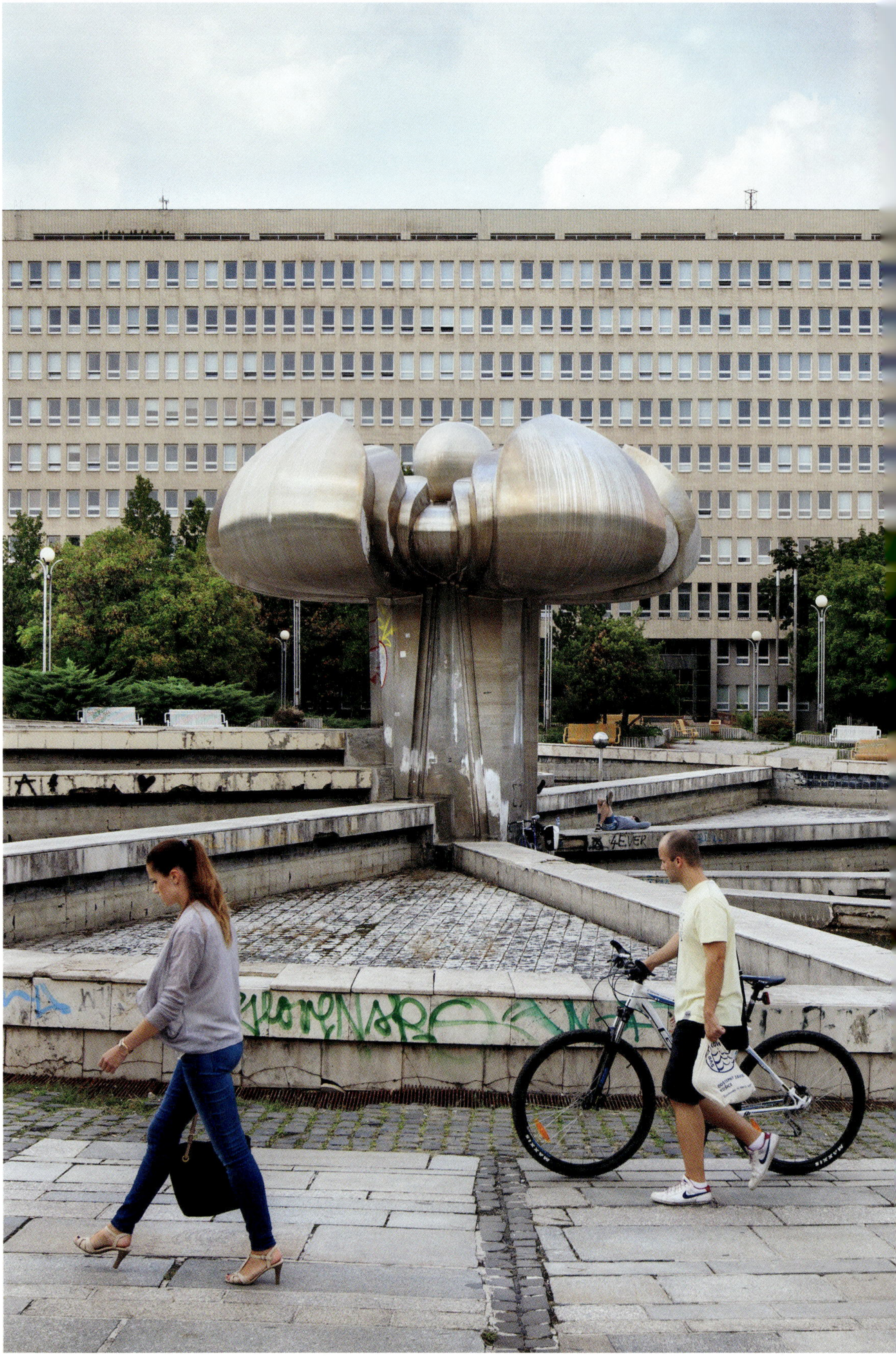
4EVER

SLOVAKIA   BRATISLAVA

THE MONOLITHS OF BRATISLAVA

So what if Communist-era architecture in Slovakia's capital city won't win prizes for beauty? Relax and enjoy the view. — BY LISA SCHWARZBAUM

Some destinations lure visitors with evocative phrases suitable for travel brochures. The fountains of Rome. The rooftops of Paris. The souks of Marrakesh. It's likely that the panelaks of Bratislava, Slovakia's capital city, will never make the list. The term, though, is potent. And the sight is a marvel — assuming, under the category of the marvelous, that you count the existence of the largest concentration of graceless concrete high-rise housing units ever to stomp across the landscape of a Central Europe country formerly under Communist control.

The word *panelak* itself is a colloquial expression in Czech and Slovak, with roots in both languages' more technical term for "panel house." Prestressed and prefabricated, panelaks were rapidly assembled and cheaply built to solve a post–World War II housing crisis. They also expressed a basic aspect of Soviet ideology, providing egalitarian habitat for humanity — even if it was a humanity that couldn't afford to complain about bad insulation, leaky windows, structural weaknesses, and mechanical failures.

Hungarians and Poles have their own related words for similar complexes; the high-rises of Central Europe were, after all, once the Eastern Bloc rage. And the impulse to provide one-size-fits-all urban shelter can be seen everywhere around the globe from London council flats to Chicago's Cabrini-Green Homes, built between 1942 and 1962 and torn down between 1995 and 2011, and St. Louis's infamous Pruitt-Igoe complex, first occupied in 1954 (designed by Minoru Yamasaki, architect of the World Trade Center) and demolished by dynamite and despair in 1972.

But in Europe, panelak prevails as the name for the buildings and all they signify, because more of

Previous Freedom Square in Bratislava. Communist-era buildings left the city a legacy of bland architecture.

Left Contrasting with utilitarian office buildings and panelaks are what Slovaks call Communist Big Weird Buildings. This one is Slovensky Rozhlas.

Opposite The Most SNP (New Bridge) with its saucerlike top is Bratislava's most visible symbol of the Communist era.

them were built in the former Czechoslovakia — in a boom that stretched from 1959 to that country's breakup in 1993 and beyond to 1995 — than anywhere else on what was once Soviet earth. Today, about a third of all Czechs and Slovaks, from all income brackets, still call their panelaks home. Some 130,000 residents live in the Bratislava complex alone, concentrated in the city's Petrzalka district.

Vaclav Havel, first post-Communist president of Czechoslovakia, and subsequently of the Czech Republic, called his country's signature housing "undignified rabbit hutches, slated for demolition." Yet the panelaks of Bratislava endure with no less determination than Bratislava Castle, their ancient Old Town neighbor across the Danube. And their inhabitants, resolutely adapting to whatever failures of promise the 21st century continues to dump on them, go about their business. Before the rabbit hutches, in 1945, the area that is now Petrzalka served as an internment camp for nearly all of the city's Hungarian population. Before that, from 1938 to 1945, it was annexed by Nazi Germany. For a time in 1944, it was a labor camp for Hungarian Jews.

I was in Vienna, just up the Danube, when I teamed up with a fellow solo traveler to take the one-hour train ride to Bratislava to see Petrzalka. I had already seen the castle and wedding-cake Hapsburg architecture that attracts most visitors to Bratislava; now I wanted to see this other side of Slovak life.

Panelaks aren't the whole story of the city's socialist architecture. There are also some striking relics of the Communist Big Weird Buildings era — architectural eruptions that regularly draw visitors with fancier cameras than mine. The essential tour includes the massive inverted pyramid called Slovensky Rozhlas, built to house Slovak Radio; the menacing 1970s extension of the Slovak National Gallery; and Namestie Slobody, or Freedom Square.

But for maximum atmospheric challenge, my walking partner and I limited our itinerary to the panelaks of Petrzalka, the bridge (*most* in Slovak) that got us there from the Old Town, and whatever ground we covered to walk between the two.

We could have easily spent an hour just gawping at the bridge, and a solid 10 minutes learning the various names for it: Most SNP, or the Bridge of the Slovak National Uprising, as the bureaucrats call it; Novy Most, or New Bridge, as the people call it; or the UFO Bridge, as new visitors are bound to call it, a natural nickname given the flying saucer-shaped folly at the top of the pylon that anchors the Petrzalka end. These days, for a fee, an elevator takes tourists up to an observation deck in the saucer, where there is also a fancy restaurant called UFO.

The masterminds of this bridge wrecked a good chunk of the city's historically important Old Town, managing to tear up nearly all of the Jewish quarter, to impose a major roadway. In a fit of what goes around comes around, the bridge's three designers were on the outs with the regime by the time the structure officially opened in August 1972, and their names were left off the dedication plaque.

We left the riverbank of everything old, on the castle side of the Danube, and walked along the lower level of the New Bridge, safe for pedestrians and bicyclists, while cars passed by on the upper level. The panelaks of Bratislava are just beyond, a mile or two over; we could see them, spread like a rash. And when we set foot on the embankment of everything new, we headed in the direction of the housing mirage ahead of us.

We walked through a homage to new capitalism — past the sprawling Aupark shopping center and through the shiny high-rise corporate complex called Digital Park. Sleek cafes beckoned at ground level. A big neon sign advertised Digital Golf. Young businessmen in jackets stood around outside, smoking. Bratislavan women checked their phones. We walked on. Finally we reached the panelak perimeter, ready to stroll around the courtyards.

One problem: There are no real courtyards. There are no natural areas for people to gather, or even pause; no shops; no services. The urban-studies matriarch Jane Jacobs, who warned the world about the alienation of high-rise sterility, would have said, "See what I'm talking about?" The architect and high-rise champion Le Corbusier would have said, "Uh-oh, my bad."

We walked for about an hour, attuned to post-Communist patches of color on selected outside walls — yellow, red, apricot, a bluish gray. Potted plants appeared in a few glass entryways. We learned that insulation had been upgraded in some buildings, and that some of the notoriously cramped flats had been reconfigured. The publishers of the home-improvement magazine called *PanelPlus* clearly know where they could find readership, and Ikea would find a natural market in the minuscule panelak kitchens.

Above Prestressed, prefabricated concrete produced uniformity, if not beauty, in the panelaks.

Below Its saucer-shaped top gave Most SNP this viewing platform as well as an unanticipated nickname, the UFO Bridge.

Opposite The Aupark shopping center is part of the new capitalism changing Slovakia.

There is no hipster irony in panelak living, no retro cool. No economic disadvantage is implied by a Petrzalka address, either, nor, at this point in the game, any political ideology. The place just *is*, extraordinary and mundane, gargantuan and invisible. On the other hand, my friend and I were keenly aware of the ironies of tourist privilege when we decided, on our way back across the New Bridge, to spring for lunch at the UFO restaurant.

The elevator took us up to a snazzy circular space, decorated in a mix of '90s restaurant cool with touches of broadly self-aware black humor; consider, at the bar, a sculpture of a Stasi-like secret policeman, spying with a long-lens camera. The meal was luxe, the tasting menu was something called "mediterasian," the service was almost unceasingly attentive, and the total bill for two, with fancy lunchtime drinks, was a bargain by New York standards. We lingered over a rich dessert, looking back across the bridge at the Old Town, Stare Mesto, where Hungarian kings were crowned in St. Martin's Cathedral beginning in the 16th century, and where river boats anchor to disgorge tourists for day trips.

Then, before we headed back to the train station and commuted back to the dispassionate elegance of

*Photographs by
Andreas Meichsner*

Vienna, we made stops in the restaurant restroom. Its window faced toward Petrzalka, with a view of all the panelaks of Bratislava spread out below and disappearing over the horizon.

    The sight was so mesmerizing that I didn't, at first, see the mordant message to the world etched on the window: "Enjoying the view?"

WHAT TO READ

Bratislava (Bradt City Guides), by Lucy Mallows. A detailed and informative guidebook from a publisher specializing in destinations that often get short shrift.

A History of Slovakia: The Struggle for Survival, by Stanislav J. Kirschbaum. The country's story from its beginnings to the current Slovak Republic.

Manufacturing a Socialist Modernity: Housing in Czechoslovakia, 1945–1960, by Kimberly Elman Zarecor. A scholarly history of the Communist-era prefab housing blocks.

With Love from Bratislava, by Christy Morgan. Memoir of a Canadian who uprooted, moved to Bratislava, and learned to love her new city and its people.

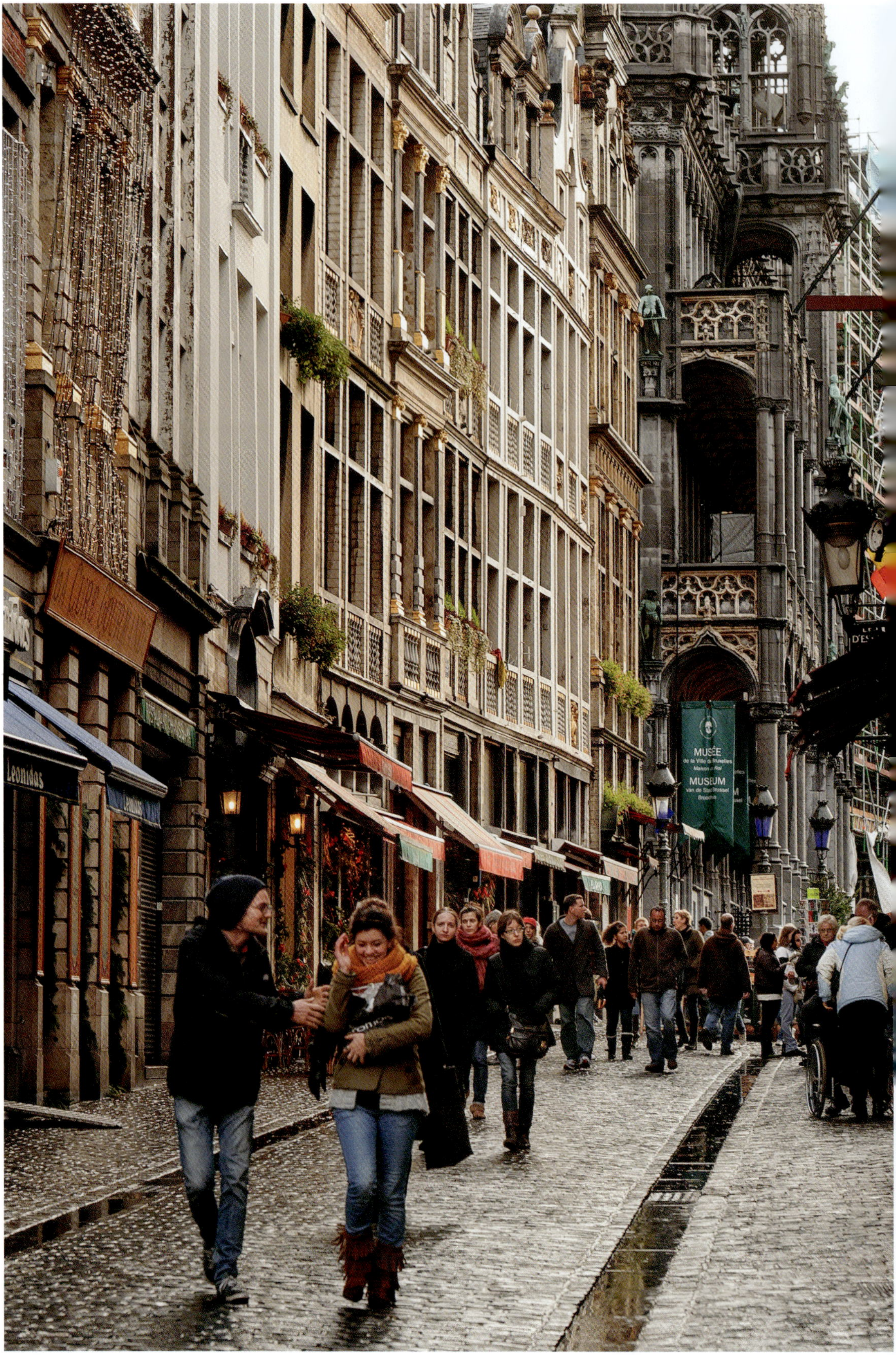
Leonidas
MUSÉE
MUSEUM

THE CUTTING EDGE OF CHOCOLATE

"Bean to bar" is just the beginning for the confectionery avant-garde, and where better to taste the latest than Brussels? — BY AMY M. THOMAS

Chocolate, like fashion, wine, and finance, has become a complex cultural phenomenon. There are basic chocolate for the masses, artisanal chocolate for purists, and avant-garde creations for connoisseurs. Brussels has it all. The capital of Belgium may be known to some as the capital of Europe, but it is also, at least as far as most chocolate aficionados are concerned, the world capital of chocolate.

Ever since the Brussels chocolatier Jean Neuhaus invented the praline more than a century ago, the city has been at the forefront of the chocolate business. Brussels has a million residents and some 500 chocolatiers, about one chocolatier for every 2,000 people. The average Belgian consumes over 15 pounds of chocolate each year, one of the highest rates in the world.

But the industry is changing. With countries like Germany and the Netherlands becoming larger exporters, Belgian chocolatiers are finding innovative ways to hold on to the chocolate crown. They are breaking away from traditional pralines, which Belgians classify as any chocolate shell filled with a soft fondant center, and infusing ganaches with exotic flavors like wasabi or lemon verbena, as well as creating imaginative pairings like black currant and cardamom or raspberry and clove.

Brussels itself is a curious mix of conservative and avant-garde. In the European quarter alone, the cylinder-shaped glass dome of the European Parliament's Paul-Henri Spaak building hovers over the neo-classical-style Place du Luxembourg while graffiti-studded beacons of Art Nouveau architecture reside nearby. The city's chocolate scene reflects that tension. The result is some wonderfully surprising creations.

Surveying the state of Belgian chocolate is an ambitious task. Brussels is home to two of the biggest

Previous If you're searching for the world's best chocolatiers, start in the heart of Brussels.

Left A bowl of melted chocolate is poured onto a marble-topped table, sending an intoxicating aroma into the air.

Opposite Jean Neuhaus put Brussels at the forefront of chocolate making by inventing the European chocolate praline.

chocolate companies in the world, Godiva and Leonidas, as well as scores of boutique chocolate-makers and haute chocolatiers. But with a few days to spend in the city, I was determined to try.

I spent the first afternoon circling the Grand Sablon, the city's central square and chocolate epicenter. I sampled golf-ball-size truffles at Godiva, molded hamster heads at Leonidas, and minty ganaches at Passion. At Neuhaus, I tried a dark chocolate truffle filled with buttercream and speculoos, a spicy Belgian cookie.

The more I strolled, the clearer it was that the level of sophistication was evolving. The packaging and presentation at newer chocolatiers were as slick as a Place Vendôme showroom, while the associated terminology — like "cru" and "domain" — was akin to what you'd hear from sommeliers. Such was the case at Pierre Marcolini's two-story flagship. Smiling saleswomen stood over the glassed-in display of small, rectangular bonbons that looked as exquisite as jewels. Backlighted shelves on the opposite wall held what Marcolini is famous for: his single-origin Grand Cru chocolate bars.

In 2004, Marcolini started scouting the globe for the best cocoa beans. He became the only chocolatier in Brussels to work directly with plantations in countries like Venezuela and Madagascar, bringing the beans back to his ateliers for roasting and grinding. It was the beginning of "bean-to-bar," the refined chocolatier's method of controlling every step of the chocolate-making process, from selecting the beans to shaping a bar.

"Most people think it's the percentage that makes a difference," said a saleswoman, speaking of the amount of cocoa in the confections. "But it's the origin of the cocoa bean that does. It's a little bit like wine." Indeed, when I bit into the Cuban cru, I could detect vibrant notes of dried cherries in the slightly acidic chocolate.

Afterward, I climbed past the Gothic Notre-Dame du Sablon church to the Place Royale. Rush-hour trams and traffic buzzed by, and the red and black roofs of "lower town" were splayed below me. Done with chocolate for the day, I was ready to experience another national specialty: art. The Royal Museums of Fine Arts offer a trove of works from Belgian and Flemish masters. The sublimely surreal flying fish, skeletal corpses, and falling angels of Delvaux and Rubens and the Brueghels seemed an appropriate counterpoint to the indulgence of the day.

My museum outing the next morning was amusingly different. Before I put my change away at the entrance, I was presented with a cookie that had been run under a spigot of molten chocolate. I was inside the rickety three-century-old building that houses Choco-Story Brussels, formerly the Museum of Cocoa and Chocolate. I had arrived just in time for the next demonstration, presided over by a bushy-browed man in a fluorescent-lighted kitchen with a vat of chocolate before him.

Europe, I learned, was introduced to cocoa beans when Spanish explorers brought them back from what is now Mexico in the late 16th century. They reached Belgium about 100 years later. When King Leopold II colonized the African Congo from 1885 to 1908, partly for the cocoa crops, the resulting horrific genocide was a dark moment in the country's history. That era was also when Belgian chocolate started earning its formidable reputation.

Outside the museum, I dodged the camera-wielding tour groups gathered before the magnificent Grand Place, with its 15th-century Town Hall and rows of guild houses, and walked down narrow streets lined with shops and stands offering frites and waffles.

I rediscovered the cavalcade of chocolatiers in the Galerie de la Reine, a graceful fin-de-siècle shopping arcade. La Belgique Gourmand, Corné, and the original Neuhaus were all there under its soaring glass ceilings.

But as big as those Belgian brands are, none are national gems the way Mary is. A century-old chocolatier, also in the Galerie, Mary is a favorite of the Belgian royal family. Its rows of caramel, marzipan, chocolate mousse, ganache, and cream-filled pralines made it easy to see why. Mary makes small batches of chocolates, so they don't have to be stored and lose their flavor. Buzzing from the caramelized hazelnut pralines the saleswoman had offered as a sample, I found myself leaving with two boxes of pralines and several chocolate bars.

Compelled to dig deeper into the chocolate of Brussels, and the city itself, I ambled down the crooked

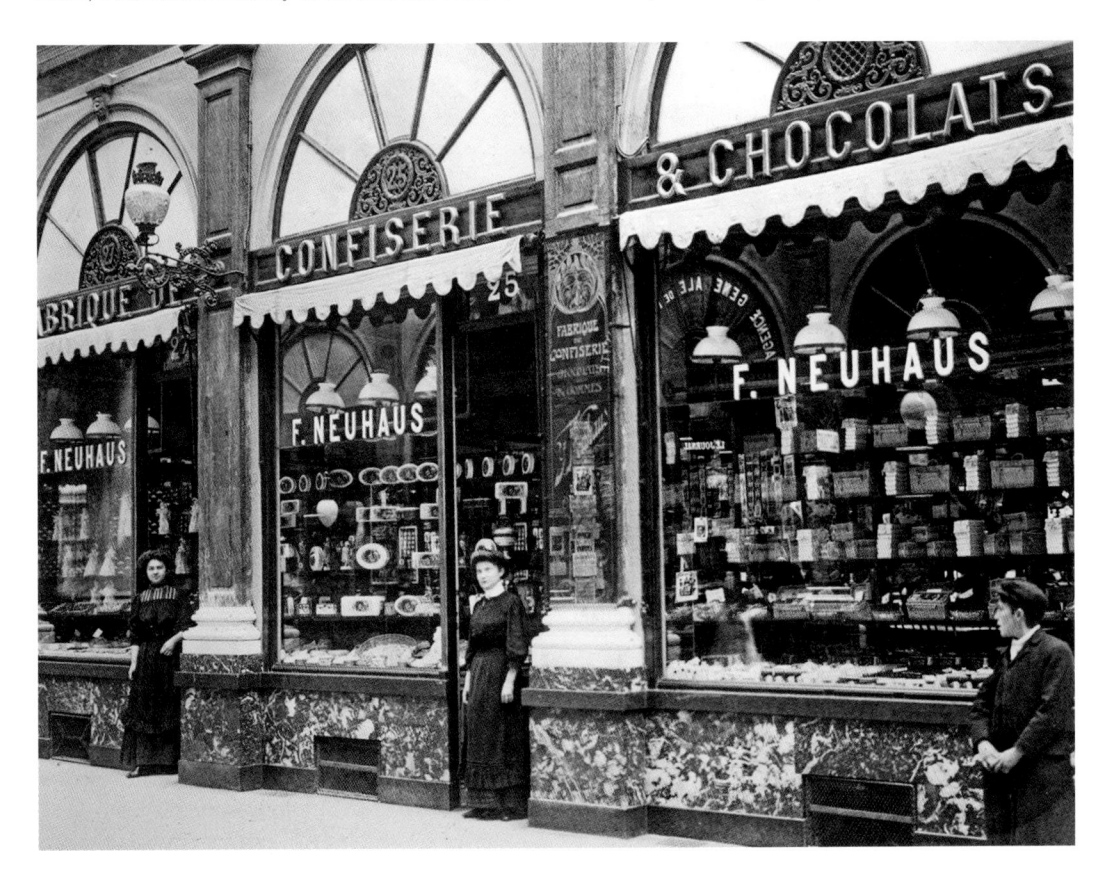

Above Molten chocolate hardens into building blocks for a complex creation by the chocolatier Ryan Stevenson.

Opposite A delicate product, painstakingly made, typifies the best Belgian chocolates, like these at Neuhaus.

Rue des Bouchers, avoiding eye contact with waiters trying to lure me into their cafes for buckets of mussels; past the big, blocky Bourse where workers in loosened ties ate sandwiches; into St.-Géry, where the canals once used for transporting building materials are now filled in and home to seafood restaurants. I veered left and found the big shop windows of Ste. Catherine, an area popular with artists and fashionistas.

I was on Rue Antoine Dansaert, which was put on the map by the radical Antwerp Six, the designers who established Belgian fashion in the 1980s. Today the neighborhood is still a bastion of cool with stylish boutiques. Any chic shopping district worth its salt has fantastic places to eat, and I found a bistro where I ordered a lunch of cod served atop polenta, just the sustenance I needed before heading to the lesser-known neighborhood of Ixelles.

The 30-minute walk across town felt like a tour of different cities. I passed comic murals and quirky second-hand shops in the gentrifying Marolles neighborhood. I gazed up at the medieval Porte de Hal, the last remains of the city walls. After I crossed the wide, looping Boulevard de Waterloo, the landscape became hillier and the architecture uniform. I was in St.-Gilles, a bonanza of Art Nouveau. Wrought-iron balconies, turrets, oriel windows: block after block, the residential facades were unique and homogenous at the same time. The neighborhood's crown jewel is the Horta Museum, once the home of the Art Nouveau architect Victor Horta.

Later I wandered through Ixelles, the farmers' market on Place du Châtelain, filled with vendors peddling pork sausages, cheeses, and jams. Wine had been uncorked, and beer was being downed. It was 7 p.m. on a Wednesday, and the crowds of young professionals extending from the market to cafe terraces lining the square told me this was the place to be. I fell into a conversation with a shopkeeper — about

Photographs by Jock Fistick

chocolate, naturally. She told me I must visit the atelier of Laurent Gerbaud.

I found it the next morning on the busy Rue Ravenstein, and inside, I understood the reason for her recommendation. I gazed at a spread of satiny bonbons with figs from Izmir, ginger from Guilin, and hazelnuts from Piedmont. Such reliance on global ingredients is what sets apart the new generation of chocolate makers. It's what produces combinations like a yuzu-flavored ganache atop a pine nut praline, or a milk chocolate caramel with lime and wildflower that's citrusy and woody, chewy and sweet.

And as they continue to push the boundaries of creativity, the chocolatiers of Brussels are also re-writing the history of Belgian chocolate.

WHAT TO READ AND WATCH

Chocolat: From the Cocoa Bean to the Chocolate Bar, by Pierre Marcolini. Chocolate philosophy and a collection of 170 recipes from a groundbreaking chocolatier.

The Art and Craft of Chocolate: An Enthusiast's Guide to Selecting, Preparing and Enjoying Artisan Chocolate at Home, by Nathan Hodge. Recipes, chocolate facts, and photographs.

The True History of Chocolate, by Sophie and Michael Coe. Two anthropologists go deep into the story of chocolate, with entertainment along the way.

Raising the Bar: The Future of Fine Chocolate, by Pam Williams and Jim Eber. A guide to help chocolate lovers choose a brand that suits their taste buds and their consciences.

Chocolat, directed by Lasse Hallstrom. A romantic comedy about a most unusual chocolate shop, starring Juliette Binoche, Judi Dench, and Alfred Molina.

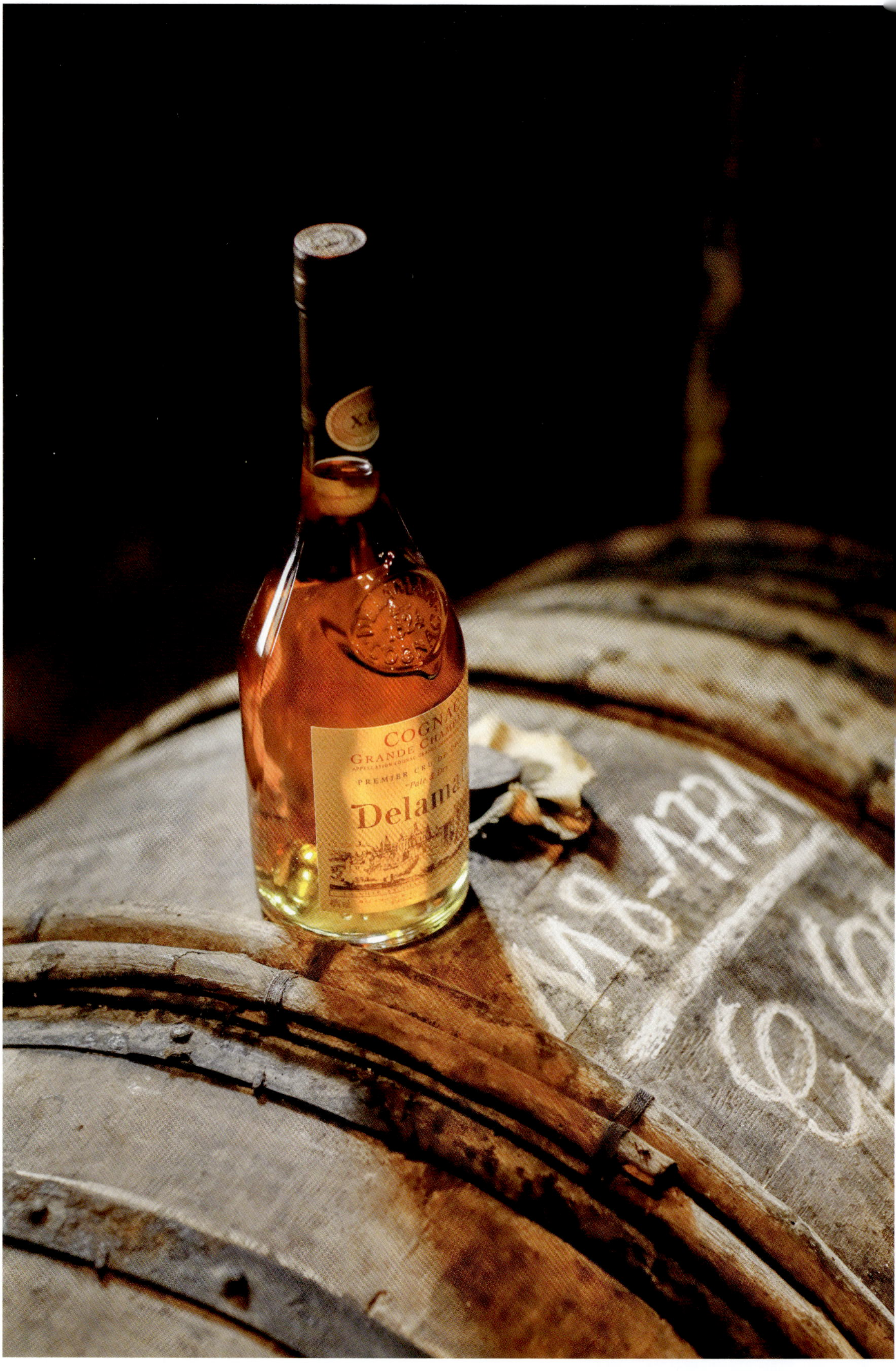

A PLACE CALLED COGNAC

In a region of southwest France, an exacting process turns grapes into the symbol of sophistication.
— BY SHIVANI VORA

With an alcohol by volume strength of 70 percent, the aroma alone of the eau-de-vie, the double-distilled brandy that would eventually be blended into a Cognac, was enough to make me feel tipsy. I stood in the 13th-century cellars of Delamain, a Cognac house in Jarnac, France, inhaling the sting of the colorless liquid and finding myself clutching an oak cask for support.

Delamain's master blender, Dominique Touteau, cautioned me against taking a taste. "Even a tiny sip will burn your throat," he said.

I had come to the Cognac region to learn more about its eponymous spirit, and understanding this essential ingredient was part of my orientation.

I'd had a longtime association with Cognac, the drink. As a child and into my teenage years, my father occasionally made me a concoction of Cognac, honey, and hot water to relieve a sore throat and clear congestion. Now my appreciation for Cognac is more fun and less medicinal. I sip it with ice as an after-dinner digestif and imbibe cocktails in which it is the primary liquor. But until I went to Cognac in southwest France, I didn't know much about the drink except that it is a brandy made with white wine grapes, primarily a variety called Ugni Blanc, and that I liked its refined taste.

My ignorance wasn't the exception, according to my guide, Madeleine Marchand, the founder of the Bordeaux-based travel company Bordeaux Excellence, who used to work at Remy Martin to distribute Cognac in eastern Asia. "There's an air of mystery around Cognac," she said. "It's a popular spirit and on every restaurant menu, but people aren't aware of its intricacies or history the way they are about wine."

Previous A bottle at Delamain. To be called Cognac, a brandy must be made in the Cognac region northeast of Bordeaux.

Left Maurice Hennessy belongs to the eighth generation of the family that founded the Hennessy brand.

Opposite Cognac advertising in 1900. The mystique of Cognac goes back centuries.

The first thing to know, she said, is that for a brandy to be called a Cognac, it must be produced in the Cognac region, comprising six subregions with a patchwork of vineyards. On a drive through these — Grande Champagne, Petite Champagne, Borderies, Fins Bois, Bons Bois, and Bois Ordinaires — she explained that while Grande and Petite Champagne are considered the finest, most of the more than 200 Cognac producers rely on eaux-de-vie made with grapes from several subregions as they craft their blends.

The landscape I saw has had vines since Roman times, but the origins of Cognac go back only to the 16th century, when Dutch merchants came to the region to buy white wines. These delicate wines were hard to preserve over the long distances they had to travel, and to keep them from spoiling, French distillers heated the liquid in copper pots and then cooled it. This process turned it into an eau-de-vie, a concentrated alcohol solution that wouldn't easily go bad.

Somehow, however, it was discovered that distilling the wine again and aging it in oak barrels — the reason for Cognac's amber hue — created an enjoyable libation. These eaux-de-vie, like the one I sniffed at Delamain, have an alcoholic strength of around 70 percent when they're first stored. Their potency drops over time, and the Cognac comes to fruition at an alcoholic strength of 40 percent as eaux-de-vie of different ages are blended.

No tour buses intruded on our scenic drive because many of the Cognac houses don't have formal tours for visitors. Many are closed on weekends. Visits to most require advance booking, most easily arranged with the help of a local tour company. But their lack of commercialism, combined with their rich history, is their appeal.

We made our way to the town of Cognac, where several larger brands are based, to see Hennessy, one of the world's biggest Cognac houses, on the left bank of the Charente River.

Hennessy had guided tours, complete with a short movie about the brand, but Marc Cordier, the director of distilling, was there to show us around. He said we would first go to the river's right bank to see the warehouses where the eau-de-vie casks age.

On the ride over, he told us that despite being part of the luxury conglomerate LVMH, the company still had family roots. Richard Hennessy, an Irishman who moved to France to serve in the French army, founded it in 1765, and Maurice Richard Hennessy — belonging to the eighth generation of the family — was the current ambassador for the brand. The current master blender, Renaud Fillioux de Gironde, was the eighth-generation Fillioux to have that title.

The warehouse was a spectacle of hundreds of casks, each labeled with a storage date and the name of the distiller, lined up in long aisles. These were a sliver of Hennessy's inventory. "We have around 350,000 casks in 50 warehouses," Cordier said. "The art of our Cognac is combining different eaux-de-vie from them to create blends for our core line that are consistent every year."

Back on the left bank, I tried three Cognacs that were part of this core line. There was the light and lively VS, short for very special, or a blend in which the youngest eau-de-vie has aged for at least two years. The VSOP, a very superior old pale where the minimum age of the youngest eau-de-vie is four years, had more boldness with notes of toasted cinnamon. But the XO, meaning extra old, with at least 10 years of aging for the youngest eau-de-vie, outdid both. This impressive blend, crafted with 100 eaux-de-vie, had a full-bodied mouthfeel and hints of cocoa.

Hennessy was only the first of the centuries-old Cognac houses I saw. Most producers in the region have been around since the 1700s and 1800s and are carrying on long-existing family traditions. Many of these smaller labels are in Jarnac, a town with a jumble of narrow streets that is a 15-minute drive from Cognac.

Louis Royer, for example, was established in 1853 by a local man who grew up in the very neighborhood where I found the company still based. Jerome Royer, a fifth-generation Royer, lived down the street, and his son Nicolas worked in the United States to promote the family's Cognac.

Rather than relying on guides, I was told, executives from the house led visits whenever they could, and in our case, it was the export manager, Jean-Cyrill Vincent. He led us on a river path to the contemporary tasting room with gleaming wood floors, which the notable French interior decorator Andrée Putman designed in 1992. Here, he poured me a generous glass of the line's highly regarded XO. An aroma of dried fruit wafted from the tulip snifter, and the drink's subtle sweetness intermingled with spice. It was like a dessert, and I couldn't leave any behind.

A doorway led to the 19th-century cellars holding a large portion of Louis Royer's 20,000 eau-de-vie casks. They didn't have a sprawling grandeur, but their honeycomb pattern arrangement, a homage to the Royer family tradition of beekeeping, was still a sight to see.

Later that afternoon, we went back in time almost 100 years further at Hine, a house founded in 1763 by the Englishman Thomas Hine, where the Cognacs were made exclusively with Grande and Petite Champagne eaux-de-vie. The brand had been based in the Hine family house since the 19th century, and with its numerous historical items, a visit was almost like having a museum to yourself.

"We're a tiny company, so our employees lead visits, but there is a time and space constraint on how many people can come here," explained Marie-Emmanuelle Febvret, a marketing and communication manager for Hine.

She led me through the interior courtyard to a room hanging with portraits, in both classic and Andy Warhol–like interpretations, of the six generations of Hine men behind the Cognac. The family no longer owned the brand, she said, but Bernard Thomas Hine

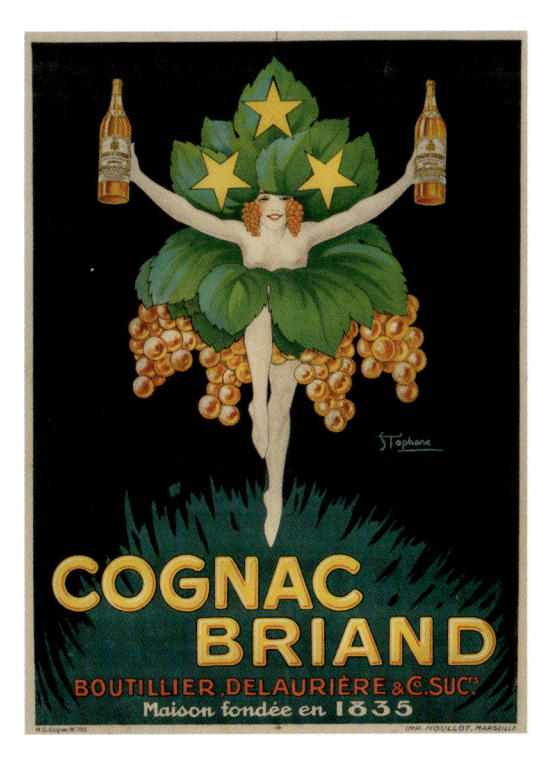

Above Distilling at Hennessy. Cognac begins with eau-de-vie, an alcohol-heavy concentrate from white wine.

Opposite Surveying samples at Delamain. Distillers keep detailed records on all of their Cognacs.

was the honorary chairman and traveled the world to promote the line.

We then went to the sumptuous former living quarters, with dark wood paneling and rich fabrics in varying shades of deep red. The family's salon had become a dining room where Hine's top customers were invited for meals, and the living room where the original Royal Warrant from 1962 designating Hine as the official Cognac supplier to Queen Elizabeth II in England hung on the wall.

This historical tour aside, the Cognac I sampled was worth the visit alone. In years when the weather leading up to the harvest is mild and sunny, Hine's cellar master may set aside some Grande Champagne eaux-de-vie casks to be aged into single vintage Cognacs. It so happened that 1978, when I was born, was a prime year. Sure, I was biased, but the drink seemed to dance, with its buttery texture and taste of fresh vanilla pods.

What could top this Cognac?

Maybe nothing, but I did have another label to visit. In an 18th-century house on a cobblestone side street, we climbed a short flight of stairs to meet Charles Braastad, a descendant of the Irishman James Delamain, who founded his storied Cognac brand in 1759. "We're small," he said. "The bigger brands produce in two days what we do in a year."

The jewel-box brand was so tiny that the production happened in one room down the hallway from his office. The scene before me there of a half-dozen employees filling, sealing, and labeling glass bottles by hand misleadingly suggested a homespun operation, not an enterprise where the least expensive Cognacs —the elegant Pale and Dry XO—cost around $130 a bottle.

It was at the medieval cellars across the street, belonging to Delamain, that I finally saw that throat-burning eau-de-vie, the basis of Cognac. Touteau, the

Photographs by Rodolphe Escher

master blender who warned me not to take a taste, explained that Delamain had a unique way to craft its brandies. "After aging the Cognacs for 25 years, we blend them and age the blend for two more years so the flavors marry," he said. "Then, I add in even more eaux-de-vie to achieve the perfect blend."

But before any of the aging, blending, or bottling figures in, all Cognac starts as that colorless eau-de-vie, so potent that the aroma alone can feel intoxicating—and so precious that its end product is known worldwide as a symbol of refinement.

WHAT TO READ

Cognac: The Seductive Saga of the World's Most Coveted Spirit, by Kyle Jarrard. The story of Cognac from its creation in the 1500s to its current status as the world's most prized brandy.

Cognac: The Story of the World's Greatest Brandy, by Nicholas Faith, a book in the Classic Wine Library series. From a longtime writer on wines and spirits; includes a directory of producers and Faith's tasting notes.

The World of Cognac, by Michelle Brachet. How Cognac is made, and how to enjoy it.

Classic After-Dinner Drinks, by Salvatore Calabrese. Recipes from a renowned European bartender, with Cognac a prominent ingredient.

Let's Drink to That: Drink Quotes for After Dinner and Other Occasions, by Robert West. An idiosyncratic little book gathering quotations from a variety of sources.

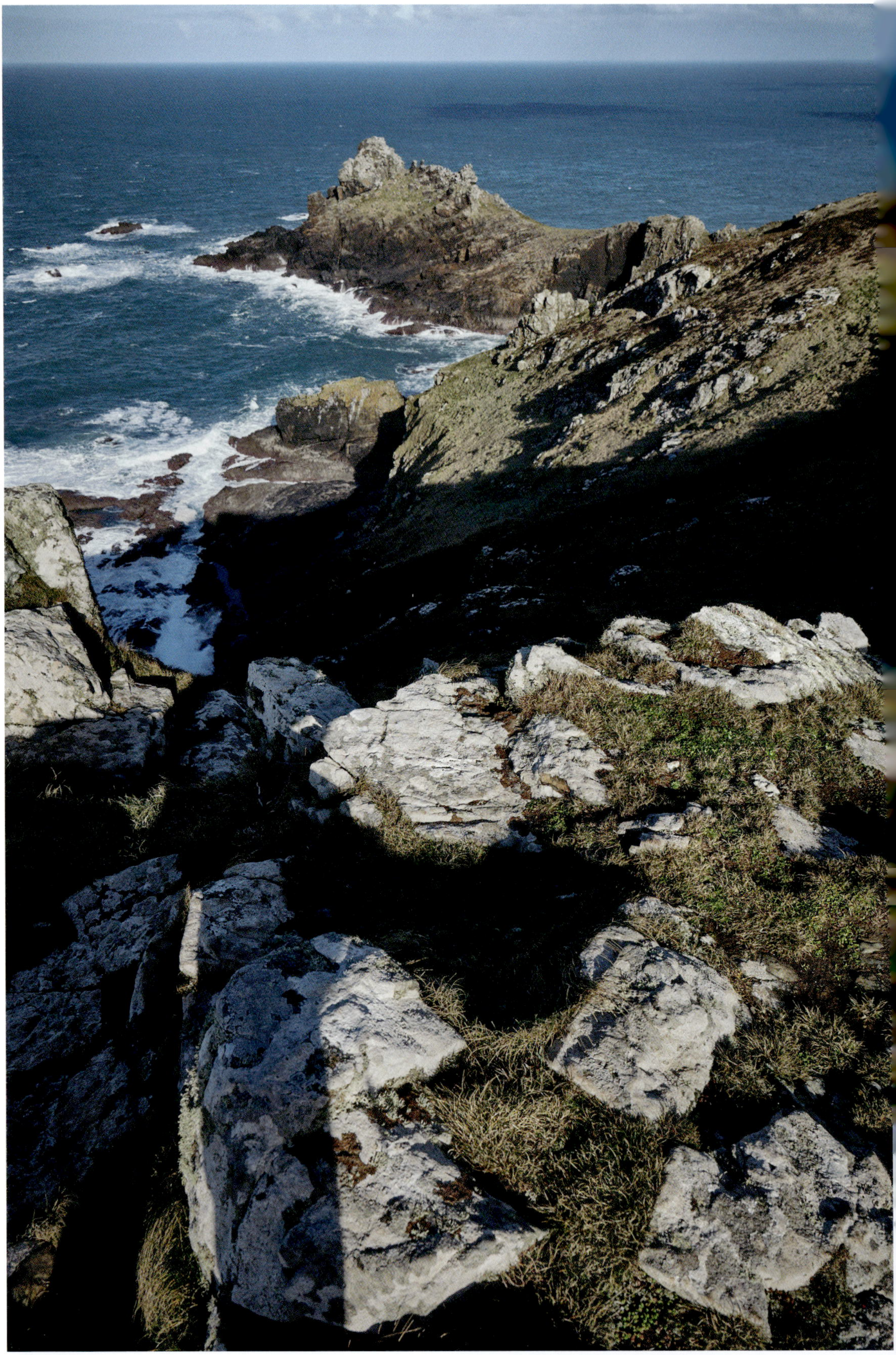

VIRGINIA WOOLF'S LOST EDEN

For a young girl with a literary future, the Cornish coast was "the country intensified." — BY RATHA TEP

Virginia Woolf wasn't always the radical we imagine today. Before the debates on truth and beauty with her circle of early 20th-century artists, intellectuals, and writers known as the Bloomsbury Group; before the polemical feminist lectures at Cambridge; and before the ever-constant push to experiment with new forms of fiction, there was the impressionable young girl, born Adeline Virginia Stephen, who spent seaside summers in Cornwall, at the rugged tip of England's South West Peninsula.

On a gray October morning, I was on the Great Western Railway, rolling along the same route that Woolf would have taken about a century before, the train hugging tight past a progression of wide swaths of golden sand and languidly sloping green cliffs. In the distance were the deep blue of St Ives Bay and the white Godrevy Lighthouse. This rail line to the coastal town of St Ives opened in 1877, causing a huge increase in tourism there, and it is easy to understand how it lured well-to-do Britons like young Virginia's family.

Long an admirer of Woolf, not only because she was a modernist literary pioneer who redefined the possibilities of the novel, but for the simple reason that no other writer has given me, sentence for sentence, such pleasure, I decided to go in search of her in her early years. Cornwall, by most accounts, had a profound effect on her future writing, making its way into the novels *Jacob's Room* and *The Waves*, and forming the basis of one of her greatest works, *To the Lighthouse*.

Woolf's girlhood summers in Cornwall were a reprieve from her upper-middle-class life in London, where, for most of the year, she spent her days in what she called "the rich red gloom" of a tall London townhouse. In Cornwall, her father, the literary critic

Previous The rocky Cornwall coast. In summers there, the young Virginia Woolf escaped "rich red gloom" in London.

Left Talland House in the late 1800s. Virginia's father, Leslie Stephen, called it a "pocket-paradise" for his family.

Opposite A first edition of *To the Lighthouse* (1927). The novel is set on the Isle of Skye, but its imagery reflects Cornwall.

and historian Sir Leslie Stephen, rented a house overlooking St Ives Bay, describing it in an 1884 letter as "a pocket-paradise with a sheltered cove of sand in easy reach (for 'Ginia even) just below." That house, that bay, that lighthouse: all would be immortalized. While *To the Lighthouse* is set on the Isle of Skye, it is laced with almost direct imagery from her time in Cornwall.

From 1882, when she was only a few months old, to 1894, when she was 12, the year before her mother died, Virginia spent a few months each year with her sister, Vanessa, and the rest of her family in Talland House, situated on the outskirts of St Ives, then a small fishing town.

It was the sheer physical freedom of Cornwall, compared to the constrictions of her London life, suggest the scholars Marion Dell and Marion Whybrow in *Virginia Woolf & Vanessa Bell: Remembering St Ives*, that helped her balk at the constructs of her day and conceive of independent achievement. She roamed free in the salty air of the sloping garden, with the expanse of the bay and its distant lighthouse before her. She swam and poked among rock pools down at the beach below, and hunted great-winged moths on rambling nighttime expeditions.

"In retrospect nothing that we had as children made as much difference, was quite so important to us, as our summer in Cornwall," she wrote in 1940 in her autobiographical essay *A Sketch of the Past*. "The country was intensified, after the months in London."

Winding my way up from the St Ives rail station, as the Stephen family would have done with cooks, servants, and mounds of luggage, I saw Talland House, a mid-19th-century stone villa. "Her family would move their entire way of life, their whole household, for two or three months out of the year to this house with a magical garden in this very remote setting, and it would become a kind of Eden for her, the place she would idealize and always remember," said Alexandra Harris, whose 2011 book *Virginia Woolf* is one of several Woolf biographies.

"In *To the Lighthouse*, Woolf, as a successful middle-aged writer, comes face to face with her mother in the garden, which is very much the garden at Talland House," Harris said. "The novel embodies the feeling of having left something unfinished through those childhood summers."

To the Lighthouse encapsulates Woolf's love and longing for her mother — as well as her conflicted view of her mother's vision of Victorian womanhood. The novel was a release of those feelings. "When it was written," Woolf wrote in *A Sketch of the Past*, "I ceased to be obsessed by my mother. I no longer hear her voice; I do not see her."

While Talland House was carved into five apartments in the 1950s and isn't open to the public, it is possible, from Talland Road above, to catch a glimpse of the cream-colored facade and sloping garden and to look across St Ives Bay to the Godrevy Lighthouse. Visitors can also walk up the paved driveway, the former "carriage drive," around the side of the garden, said Peter Eddy, the house's longtime owner (with his brother, John Eddy), who met me there.

I walked around, soaking up the spirit of the place.

The garden is more manicured now, lacking the fiery red-hot poker flowers and the pockets of charm — "love corner," "coffee garden," and "lookout place" — that defined the space for the Stephens. Yet a few relics remain, including feathery spears of pampas grass near where Woolf would have played evening games of cricket, and mixed hedging around the garden's bottom border that included her beloved escallonia, "whose leaves, pressed, gave out a very sweet smell."

Looking across the bay from the garden, I recalled one of the best-known lines from *To the Lighthouse*: "For the great plateful of blue water was before her; the hoary Lighthouse, distant, austere, in the midst..."

Just minutes' walk away is Primrose Valley, once blanketed with apple orchards. A little dirt path there would have taken Virginia and her siblings down to Porthminster Beach. Now, sprawling houses with gray-shingled mansard roofs edge up to one another, with hedging and moss-covered stone lining a paved route. The beach, though, a wide crescent of smooth, powdery sand on the turquoise bay, retains its essential, sweeping majesty.

In the center of St Ives, I got lost amid the labyrinth of cobbled streets, but I couldn't find much left of the "windy, noisy, fishy, vociferous, narrow-streeted town" that Woolf recalled. All that has been replaced with a more tourist-friendly image: St Ives, the arts haven by the sea. The town even has a branch of London's Tate Museum.

In adulthood, Woolf would return many times to Cornwall. Her sister, Vanessa Bell, received a rather alarming letter, written on Christmas Day, 1909. "I went for a walk in Regents Park yesterday morning," Woolf wrote, "and it suddenly struck me how absurd it was to stay in London, with Cornwall going on all the time." She impulsively purchased a train ticket, and arrived at the village of Lelant, near St Ives, at 10:30 p.m. without "spectacles, cheque book, looking glass, or coat." Pacing the platform at that Lelant station, I was struck by how she might have chosen her lodging, the Lelant Hotel. Now the Badger Inn, it was the nearest accommodation, a short, steep walk away at the top of Station Hill.

It's about seven miles farther to Godrevy, a beach and headland that is now part of the National Trust. There, sunlight streamed down through the clouds and seemed to reflect the golden sands, lighting up the whole place in the area's characteristic soft glow. I walked past wild flowing grasses before reaching the closest point on shore to Godrevy Island. And then the lighthouse, a literary landmark because of Woolf's famous book, stood before me: stark, solid, sacrosanct.

Her next trip to Cornwall, at age 28, was more scripted. Back in London and nearing completion of her first novel, *The Voyage Out*, she spiraled into a

Above The Stephens could easily see Godrevy Lighthouse. Woolf wrote of a "hoary Lighthouse, distant, austere…"

Opposite St Ives, once a fishing village, now cultivates its image as a getaway for vacationers and artists.

mental breakdown so severe it landed her in Burley Park, a home for mentally ill women. (Hermione Lee, arguably the foremost Woolf expert, associated the symptoms with what would now be recognized as manic-depressive illness or bipolar disorder.) Part of her recuperation that summer was a walking tour around Zennor, a tiny village and parish just southwest of St Ives, with a nurse, Jean Thomas.

Tramping through a light mist, I found my way to the handsome stone farmhouse where they stayed, now a private residence. Two nearby structures have been turned into holiday accommodations called Porthmeor Cottages. Chickens pecked outside a coop, and in the distance, cattle grazed open pastureland that seemed to drop off into the sea below.

Three years later, in 1913, Woolf sank into periods of severe depression and was again admitted to Burley Park. In September she attempted suicide. After a period of rest she slowly improved, and with her husband, Leonard Woolf, she headed to Cornwall again in 1914.

They spent a portion of their stay at Carbis Bay, a seaside resort village about a mile and a half up the coast from St Ives. I found its beach dotted with surfers in wet suits and, above them, whitewashed, glass-fronted villas.

The Carbis Bay Hotel & Estate, where the Woolfs stayed, seemed to me more Caribbean than Cornish, with palm-tree-fringed views of the sweeping turquoise bay. But there, in the distance, was the Godrevy Lighthouse, and in a hallway off a glass conservatory inside the hotel hung a photo of the Woolfs, with Woolf's guest signature in purple.

During the 1920s and 1930s, a creatively fruitful time for Woolf, she worked on her three novels most closely associated with Cornwall. When she and Leonard visited in those years, they stayed mostly in the Zennor area. As I made my way around its

Photographs by
Andy Haslam

medieval farming tracts, sweeping moors, and winding coastal paths, I understood why. It was an antidote not just to the frenzy of London, but also to the rapid growth of St Ives and Carbis Bay.

In the tiny hamlet of Poniou, a longtime resident told me the Woolfs had stayed there in 1921. They stayed there again in May 1936, Virginia's last trip, at age 54, to Cornwall, an attempt to keep yet another breakdown at bay. They wandered around St Ives and crept into the garden of Talland House, and in the dusk, Leonard wrote, "Virginia peered through the ground-floor windows to see the ghosts of her childhood."

When I peered through those same windows, I imagined her there, leaning toward the glass and trying to recapture a vanished past when life had felt so new.

WHAT TO READ AND WATCH

To the Lighthouse, **Jacob's Room**, and **The Waves**, by Virginia Woolf, all novels influenced by Woolf's experiences in Cornwall.

Virginia Woolf, by Hermione Lee. A widely praised biography.

Virginia Woolf and Vanessa Bell: Remembering St Ives, by Marion Dell and Marion Whybrow. Focuses on the sisters' summers at Talland House.

Virginia Woolf, by Quentin Bell, Woolf's nephew. An authoritative biography with occasional personal observations like, "She had lost whatever prettiness she may have possessed; but certainly she continued to be very beautiful."

The Hours, directed by Stephen Daldry. Based on the Pulitzer Prize–winning novel by Michael Cunningham. Nicole Kidman plays Virginia Woolf.

CHARLIE'S SHOES

A CHARLIE CHAPLIN HOME MOVIE

A house on the Swiss Riviera opens to an intimate view of a comic artist's life and work. — BY ELAINE GLUSAC

Charlie Chaplin appeared in more than 80 films over the course of his roughly 75-year career. But I had to travel to Switzerland to see this one from the 1960s: White-haired and in his 70s, Chaplin skips playfully on the front lawn of his estate, holding hands with two of his young children. The black-and-white scene jumps to the great comedian dining with several of his brood, each spooning soup in comic unison, then to Chaplin, wide-eyed, a hat levitating magically above his head to the family's delight. In these home movies shot by his fourth and last wife, Oona, he is rounder than his familiar film character, the Little Tramp, but he remains impish, a child among his own children.

That is the personal portrait that emerges from Chaplin's last home, a 37-acre estate called Manoir de Ban. From 1953 until his death in 1977, he and his family lived here in the small town of Corsier-sur-Vevey, within sight of Lake Geneva. Restored and re-fashioned into a museum complex known as Chaplin's World, the property includes the manor house, an immersive cinema museum devoted to his professional achievements, and a restaurant called The Tramp.

It seems fitting that Chaplin, a perfectionist and multitasker, chose Switzerland, a country famous for precision in everything from luxury watches to Roger Federer's backhand, as his retirement home.

"A friend suggested Switzerland," he wrote opaquely in his 1964 memoir, *My Autobiography*. On an ocean liner bound for Europe with his family in 1952, Chaplin learned he was prohibited from returning to his home in the United States without submitting to an interrogation regarding his politics and morals. For several years prior, the FBI and the House Un-American Activities Committee had been

Previous Chocolate "Charlie's Shoes" in a box shaped like a film reel, at the Läderach chocolate shop in Vevey.

Left Chaplin and his family at Manoir de Ban. In old age, he delighted in his life as a family man.

Opposite Rooms set up to mimic movie sets take cinephiles on a trip into the past at Chaplin's World.

investigating his links to Communism — "I am a peace-monger," he told them. The author Peter Ackroyd, in his biography *Charlie Chaplin*, suggests that Switzerland's appeal lay in its lenient tax code.

Or, perhaps, like generations before him, Chaplin came for the peace and quiet. By the 18th century, Lac Léman, a.k.a. Lake Geneva, was already a haven for travelers who found respite between their tours of the great European capitals in slow walks along the shore, especially the 19-mile stretch between Lausanne and Montreux known as the Swiss Riviera.

In the early 20th century, Clinique La Prairie spa began dispensing rejuvenating treatments there, and the wealthy continued to spend seasons in formal lakefront hotels, as captured in Anita Brookner's *Hotel du Lac*, a low-key 1984 novel set in the Vevey hotel that is now called the Grand Hôtel du Lac.

The snow-capped Alps of France and Switzerland that rose up beyond the far shore of the placid lake provided the mountainous backdrop that Chaplin could see from his front yard at Manoir de Ban, a 13-minute uphill bus ride from lakeside Vevey.

I arrived at Chaplin's World with a keen interest in Chaplin the artist — the comic genius and cinematic innovator who worked on both sides of the camera. That artistry is the subject of the Studio film museum, while the mansion, where I started my visit, explores his personal life.

Nearly leaping, a lifelike wax figure of a waving Chaplin greeted me in the foyer of the neoclassical mansion. The first floor has been restored to its appearance in Chaplin's day, down to the family furniture, including the cozy jacquard-print sofa on which I was invited to sit in the ornate living room.

"We think we are not precisely a museum, but we haven't found the word for it yet," said Annick Barbezat, the communications director for Chaplin's World, as she guided me on a summer visit. "People say, 'It's dangerous to sit on the sofa — it could stain.' We counter, 'We'll wash it and put it back.'"

Chaplin served as an actor, writer, director, and composer on many of his films; and original scores, letters, and scripts lie on his desk as if he had just left the room. "Chaplin had a lifelong compulsion to do everything himself, even down to wanting to play every role in each of his films," the film critic and author David Robinson wrote in the foreword to Chaplin's *My Autobiography*.

He was also scandal-prone. A library in the house is wallpapered in newspaper clippings about incidents including allegations of tax evasion and, more damning, affairs with young women, some only teenagers when they met Chaplin and starred in his films.

Somewhat incongruously, a wax figure of his friend Winston Churchill presides in this room, one of a series of celebrity references in the house that remind visitors of the breadth of Chaplin's worldwide fame in the early 20th century. Black-and-white photos of past overnight guests, ranging from Salvador Dalí to Sophia Loren, fill one former bedroom.

But the most moving rooms attest to the private man. In another bedroom, the visitor sees the home movies made by Oona (who was also the daughter of Eugene O'Neill). Her camera caught a joyful Chaplin waltzing with one of his children — he had eight with Oona, 36 years his junior — in his arms and lying on the floor mimicking another, a thumb-sucking infant, beside him.

If the house embodies the personal Chaplin, the Studio film museum on the grounds is the true attraction for cinephiles, featuring an immersive journey through his career via a series of rooms set up to mimic movie sets. Each conjures one of his most famous films with wax figures, props, and looping clips. A baleful Jackie Coogan, dressed for his title role in *The Kid*, anchors a cobblestone street corner. A laughing Paulette Goddard holds a bunch of bananas in an allusion to her scene in *Modern Times*, with the film running behind her.

Michael Jackson, a fan and friend, is also here, in an exhibit suggesting that Chaplin's dance moves in *Modern Times* inspired Jackson's signature moonwalk.

With the exception of a static room devoted to the most valuable artifacts, like Chaplin's trademark bowler hat and cane and his Oscar statues, the Studio encourages playful interaction. During my visit, visitors took selfies in a barbershop chair like the one in *The Great Dictator*. In a reproduction of the Yukon cabin, poised on a fulcrum, used in the 1925 film *The Gold Rush*, I shuffled side to side to make the cabin tilt as it did in the movie.

"Chaplin said, 'If you want to know me, see my movies,'" Barbezat told me. "You can read his humanity in movies like *The Great Dictator* and *The Kid*. We hope to do what he did. He made people think and feel."

On the Swiss Riviera, Chaplin's world isn't limited to Chaplin's World. Just beyond his estate, the Modern

Above The Fork of Vevey, installed long after Chaplin's death, captures the spirit of the zany humor of his films.

Below The Château de Chillon, a much-visited tourist site near Montreux, Vevey's sister town on Lake Geneva.

Opposite The Grand Hôtel du Lac is the setting of Anita Brookner's novel *Hotel du Lac* about wealthy visitors to Vevey.

Times Hotel salutes the Little Tramp with film clips and Chaplin portraits. In Vevey, where Oona pushed the wheelchair-bound Chaplin along the lakefront path in his last years, a bronze statue of the Little Tramp gazes wistfully out over the water.

Though the family maintains tight control of Chaplin's image, I saw several sites in Vevey that paid homage to him, including most notably the Läderach chocolate shop. Many years ago its chief chocolatier, Blaise Poyet, approached the family about making a confection in Chaplin's honor. He modeled it on the Little Tramp's oversize shoes and rendered them in chocolate.

"They have three characteristics based on Charlie," said Poyet, seated in the shop's kitchen. "First, he was strong, hard. So I use dark chocolate. Second, he was very romantic, and for that I use caramel. And third, he was original, so I use pine nuts, which is unusual."

A cafe down the street bore Chaplin's French pet name, Le Charlot, and a women's shop had a window decorated with a bowler hat, a cane, a red rose, and a number of film stills that harmonized with the vintage-inspired dresses on sale. "It's a homage to the museum," said a salesclerk. "He was a romantic."

Photographs by Clara Tuma

My own Chaplinesque—which is to say mischievous—moment occurred after I had an overpriced 10-franc beer on the lakefront terrace of the aristocratic Hotel des Trois Couronnes in Vevey. I put a 20-franc bill down to pay for it and pocketed the unfamiliar change, only to discover later that the waiter had exchanged it for smaller notes and not deducted the tab.

What to do? Did I have to go back to the hotel, or should I just call it a lucky break?

I knew Chaplin's answer. If it happened to the Little Tramp, he'd twirl a cane and wobble lakeward into the sunset.

WHAT TO READ AND WATCH

Charlie Chaplin: A Brief Life, by Peter Ackroyd. Respectful of Chaplin as an artist while documenting his flaws and obsessions.

My Autobiography, by Charlie Chaplin, with David Robinson. Written when Chaplin was in his 70s and living at Manoir de Ban; praised as a fine theatrical autobiography.

The Real Charlie Chaplin, directed by Peter Middleton and James Spinney. A Showtime documentary. "This introduction to Chaplin shines whenever he performs, displaying his comic genius for doing everything wrong to absolute perfection." — Nicolas Rapold in *The New York Times*.

Chaplin, directed by Richard Attenborough. Robert Downey Jr. stars as Chaplin. Geraldine Chaplin, Charlie's daughter, plays her own grandmother, the troubled Hannah Chaplin.

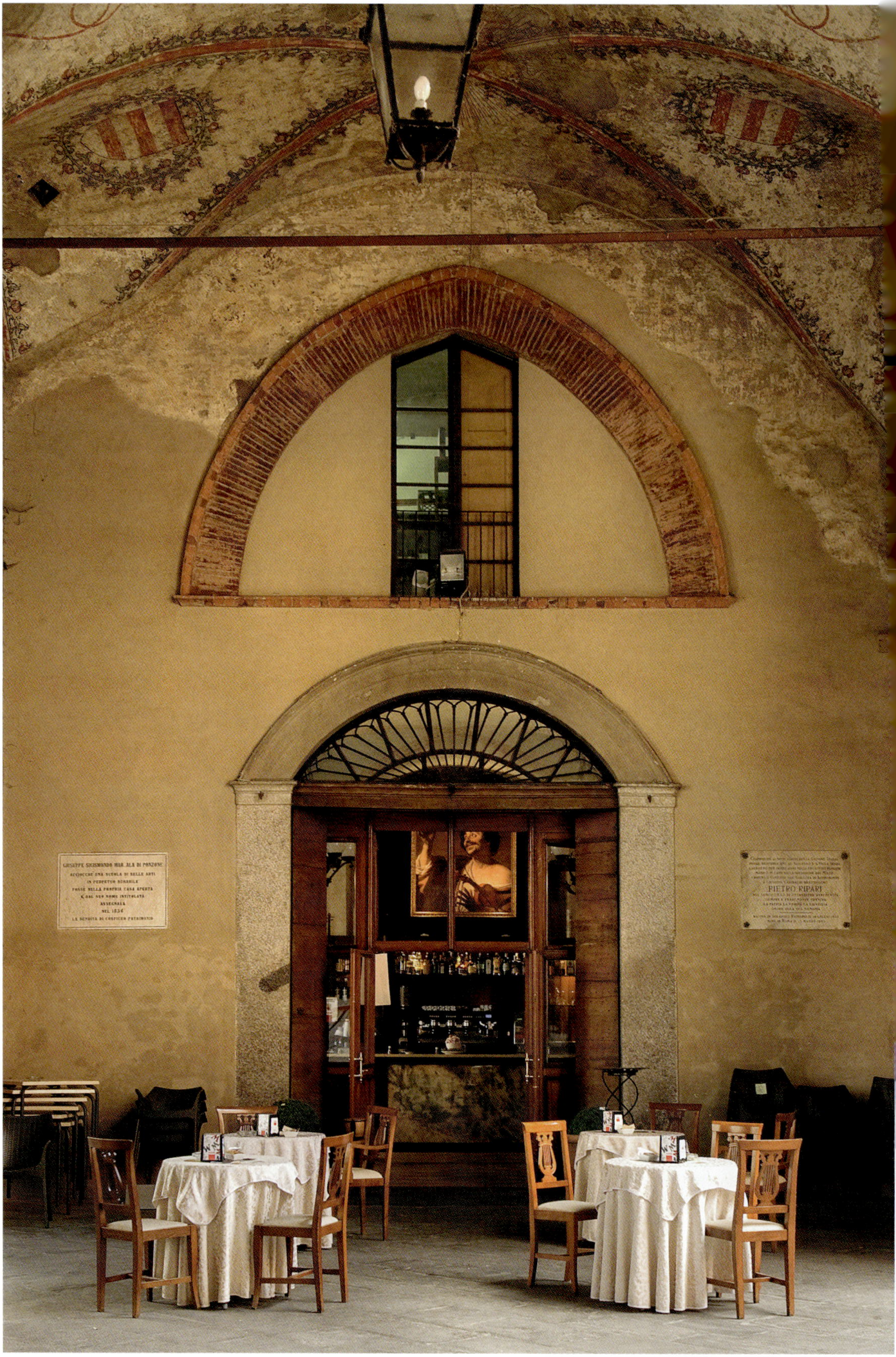
PIETRO RIPARI

THE CITY OF THE STRADIVARIUS

"You can make a violin with a machine or a computer,"
says one violin maker in Cremona. "But you can't put
your heart inside of it." — BY JASON WILSON

Cremona is a small, pretty, well-kept, bourgeois, mercantile city in the fertile Po Valley of Italy. There is no local wine region. There is no city university. There are no grandiose must-see sights. Yet Cremona is famous, and for an appealing reason. It owes its fame to music.

As I've traveled around Italy over the last 25 years speaking grammatically challenged Italian, I'm often asked where I learned the language. When I answer Cremona, where I was a 19-year-old exchange student, the confused, incredulous response is generally: "Cremona? Why Cremona? Of all the cities in Italy?" Before I can answer, the next question is almost always, "Do you play the violin?"

I do not, in fact, play the violin. But the history of this sleepy city of 70,000 on the Po River, just over an hour south of Milan by train, is inexorably intertwined with violins and other stringed instruments. At a dinner during my first weekend in town, half a lifetime ago, I sat next to a man named Fulvio, who told me he made violins for a living. He'd gone to school at age 13 to learn violin-making and then had apprenticed for years, and now he had his own violin workshop, where he made stringed instruments by hand for musicians and collectors around the world. "This city is the birthplace of Stradivarius," he said, and explained that there were dozens of luthiers — makers of stringed instruments — just like him working in the city center.

Fulvio invited me into his workshop, where over several weeks and months he shaped, carved, chiseled, sanded, and varnished very special pieces of wood

Previous Cremona offers good food, fine architecture, largely tourist-free streets, and, above all, a unique musical heritage.

Left The Academia Cremonensis teaches the Cremonese method of making stringed instruments.

Opposite A Stradivarius violin at the Metropolitan Museum of Art in New York.

into instruments that he sold for tens of thousands of dollars. No other place in the world made violins like Cremona, Fulvio said. The Cremonese method — one that dates back to Andrea Amati, "father of the violin" in the 16th century; to the Guarneri family in the 17th and 18th centuries; and of course to Stradivarius — takes longer and is more difficult than other methods, and creates one-of-a-kind instruments.

More than 140 *liutai*, as the luthiers are called in Italian, currently ply their trade in the city. Wandering the narrow streets around the Piazza del Comune, you can watch dozens of violinmakers at their workbenches through their storefront windows. If they're not busy or if they're in the right mood, some of them may wave you inside to have a look.

"This is an antique job. Nothing has changed for centuries," the violinmaker Philippe Devanneaux, who came to Cremona from Paris decades ago, told me when I visited him. "Of course, you can make a violin with a machine or a computer, but you can't put your heart inside of it."

That makes Cremona a must-visit for music lovers, especially during the annual Stradivari Festival. But it's also a perfect overnight trip from Milan, where even those without a passion for stringed instruments can look forward to some of the best food in northern Italy, impressive architecture, and streets that are largely tourist-free.

In her 1954 book *The Surprise of Cremona*, Edith Templeton calls the city a "strange provincial town" and, oddly, does not mention a word about violins. She recounts a meeting with the editor of the local newspaper who tells her, "There is nothing interesting in Cremona...nothing, nothing, nothing." She ends up enjoying Cremona. "It is a wonderful relief to come to a town where there is no first-class hotel," she writes. While there are certainly a couple of nice hotels to stay in these days, I couldn't agree more with the sentiment: Cremona's virtue lies in how far off the tourist path it remains.

Decades after her visit, I've found a similar self-deprecating attitude among the Cremonese. Since they don't like to boast, allow me to do it for them: Cremona has one of the most beautiful piazzas in northern Italy. Twelve streets converge on the haunting Piazza del Comune, marked by its majestic 14th-century, 367-foot-tall bell tower, called simply the Torrazzo (for which Cremona's famed torrone nougat is named).

Gothic palazzi and the Romanesque cathedral cut dramatic shadows against the arcades and the octagonal 12th-century baptistery, an architectural gem.

The 268-year-old Teatro Ponchielli (where Mozart once performed) has one of the largest stages in Italy and is still a magnet for international performances. The sprawling markets in the Piazza Stradivari and Piazza Pace are as lively as any in Lombardy.

And then there's the food. Cremona's location at the border of Lombardy and Emilia-Romagna brings influences from both: charcuterie like *cotechino* and *salame*; Grana Padano cheese; stuffed-pasta specialties like *marubini* and *tortelli di zucca*; and the famed Mostarda di Cremona, a sweet and gently spiced fruit preserve, served with the classic stew called *bollito misto*.

But perhaps the crowning food achievement of Cremona is its perfection of the *tramezzini* sandwich, spongy, perfectly triangled white bread stuffed with myriad varieties of ham, tuna, eggs, and artichokes and slathered with mayonnaise. They are always served with the question, "Mangia subito?" —to which the answer can only be, "Yes, I am eating this immediately."

Ugo Grill, which closely guards the recipe for its mayonnaise, has served the tramezzini gold standard for decades. But there are new challengers, like Tramezzo 1925, where I ate a sandwich that was transcendent, made with fresh-sliced homemade prosciutto cotto and artichokes.

But it would be folly to visit Cremona and not revel in its music heritage. Unesco has decreed that traditional violin craftsmanship in Cremona deserves protection on its list of Intangible Cultural Heritage of Humanity. Then there is the gorgeous, high-tech Museo del Violino, in the city center, which was financed by more than 10 million euros from the local steel magnate Giovanni Arvedi.

I took the museum's audio tour (available in several languages), which offers fascinating details about the origins of the violin, the Cremona school of violin-making, and the many esoteric steps in the process of creating Cremonese-style violins, violas, and cellos.

But then I arrived in a darkened space entitled the Treasure Box, where spotlights illuminated the dozen or so most important stringed instruments in Europe, including Antonio Stradivari's 1715 "Il Cremonese" violin and others by Guarneri and Amati. At that point, my audio guide strangely seemed at a loss for words. "You are standing before the masterpieces of classic violin-making," the narrator said. "We shall add nothing else but leave you to the contemplation of this musical treasure chest." In fact, visitors can go further, as the instruments are regularly played during small recitals that are open to the public, generally held at noon several days each week.

In an adjoining room hung my favorite exhibition, a collection of contemporary instruments that have won various Milan Triennale awards over the years. Type in a corresponding number on the audio guide, and you can listen to each instrument being played. I particularly enjoyed listening to a viola numbered 813, made by Dante Fulvio Lazzari—the same Fulvio who sat next to me at dinner so many years before.

After leaving the Museo del Violino, I walked a few blocks to visit the Academia Cremonensis, set in a beautiful, grand palazzo, which teaches the Cremonese method of making stringed instruments, as well as bow-making, to students from around the world. "The secret of the Cremona violin is the weight," said Giovanni Colonna, violinmaker and

Above Violins in the workspace of Philippe Devanneaux, one of the many luthiers attracted to Cremona.

Below Torrone nougat, a famed Cremona specialty, is named for the Torrazzo, a 14th-century bell tower.

Opposite An aperitivo-hour crowd in front of the 12th-century Cremona Baptistery.

lutherie director at the Academia Cremonensis. "It's light, but not too light."

He continued: "In our method, we start from the inside and the whole instrument grows together. There is no pattern, so you do it all with your eyes."

After a few tramezzini pit stops, I found myself inside a more intimate workshop, tucked around the corner from the Torrazzo. When Yael Rosenblum greeted me, she offered to wash her hands, which were covered with black shavings. "This is ebony," she said. "You don't want this on your hands."

She gave up a career as a professional violinist in Israel and moved to Cremona to study violin-making and to make violins. Professionals around the world play her violins, violas, and cellos; one of her first instruments is played regularly at La Scala.

"To be a violinmaker, living in Cremona is excellent," she said. "You can find all the raw materials, the setup, the tools."

*Photographs by
Andrea Wyner*

I told her about my long relationship with Cremona, and I asked her the question many people have asked me: Why Cremona? Besides the violins, how did she find living in Cremona?

"Well," she said, channeling the city's habit of self-deprecation. "Put it this way. Not everyone can live in New York. Some people have to live in New Jersey."

I shot her a disappointed look, and she laughed. "No, no," she said. "It's really inspiring to live here."

WHAT TO READ AND WATCH

The Surprise of Cremona: One Woman's Adventures in Cremona, Parma, Mantua, Ravenna, Urbino, and Arezzo, by Edith Templeton, with an introduction by Anita Brookner. A charming 1954 travel memoir reissued in 2003.

Stradivari's Genius: Five Violins, One Cello, and Three Centuries of Enduring Perfection, by Toby Faber. Traces the history of six instruments over centuries of being bought, sold, lost, and sometimes superbly played.

The Violin Maker: A Search for the Secrets of Craftsmanship, Sound, and Stradivari, by John Marchese. An impassioned account of how a master craftsman turns a block of wood into a magical instrument.

Stradivari: Search for Perfection, directed by Sven Hartung. A documentary following a talented young violinist on his global search for the perfect violin.

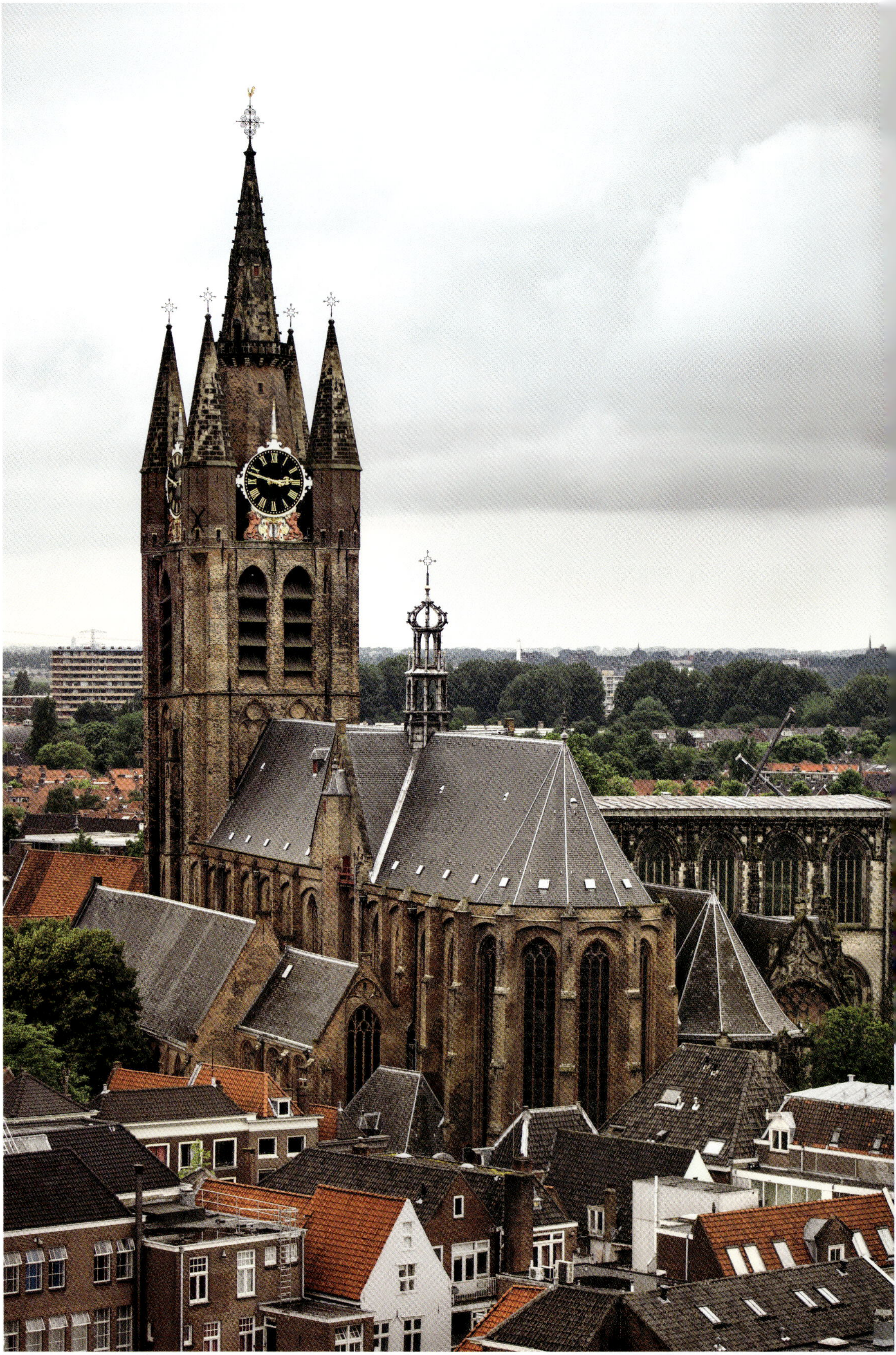

IN THE LIGHT OF DELFT, A GLEAM OF VERMEER

The Dutch city where the artist lived and painted still looks enough like its 17th-century self to conjure a picture of his life. — BY NINA SIEGAL AND CHRISTOPHER F. SCHUETZE

The view from the top of the twisting, 376-step staircase in the tower of Delft's 15th-century Nieuwe Kerk is worth the climb. On a clear day, the panorama seems to encompass all of South Holland: the Rotterdam skyline, The Hague and its port, and, just beyond the horizon, Keukenhof and its tulips. Down below is Delft itself, a city of canals and cobblestones, medieval churches, and an ancient trading tradition. This is the world of Johannes Vermeer.

To see Vermeer's luminous and evocative paintings, full of nuanced light and haunting, timeless human faces, Delft is not the place to go. They are scattered in museums around the world. None are in Delft itself, although several are only a few miles away in The Hague and a bit farther in Amsterdam. But to find Vermeer himself, as well as we can capture him 350 years after his own time, one must go to Delft.

Little is known about Vermeer's life, although some of his masterpieces, like *Girl with a Pearl Earring* and *The Milkmaid*, are among the most beloved paintings in our own era. We do know that he lived and worked his entire life in Delft; and today the city remains virtually unchanged in shape and hue from his time, offering the disorienting sensation that one is walking into a 17th-century painting.

On Delft's cobblestone streets, along its curving canals lined with tidy brick and half-timbered houses, past its original windmill and churches dating to the Middle Ages, we can imagine Vermeer purchasing his pigments or his canvases. Somewhere inside one of these houses, he is at work on scenes of domestic

DELFT   NETHERLANDS

Previous The Oude Kerk (Old Church), where Vermeer and four of his children are buried in the family crypt.

Left Whimsy rules at this cheese shop on the market square in Delft.

Opposite With its canals and cobblestones, Delft remains evocative of Vermeer's world.

intimacy, inviting us inside muted chambers with checkerboard floors, high-back chairs, and light slanting through stained-glass windows.

In the city's antique shops it's still possible to buy heavy ceramic milk jugs and pewter tableware like those in Vermeer's paintings, and the city's signature blue-and-white delftware tiles can be bought at the still-functioning Royal Delft pottery factory. (The factory also has a museum including a reconstruction of what Vermeer's kitchen would have looked like.)

At the Oude Kerk (Old Church), a 13th-century Gothic church with a 250-foot tilting tower known as "the crooked John," Vermeer and four of his children are buried in a family crypt. In the Raedhuijs, or town hall, on the Grand Market Square, he was officially betrothed to the love of his life, Catharina Bolnes. They were married across the square, at the 14th-century Protestant Nieuwe Kerk (New Church), with its 350-foot spire, the same church where Vermeer had been baptized.

It's more difficult to identify the landmarks of Vermeer's day-to-day life or the locations that were most familiar to him. That is partly because he rarely painted outdoors, so his work offers almost no clues about his personal terrain. But in 2015, a significant discovery was made about the location of one of his most famous paintings, *The Little Street*, which is considered by Vermeer scholars to be the most naturalistic townscape in all of Dutch painting. The painting itself is in the Rijksmuseum in Amsterdam, but its setting is in Delft, and finding it reordered some of the art world's thinking about Vermeer and also changed the way this tranquil city of 96,000 viewed its already much-loved son.

After about a year and a half of research, Frans Grijzenhout, an art history professor at the University of Amsterdam, found data in a 17th-century tax registry from the Delft archives that allowed him to pinpoint the location of the house in *The Little Street*. The site is on the east side of town, near the main square, at Vlamingstraat 40–42. The house, it turns out, was owned by Vermeer's widowed aunt, Ariaentgen Claes van der Minne, or Ariaantje.

Finding the location of the painting, Grijzenhout said when I interviewed him in Amsterdam, offers Vermeer devotees a new perspective on how his relationships might have evolved during his life, and how he chose what to paint.

The Little Street, in spite of its title, is not a depiction of a street as much as it is a portrait of two houses: one large 15th-century brick house with crow-stepped gables and green and red shutters on its iron-grilled

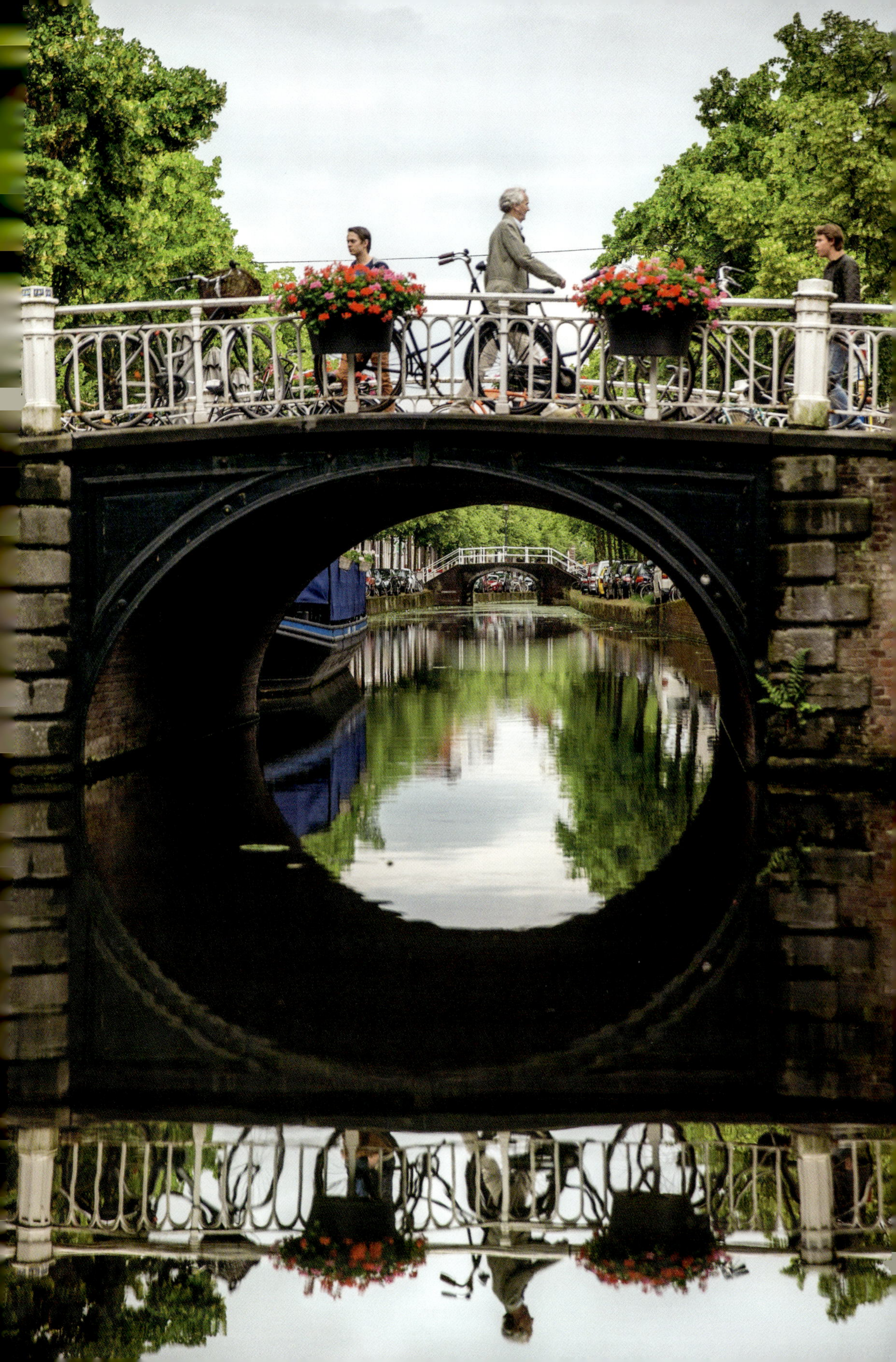

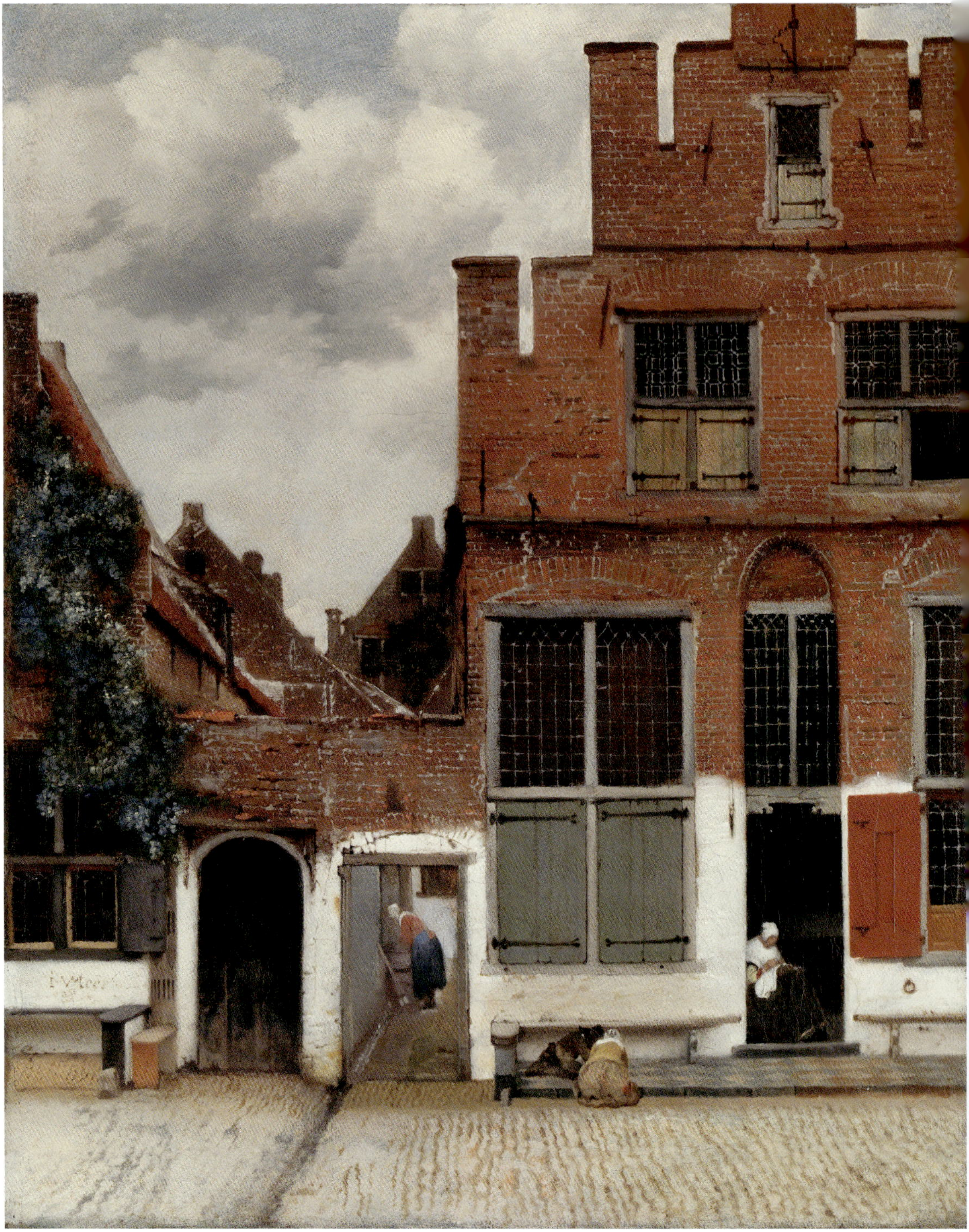

windows, and part of a smaller house, as well as two adjoining doorways leading into two byways. Through the doors, we see women busy at work, one with needlework and the other washing laundry over a wooden barrel. A boy and girl are crouched on the pavement, absorbed in a game.

Both houses in the painting are gone now, replaced by others built later. But knowing that *The Little Street* was a real place in Delft brings Vermeer into sharper focus in the city where he was born and raised, married, fathered 15 children, painted about 45 exquisite works of art, and died at 43 in 1675.

Born the son of a Protestant art dealer and innkeeper, Vermeer converted to Catholicism when he married Catharina, who was an heiress from a Roman Catholic family. It was a rare mixed marriage for their times. They moved in with his mother-in-law on the west side of town, and his social milieu shifted.

"Vermeer changed from a very average, simple, lower-middle-class surrounding into a definitely higher social circle," Grijzenhout said. "Until now, we thought that meant that he turned his back on the eastern part of the city, which was the poorer region." Learning that Vermeer painted *The Little Street* in his former neighborhood indicates that he didn't renounce his past life at all. "We can now say that, at least in this painting, he lovingly registered a part of life in that poorer neighborhood in the east."

At the Prinsenhof Museum in Delft, I met the art historian Anita Jansen, the curator of its old masters collection. Although it owns no Vermeers, the Prinsenhof has an impressive permanent collection of paintings from the 16th and 17th centuries. From the museum, Jansen walked with me into Vermeer's Delft; it was like stepping onto one of the 400-year-old city maps hanging on the Prinsenhof's wall.

We went first to the Oude Kerk, and then, heading down the cobblestone Oude Delft street alongside one of the city's old canals, we saw the wealthier section of town where Vermeer lived with his in-laws. Some of its monumental patrician canal houses still feature ornate sandstone family shields. We passed the location of the home of Vermeer's only real patron, the son of a brewer, Pieter van Ruijven, and his wife, Maria de Knuijt. They bought 21 of Vermeer's paintings, and the collection remained in their family until 1696.

Turning onto Boterbrug, we quickly arrived on the Grand Market Square, a sprawling open cobblestone space, where we gazed up at the Nieuwe Kerk. When Vermeer and Catharina married here, they did so over the protestations of her parents, Reynier Bolnes, a successful brickmaker, and Maria Thins, who came from a well-to-do patrician family in Gouda (the town in the southern Netherlands that is famous for its cheese).

To the west of town hall, in an area called "Papists' Corner," is the mansion where Maria Thins lived after she left Bolnes, who had reportedly been abusive to her and their children. Vermeer and Catharina not only moved in with her after their marriage, but stayed there as they raised their own children. His conversion not only prompted him to move from his old neighborhood, but also apparently erased him from the civic records. (After Protestants deposed the Catholics in the province of Holland in the late 1500s, the public practice of Catholicism was banned in Delft and other cities for about 200 years.) From his

Page 234 *The Little Street,* painted in 1658, is now in the Rijksmuseum in Amsterdam, but the street in Delft remains.

Page 235 The location of the house in Johannes Vermeer's painting *The Little Street*. He was born nearby.

Above Delft, like Amsterdam, is a city of cobblestones and canals, but fewer tourists frequent it.

Opposite Inside the Nieuwe Kerk, the New Church, where Vermeer and his wife were married.

mother-in-law's house, Vermeer painted, dealt in art, and later ran an inn that he inherited from his father.

Passing the cafes and shops that encircle the lovely square, we saw a plaque that read "Vermeer was born here" at the site of a long-gone inn and tavern, Huis Mechelen. Jansen said the information is no longer considered accurate. Though Vermeer did live at the inn, from about the age of 9, historians now believe that he was born around the corner at Voldersgracht 25, at another inn called De Vliegende Vos, or the Flying Fox, which Vermeer's father and mother ran.

The local St. Lucas Guild of artists, artisans, and art merchants, which Vermeer joined in 1653, was close by at No. 21. The site is now occupied by the headquarters of Vermeer Centrum Delft, which has an interesting Vermeer museum, runs Vermeer-themed guided tours, and has audio tours in multiple languages. The museum even offers a guide to "love messages" Vermeer is thought to have inserted in his paintings, which are reproduced in its displays. A combination ticket covers this museum, the Prinsenhof, and the churches that were important in Vermeer's life.

It turns out that if you walk northeast on the Voldersgracht, along the narrow canal with its olive-green waters, the street name changes to Vlamingstraat, which Grijzenhout, through his research, identified as the location of *The Little Street*. So, I realized, Vermeer painted the image, essentially, on the street where he was born — very close to home. We continued onto Vlamingstraat and stopped in front of No. 42, the former home of Vermeer's Aunt Ariaantje. Two much more recent homes have replaced the ones in the painting.

What was the same was the rhythm of the structures — a house, then two doorways, and then another house. After the discovery that this was the location of *The Little Street*, a life-size detail from the painting, showing a woman at work, was added outside. But

*Photographs by
Ilvy Njiokiktjien*

even without that, it was easy to overlay the painting mentally on the scene and picture Vermeer observing the life around it, the daily life of Delft.

That trick of the imagination is helped in Delft by the absence of hordes of tourists. Unlike Amsterdam, which finds itself crushed under the weight of its own popularity, Delft remains relatively quiet, an attractive alternative for the traveler who wants to see an Amsterdam-like city without Amsterdam's crowds.

Delft is also about 10 miles from The Hague, making it easy to plan a trip that combines visits to both cities. The Hague is where the seeker of Vermeer can see what has probably become his most famous painting, *Girl with a Pearl Earring*, given added fame by the book and Hollywood film of the same title. The painting is in the Hague Mauritshuis museum, along with two other Vermeers: *Diana and Her Companions* and —appropriately, for the traveler who has just come from the artist's hometown—*View of Delft*.

WHAT TO READ AND WATCH

Vermeer, the Complete Works, by Karl Schütz. A coffee-table book with fine reproductions of all 35 of Vermeer's paintings currently in existence.

Vermeer's Hat: The Seventeenth Century and the Dawn of the Global World, by Timothy Brook. A clever exploration of a world in the midst of change, and Holland's role in it, as revealed through details in Vermeer's paintings.

Girl with a Pearl Earring, directed by Peter Webber and based on the novel by Tracy Chevalier. An imagined story of Vermeer's interaction with his model. Praised for its beauty, the film attempts to mirror Vermeer's visual sensibility.

Tim's Vermeer, directed by Teller. A documentary about a man who recreated a Vermeer painting by inventing optical devices with technology available in Vermeer's time. You will come away convinced that Vermeer was as much a technical wizard as a gifted painter.

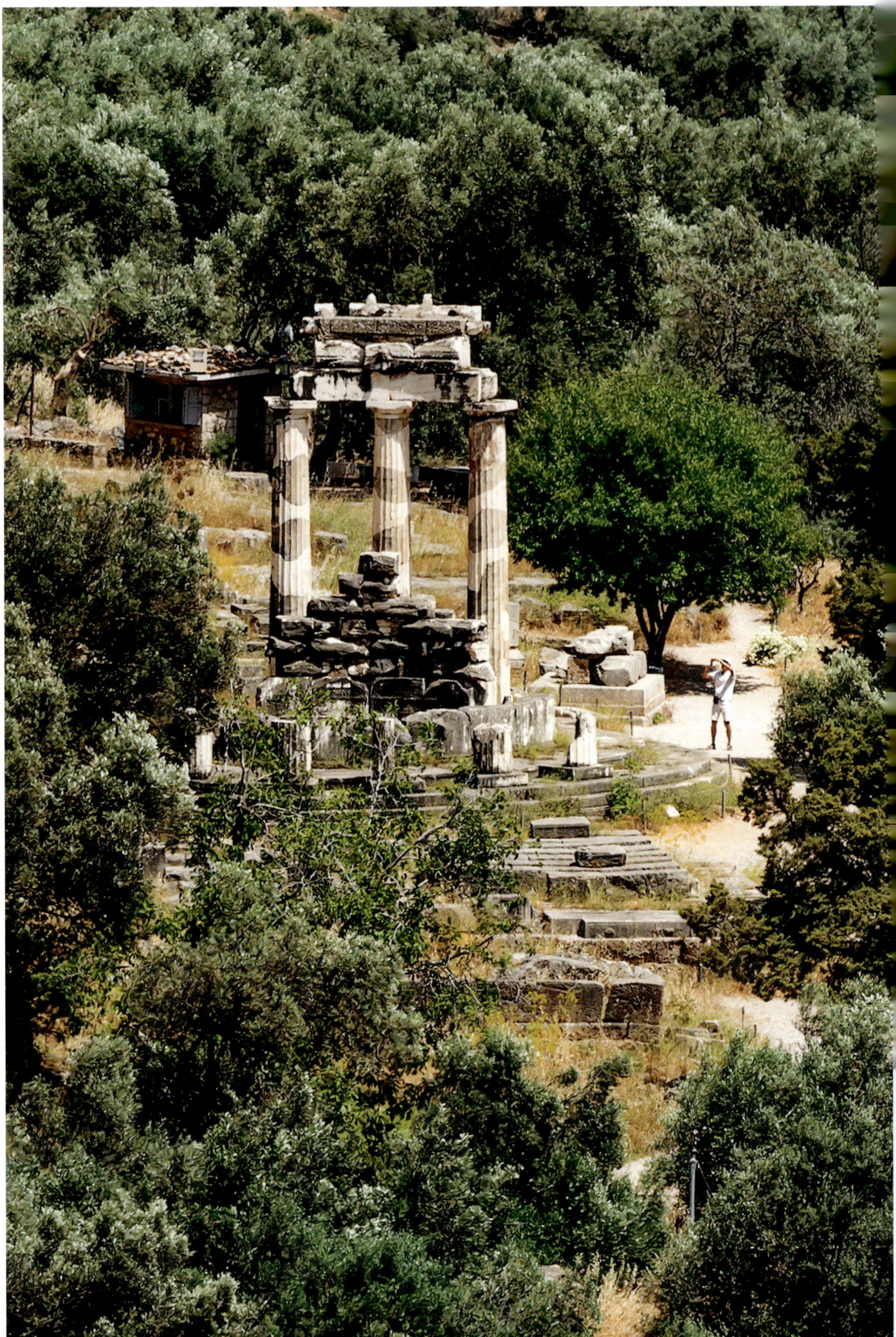

THE ORACLE AT THE CENTER OF THE WORLD

Delphi was the trip of a lifetime for the ancients, and it's still a good one now. — BY LIZ ALDERMAN

The peaks of Mount Parnassus shimmered on a warm spring afternoon above the temples of ancient Delphi. In a verdant valley below, silver-tipped olive trees stretched to the sea. The sun traced a golden arc in the azure sky. On a flat plateau surrounded by this natural theater, I looked up to find myself standing at the center of the world.

At least, the center of all things as the ancient Greeks knew it. In front of me was a black ovoid stone, known as the omphalos, set on the spot in Greek mythology where two eagles loosed by Zeus crossed paths at the earth's nexus. It marked Delphi as one of the greatest enigmas of the ancient universe.

I had come for what was supposed to be an afternoon visit during a trip to Athens. Delphi is best known as the home of the famous Oracle — a powerful priestess who saw the future of kings and nations — and I wanted a glimpse of the mystery. But as I stood on the archaic plateau, I was riveted.

The broken columns of once-mighty altars rose like spirits in the pure air. A timeworn stadium and a prodigious stone amphitheater reigned silently over the mountain. The Temple of Apollo, where the Oracle dispensed her cryptic prophecies, was ringed with paths trod by truth-seekers who had labored up the steep valley from the Corinthian Gulf. Clearly, taking in this soul-stirring experience would require time.

While most travelers tend to use Athens as their base for seeing Greece's classical highlights, reversing that pattern by choosing Delphi as the hub for a multi-day tour can bring unexpected rewards. After all, for ancient visitors, Delphi was the trip of a lifetime.

A Unesco World Heritage Site, Delphi alone merits a full day to wander the extensive marble ruins and the fine Archaeological Museum of Delphi

Previous Delphi, where King Oedipus, Alexander the Great, and Nero went to consult the Oracle.

Left Strong Greek coffee with candied baby vegetables in sugary syrup, a specialty in Chrisso, near Delphi.

Opposite Galaxidi on the Corinthian Gulf, where ancient visitors sailed in and began their trek to Delphi.

showcasing sublime sculptures, delicate friezes, and other excavated gems. A second day can be spent touring mythological caves and springs, accompanied by birdsong, during a hike in Delphi's lush forests.

The town of Delphi, with terraced hotels, rustic tavernas, and sunning cats, is a charming and convenient base. It has uninterrupted views over the immense valley of ancient olive trees, the largest grove in all of Greece, to the azure waters of the Corinthian Gulf.

You can get to the gulf in less than half an hour by car. But that drive should be turned into a third full day of discovery, visiting scenic villages that antiquity's travelers would have passed on their way to Delphi from the sea. In springtime, the villages bolt to life with Carnival festivals celebrating pagan customs.

Ancient Delphi is a short bus ride or a pleasant walk from town. A wide road hemmed in by pines, laurels, and cypresses leads to the entrance and up toward the Sacred Way — the path taken by King Oedipus, Alexander the Great, the Roman Emperor Nero, and countless less exalted men and women determined to hear the Oracle's pronouncements.

With Apollo's priestess as the main attraction, Delphi's renown grew as Greece's wealthy city-states, and powerful conquerors, built sumptuous treasuries filled with rich offerings to encourage the sun god to favor them in war and politics. Many paid tribute to victories gained through the Oracle's guidance — and Apollo's help — with grandiose sculptures, including a giant silver bull and a replica of the Trojan Horse.

Despite the ancient bling, Delphi's supremacy as a sacred power center was epitomized by the simple black stone omphalos that had riveted me — what the Greeks called the "navel of the world." While the temples have crumbled, seeing the omphalos gave me goose bumps and left me awestruck over Delphi's sublime place in history.

At the top of the Sacred Way, the Temple of Apollo, now razed to its foundations, greeted visitors with these wise words: "Know Yourself," and "Nothing in Excess." Inside, the Oracle, a woman older than 50, would sit entranced over a crack in the earth, answering questions. A centuries-old debate still rages over whether her divine inspiration came from an ether-like vapor formed by an ancient water source, the nearby Castalian Spring.

Whatever the truth, visitors can explore the remains of the spring in a rocky crag near the Delphi museum, an archaeological time capsule whose centerpiece is an exquisite life-size bronze statue from 475 B.C. known as *The Charioteer*. With flowing robes, gems for eyes, and regal poise, this masterpiece by an unknown artist embodies the mystery of Delphic lore.

The next day should be spent visiting the Corycian Cave, an obligatory stop for ancient supplicants after encountering the Oracle. A three-and-a-half-hour trek (each way) from the ruins, this sanctuary for the nature god Pan dates to the neolithic era. The hike starts above Delphi's marble amphitheater and winds through lovely pine forests. At each turn, there are outstanding views over the ancient site. In hot summer months, those preferring not to sweat it out can drive.

After a long day, it's essential to refuel at a traditional Delphi taverna. I found a lively spot called To Patriko Mas, with a stunning position overlooking the valley and a menu dominated by charcoal-grilled meat and fish.

Head out on the third day to explore the path that ancient visitors took to get to the Sacred Way, taking it in reverse order: Start in Delphi and end with dinner at Galaxidi, a charming fishing village on the Corinthian Gulf.

I left Delphi by car and headed down the mountain to Chrisso, a once-powerful city-state that dates to the 12th century B.C. Now a small stone village, Chrisso sparkles with tiny churches and water gurgling through granite gutters from a spring sourced in Mount Parnassus. Locals divert the water to their gardens to grow a local treat—baby vegetables, which are candied in sugared syrup. These should be sampled with a strong Greek coffee at one of the tavernas in the central square.

I continued toward the cliffside town of Amfissa, a prominent citadel in Delphic times. Named for Apollo's lover, it had its own Acropolis and a stretch of Cyclopean walls (constructed without mortar in an ancient Greek technique). Today, old ladies wearing kerchiefs and crocheted skirts navigate the road with canes and a slow step.

A castle was built atop the ancient wall during Ottoman rule, with a view of the valley. When I visited, the almond trees were in bloom. Slow-moving honeybees filled the air with a low hum, drawn by the sweet perfume of the blossoms. Nearby, an old tannery is said to be protected by the spirit of a youth whose

Above The amphitheater is an uphill walk from the temple where the Oracle of Delphi delivered her strange prophecies.

Below A remnant of an Ionian column from the days when Delphi was the center of the world.

Opposite The small stone village of Chrisso was once a powerful city-state dating to the 12th century B.C.

quest for love ended in tragedy. In spring, the villagers put on a raucous nighttime carnival in his honor, dressed as ghosts and fairies with elaborate masks and animal bells.

I paused to sample local wines, cheeses, and olives in Amfissa and then continued toward Itea, a modern port located next to the ancient harbor of Kirra, where travelers from around the Mediterranean world once disembarked to start their journey to see the Oracle.

Today international cruise ships disgorge crowds onto tour buses that make a beeline for Delphi. At a clutch of tavernas on the waterfront, locals nibble freshly caught shrimp and anchovies with a shot of raki in the Corinthian Gulf's briny air.

Hug the gulf to continue to picturesque Galaxidi, with stout stone mansions, swaying palm trees, and a snug harbor. An important center for sailing ships until steam engines came along, Galaxidi is believed to have once had a temple to Apollo. The church of St. Nicholas, the patron saint of sailors, now sits in its place, adorned with a rare solar calendar that tracks the zodiac cycle. A nautical museum holds a unique collection of ship paintings and priceless artifacts, including prehistoric obsidian tools and a 4,000-year-old urn pulled from an ancient shipwreck.

*Photographs by
Maria Mavropoulou*

After a taverna dinner of fresh seafood, I strolled along the waterfront and looked back across the gulf to catch the sunset. There, as the sky faded to a golden pink, the peaks of Mount Parnassus towered in the distance over the modern town of Delphi, where gray stone houses clung under orange-tiled roofs to the cliffs.

Rising above it, ancient Delphi glimmered from the mountainside like a polished gem — as smooth and simple as the stone at its very heart that once marked the center of the world.

WHAT TO READ AND WATCH

Delphi: A History of the Center of the Ancient World, by Michael Scott. A valuable and entertaining companion book to a visit at Delphi.

The Oracle: Ancient Delphi and the Science Behind Its Lost Secrets, by William J. Broad. A Pulitzer Prize–winning journalist follows researchers looking for clues to the source of the Oracle's visions.

Secrets of the Ancient World: Oracle of Delphi. A documentary film based on the same scholarship that informed William J. Broad's book.

Blue Guide Greece: The Mainland, by Sherry Marker and James Pettifer. A spot-on guidebook for travelers interested in the ancient sites.

See Delphi and Die, by Lindsey Davis. Marcus Didius Falco, Davis's resourceful ancient detective, goes crime-solving in Greece. Arriving in A.D. 76, he comments: "Nothing prepares the traveler for Delphi. In its heyday it must have been staggering."

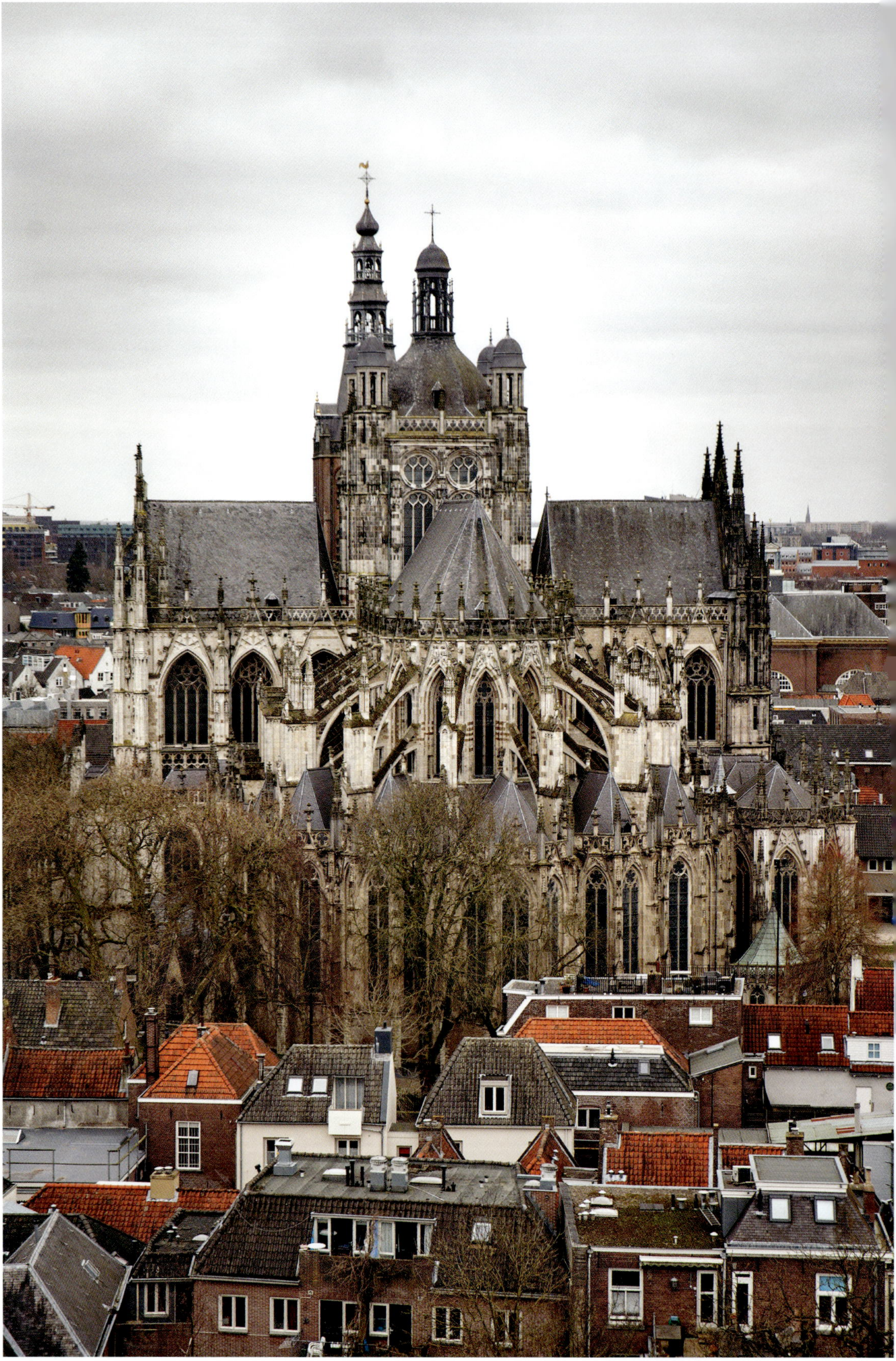

FROM HELL TO HEAVEN IN HIERONYMUS'S HOMETOWN

The easy charm of Hieronymus Bosch's city may not jibe with the bizarre images in his paintings, but the town is happy to honor him. — BY NINA SIEGAL

Hieronymus Bosch is a kind of populist superstar among the old master painters. His fans relish his surreal, inventive images of the afterlife, but particularly his vivid visions of hell: sinners straddling giant knife-blades, egg-shaped machines churning miscreants into their bellies, cruel hybrid frog-devils and dog-faced lizard birds.

More than 500 years since Bosch's death, it's believed that only a tiny fraction of his output survives — about two dozen paintings and some 20 drawings — but the fascination with his oeuvre hasn't abated. In all that time, aficionados have asked the same question: How did he come up with his amazing imagery? Where did he get the inspiration for these strange little monsters?

Very little is known about Bosch the man. We have no letters or diaries, and written information in archives tends to be about transactions: who bought what and when. I wondered what I could discover about his mind and his artistry by going back to the place where he was born, lived, and worked.

I headed to the city of 's-Hertogenbosch, known popularly as Den Bosch, whose name the artist eventually took as his own. An hour south of Amsterdam by train, it is a picturesque medieval city that's not on a typical tourist itinerary, though it has the largest cathedral in the Netherlands and boat trips in an underground network of natural waterways.

Although only a handful of landmark buildings from before the 16th century survive, the city is still laid out almost exactly as it was in the late Middle Ages and early Renaissance — Bosch's time — because all the new structures have been built on plots that were established in the 15th century. The skyline has barely changed, and a visitor can still get a pretty good sense of how it felt to live in the old city in Bosch's day. The key physical landmarks of Bosch's life are positioned along a single red brick street, the Hinthamerstraat, so that you can follow his life along a straight and narrow route. What an apt metaphor for Bosch, a devout Catholic whose paintings often centered on the figure of the Wayfarer, a traveler torn between the righteous and the sinful paths.

Local guides offer city tours, but I planned my excursion with the art historian Gary Schwartz, who was born in Brooklyn but has lived in the Netherlands for decades. He is the author of *Jheronimus: The Road to Heaven and Hell*.

We met at what's known as a "brown cafe," a kind of living room pub. This one, at 10 Markt—No. 10 in the market square—was called In de Kleine Werelt and had a spacious terrace under umbrellas. Before he began telling me about Bosch's early life, Gary ordered us each a pastry known as a *Bossche bol*, the city's signature treat, a kind of doughnut filled with whipped cream and smothered in chocolate. From where we sat, we could see the verdigris bronze statue of Bosch in the city square and two of the three houses where the artist once lived.

Bosch, born Jheronimus van Aken sometime around 1450, was part of a family of painters. Their house at the time was also on this square, but it most likely burned down during a devastating fire in 1463 that destroyed much of the medieval city. The fire itself, many historians suggest, may have been an inspiration for Bosch's vivid depictions of hellfire, since it may have made a strong impression on him as a teenager.

From about the age of 12 until 30, Bosch lived at a house that does still exist, at 29 Markt. Now a national monument, it is under restoration as the Huis van Bosch, or House of Bosch. For many years, this three-story building served as the Bosch family home, workshop, and studio, where his family ran a very active art operation. His grandfather, Jan van Aken, from Aachen, Germany, was a painter and the father of four sons who were also painters. This house is where the young Hieronymus learned to paint and probably where he adopted his artistic pseudonym, Bosch, taking the name of his own city as a kind of calling card.

At around age 30 Bosch married Aleid van de Meerveen, who had inherited land, houses, and income from her parents and grandparents, including her home at 61 Markt. He moved in with her, and while the couple had no children, they took in Aleid's orphaned nephew. They lived in this house from 1483 until Bosch's death in 1516.

During Bosch's lifetime, Den Bosch was a home to prestigious monasteries. According to Gary, one of every 20 inhabitants was either a monk or a nun. Bosch was not a monk, but he did become the first artist to be accepted into the Illustrious Brotherhood of Our Dear Lady, a fraternal order devoted to worshipping the Madonna that received its charter in the 14th century. "This order had a certain religious glamour, and there were more people who wanted to be part of it, so they started taking members who weren't clergy — dues-paying members," Gary said. "But at the core they were sworn brothers. They were 'made men,' and they belonged to the church hierarchy."

To become a "sworn brother," Bosch would have had to qualify as one of the four grades of minor orders, which were doorkeeper, reader, acolyte, and exorcist. Gary said he suspected Bosch may have qualified as an exorcist. This naturally made me wonder: Could he have seen the demons he depicted?

"It didn't mean that he was allowed by the church to exorcise demons in people. That was only done by full priests," Gary explained.

Leaving the crowded, noisy market square and heading east along the Hinthamerstraat, we came to No. 94, the Home of the Illustrious Brotherhood, with a mustard yellow facade and Gothic-looking spires. The brotherhood still exists, functioning now as a sort of Christian-based and ecumenical civic organization.

Across the narrow street and through the cobblestone plaza is the immense Gothic Sint-Janskathedraal (Cathedral of St. John), built in the 13th century originally as a parish church and now the largest cathedral in the Netherlands. Just inside the front door of the cathedral, to the left, is the Brotherhood Chapel, where all the members of Bosch's order would gather for their more exclusive services and rites. Once this church was full of artworks by Bosch, Gary said, commissioned by his friends and brothers in the clergy. Even the church's main altar was a Bosch work, which apparently remained in place until 1629, when the city fell to the Protestant army of the Reformed Dutch Republic in the Eighty Years' War. This is also where Bosch's funeral Mass was held.

At the end of the Hinthamerstraat, we stopped before the chapel of St. Anthony and what was once an asylum for the insane, which Gary told me was established in the Middle Ages to treat those suffering from St. Anthony's Fire. Known today as ergotism or erysipelas, this disease causes fever, chills, convulsions, loss of limbs, hallucinations, and, ultimately, death.

One of Bosch's favorite subjects was St. Anthony, who was tempted by demons and whom he depicted

Page 244 The Cathedral of St. John, where the funeral of Hieronymus Bosch was held in 1516.

Previous An antique map of Den Bosch. The town's full name is 's-Hertogenbosch.

Above A fantastical stone creature on the Cathedral of St. John.

Opposite A poster shows some of Bosch's unique creatures. Den Bosch celebrates him at its Jheronimus Bosch Art Center.

as a dour-faced abbot hunched over in a heavy brown monk's robe. I always assumed that Bosch chose this theme because it gave him a chance to paint his beloved little monsters, but learning about St. Anthony's Fire puts a new spin on it: Could it be that Bosch was also depicting the hallucinatory terrors of the disease's sufferers, perhaps described to him?

As dark clouds started to loom in the ever-changing Dutch horizon, we headed toward the last stop on our walking tour: the Jheronimus Bosch Art Center, where I said farewell to my guide. This former church and its annexes are now a permanent destination for Bosch aficionados to explore his works. Inside, the display includes all of Bosch's known works presented in large-format poster reproduction, in frames that you can open and close to see his triptychs, for example, up close and from all sides. Also on display are modern works inspired by Bosch's mind-bending images. The museum offers guided tours of its collection and a commanding city view from a 120-foot-high tower.

Den Bosch also has several other museums, but for my final activity in town, I took a boat tour on the city's waterway. My guide was Hugo Groeneveld, a retired coastal engineer who narrated a bit of city history as he motored our small skiff on placid canals and through winding, watery tunnels. The open-air stretches were bucolic and lovely, while the tunnels at times were dank and eerie. Along the way we encountered various life-size figures from Bosch's *Garden of Earthly Delights* on the banks and popping out from walls of the tunnels. These figures are part of the city's celebration of Bosch, but I would have been just as content without them.

Just being below the city in the boat, with the quiet ripple of the waves and the soothing purr of the skiff's motor, suggested a different element of Bosch's universe, the more positive side. The sense of peace

Photographs by
Ilvy Njiokiktjien

one gets so close to the water—and yet so close to the city—seems to me a kind of paradise. The tunnel walls multiplied ahead of us, suggesting a kind of circular infinity. I gazed through the darkness until there was a hint of daylight, indicating the way forward. When at one point our captain shut off the boat's lights and we floated onward in the dark, I was reminded of another Bosch picture, *Ascent of the Blessed*, now in the Accademia Gallery in Venice. In that image, the lucky souls who have followed the righteous path and have been delivered from purgatory into salvation float upward into a circle of light. There, in the center, is a faint figure, barely distinguishable by the suggestion of a pair of white wings, offering them welcome. It's nice to think that Bosch, so famous for his visions of hell, surely enjoyed this bit of heaven on earth.

WHAT TO READ AND WATCH

Hieronymus Bosch: The Complete Works, by Stefan Fischer. A TASCHEN coffee-table book with reproductions of the paintings, interpretive text, and a foldout of *The Last Judgment*. The cover image is *Ascent of the Blessed*.

Hieronymus Bosch: Visions and Nightmares, by Nils Büttner. "An attractive little hardbound book with good color illustrations providing an inviting, judicious overview of Bosch in his historical environment." —*New York Review of Books*.

Jheronimus Bosch: The Road to Heaven and Hell, by Gary Schwartz. This biographer relieves viewers of the burden of trying to interpret Bosch's strange images by suggesting that they are not meant to be deciphered, but to "confuse, worry, and disturb."

Bosch: The Garden of Dreams, directed by José Luis López-Linares. A documentary with art experts analyzing *The Garden of Earthly Delights*.

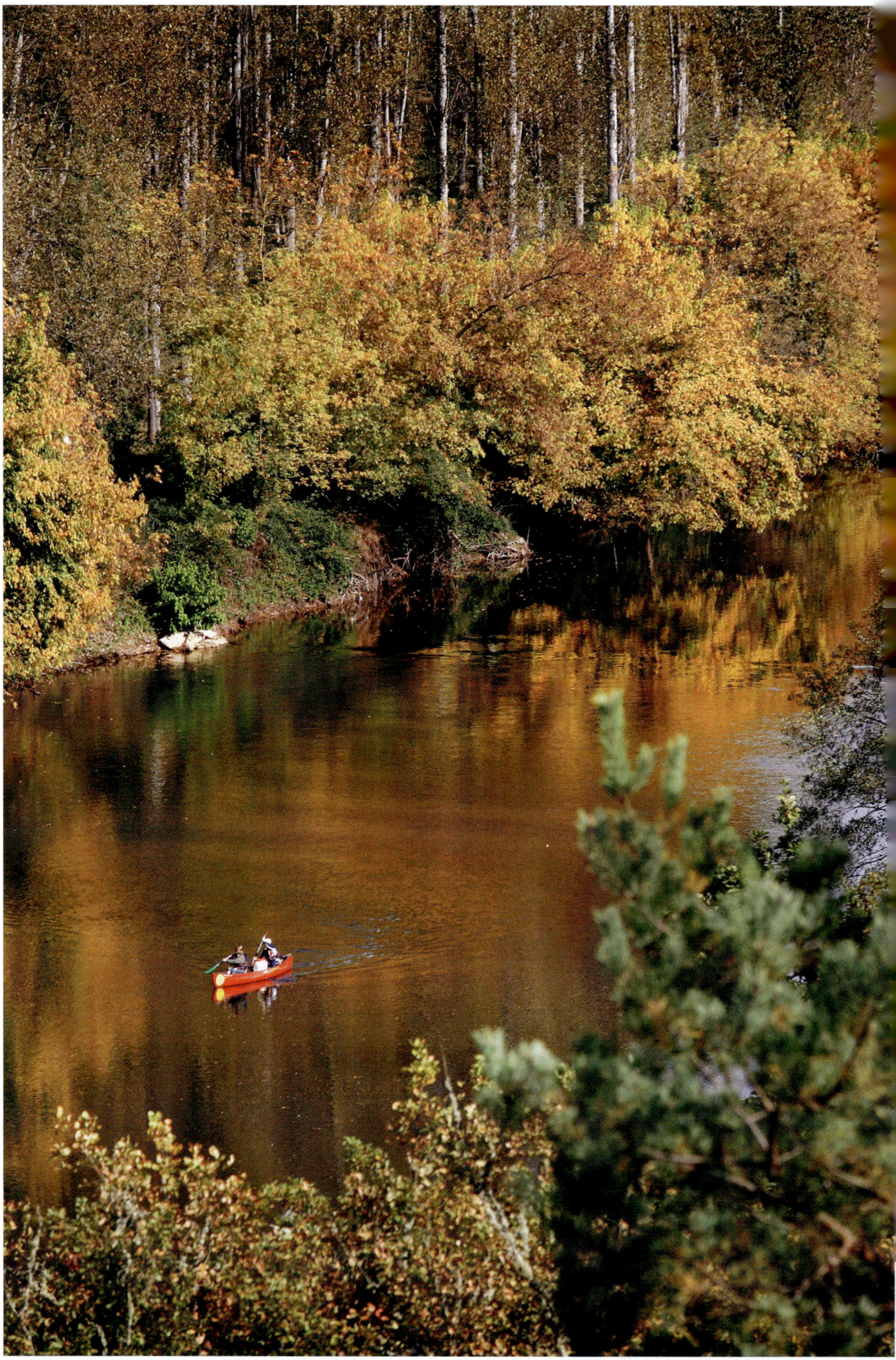

FRANCE DORDOGNE

CANOEING INTO PREHISTORY

Rivers of the Dordogne flow to grottoes and cliffs that sheltered cave painters 20,000 years ago.
— BY CHRISTOPHER SHAW

Far below the clifftop terrace where we were savoring a wild boar stew, the Vézère River curved silky and dark under a steep cliff, carrying three canoes and a kayak. The paddlers passed smoothly over the water, around a bend and out of sight. Reports had been right — the canoeing would be good here in the Dordogne, an area in Aquitaine where the rivers have invited exploration and settlement since the days of the Neanderthals.

My wife, Sue, and I were dining at the Auberge de Castel-Merle, a small hotel atop a limestone knob that once held a castle of the Knights Templar. It was the base we had chosen for the first few days of our trip. The auberge overlooks the Vézère and the tiny medieval village of Sergeac in a landscape that harbors hundreds of caves and overhanging rock shelters. Within them are the prehistoric creations for which the Dordogne is known: paintings and engravings of bison, reindeer, and other animals made by people who lived 10,000 to 45,000 years ago.

On this evening, light struck the 12th-century fortified church of Sergeac and the wheat, bean fields, and grazing cattle on the rich floodplain across the river. Beyond rose hills covered with green oak and pine, habitat for wild boar, truffles, and nightingales.

After the glaciers retreated at the end of the last ice age, this valley was a cold, dry steppe where reindeer, bison, and horses grazed. Among the predators hunting them were humans who were probably the direct ancestors of many Europeans. Like others before us, we had come to the Dordogne hoping to grasp the moment when the light of full-spectrum human

Previous The Vézère River hugs a landscape where prehistoric people left behind stone tools and cave art.

Left A horse carving discovered at a dig near the village of Sergeac. Prehistoric hunters wintered in caves.

Below Both Neanderthals and early modern humans sheltered in the caves at Castel-Merle.

Opposite The discovery of art in the Lascaux caves thrilled archaeologists and paleontologists, like these in 1948.

awareness blinked on, manifesting itself in a tangible, viewable record. The rivers promised to provide the fastest and best route to the region's character.

The next day, a shuttle conveyed us to an embarkation point several miles upstream on the Vézère, and we set out in a rented canoe. It was a good summer for rain, and a swollen current rushed us through the village of Montignac, past narrow medieval lanes and foie gras shops, and then beneath the nearby hill of Lascaux — more than a mile above us — which has been called the Sistine Chapel of the Upper Paleolithic. The Cave of Lascaux contains 16,000-year-old images of animals, and although it is now closed to the public to preserve the art, a replica called Lascaux II was opened in 1983 near the original and is a favorite (and moving) tourist site. We swept on past. Our goal for this trip was to encounter the seam where land and art were joined, so the river held us in its grip for now.

The river carried us under overhanging grottoes gouged out of limestone by the current; the 16th-century Château de Losse sits on top of one of them. Gardens of ferns and mosses dangled from their ceilings, and swifts darted in and out. On the river, black kites swooped overhead and anglers fished for pike.

The overhanging grottoes were our first sign of the caves and natural rock shelters that fostered and preserved this region's outpouring of prehistoric art, which has long fascinated archaeologists. They have rival theories about the motivation of the cave painters: shamanic or religious rites, fertility rituals, magic to ensure a good hunt, or perhaps just the artists' impulse to paint and their contemporaries' desire to see what they could do.

Farther on, we pulled out our canoe at a boat landing and walked a few minutes to a narrow vallon, a small side canyon. Students were working under a shed roof, excavating a thin layer of a floor 33,000 years old in a natural rock shelter called Abri Castanet. Abri means shelter in French, and this vallon, about

100 yards across and 300 yards long, has at the bases of its cliffs a dozen such shelters, containing some of the oldest known carvings and paintings as well as cruder artifacts going much farther back. Marcel Castanet, the first excavator at this spot, is the source of the name for Abri Castanet.

The nomadic hunters called the Cro-Magnon, who were, like us, Homo sapiens, existed here from about 40,000 to 10,000 years ago, and wintered in this vallon sporadically over that time. It is thought that different groups met in those cold months and shared materials, techniques, and genes before separating to go to their summer hunting grounds. Their own ancestors had come to Dordogne from Africa, taking thousands of years to get there only to find another human species already in residence—the Neanderthal.

The next day we paddled on downstream. The valley narrowed under limestone cliffs, called *falaises*, that have yielded evidence of human occupation from the 19th century back 400,000 years to the early days of the Neanderthals. Only a millennium or so before our own era, villages with stone churches and battlements began to be built into some of these cliff walls:

In the eighth and ninth centuries residents took to the rocks to evade river-borne Viking raids, and in the 15th century, peasants took refuge there from the English during the Hundred Years' War. Two of these sites with evidence of long habitation are La Roque St.-Christophe and La Madeleine, both open to the public.

We ended our touring on this part of the Vézère at Les Eyzies-de-Tayac. The epicenter of prehistoric France, it is the site of the shelter called Cro-Magnon, where the first Upper Paleolithic remains were identified in the 19th century and were given the Cro-Magnon name. The comprehensive National Museum of Prehistory, one of the finest of its kind in the world, is there now. Inside are vast collections of stone tools found in the region, along with carvings extracted from caves and shelters.

From the museum we drove our rental car outside town to the Font-de-Gaume cave, one of the earliest decorated caves explored in the 19th century. Open to the public, it is, like many caves in the area, operated by the French Ministry of Culture, and visits are kept brief and strictly controlled to protect the art. We followed the guide down a narrow passage to paintings

Above Houses in a cliff at Les Eyzies. Human remains discovered in this area in the 19th century were named Cro-Magnon, after the rock shelter where they were found.

Opposite A view of the village of Sergeac from the terrace of the Auberge de Castel-Merle.

of mammoths, bison, and horses and to a famous and graceful portrait, 14,000 years old, of a male and a female reindeer.

Later we drove south for more canoeing, this time on the Célé River. It runs southwest into the upper Lot River, near Cahors, through the high karst plateaus and deep, narrow valleys of the Causses du Quercy, now a designated natural area of almost half a million acres. Many of the region's remote villages are connected by hiking trails, and its inky, deep Cahors wines were the preferred appellation for British import in the days of Eleanor of Aquitaine.

For three days we paddled under 1,500-foot falaises pocked with caves and shelters. The valley, not quite narrow enough to be called a canyon, would have made a natural funnel for prey species, with plenty of places for prehistoric hunters to ambush them.

As a canoeing river, the Célé is swifter and more engaging than the Vézère or Dordogne, with sporty Class 1 mini-rapids and only occasional portages of a few dozen feet around old dams or bridges. At the end of each day, we landed in one of the villages under steep canyon walls, left our canoe on shore, and carried our things to a pension or hotel.

On the last morning, we left our hotel in Cabrerets and climbed half a mile out of the village to the Pech Merle cave. Pech Merle, open to the public and operated by the Ministry of Culture, contains all the archetypes of Upper Paleolithic European art—charcoal drawings of horses, reindeer, mammoths, and a rare "wounded man" that many interpret as a trancing shaman. We saw children's footprints left 25,000 years ago and preserved in hardened clay on the cave floor.

Most riveting were the "twin horses," two life-size horses painted in black and dull rust with heavy outlines and facing in opposite directions, one behind the other, their transparent hindquarters arranged

Photographs by
Ed Alcock

in convincing perspective and their equine forms wedded to the rock's natural shapes. They have been on a freestanding boulder in this cave for 26,000 years.

Large spots made by prehistoric artists who painted the palms of their hands and then slapped them onto the rock, and negative handprints made by blowing pigment over the hand and onto the rock, made the horses shimmer with life. A spectral fish, probably a pike, was superimposed over the horses like a Chagall angel, fusing the ephemeral with the substantial.

It was hard to view this painting as primitive. We came out into the sunlight seeing the world differently, and made our way, blinking and speechless, back down the trail to the river.

WHAT TO READ AND WATCH

The Cave Painters: Probing the Mysteries of the World's First Artists, by Gregory Curtis. Tells the stories of the cave paintings in France and Spain and what we know and don't know about their creators.

Stepping-Stones: A Journey through the Ice Age Caves of the Dordogne, by Christine Desdemaines-Hugon. Focuses on five sites with Paleolithic paintings, noting some similarities with the work of modern artists.

Dordogne in the Perigord, directed by John Woods. A travel video of the region with historical context, covering cave paintings, Roman ruins, castles, chateaux, and more.

Cave of Forgotten Dreams, directed by Werner Herzog. A documentary about the Chauvet cave in another part of southern France and its 32,000-year-old paintings. Herzog is "an agreeable, sometimes characteristically funny guide," Manohla Dargis wrote in a 2011 review.

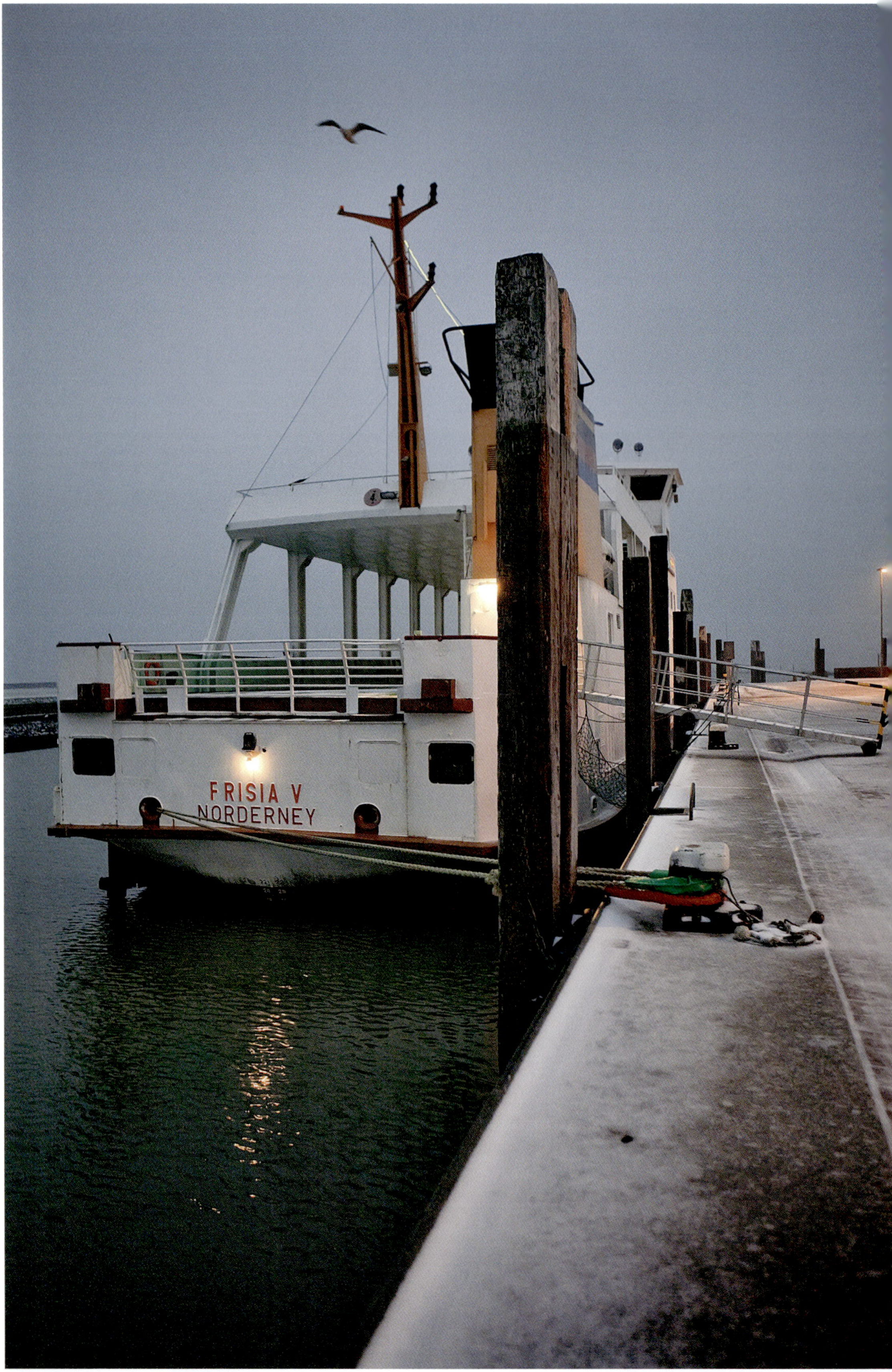
FRISIA V
NORDERNEY

EAST FRISIAN TEA, A CUP TO REMEMBER

In a German region of windmills and farms, the water is soft, the tea is bold, and the ritual deepens the pleasure. — BY IAN JOHNSON

For years, I was a green-tea snob who would drink only the freshest Dragon Well or Azure Conch Spring. And as a longtime Sinophile living in Beijing, I aped Asian cultural practices; when it came to tea, that meant fanatically seeking out the tender shoots harvested right after the first flush, usually in early April, and adding nothing but hot water. Everything else was taboo. Black teas, especially with cream and sugar, never crossed my tongue.

Then I moved to Berlin, where I had first gone to study, and made it my hometown. And there I met Albrecht Ude, a German who had studied Sinology and was deeply interested in tea. Excited to find another tea aficionado in Berlin, I visited him in his apartment. It was an homage to tea, full of manuals on tea plantations, tea import ledgers, and rare works on tea botany.

When I first went to see him, he was studying *sado*, the Japanese tea ceremony, but our drink that afternoon was something else: a thick, dark, malty tea served in espresso-size porcelain cups, a piece of rock sugar in the bottom and heavy cream carefully poured down the side from a flat, shell-like spoon. Stirring was taboo. The cream hit the bottom and mushroomed up, creating what Ude called a "tea cloud."

"East Frisian tea," Ude said with pride — he'd grown up in East Frisia (Ostfriesland), and the tea was blended by a tea seller there. "It is special."

I stared at the strange mixture and sipped. It was strong and biting, mostly dark Assam leaves leavened only by a bit of Darjeeling. But as the sugar and

Previous In a corner of Germany near the Netherlands, East Frisia is a land of North Sea coast, tidal flats, dikes, and canals.

Left An expert advised going to East Frisia for its powerful, flavorful brew: "You can only truly drink it there."

Opposite Willem Hedemann buys tea from wholesalers and mixes the leaves in his home to create his own brand.

cream rushed up from the bottom of the cup, the brew softened. That afternoon, I indefinitely lifted my ban; some black teas were evidently worth drinking.

At the end of my visit, Ude showed me the source of the tea. The leaves came in a half-kilo package — a simple white bag with a faded blue picture of peasants in a field. Below it was the brand, Hedemann, and an address in East Frisia, which is in the state of Lower Saxony in northern Germany.

"Go there and drink it," he advised. "You can only truly drink it there." I asked why, but he shook his head; it was a question I'd have to answer myself. I followed his advice, and was soon on my way.

East Frisia is best reached by car. It has no major airport and is so sparsely populated that it has infrequent train service. So I drove five hours northwest of Berlin, heading to Hedemann's base in Ostgrossefehn, which could be translated as East Great Fens. That meant flat rural countryside — fens are undrained marshes — popular with tourists who bicycle.

The landscape isn't spectacular, but it is scenic. Just like the Netherlands, its neighbor to the west, East Frisia is flat, with dikes protecting green pastures that swoop down below sea level. Holstein cows, windmills, and marshy, canal-crossed fields dominate the view.

The region bulges out into the North Sea, its coastline dotted with islands for 60 miles. Huge tides empty the shoreline and drain down the creeks and canals, leaving the mud flats, called the Wadden Sea, to worms, crabs, birds, and seals. The area's biodiversity has made it one of Unesco's World Heritage Sites.

That geography has defined East Frisia, isolating it from the rest of Germany for much of its history. Frisians looked to the Netherlands or England for cultural traditions rather than to their own countrymen. Starting in the 17th century, that culture included importing and drinking tea.

Today, according to the German Tea Association, if East Frisia were a country its annual per capita tea consumption of 300 liters would be the highest in the world, ahead of Kuwait's 290 liters, Ireland's 257, and Turkey's 225.

When coffee took off in Germany and other parts of Europe in the 19th century, East Frisians kept to tea because it was economical. Tea leaves can be used over and over again, and they do not require grinders and filters. When guests came, East Frisians showed their hospitality by throwing more leaves in the pot. Over time, a heavy brew became the standard.

I first stopped at the charming East Frisian Tea Museum, in the Renaissance-era city hall of

Norden. The building itself, a rare Renaissance Rathaus (town hall), was worth the stop; but for a tea lover, the treasures were inside. The museum displays all sorts of tea-related items and a collection of regional artifacts.

It also offers tea-serving demonstrations. The rituals are a big part of East Frisian tea culture. The small cups, the rock sugar, the cream that is never stirred — it all took shape in the 19th century, when Germany was industrializing and urbanizing. In response to the economic upheaval, local histories were written and traditions set down in an effort to keep them from disappearing. East Frisian tea became integral to locals' sense of identity. Even the porcelain used in the area had distinct rose patterns; the museum has display cases filled with teapots, cups, and saucers. Its gift shop sells both the local tea and antique teapots in the East Frisian design.

And the culture has remained very local. Four companies — Bünting, Onno Behrends, Thiele, and Uwe Rolf — support the tea museum, but at the time I was visiting, only Bünting was marketing its brand nationally in stores; the rest could be bought only in the region, although online marketing has expanded these companies' reach.

A few East Frisians own tiny companies that produce the equivalent of craft brews. Willem Hedemann, the maker of Ude's tea, was one of those small-batch producers who buy tea from wholesalers and mix it.

The packet that Ude had shown me had a number on the bottom, so I called and received an invitation from Willem Hedemann himself for afternoon tea. On the way there I drove along the coast, trying various brands. One scenic stop was the port of Neuharlingersiel, where I sampled a stiff pot of Bünting tea at Cafe Rodenbäck. I picked up tea from the other producers as well. Almost all of the blends are dominated by leaves from Assam in northeastern India, known for its dark, rich tea. The exact leaves and mixtures are trade secrets, but about 90 percent of the local blends are Assam, leavened with as little as 10 percent of the lighter, fruitier tea from Sri Lanka (Ceylon, in classical tea parlance).

All of these were good but not quite what I had in mind. In midafternoon I arrived in Ostgrossefehn, wired but ready for more.

Above A quiet moment on a canal in Greetsiel. The charming East Frisian Tea Museum is nearby in Norden.

Below Spotlights illuminate a windmill on a foggy night in Greetsiel.

Opposite Houses in Greetsiel. Frisians owe much of their cultural inspiration to the Netherlands and England.

Hedemann, a tall, fit man in his 70s, had been in the business since his father, a tea merchant, took him along on door-to-door visits when he was 14.

"I had an unbelievable tongue," he said as we sat at his backyard picnic table with tea and cake. "People used to test me, blind tests, and I could tell what they were. I'd chew the tea and say what's the best and what price groups they should be in."

We also talked about the water. Ude had wanted me to visit East Frisia because the water there is exceptionally soft and sweet. The effect on tea is amazing, addictive, the tones softer and more complex than the tea I had in Berlin.

Hedemann and I talked for a couple of hours, the winds whipping his tablecloth and bringing rain clouds. His tea really was distinctive, more biting than the local commercial brands and much more challenging than anything I'd bought in a store. It was the difference between a peaty single malt whisky

Photographs by Djamila Grossman

from Islay and a smooth blend. He showed me some prized older teas he had mixed in previous years.

In the end, I began to associate the taste with a color. At its best, steeped in soft water and served in the small, thin porcelain cups, East Frisian tea is golden and almost transparent, the cream glistening slightly on the surface.

"When it's like that," Hedemann said, leaving the tea on his tongue for a moment, "then it's right. Then it's real East Frisian."

WHAT TO READ AND WATCH

The Story of Tea: A Cultural History and Drinking Guide, by Mary Lou Heiss and Robert J. Heiss. An entertaining and well-researched narrative by authors described in *The New York Times* as "the professors of tea."

Tea: History, Terroirs, Varieties, by Kevin Gascoyne, François Marchand, Jasmin Desharnais, and Hugo Américi. Tea facts in depth.

The True History of Tea, by Erling Hoh and Victor H. Mair. Chronicles the story of tea around the world, with particular emphasis on its Asian origins.

Journey through East Frisia, by Ulf Buschmann with photographs by Günter Franz. A regional guidebook.

Teemuseum.de, the website of the East Frisian Tea Museum, includes a link to a short video (described as a trailer) with a tempting image of the region's tea taking shape in a cup. For those who can't follow the German narration, the pictures tell the story.

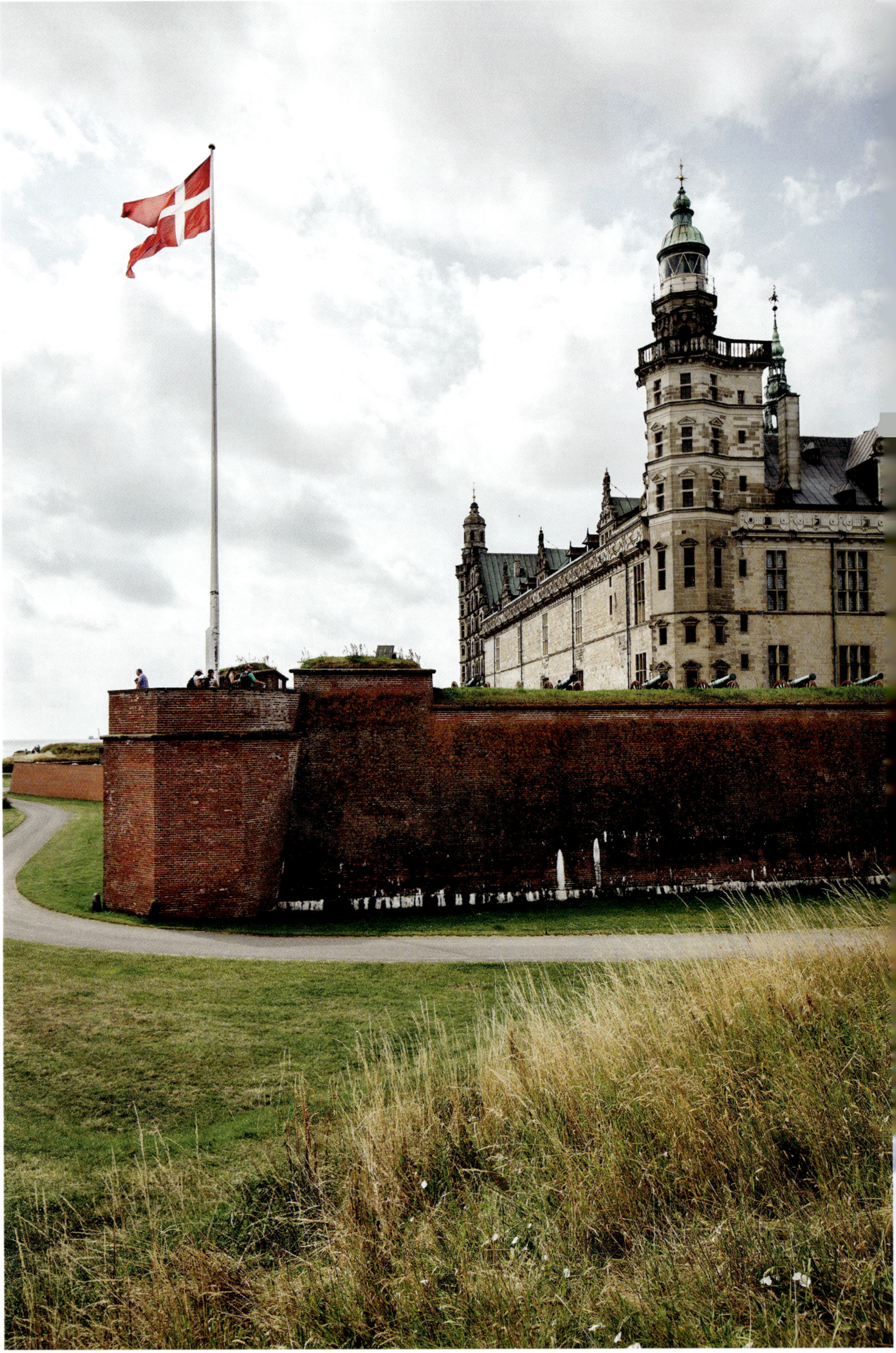

AT HOME WITH HAMLET IN ELSINORE

Shakespeare probably never saw it, but the castle where he set his most famous play still brings his brooding prince to life. — BY SETH SHERWOOD

One autumn afternoon, I walked along the coast of a chilly northern sea in search of a ghost. Admittedly, the bucolic spot where I was searching felt incongruously cheerful for a paranormal encounter. A low sun splayed its rays over the blue water and the majestic red brick walls of the Renaissance castle next to me. Couples with ice cream strolled around the embankment and seagulls floated above.

No phantoms materialized. I was probably several centuries too late.

For it was there, along the ramparts of Kronborg Castle, that Hamlet, prince of Denmark, encountered the ghost of his murdered father, setting in motion the revenge story that propels what is perhaps the most famous literary work in the English language.

A devotee of *Hamlet*, I had taken the 45-minute train ride up the coast from Copenhagen to the town of Elsinore (called Helsingor in Denmark) to immerse myself in the Renaissance-era "Elsinore" Castle—as Shakespeare called it—and stroll among the town's centuries-old edifices.

I was also keen to witness Elsinore's recent renaissance. Though the town enjoyed centuries as a prosperous royal outpost (thanks mainly to taxes levied on foreign trade ships passing through the adjacent sound that separates Denmark from Sweden), its fortunes ebbed in the 1980s with the collapse of its shipbuilding industry. The docklands wasted away. The venerable Shakespeare Festival at Kronborg Castle (Kronborg Slot) has long brought Elsinore alive for a couple of weeks every summer, but for the rest of the year, the town's income became dependent on Swedish day-trippers who ferried over to buy cheap booze.

ELSINORE   DENMARK

Previous Kronborg Castle in Helsingor, Denmark, is the Elsinore of Shakespeare's *Hamlet*.

Left Helsingor embraces its Shakespearean role. This statue of Hamlet is outside the train station.

Opposite Hamlet at Kronborg Castle in 1937. Laurence Olivier played the lead that year.

In the new millennium, however, Elsinore has experienced a resurgence. After a major municipal effort, the town now has cutting-edge cultural venues, public artworks, and more cultural festivals to augment its time-honored appeal.

From the train station, I threaded my way past churches with green copper spires and gabled, half-timbered houses in fanciful colors—peach, mustard, sage. But eventually, all paths lead to the iconic Kronborg Castle, a sober four-sided fortress bedecked with ornate spires and scrolled architectural flourishes, a curious marriage of Lutheran restraint and Renaissance pomp.

Shakespearean history lurks inside the castle, a Unesco World Heritage Site that can be visited solo or as part of group tours on such themes as "Introduction to Kronborg Castle" and "In Hamlet's Footsteps."

An actor in period costume led my tour group through the castle rooms as he alternately narrated, reenacted, and provided background to *Hamlet*. Assuming the role of Horatio, the prince's confidant, he brought the play's celebrated scenes to life. He shepherded us along the ramparts and bastion, where we could imagine Hamlet's encounter with his father's ghost; into the cellars, where Gertrude and Claudius could have stored their fine wines; and through various stately rooms where they might have strolled in their flowing robes—the royal chambers, the palace chapel, the immense ballroom.

None of this actually happened, of course, because the play is fictional. But real royalty did live in Kronborg, which Unesco describes as an especially well-preserved example of a Renaissance castle. There also was, apparently, an actual Prince Hamlet in some previous era, although the history is a bit misty. For Shakespeare, who routinely based his plays on histories and legends found in books, the story was what mattered. He knew a setup for a good plot when he saw one.

He took the Hamlet story and created a play that had everything (and still has): a mysterious crime, supernatural encounters, romance, comic relief, sword fights, a mad scene, a despicable villain, lurking eavesdroppers, and an emotionally overwhelmed main character who must cope with it all. Not to mention timeless poetry and insights into the human condition that have kept people reflecting for several hundred years on what Shakespeare had Hamlet say.

Shakespeare experts have uncovered evidence that even though he probably never saw Kronborg Castle himself, he may have heard detailed descriptions of it from people he knew who traveled more widely. It was not unusual for traveling English theater troupes to put on plays in many European countries, and one such group may well have included actors who were close associates of Shakespeare's. Perhaps they performed in Elsinore, where the castle had recently been rebuilt, and returned to England with colorful stories of a fortified edifice on a wind-whipped promontory. It's not a stretch to assume that Kronborg Castle would have been a strategic point of considerable interest to warring kings like Hamlet's father and the forbidding Fortinbras, an offstage threat for most of the play who arrives at the castle just in time to count the bodies from Hamlet's final confrontation with his father's killer.

After my tour, I chatted with the actor-guide, William Jansen, alongside the castle courtyard where Elsinore holds its Shakespeare festival every August. A mix of performances, films, and concerts, the festival has drawn some of the modern era's most celebrated actors to play Hamlet. Laurence Olivier, Derek Jacobi, Richard Burton, Kenneth Branagh, and Jude Law have all held Yorick's skull on that very spot.

Back in Elsinore, I walked through town toward one of the new Hamlet-free attractions, the M/S Maritime Museum of Denmark. Everywhere, the town flaunted its nautical past. Model ships and sailor hats peeked out from boutique windows. On a wall, a mural depicted a cartoonish vision of the harbor, replete with three-masted ships, buccaneers, sailors, fishmongers, and spyglass-toting explorers.

Things took a turn for the strange along the docks, where a giant fish had been assembled from colorful plastic flotsam and jetsam, like watering cans, dish racks, garden tools, and children's toys. Nearby, a silvery boy sat on a silvery rock and stared forlornly out to sea. A male counterpart to the famous Little Mermaid statue in Copenhagen, this highly polished stainless-steel statue of *Han* ("Him" in Danish) was unveiled in 2012 by Elmgreen and Dragset, a contemporary art pair known for their sometimes provocative public art installations around the world.

A descending gangplank-like walkway took me into the museum, which traces the seafaring history of the Danes from the Vikings to the Maersk global shipping empire. Its subterranean space is built into the U-shaped perimeter of a disused dry dock where large ships were once serviced. The design came from the Bjarke Ingels Group (a.k.a. BIG), an envelope-

Kronborg 1937
The performance of "Hamlet"
by the "Old Vic" company

Above *Han*, a contemporary statue in Helsingor, is a male version of the classic *Little Mermaid* statue in Copenhagen.

Opposite Set in an old shipyard, the Maritime Museum of Denmark appears stark but, once inside, is a strongly sensory experience.

pushing young Danish architectural firm that has built an impressive international portfolio and racked up abundant awards.

The result is an enveloping sensory experience, part nautical fun house and part time capsule. Ambling along uneven floors (which mimic being at sea), I was subsumed in cinematic music, colored lights, projected films, and noises of boat horns and seagulls. Display cases resembling old portholes and stacked chests revealed the accouterments of old-time shipboard journeys, from "hardtack" sailor biscuits to sextants and sundials.

The interactive exhibits revealed something else: my unfitness for maritime life. In an ersatz old-world tattoo parlor, I stenciled the word *Mor* (Mother) on my forearm with a buzzing pen meant to mimic a needle. The shaky, amateurish result would have left any mother ashamed. In a soaring hall dedicated to contemporary global shipping, equipped with computer terminals and a huge projected map of seaborne transport lanes, my attempts to route a container ship from Australia to Bangladesh resulted in a half-million-dollar loss for my "company."

Exposed as a landlubber, I consoled myself with fish and chips in the atrium-like restaurant of the Culture Yard next door. Formerly part of the town shipyard, it's a fully overhauled industrial building outfitted with a jagged glass facade suggesting transparent origami. It houses auditoriums, exhibition areas, a multimedia library, and other spaces to host an annual roster of concerts, theater, and cinema.

That evening's entertainment was provided by bands participating in the Knejpe Festival, a two-night gala in numerous nautical-themed bars and old-world taverns. Valorizing sea shanties and world music — Greek blues, Cuban folk, Afrobeat — the event paid homage to Elsinore's past as an international port. (Another annual event, the multimedia Click Festival,

*Photographs by
Linus Sundahl-Djerf*

looks instead to the future, exploring "the field between art, science, and technology.")

Within Holger Danske, a stony cavern, a gray-haired man and woman called Duo Visti worked a banjo and accordion, strumming and squeezing out minor-key Danish drinking songs while the boisterous crowds swallowed local Wiibroe lager. Down the street, a band called Klepti Klepti summoned rollicking Balkan Gypsy music that shook the walls of Hald An, a smoky tavern decorated with a faded seascape mural.

"Hundreds of years ago there were bars everywhere" in Elsinore, said Kirsten Dalsgaard, a self-described regular of Kobenhavneren tavern, a cottage-like warren of small rooms decorated with beer steins and paintings. On this festival night, she added, "We are trying to relive it."

WHAT TO READ AND WATCH

Hamlet (full title: The Tragedy of Hamlet, Prince of Denmark), by William Shakespeare. One reliable edition is published by the Folger Shakespeare Library.

Hamlet at Elsinore, DVD released in 2011. Filmed in 1966 at Kronborg Castle, with Christopher Plummer, Michael Caine, and Donald Sutherland. Indoors and out, the castle is an atmospheric backdrop.

Hamlet, directed by Peter Brook in 2000. This production is worth an Internet search to find. The actors' unusually clear diction brings the play alive for modern audiences, and Adrian Lester's performance in the title role is a revelation.

Performing Hamlet: Actors in the Modern Age, by Jonathan Croall. An informed look at what goes into staging and acting Hamlet. Performers who comment include Jude Law, David Tennant, and Adrian Lester.

Hamletscenen, the annual Shakespeare festival at Kronborg Castle. The website is hamletscenen.dk.

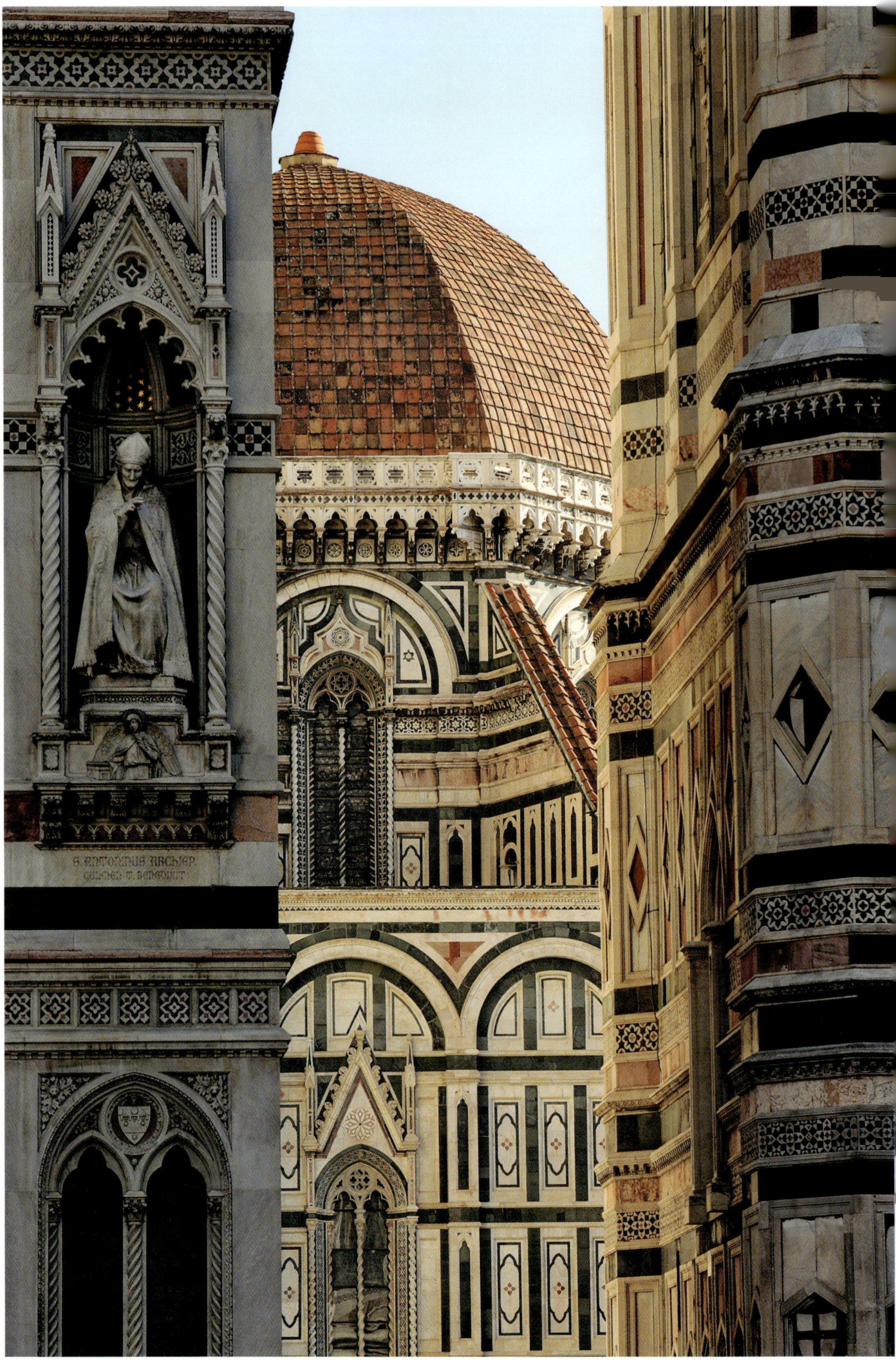

FLORENCE WITHOUT YOUR BAEDEKER

How to be a happy tourist in a city that overwhelms? Take along Forster's A Room with a View, *and keep an eye out for irony.* — BY ADAM BEGLEY

Here's what you do first in Florence: complain about the tourists. It's a time-honored tradition and there's no avoiding it — or them, as they squeeze down the narrow streets. They choke the majestic Piazza Signoria; they overwhelm the Uffizi Gallery — so go ahead and get the grumbling over with. Hordes of them! A year-round blight! Why can't they just stay home! Or, if you're like E. M. Forster's "clever" lady novelist in *A Room with a View*, the one who exclaims in dismay over the bovine "Britisher abroad," admit that you'd like to administer an exam "and turn back every tourist who couldn't pass it."

Snobbery is part of the sophisticated traveler's baggage — that hasn't changed at all in the century and more since Forster, in his charming novel, skewered the supercilious "good taste" of those who look down on the "ill-bred people whom one does meet abroad." Nowadays, when everyone in the ill-bred crowd is snapping photos of the Duomo with a phone, or swarming the Ponte Vecchio, plastic water bottle in hand, the urge to override touristic self-loathing by claiming for oneself a spurious superiority is pretty much irresistible; Forster, were he still around, would poke fun at that snobbish impulse with puckish glee. (But don't let that stop you from grousing about the sheer number of bodies blocking the view of the Arno.)

The next thing to do in Florence, according to Forster, is throw away your guidebook. Chapter II of *A Room with a View* is called "In Santa Croce with No Baedeker," and it's a gently comic interlude every honest visitor to that great Franciscan basilica will recognize as a mocking portrait of himself. Or herself, in the case of our young heroine, Lucy Honeychurch,

Previous In Florence as seen by E. M. Forster, you can put down your guidebook to explore with no agenda. You won't miss the Duomo, the city's famous cathedral.

Left The Piazza Signoria, where Forster's heroine, Lucy Honeychurch, witnesses a stabbing and finds love.

Opposite A 1923 paperback copy of *A Room with a View*.

who winds up alone in the vast interior of Santa Croce without her Baedeker *Handbook to Northern Italy*.

On the way in, she noted "the black-and-white facade of surpassing ugliness" (the marble was added in the 19th century—paid for by an Englishman, by the way); now she's rattling around in the vast nave, wondering which of all the tombs was "the one that was really beautiful," the one most praised by Ruskin. With no cultural authority to tell her what to think, she thinks for herself: "Of course it must be a wonderful building. But how like a barn! And how very cold!" And then, just like that, her mood changes: "the pernicious charm of Italy worked on her, and, instead of acquiring information, she began to be happy." We all want to be happy tourists, so here's the question: Is Forster's early 20th-century advice—toss the guidebook aside and let the pernicious Florentine charm seduce you—still viable in the 21st?

Enjoying *A Room with a View* is easy. A love story that begins and ends in Florence, with complications in England sandwiched in between, it's short, cheerful, and delightfully sly. Besides, there are two excellent and generally faithful film adaptations, the classic 1986 Merchant-Ivory production and a PBS version released in 2008, with enticing shots of Florence and a weird, unwarranted twist at the end. Once Lucy Honeychurch and George Emerson have kissed in a field of violets in the hills above the city (near Fiesole, about which more later), you know (spoiler alert) you're going to hear wedding bells at the end, no matter how many plot twists the crafty author engineers.

Enjoying Florence—a hard, forbidding city ("a city of endurance," Mary McCarthy called it, "a city of stone"), handsome but not pretty, a challenge even if you could siphon off the tourists and replace them with picturesque Italians energetically engaged in producing local color—enjoying Florence takes more time and more effort. But if you have with you your copy of *A Room with a View*, you'll find it easier to get along. Forster's supple, forgiving irony, his ability to satirize lovingly, combined with his firm but regretful insistence on not confusing art and life, is exactly what you need if you plan to share this intensely urban town with tens of thousands of sightseers for the five or six days it will take you to do just like them and see the sights.

Forster reminds us that though Florence is a capital of art (is it ever!), it's not just an overcrowded museum. When Lucy leans out of her window in the Pensione Bertolini and gazes out across the Arno at the marble churches on the hill opposite, and watches with dreamy curiosity as the world trips by, the author notes approvingly, with his usual mild irony, "Over such trivialities as these many a valuable hour may slip away, and the traveler who has gone to Italy to study the tactile values of Giotto, or the corruption of the Papacy, may return remembering nothing but the blue sky and the men and women who live under it." He's not suggesting that you ignore Giotto or the magnificence of the city's turbulent history, but that the hours spent soaking up the dazzling Florentine sunshine with no cultural agenda may be valuable after all.

When Forster himself first came to Florence in October of 1901, he stayed as Lucy did in a pensione on the Lungarno delle Grazie, with a view over the Arno to the Basilica di San Miniato al Monte and the dark hills beyond. He was on a grand tour, traveling with his mother, and was a dutiful sightseer. He wrote to a friend back home, "the orthodox Baedeker-bestarred Italy—which is all I have yet seen—delights me so much that I can well afford to leave Italian Italy for another time." He was back the following year, at the same pensione, and by the time he'd finished *A Room with a View*, he had struck a happy balance.

In and around the Basilica di Santa Croce is everything that's delightful and appalling about Florence today. The neo-Gothic facade is still ugly, the long square in front of it dusty, bland, pigeon-infested, and lousy with tourists. The interior is still cavernous, austere, and chilly, impressive but somehow dispiriting. Even if you've ditched your guidebook, you're reminded at every step of the city's vast cultural riches: here are the tombs of Michelangelo, Galileo, and Lorenzo Ghiberti, whose bronze baptistery doors opposite the Duomo were so perfect, according to Michelangelo, they could have been the gates of paradise; here are the memorials to Dante and Machiavelli. Crowds are waiting to get into the small, high-ceilinged chapels to the right of the high altar—that's where you can admire the tactile values of Giotto, whose early 14th-century frescoes grace the walls.

Just outside the basilica in the main cloister is the Pazzi Chapel, a perfectly proportioned Renaissance gem designed by the great Florentine architect Filippo Brunelleschi (who gave the Duomo its dome). The chapel, its white walls decorated with glazed terra-cotta medallions by Luca della Robbia (one of young Lucy's favorite artists), looks best when it's empty, filled to its noble height with nothing but chalky light from the lantern and the oculi in the dome. In other words, if a tour guide and his flock are in there, wait till they've gone.

If you stroll a few dozen yards past the Pazzi Chapel, you'll find yourself in a second cloister, also designed by Brunelleschi in 1446, the last year of his life. It's a place of great beauty and calm, usually deserted, and you don't need to know a thing about it to fall in love. The simple, elegant two-story cloister with its slender columns shelters you from the rigors and confusions of Florence and gives you instead the tranquil harmony of the Renaissance without pomp or grandeur, washed by bright Tuscan sun. I like to imagine, though Forster doesn't suggest it, that Lucy loitered there without her Baedeker, and that's why she began to be happy. At the very least, a quiet moment in the cloisters will give you strength to confront the multitudes and the immortal works of art remaining on your list.

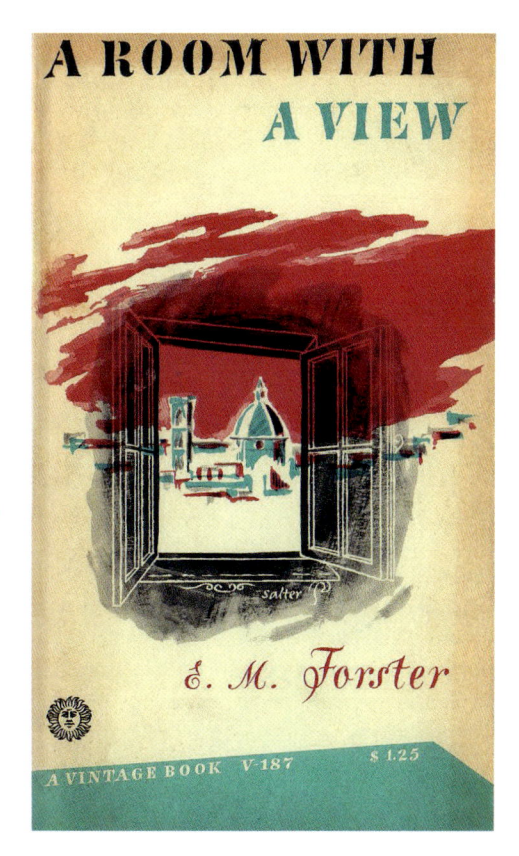

Above A view of the Ponte Vecchio over the river Arno.

Opposite A cloister at Santa Croce. Forster's Lucy arrives there without her Baedeker guidebook.

And so will loitering over lunch. And dinner. One eats very well in Florence, and in general the simpler the restaurant, the better the food. If you can visit one church and one museum before lunch and one more church or another museum after lunch (whatever you do, don't miss the wealth of paintings piled higgledy-piggledy in the Palatine Gallery of the Palazzo Pitti), and then take a nap (Tuscan wine is cheap and abundant), and then stroll to dinner, perhaps along the Via de' Tornabuoni, under the looming, illuminated facades of great, stern palazzi, and stroll some more after dinner when the crowds have thinned and Florence seems gentler and the multicolor Duomo seems less garish but just as huge and astonishing — you'll find that after a few days of this routine, all your complaints will be forgotten, replaced with amazement and gratitude.

Unless of course you stray into the Piazza Signoria, where the replica of Michelangelo's giant David attracts a sizable contingent of art lovers with camera phones night and day. This is where Lucy wanders one evening, unaccompanied:

"'Nothing ever happens to me,' she reflected, as she entered the Piazza Signoria and looked nonchalantly at its marvels, now fairly familiar to her. The great square was in shadow; the sunshine had come too late to strike it. Neptune was already unsubstantial in the twilight, half god, half ghost, and his fountain plashed dreamily to the men and satyrs who idled together on its marge. The Loggia showed as the triple entrance of a cave, wherein dwelt many a deity, shadowy but immortal, looking forth upon the arrivals and departures of mankind. It was the hour of unreality — the hour, that is, when unfamiliar things are real. An older person at such an hour and in such a place might think that sufficient was happening to him, and rest content. Lucy desired more."

*Photographs by
Chris Warde-Jones*

And then something does happen to her: Two Italians quarrel, one stabs the other in the chest, and Lucy, who sees the blood come trickling out of the fatally wounded man's mouth, swoons—into the arms of George Emerson, as luck would have it.

Nothing so dramatic is likely to occur to the 21st-century visitor. But if it does, head for Fiesole, the little hill town no more than a few miles from the Piazza Signoria.

Once you've arrived, you realize that the chief virtue of this modest town, aside from the fresh air, is the panoramic view of the Arno Valley and the extraordinary, maddening city you've just left, its Duomo vast and proud even at this distance. And the wisdom of the structure of *A Room with a View* is suddenly as clear as the bright Tuscan sky: You will return to Florence, and next time it will be a honeymoon.

WHAT TO READ AND WATCH

A Room with a View, by E. M. Forster. Look for the Penguin Modern Classics edition including "A View without a Room," an essay written by Forster for the novel's 50th anniversary and published in *The New York Times* on July 27, 1958.

A Room with a View, directed by James Ivory. Widely acclaimed 1986 film adaptation starring Helena Bonham Carter and Daniel Day-Lewis. A more recent film version, written by Andrew Davies and directed by Nicholas Renton, was a PBS 2007 Masterpiece production.

Rick Steves Pocket Florence, by Rick Steves and Gene Openshaw. A practical and portable guidebook in the popular Rick Steves library of travel guides.

E. M. Forster: A Life, by P. N. Furbank. First published in 1978, and still a fine account of the author's long, remarkable life.

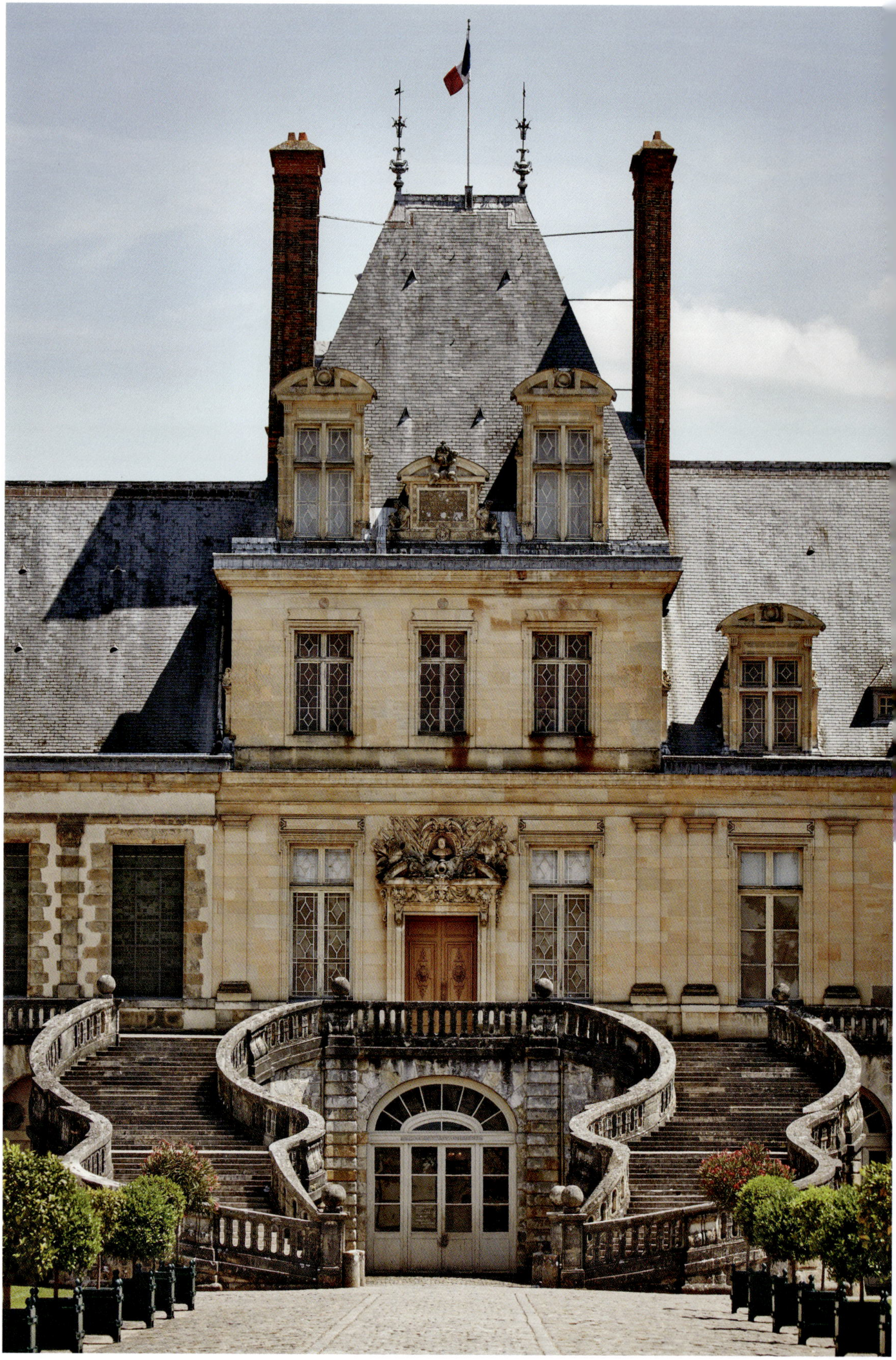

THE PALACE IN THE FOREST

The royal hunting lodge at Fontainebleau grew over eight centuries into a chateau to rival Versailles.
— BY THAD CARHART

You've visited the Louvre, Notre Dame, Sainte-Chapelle. You've been to Versailles and perhaps even made a trip to the chateaux of the Loire Valley. Is there anything else of the same caliber near Paris for those who love the classic ideals of French architecture and decorative arts? The answer is a resounding yes: the Château de Fontainebleau.

Though far less familiar to travelers than Versailles — and drawing fewer than one-seventh the number of visitors — Fontainebleau, 45 miles south of Paris, isn't exactly unknown. But given its centuries of history at the center of the French monarchy, and the richness and variety of its buildings, inside and out, its relative obscurity is something of a mystery. No site in France can compare as a royal residence: It predates the Louvre itself by 50 years, and Versailles by five centuries.

Fontainebleau's singular attraction to an unbroken line of French kings spanning eight centuries was originally as a hunting lodge, perfectly situated at the edge of the ancient Forest of Fontainebleau—in effect, a royal game preserve. But as each king took up residence for two months of hunting every fall, the relatively modest medieval structure was added to, then added to again, by the sovereigns who brought their court with them to the vast forest. They developed a succession of structures and styles that span many centuries and yet — magically, convincingly — cohere in a pleasing whole.

Some of France's greatest architects — Philibert de l'Orme, Ange-Jacques Gabriel, and André Le Nôtre among them — fashioned buildings, courtyards, interiors, and elaborate grounds, adding to what they found while resisting the impulse to replace or destroy.

Previous The horseshoe-shaped staircase that leads into the Château de Fontainebleau was built for Louis XIII.

Left The kings brought the work of great architects and artists to their royal getaway in the forest.

Opposite A 19th-century engraving pictures a glittering crowd at Fontainebleau.

What greets the visitor today is the single greatest assemblage over time of French architecture and décor still in its original state.

A word of caution: Fontainebleau is immense and immensely varied. The roof alone has a surface area of five acres, and it covers more than 1,500 rooms. The gardens and outer grounds extend over 230 acres. In addition to the main sights, there are special guided tours. Trying to "do it all" in a single day is likely to lead to frustration, and it's best to plan ahead.

The chateau dates from 1137. Thomas Becket consecrated its original chapel in 1169, and Saint Louis himself (Louis IX, who was canonized by the church) founded a convent there in 1259 whose charge was to arrange for the ransom of Christian prisoners captured in Egypt during the ill-fated Seventh Crusade.

In the early 1500s, François I transformed the medieval fortress and hunting lodge into a royal palace, bringing the arts of the Italian Renaissance to northern France. The result is a unique amalgam of Italian exuberance and artistic genius joined to French subtlety and classical restraint. The rooms that date from the 16th century are among the most breathtaking in France, but their richness can be overwhelming, with elaborate frescoes and paintings, sculpted frames, coffered ceilings, carved wall paneling, and faceted doors. Every single part of the environment was imagined as part of a pleasing whole, expressing a decidedly French notion of elegance suitable to its time.

The Galerie François I, a remarkable passage 200 feet long by 20 feet wide, leads from what is now the front of the chateau to its inner recesses. (It is said that the king kept the key to the private sanctum around his neck.) It would be a mistake to walk through as if this were just a fancy hallway. The work of Italian artists, including the architect Sebastiano Serlio and the master woodcarver Francesco Scibec da Carpi, the Galerie François I combines masterly frescoes, life-size stucco figures, elaborate wainscoting, delicate painting, and gold leaf detailing. A series of powerful frescoes by Rosso Fiorentino illustrates stories from antiquity, drawing allegorical parallels to François as a great king. His emblem, the salamander, is everywhere, as is his royal monogram, "F." Each panel is surrounded by sumptuous stucco figures in white plaster that mix female nudes, winged angels, satyrs, muscled heroes; the effect is both sensual and entirely captivating. Views from the windows look across the pond to the forest in the middle distance. One can imagine the effect of all this in a France only recently emerging from the Late Middle

Ages. It is one of the defining works of what is now known as the First School of Fontainebleau, and a recognized masterpiece of the Renaissance in northern Europe.

The other 16th-century masterwork at Fontainebleau is the Salle de Bal, the ballroom, built by François's son, Henri II, in 1558. Its decoration is a startling mix of dramatic color (Italian frescoes again) and the exquisite reserve of the glorious woodwork on the ceiling and the walls and the vast patterned oak floor. Perfectly proportioned at the heart of the chateau, it looks out on the cobbled Oval Courtyard on one side and, on the other, across colorful beds of flowering plants worked in symmetrical patterns called *broderie* (embroidery) to the ever-present forest.

The walls and ceiling bear the coats of arms of Henri II and his wife, Catherine de' Medici. Also present in thinly disguised form is the monogram "D" for the king's mistress of more than 20 years, Diane de Poitiers. When Henri was fatally wounded in a jousting accident, he languished for 11 days before dying. Diane was kept from him by the queen and exiled from court at the moment of his death.

The intrigues must have been endless, but the beauty of the surroundings may have overwhelmed them when the king was entertaining in this room. For centuries now it has been used for ceremonies, parties, and dinners. Even an occupying army found it appealing: The Germans, who requisitioned the chateau during World War II, used it for concerts by the Berlin Philharmonic, then quickly sent film back home to show off their conquest.

The figure most closely associated with Fontainebleau in our day is among the last in the long line of monarchs who lived there, Napoleon Bonaparte. His golden "N" blazes from the iron gate at the entrance; in fact it was he who pulled down a wing of the chateau to open up the formal courtyard and make it more clearly the stately entrance to his palace. Among his many attributes can certainly be counted a showman's flair for the dramatic.

In the days of the kings, men and women of the royal court generally savored their annual visits to Fontainebleau. Protocol was greatly relaxed, the stables and forest were right out the back door, and a tradition of voluptuary delights—hunting for boar

Above Built in 1558, the over-the-top ballroom overflows with Italian frescoes and intricate woodwork.

Opposite A winding staircase in an old part of the chateau. Fontainebleau is immense—and immensely varied.

and deer, lovemaking, comfortable rooms—must have made it more of a true home for the king and his courtiers than Versailles could be.

For Marie Antoinette, it was an escape like no other available. She left two small, deeply personal spaces here. The first is the Turkish boudoir, built for her in 1777, an Orientalist confection of a room set well away from the other royal apartments. Here she would entertain an inner circle of friends, enjoying her private retreat from court life. Napoleon's Empress Josephine also loved this room, and had it refurnished after Marie Antoinette's items were lost in the Revolution. You can visit it on private tours only.

The other, sometimes called the silver boudoir, was offered to the queen by her husband, Louis XVI, in 1787, a mere two years before France drove the Bourbons from the throne. It, too, is rich in its details, though the conceit here is classical antiquity rather than exoticism. Coming near the end of the self-guided tour of the royal apartments, it is too often overlooked because it is small and not overly showy.

The list of rooms and of the kings who built them is very long: Henri IV's wing, as well as one of the few remaining intact indoor tennis courts in France; Napoleon I's opulent throne room; Napoleon III's jewel box of a theater; and many others.

The forest of Fontainebleau, the vast reserve where the kings hunted game, is a national forest with trails for hiking and biking, as well as boulders and crags beloved by rock climbers. But most visitors to the chateau will concentrate their outdoor explorations on its formal grounds.

Louis XIV's Grand Parterre, the orderly gardens that are said to be the largest in Europe, provides the perfect vantage point for looking back at the long and irregular mass of the chateau's linked buildings. At once you see how grandeur need not

*Photographs by
Andy Haslam*

develop from a unified vision, but can evolve as an accretion of architectural detail over time, both varying and enriching the overall effect. This is part of Fontainebleau's particular genius.

On the other side of the distant wall of buildings lies a small, hidden garden that is less grand, more mysterious, and unapologetically feminine: the Garden of Diana. Its scope is intimate and lovely; its paths meander. Maples and willows grace the asymmetric stretches of perfect lawn, and mature pines flank its edges.

At the focal point sits a fountain that could only be French, over which Diana the Huntress presides. Her bronze likeness, set above a stone basin, pulls an arrow from the quiver as she strides forward, a small deer bounding at her side. Four hounds and four stag heads are arranged above the pool. A sense of the tutelary spirit prevails — not just of the hunt, but of the ancient forest itself. This, too, is Fontainebleau.

WHAT TO READ AND WATCH

Finding Fontainebleau: An American Boy in France, by Thad Carhart. In this semi-autobiographical book, the author of this article invites readers to share the fascination with the chateau.

In the Forest of Fontainebleau: Painters and Photographers from Corot to Monet, by Kimberly Jones, Simon Kelly, Sarah Kennel, and Helga Aurisch. Through the artists who painted there, traces the connections of Fontainebleau to the advent of Impressionism.

Fontainebleau, France: Royal Château, a Rick Steves video. A three-minute tour led by the popular travel writer Rick Steves, with particular emphasis on Napoleon.

The Seine: The River That Made Paris, by Elaine Sciolino. The Seine connected the monarchs to Fontainebleau, and although the chateau and forest play only a cameo role in this book, it provides rich cultural context.

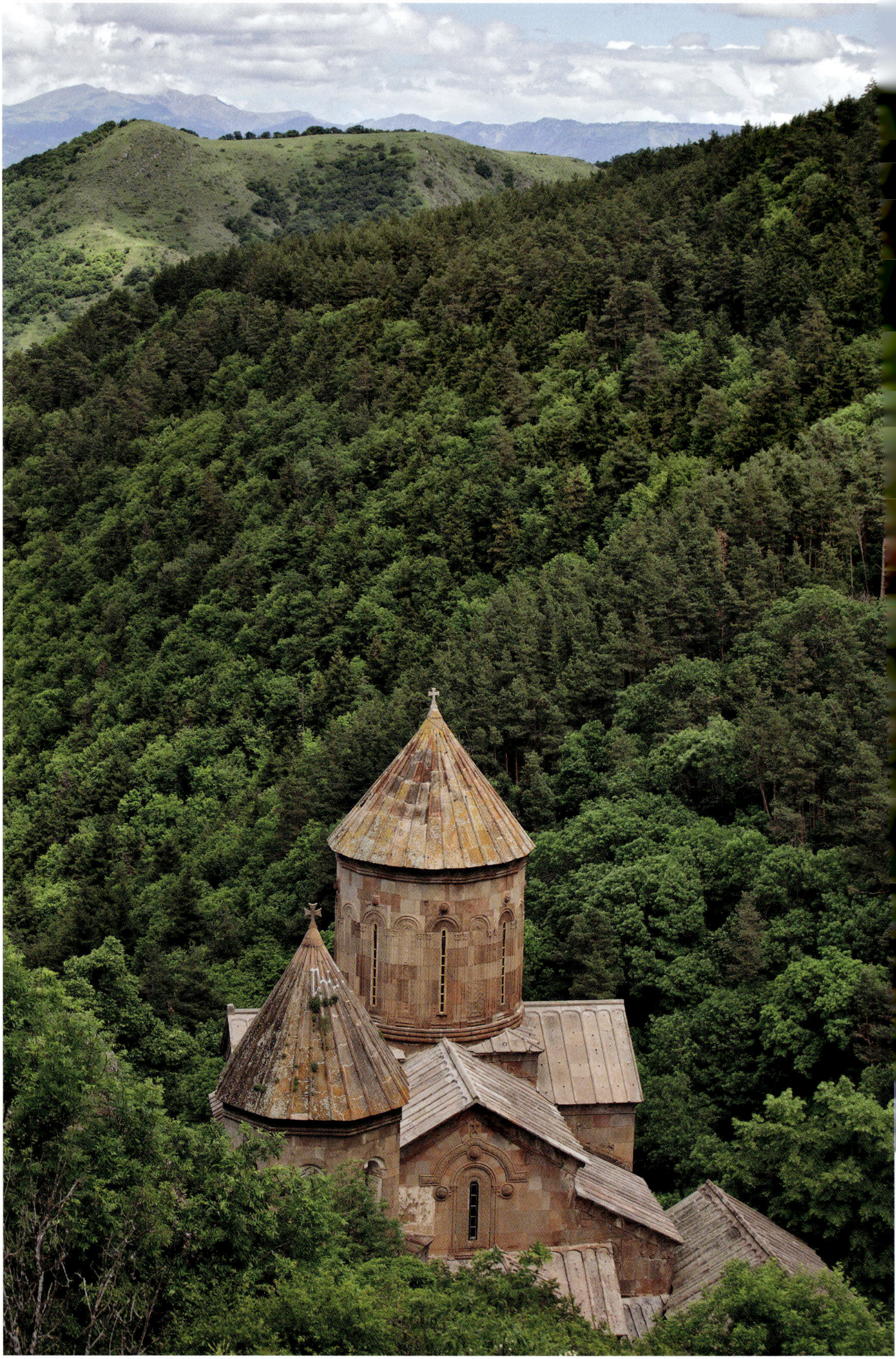

GEORGIA & TURKEY

CHANTING AND CLIMBING IN THE VANISHED KINGDOM OF TAO

Ancient churches, ruined monasteries, and haunting music link the splinters of a shattered realm.
— BY CÉLESTINE BOHLEN

The idea was to take a trip with my 22-year-old daughter, Liza, an adventure worthy of a college graduation present. We settled on a 10-day journey through the small Caucasus country of Georgia, with a swing through neighboring Turkey, in search of the long-lost kingdom of Tao.

It sounded vaguely Chinese, and the scenery did look at times like Chinese scroll paintings: rocky, pine-covered mountains cut through by waterfalls, fast-moving rivers, and vast upland plateaus with alternating patches of snow and wildflowers.

But the stunning landscape was just the backdrop for the trip. Although the boundaries of the Tao-Klarjeti kingdom, as it is sometimes called, once part of a larger realm ruled by the Bagratid dynasty, had vanished from the map by the 11th century, its Georgian rulers left behind an astonishing collection of churches, monasteries, and fortresses. Said to number 300, they are scattered across territory later disputed by, notably, the Byzantines, the Mongols, the Persians, the Seljuk Turks, the Ottomans, and the Russians.

These remnants of ancient Georgian culture were what drew us to join John Graham, an American musicologist and tour leader who lives in Tbilisi, the Georgian capital, and seven other travelers on a journey that began in the Black Sea city of Batumi, Georgia's second-largest urban center. Then we circled through the Turkish cities of Kars, Yusufeli, and Ardanuc before ending in Tbilisi.

Previous The remote Sapara Monastery. Its church of St. Saba, added in the 13th to 14th century, is largely intact.

Left Georgian polyphonic chant, haunting and unforgettable, was preserved with the help of the Karbelashvili family, pictured here.

Opposite A 17th-century Georgian manuscript depicting St. George's life and martyrdom.

John himself, whom I had met in Paris when he was touring with a choir of Georgian singers, provided another lure. An academic expert in Georgian polyphonic chant, with a doctorate from Princeton, he had promised us music along the trip, and over and over, he delivered.

On our first evening in Batumi, three professional singers from the Adjarian State Song and Dance Ensemble sat down at our table and burst into song, working their way through a powerful repertory of sacred, folk, and "urban" chants. The men sang without accompaniment, without notes, their eyes focused on a space above a feast of Georgian dishes.

As John explained, the typical Georgian men's choir sings in three-part harmony, with a tenor who leads the song and two other voices improvising backup. During the trip, we had our own trio of singers: John managed to corral two of our members — Alex, a college classmate of Liza's and a jazz pianist, and Tom, a British arts administrator — to join him in liturgical chants.

Inside Georgia, all the churches we visited had been restored and returned to the Georgian Orthodox church since 1991, when the country won independence from the Soviet Union. In Turkey, most of the churches were in ruins, their vaulted ceilings now rubble, with battered carvings and faint traces of once-colorful frescoes. Many had been converted into mosques during Ottoman rule and then abandoned.

Ruined or restored, these churches have maintained a haunting serenity. Our trio's solemn, melodic chants — wedding songs, Easter and other liturgical hymns — conjured up their original purpose as places of worship, learning, and reflection, monuments to the glory of God and the Georgian kings and monks who built them.

"The development of multivoice chanting in Georgia in the Middle Ages was unique in the region; almost all of the surrounding countries were then singing in monophonic music styles," John explained. In other Orthodox churches, like the Russian and Greek, monophonic chant remained the dominant style until at least the 16th century.

Some of the monasteries we visited in Tao were the very sites where medieval chantbooks called *iadgari* (heirmologions) were collated by 10th-century scribal monks. But for many centuries, it was mostly an oral tradition; it wasn't until the late 19th century that this polyphonic music was transcribed into Western notation. This required adapting the dissonances and harmonies peculiar to Georgian music to five-line notation, and deciphering the cryptic shorthand used by medieval monks to guide singers through melodies they already knew.

At almost every stop, John had a story about the monks and church leaders who had left their mark on these mountainsides. Manuscripts from the monastery at Otkhta, near Yusufeli, eventually made their way to the St. Catherine monastery in Egypt. St. George the Athonite, who wrote some of the texts we heard, was educated at another monastery outside Yusufeli that is now a mosque buried in brambles. St. Gregory of Khandztha, a leading church figure in the eighth century, founded a monastery in Klarjeti (now in Turkey) and helped his disciples establish others. "They were crawling all over these hills building churches," John said.

Our trip wasn't just about churches. A determined hiker, John led us up scraggly paths to explore mountain fortresses: one built in the fifth century above the Turkish city of Artanuc, another above Borjomi, an old Soviet spa town in Georgia. We scrambled through Hell's Canyon, outside Artanuc, whose soaring cliffs provided good acoustics for our singers to exercise their vocal cords. We visited two cave complexes, one at Uplistsikhe, built in 1500 B.C., and the other at Vardzia, about 35 miles from the Georgian border city of Akhaltsikhe.

The honeycomb cave complex at Vardzia, built in the 12th century as a haven during a time of Persian invasions, is associated with Georgia's famed Queen Tamara, a charismatic ruler who can be seen there in a fresco in the Church of the Dormition, itself carved out of soft rock. Legend has it that when an earthquake struck in 1283, crumbling the rock face that hid the caves, the population and resident monks were safe inside the church, celebrating Easter; it was deemed a miracle.

Looking out over the valley below from a newly installed safety barrier, Liza compared the view to a scene from *The Lord of the Rings*. Another group member, Michael, an intrepid Australian, said as he crouched through a low tunnel that it reminded him of the mountains of Ethiopia.

Farther south, our bus climbed up a steep dirt road to the monastery of Sapara, nestled in the woods below a ruined fortress. Used as a summer music camp during the Soviet era, the church of St. Saba, added to the monastery in the 14th century, is largely intact, with vivid wall paintings of apostles and the local noble families. A young monk was so moved by our trio's chants that he gave us souvenir icons in gratitude.

We were often alone on our visits, particularly in Turkey, a predominantly Muslim country with an ambiguous attitude toward monuments of other cultures. At some stops, villagers came out to chat, curious about how our crew had managed to make our way up to their isolated mountaintop.

We even had all of the empty vastness of Ani, a former Armenian capital poised on a high riverbank on the now-closed Turkish-Armenian border, about 24 miles from Kars, to ourselves. Once said to rival Constantinople with a population of 100,000, Ani fell prey to invasions and earthquakes; by the 15th century, its dozens of churches, including one built by Georgians during a brief occupation by Queen Tamara, were abandoned "to the owl and the jackal," as one guidebook put it.

When we did see crowds in Turkey, they were typically Georgians, making the cross-border pilgrimages to their now-abandoned holy places. At Bana,

Above A staircase at Vardzia. Visitors can enter the Church of the Dormition, which is carved into the rocky cliff.

Below Candles in the Vardzia cave complex in Georgia.

Opposite The honeycomb of shelters at Vardzia was built in the 12th century as a haven during a time of Persian invasions.

near the Turkish village of Benek, priests led their flock through high grasses to the giant ruins of a cathedral, site of a Georgian king's wedding to a Byzantine princess, later used as an Ottoman arms depot until it was blown up by the Russians in the 19th century.

At the 10th-century Tbeti church in the Turkish province of Artvin, we ran into a festive group of Georgian schoolteachers from Batumi, who were surprised and thrilled by our trio's chants. They soon joined in, adding their voices to music that filled the ruined cathedral. The teachers invited us to share their ample picnic, complete with homemade wine and *khachapuri*, the delicious Georgian cheese bread. Asked why they had made the arduous day trip, one teacher, Nona Akhaladze, said, "This was all ours before the Turks stole it from us." She was corrected by a fellow teacher who reminded us that, in fact, it was Lenin who ceded the Tao-Klarjeti region, then part of the Russian Soviet Republic, to the Turks as part of the Brest Litovsk peace treaty signed before the end of World War I.

The music John had promised us kept popping up, sometime planned, sometime spontaneous. After our picnic at Tbeti, the teachers began a medley of folk

Photographs by Danielle Villasana

songs, punctuated with solos by a part-time opera singer. A couple of days before, when we were staying in Kars, a city made famous by the Turkish writer Orhan Pamuk's evocative novel *Snow* but also known for czarist-era Russian buildings and its version of Gruyère cheese, we stopped by a local tearoom known as a gathering place for bards from all over Turkey. People sat on benches along the walls, listening to performers whose long narrative songs (their lyrics sadly lost on us) were accompanied by strumming on long-necked lutes, or *saz*.

On our last day, we arrived in Tbilisi on a steamy summer evening in time for a lively concert in a city park where Alex had been invited to jam with a jazz quintet headed by the director of the Tbilisi music conservatory. It was a fitting musical finale to our trip — a modern take on the improvisation we had heard in the lonely churches of what was once the Tao kingdom.

WHAT TO READ AND WATCH

Bread and Ashes: A Walk through the Mountains of Georgia, by Tony Anderson. The author's account of a revealing trek in 1998.

Georgia (Bradt Travel Guide), by Tim Burford. One of the few guidebooks in English dedicated solely to the country of Georgia.

Sacred Georgian Chants sung by the Georgian Harmony Choir. One of the short videos featuring Georgian chant that are often available on YouTube or other streaming services.

The Making of the Georgian Nation, by Ronald Grigor Suny. Described by *The American Historical Review* as "the standard account of Georgian history in English."

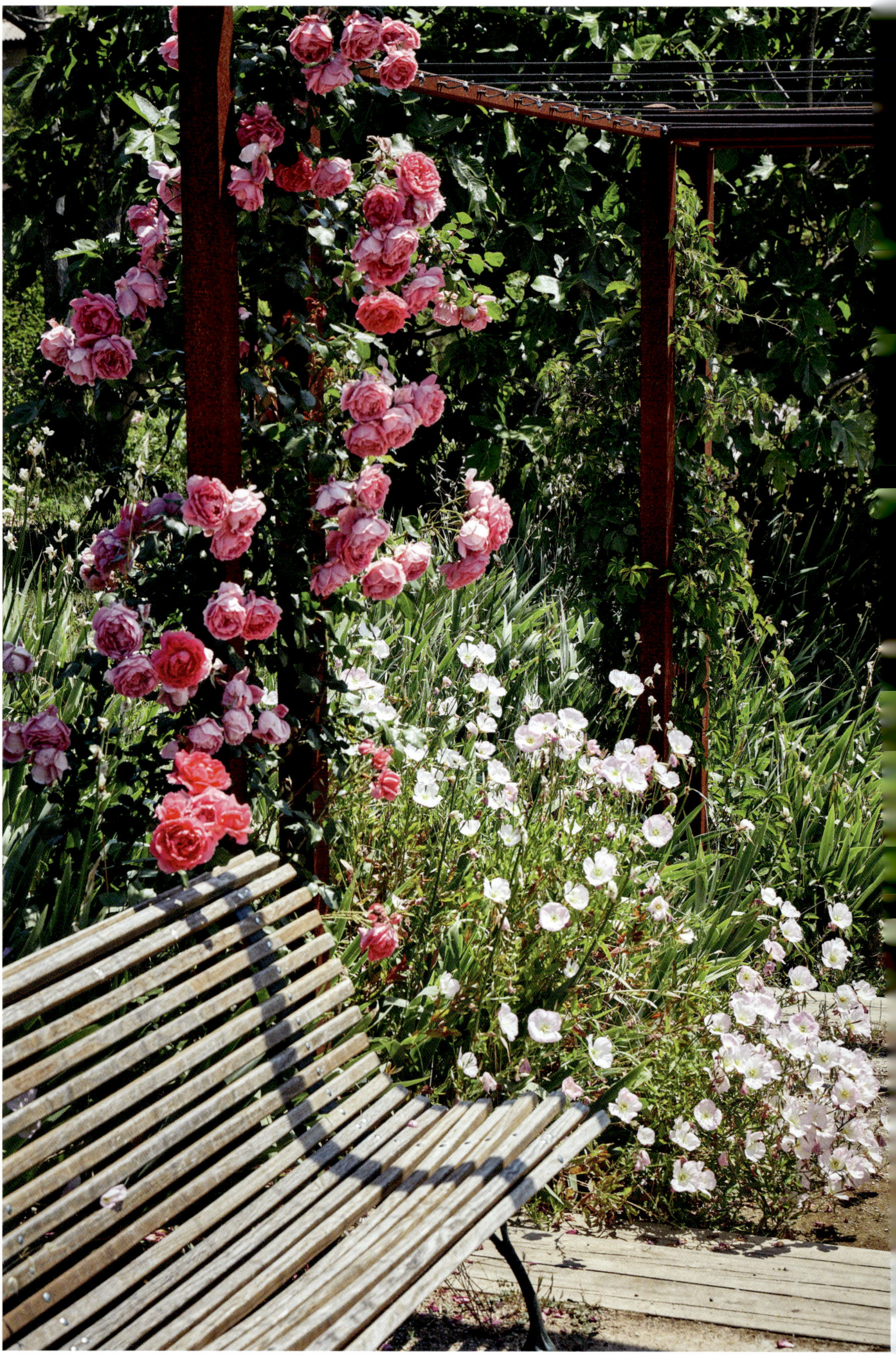

THE PERFUME CAPITAL OF THE WORLD

Start with a field of flowers, add the artisans of Grasse, and you just might get Chanel No. 5.
— BY COLLEEN CREAMER

Before I became a perfume devotee a dozen years ago, my lexicon for describing scent was limited to words like "woodsy" or "flowery." Later I found myself craving the dexterity of language that could match the increasingly complex perfumes arriving at my house in tiny decanted samples.

At the time, perfume blogs and a few books were lifting the veil off a closely guarded industry. I had fallen in love not only with perfume, but also with the deft and curious descriptions of fragrance at the hands of gifted perfume critics, particularly Luca Turin and Tania Sanchez, who together wrote the vastly entertaining *Perfumes: The Guide*. I felt as though I had discovered two new strains of art, perfumery and the translation of scent to words—not to mention the most underrated of the five senses.

When I decided to take a deeper look into the fragrance industry, there was no better place to do it than Grasse, a city about 10 miles north of Cannes in southern Provence that is known as the perfume capital of the world. In this medieval town and its environs, which are sufficiently inland to be sheltered from the sea air, a confluence of soil, sun, and temperature nurtured the rose, jasmine, lavender, myrtle, wild mimosa, and other flowers that were the genesis of the French perfume industry. Grasse is especially known for its fragrant May rose, the pale pink flower that blooms in May, and jasmine, both flowers at the heart of more than a few famous fragrances, including Chanel's breathtaking star, No. 5.

The short version of Grasse's place in the history of perfume begins with a foul odor. In medieval times, the town had a thriving leather business, but the tanning process made for pungent merchandise that didn't sit well with the gloved nobility. A Grasse tanner presented a pair of scented leather gloves to

Previous Vividly fragrant roses at the International Perfume Museum in Grasse.

Left Heirloom perfume bottles at Parfumerie Galimard. The company was founded in 1747.

Opposite Sorting roses in a perfumery workshop in the Grasse area, circa 1895.

Catherine de' Medici, the queen of France from 1547 until 1559, and an infant industry was born.

In and around Grasse to this day, Dior, Hermès, and Chanel all grow May roses and jasmine in protected flower fields. Every year the town exuberantly celebrates its fragrant blossoms with festivals. There is an International Museum of Perfume; and year-round, perfumeries offer tours in many languages and workshops for visitors who want to blend fragrances of their own.

Many renowned "noses" (or perfumers) work in Grasse and find inspiration there. The town is so associated with perfume and its history that Unesco has placed it and its skills on the Intangible Cultural Heritage list.

On my first morning in Grasse, I roamed through winding cobblestone streets to get a taste of the old city at its historical center. Small, colorful cafes, brasseries, and shops blended with russet-hued villas that were embellished with every color in the Provençal palette. Gift shops selling pastel soaps, sachets, and, of course, perfume lured shoppers.

I made my way to Notre-Dame du Puy Cathedral, a Romanesque church dating from 1244 that is home to three paintings by Peter Paul Rubens and one by Jean-Honoré Fragonard, the 18th-century painter who is Grasse's most famous artist. One of the city's big fragrance houses is named for Fragonard, and I made the relatively short hike there from the church. It was a circuitous trek, and I stood outside to catch my breath in the temperate spring air before going inside the multilevel ocher Fragonard building—a parfait of shop, small unpretentious museum, and working perfume manufacturer.

Although the building dates to 1782, the perfumery has no direct connection to the painter; it was opened in 1926. I wandered around its displays while waiting for the next English-speaking tour and was reminded that although the origins of perfume stretch back to ancient civilization, it was in the 18th century that France made it an industry. Louis XV, the monarch from 1715 to 1774, became known for his love of fragrance, and his court was celebrated as *la cour parfumée* (the perfumed court).

On the tour, a guide named Jessica led a small group of us through rooms with massive stainless-steel vats. We passed staff members who were used to the intrusion. Jessica explained that after the jasmine, orange blossom, lavender, and other flowers are picked, the blossoms are placed on trays in the upper part of a still, over water that is brought to a boil. As the steam rises, it captures the scent-bearing components and carries them into a glass cooler where the mixture of water and essential oils is then collected.

"We need three tons of flowers to get one liter of oil," Jessica told us. This elicited an audible gasp from the gaggle of tourgoers, mostly from the British Isles. We were one excited group of perfume lovers. Jessica tested us on which scents—lime, apple, and lemon among them—we could recognize. Then I sneaked off to Fragonard's little shop and purchased an orange blossom soap to take home.

Perfumers in Grasse, along with those in the rest of the perfume world, have had to change with the times. Around the turn of the 20th century, a blast of new olfactory chemicals was discovered, creating cheap competition. Grasse is still known for natural botanical components, but its flower production has been scaled back. The rising price of property around Grasse has caused disruption as well; much of the land has simply become too expensive for farming.

Still, Grasse's influence and relevance in the fragrance industry remain almost unmatched based on its history, the quality produced by its growers, and the creative gifts of the perfumers who live there. Small-scale flower producers are also benefiting from the worldwide organic movement, with its demand for natural ingredients.

That evening, after I drove my rented Fiat back to my Airbnb rental, my host told me that she and her husband were both chemical engineers and that he is in the perfume industry. She added that he "hates to talk shop at home." I internally swore to honor that request; for a gratifyingly low price, I was getting a comfortable room, a great breakfast, and a view over Grasse's rolling slopes of terra-cotta rooftops. I was already planning my return.

The following morning, I drove to the Musée International de la Parfumerie, in the heart of the old city. It traces 3,000 years of perfume history, from ancient Greece through modernity, with artifacts, videos, olfactory installations, and explanatory panels. A few miles away is its plant conservatory, nearly five acres of gardens that give visitors a chance to smell and touch many of the botanical ingredients involved in perfumery. Several large areas focus on how roses, jasmine, and lavender are grown

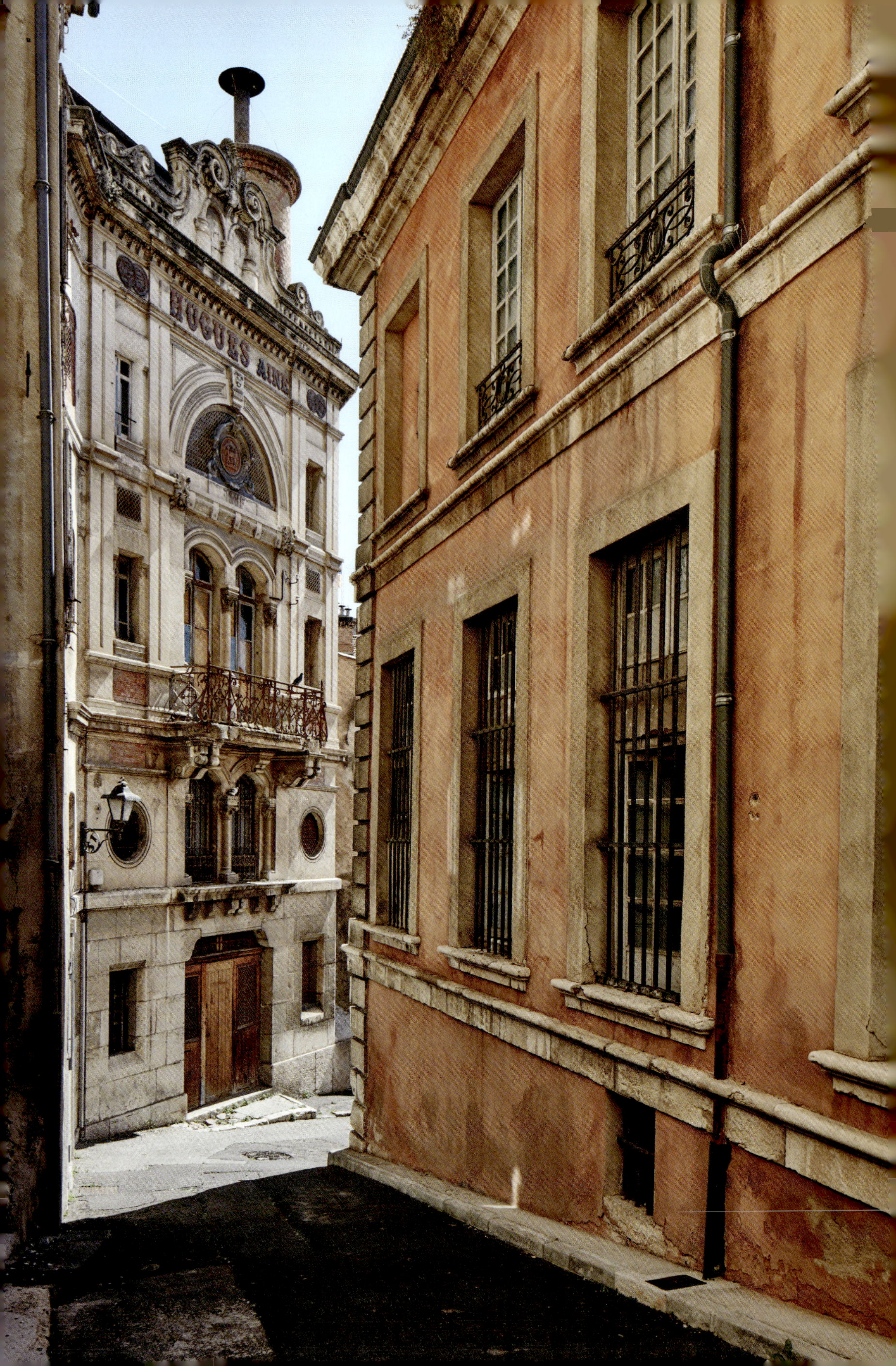
HUGUES AINE

Opposite The old city at the historical center of Grasse. Flowers for perfume grow in protected fields nearby.

Above Named for Jean-Honoré Fragonard, the 18th-century Grasse-born painter, this perfumery is one of the commune's oldest.

regionally; another area is catalogued by olfactory families: floral, fruity, and so on. There are places on the grounds to spread out a prepacked lunch and picnic, or just to sit and breathe in the fragrances.

At Café des Musées, a contemporary cafe near Fragonard, I met with Jessica Buchanan, whose boutique perfume line, 1000 Flowers, I had found online. In 2007, she sold her house in western Canada to study at the Grasse Institute of Perfumery, and she now offers personalized perfumes as well as her own line of fragrances. She lives in Grasse and has a boutique there.

At one time there were many small perfumers in the city, she told me, and although there are fewer now, the growers and perfumers of Grasse consider themselves a family. "There are quite a lot of perfumers here, and then there are the big rock-star perfumers associated with the big brands, but we are all part of this community," she said. "There are perfumers you would never know who work in the big companies and who work on functional products. Their work is just as important as that of big-name perfumers; it's just different."

My next visit was to Molinard, one of the most beautiful old perfumeries in Grasse. It was established in 1849, when the company produced and sold floral waters in a small shop in Grasse's center. The interior blends natural light from skylights with illumination from chandeliers to a royal effect—fitting, since Molinard's color theme is threaded with purple. I was greeted by a raven-haired receptionist who told me a little more about the history of Molinard, and I was reminded of my small bottle of Nirmala, an unusual fragrance the company introduced in 1955.

The oldest perfumery in Grasse is Galimard, which dates to 1747, when Jean de Galimard supplied the French court with olive oils, pomades, and perfumes. I knew I wanted to have my own fragrance

Above A museum of perfume is inevitably also a museum of flowers. This variety is the California poppy.

Below Rose petals at Parfumerie Galimard. Extracting their aroma is big business in Grasse.

Opposite Despite competition from cheap synthetic fragrances, Grasse and its flowers remain the gold standard.

blended while in Grasse, and for this I signed up for a Galimard workshop. Bespoke fragrances involve a considerable amount of time and deliberation, so realistically, I understood I wasn't going to get something spectacular with zero skills; I just wanted to have some fun.

While waiting for the workshop to begin, I inhaled what Galimard had to sell — single fragrances, home scents, and other fragrance-related items — until the friendly woman attending the counter tapped her nose: a gentle suggestion that I stop. She was aware that I was in the next group of budding perfumers, and she wanted my olfactory facility unconfused.

My small workshop group was seated at individual "perfume organs" — each a half circle of small bottles of essential oils and an empty 100-milliliter glass beaker. I felt a twinge of acute uncertainty. I knew what I liked but had no idea what fusion of chemicals would deliver it.

Our chic facilitator, Manon, explained the functions of the top note, the heart note (the dominant character), and the base note, the three stages of a perfume's scent across time. With a little guidance, she helped us establish a rough estimate of what we desired. Beside me, twin girls were fulfilling a birthday wish.

Photographs by Andy Haslam

Direction was offered during the measuring, testing, and smelling. Manon kept an eye out for potential epic fails that occur when using too much of this or that. Two hours later, after I made what seemed like life-threatening decisions, "Lark" was born, and it was far better than I had any right to imagine, at once light and dark (a few of the notes included lotus, bergamot, bois de santal, gardenia, bamboo, and sandalwood).

The sense of smell has a deep drawer and a quick retrieval system. Now back at home, when I wear my almost-homemade fragrance I am transported back to the time when I was in a lovely French town with equally lovely inhabitants who let me sit at their table while they discussed the magical alchemy of perfume.

WHAT TO READ AND WATCH

Perfumes: The Guide, by Luca Turin and Tania Sanchez. A useful guide categorizing scents into groups like "best citrus" and "best bang for the buck," with a glossary of ingredients.

The Perfect Scent: A Year Inside the Perfume Industry in Paris and New York, by Chandler Burr. An insider account by the former perfume critic for *The New York Times*.

The Secret of Chanel No. 5: The Intimate History of the World's Most Famous Perfume, by Tilar J. Mazzeo. A look at the life of Coco Chanel and her best-selling signature scent.

Coco Before Chanel, directed by Anne Fontaine. Audrey Tautou stars as the young Coco Chanel.

The Secret Ways of Perfume, by Cristina Caboni. A popular novel, originally in Italian, whose central character was born gifted with an unusual ability to detect and interpret scent.

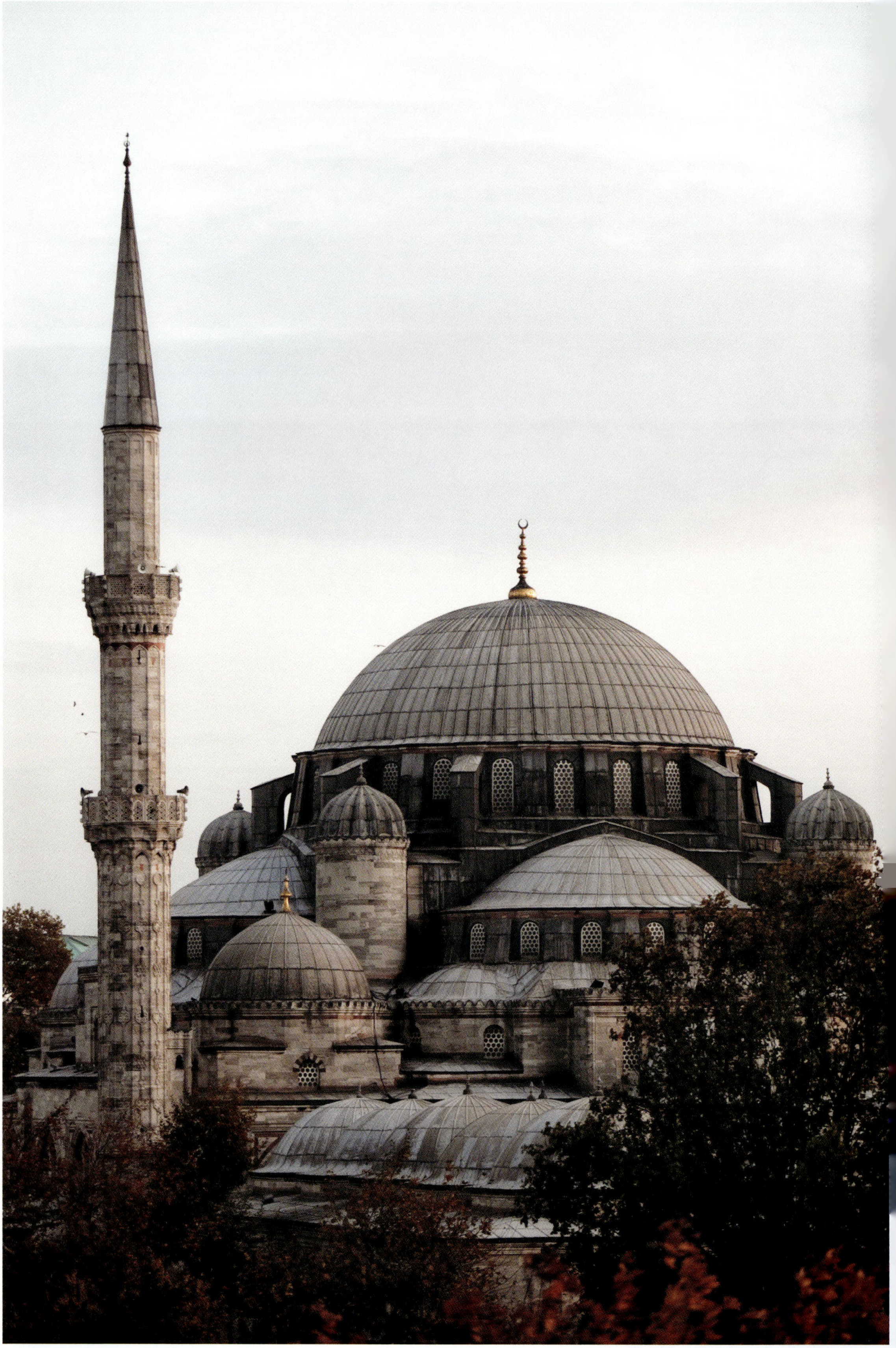

TURKEY   ISTANBUL

THE MOSQUES OF SINAN

The star architect of Istanbul's Ottoman heyday left monumental works all over town. — BY ANDREW FERREN

"The only way to arrive at Semsi Pasha Mosque is by water," my guide said as our little boat dodged two tankers on the Bosporus. On every shore around us, the domes and minarets of some of Istanbul's nearly 3,000 mosques delineated the skyline of a city that looks like no other.

Soon the captain made the first of several attempts to part the row of fishermen casting offshore. Minutes later, amid the cries of seagulls, we disembarked in Uskudar on the Asia side and stood before the 16th-century Semsi Pasha, one of the city's most diminutive mosques, a micro-version of massive temples like the famous Blue Mosque. With its simple stone walls and just a whisper of stained glass in the windows, its understated interior is an elegantly restrained evocation of paradise on earth.

I had come to Turkey on an architectural pilgrimage. After several recent visits to explore the country's contemporary art and design, I yearned to know more about the work of a 16th-century architect and engineer named Sinan. He was hardly just any architect and engineer. Sinan (c. 1490–1588) was chief architect and civil engineer of the Ottoman Empire, working when the empire was at its apogee; his employers, Sultan Suleyman the Magnificent and his heirs, were the most powerful men on earth.

In a career that began when he was 40 and spanned five decades, Sinan built some 300 structures across Eastern Europe and the Middle East. Since most Western visitors to Turkey have never heard of Sinan, guides often compare him to his contemporary, Michelangelo. But given the scope, scale, and sheer quantity of his buildings, that's something of an insult to Sinan, at least where architecture is concerned. Michelangelo made spectacular contributions

Previous The Sehzade Mosque, completed in 1548, was an early work by Mimar Sinan, Ottoman Empire architect for three sultans.

Left The Sultan Suleyman Bridge, built by Sinan in 1567, spans Lake Buyukcekmece outside Istanbul.

Opposite Sinan was a civil engineer as well as an architect. He expanded this Roman aqueduct to bring in more water.

to a few buildings in Rome and Florence. Sinan has hundreds of monumental structures still in daily use, from Belgrade to Mecca. You might say that Sinan was the world's first "starchitect."

Sinan was an innovator of spatial design, "the Euclid of his day," said Dogan Kuban, author of more than 70 books on Islamic architecture. "At St. Peter's in Rome, your eye is drawn to the dome itself," he told me when I contacted him. "Sinan's shallow domes, however, with their abstract painted decoration, seem to magically float overhead. Instead of the structure, you contemplate the space."

I asked the bespoke travel agency Sea Song Tours in Istanbul to provide me with a three-day crash course in Sinan. I wanted to learn how his experimentation with complex geometric compositions transformed thick stone walls into columns, arches, domes, and half domes — and things called spandrels and squinches — as he made the vertical transition from the mosques' square floors to their round ceilings.

My guide, the aptly named Sinan Yalcin, brilliantly zeroed in on the salient details of each building in 20- to 30-minute visits as we zigzagged through Istanbul, crossing back and forth from Europe to Asia by car and boat. Though we moved quickly, ate cheaply and fast in local lunch spots, and nearly froze standing shoeless in vast stone structures in mid-March, it was perhaps the most luxurious trip I've ever taken — 72 hours dedicated to one architectural marvel after another.

The first stop was Sehzade Mosque in the Edirnekapi quarter of Istanbul, built early in Sinan's career. When it was finished in 1548, the architect recognized that he still had something to learn. On the mosque's exterior lateral walls, he cleverly organized the buttresses that support the weight of the dome into orderly colonnades. To create symmetry, he placed doors in the center of those colonnades. But inside the mosque, the doors meant worshippers now came and went from the middle of the room rather than from the back. "A sacred space meant for prayer and contemplation became a passageway," Sinan the guide explained. "It was a mistake he would never repeat."

Nearby is Sinan's most important mosque in Istanbul. Commissioned by Suleyman for his own tomb and completed in 1558, the Suleymaniye Mosque sits atop the most prominent hill above the Golden Horn and remains among the most visible monuments in the city. Sinan artfully modulated the height of the four minarets, enhancing the illusion that the mosque floats above the city. Renewed in a three-year restoration, the vast complex gleams. Still, its monumentality left me a little cold.

To get the blood flowing back into our frozen feet, we walked to our next stop, Rustem Pasha Mosque, nestled in the city's bustling spice market, where merchants crowd the sidewalk and rivers of mostly female shoppers flow through the streets. Sinan solved the problems of placing a house of worship in this less-than-tranquil site by raising the entire complex above street level. Two unassuming staircases lead to a serene plaza floating above the hubbub, but the real treasure awaits within, where brilliant 16th-century Iznik tile work provides worshippers with a garden of cobalt, turquoise, and carnelian tulips and emerald-green leaves.

The next day began early at Mihrimah Sultan II Mosque, which was commissioned by Suleyman's daughter Mihrimah. Entering just after prayers on a gray March morning was like stepping into a box of light. Laced with clear and stained-glass windows, the walls of the mosque are a marvel of 16th-century masonry. Sinan was said to be in love with Mihrimah, but as she was married to Rustem Pasha, Suleyman's grand vizier, he contented himself with making the mosque as luminous as possible to reflect her name, which means "sun and moon." On the summer solstice, it is an ideal place to watch the sun set and the moon rise on opposite sides of the sky.

Sinan the guide was full of juicy tidbits about life in Sinan the architect's day. For instance, despite the Ottomans' highly patriarchal society, daughters like Mihrimah often enjoyed greater wealth and longer life than many of the sultans' sons. On the day a new sultan was proclaimed, his brothers would be killed to avoid power struggles.

This latter point was made as we admired the Selim II tombs situated between the Hagia Sofia and the Blue Mosque, where stylized turbans made of white cloth adorn the caskets containing the bodies of men of the sultan's family. Next door are the restored Hurrem baths, commissioned by Suleyman's beloved Slavic wife Roxelana.

After a fabulously no-fuss lunch of kofte (spiced ground meat patties) and red beans at a local lunch counter, we walked 10 minutes to Sokollu Pasha Mosque, also famous for its gorgeous Iznik tiles. The

Above Men perform ritual washing at the ablutions fountain at the Suleymaniye Mosque in Istanbul.

Opposite Noon prayer at the Mihrimah Sultan I Mosque, completed in 1549.

approach offers a dramatic and ever-expanding view of the sweeping roof that shelters the ablutions fountain in the foreground and the seemingly infinite repetition of domes and arches of the mosque itself. In the middle of the afternoon, we were the only visitors.

It was after this that we took the boat over to Uskudar to see the diminutive Semsi Pasha. From there we walked to the Mihrimah Sultan I Mosque (1549), where Sinan tweaked the double porch—the broad overhang that covers the area where the faithful take their shoes off and where latecomers can kneel in prayer—widening it in a design innovation that was then employed in rural mosques all over the Middle East.

I still had a day to pursue the holy grail of my pilgrimage, Sinan's Selimiye Mosque, a three-hour drive northwest of Istanbul in the city of Edirne, a former Ottoman capital near the Turkish border with Bulgaria and Greece. Sinan considered Selimiye his masterpiece, and in 2011 Unesco agreed with him, declaring the entire mosque complex, known in Turkish as a *kulliye* and featuring schools, almshouses, hospitals, baths, and a covered bazaar, a World Heritage Site.

Sinan's elegantly slender minarets first come into view miles outside of town. As one gets closer, the mosque appears as a tautly composed jumble of shapes—spheres, cones, and cylinders—wrapped in honey-colored sandstone or clad in matte gray lead. However, once past the heavy green curtain that shelters the entrance of virtually all mosques, the artful complexity of the exterior's seemingly impenetrable walls dissolves into a tracery of stone columns and arches embracing one vast, harmonious space.

Despite its astonishing scale—the dome of Selimiye surpasses by a few inches that of the Hagia Sofia—no detail was too small to escape Sinan's attention, from the intricate carving of the *minbar*, or

*Photographs by
Piotr Redlinski*

stepped pulpit, to the hidden relief of an upside-down tulip carved into a column.

Beyond history and architecture, Edirne is known to Turks today as Liver Town—all restaurants serve the stuff, sliced into strips, breaded and fried, and little else. After consulting with several shop owners, Sinan the guide found a place he liked, and we squeezed in amid the locals for a hearty lunch.

Afterward we strolled through the sprawling Rustem Pasha Caravanserai, part of which is now a hotel, en route to the car. On the drive back, we stopped about an hour outside of Istanbul to admire the long and graceful arched stone Sultan Suleyman Bridge. Built by Sinan in 1567, it still holds its own against time and the industrial skyline behind. Then, as darkness fell, we slipped back into the city that five centuries later still belongs to Sinan.

WHAT TO READ

Sinan: The Architect and His Works, by Reha Gunay and Ali Ottoman. Describes Sinan's buildings with photos, floor plans, and a guide to their locations. Gunay has also written a detailed guidebook, *Sinan's Istanbul*.

Istanbul: City of Majesty at the Crossroads of the World, by Thomas F. Madden. A readable history of the city and its role at the center of civilizations from the ancient past to the present.

Sinan Diaryz: A Walking Tour of Mimar Sinan's Monuments, by Ann Pierpont. A guidebook written in part as Sinan's imagined diary.

The Architect's Apprentice: A Novel, by Elif Shafak. Sinan is a prominent character in this vibrant story of Ottoman Istanbul and a young apprentice's quest to find his destiny there.

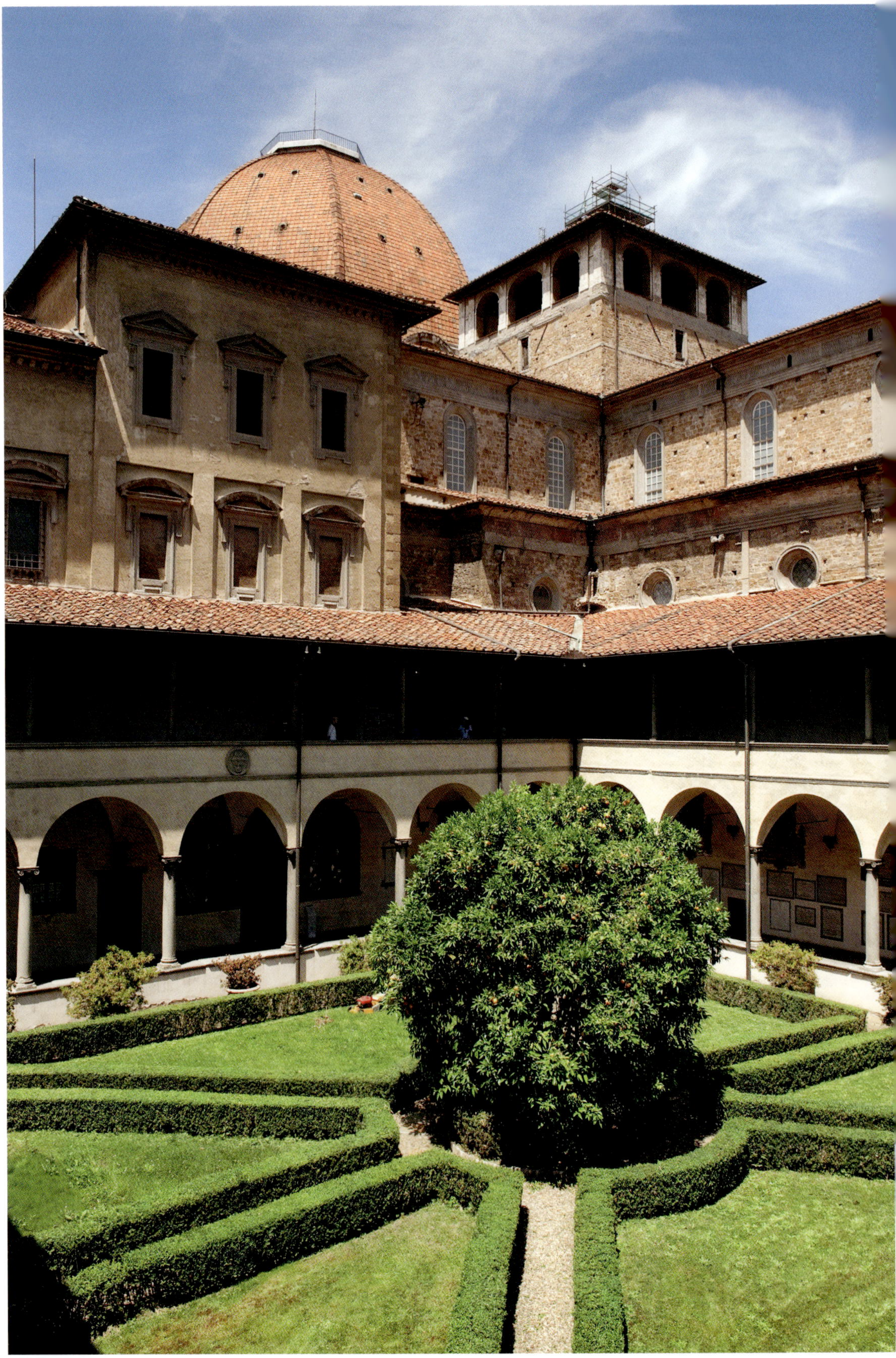

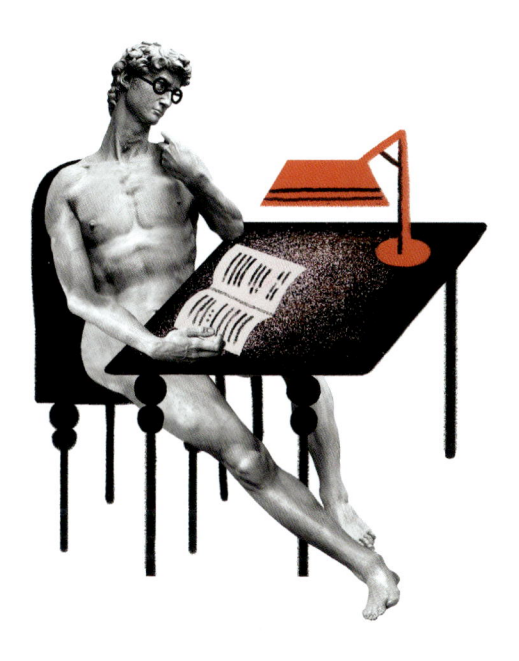

MEETING MICHELANGELO AT THE LIBRARY

The Medici, the doges of Venice, and the scholars of Renaissance Rome knew how to shelve a book in style.
— BY DAVID LASKIN

In the madness of late spring at San Marco Square in Venice, amid the hordes pouring in from land and sea, hard by the hissing espresso machines and sizzling panini presses of overpriced cafes, I found the still point of the turning world.

I found it in the library.

It was 10 in the morning and I was standing, alone and enthralled, on the second-floor balcony of the Biblioteca Nazionale Marciana. Across the Piazzetta rose the Doge's Palace. At my feet, tourist insanity. At my back, an immense, hushed, empty reading room designed by Jacopo Sansovino, a 16th-century Venetian architect and sculptor, and decorated by his contemporaries Titian, Veronese, and Tintoretto.

Why go to the library in Italy when all around you there is fantastic art, exalted architecture, deep history, and intense, passionate people? Because, as I discovered in the course of a rushed but illuminating week dashing from Venice to Rome, Florence, and Milan, Italy's historic libraries contain all of those without the crowds. I hit six libraries in my literary Giro d'Italia, and not once was I shushed or told not to touch.

Carlo Campana, the librarian on duty in the Marciana manuscript room, was typical in his affable erudition. Bald, voluble, with a pirate's flashing grin, he took me on a quick tour of the library's monumental public rooms. Joining me on the balcony off the *salone*, as the palatial reading room is called, he explained that the library was part of a project to create a triumphal entry to the city from the Venetian Lagoon. When the Marciana opened in 1570, Andrea Palladio, the most famous Venetian

Previous A serene cloister at the San Lorenzo Church, the complex that also houses the Laurentian Library.

Left Saint Filippo Neri founded the Oratorians Catholic society and its library, the Biblioteca Vallicelliana, in Rome.

Opposite Drawings by Leonardo da Vinci in the Biblioteca Ambrosiana in Milan.

architect, hailed it as the richest and most ornate building "since Antiquity."

"Situating the library in the most important place in Venice reflects the prestige of the book in the culture of the city," Campana said. Today the library has a million books.

Originally, the salone was filled with walnut desks to which codices (ancient bound manuscripts) were chained, but in 1904 it was converted to an exhibition and lecture space. Today you can visit the salone using the same admission ticket that gives you access to the Doge's Palace and the nearby Correr Museum, or you can ogle the room during a show, talk, or concert. The reading rooms on the ground floor are reserved for scholars.

Most of Italy's splendid old libraries began as the private collections of humanist nobles or cardinals. The Marciana's nucleus was 750 Greek and Latin manuscripts donated to the Venetian Republic in 1468 by the Greek cardinal Basilios Bessarion. With rare exceptions, these Renaissance libraries were originally restricted to elite circles of local aristocrats and scholars. Since Italy was so fragmented politically for much of its history, there was no Italian equivalent of a comprehensive national library until the Biblioteca Nazionale Centrale di Roma was founded in 1876.

When I arrived in Rome, I had two days to squeeze in as many libraries as possible, but after scoping out the Biblioteca Nazionale online I crossed it off my list. With some seven million volumes and 8,000 manuscripts housed in a modernist 1970s-era building in the decidedly uncharming environs of the Termini rail station, this is clearly a place for serious scholars, not dreamy bookish tourists.

I also skipped the Vatican Library—not because I deemed it insufficiently aesthetic, but because it deemed me insufficiently qualified. The library's website states that only "researchers and scholars with appropriate academic qualifications" are allowed access. In the film *Angels & Demons*, the Harvard "symbologist" Robert Langdon (played by Tom Hanks) had no trouble penetrating the Vatican Library and its "secret archives." But I had to content myself with looking over Hanks's shoulder at the (entirely fabricated) bulletproof glass barriers and glinting steel elevator doors that he confronts while battling the forces of evil.

Luckily, Rome has no shortage of important, and stunning, libraries open to the public. I managed to squeeze in three, all in the part of Rome I know and love best—the historic center anchored by Piazza Navona. Now run by the state, they were originally associated with different religious orders and retain some of the unique spirit of the clerics who established them.

To my mind the most fascinating of these clerics was the 16th-century priest (and saint) Filippo Neri, the charismatic founder of the Oratorians and their library, the Biblioteca Vallicelliana. In the tumultuous world of Rome in the Counter-Reformation, Neri was something of a folk hero, a street preacher who devoted his life to the poor and paradoxically won a following among the rich and powerful. The end of Neri's life overlapped with the early career of Caravaggio, and the two shared some of the same unconventional religious fire. Neri's Oratorians took no vows and were bound by no formal rules aside from a commitment to humility and charity, and yet they dwelt here in a gorgeous convent designed by Francesco Borromini, the most sought-after architect in Baroque Rome after Bernini.

"Neri was a mystic of happiness who believed that music was a great 'fisher of souls,'" Paola Paesano, the Vallicelliana Library's stylish young director, told me. "I like to think that the library gives architectural expression to Baroque music."

I grasped what she meant by this when I entered the great reading room. On the coffered ceiling, garlands, stars, and swoops of stucco harmonized in intricate patterns. White pilasters rising at intervals set up a pleasing counterpoint to the walnut tracery of the bookshelves holding Neri's collection. Goethe, who admired Neri and wrote a biography of him, said that "architecture is frozen music." Never before had that old chestnut struck such a resonant chord with me.

I exited the Oratorian convent into the roar of tour buses and scooters on Corso Vittorio Emanuele II. But I was still under Neri's spell, and I ducked into Chiesa Nuova, the superb Baroque church he built beside the convent, to pay my respects at his tomb, where his body lies incorrupt in a gem-encrusted glass case.

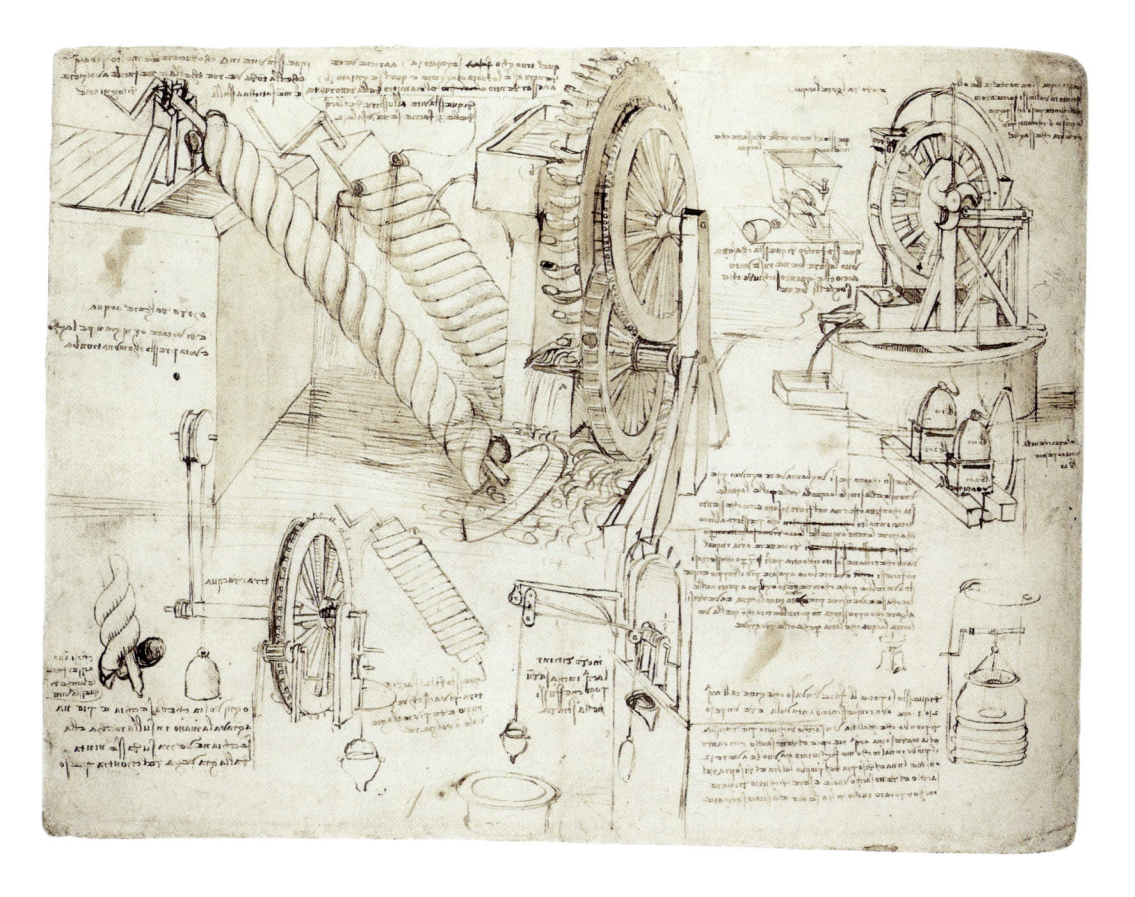

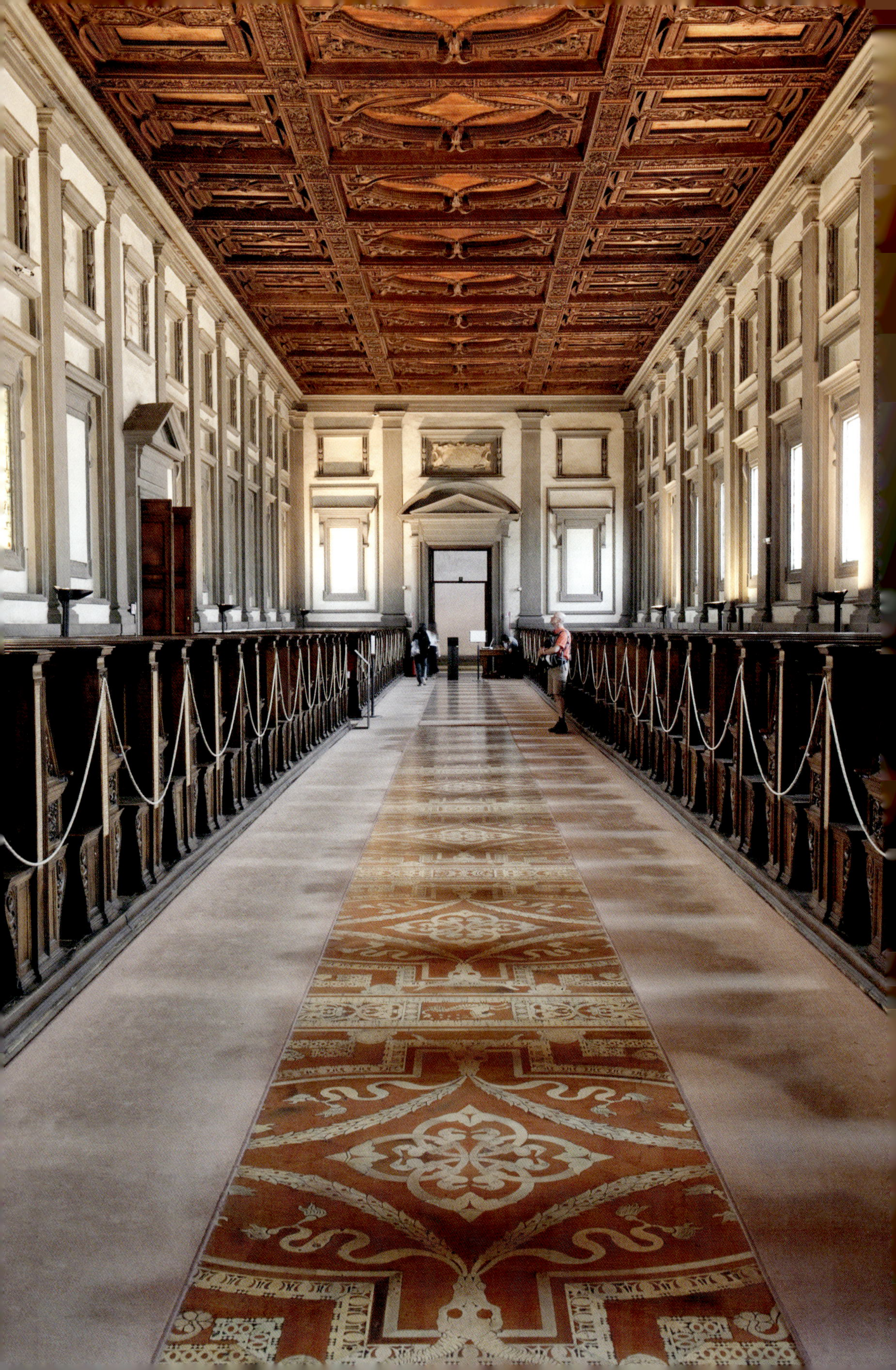

Opposite Michelangelo designed the Laurentian Library in Florence to hold the book collections of the Medici.

Right Sixteenth-century globes at the Biblioteca Vallicelliana in Rome.

The two libraries I visited the next day were a fine study in contrasts. The Angelica, founded by the Augustinian order in 1604 and reckoned by some to have been Europe's first public library, is small, plush, and perfectly faceted, reflecting the wealth of the Augustinians. The Casanatense, founded by the Dominicans, is spartan and muscular, showing its roots in its deep collection of books and codices on doctrine and natural history. Between them is a 10-minute stroll through the densest and most history-encrusted area of Rome.

Were I a resident of Rome instead of a tourist, my dream day would begin in the Basilica di Sant'Agostino, adjacent to the Angelica, with a moment of reverence before Caravaggio's humbly ravishing *Madonna di Loreto*. Then I would settle into a leather chair in the Angelica's main reading room. I'd ask the staff to fetch me Cicero's *De Oratore*, just so I could breathe in the scent of the first volume printed in Italy (1465), and then I'd peek into the precious early edition of Dante's *Divine Comedy*.

"The salone of the Angelica is a kind of *vaso dei libri* — a vessel of books," the library's brisk director, Fiammetta Terlizzi, told me proudly as we surveyed the four tiers of bookshelves lining the walls of this splendid chamber. "The room has the height and perspective of a cathedral." For all its loftiness, it has space for only a couple of dozen readers, all of them seated in chairs facing in the same direction. When these lucky few look up from the page, their eyes rest on a soaring altar of books bathed in celestial light.

The elegantly spare reading room at the Casanatense is the perfect antidote for what the writer Eleanor Clark called the "too-muchness" of Rome. Whitewashed, cavernous, and presided over by a pair of enormous 18th-century globes, it is now used for exhibits and lectures. The rest of the library is a delightful warren of more whimsically decorated chambers — an alcove for the card catalog; the frescoed Saletta di Cardinale, or "little hall," of Cardinal Girolamo Casanate, who founded the library in 1700; an airy corner room reserved for laptop-wielding students; a hushed darker space for scholars consulting manuscripts. Among the Casanatense's most prized holdings are the personal papers of the composer Niccolò Paganini and an illuminated 14th-century *Teatrum Sanitatis* with vivid depictions of medieval daily life.

After my two days in Rome, I headed to Florence to check out the only library designed by Michelangelo, the Biblioteca Medicea Laurenziana, or Laurentian Library, built to house the book collections of the Medici. Though summer was still a month away,

Above The Biblioteca Casanatense in Rome. Among its holdings are the papers of the violinist and composer Niccolò Paganini.

Opposite The Biblioteca Angelica in Rome. Each of Italy's splendid old libraries has its own beauty and character.

Florence was already dense with tourists. But the cloister of the Church of San Lorenzo, which houses the Laurenziana, was so deserted when I arrived at 11 a.m. that I wondered if I had come to the right place. I bought my ticket, followed the signs, and pushed open the door, and for the next hour I had Michelangelo pretty much to myself.

"Austere" was the word that came to mind as I ascended a flight of oval steps carved from a somber, gray stone. But no adjective I know does justice to the reading room. Rows of walnut benches that ingeniously double as lecterns — *plutei*, they are called — flank the sides of a central corridor paved in intricately patterned rose and cream terra-cotta. Along the two lateral walls, stained glass windows face each other in precise rectangular alignment, illuminating the benches. The heavily carved wooden ceiling seems to flatten and deepen the space to infinity, like the vanishing point in a Renaissance landscape painting.

Michelangelo's library is so rational, so resolute, so majestically realized that not in my wildest dreams could I imagine working here. It is now primarily a showpiece, with side rooms of a later and lesser vintage used for lectures and exhibits. Scholars from all over the world labor in less imposing spaces tucked away in the cloister.

"There is a small club of libraries with truly deep holdings, and we are part of it," said Giovanna Rao, the director of the library, when we met in her office, a former monastic cell. "Our manuscript collection, which runs to 11,000 items, rivals that of the British Library or the National Library of France, though we are not a national library. And of course, no other library enjoys the good fortune of having Michelangelo as its architect."

There was one more library on my itinerary, the Biblioteca Ambrosiana in Milan. With a collection of ancient manuscripts rivaling the Vatican's, the

Photographs by Susan Wright

Ambrosian Library is world-class. But nonscholars like me are not deprived of its riches. Its ornate 17th-century reading room, the Sala Federiciana, is used to display its greatest treasure: Leonardo's Codex Atlanticus, a collection of 1,119 sheets of drawings and captions on subjects ranging from botany to warfare.

Surrounded by the gilded and sepia spines that line this mellow chamber, and dwarfed by its white barrel-vaulted ceiling, I lost myself for half an hour in Leonardo's inspired doodles of catapults, primordial pontoon bridges, and tripod-mounted cannons — ingenious improvisations of a relentless polymath.

Only in Italy, I reflected, and only in a library, could I stand alone and undisturbed in the center of a great city and peer into the mind of genius.

WHAT TO READ AND WATCH

The Library at Night, by Alberto Manguel. An author's exploration of the meaning of libraries through history.

The World's Most Beautiful Libraries, by Massimo Listri. A photographic journey published by TASCHEN.

The Library Book, by Susan Orlean. For lovers of libraries, a collection of facts and curious stories about their meaning in people's lives.

The Bookseller of Florence, by Ross King. The flowering of the Renaissance as experienced by Vespasiano da Bisticci, "a maker of books and a merchant of knowledge" whose wares enriched the libraries of popes and princes.

Angels & Demons, directed by Ron Howard. Tom Hanks confronts the Vatican Library in this film adaptation of the novel by Dan Brown.

THE SHIP

FLAXMAN COURT W1
CITY OF WESTMINSTER

FOR JIMI HENDRIX FANS, A MUST-SEE SPOT IN LONDON

Improbably, a rock icon shares museum space with a star of the Baroque, G. F. Handel. — BY JUSTIN SABLICH

As the story goes, one fateful night in the late 1960s Jimi Hendrix, best known for changing the music world with his guitar playing, set free two ring-necked parakeets on Carnaby Street, and that's why thousands of the nonnative birds haunt London's parks to this day.

"Absolute rubbish," Christian Lloyd, a musicologist at Queen's University in Kingston, Ontario, said in an interview. "It's the kind of thing people want to be true, but it's just not true."

Lloyd would know. His research, along with relics that Hendrix fans would drool over, like Hendrix's broken Fender Stratocaster from a 1969 Royal Albert Hall performance, is on display at Handel & Hendrix in London, a residence-turned-museum dedicated to the two musical giants who lived there about 200 years apart: Hendrix and George Frideric Handel.

Parakeets may not be part of Hendrix's legacy in London, but he nevertheless left his mark. The several months he spent there, spread throughout the final five years of his life, were pivotal in his meteoric rise. During some of that time he lived, entertained friends, and made music in a flat at 23 Brook Street in Mayfair. In the 18th century, Handel lived next door at No. 25, and the two houses, which date from the early 1700s, are now joined as Handel & Hendrix.

Hendrix fans may or may not be surprised to be rubbing elbows with Handel devotees, and vice versa, but the museum is dedicated to both, and the mix seems to work. The Hendrix apartment is smaller than the formal Handel rooms, but it is deeply atmospheric. Decorated just as he and his girlfriend at the time, Kathy Etchingham, had it, the flat evokes both Hendrix himself and the music scene of the '60s.

London was where the nomadic Hendrix found the closest thing to "a real home," as he put it, and where

LONDON   ENGLAND

Previous The Ship, one of Hendrix's favorite London pubs, remains a popular music-business hangout.

Left Hendrix in his flat at 23 Brook Street. A couple of centuries earlier, Handel, the Baroque music star, lived at No. 25.

Opposite The album cover for *Are You Experienced*, released in 1967. Hendrix's time in London was pivotal in his career.

his life was cut short at the age of 27. Along with the apartment, today's London also retains enough of what appealed to him personally to make for a proper Jimi Hendrix experience more than 50 years since he last called it home.

The concept of home was a complicated one for Johnny Allen Hendrix, born in Seattle in 1942. He was sent to live with his grandmother in Canada when he was 6, and his parents divorced two years later. His mother died of alcohol-related illness when he was 15. After a year in California with the United States Army at age 18, he found his true calling in 1962 as a touring musician.

By the time he ended up in New York in September 1966, performing in small cafes under the name "Jimmy James," he had developed a "fugitive kind of mentality," according to Lloyd. This is where Chas Chandler, who had recently quit the Animals and wanted to begin a new career as a manager, was blown away by what he saw and asked Hendrix if he'd come with him to London.

"I'm in England, Dad," Hendrix told his father over the phone. "I met some people, and they're going to make me a big star. We changed my name to J-I-M-I," The decision on the name change was made on the flight over.

On his first night in London he met Etchingham, a former DJ and a familiar face around the city's thriving rock scene, and thus began what would be the most significant romantic relationship of his life. Before living at Brook Street, they moved into an apartment owned by Ringo Starr at 34 Montagu Square.

"During our first weeks together, we did a little shopping and sightseeing and I introduced him to friends," Etchingham wrote in her memoir, *Through Gypsy Eyes*. "Because we didn't have much money we went everywhere on the Underground." Hendrix had never been outside of North America before, and like any other first-time visitor to London, he was drawn to attractions like Buckingham Palace and the Houses of Parliament.

"It's a different kind of atmosphere here. People are more mild-mannered. I like all the little streets and the boutiques. It's like a kind of fairyland," Hendrix would later say of London.

His flamboyant style, from his fashion sense to his approach to rock and blues, was a perfect match for mid-1960s London, as "everyone is starting to experiment: in fashion, in art, in lifestyles," Lloyd said.

Hendrix accentuated his look with accessories from Portobello Road, which today claims to be the world's largest antiques market. While most of his favorite London stores have since closed, Lloyd said Pretty Green on Carnaby Street, owned by Liam Gallagher of Oasis fame, would have drawn Hendrix in and has even released its own Hendrix-themed line of shirts.

"I arrived here with just the suit I stood up in. I'm going back with the best wardrobe of gear that Carnaby Street can offer," Hendrix said before his first stint in London ended.

His scope of the city expanded dramatically after forming the Jimi Hendrix Experience in October 1966 — with bassist Noel Redding and drummer Mitch Mitchell — as relentless performing led him to all corners of London. Some of the venues where he played can still be visited.

"He played Chislehurst Caves, which is literally a cave," Lloyd said. "God knows what the sound was like in there." Other bands that performed there include the Rolling Stones, the Who, and the Yardbirds. The caves, a labyrinth of tunnels under southeast London, were originally dug for mining flint and chalk, dating all the way back to the 13th century. They have been used for various purposes, including the cultivation of mushrooms, a bomb shelter during World War II, and, for some reason, a music venue during the 1950s and 1960s. Today, you can take a guided tour.

The venues would get bigger after the British release of the band's first album, *Are You Experienced*, in May 1967. It spent 33 weeks on the charts, reaching No. 2. The album's cover, now a staple of psychedelic rock era art, included a fish-eye lens photograph of the band taken by Karl Ferris in Kew Gardens, the botanical garden in southwest London.

"After the session, to celebrate, we walked across the road to an ancient Elizabethan pub and downed many ales and smoked joints in the garden," Ferris said. "It was a good thing that we had a chauffeur to drive us back to London." The pub was the Flower and Firkin, now called the Tap on the Line.

Another pub for Hendrix fans is the Ship on Wardour Street, close to where the Marquee Club once was. It remains a popular music business hangout. "He would walk in there and recognize it instantly," Lloyd said of Hendrix.

By the time Hendrix returned to London in July 1968, he was a major star. Etchingham chose the Brook Street flat, and they moved in. Hendrix lived there between tours in 1968 and more steadily during the first three months of 1969. The space was a "bed-sit," a studio apartment, but the couple partied with friends and Hendrix jammed with fellow musicians. He also hosted members of the media for interviews.

"He sat on the bed, holding forth and rolling joints," Lloyd said. "What rock star's bedroom would you get into these days? You wouldn't even get near the house."

In the apartment now, the turquoise velvet curtains (originally purchased from John Lewis on nearby Oxford Street), red Persian rugs, Bohemian knick-knacks, and piles of vintage vinyl appear at first glance to be the actual artifacts, but almost all of the items in the room are replicas. Hendrix requested that most of his possessions be destroyed after the couple had separated later in 1969.

Thanks to Etchingham's involvement and enough old photos to go by, replacement items were acquired through 1960s memorabilia auctions while others, like the pink-and-orange striped bedspread, were remade to match the originals.

"She was able to recollect an incredible amount of colors and textures that the black-and-white photographs couldn't give us; gradually the room was restored back to its former glory," Claire Davies, Handel & Hendrix's deputy director, said. "She also had so many stories about Jimi's brief moment of

Above The restored Hendrix flat. Kathy Etchingham, who shared it with him, helped bring back its 1960s appearance.

Opposite The Flower and Firkin, now called the Tap on the Line, was one of the pubs where Hendrix relaxed with friends.

domesticity with her in the flat that helped to shape our narrative."

Elsewhere in the exhibit, visitors can sift through a re-creation of Hendrix's record collection, mainly a mix of blues (Muddy Waters, Howlin' Wolf) and rock (the Beatles, Bob Dylan, and Cream). He also owned two copies of Handel's *Messiah*.

Upscale Mayfair may have seemed like an odd area for a counterculture rock star to live, but it drew many industry types and was close to several clubs and studios. Venues that still exist include the Court (formerly Bag O'Nails) and the Scotch of St. James on Mason's Yard, where Hendrix and others of London's rock elite performed and socialized, including members of the Beatles and the Who. The Court is for members only, but a blue plaque commemorating Hendrix's first performance there is outside.

When it came to food, Mr. Love, a restaurant on the ground floor of the apartment building, was the go-to, with steak and chips a recurring order. Hendrix was not particularly fond of traditional English food.

"See, English food, it's difficult to explain," he told *Melody Maker* magazine. "You get mashed potatoes with just about everything, and I ain't gonna say anything good about that."

Ultimately, Hendrix's time in Mayfair was short but meaningful.

"When you think of how short his adult life was, it's actually a fairly significant chunk," Lloyd said. "It's also the part where it all starts going wrong for him in some ways."

Hendrix's career took him back to the United States in March 1969. Etchingham joined him briefly, but Hendrix wouldn't commit to moving back to London, so the couple split in April.

Shortly afterward, the Experience broke up as well, and while Hendrix continued performing, he never would put out another official studio album.

Photographs by Andy Haslam

His final major performance in England was in August 1970 at the Isle of Wight Festival, and on September 18 he was found dead of an apparent drug overdose in Room 507 of London's Samarkand Hotel on Lansdowne Crescent.

While something may have kept bringing him back to London, there's no telling if a roamer like Hendrix would have ever truly laid roots down, had he lived longer.

"I'm scared of vegetating." Hendrix said. "I have to move on. I dig Britain, but I haven't really got a home anywhere. The Earth's my home."

WHAT TO READ AND WATCH

Room Full of Mirrors: A Biography of Jimi Hendrix, by Charles R. Cross, Lloyd James, and others. "The perfect nostalgia item.... But it works equally well for readers who need to be told why *Time* magazine did a 'Swinging London' cover story in 1966." — Janet Maslin in *The New York Times*.

American Masters: Jimi Hendrix — Hear My Train a Comin' directed by Bob Smeaton. A PBS biographical documentary. Exhaustive and well produced, with performance footage, home movies, and more.

Jimi: All Is by My Side, directed by John Ridley. Biopic focusing on Hendrix's experiences in 1966 and 1967, including time in London. Starring André Benjamin of Outkast as Hendrix.

Jimi Hendrix: Live at Woodstock, directed by Michael Wadley. Hendrix's hourlong performance at the Woodstock festival in 1969, including his strikingly original rendition of "The Star-Spangled Banner."

CHARLES
DE GAULLE

1890–1970

THE LONDON LEGACY OF CHARLES DE GAULLE

After the Nazis took France, de Gaulle operated from Britain, marshaling the will of the French to resist and survive. — BY ANN MAH

With its bland architecture and gray concrete pavement, little distinguishes Curzon Square from its surroundings in the heart of London's Mayfair district. But it was here that Charles de Gaulle wrote a speech that would change his country's fate and, he believed, fulfill his destiny.

On June 17, 1940, still reeling from France's fall to Nazi Germany three days earlier, de Gaulle fled to London, where he borrowed a friend's apartment at 3 Curzon Square (then called Seamore Grove) and drafted a passionate call to arms. The next day he broadcast a message on BBC radio — a direct, clarion appeal to the French people:

"I, General de Gaulle, now in London, call on all French officers and men who are at present on British soil, or may be in the future, with or without their arms; I call on all engineers and skilled workmen from the armaments factories who are at present on British soil, or may be in the future, to get in touch with me."

De Gaulle's initial broadcast reached only a few parts of occupied France. (Subsequent transmissions on June 19 and 22 reached greater swaths of Vichy territory.) But today it is considered one of the most significant moments in French history, even honored with its own square in Paris, Place du 18 Juin 1940.

The building that held de Gaulle's borrowed apartment is gone, replaced by another. But the site where it stood is still a place to contemplate the final words of that speech: "Whatever happens, the flame of French resistance must not and shall not die."

The scars of World War II have largely faded from central London, but the memory of Britain's finest hour, as Winston Churchill unforgettably called it,

Previous A statue of Charles de Gaulle near 4 Carlton Gardens, where the Free French Forces had their headquarters.

Left De Gaulle with Queen Elizabeth, the wife of King George VI and mother of Elizabeth II, in 1941.

Opposite The Royal Automobile Club, where Free French soldiers mingled with English officers.

lingers in a seemingly endless parade of popular books, television shows, and films. Amid these stories of British resilience, the history of the Free French in London is often overlooked. But de Gaulle's three years in exile there, defined by isolation, determination, and a sense of destiny, were crucial both to him and to France.

In 1940, as now, Mayfair had an air of starchy establishment, anchored by embassies, banks, and gentlemen's clubs, which served as social hubs for an elite membership. Into this rarefied world dropped Charles de Gaulle, a tall, awkward man of 49, recently promoted to the rank of general. He brought with him his aide-de-camp Geoffroy Chodron de Courcel and 100,000 francs of secret government funds.

"On the 18th of June, he was a man alone," said Hubert Rault, who leads walking tours with his company, de Gaulle in London, as I stood with him on Curzon Square. "He didn't even speak English. But he came to England because he needed support from Churchill. He knew without English support, there would be no Free French."

Churchill, an early advocate of de Gaulle, overruled objections in his cabinet to allow the June 18 radio address. Ten days later, he officially recognized de Gaulle as the head of the Free French Forces. As he later wrote in his memoirs, Churchill believed de Gaulle was *l'homme du destin* — the man of destiny.

With Rault as my guide, I set out to find de Gaulle's haunts among the elite addresses of London's West End. At St. James's Square we stopped to admire a pretty Georgian building that once housed the Petit Club Français, a wartime watering hole for French exiles and their friends; it is now the Royal Naval and Military Club. A few steps away is Norfolk House, a wide brick building where General Dwight D. Eisenhower planned the Allied invasion of Normandy. Along Pall Mall, the Royal Automobile Club looms in Beaux-Arts splendor; during the war, it offered free membership to Free French soldiers, who frequented the dining room as their canteen.

The back of the Royal Automobile Club faces Carlton Gardens, a quiet dead-end street where, at No. 4, a tall, plain building served as the headquarters of the Free French Forces. A small blue plaque honors de Gaulle, while a second, larger panel displays a version of his famous appeal, embellished with French flags, the Lorraine Cross (the symbol of the Free French), and, running across the bottom, the words "Vive La France!"

Today the building houses the offices of a financial firm and is closed to the public. At Rault's urging,

I peered closely at third-floor corner windows, glimpsing a second set of dark wood window frames behind the newer facade. "That was de Gaulle's office," he said. "I was invited inside a few years ago, and they've kept it exactly as it was." A photograph of de Gaulle shot by Cecil Beaton at Carlton Gardens shows a solitary man standing before his desk with crossed arms, his features only half illuminated by the light from the windows.

Across the street, a life-size bronze statue, unveiled by Queen Elizabeth in 1993, depicts de Gaulle standing with an outstretched hand. Though it is ringed with fencing, I saw that someone had managed to tuck a bouquet of silk flowers at the bottom of the pedestal, adorned with a tricolor ribbon that read "Forces Navales Françaises Libres" — Free French Naval Forces — and "en souvenir" — in remembrance.

In 1940, a small and motley group of volunteers worked at Carlton Gardens. (By D-Day, they numbered 600.) Some were French soldiers who had been serving in Britain when France fell; others had heard de Gaulle's radio appeal and braved incredible odds to join him. These men and women soon found themselves in the eye of the Blitz. The near-daily air raids drove people into shelters like the Down Street Tube station, a brisk walk from Carlton Gardens. De Gaulle may have visited this station, which was Churchill's first bunker meeting room. Today it is out of use, and only a shiny, red-tiled facade hints at its history as a Tube stop.

But what of de Gaulle's personal life? How, if at all, did he relax? I found my way to the French House in Soho, a former favorite pub of Free French Forces. One tall tale claims that de Gaulle wrote his famous June 18 appeal here, and even though I knew that wasn't true, the pub's old-fashioned atmosphere — with its wooden bar, paneled walls papered in black-and-white photos, and low-wattage globe sconces — did have a feeling of the 1940s. Still, as I sat at a sticky table sipping a Kir amid a boisterous after-work

IMPERIAL
WAR MUSEUM

HEN·VIII·REGE·FVNDATVM·CIVIVM·LARGITAS·PERFECIT

Opposite The Imperial War Museum in London includes the stories of French men and women who fought for Britain.

Above The atrium of the Imperial War Museum. Some French citizens received British military decorations for valor.

crowd, I had a hard time picturing the general here. "He wasn't really a pub man," Rault had told me.

Presumably he was more comfortable at Berry Bros. & Rudd, a London wine and spirits merchant, where he kept an account. Founded in 1698, the family business still occupies its original 17th-century storefront, a room with wide-planked floors and timber-framed walls that "looks very much like de Gaulle would have seen it," said Maggie Huntingford, who was behind the front desk during my visit. Today this building is used as offices while, around the corner, a bright and modern retail shop sells an impressive array of bottles. I looked for de Gaulle's favorite drink, Armagnac, and found a range spanning over a hundred years, beginning with 1897.

Back on Pall Mall, I strolled past some of de Gaulle's frequent lunch spots: the Carlton Club, an exclusive establishment where Churchill was a member; the Ritz; and the Cavalry and Guards Club. At the grand Connaught hotel he dined regularly on roast beef and Yorkshire pudding, which he referred to as "island specialties." He also kept rooms on the hotel's top floor and lived there during the Blitz while his family took shelter near the Welsh border.

De Gaulle's wife and three children — who had endured a harrowing escape across the English Channel in June 1940 — spent long periods apart from him, tucked away in different corners of rural England. After the Blitz, they joined him in a house in Hampstead, in north London.

Compared with Mayfair's stately grandeur, Hampstead twinkles with village charm. Amid a web of narrow lanes edged with trees, hedgerows, and attached houses, the general's house stands at 99 Frognal Road, an elegant three-story brick villa with tall French windows. A brick wall surrounded the garden where Yvonne de Gaulle kept chickens so that their youngest daughter, Anne, could have fresh

Above De Gaulle liked the Connaught Hotel's roast beef and Yorkshire pudding, which he called "island specialties."

Opposite Tables set at the Ritz Hotel for afternoon tea. De Gaulle often went there for lunch.

eggs. Now called St. Dorothy's Convent, the house is a residence for international women students. A plaque honoring de Gaulle is almost hidden by the garden wall.

Nearby is St. Mary's Hampstead, a slender white church established in 1816 by the Abbé Jean Jacques Morel, a priest who fled France after the 1789 revolution. De Gaulle worshipped there regularly — a sign near the door said "his tall and impressive figure was always to be seen in the front bench at the 11 o'clock Mass whenever he was home."

By the time de Gaulle moved to Hampstead in September 1942, his relationship with Churchill had grown contentious. Though they shared a mutual respect, they clashed frequently. In May 1943 de Gaulle moved his headquarters to Algiers, which had just been liberated from Nazi control by the Allied invasion of North Africa. In departure, he left a letter for Churchill, who was in Washington meeting President Franklin D. Roosevelt, in which he expressed no thanks for British help. (At the same time, Churchill was unsuccessfully lobbying the British cabinet to end its support of de Gaulle.) In the years since the liberation of Paris, the story of the Free French Forces in London has slipped away, and French gratitude to Britain has gone unmarked by an official monument.

Or has it?

On my last afternoon in London, I visited old Broadcasting House, the BBC's original headquarters. Built in 1932, the building is an Art Deco icon, a round tower adorned with the works of the sculptor Eric Gill. I was there to see the place where de Gaulle made his June 18 appeal and went on to speak in dozens more broadcasts.

Robert Seatter, the head of BBC history, led me to the Artists' Lobby, once the green room for visiting performers. After showing me an enormous wartime microphone, he paused before a gold-and-black

Photographs by
Tom Jamieson

tapestry, *Le Poète*, which was created by the French artist Jean Lurçat as homage to the poem "Liberté," written by Paul Éluard during the Nazi occupation.

"A lot of people don't realize how important the BBC was to landlocked Europe," Seatter said. At the beginning of the war, the BBC's wartime foreign-language programming—the only reliable news source for many in France and other countries of occupied Europe—was broadcast in eight languages; by the end, that had grown to 48. "If you could only see us listening to your broadcasts," wrote one French listener at the time. "We only live for that." In 1949, the French government gave the tapestry to the BBC to express thanks for its wartime service.

I gazed at the tapestry, which depicts a male silhouette hidden behind a screen of leaves. It was a metaphor of liberty, a symbol of gratitude never forgotten.

WHAT TO READ AND WATCH

The General: Charles de Gaulle and the France He Saved, by Jonathan Fenby. A thorough and detailed biography. "Dare I call a 707-page biography a page-turner?" — Josef Joffe in *The New York Times*.

De Gaulle, by Julian Jackson. A 2018 biography placing Charles de Gaulle in context as the leading French figure of the 20th century.

The Liberation of Paris: How Eisenhower, de Gaulle, and von Choltitz Saved the City of Light, by Jean Edward Smith. Clear, concise, and vivid storytelling from a respected historian and biographer.

Charles de Gaulle: The Last King of France, directed by Patrick Rotman. A documentary of de Gaulle's years as president of France, revealing of his character and powers of persuasion.

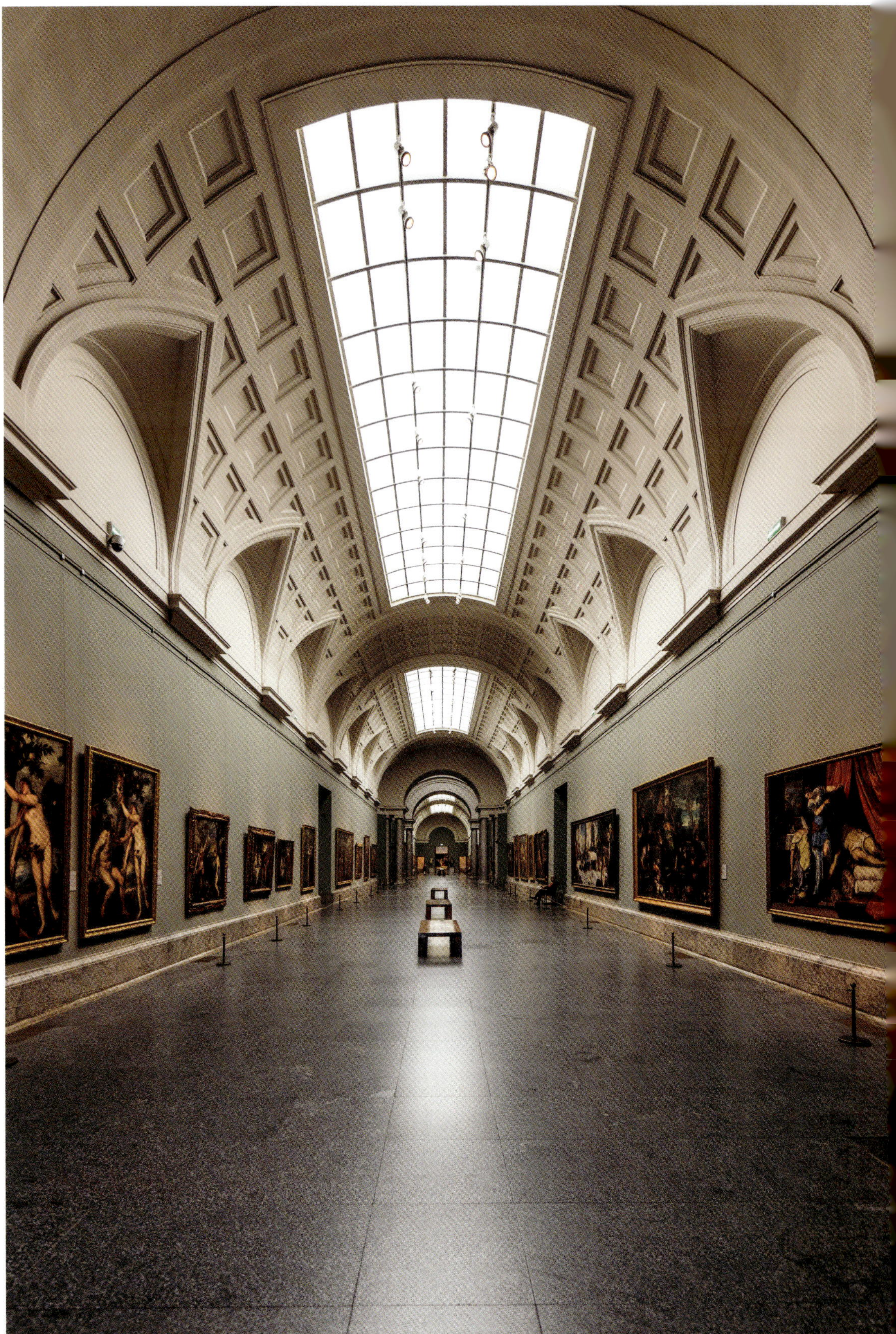

SEVEN HOURS IN THE PRADO

When you've gotten a little too used to your neighborhood world-class art gallery, there's a way to keep from taking it for granted. — BY ANDREW FERREN

It's often said that we don't appreciate what we have until it's gone. In the early 19th century, Spain's royal family had time to ruminate on that axiom when they lost not only their throne — to Napoleon's brother, Joseph Bonaparte — but also hundreds of priceless paintings and other treasures that were stripped from Spanish palaces, monasteries, and churches and carted off to Paris by the French army.

With Napoleon's defeat in 1814, both the throne and the artworks were returned to the restored Spanish monarch, Ferdinand VII, who had used his time off as ruler to hatch a plan for safeguarding his collection for future generations. Spurred by his culturally enlightened second wife, Maria Isabel de Braganza, Ferdinand created the Royal Museum of Paintings in Madrid in 1819. Beginning with about 300 masterpieces from the so-called Golden Age of Spanish painting in the 16th and 17th centuries, the museum grew to include art from across Europe. Today, vastly expanded and known as the Prado, it is one of the world's great repositories of Western art.

All of Spain honors this magnificent museum, but for the individual who discovers it, the Prado experience is personal too. It was part of the reason I chose to live in Madrid. But after 17 years and more than 200 visits I began to wonder if it was too familiar. Was I, like the pre-Napoleon Ferdinand VII, beginning to take something I loved for granted? It was time, I decided, to renew my knowledge of the entire museum — every gallery, vestibule, and passageway in which art is displayed.

I began my project on a chilly Tuesday, envisioning myself back home by 2 p.m. But once inside, circumstances quickly intervened. By circumstances I mean

Previous If you have just one day in Madrid and want to see the Prado, you need a strategy.

Left Amid all the highlights there's still room for a surprise, perhaps this glassware, part of the 16th- and 17th-century Dauphin's Treasure collection.

Opposite The Prado, pictured in 1890, began as a museum for natural sciences, but in 1819 it opened as a public art gallery.

lingering in galleries I'd been accustomed to breezing through; resting on a bench while surreptitiously listening to elementary school children decide which baby is Jesus (he's the one with the halo in the *Adoration of the Magi*, by Rubens); getting to know a bevy of sexy Greek and Roman mythological figures; and discovering some new (to me) Spanish artists of astonishing talent. I ended up staying—thirsty, hungry, and exhausted at times, but blissfully happy—until 5 p.m.

If you have just one day and want to see the whole Prado, you need a strategy. The numbering of the museum's 120 galleries isn't much help. Gallery 1, for example, connects to Galleries 4, 24, and 42 but not to Gallery 2.

I began in Gallery 75 on the ground level, one of the 19th-century galleries. In the art world, there is not much love for Spanish 19th-century painting after the great Francisco de Goya, who died in 1828. But these galleries handily illustrate the period of the museum's founding, starting with a regal portrait by Goya of a distrustful-looking King Ferdinand VII.

Known as *el Rey Felón* (the Felon King), he was something of a retrograde despot who as crown prince conspired against his father and as king abolished Spain's first constitution. If the Prado was his great gift to Spain, then perhaps Goya's great gift to posterity was the ability to convey Ferdinand's devious character in this portrait that the king himself would approve. Ferdinand's pro-museum wife, Maria Isabel de Braganza, is here as well, sculpted in marble in the style of a Roman empress by José Álvarez Cubero. And there's a marvelously large 1787 wooden architectural model of the Prado itself that looks like an elaborate royal toy.

The neighboring galleries display pastoral landscapes, portraits of bourgeois matrons, and melodramatic history paintings. On my visit, one group of high school students sat on the floor in front of Goya's *The Second of May*, 1808, discussing the swirling street battle it shows, while others tried to decipher his enigmatic "black paintings," images of witchcraft and raw human brutality painted in the turbulent aftermath of the Napoleonic wars.

After those unsettling works, Galleries 71 through 74 provide a welcome intermezzo of gleaming Greek and Roman sculptures. Though it's little known, the Prado displays more than 250 sculptures, including several purchased in Rome by Velázquez on behalf of King Philip IV in the 17th century.

Back toward the center of the museum, the tour takes on more chronological coherence, starting with the Italian Renaissance. With wealth pouring in from the American colonies from the 16th century onward, Spain's rulers had deep pockets for buying art. The first Hapsburg emperor, Charles V, and his son Philip II had the taste to match their resources and acquired the best of the best. Exploring Galleries 49 and 56B is like stepping into a textbook of Italian Renaissance and Mannerist art, with no fewer than seven glorious Raphaels as well as works by Mantegna, Fra Angelico, Botticelli, Correggio, Andrea del Sarto, Bronzino, and Parmigianino. With so many beloved masterpieces, it's easy to just ricochet from painting to painting.

Under Charles V, the Flanders region became linked to the Spanish crown, and Flemish paintings began making their way to Spain. One work not to be missed is Rogier van der Weyden's *Descent from the Cross*. The artist's shallow pictorial space pushes the nearly life-size figures taking Christ's body off the cross into our world, making the pathos — translucent tears stream down several faces — all the more powerful. It's so moving that people often drift away from it without noticing that hanging nearby are paintings by artists like Robert Campin and Hans Memling.

While the school groups slipped off for lunch, the throngs of grown-ups in the Flemish galleries were thickening. I didn't get into the melee in front of Hieronymus Bosch's famous triptych *The Garden of Earthly Delights*, a cinematic and fantastically freakish portrayal of the fall from paradise to hell, but went instead to his other works, like *The Haywain*, and to paintings by Pieter Bruegel the Elder, Albrecht Dürer, and Joachim Patinir, the latter a painter of luminous landscapes with scarcely a penitent saint or writhing sinner in sight.

It was 1 p.m., my iPhone had already clocked 7,600 steps, and I still had two floors to go. At this point, I would typically have headed to the main level where the art shifts gear to the dramatic Baroque. On this day, however, I had promised to first reacquaint

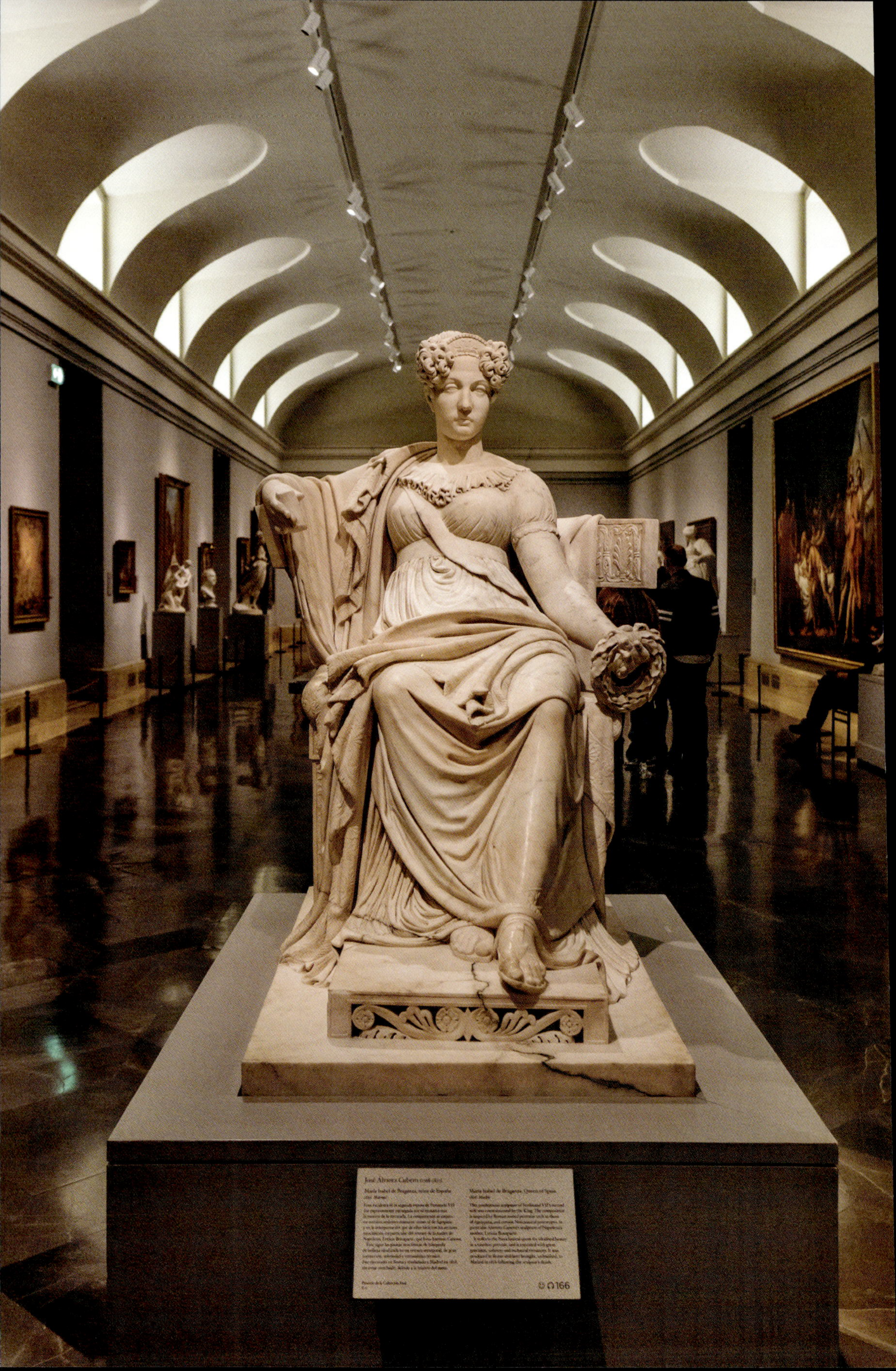
José Álvarez Cubero
166

Opposite In Gallery 75, meet a Prado founder, Queen María Isabel de Braganza, who is present in marble.

Right Art lovers come and go at the Prado, one of the world's great repositories of Western art.

myself with the Renaissance in Spain at the building's far northern end. There I found Luis de Morales, Bartolomé Bermejo, and Juan de Juanes, whose six exquisite panels created for the altar of Valencia's Church of St. Stephen are given pride of place.

One flight up from there is Gallery 1, displaying a single work: Leone Leoni's imposing 1551 bronze sculpture *Emperor Charles V and the Fury*. The emperor's exquisitely made suit of armor comes off to reveal a heroic nude beneath. Leoni was a favorite of the Hapsburgs, and sculptures of other family members (though none that bare it all) are displayed in the cloister gallery of the Jeronimos wing.

From Gallery 1, the masterpieces come fast and furious. Galleries 40 to 44 reveal, in sometimes overwhelming abundance, the sensuality and lush colors of Giovanni Bellini, Lorenzo Lotto, Veronese, and other masters of the Venetian School of painting. The Prado has more paintings by Titian, the godfather of Venetian painting, than any other museum — most of them emblematic works like *The Andrians*, *Venus and Adonis*, and *Virgin Dolorosa* that influenced generations of artists.

The Flemish painter Peter Paul Rubens came to Madrid in the 17th century as both a diplomat and an artist, frequently copying works in the royal collection by Titian and others. He also painted works of his own for the Spanish kings. Many of them line the 367-foot-long central gallery that forms the spine of the Prado and creates a visual nexus, revealing the links between the great masters of Spanish painting — El Greco, Ribera, Zurbarán, Maíno, Velázquez, and Murillo — and their Italian and Flemish forebears.

By now any art lover needs a break, and there's one to be had in the museum's cafe. In warm weather there are lovely outdoor tables with yummy sandwiches and yummier sangria that might have kept me from going back inside to finish my mission, but fortunately it was January.

Refreshed, I focused on my quest for surprises. Several presented themselves in the form of a gallery with more than a dozen paintings by the French painters Nicolas Poussin and Claude Lorrain that I never knew existed here. Ditto for another gallery of paintings by Anthony Van Dyck that I had somehow walked past for 17 years.

And now, at last, the 17th-century Spanish superstars. "Velázquez alone is worth the whole trip," wrote the French painter Édouard Manet of his Prado visit in 1865. Velázquez, he said, is the "painters' painter," so little wonder that the likes of John Singer Sargent, Pablo Picasso, and Francis Bacon would make similar

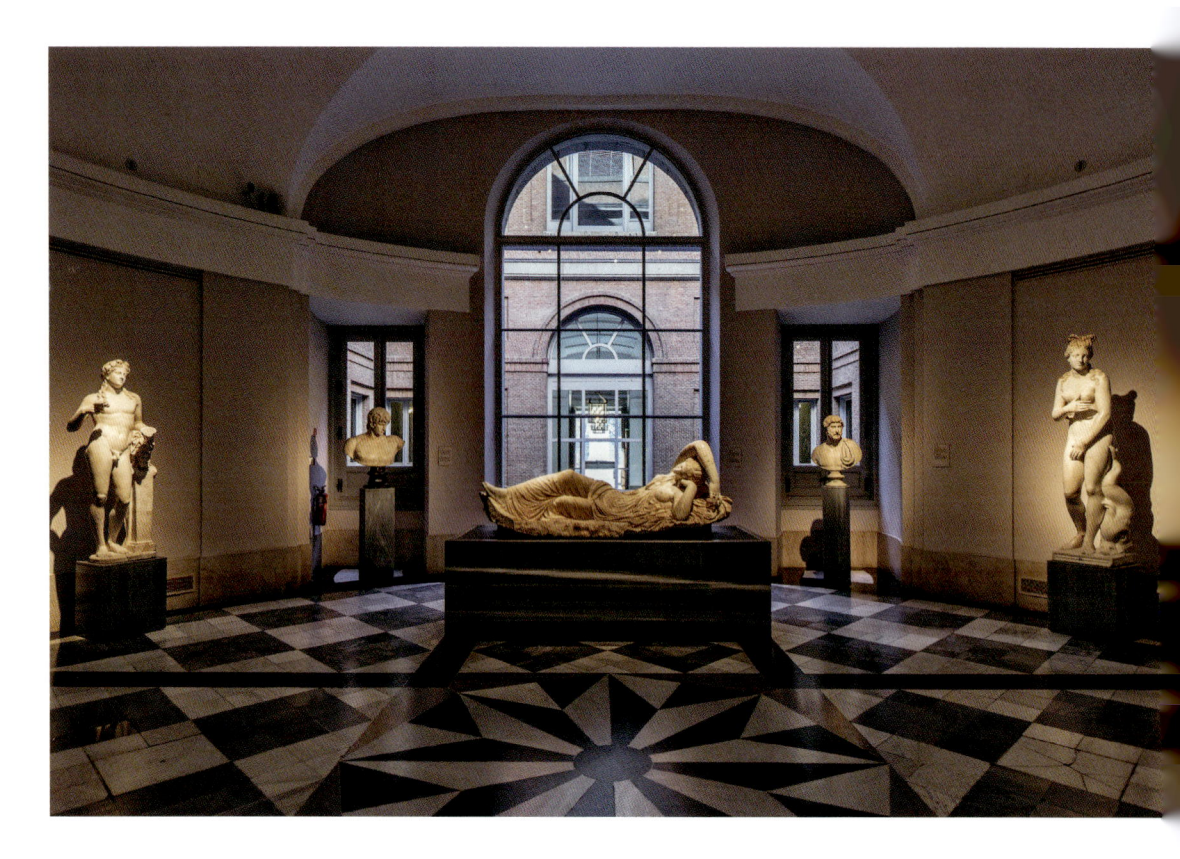

Above The Prado has more than 250 sculptures. Some were bought in Rome by Velázquez on behalf of King Philip IV.

Opposite Velázquez paintings at the Prado. "Velázquez alone is worth the whole trip," Édouard Manet wrote.

pilgrimages to study the works displayed in Galleries 7 through 18. Artists of his era, the Spanish "golden age," manipulated paint on the canvas to create dazzlingly realistic effects, like the light shimmering on silk gowns in Velázquez's *Las Meninas* or the churning clouds in the apricot-and-lavender skies of El Greco. But their naturalism can have a deeper emotional impact, as in the candor and humanity of Velázquez's portraits of buffoons or the austerity of Zurbarán's nearly all black-and-white painting *Agnus Dei*, which conveys the solemnity of Catholic Spain.

By the dawn of the 18th century, Spain had a new ruling dynasty, the Bourbons, but the pace of royal collecting and commissioning remained apace. The Prado's large collection of Goya's portraits—including one of King Charles IV and his family that features his already devious-looking son Fernando—are reminders that his canny ability to reveal a subject's hapless or sinister character speaks across the centuries.

Before heading to the third floor to delight in the frolic of Goya's tapestry cartoons, I got a whiff of fresh coffee and followed my nose into the tiny coffee and cookie shop tucked behind the central gallery. Sipping and chewing in surprising proximity to Rubens's *Three Graces*, I mused on how much had changed since I arrived in Madrid, when the Prado was among the most old-school of the world's big-name museums, with surprisingly limited hours, endless lines, and a lackluster shop and cafe. Now it had become a model of accessibility, open a minimum of nine hours a day (two of them with free admission), with online ticket sales, hands-on exhibitions for the vision-impaired, a guide for the LGBTQ+ community, and free online courses.

After nearly 12,000 steps (about six miles), my final stop was an almost vault-like gallery tucked under the eaves in the North Tower, showcasing one final surprise: a collection of nearly 150 exquisite

*Photographs by
Emilio Parra Doiztua*

hardstone-and-rock-crystal goblets, platters, and other objects adorned with gold and silver and known as the Dauphin's Treasure.

Maybe I was delirious at this point, but these stunning and delicate objects displayed next to the extraordinary padded leather cases that perfectly mimic the shape of the objects they carry — and are also centuries old — seemed like a fitting metaphor for the Prado itself: artistic perfection inside and out.

WHAT TO READ

The Prado Masterpieces, by Museo Nacional del Prado. A comprehensive overview of the museum's permanent collection, from ancient sculpture to 19th-century paintings.

Madrid and the Prado: Art and Architecture, by Barbara Borngässer, David Sanchez, and Felix Scheffler. A guidebook to the museum, its building, and its place in the life of Madrid.

Velázquez, by Norbert Wolf, and ***El Greco***, by Michael Scholz-Hänsel. Informative and affordable books from TASCHEN's Basic Art series, illustrated with the painters' work.

The Master of the Prado: A Novel, by Javier Sierra. A page-turner of a novel with the Prado front and center. By the same author who brought Leonardo da Vinci and his world alive in *The Secret Supper*.

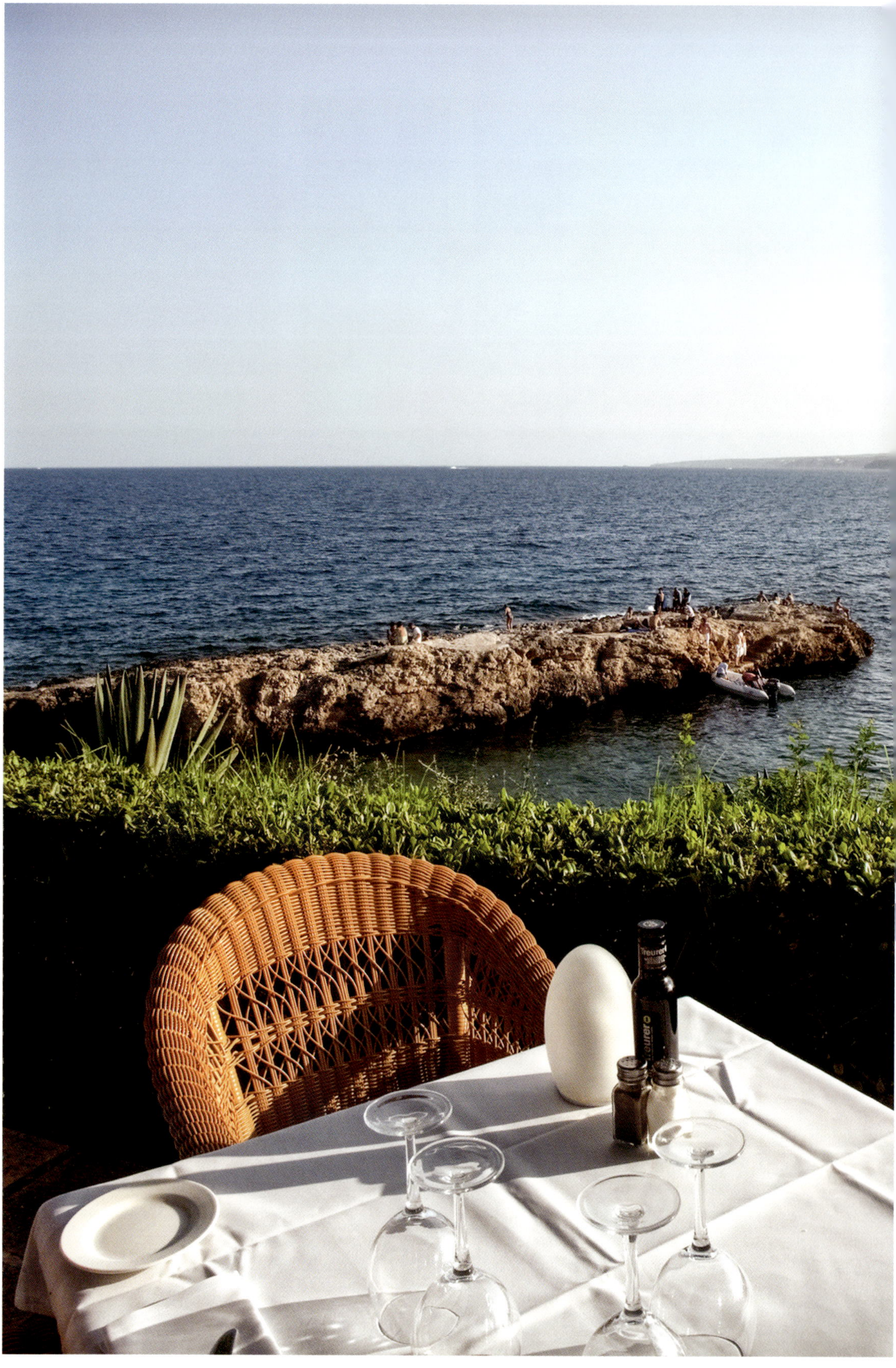

MIRÓ'S MEDITERRANEAN REFUGE

Spend a little time on the island of Majorca, and the casual placement of Joan Miró artwork tells a larger story. — BY SARAH WILDMAN

A bronze Miró sculpture interrupts the sidewalk below the grand Cathedral of Palma de Mallorca. It stretches up, the height of two men, a hollowed concave rectangle topped by a large egg-shaped nugget tilted toward the Mediterranean. Day after day tourists rush past it in a hustle, descending from the steep side street that winds down to the shaded Passeig de Born, a busy thoroughfare filled with clothing stores and mopeds.

No fanfare announces the sculpture's presence. It would be easy simply to glide past *Femme*, as the bronze is called, without pausing to appreciate this work by one of Spain's, indeed one of the world's, most renowned artists. But spend a little time on Majorca and the casual, almost offhand, placement of the artwork reveals itself as part of a much larger story—about an artist who was sheltered and inspired by this island, but who, surprisingly, only posthumously received the kind of recognition here that he was given elsewhere.

I arrived in Palma, the largest city on Majorca (spelled Mallorca in Spain), hoping to understand the story of Miró's life and work here; to see and feel the island's rugged landscape of scrubby trees and mountains, surrounded by the sea; to watch the way the early morning light filters down into Palma's Gothic quarter and glances off the tops of centuries-old buildings.

Joan Miró was born in Barcelona in 1893, and though his work had already earned an international audience when he settled in Palma in the mid-1950s, few here, it seemed, had heard of him. Miró embraced this anonymity, setting up studios well outside the city where he would create some of his most important works, including the triptych *Bleu I, II, III* (1961),

Previous Majorca is rich in sea views, but Joan Miró arrived in 1940 looking more for safety than for vistas.

Left A ceramic mural, in Palma, *Mur pour David Fernández Miró,* is named for one of the artist's grandsons.

Opposite Miró's style was mature before he found Majorca, as in *Ciphers and Constellations, in Love with a Woman,* from 1941.

which was, according to the German art critic Barbara Catoir, a paean to the color of Majorca's sky and the sea that surrounds the island.

As the Catalan landscape of his childhood found its way into Miró's paintings, so, too, did Majorca: the white plaster walls of the fishermen's cottages, the gourdlike urns and brightly painted folk-art figures, the crescent-shaped vestiges of Moorish architecture, and the rhythms of the Santa Catalina market, with its fishmongers and rough-handed fishermen drinking coffee out of tiny glass tumblers.

"I invent nothing, it's all here! That is why I have to live here!" Miró told Walter Erben, a German writer who visited him at his studio outside Palma in 1956.

Since 2004, Palma has also had a modern art museum, Es Baluard, in a repurposed space in a fortress built into the old city walls. Inside, the Sala Miró contains a small permanent collection of Miró works. Lining the walls are paintings from his *Série Mallorca,* 1973, a set of primarily black-and-white etchings illuminated with orbs of blue, orange, and red, and strips of green.

Outside the museum, a quiet, expansive terraza overlooks the city and the port, with a breathtaking view of the Bay of Palma. A clutch of locals sat there when I arrived, cheekily ignoring the art, eating olives and drinking beer. The afternoon sun warmed the terra-cotta buildings, setting the city afire with the Mediterranean light that Miró admired. In the distance, hundreds of boats dotted the water.

Miró's mother was from the Majorcan mountain town of Sóller. Each summer, as a boy, Miró would visit, toggling frequently between Palma and Sóller, 90 minutes away, where he spent time with his grandmother. I found the train to Sóller nearly as it was then. Made of wood and dating from 1912, it ran on a claustrophobically narrow track, swaying and clicking as it wound its way from the scrappy outer suburbs of Palma up into the fragrant, forested mountainside, through skinny tunnel after tunnel. In the Sóller train station, reproductions of a handful of works by Miró were on display, alongside some by his good friend Picasso.

But it was Palma, not Sóller, where Miró spent the most time. In those early years, he sketched Palma landmarks—the cathedral; the 700-year-old Bellver Castle at the edge of the city; Sa Llotja, the 15th-century stock exchange. Over time, the landscape of Palma and its surroundings would prove to be among Miró's most consistent influences.

It is an odd paradox that, until recently, his fondness for the island was not entirely reciprocated. He

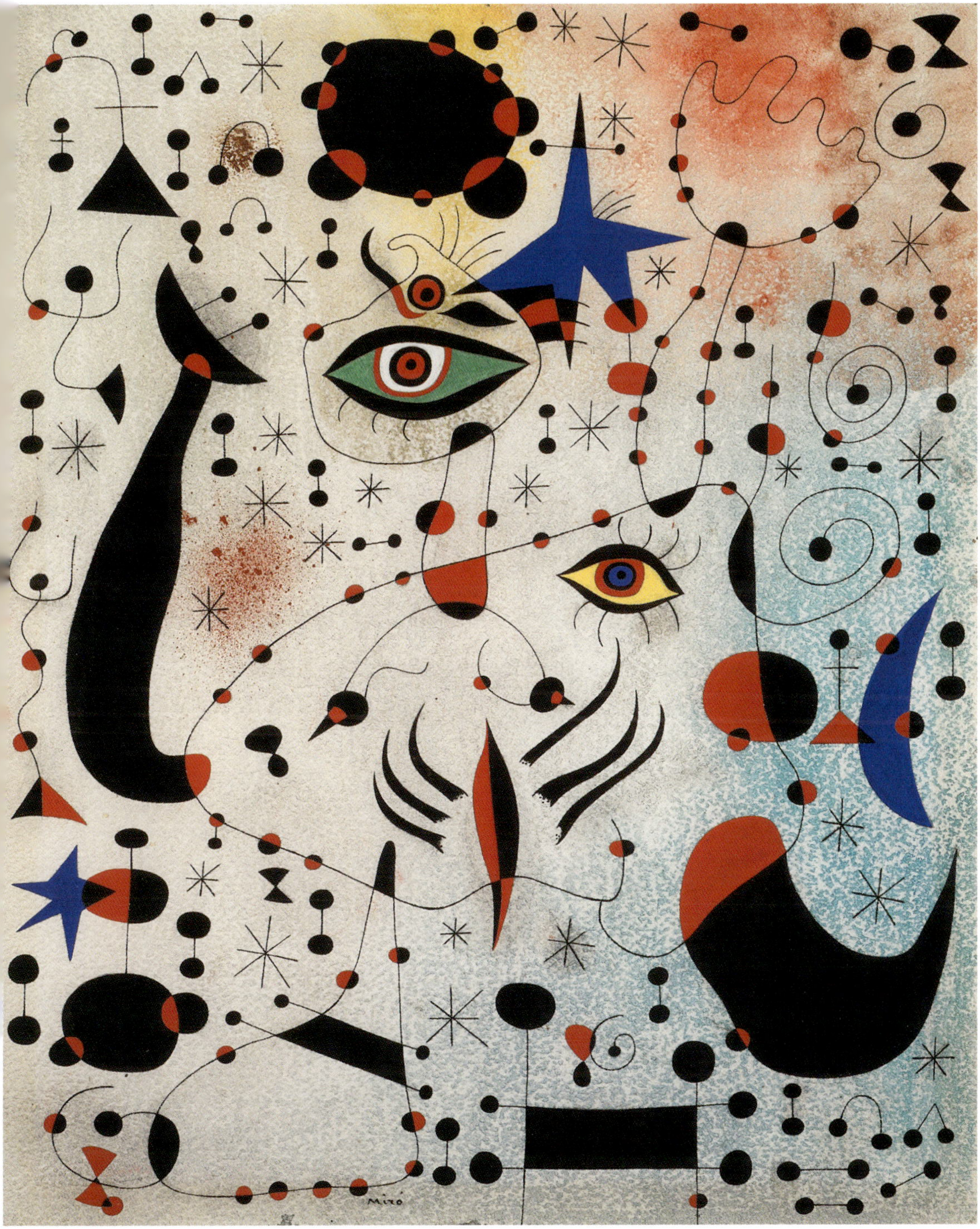

Above From Palma, a train ride through fragrant forest leads to this station at Sóller, a town frequented by Miró.

Opposite Fish for sale at Santa Catalina market, in Palma, where Miró's wife used to do the shopping.

hoped to create stained-glass windows for Palma's cathedral but was rebuffed. He tried to give Palma several sculptures to welcome visitors to the city, according to his grandson, Joan Punyet Miró, and that offer, too, was refused. Now the few pieces of Miró's art in the city's public spaces seem disconnected, appearing out of nowhere.

"My grandfather moved to Majorca in 1956 when he was 63 years old; he passed away here in 1983 at the age of 90," Punyet said. We were in the offices of the Successió Miró, which administers rights for Miró's works on behalf of his heirs and is located in Palma. The office was filled with remarkable photographs: Miró with Picasso, Miró's portrait taken by Man Ray. Large binders were filled with original black-and-white pictures from every era of Miró's life.

"Majorca was a place that would shelter his soul," Punyet said.

It was also, for a time, a place that sheltered him from war and political repression. In 1936, as the Spanish Civil War broke out, Miró, who was an outspoken critic of Fascism, fled Barcelona with his wife, Pilar, and daughter, María Dolores, for Paris. The family remained in France until 1940, when the Nazi occupation of Paris pushed them back to Spain and into hiding from Franco's mainland Fascist forces. They went to Majorca and took up residence in a tiny apartment on a slip of a street called Carrer de les Minyones, in the shadow of the cathedral.

"He remembered what happened to Federico García Lorca, that he got shot," his grandson said, referring to the playwright who was executed by firing squad in Granada in the early days of the Spanish Civil War.

On Carrer de les Minyones, Miró was known only as "Pilar's husband." He worked on *Constellations*, one of his best-known series, and only occasionally ventured out. "I took refuge in the cathedral," he wrote a friend, recalling how he would sit in the early morning, listening to the organist practice. "Who was I then? Almost no one, a poor man, a little crazy, someone who wanted to paint things in a manner that, here, no one understood. No one."

Even in 1956, when Miró settled for good in Majorca, in Cala Mayor on the western outskirts of Palma, he rarely went into the city, several people told me, other than to hear the organist at the cathedral, or to have an occasional traditional Majorcan *ensaimada* pastry at C'an Joan de S'aigo, the oldest ice-cream shop in Palma, in the labyrinthine heart of the old city center.

But the same was not true for his wife. Pilar interacted with Palma, coming in each day to the Santa Catalina market, shopping for provisions, chatting with her neighbors. In 1995, an obituary in the Spanish national newspaper *El País* called her Miró's door to the world. It was she who received his visitors and who, after his death, sold off some 40 pieces of art to raise money for a museum on the site of the studios the couple had already donated to the city.

"I dream of a grand atelier," Miró explained in the French magazine *XXe Siècle* in 1938. That dream was realized in 1956 on the Majorcan property Son Abrines, where he then had his home. The Catalan architect Josep Lluís Sert (who was also for many years dean of the Harvard School of Design) created for Miró a light-filled space with a remarkable system of cooling and light. The building's shutters function like the gills of a fish, allowing the room to breathe through the walls and ceiling. Now Miró could turn to his most ambitious works—large-scale paintings, triptychs, sculpture, lithographs, and etchings.

Three years after moving into the Sert studio, Miró purchased Son Boter, a traditional Majorcan country home on the hillside above. That, too, he used as a working space.

Open to the public since 1992, these two studios are now part of the Fundació Pilar i Joan Miró a Mallorca, which also includes a Modernist cube museum designed by Rafael Moneo. In an open breezeway between the museum and the studios, Moneo installed an infinity pool, set dramatically against the sky,

Above The view across reflective water toward Palma landmarks: the Royal Palace of La Almudaina, left, and the Majorca Cathedral.

Below Showing off a *sobrassada*, a pork sausage known as a Majorca specialty, at L'Olivar Market in Palma.

Opposite Miró's studio, designed by the Catalan architect Josep Lluís Sert, is now open to the public.

as a way of bringing in the element of water, since much of the view of the sea has been obscured by buildings since the 1950s. It was in response to the development in those years that Miró and his wife created the foundation and gave the studios to the city. "I do not want them someday to build one of those horrendous skyscrapers which I see all around me," Miró said.

In the museum are dozens of important works: enormous, captivating canvases splashed with color, or darkened with bold black paint, all hung in a cool cavern of sandstone. The Sert studio, on the other hand, has been left almost as it was in the artist's day, with dozens of paintings propped against walls, set up on easels, or lying on the floor.

Outside Son Abrines, the hill slopes upward and a landscaped stone walkway leads to Son Boter, a 17th-century manor that was once a boardinghouse run by the Baroness von Münchhausen. When Miró acquired the building in 1959, he began drawing on the walls, like a genius cave man, sketching out his enormous sculptures. The morning I visited, a freak storm began, rolling in from the mountains. I looked out the front door. A wall of water had formed between me and the rest of the grounds, preventing anyone

Photographs by Lourdes Segade

from entering and me from leaving. I understood then the isolation Miró had found here.

Later I caught a bus to Ses Illetes, the beach Joan Punyet had told me Miró would walk on, collecting his thoughts, as well as driftwood, stones, and shells. It is still lovely. The water is crystal clear, and there are rocks to climb on, a jetty that stretches out into the sea. It is no longer, by any stretch of the imagination, isolated. There are restaurants, hotels, and shops.

But looking out at the sea, beyond all the modernity, I saw the endless Majorcan sky meeting the Mediterranean, blue upon blue. I thought of the expression that Miró had for the intensity of that horizon, which so inspired him and which could only be found here, on Majorca. He called it "eloquent silence."

WHAT TO READ AND WATCH

Miró, by Janis Mink. A biography of Miró, including a review of his artistic importance and many photographs of his works. Part of TASCHEN's Basic Art series.

Joan Miró: I Work Like a Gardener, a book from a 1958 interview with Miró by Yvon Taillandier. The artist speaks about his creative process.

Miró on Mallorca, by Barbara Catoir. A critic's exploration of Miró's art in the years when he lived on Majorca, working in its clear light, surrounded by blue skies and sea.

Miró: Round Trip, by Francisco Copado, Robert Lubar Messer, and Enric Juncosa Darder. Companion book, published in 2018, to an exhibition of Miró works created on Majorca.

Joan Miró: Ladder of Escape, directed by Carroll Moore, narrated by Ed Harris. A video produced by the United States National Gallery of Art.

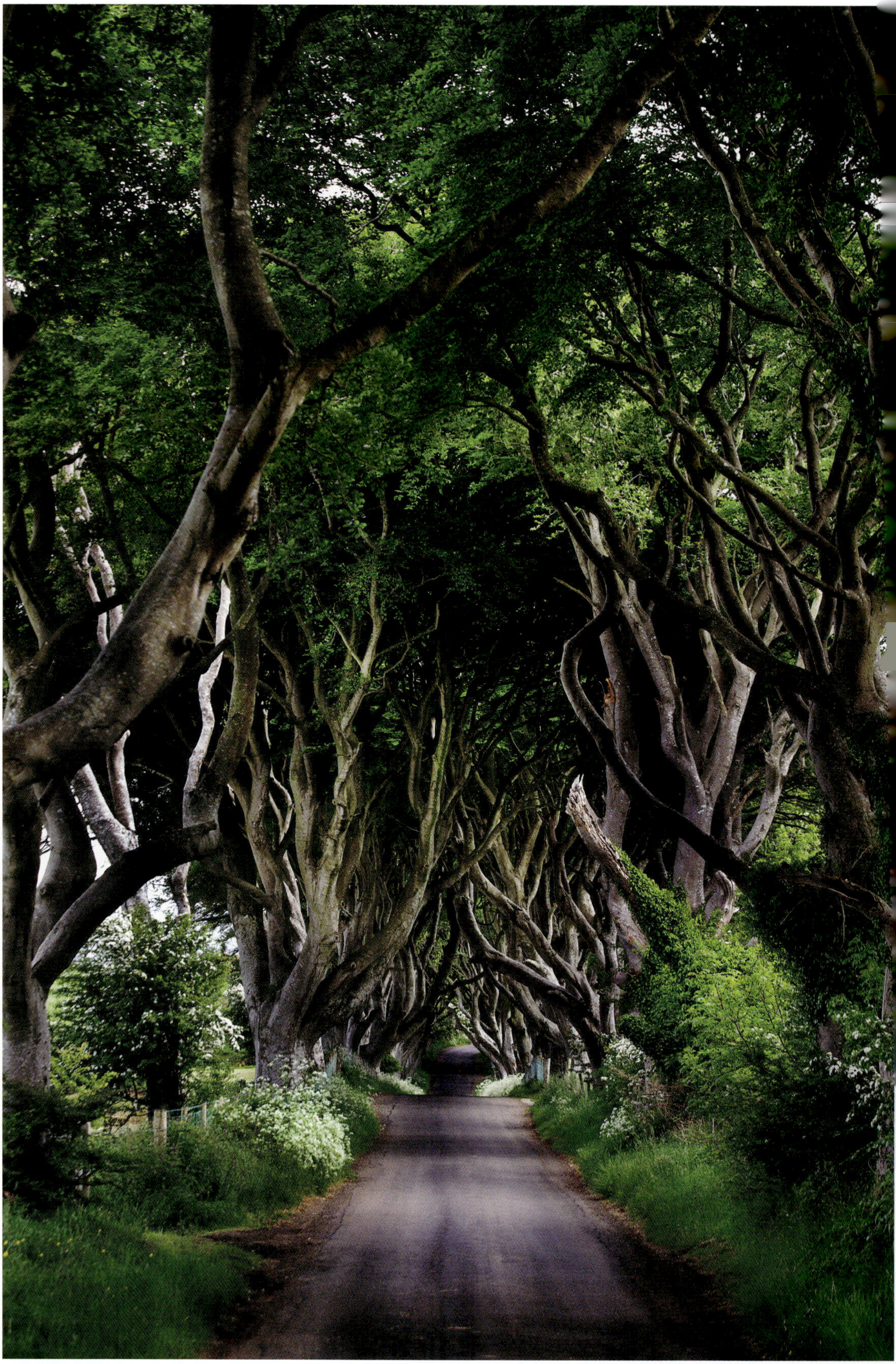

NORTHERN IRELAND

THE ROAD TO WESTEROS

A search for settings in Game of Thrones *leads to fantastical landscapes and epic selfie bait.*
— BY JEREMY EGNER

The many marvels dotting the dramatic Antrim Coast of Northern Ireland include a cluster of eerily beautiful caves in Cushendun, a tidy village around 45 miles north of Belfast. Formed by 400 million years of shifting red stone and the surging slate-blue Irish Sea, the caves inspire awed reflection upon the raw power of nature and the irresistible imprint of time, among other musings on the mystic.

A voice whispered into my ear: "That's where Melisandre gave birth to the shadow monster."

So it was — I knew it was around there somewhere, as did the dozens of *Game of Thrones* fans surrounding me, feverishly snapping selfies before returning to their tour bus in a nearby parking lot.

The voice belonged to my own guide, Flip Robinson, a 6-foot-8, magnificently bearded man who became a part of *Game of Thrones* by parlaying his stature into a gig as a stand-in for behemoth characters like Hodor and the Mountain. He waved to a colleague as she led her group away as suddenly as it had arrived, off toward Braavos or the Iron Islands or some other *Thrones* location down the road.

The *Game of Thrones* HBO television series, one of the world's most influential pop-culture franchises, left a dragon-size footprint on everything it touched. Nowhere is that dynamic more visible and tangible than in Northern Ireland, the production's former home. *Thrones* eventually filmed in Croatia, Spain, Morocco, Iceland, Malta, and other locations. But as the home of not only the production, in Belfast's Titanic Studios, but also Westeros itself, Northern Ireland has been transformed in fact and figment. As

Previous The much-photographed Dark Hedges provided an atmospheric backdrop for the *Game of Thrones* television series.

Left A first edition copy of *A Game of Thrones* by George R. R. Martin, the book that started it all.

Opposite Titanic Belfast, a museum about the doomed ship, anchors the city's Titanic Quarter, home of the *Thrones* studio.

the series altered the TV landscape, it also altered actual landscapes: For millions of viewers all over the world, Northern Ireland has been redefined and remade in the show's image.

In the process, Belfast's filmmaking industry went from a sleepy endeavor to a powerhouse. "*Game of Thrones* changed everything," said Richard Williams, the chief executive of Northern Ireland Screen, which promotes film and television production in the country. "We are relevant — it is basically night and day."

The region extends a warm welcome to tourists who come to see the landscape of the show. The majestic stretch of coastal landscape called the Causeway Coastal Route is now crisscrossed with motor coaches bearing *Thrones* pilgrims. Elsewhere, spots like the Castle Ward estate, near Strangford, site of the original Winterfell, now open their doors to thousands of fans each year.

Besides providing legions of fans with an experience that layers fantasy on fantasy, *Thrones* has funneled hundreds of millions of dollars into Northern Ireland. But the financial benefit might actually pale compared with a more existential one in a place that for decades was known internationally mostly for sectarian violence.

"Twenty years ago, you would have been here writing about the Troubles, not a TV show," Gary Hawthorne, one of my drivers, told me during my visit.

Robinson said, "Fake violence has helped bring us back from the real violence."

Part of the outsize impact *Thrones* has had on Northern Ireland comes from the size of the production relative to the size of the place, which was a main reason it was such an ideal home base. At 5,460 square miles, the country is about half the size of Belgium (with about a sixth as many residents, at around 1.9 million). But within that area is an astounding array of scenery that is particularly suited to a medieval fantasy saga.

"We had 63 locations in 10 years, every single one of them within an hour and a half of Belfast," said Robert Boake, the supervising location manager in Northern Ireland.

This became apparent on the afternoon I spent driving with Robinson along the causeway, a twisting roadway that hugs the U-shaped glens of the coast, the Irish Sea on one side and villages and vertiginous green hillsides, strewn with sheep, on the other.

In mere hours, we spanned Westeros and beyond, moving from the Wall and Castle Black

(Magheramorne quarry) to the stairs where Arya crawled out of the Braavos canal (Carnlough Harbor) to the rocky shoreline in Pyke (Ballintoy) where the Greyjoys did nutty Greyjoy stuff. We also closed the shadow-baby loop, strolling around the Stormlands meadow (near Murlough Bay) where Renly made camp until Melisandre's monster got hold of him. Occasionally we stopped to walk around and by turns get lashed with rain, pummeled by wind, and caressed by crystalline sunshine. ("In Northern Ireland, you get four seasons in one day," Robinson told me, and I eventually came to recognize this as a national slogan.)

At Fair Head outside Ballycastle, we parked in a muddy lot, dropped some cash in an honor box, and walked uphill through a horizontal downpour. About 20 minutes later, the rain was gone and the sun dried our faces as gale-force gusts threatened to blow us over the edge of a sheer cliff dropping hundreds of feet to the rocky coast.

We had arrived at Dragonstone, or the dazzling headland the Targaryen family stronghold was superimposed on by computer imagery, anyway. To stand where the impossibly green meadow gives way to gray granite cliffs plummeting toward the sea, as you note the spot where Tyrion and Daenerys argued over strategy, where Jon Snow met Drogon, is to feel the frisson of an epic story meeting an epic landscape.

This reciprocity between project and place extends beyond the countryside. Another reason the marriage between *Thrones* and the region was happier than any on the show is that the production's material needs — armor, medieval weapons, elaborate costumes, and jewelry — meshed well with the area's longstanding artisanal traditions. "We're good at that stuff," Williams said.

Even when a fight was filmed in a place like Morocco, the spears were almost always built in Belfast. Fans who would like to try on a replica of Cersei's crown can often do so at Steensons jewelers in Ballymena, because that's where the original and other Westerosi finery were designed and made.

"There are not many people in this country who haven't been involved in some direct capacity," Boake said. "Their brother made something for the show, or their sister was an extra, or their cousin worked on an episode."

Above Dunluce Castle on the Antrim Coast dates back to the 14th century. In *Thrones*, it was Castle Greyjoy.

Opposite *Thrones*-themed tours bring eager tourists to this landscape near Cushendun.

As we drove along the coast, Robinson reminisced about his time as Hodor's double, dodging White Walker stuntmen in the Three-Eyed Raven's cave as he dragged Bran's double toward a green screen, in one of the show's most famous scenes. "Then Kristian Nairn held the door," he said. "He did the easy bit."

Robinson was a former carpenter laid low by the global financial crisis, working as a tour guide, when he applied to be a *Thrones* extra. Soon he was facing off with the likes of Lena Headey and Nikolaj Coster-Waldau as a stand-in for the undead Mountain, a stint that became the hook for his Giant Tours, which takes small groups of *Thrones* fans up and down the coast. "It changed my life around," he said.

The most common analogy holds that *Thrones* is to Northern Ireland what the *Lord of the Rings* movies were to New Zealand—a pop-culture phenomenon that showcased a wondrous land for a global audience. But *Thrones* also helped to redefine Belfast, once known as one of the most dangerous places on earth. From the late 1960s to the late 1990s, the Troubles, which pitted Protestant paramilitary groups loyal to the British Crown against Catholic ones in favor of a unified, independent Ireland, claimed some 3,600 lives in bombings, sniper attacks, and bloody street battles that ripped Belfast apart. There are still rifts, but the show has helped "continue our peace process," said Conleth Hill, better known to *Thrones* fans as the cunning Varys. As one of the few actors from Northern Ireland in the cast—he grew up and still lives in Ballycastle—Hill observed the show's impact from both inside and out. "Before the Troubles, there was loads of tourists coming through my town," he said. "Now they're coming again."

Tourism NI has created a locations app and outfitted filming sites with information plaques for self-guided pilgrims. It also sponsors projects like the enormous Game of Thrones Tapestry, based on

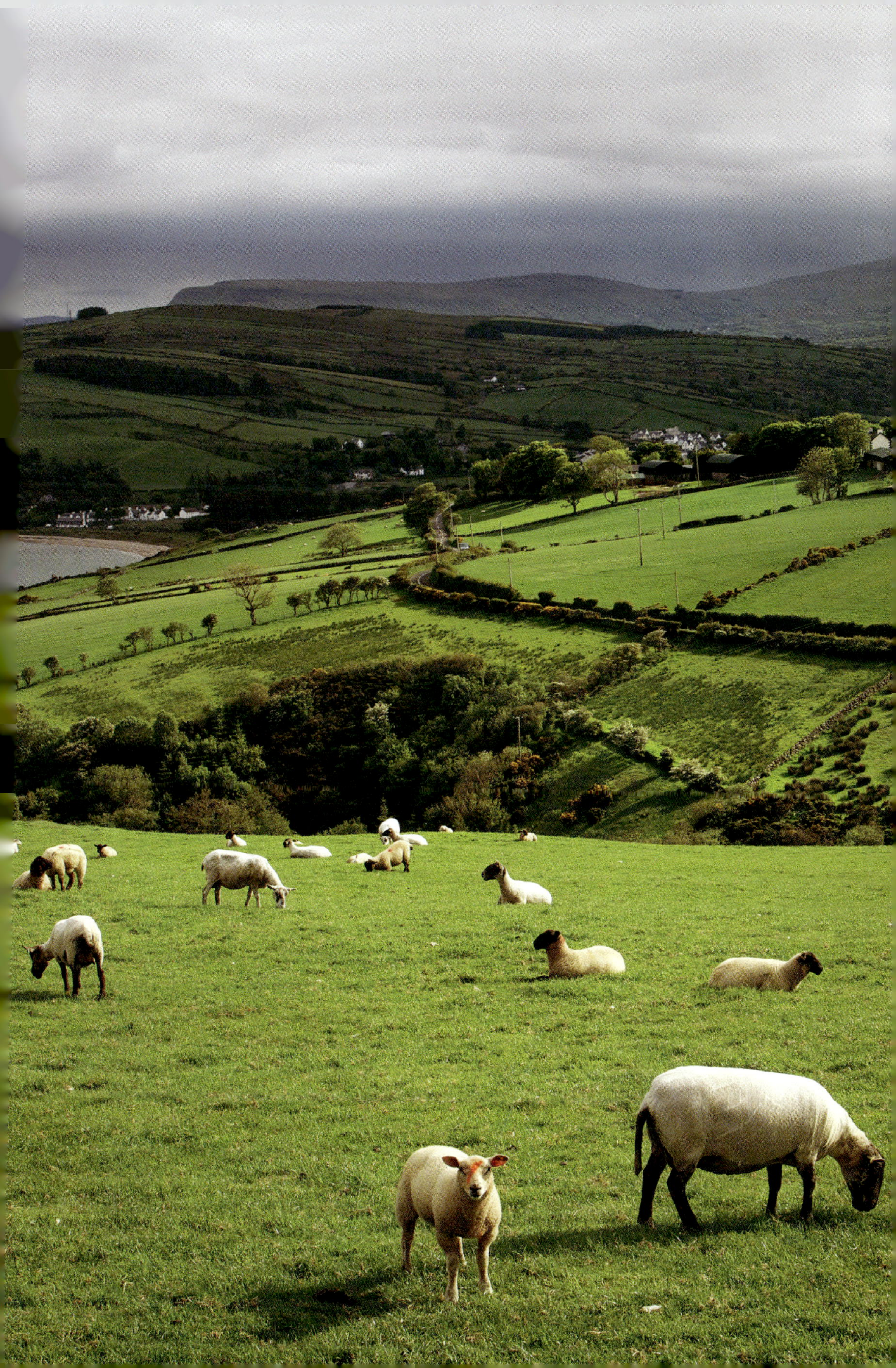

Above Ballintoy beach plays the role of a windswept shore called the fictional Iron Islands.

Below Audley's Castle in County Down was the film location for Winterfell.

Opposite Stone walls on the 18th-century Castle Ward estate also had their moment in *Game of Thrones*.

the Bayeux Tapestry in France; it uses Belfast's world-famous linen-weaving expertise to depict the *Thrones* story. I saw it at the Ulster Museum, a few floors above an exhibition about the Troubles. The 217-foot-long tapestry recaps the entire tale. Much like the show itself, the tapestry is fundamentally bonkers but astounding in scale and execution, and a tremendous kick to experience.

HBO is offering tourism experiences, too, by turning several former *Thrones* sets into immersive attractions featuring costumes, weapons, and other artifacts from the show.

Another wallow in *Thrones*-dom awaited me at Castle Ward, a longtime National Trust site about an hour south of the city. William Van der Kells, a guide, greeted me in full Northern regalia: a black cloak and faux fur collar with a shiny gauntlet on one hand, holding a large sword made of "the finest Valyrian rubber." Castle Ward added its "Winterfell tour" after the show shot much of its first season on the property.

The Stark castle was based around the 1610 tower house, the same one Bran climbed to discover Jaime and Cersei in flagrante twincestus. We shot arrows on the spot in the courtyard where the Stark children did in one of the first scenes of the series, a few yards

Photographs by Robert Ormerod

from where Tyrion smacked Joffrey. Then we drove through a driving rain to other locations on the property, like the tree where Robb Stark and Talisa fatefully tied the knot, before taking cover beneath an old castle near the site of Walder Frey's (digitally projected) one, where it all ended badly. "Around here you get all four seasons in a day," Van der Kells said.

By then, I was wearing the cloak and snapping my own selfies to send to my daughter. The only shadow monster in evidence was the storm cloud dumping rain on me. But as I peered through the gloom and fog at the choppy Strangford Lough, it occurred to me that while I'd come to see how *Game of Thrones* had redefined Northern Ireland, what struck me most was how Northern Ireland had defined *Game of Thrones*.

WHAT TO READ AND WATCH

A Song of Ice and Fire, by George R.R. Martin. The series of novels that started it all. (*A Game of Thrones* was the title of the first volume.)

Game of Thrones, the HBO television series. Sure to have a long life in streaming and DVD incarnations.

A Game of Thrones: The Graphic Novel. An adaptation by Daniel Abraham and Tommy Patterson.

Discovernorthernireland.com. The website of the Northern Ireland tourism agency has extensive information for *Game of Thrones* tourists, accessible through a prominent link on its home page.

A Feast of Ice and Fire: The Official Game of Thrones Companion Cookbook, by Chelsea Monroe-Cassel and Sariann Lehrer. Cuisine from across the Seven Kingdoms. Foreword by George R.R. Martin.

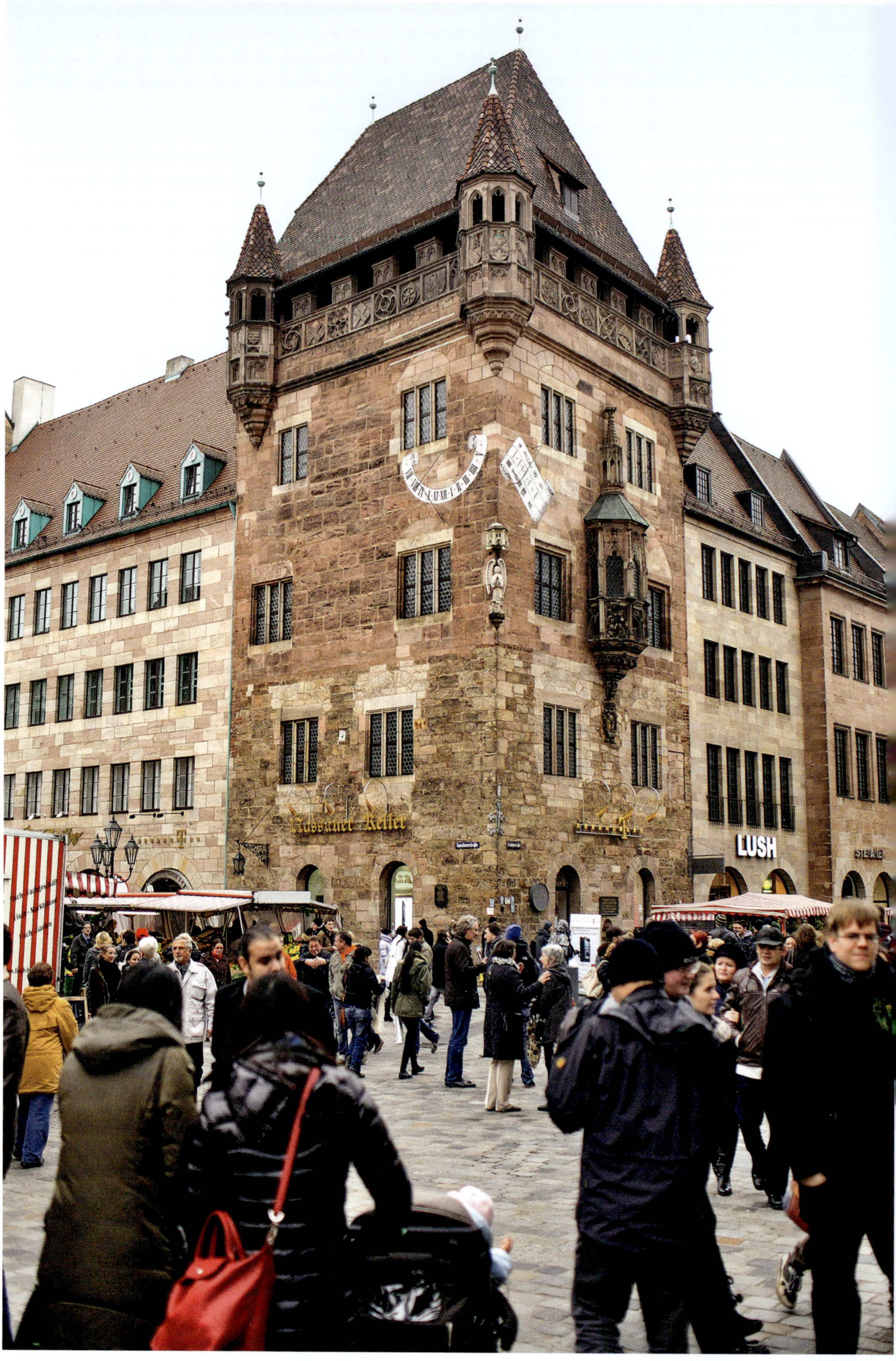
Nassauer Keller
LUSH

THEN AND NOW IN NUREMBERG

Hitler left his stain, but there's much more to discover in this city of lebkuchen, red beer, and Dürer.
— BY RUSS JUSKALIAN

"This will be easy to see," said Annelise, my guide, flipping off the lights in the chilly sandstone beer cellar that had been converted to an air-raid shelter during World War II. A small plaque on the wall glowed with electric-lime phosphorescence. It was, she told us, an emergency exit sign for the 50,000 civilians who sheltered — two to a square meter — in these cellars during Allied firebombings.

The sign was a small but poignant reminder of how hundreds of years of beer brewing in Nuremberg — a city that was 90 percent destroyed during the war — linked past and present.

Just over an hour from Munich by direct train, Nuremberg, with a population of about half a million, is Bavaria's often-overlooked second city. Of course, the locals say Bavaria has little to do with the place; a greater allegiance is owed to the smaller administrative district of Middle Franconia, which has its own dialect, history, and cuisine. Not to mention beer.

Many outsiders think of Nuremberg only in terms of its World War II significance. This was where Hitler spoke at huge rallies — one of which, in 1934, was recorded for the propaganda film *Triumph of the Will* — and where, after the war, Allied military tribunals tried leading Nazis for war crimes.

But the city is more than its Third Reich history. Visitors find a magnificent Holy Roman Empire–era castle; a rich brewing and beer tradition; perhaps the best gingerbread in the world; and, if they visit in December, Germany's most celebrated Christmas market.

A good place to begin exploring here is underground. Starting more than 700 years ago, local breweries were required to maintain extensive cellars

Previous Nuremburg was 90 percent destroyed in World War II. Its Old Town was carefully reconstructed.

Left *Adam and Eve,* a woodcut by the 16th-century celebrity artist Albrecht Dürer. His art still helps keep Nuremburg on the map.

Opposite A walk through Nuremberg's Old Town reveals cobblestone streets and half-timber buildings.

for brewing the low-temperature-loving, bottom-fermenting lagers favored in this region, and those cellars currently cover more than six acres snaking beneath much of the old city center.

The combination of brewing's importance in the Holy Roman Empire (where it was a privileged craft), the city's easily excavated sandstone layers, and the relative safety of beer as a beverage (water was frequently contaminated) allowed brewing to thrive here. Until the 1600s, "everyone drank the beer, even small children," Annelise told us on an hourlong tour.

With the widespread adoption of refrigeration in the late 19th century, the brewers no longer needed the cool sandstone cellars, and they were taken over by the pickling industry. Then came World War II, and the cellars, some up to 80 feet deep, were connected by narrow tunnels into a spider-web network of bomb shelters and hideouts, complete with ventilation systems, hidden escape routes, and fortified entrances. Art and stained-glass windows from the nearby churches survived in these makeshift bunkers, too.

Hausbrauerei Altstadthof, a brewer operating since 1984 in Nuremberg's Old Town, uses the old methods to produce *Rotbier,* the sweet and malty red beer that was once synonymous with Nuremberg and isn't easy to find today. Altstadthof's restaurant is the place to sample both the beer and the local cheeses and sausages that go with it.

A walk in the Old Town feels like a step into a medieval world, with cobblestones, tall and narrow half-timbered buildings, and the Gothic St. Lorenz Church. It can be hard to remember that it is almost entirely a reconstruction, faithfully rebuilt after the war. Museums and museum-like antiques shops occupy many of the storefronts.

Nuremberg was the home of Albrecht Dürer, the influential early 16th-century artist who was a multinational success in his day and is considered a revolutionary master of the woodcut. The printing press was still a recent invention then, and Nuremberg was a busy center of printing that produced books for distribution in many parts of Europe. Dürer's uncle was the town's leading printer. Dürer refined the woodcut technique to produce nuanced images.

His house somehow escaped the bombing, and the tour there includes a free audio guide narrated by an actress playing his wife. Their marriage was arranged and reportedly not very happy, but she helped him market his paintings and sometimes served as a model.

No matter what your age, if you are in Nuremberg don't miss the Toy Museum, with exhibits on the craft- and engineering-based toys that the city has been known for. At the City Museum Fembohaus, the star exhibition is the Renaissance-era merchant's home that houses the museum. And the tiny executioner's house, built into a bridge over the Pegnitz River, reveals the day-to-day life of the city executioner of 1600, Franz Schmidt.

The castle district, on the northern edge of the Old Town, is a place to meander along cobblestone streets beneath the old city walls. Overlooking Nuremberg from a small hill, the castle itself — a stone and half-timbered redoubt made up of a number of separate buildings and iconic towers, some dating to at least the 13th century — reminded me of a modest version of the castle in Prague.

Nuremberg is home to the former Third Reich rally grounds, designed by the architect Albert Speer, where hundreds of thousands of Nazis and spectators came to see Hitler speak in huge propaganda events. Not much remains of the few structures that were actually built, but it's just a short bus ride out of the city center to see those forceful reminders of a terrible time: the crumbling ruins of the Zeppelinfeld, an open space with grandstands, and the Kongresshalle, a U-shaped, Colosseum-like building that was intended as a center for Nazi party convocations.

Today the Kongresshalle stands in a poor state of repair, except for its head buildings — the serif-like blocks at the top of the U-shaped complex — which house the Nuremberg Symphony and Documentation Center Nazi Party Rally Grounds. The documentation center is a museum that charts the mythology and propaganda that facilitated Hitler's rise.

When I visited, it was unnerving to walk around the nearly empty grounds. But the museum, which is reimagined with metal and glass at Escheresque angles, is a complete counterpoint to the blockiness of the Third Reich's original vision. Nonetheless, I was happy to move on to lighter experiences.

These included sampling Nuremberg's famous culinary treats: Nürnberger bratwurst and Nürnberger lebkuchen. These foods are protected under European Union law, meaning they can't be labeled

Above A sausage stand in central Nuremberg. Sausages are everywhere, but the famous red beer can be harder to find.

Opposite The Documentation Center, at the site of Nazi rallies, shows the myths and propaganda that Hitler used to gain power.

"Nürnberger" unless produced within the region using traditional means.

Short and thin—about "the size of a finger," in the words of one waitress—the Nürnberger bratwurst is a sausage often served three to a bun. Some of the best I had came from open-air grill stands. But there was also a good experience at the Historische Bratwurstküche zum Gulden Stern, a half-timbered restaurant that claims to be the oldest sausage kitchen in the world. Nürnberger Bratwurst there arrived on a plate of pungent sauerkraut cooked over a beechwood fire.

Bakeries all over town sell lebkuchen, a type of gingerbread made with ground hazelnuts, almonds, and walnuts; sweetened with honey; and spiced with cloves, ginger, and cardamom. The most decadent, called *Elisenlebkuchen*, is made without flour.

Many of the restaurants in touristy central Nuremberg offered uninspiring food served by world-weary servers, but I also found some excellent exceptions. One of them, Schäufelewärtschaft, was the kind of place that alone makes Nuremberg worth visiting. It had a country-kitchen aura of whimsy, with simple wood tables, a beer of the day, and photos on the wall of inquisitive-looking pigs peering down at the diners.

The namesake dish, *Schäufele*, a Franconian specialty of roasted pork shoulder, was like a geological cutaway: lighter meat striated with fat sitting below, and barely clinging onto, a submerging tectonic plate of scapula; followed above the bone by a darker, denser meat layer deposited with veins of slow-cook-induced fat-turned-jelly; capped by an inch of pure pork-fat crust. Served with a fist-size potato dumpling, sitting in a pool of red-brown beer-and-pork stock, it made this eater—well versed in the ways of southern German cooking—almost giddy.

That this dish was so delectable makes sense. The restaurant was opened in 2005 by a club of 36

Photographs by Russ Juskalian

pork-lovers whose name translated to English as Friends of the Franconian Schäufele.

Night life in Nuremberg takes place in the beer halls and *Stüberl*, or pubs, which are liberally sprinkled around the city center, and there are places to eat in the open air. If sipping a beer, snacking on pinkie-size sausages in a roll, and standing in the center of a medieval city under the stars — with the nearby castle illuminated for display — doesn't transport you to another time, I'm not sure what will.

WHAT TO READ AND WATCH

Visit the City — Nuremberg (3 Days In), by Brigitte Hintzen-Bohlen. A BKB travel guide covering the basics, from museums to gingerbread.

Discover Great Cities — Nuremberg, directed by Frank Ullman. A conventionally constructed but informative travel video available on Amazon.

Dürer, by Norbert Wolf, from TASCHEN's Basic Art series. The life and celebrated art of Albrecht Dürer, the Nuremberg artist who revolutionized woodcut illustration, engraving, and printmaking.

Medieval Woodcut Illustrations: City Views and Decorations from the Nuremberg Chronicle, edited by Carol Belanger Grafton. Offers glimpses into the European mindset of 1493.

The Nutcracker of Nuremberg, by Alexandre Dumas, illustrations by Else Hasselriis. Before Tchaikovsky's ballet, Dumas's version was a popular telling of the classic Christmas story.

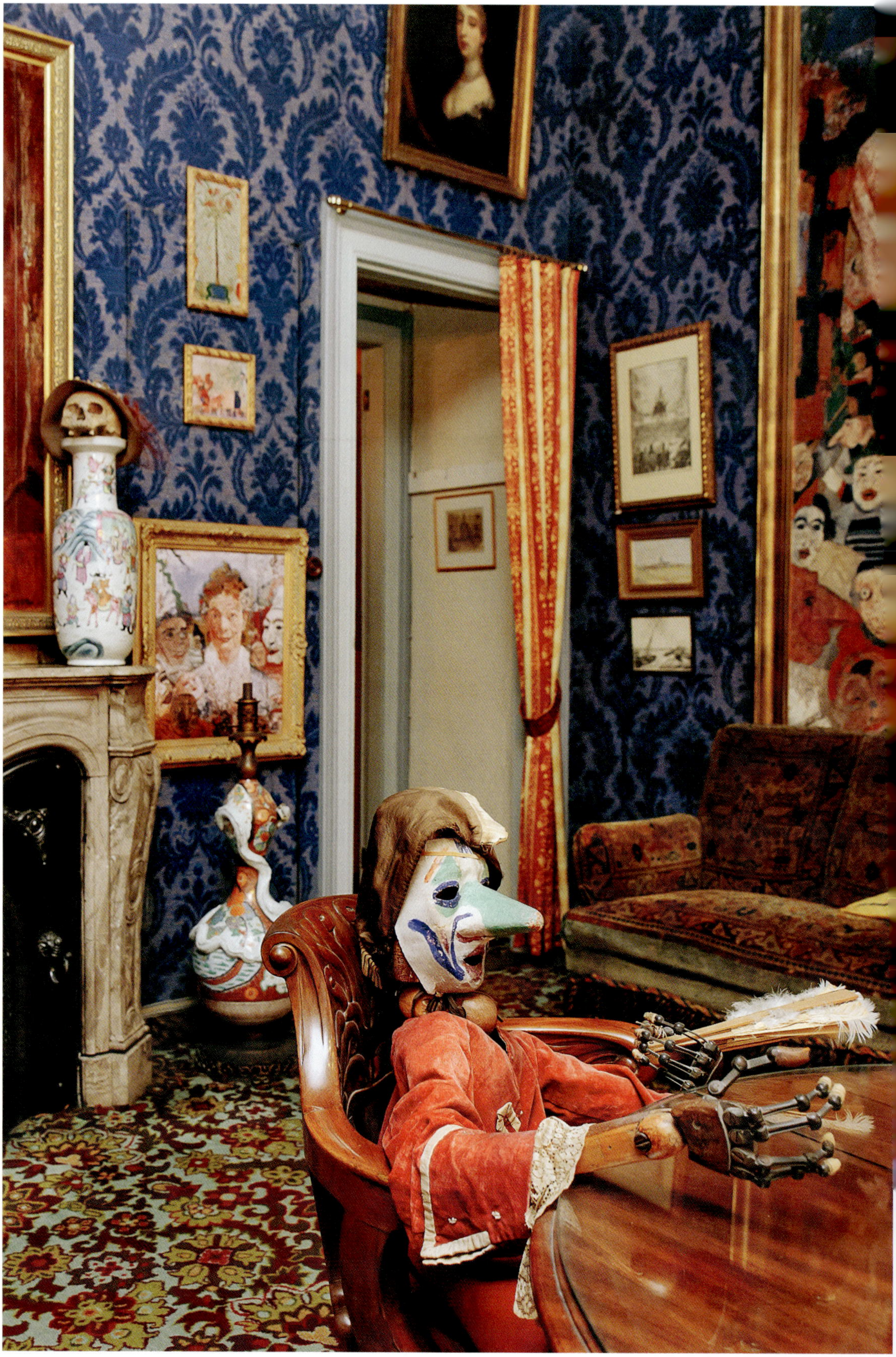

JAMES ENSOR'S TWO-SIDED HOMETOWN

The contradictions of Ostend, Belgium — gritty and grand, briny and elegant — are clues to the painter's funny, scary, and weirdly wondrous art.
— BY ALEXANDER LOBRANO

The monumental, imperial ambitions that once transformed Ostend — where the painter James Ensor was born, lived, and worked his entire life — first become visible on its outskirts, as the road leaves behind the tidy, low-lying green polders of Flanders. Huge railway viaducts leading into town along the industrial harbor are bordered by elegant granite balustrades ornamented by finials and huge carved balls of stone. The train station itself is a bombastically beautiful 1913 structure, an arched concourse flanked by a pair of monumental buildings with huge slate-covered mansard roofs. It was the railroad — and aspiring 19th-century kings — that changed Ostend from a modest fishing port surrounded by dunes and marshes on the short, flat coast of Belgium into one of Europe's grandest seaside resorts.

The Pharaonic seriousness of King Albert I's rail works and the station still accomplish what they were intended to do, which is suggest that you've reached an important destination, a splendid place conjured up out of the sand by a royal house of power and permanence. Yet the Belgian throne had only been created in 1831, and the ostentation has a certain operetta-set quality. Ostend is not Versailles.

Greeted by the sharp cries of seagulls overhead and invigorated by the iodine-rich North Sea air, I had the impression of having accidentally blundered backstage as I walked along the stone-lined quays of its working fishing port, lined with snug brick houses. The atmosphere was appealingly bluff and briny, and the fish market next to the port was busy selling piles

Previous James Ensor's unique sensibility permeates Ensorhuis, a museum in the Ostend house where he lived.

Left Fascinated by faces and the daily pageant of humanity in Ostend, Ensor was drawn to the expressiveness of masks.

Opposite *The Intrigue* is in the Royal Museum of Fine Arts Antwerp. To understand Ensor, a guard there advised, "You'll have to go to Ostend."

of tiny gray North Sea shrimp (one of Ensor's favorite foods when prepared in deep-fried croquettes), and huge flat-winged skates like the one he painted in his bluntly erotic *The Skate*, now in the Royal Museums of Fine Arts of Belgium in Brussels.

I bought a cup of sea snails cooked in court bouillon and ate them while sitting on a bench in Zeeheldenplein, an open-air square overlooking the English Channel and the port, dominated by a statue of a fisherman. Watching the drama of the sunlight suddenly piercing the thick gray clouds over the Channel, creating fleeting wells of silvery light that briefly polished the flinty-looking sea, I thought about how essential this town had been to Ensor's art.

He was deeply nourished by the sea, the constant emotional scouring of Ostend's beaches by North Sea breakers and the daily absolution offered by the tides. "I was guided by a secret instinct, a feeling for the atmosphere of the seacoast, which I had imbibed with the breeze, inhaled with the pearly mists, soaked up in the waves, heard in the wind," he wrote to a friend.

But where was the grande dame I'd read about, the opulent Queen of Beaches that attracted the crowned heads of Europe, not to mention Mozaffar ed-Din Shah Kadjar, ruler of Persia, who spent the month of August here in 1900? The streets I walked through to get there gave me a first insight into why the town was the lifelong muse and subject of Ensor, its most famous son, who was born here in 1860.

Ostend has two personalities. With a harmless layer of humdrum and honky-tonk as the mortar between them, it's both a busy, bawdy working-class port and a genteel beach resort. The tensions of that dual identity are mirrored in Ensor's work, with its finely developed sense of social satire. Here, too, he would have observed the joyous summertime vulgarity of any great seaside destination, where dozens of different definitions of pleasure are both on display and hidden. And here was a fresh daily pageant of strangers' faces, both bizarre and beautiful.

Within just a few hours of arriving, I understood that the art of James Ensor is as inextricably linked to Ostend as the fiction of James Joyce is to Dublin or the poetry of Fernando Pessoa is to Lisbon.

My fascination with Ensor began decades earlier, on a snowy morning in Antwerp. I'd gone to the Royal Museum of Fine Arts Antwerp to see *The Dance of the Bride* by Pieter Bruegel and whatever other treasures I might find. I had the galleries all to myself aside from the tall, bald museum guard with a red beard and a gray flannel suit who shadowed me from room to room.

Then I came around a corner and was stopped in my tracks by *The Intrigue*, a big, raw colorful canvas of demented-looking figures. Who were these people, and why had the artist depicted them in such a grotesque way? It was a disturbing painting, which made it perversely irresistible, so I kept returning to it. I'd just decided the faces weren't really faces at all, but maybe masks of some kind, when the museum guard spoke to me: "Sir, if you really want to understand Ensor, you'll have to go to Ostend. It was the prism through which he saw the world."

"Thank you," I said. "Maybe someday I will."

Now that day had finally come, but to know where to track Ensor in Ostend, I met Xavier Tricot, an artist, writer, and one of the world's preeminent Ensor scholars, for a coffee in the cafe at De Grote Post. This popular cultural center was created from the town's beautiful former main post office and has become a gathering spot for an arty, free-spirited crowd where Ensor would have fit right in.

"People ask why Ensor stayed in Ostend instead of moving to Brussels or Paris, but I think he felt safe here because it was a small place which he knew, and where he was known," said Tricot, himself an Ostend native and resident. "Ensor also loved being by the sea, and the light here, and the implicit eccentricity of the town." Ostend also embodied a paradox. "Even after King Leopold II transformed the town into a resort for the nouveau-riche bourgeoisie, at heart it was still the same salty old port it had always been," Tricot said.

Tricot saw a similar duality in Ensor himself. "He was an elegant man who was very conscious of his social status. When he was young he witnessed the political and social upheavals in Belgium, and sympathized with the anarchists and the socialists. But he also identified a lot with his English father, who was well-born and had studied medicine in Germany, as opposed to his rather dour mother, who came from a simple Flemish family and ran a souvenir shop."

Ensor also had a complicated relationship with Ostend. "He was a pariah until he had his first solo exhibit in Brussels in 1895," Tricot said. "Then his genius was finally recognized by the local bourgeoisie, and the Belgian king made him a baron in 1929. He was very proud of that."

To best put Ensor in the context of his times, Tricot advised visiting the De Plate Ostend Historical Museum in the former royal residence at Langestraat 69. Intimate and atmospheric, with creaky

Above Ensor in old age, displayed alongside masks and mementoes at the Ensor Museum.

Opposite Some of Ostend's buildings date to the times Ensor lived in and remembered.

parquet floors, the museum shows how the town changed completely after 1838, when it became the terminus of a new rail line from Brussels. Across the English Channel, a rail line from London to Dover had also just opened, and in 1846 a Belgian steamship company began cross-Channel service with the purpose of attracting British tourists to the Belgian coast. More important, the little port had found favor with King Leopold I, the first regent of Belgium, who built this handsome villa and spent his holidays here with his French-born queen, Louise-Marie d'Orleans. Slightly creepy in a way that Ensor would probably have relished, her deathbed room is preserved intact.

Also on display were old travel posters and black-and-white photographs of grand hotels and a casino from the town's resort heyday. Ensor was something of a voyeur in relation to all this splendor. "I can give you some more information on my childhood and family," he wrote to a friend. "A picturesque detail to note. My grandparents had a shop in Ostend in the Rue des Capuchins that sold seashells, lace, stuffed rare fish…Chinese porcelain, guns, a mess of strange objects that were always being knocked over by several cats, parrots with deafening voices, and a monkey. I spent many long hours in the company of the cats, parrots, and monkey. The shop smelled of mold and the monkey's sour urine…while the cats walked on the precious lace. However, during the summer season, this strange place was frequented by the most distinguished foreigners, including William I Prince of Prussia, Leopold I King of the Belgians, the Duke of Brabant, the Duke of Flanders, etc."

The house at the corner of Vlaanderenstraat and Van Iseghemlaan, where the shop was located and Ensor grew up, was demolished in 1999. But the one at Vlaanderenstraat 27, where he moved in 1917 and lived until his death in 1949, is now the Ensor House,

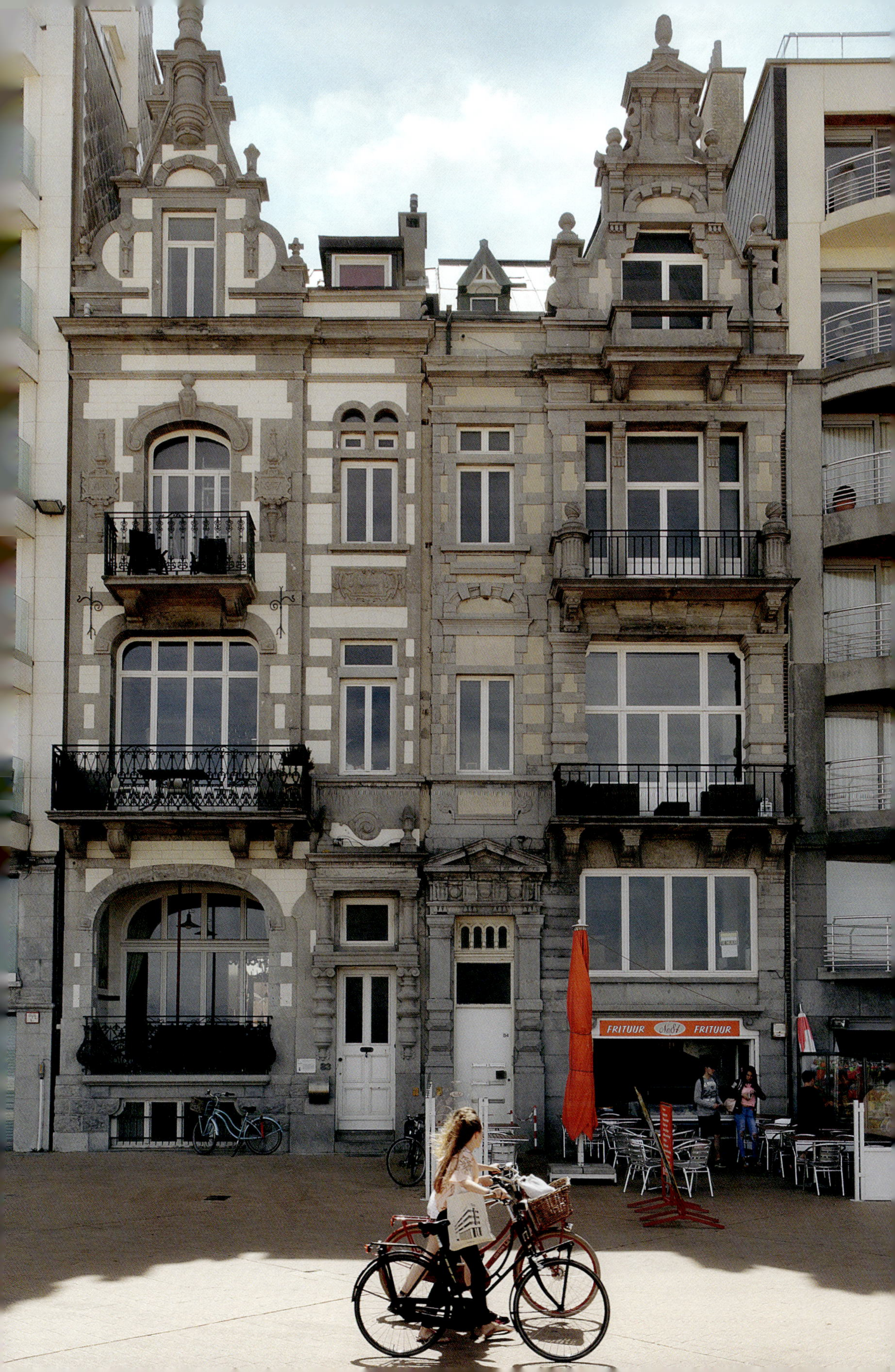
FRITUUR
FRITUUR

Above Broad beaches, crisp North Sea air, and royal favor made Ostend a favorite getaway.

Below Ensor's attachment to Ostend continued to his death. This is his tomb at Notre Dame des Dunes Church.

Opposite A sculpture of Ensor in Leopold Park. Ostend is both a working-class port and a genteel beach resort.

part of the Mu.ZEE, the city's major art museum. None of the painter's original works are displayed, but the house is scrupulously preserved as the painter lived in it. From the souvenir shop on the ground floor, with its wooden cases of shells, toy boats, and leering papier-mâché masks sold for Ostend's springtime carnival, to the stuffy parlors with vases of feathers, elaborately patterned wall-to-wall Brussels carpeting, damask curtains, and bric-a-brac everywhere, it's a stifling terrarium-like place. It's easy to imagine Ensor, in his waistcoat and with his waxed mustache, playing his harmonium in front of one of his best-known works, *Christ's Entry into Brussels*—a vivid agglomeration of religious, political, and military imagery surrounding a carnivalesque crowd of mostly grotesque faces—which today hangs at the J. Paul Getty Museum in Los Angeles.

The Albert I Promenade, overlooking Ostend's broad beaches, is lined today with structures built after World War II; but the long, colonnaded King Boudewijn Promenade, with its harlequin floor, survives. The Brasserie Albert at the Art Deco–era Thermae Palace Hotel offers the well-made Belgian comfort food that Ensor enjoyed, along with fine views of the North Sea.

Photographs by
Alex Crétey Systermans

Eager to see some of Ensor's work again, I headed for the Mu.ZEE. It was empty on a weekday, so I had the Ensor gallery to myself as I contemplated one of the artist's oddest paintings, *Ma Mère Morte (My Dead Mother)*, depicting, behind a foreground of medicine bottles on a tray, his mother on her deathbed, with the same cool delectation he might have felt painting it.

Then I moved along to a canvas that I consider the museum's Ensor masterpiece, *Self-Portrait with a Flowered Hat*. In this 1883 painting, the artist impassively returns the viewer's gaze, as if to say, "Yes, I am wearing a flowered hat with a big feather, and what of it?" And I concluded that it was this very pose, of frank but well-mannered iconoclasm, that made James Ensor Ostend's perfect son.

WHAT TO READ AND WATCH

James Ensor: The Complete Paintings, by Xavier Tricot. A definitive volume of Ensor's work.

Ensor, by Ulrike Becks-Malorny. A detailed survey with art and analysis. Part of TASCHEN's affordable Basic Art series.

Ostend: Stefan Zweig, Joseph Roth, and the Summer Before the Dark, by Volker Weidermann. A novelistic view of Ostend and a bohemian coterie trapped there at the outset of World War II.

James Ensor's World, Royal Academy of Arts, London. A two-minute video summary of Ensor and his relationship with Ostend, with narration in Ensor's own words.

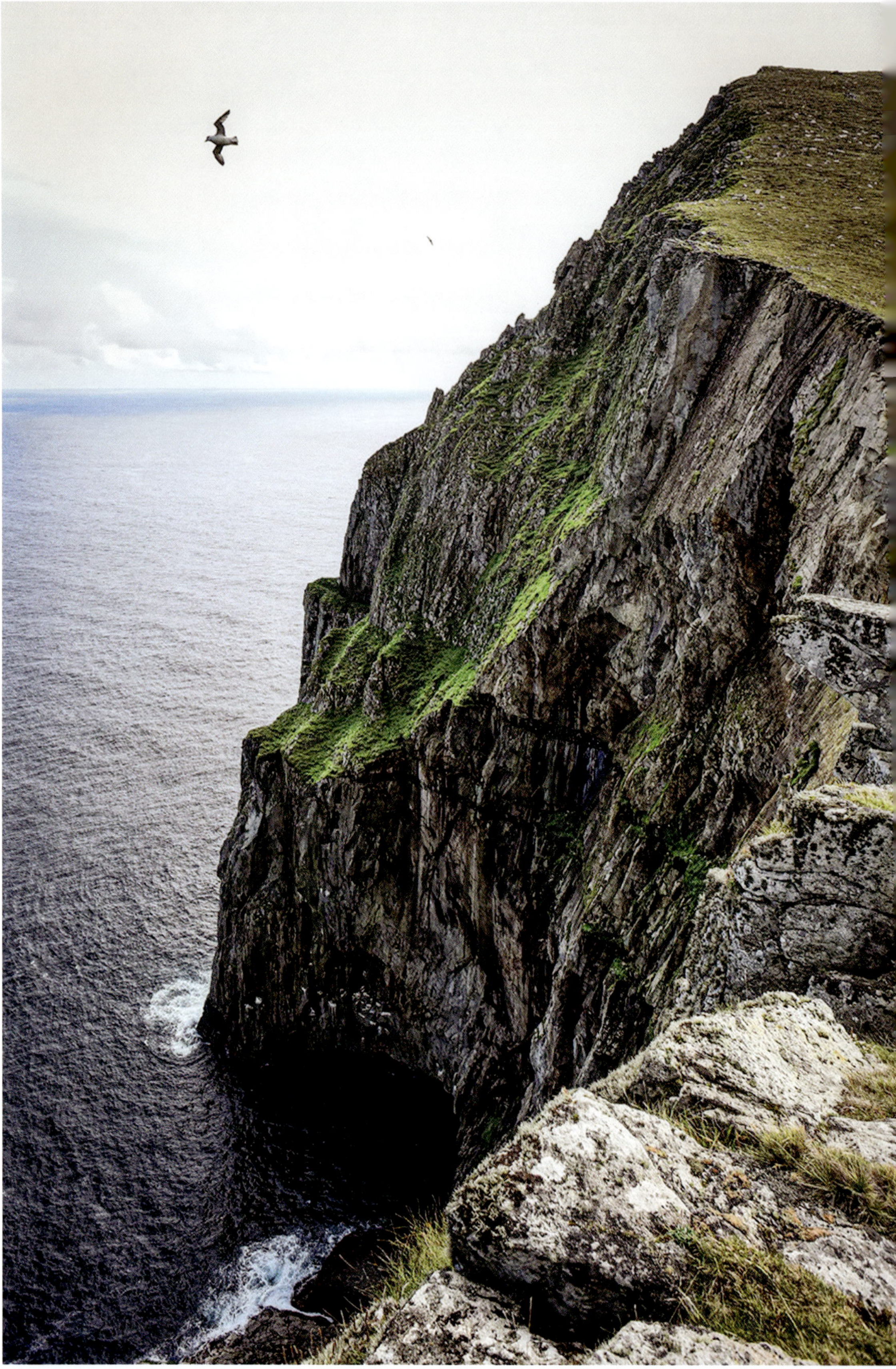

SCOTLAND • OUTER HEBRIDES

HAUNTING STORIES ON A STONY ISLAND

From prehistory to one last day in 1930, independent-minded islanders eked out a living in remote St. Kilda.
— BY STEPHEN HILTNER

For the first hour or so, the water was relatively calm. After departing from the small fishing village of Stein on the Isle of Skye, we sped through a strait known as the Little Minch toward the main band of the Outer Hebrides, the thick curl of rocky skerries that hovers like an apostrophe over the northwestern coast of mainland Scotland.

But as we pressed onward, traveling west beyond the islands of North Uist and Lewis and Harris, the water suddenly grew rougher. Here, fully exposed in the North Atlantic Ocean, we had no refuge from the swells: Every few seconds, for more than two hours, the hull of our tour boat slammed against the oncoming waves with enough force to rattle the passengers' teeth.

I looked to my right, across the boat's narrow aisle, and saw my brother and sister huddled uncomfortably in their seats. Altogether there were about a dozen of us crammed into a surprisingly small boat, including our guides, Harvey and Willie. No one looked comfortable.

At last Hirta, the largest island in the archipelago of St. Kilda, came into view in the distance — between Boreray, a smaller island, and the sea stack known as Stac an Armin. Another sea stack, Stac Lee, was in front of Hirta. When our boat had closed the distance and we finally arrived, an inflatable dinghy ferried us to Hirta's shore.

For centuries, St. Kilda, one of the most remote and unforgiving outposts in the British Isles, has electrified the imaginations of writers, historians, artists, scientists, and adventurers. Some 40 miles west of the chief islands of the Outer Hebrides, St. Kilda has a tantalizing history, complete with a rich cultural

Previous "Remote" only begins to describe St. Kilda, a group of rugged islands chilled by North Atlantic winds.

Left A tiny population of isolated islanders stuck it out on St. Kilda until 1930.

Opposite above A gun was installed near Hirta village after an attack by a German submarine in World War I.

Opposite below Small groups of tourists reach St. Kilda on day trips from the Isle of Skye.

heritage, fiercely independent people, distinctive architecture, and haunting isolation, as well as disease, famine, and exile.

Recent archaeological research suggests that Hirta, the main island, which is around 2.5 square miles in area, was inhabited as far back as 2,000 years ago. Its last full-time residents, 36 in total, were evacuated to the mainland on August 29, 1930, their community and their way of life having become unsustainable.

Designated as a dual Unesco World Heritage Site, with both natural and cultural significance, St. Kilda is now owned, managed, and protected by the National Trust for Scotland. Members of its staff, occasionally alongside other volunteers and researchers, occupy Hirta for several months of the year. Contractors for the British Ministry of Defense also spend time on the island, where they operate a radar station.

For much of its inhabited history, reaching St. Kilda required a multiday journey across the open ocean in a boat powered only by sails or oars. The threat of violent storms—especially common between September and March—made the voyage daunting at the best of times and unthinkable at the worst.

Even today, boat schedules are subject to the whims of the weather forecast, and cancellations by tour companies aren't unusual. When my siblings and I visited in late August, we had to preemptively shift our trip up by a day to avoid an impending spell of ominous weather arriving later that week.

St. Kilda's natural features are almost comical in their splendor. Jagged sea stacks rise like bundled knives from the opaque water; clamoring seabirds float nonchalantly above precipitous cliffs; swooping fields blanket an otherworldly landscape utterly devoid of trees. Precipitous cliffs abut grassy slopes. The archipelago of St. Kilda is one of the most important breeding grounds for seabirds, including northern gannets, Atlantic puffins, and northern fulmars, in the North Atlantic.

And yet it was St. Kilda's architectural remnants that hinted at the most dramatic elements of its history. With no trees to supply building materials or fuel, the islanders built in stone and burned peat. In the small abandoned village on Hirta, a handful of houses have been restored, simple structures of irregularly shaped rough stones piled together. Stone sheepfolds and igloo-shaped stone storage huts called *cleitean* remain nearby. The cleitean, unique to St. Kilda, were used to dry and store a range of food and goods, including seabirds, rope, eggs, peat fuel, and potatoes. More than 1,300 cleitean have been identified on St. Kilda, a vast majority of which are on Hirta.

Their roofs were topped with turf, and wind passing through the structures facilitated the preservation of stored goods.

Wild sheep remain on the islands, descendants of livestock first brought to the islands at least 4,000 years ago. We saw Soay sheep, an ancient and exceptionally hardy breed, dotting the landscape on Hirta. They share their name with the adjacent island of Soay; the word *Soay* likely derives from a Norse term for "sheep island."

With a population that peaked at around 180 in the late 17th century, St. Kilda has never made for a convenient home. Its inhabitants raised sheep and a few cattle and were often able to grow simple crops like barley and potatoes. But the mainstays of their diet came from seafowl: the birds' eggs and the birds themselves, which were consumed both fresh and cured. Fishing was often impractical because of the treachery of the surrounding waters; islanders also expressed a distinct preference for gannet, fulmar, and puffin over fish.

Before looking around the village, we hiked to Conachair, the island's highest point at 1,400 feet and a good vantage point. We came up on the grassy side; the ocean-facing north side is a vertical cliff dropping into the sea. Cliffs are integral to the islands of St. Kilda, and the islanders learned to take advantage of them. The rough rock attracts the seabirds, which nest in crevices or on inaccessible heights. The St. Kildans collected the birds and their eggs using long poles and their bare hands — by lowering themselves on ropes from atop cliffs, or by climbing up the rock faces from the water below. Looking at those cliffs and sea stacks, I tried to envision the circumstances under which such extremes would be necessary simply to enjoy a monotonous meal. It tested the limits of my imagination.

Life on St. Kilda was an agonizing experiment in precarity. Stormy weather spoiled crops, threatened food stores, prevented fowling, and delayed necessary work. Landing a boat at Hirta's Village Bay could be difficult even in ideal weather. When ships did arrive, they sometimes brought diseases, including smallpox, cholera, leprosy, and influenza, that spread quickly and with devastating effect. For decades, St. Kildans sometimes launched their mail blindly into the sea in small waterproof containers; the hope was that their "mailboats," as they were called, might by chance reach a populated place or be picked up and sent along by a passing ship.

The islanders' extreme isolation also bred a particular kind of cultural disconnection. In his 1965 book *The Life and Death of St. Kilda*, the author Tom Steel describes this scene in which a St. Kildan washed ashore on the nearby Flannan Isles:

"He entered what he thought was a house and began to climb the stairs — stone objects which he had never before seen in his life, but which he took to be Jacob's ladder. He reached the top and entered the brightly lit room. 'Are you God Almighty?' he asked the lighthouse keeper. 'Yes,' came the stern reply, 'and who the Devil are you?'"

Despite the remoteness, in the 20th century St. Kilda was reached, if only peripherally, by war. A four-inch gun was installed near Hirta village in 1918 after an attack by a German submarine, and remains in place, a relic facing the sea. The submarine's target was a British Navy signal station that

Above In a treeless landscape, the islanders built in stone and burned peat. Some of the deserted houses are restored.

Opposite Seabirds nesting in craggy cliffs were a food source for the St. Kildans, who used long poles to collect them.

had been built a short time before as part of World War I defenses. The station was destroyed and the village church was damaged, but no one was hurt. During World War II, when the islands were no longer inhabited, military planes flew overhead, though none apparently in combat. Near the summit of Conachair we saw the remains of a British Beaufighter aircraft that crashed there in June 1943.

Surprisingly, St. Kildans were often described by those who visited them as uniquely cheerful. Crime was virtually nonexistent. Supplies and donations brought in from the outside world—along with much of the food gathered on the islands—were divided equitably among the islanders. Items such as boats and ropes, upon which the survival of the settlement depended, were owned and maintained communally.

When the Scottish writer Martin Martin visited the archipelago in 1697, he saw the people as joyous. "The inhabitants of St. Kilda are much happier than the generality of mankind," he wrote, "as being almost the only people in the world who feel the sweetness of true liberty."

In the end, though, life on St. Kilda proved untenable. The market for the islanders' exports—feathers, tweed, sheep, seabird oil—gradually waned. Infant mortality rates were astonishingly high. Failing to keep pace with the comforts and technologies of the mainland, the islands became increasingly anachronistic. A particularly harsh winter in 1929 and 1930 sealed the St. Kildans' fate. Fearing starvation, they petitioned the government to be evacuated.

Even that, however, wasn't enough to break the spell for Alexander Ferguson, one of the evacuees, who, years later, describing St. Kilda in a letter, wrote that "there is no paradise on earth like it."

"To me it was peace living in St. Kilda," Malcolm Macdonald, another longtime resident, once said. "And to me it was happiness, dear happiness."

**Photographs by
Stephen Hiltner**

Four hours after arriving, having wandered over Hirta's rolling terrain and strolled quietly along its hollow shell of a village, our group enjoyed a snack and a hot drink before lining up along the jetty to board a dinghy and return to our boat. Our return voyage was smoother, quieter, calmer. For a long stretch, a pod of dolphins swam alongside us, as if escorting us through the water.

When we finally reached Stein, I felt a tinge of loss. Only then did I begin to understand what it was that compelled several of the 36 islanders, who left in desperation in 1930, to return to and temporarily live on Hirta in the summer of 1931: a mounting certainty that the pleasure of wandering free among the islands, surrounded by the boundless ocean, was worth the trouble of getting — and being — there.

WHAT TO READ AND WATCH

The Life and Death of St. Kilda: The Moving Story of a Vanished Island Community, by Tom Steel. A readable history of St. Kilda and its abandonment.

The Truth About St. Kilda: An Islander's Memoir, by Donald Gillies. An autobiographical account of the author's life on Hirta in the early 20th century, based on the author's handwritten notebooks.

The Prisoner of St Kilda: The True Story of the Unfortunate Lady Grange, by Margaret Macauley. In the ultimate bad breakup, an 18th-century Scottish nobleman had his wife kidnapped and spirited off to lead a miserable life in St. Kilda. The author explores how and why.

The Edge of the World, directed by Michael Powell. A 1937 film based on the evacuation of St. Kilda in 1930. Though filming on Hirta was not allowed and the production had to be relocated to the Orkneys, the movie dramatizes St. Kilda's actual plight.

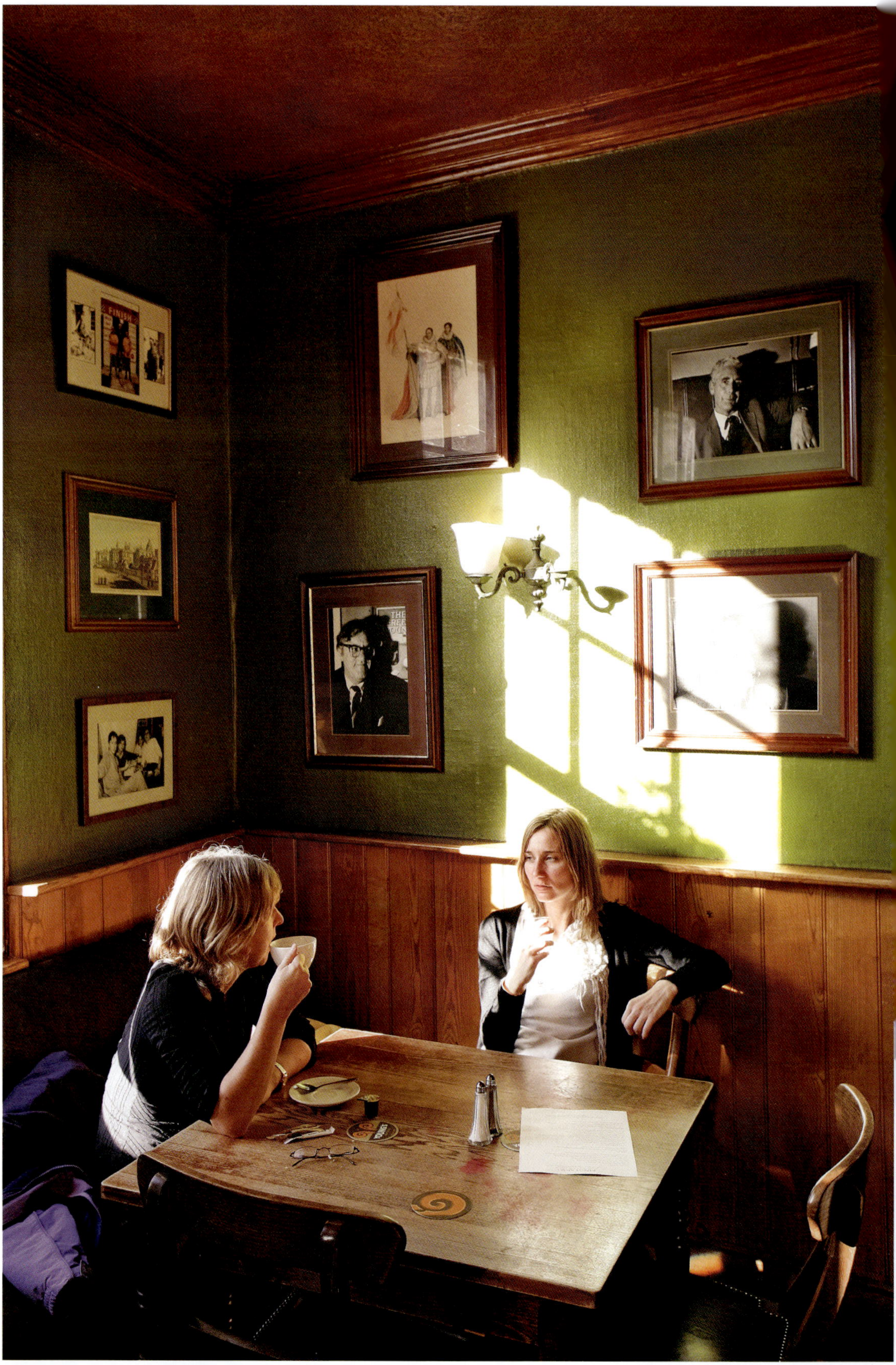

A PUB CRAWL THROUGH THE CENTURIES

In Oxford, where J. R. R. Tolkien and the Inklings once convened, a pint of ale comes with a gallon of tradition.
— BY HENRY SHUKMAN

Samuel Johnson declared a tavern seat "the throne of human felicity." The Frenchman Hilaire Belloc, who spent his life in England, said, "When you have lost your inns, drown your empty selves. For you will have lost the last of England."

A good pub is a ready-made party, a home away from home, a club anyone can join. Some British pubs began as simple meeting places, some as coaching inns — hostelries where stagecoaches stopped for the night for fodder, bed, and a stable. Generally these were larger and had a secondary pub at the back for ostlers, farriers, and other riffraff.

In Oxford, which has some pubs — like the Bear, on Blue Boar Lane, and the Mitre, on the High Street — that date back to the 1200s, many of the names echo the Middle Ages. The White Hart (a stag, Richard II's heraldic emblem), the Kings Arms (named for James I, during whose reign neighboring Wadham College was founded), the Bear, the Wheatsheaf: all are names that call up a past of knights, farms, and forests.

The pubs of Oxford serve locals and travelers, increasingly with food as well as drink. They also did and do serve the students and faculty of Oxford's famous university, whose spires and pinnacles carry their own aura of the distant past. From the quadrangles and college halls, it has long been an easy walk to refreshment.

What is this link between alcohol and academia, books and beer? One 20th-century student reputedly demanded a flagon of claret during his exams, having discovered an ancient rule in the University Statute Book entitling him to it. The invigilator was able to annul the request because the student was improperly

Previous The Kings Arms, in the heart of Oxford, was founded in the early 1600s, during James I's reign.

Left One of the gardens of the Turf Tavern is in the shade of an ancient wall built to keep the Vikings out.

Opposite A quiet hour at the Old Bookbinders. At Oxford's pubs, students, workers, and anyone else might mingle.

dressed — according to another statute, he should have been wearing a saber.

Yet the pub is fundamentally a great leveler — not just a students' hangout or a workingman's club, but an everyman's club. The best pubs are filled not only with the scent of yeast and hops, but also with banter and wit. Back in 1954, when the Rose & Crown on North Parade Avenue in Oxford was threatened with closure (inadequate toilet facilities), the defense that won the day called it a "home of cultured, witty, and flippant conversation."

Whether the question is how to warm plates swiftly or how to use the hyphen correctly, there's no talk like pub talk.

Some pubs, like the Rose & Crown, are a kind of family where the landlord knows exactly how much to know of his regulars' business but every well-behaved person who is neither a dog nor a politician is welcome, too. The Rose & Crown is an ideal pub. Half a mile north of the Oxford city center, it's only 150 years old, but the three small wood-paneled rooms and the affable proprietors make it a home away from home. It also keeps the best pint of Old Hooky in town. Brewed about 20 miles away at Hook Norton, a brewery that hasn't changed much of its process since it opened in 1849, Old Hooky is a legend in the annals of real ale, a vessel of hazel clarity, redolent of harvest stubble lit by an evening sun, of woods drenched in rain, of dewy meadows at dawn, of cattle in dells, of Thomas Hardy and sandy-gray churches nestled in the nooks of sheep-studded hills. If this isn't the drinkable essence of England, nothing is.

Some say the pub is in crisis. Several years ago *The Guardian* reported that for the first time since the Norman Conquest fewer than half the villages of England had a pub, and pub closures have continued since then. Chains of horrendous corporate-owned "vertical drinking establishments" — giant Identikit bars — threaten the remaining real pubs, and the real pubs themselves are mostly owned by equally horrendous "pubcos," companies invented to dodge laws against brewing monopolies. Yet somehow real ale (championed by a group called Camra, the Campaign for Real Ale) and real pubs do survive.

A chap at the back bar of the Kings Arms, with long hair, sports jacket (slight rip in shoulder seam) and a pint of Waggle Dance at his elbow, was holding forth one afternoon about Bulgaria — "I've always loved the country," he drawled — and then about Falstaff. Some say the death of Falstaff in Shakespeare's *Henry V* symbolizes the death of merry old England. In come the Protestants; out go the bibulous friars, jolly yeomen, and Mother Mary. After that, only in the public house did the Middle Ages continue to find shelter.

The Kings Arms is a linchpin of Oxford life. Situated at a junction in the heart of the city, it has spacious, airy front rooms, and at the rear three or four small rooms, all thick with honey-colored wood and irregular in shape. It was founded in the early 17th century when adjacent Wadham College was being built (the landlord presumably hoping for trade with the masons). It used to host bare-knuckle and cudgel fights, almost to the death, in its courtyard.

The much less capacious Bear, tucked down Blue Boar Lane at the back of Christ Church, dates to 1242 and has only two tiny wood rooms. They are covered, wall and ceiling, with picture frames containing short pieces of ties. Ties of clubs, regiments, schools — the Royal Gloucester Hussars, the Imperial Yeomanry, the Punjab Frontier Force, Lloyd's of London Croquet Club — telling of an older, more powerful, more sedate England. Croquet, beer, cricket, empire, and P. G. Wodehouse: A snip off your tie, and you'll get a free half-pint.

The small Eagle and Child on the broad boulevard of St. Giles' was for decades distinguished mostly by the coziness of its nooks, and by the fact that — like its counterpart across the road, the Lamb & Flag, where Graham Greene liked to drink — it has long been owned by St. John's, a college of spectacular wealth. But since the *Lord of the Rings* movies, it has become a celebrity among pubs. It was here that the Inklings — J. R. R. Tolkien, who wrote *The Hobbit* and the *Rings*, C. S. Lewis, inventor of Narnia, and others — would meet on a Tuesday to drink, talk, and smoke. Lewis recalled the "golden sessions" they enjoyed by the fire. Tolkien lived around the corner on St. John's Street.

On a summer evening, when green-filtered light from the trees floods in through the front windows and the sheen on its paneling is restful on the eye, the Eagle and Child is dark as a hovel, yet struck through with daylight. The nooks were clearly made for smoking, now banned. These oak rooms without smoke? Any male writer of the 19th or 20th century — Tolkien, Lewis, or whoever—without pipe, cigar, or cigarette? Unthinkable. Unwritable.

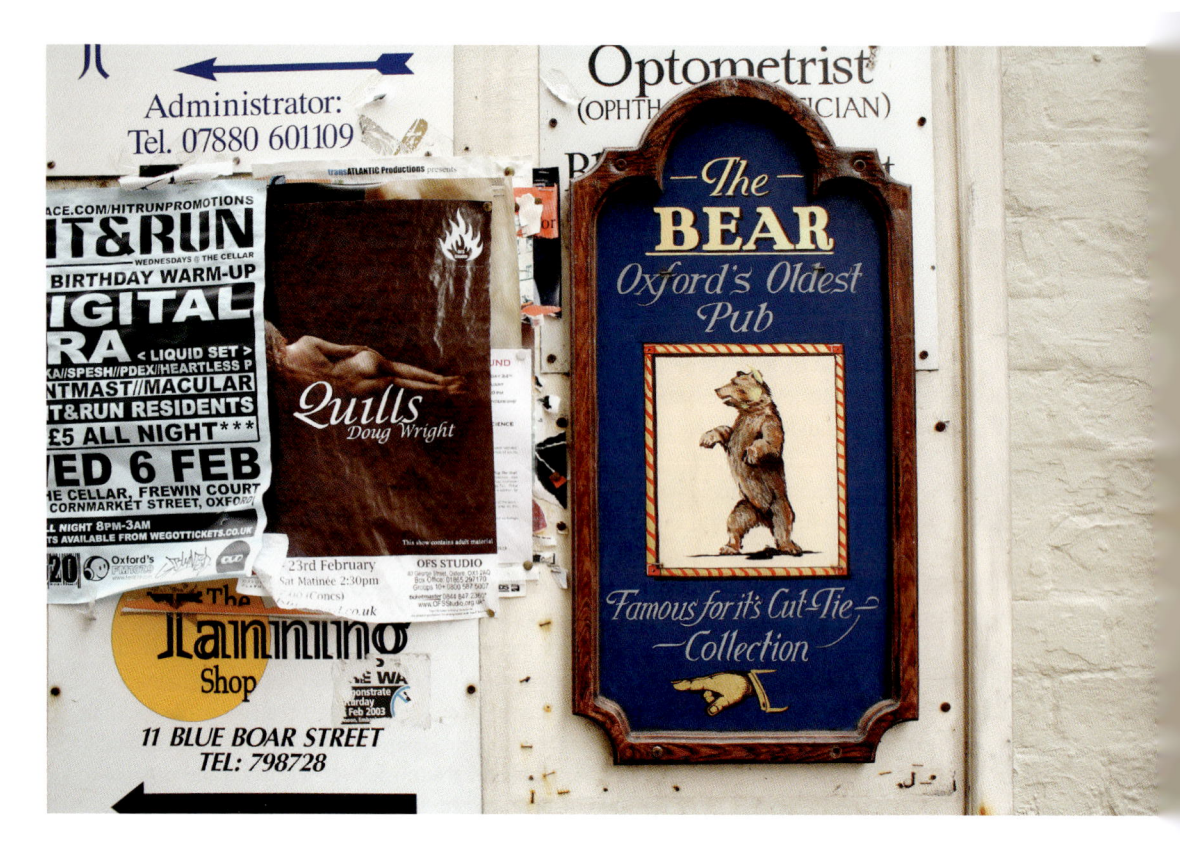

Above The Bear, dating to 1242, is the oldest pub in Oxford.

Below The Old Bookbinders in Jericho, a canal-side neighborhood in Oxford.

Opposite The Rose & Crown honors tradition in the choice of its ales.

There's no mistaking the aged authenticity of the Turf Tavern. Its string of low-beamed, stone-walled rooms could be straight out of Chaucer. But what really makes it is its three gardens. In one, beside the cottages of Bath Close, you could be in a Cotswold village, with flower boxes and black beams. On the other side, you're deep in the shade of the ancient city wall, erected against the Vikings. You can hardly tell if it's the 21st century or the 15th. How many centuries have people hungry for learning, for the book, sat here under the walls swigging jars of ale? On a summer night, with the sky stretched over the stones of Oxford, history becomes a living stream of ale: Ruddles and Theakstons, Hook Norton and Feathers.

Here, allegedly, Bill Clinton didn't inhale. Here, too, Bob Hawke most affirmatively did swallow a yard of ale (two and a half pints) in 11 seconds, securing a place in the Guinness World Records, as well as (later) the Australian premiership.

One could crawl on and on. There's Old Bookbinders down in the canal-side neighborhood of Jericho, a stone's throw from where the Castle Mill boatyard inspired Philip Pullman to create the Gyptians boat people in *The Golden Compass*. At Bookbinders, the ales are kept in barrels behind the bar, and you can

Photographs by Jonathan Player

reach into a tub for free handfuls of ground nuts. There's the Gardeners Arms of Plantation Road, with its old wood rooms and some of the best vegetarian food in town. Not to mention the Trout on the river, the Grapes in the center, the White Horse, and the little Half Moon by Magdalen Bridge.

Oxford. What a surfeit of good will in its honey-gold stone and nut-brown glasses.

WHAT TO READ AND WATCH

The Good Pub Guide, by Fiona Stapley. Guidebook to pubs all over England, with reader recommendations. First published in 1982 and updated annually.

The Pub: A Cultural Institution, from Country Inns to Craft Beer Bars and Corner Locals, by Pete Brown. A personal survey of 300 British pubs by a writer drawn to appealing or unusual atmospheres.

The Inklings, by Humphrey Carpenter. A picture of C.S. Lewis, J.R.R. Tolkien, and others as they interacted in their genial circle of Oxford writers, written by an author who knew some of them.

Inspector Morse. A multiseason British television series about a brilliant Oxford detective, based on novels by Colin Dexter and aired by the BBC. The subsequent series *Endeavour* is a prequel.

Insight Guides Great Breaks Oxford. A collection of walks and tours in Oxford, with historical background and information for travelers.

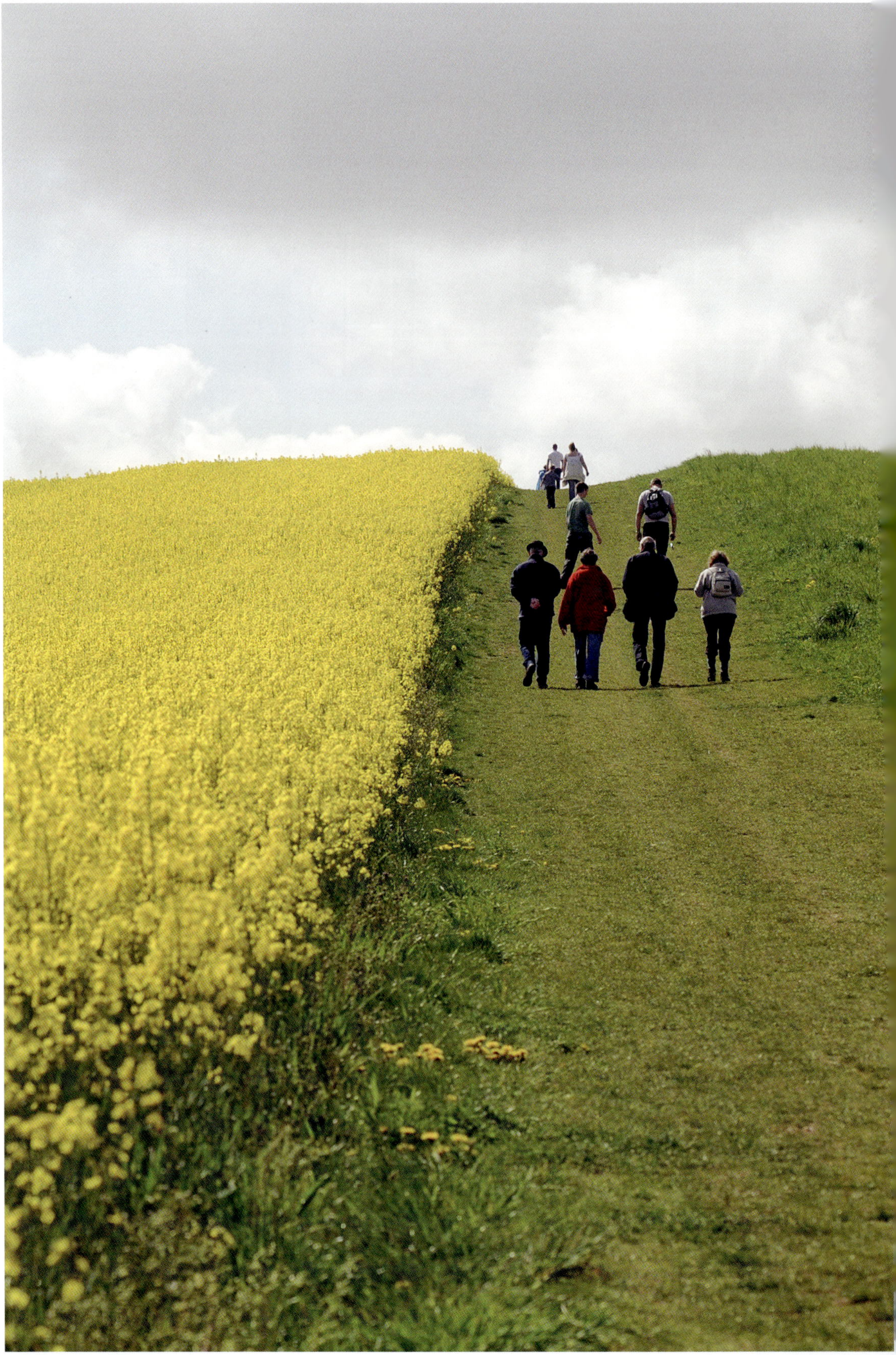

A TREK ON EUROPE'S OLDEST ROAD

England's Ridgeway trail is a route that people have traveled for 5,000 years. — BY HENRY SHUKMAN

The Ridgeway is the oldest continuously used road in Europe, dating back to the Stone Age. Situated in southern England, built by Britain's Neolithic ancestors, it's at least 5,000 years old, and may even have existed when England was still connected to continental Europe and the Thames was a tributary of the Rhine.

Once it probably ran all the way from Dorset in the southwest to Lincolnshire in the northeast, following the line of a chalk escarpment — a ridge rising from the land — that diagonally bisects southern England. Long ago it wasn't just a road following the high ground, away from the woods and swamps lower down, but a defensive barrier, a bulwark against marauders from the north, whoever they may have been. At some point in the Bronze Age (perhaps around 2500 B.C.), a series of forts were built — ringed dikes protecting villages — so the whole thing became a kind of prototype of Hadrian's Wall in the north of England.

The land here is downland, somewhere between moorland and farmland, hill after hill curving to the horizon in chalk slopes (the word "down" is related to "dune"). On these pale rolling hills, the plowed fields, littered with white hunks of rock, sweep away in gradations of color from creamy white to dark chocolate. The grassland becomes silvery as it arches into the distance. The wind always seems to be blowing. The landscape is elemental, austere, with a kind of monumental elegance. The formal lines of the fields and hills not only speak of the severity of life in the prehistoric past, but would also match some well-tended parkland belonging to an earl.

I used to come here as a child. The Ridgeway, now officially called the Ridgeway National Trail, was a

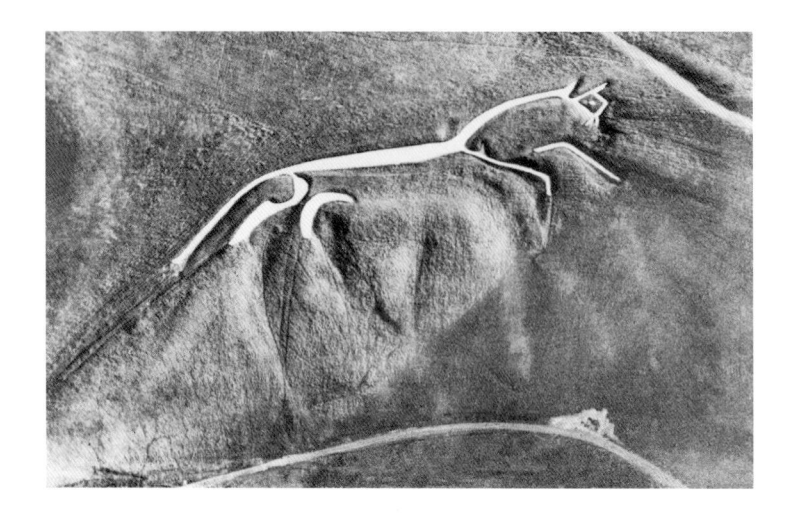

Previous About half of today's Ridgeway is made up of footpaths connecting the original old track, which follows a ridge.

Left The White Horse, a chalk figure scratched and dug into the grass, is 3,000 years old. This photo is from 1950.

Opposite above A road sign along the Ridgeway between Broad Hinton and Marlborough.

Opposite below Part of a circle of monoliths at Avebury, one of the prehistoric sites along the Ridgeway National Trail.

favorite Sunday outing. Just half an hour south of Oxford, my family's home back then, its steep turfy hillsides were the best place in the world for rolling downhill. We'd lie across the grassy slopes and roll down sideways. You could go for hundreds of feet, until dizziness got the better of you, and you got up with the ground spinning before tackling the long scramble back up to do it again. Maybe we didn't get quite the thrill from the huge views over southern England that our parents did, but we loved the wind coming up fresh from the southwest, and the big clouds scudding by, and the sense of space and openness.

We also loved the Uffington White Horse, the most famous chalk drawing in England, a huge, graceful, serpent-like beast scratched and dug into the grass just below the top of the escarpment the Ridgeway follows, made 3,000 or so years ago by the same people who built the stone circles of southern England, the so-called Beaker people, named after the beakers they were buried with. We used to walk along the White Horse, over its chalk surface.

But I never knew what exactly the Ridgeway was, or the White Horse for that matter. So decades later, when a friend suggested a walk along the trail, I jumped at the chance. Southern England is built up, and a long-distance footpath that navigates a route straight through it — for the most part avoiding roads and settlements, one that takes you past some of the best Neolithic monuments on earth, and through ancient landscapes — was surely worth checking out.

The Ridgeway of today is 87 miles long, about half of it a series of footpaths that connect the original old track following the ridge up on the chalk escarpment. It can easily be traveled in shorter segments, depending on time available. My friend Rory and I decided to walk only the old western half of the trail — about 40 miles entirely on the ancient road— from the market town of Wantage (where King Alfred was born) to Avebury, famous for its huge circles of monolithic standing stones.

We set out on a chilly March morning intending to cover the distance over the next two days. Equipped with light daypacks containing rain gear, lunch, and snacks, and wearing good athletic shoes, we bounced up the lane toward the tremendous escarpment of chalky turf looming ahead of us, a great green tidal wave we would have to scale. This is the "ridge" of the Ridgeway, and the old road runs along the top of it, connecting the series of ancient forts.

By the time we had made our way up, the spring in our step had long since wilted, and we had shed our fleeces and sweaters in spite of the cold overcast weather. The "road" looked like an old farm track and made for wonderful walking as it undulated smoothly over the level ground at the top of the ridge. It was close to silent up there. We moved back into a world of bleats and birdsong, and soughing wind.

"This is what I'm after," Rory said. "To get away from the sounds of petrol."

"Escape the carbon age?"

"Back to the Neolithic. Where it's quieter."

We strained our ears. Sure enough, away in the distance we could just hear a tractor growling faintly.

Every so often we passed one of the distinctive clumps of beech trees that dot the landscape. There's something about these copses: When you're in one, its whistling shade is eerie and beautiful, steeped in a sense of another time, of history, of the age of the landscape. When you're looking at them from far away, they form thick dashes and hyphens on the sweeping page of the land. The grasslands up here, beloved of sheep and horses, curve away in sculptural lines, creating deep bowls and broad gullies. It's a landscape that exhales prehistory, littered with burial mounds, standing stones, and hill forts.

Maybe it was England's chilly spring or maybe the fact that it was a weekday, but over the course of the walk we met a total of only four other walkers.

The first major site we reached was the White Horse. This Neolithic marvel, a 374-foot serpentine line of gritty chalk, dug into the hillside below the ridge, visible from many miles away — in fact only really visible from a distance — has the graceful lines of the Lascaux cave paintings in France. The way it's embedded in the very land has made it a talisman of southern England over the centuries. Below it the ground drops away steeply to a flat-topped knoll like a platform or stage, on which St. George is alleged to have slain the original dragon. (Some say the chalk horse is actually a dragon.)

After a rest of half an hour, we heaved ourselves back up to the track and marched onward, always with the land falling away to one side, and always with the skylarks, those quintessential English songsters, warbling away above us.

The next major site, Wayland's Smithy, was a long barrow, or burial mound, guarded by several large gray stones at its entrance and by an encircling ring of rustling beech trees.

Rory laughed. "Spooky, no?"

It is. It could be one of those portals to another dimension beloved of contemporary children's literature. Something in the DNA seems to wake up, as if somehow recognizing the ceremonials of another time. No wonder there has been a long tradition in England of people devoting themselves to unearthing the secrets of the lost religions of pagan times.

Every five or six miles we reached one of the turfy hill forts, each a ring of dike and ditch, which made this whole ridge such a formidable defensive barrier. It protected King Arthur's Britons from the invading Saxons, then the Saxons from the marauding Vikings. Today the forts make good places to break the journey with a snack, meal, or drink. If you need something more substantial, occasional roads cross the Ridgeway and will take you down to the villages strung along the foot of the high ground.

Late in the afternoon, we made our way down to the Inn with the Well (named after the deep glass-covered well in its bar) in Ogbourne St. George, ready

Above Hikers can dip down to villages or see them from the trail's heights. This church is in Fyfield.

Opposite A new generation takes its turn exploring at the White Horse.

for a pint. In the bar we met a party of three other walkers doing the Ridgeway the opposite way from ours. We all raised a glass before having dinner and going to our rooms for the night.

The next morning we wound back up the formidable face of green hillside and made our first stop at Fyfield Down, a vale studded with gorse, with ancient "strip lynchet" field terraces marking the land in italic lines. The turf was littered with giant gray stones. It's from here that many of the standing stones in the nearby monuments came. The so-called Grey Wethers (gray sheep), or Sarsen stones — the monoliths of many stone circles — still lie strewn over the slopes here, left behind by glacial action, looking like the rubble from some giant blast. In medieval times, when the original erectors of the stone monuments were long since gone, these monoliths were thought to be magical in and of themselves. Hence the name Sarsen, a corruption of Saracen — or Arab. In those days, Arabs were considered magicians and wizards, perhaps because their knowledge of math and science far outstripped that of the comparatively crude Christian North.

On we went, from one Neolithic site to the next, past dramatic trees, past views down onto villages, dropping into a walking rhythm outside normal time. It seemed we were moving through a far larger context, one that sweeps across time. Conversation deepened. We pondered the lives we were leading, and how they measured up to what we had hoped for as young men. What influence did this land we grew up in — gray above, green below — have on us? England has been the epicenter of logical positivism, rationalism, empiricism, not to mention having been a violent colonial machine. Yet it is also a land of mystery — of Avalon, Arthur, Merlin, Druids, and standing stones.

It was late afternoon when we dropped down to Avebury, the largest of all megalithic sites in Britain.

*Photographs by
Chris Warde-Jones*

Trees, stones, hills, and chalk: These were the things with which the ancient people made their art. And they made huge art pieces. At Avebury, two giant earth banks surround a circle of stones more than 300 yards across. This in turn encloses two inner rings of stones. Many are gone, broken up in the 1700s to create building materials for the village that now stands right in the center of the complex. It's a strange sight, the English village houses cheek by jowl with ancient monoliths, but it's a poignant expression of what this whole area is about: successive layers of human history hard up against each other.

It's only around 60 miles from London and a few miles from the M4 motorway, but it could be thousands of years and a million miles away. After a stroll among the huge stones, we headed for the Red Lion pub in the middle of the village and killed time with a genteel English cream tea as we waited for our bus back to the city.

WHAT TO READ AND WATCH

Ridgeway: National Trail Guide, by Anthony Burton. A guidebook published in association with Natural England, the official body charged with developing and maintaining England's National Trails. The trail's website is nationaltrail.co.uk/ridgeway.

The Ridgeway: Avebury to Ivinghoe Beacon, by Nick Hill and Henry Stedman. A Trailblazer guidebook, including detailed walking maps.

The Ridgeway, by Max Landsberg. From Rucksack Readers, which publishes waterproof, easy-to-carry guidebooks.

The Ridgeway in Three Minutes, by Abbie Barnes. A clever overview video available on YouTube.

Stonehenge: A Novel of 2000 B.C., by Bernard Cornwell. The England of 4,000 years ago, imagined by a popular and prolific author. Described by *Publishers Weekly* as a "wild tale, rich with sorcery, pagan ritual, greed, and intrigue."

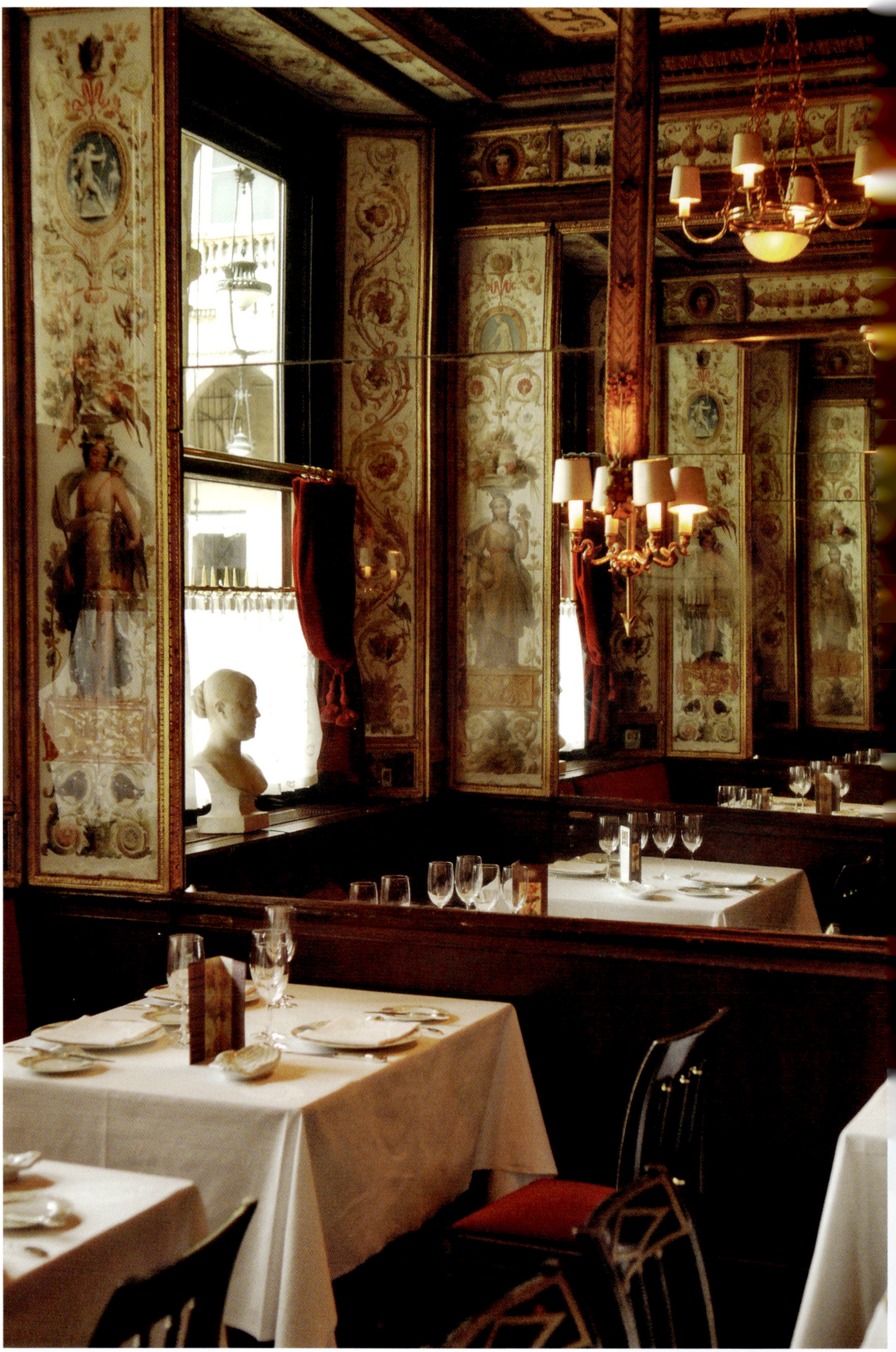

LIBERTY, EQUALITY, GASTRONOMY

Two centuries ago, a discriminating gourmand wrote restaurant guides for Parisians. How good a critic was he? Several of his favorites are still open.
— BY TONY PERROTTET

A marvelous painting of a gourmand at his table hangs in the Musée Carnavalet in Paris — a portly, pink-faced figure happily gorging on a regal casserole, with a bottle of wine at one elbow and a luscious-looking soufflé at the other. It is traditionally believed to be a portrait of Alexandre-Balthazar-Laurent Grimod de la Reynière, an aristocrat notorious in Napoleonic France for gratifying his palate with the same abandon as his contemporary the Marquis de Sade showed in indulging carnal desires. Whether or not the painting is actually Grimod's likeness, it captures the eccentric, omnivorous spirit that made him not only a gustatory symbol in the Paris of his day, but the grand-père of all modern food writers.

Starting in 1803, Grimod, whose family fortune had largely been lost during the Revolution, financed his voracious appetite by writing a series of best-selling guidebooks to the culinary wonders of Paris — its famous delicatessens, pâtissiers, and chocolatiers — including the first reviews of an alluring new institution called le restaurant. His *Almanachs des Gourmands* were something new, the Michelins and Zagats of his era.

Grimod was born in 1758. His family mansion on the Place de la Concorde stood on the site occupied today by the United States Embassy. A social butterfly, he became a successful theater critic before the Revolution, survived the Terror, and amused himself later by hosting literary salons in the cafes. And, of course, eating.

I discovered Grimod in the New York Public Library. I was researching a book on Napoleon and came across two pocket-size, leather-bound volumes,

Previous Le Grand Véfour dates to 1784. "Nowhere else can one find a better sauté," Grimod wrote in 1820.

Left A painting thought to be of Grimod de la Reynière, hanging in the Carnavalet Museum in Paris.

Opposite Escargots at Le Procope, a Left Bank restaurant once frequented by leaders of the French Revolution.

the 1805 and 1810 editions of the *Almanach*. They made fascinating reading: idiosyncratic and outlandish, filled with arcane gossip about forgotten chefs and digressions on the best way to cook calf's head in aspic or quails in sarcophagi (the birds lie in tiny pastry "coffins," with their heads intact; a version of the dish appears in the film *Babette's Feast*). At various points, Grimod even includes the names and addresses of actresses he is wooing, like the comely Augusta, cited for her "grace and freshness."

The *Almanachs* also include detailed gastronomic walking tours of Paris, called "nutritional itineraries" — each one a vivid window onto the past. The more I read, the more interested I became in finding out what remains today of Grimod's Paris. So I flew to Paris to find out.

I assumed that recreating a 200-year-old trail would require something of a creative leap, but on the first day, when I passed through the vaulted arches of the Palais Royal, I realized what a challenge I actually faced. In Grimod's day this was the heart and soul of Paris, a rowdy entertainment center filled with brothels and sideshows that, despite its louche ambience, also boasted some of his favorite specialty food stores and restaurants. Now it presented itself as a serene park, quaint and genteel as a fashionable graveyard.

Its splendid arches were intact, but they were lined with clothing boutiques. I pored feverishly over my 1810 guide. Where was Corcellet, the most revered épicerie in France, with its rich pâtés, delicious sausages, and succulent hams? (The painting in the Carnavalet was actually commissioned as a sign by the owner of Corcellet in 1804, after Grimod gave it a rave review in the *Almanach*.) Or the dining hall of the so-called Three Brothers from Provence, "renowned for their garlic râgouts and excellent brandades de merluche"?

I knew that at least one survivor did remain: Le Grand Véfour, the oldest continually operating restaurant in Paris. I found it tucked like a jewel box in the Palais Royal's quietest corner.

Le Grand Véfour was founded in 1784 as the Café de Chartres, and Napoleon and Josephine used to meet there on trysts. After it was purchased by Jean Véfour in 1820, Grimod praised its cuisine: "Nowhere else can one find a better sauté, chicken Marengo, or mayonnaise de volaille," he wrote.

The moment I stepped through the door, I was swept into a romantic fantasia of the 19th century. The décor was original and exquisite. Long mirrors reflected sparkling chandeliers and plush crimson upholstery. The gold-framed glass panels that stretched to the ceiling were lavishly painted with classical beauties.

A phalanx of tuxedoed professionals briskly whisked me to my table, where a large menu materialized before my eyes. After noticing with a gulp that Le Grand Véfour had also inherited the tradition of the mind-boggling price tag, I ordered the relatively affordable fixed-price lunch special. Then I spent three hours working through it. At a steady, dreamlike pace I received what seemed like a dozen courses, with amuse-bouches, sorbets, cheeses, and confections providing the backdrop to the more substantial shredded crab and radish salad and monkfish on mango with coriander mousse.

A few days of this and I'd be more rotund than the great gourmand himself.

Grimod wrote his guides at a pivotal culinary moment, when Paris was flush with money from Napoleon's conquests and establishing itself as the gourmet capital of Europe. It was also incubating the new culture of the restaurant, named for the soups called "restaurants" (restoratives) that were initially the new dining places' staple. Unlike the old inns and taverns, restaurants offered patrons private tables and the chance to choose fine meals individually prepared. They became tourist attractions in themselves, vying with one another in their opulent décor and presenting Parisians with dozens of fresh and exciting dishes printed on menus the size of newspapers. It was the perfect environment for the blossoming of Grimod's peculiar talents.

As I made my way through the streets he had known, I was constantly surprised at how much remains from the Parisian culinary past. I tracked down the oldest remaining pâtisserie of Paris, Stohrer, whose 1730 shop a few blocks from the Palais Royal is an irresistible palace of sweet delicacies, with original lead mirrors reflecting a multicolored array of pastries and glazed fruits. I found the mustard emporium of Maille on the Place de la Madeleine. Although the premises are modern, Maille has been a fixture in Paris since 1757, and you can still sample Grimod's favorite mustards ("famous from pole to pole," he enthused).

The disappearance of Les Halles, the old market, would bring a bitter tear to Grimod's eye. In 1810, he wrote page after page assessing the vendors' wares, ending in a shopaholic ecstasy: "One would like to invade every stall, carry away everything to stock one's kitchen." But he could have taken consolation nearby on one of his favorite streets, Rue Montorgueil. In the *Almanach* he drools over its oyster vendors, whose shells were piled as high as the roofs of the houses. Here also stood one of his favorite restaurants, Au Rocher de Cancale, which he cites as having the best seafood and poultry in Paris, not to mention a quail pâté cooked in Malaga wine that was "suitable for the table of the gods." Today, Rue Montorgueil is a fashionable pedestrian street filled with upscale vendors. Not only were fresh oysters still on sale at pricey seafood markets, but I was delighted to find Au Rocher de Cancale still going strong as a lively lunchtime bistro.

The florid exterior was unmistakably of the period, although a plaque noted that the establishment had moved from one side of the street to the other in 1846. No matter! It was lunchtime. In the upstairs dining room, I spied a series of unique frescoes salvaged from the 1846 restaurant and preserved under plexiglass like archaeological finds from Pompeii. They had been discovered, the waitress told me, when the room was renovated in the 1980s.

Together, they told the story of a Grimodesque gourmand tackling a meal. In the first image, the diner savors an aperitif of Champagne. In the second, he sucks down oysters. In the third, he is enjoying the main course with a wicked grin. Next, he waves away a waiter, unwilling to be bothered. In the last, he holds the bill and ruefully weighs his coins.

I'm not sure what Grimod would have made of my tandoori cod over fennel and rice, but I personally

Above The ice creams at Le Procope are still as good as Grimod described them in 1810.

Opposite Diners at Le Procope. When Grimod wrote his restaurant guides, Paris was rich from Napoleon's conquests.

thought that it would not be out of place on the gods' table.

On the Left Bank, one of Grimod's remaining favorites is the venerable Le Procope, once frequented by revolutionary heroes like Danton and Marat. By 1810, it had been renamed the Café Zoppi, but Grimod still heartily recommended it for "the best ice creams in Faubourg St.-Germain, and also the most copious." He would be happy to know that when I dropped by, the sorbets and ice creams were still lethally good.

Ten minutes' walk away, Debauve & Gallais, official chocolatier to Napoleon, is also alive and well. This aromatic relic, founded in 1800, still has its original semicircular counter covered with fabulous treats. Grimod was particularly fond of the shop's so-called health chocolates, which were regarded by Parisians as multivitamins are today. Consume them daily, he observes, and "an Adonis can acquire all the virtues of a Hercules."

At the Quai des Grands-Augustins I came across a lavishly decorated old restaurant called Lapérouse. In Grimod's day this was a popular wine shop and bar, but it was taken over in 1840 as a restaurant by Jules Lapérouse, who had the brilliant idea of maintaining private rooms upstairs for married gentlemen to discreetly entertain the courtesans of Paris with Champagne, delicacies, and expensive gifts. After I consumed yet another excellent, over-the-top lunch, a waiter took me to visit those notorious chambres particuliers. I observed that the antique mirrors were covered with etched marks, made, according to tradition, by women testing the authenticity of their diamonds.

On my last day in Paris, I was strolling the Rue St.-Honoré when I noticed a tiny row of medieval structures attached to the Church of St.-Roch. One was a minuscule restaurant called La Cordonnerie (the Shoemaker's) and, according to the blackboard, it served *cuisine de marché*, fresh market food.

Photographs by
Andrew Testa

There were fewer than 20 seats in its intimate space, which dated from 1690, with blackened beams against the low white ceiling. I felt sure that Grimod must have eaten here at some time or another.

The chef was a maestro in his cramped workplace, preparing alone the day's menu of foie gras in homemade chocolate sauce and roast pork with field mushrooms.

I eagerly took a seat in the farthest corner, ordered without restraint, as Grimod might have done, and chatted, between sips of muscadet, with an elderly couple at a nearby table. They said they lived around the corner and came here at least once a week. "Always the full three courses at lunch," giggled Madame. "Then a nap—and no dinner!"

No dinner? I wasn't sure Grimod would have approved.

WHAT TO READ

Almanach des Gourmands, by Grimod de la Reynière. Amazon sells a paperback edition published in 2003. There is no English translation.

The Invention of the Restaurant: Paris and Modern Gastronomic Culture, by Rebecca L. Spang. "[A] pleasingly spiced history of the restaurant." —Edward Rothstein, *The New York Times*.

Alexandre Dumas' Dictionary of Cuisine. Somewhere between writing *The Count of Monte Cristo*, *The Three Musketeers*, and his other novels, Dumas learned to be an expert cook and wrote about it.

The Physiology of Taste, by Jean Anthelme Brillat-Savarin, edited by M. F. K. Fisher. First published in 1825, and never out of print, a collection of recipes and witty observations about food from a contemporary of Grimod.

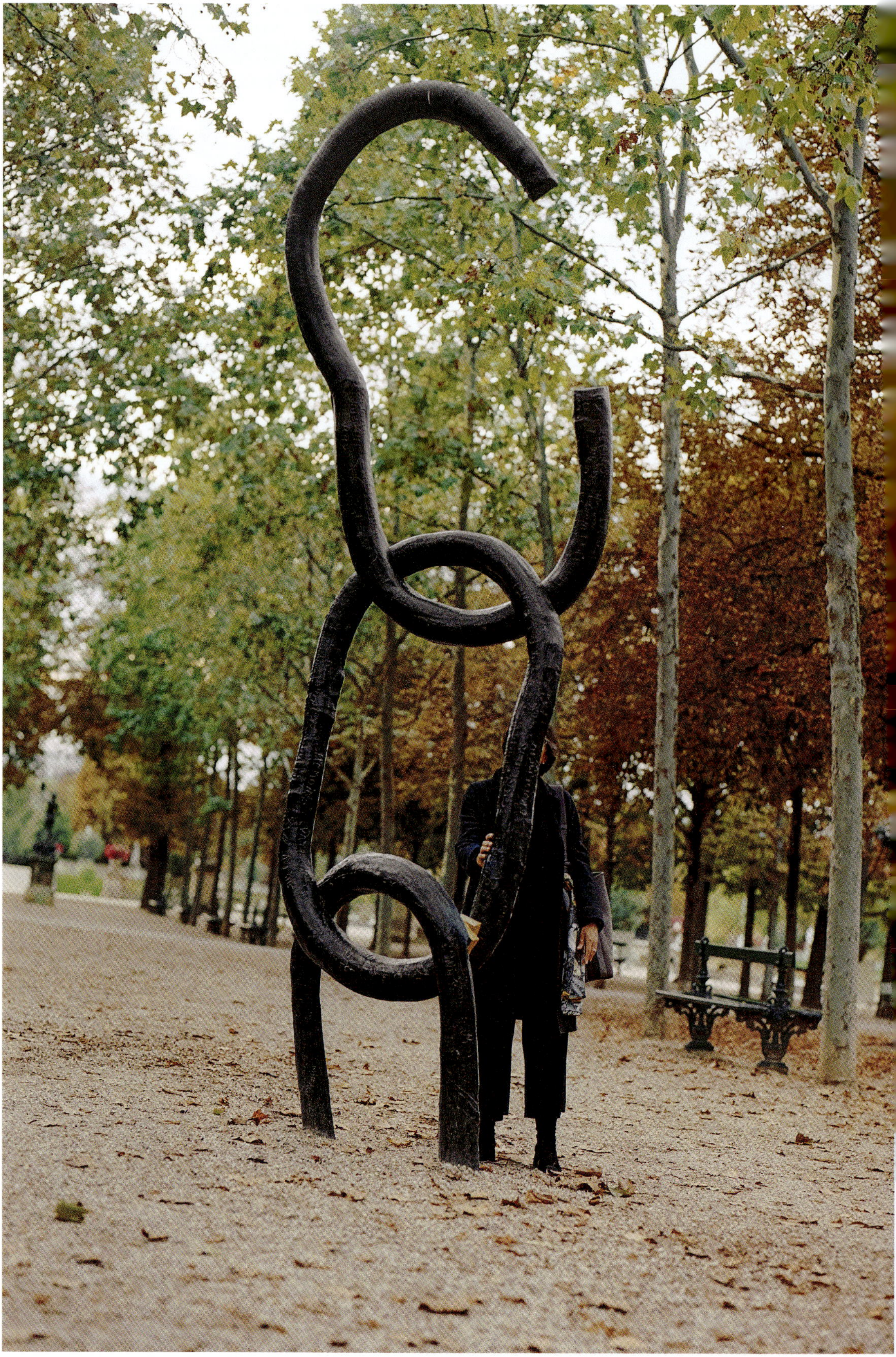

ON THE TRAIL OF A FREEDOM SEEKER IN PARIS

History remembers John Jay's work to negotiate American liberty, but not the enslaved woman he refused to free. — BY MARTHA S. JONES

There are some stories about the past that Paris does not tell. One of them is the experience of an enslaved woman I know by only one name, Abigail. Taken from America to Paris by one of America's founders, John Jay of New York, she died there in a failed attempt to win her liberty. The city's markers of memory — *lieux des memoires* — readily tell of Jay and the other famous men who signed the Treaty of Paris, which settled the American Revolutionary War. But Abigail's story remains easy to overlook.

I first puzzled over her life and death when as a newcomer to Paris I stumbled upon the city's tributes to American founders. Exiting the Musée d'Orsay and heading to the Right Bank across the Passerelle Léopold-Sédar-Senghor footbridge, I met up with a 10-foot-tall bronze likeness of Thomas Jefferson with plans for his estate, Monticello, in his hand. Hiking along the Rue Benjamin-Franklin in the 16th Arrondissement, I ventured to the tiny Square de Yorktown to discover that the figure seated high atop a stone plinth was Franklin himself. Fresh from people-watching at the cafe Les Deux Magots, once the haunt of James Baldwin and Richard Wright, I made my way around the corner on Rue Jacob and, pausing at No. 56, read the pink marble plaque that marks the site of the Hôtel d'York, where peace commissioners Benjamin Franklin, John Adams, and John Jay signed the treaty.

These fabled places are, I recognized, whitewashed. There is no mention of the enslaved people who labored in the founders' Parisian households. No site explains that while Jay brokered the new nation's freedom, he also dealt in the unfreedom of others.

Abigail comes to us refracted through the concerns of those who conspired to keep her bound to the Jay

Previous In the Jardin du Luxembourg, the sculpture *Le Cri, l'Écrit* acknowledges France's role in the slave trade.

Left Ruins of La Force in 1851. Abigail, enslaved by John Jay, was held in this prison after trying to escape in Paris.

Opposite "Libre," or free, is written on the monument in the Luxembourg Gardens.

family, and recovering her distinct voice is difficult to accomplish through records that she, as an enslaved woman, had little hand in constructing. Still, I have collected small shards of the past that bring her more clearly into view. As a historian, I worry that I won't ever learn enough about her, yet still I am sure that Abigail, along with John Jay, must be remembered.

Much of what we know about Abigail's 18 months in Paris comes from the efforts of Jay, Franklin, and their families to thwart her attempts to get free. Letters that refer to her passed between households in the villages of Passy and Chaillot, both now parts of Paris, and between Paris and London, where Jay attended to his health and family business.

Abigail had been bound to the Jay family since at least 1776, and nothing in the Declaration of Independence changed her status. Nor was she protected by living in the North. Slavery was still legal, and common, in New York in her day. The New York Slavery Records Index reports how John Jay's father and grandfather invested in the slave trade to New York. John Jay himself held at least 17 people over his lifetime.

In 1779 Abigail found herself along on a journey that intersected with old slave-trading routes, accompanying the Jay household when it departed for Europe. Their party stopped over in Martinique, a French Caribbean sugar colony driven by enslaved labor. Jay purchased a boy named Benoit before proceeding to a diplomatic assignment in Madrid, the onetime capital of Spain's slaveholding empire. By 1782, the Jays were on their way to Paris, the hub of an empire in which the slave trade and a ruthless plantation regime filled the coffers of French families. In the 18th century, slavery knitted together the Americas and Europe with casual and callous disregard.

When Jay headed to London in October 1783, his wife, Sarah, and nephew Peter Jay Munro managed the family's affairs. Abigail attended Sarah, who gave birth to three children far from home. Sarah wrote appreciatively to her mother: "The attention & proofs of fidelity which we have receiv'd from Abbe, demand, & ever shall have my acknowledgments, you can hardly imagine how useful she is to us."

In Paris, isolation imposed a special strain on Abigail. She was the only enslaved person to accompany the Jays from North America, made too few friends, and longed for her own loved ones back across the Atlantic. Only later, in 1784, would James Hemings arrive in Paris, held enslaved by Thomas Jefferson. James's sister Sally followed in 1787. Abigail, having died in 1783, never had an opportunity to meet up with them.

In spring 1783 Sarah Jay wrote tellingly to her own sister Kitty: "Abbe is well & would be glad to know if she is mistress of a husband still." Abigail, we learn, was married, and worried that her ties to her husband might have frayed during years spent apart.

Nothing in the surviving records describes Abigail; we're left to imagine her. Was she tall or short, slight or round, dark or light? Did she walk with assurance, or was she wary much of the time? We do not know her age. Still, we can say how she felt. By summer 1783, Abigail was unwell. Mrs. Jay reported that a toothache and rheumatism kept her confined much of the time. But Abigail was also unsettled in her mind. Perhaps it was too many years away from friends and family. Or, Mrs. Jay suggested, she might have become jealous of a French member of the household staff or been influenced by an "English" washerwoman who enticed her with the promise of wages. In Paris, slavery's bonds loosened just enough to permit Abigail to rethink her future.

It was late October when Abigail determined to test slavery's hold on her and headed onto the streets of Paris not intending to return. At Mrs. Jay's request, William Temple Franklin, companion to his grandfather Benjamin Franklin, sought the assistance of Paris police by a lettre de cachet, a request sometimes used to discipline household members deemed out of step. The police soon found Abigail in the company of the washerwoman, and they took her to the Hôtel de la Force, a city jail whose women's quarters were called La Petite Force. She could be detained indefinitely, the Jays were assured, if they agreed to pay a modest amount for her meals.

Mrs. Jay wrote to her husband, worried about Abigail's health were she to remain in prison. Peter Jay Munro explained to his aunt that during his visits with Abigail, she refused to return to the family's house unless she was promised passage back to America.

John Jay dismissed Abigail's concerns and wrote to Munro, encouraging that she be coerced: "I think it would be best to postpone your visit to the Hotel de la Force for some weeks." Jay believed Munro's calls "would then probably be more gratefully received," and then went on to belittle Abigail, remarking, "Little minds cannot bear attentions & to Persons of that Class they should rather be granted than offered." Jay advised that the family should follow Benjamin Franklin's advice and let Abigail remain in jail for a longer time; Franklin had suggested 15 to 20 days of confinement would have the desired effect. It was a form of discipline intended to bend Abigail's will.

Over the coming weeks, winter approached while Abigail remained confined. An illness sent her to the infirmary, and she then turned "penitent," Munro reported, and asked to return to the Jays. William Temple Franklin arranged for her release, and Mrs. Jay made a note that he had fronted 60 livres, likely the charge for Abigail's meals, to secure her return.

Back at the Jay residence, Abigail almost immediately took to her bed. "We hope she'll recover," Sarah Jay wrote to her husband. But within two weeks, Abigail was dead. What happened then, neither the Jay nor the Franklin family letters confess.

I hoped that signs of Abigail's time in Paris had survived. Could I find anything like a monument to her? I started looking in Passy and Chaillot. Today the area is fashionable, with streets lined by high-end boutiques. A rare-book shop on the Rue Benjamin-Franklin displayed a copy of Jean-Paul Marat's *The Chains of Slavery* in its front window, as if to encourage my quest. It's just a short walk to the Trocadero, where a postcard-perfect view of the Eiffel Tower emerges between 19th-century buildings.

Perhaps Abigail was buried nearby. I headed to the site of Passy's 18th-century cemetery, along the narrow rue de l'Annonciation, where a few of the

Above The author's reflection in a store window on Rue Benjamin-Franklin. Franklin and John Jay went to Paris as diplomats.

Opposite A statue of Benjamin Franklin in Paris. Franklin's grandson helped to thwart Abigail's attempt at freedom.

one- and two-story elite homes of Abigail's time still stand, painted now in muted pastels and secured by walls and gates. The street was busy with cafe chatter and darting shoppers. Things were quieter on the Rue Lekain, where Passy's cemetery was located in the 18th century. There is no sign of it now. The bodies were long ago removed and reinterred or stored in the city's catacombs.

Perhaps there were clues about the weeks of Abigail's detention in the records at the archives of the Préfecture de Police. I searched through ancient lettres de cachet preserved in rooms set aside in a working police precinct. It's an imposing place, constructed from late 20th-century steel and iron, with small windows that heighten the penal feel. I sifted through hundreds of records that recount the lives of the many unfortunates caught in contests over their wayward conduct — husbands versus wives, parents against children, and masters versus servants — many of whom landed in the cells of places like the Hôtel de la Force. I found not a single document bearing Abigail's name. Even that absence might have been a monument of sorts to her ordeal.

Finding some trace of Abigail at the site of La Petite Force proved more promising. One wall of the jail remains standing where Rue Pavée and Rue Malher meet in the Marais neighborhood. I wended through the narrow streets and then, looking up, recognized the outline of the wall, which marked the northernmost boundary of the jail. The place was once the home of the Duke de la Force, whose name was preserved when the city built the jail there, a model for penal reform with windows, separate quarters for women, and an infirmary, all of which Abigail came to know.

On one side of the jail wall still stands the Hôtel de Lamoignon, today's Bibliothèque Historique de la Ville de Paris. I headed there to get a better look at its

*Photographs by
Cédrine Scheidig*

courtyard, only to meet up with a reference librarian who was happy to search the library's digital collection for images of La Petite Force. There it was, on her screen: three stories of stone and iron, a gated archway for an entrance. I sat for a long moment, imagining Abigail: arriving there, first insisting upon staying, and finally falling fatally ill.

I knew I had to make one final stop: the Jardin du Luxembourg, where the roses were in bloom. There, just behind the meeting place of France's national senate, stands a tribute to the enslaved people of France who lived and died in bondage, an experience that the nation declared a crime against humanity in 2001. Here, enslaved people are honored as among France's founders. For Abigail, and for others bound by American founders during their mission to Paris for freedom, a similar tribute feels long overdue.

For now, this tour of Abigail's Paris will have to suffice.

WHAT TO READ

Vanguard: How Black Women Broke Barriers, Won the Vote and Insisted on Equality for All, by Martha S. Jones. Henry Louis Gates Jr. called *Vanguard*, by the author of this article, "a sweeping narrative for our times."

Ties That Bound: Founding First Ladies and Slaves, by Marie Jenkins Schwartz. "...rich details about the daily lives of this group of Founding First Ladies and the enslaved people who made their privileged lifestyles possible." — *North Carolina Historical Review*.

The Half Has Never Been Told: Slavery and the Making of American Capitalism, by Edward E. Baptist. Exposes how tightly the development of the US economy was entwined with enslaved labor.

The 1619 Project: A New Origin Story, by Nikole Hannah-Jones and other writers for *The New York Times Magazine*. Through articles in a variety of genres, places slavery and Black Americans at the heart of the nation's development.

PALAIS
DE LA PORTE DORÉE

PARIS FROM THE OUTSIDE IN

Exploring at the edges reveals a city at once familiar and startlingly new. — BY DAVID MCANINCH

All tourists walk around Paris, but not the way I did on six gloriously cloudless May days. Wearing a pair of beat-up sneakers and carrying a notebook, I walked all around Paris, counterclockwise along its boundaries for 35 miles, making centrifugal excursions into the closed-in suburbs and occasional dips into the outer arrondissements of the city itself. Each morning I took the Métro roughly to where I'd left off the previous day and began again.

I hiked in a forest, had a close encounter with the actual embalmed heart of Louis XVII, and in an immense former marble factory listened to a cumbia band alongside French hipsters drinking American IPAs. I gazed in awe at some of the most ugly-beautiful Brutalist buildings I'd ever seen, ate an exquisitely poached filet of whiting with spring peas at a serene restaurant where the bread came in a miniature burlap sack, and ambled around an empty museum filled with sleek 1930s furniture that, in the absence of any other visitors or even (as far as I could tell) a guard, I found exceedingly hard not to sit on.

I saw a Paris that was at turns familiar — the workaday brasseries and tabacs, the bakeries with their yeasty aromas and morning chitchat, the busy traffic circles — and eye-poppingly new to me: a vast and messy urban agglomeration that's home to the great majority of metropolitan Paris's 10 million residents.

The walk was conceived as a lark, a way of seeing the city with fresh eyes. But I soon found I'd stumbled into a full-fledged civic movement whose leaders want to redraw the political, social, and cultural boundaries of Paris. They hope to explode what the author Mira

Previous The Musée de l'Histoire de l'Immigration hugs the Paris city line at the edge of the Bois de Vincennes.

Left A historic photo of the Thiers City Wall. Its last vestiges disappeared during construction of the Périphérique highway.

Opposite La Marbrerie, a place to catch live music in the eastern suburb of Montreuil.

Kamdar, who lives in the suburb of Pantin, has called "the implacable logic of center and periphery, of included and excluded."

Anyone who has taken a cab into the city from the airport has seen the clogged multilane ring road known as the Boulevard Périphérique, which in the 1970s replaced the last vestiges of Paris's 19th-century Thiers Wall and has arguably become a more impenetrable barrier. Inside the Périph reside the picturesque splendors of the City of Light. Outside it: la banlieue, as the suburbs are collectively known, with their housing projects and cheap kebab shops and social unrest. Or so things often appear in the public imagination.

The reality is more complicated. The edges of Paris and the patchwork of towns just beyond them range from dense immigrant enclaves and repurposed industrial sites to leafy bastions of bourgeois comfort. I encountered imposing high-rise apartment blocks, but just as often I found myself strolling along a disused rail line reclaimed as a pedestrian thoroughfare, or down a sleepy main street that could have belonged to a market village in rural France.

I arranged to meet two of the activists championing what's popularly known as Le Grand Paris (essentially, Greater Paris), Renaud Charles and Vianney Delourme. Both bearded 40-somethings, they are the founders of the cheekily named website Enlarge Your Paris. Over two hours at their "temporary offices in petit Paris," which turned out to be a cafe on Rue du Faubourg Saint-Denis, they spoke of the signs of a new era for Le Grand Paris: public transportation projects underway, the new Jean Nouvel–designed Paris Philharmonic in the shadow of the Périph, a massive government reshuffling called Le Métropole du Grand Paris that has given outer municipalities a greater voice. They also heaped me with dozens of suggestions for my exploration, some of which I followed.

Here's one thing to know before trying to walk the perimeter of Paris in a week: The city and its pleasures will conspire against you. On my very first day, after a morning spent pushing north along the Boulevard Soult past everyday businesses like a locksmith shop, a car insurance agency, and a shoe repair place, and after a foray into the unlovely suburb of Bagnolet, I stopped for lunch at La Pelouse, a cafe in the 19th Arrondissement. One 11-euro plat du jour, a carafe of chilled Brouilly, and a crème caramel later, I found my motivation weakening, especially with the ever-entertaining human pageant to sit and watch on this busy corner in Belleville. After that, I made a promise to myself to exclude wine from lunch for the rest of the week (a promise I would fail to keep).

If a single observation stands out from that first day's walk, which ended just before sunset alongside the promenade-lined Canal de l'Ourcq in Pantin, it's that Paris's edge areas have served as a vast laboratory for bold and occasionally bonkers architecture.

Beyond the Boulevards des Maréchaux, the inner ring of surface streets that mark the limits of the Paris most visitors know, the uniform ranks of Haussman-era buildings give way to a crazy quilt of styles and eras, from the orange-brick HBMs (Habitations à Bon Marché) erected in the 1920s and '30s as affordable dwellings — and no longer very affordable at all — to their much-maligned successors, the megalithic postwar housing projects known as HLMs (Habitations à Loyer Modéré). The latter represent the most visible legacy of the architect and urban planner Le Corbusier, although strangely, on the fourth day of my walk I happened on his home and studio and found it perfectly human-scale and pleasant.

Sitting by the canal as the sky darkened, I stared at the modular-looking neo-Brutalist structure housing the Centre National de la Danse, a gray concrete behemoth that somehow radiated both childlike exuberance and dystopian menace. A few days later, I would be similarly blown away by Édouard François's much newer M6B2, a 17-story balconied residential building at the edge of the 13th Arrondissement that's wrapped entirely in mesh, onto which hanging plants have been encouraged to grow.

Certainly, picturesque churches and other jewels of France's historical patrimony can be found outside central Paris. On my second day I followed a market street bustling with vendors hawking iPhone cases and the like, and emerged onto the vast parvis of the Basilique Cathédrale de Saint-Denis.

Inside, I explored the church's magnificently creepy necropolis, which houses the crypts of France's kings dating back to Dagobert I in the seventh century. I found being surrounded by the sarcophogi of hundreds of dead monarchs to be exponentially more interesting than my past visits to the renowned Sacré Coeur, which receives 10.5 million visitors a year in comparison to Saint-Denis's mere 134,000. I was even able to enjoy several uninterrupted minutes in the presence of the child-king Louis XVII's shriveled heart, so close my breath was fogging the vitrine.

Not every segment of my walk was filled with such memorable moments. Day 3 was pretty much devoid of them: a sun-hammered slog along warehouse-lined streets and finally my arrival at La Défense, its sparkling glass towers rising above me with monolithic indifference.

By comparison, the next day brought abundant splendors and comforts. Foremost among them: the Bois de Boulogne. What a tonic this 2,000-acre urban forest and prairie is, with its coolly shaded footpaths snaking through stands of Austrian pine.

And what a strangely exhilarating sensation it is to emerge from those woods and behold the Fondation Louis Vuitton, a Frank Gehry–designed art museum. Completed in 2014 at a reported cost of $900 million, it thrusts skyward from its bucolic surroundings like a hallucinatory yacht. Inside I wandered through white rooms featuring the works of superstar contemporary artists, but my favorite part was the roof deck, where I peered past Gehry's sail-like glass-and-steel panels at the Bois de Boulogne's ocean of trees, the Eiffel Tower, and La Défense.

On the recommendation of the Enlarge Your Paris guys, I had lunch that day at La Table de Cybèle, an airy restaurant on a quiet street in the staid suburb of Boulogne-Billancourt. It was here that my moratorium on midday wine came to its premature end with a taut Lirac, poured by a willowy server. Later the chef — she of the miniature burlap sack of bread — came around and introduced herself to guests, in the American fashion. Which made sense, since she actually was from Northern California.

Above The Philharmonie de Paris, just inside the Périphérique, attracts music lovers to the city's outer limits.

Opposite La Cité de Refuge was one of Le Corbusier's first urban housing projects.

I wandered somewhat aimlessly around Boulogne-Billancourt, which is how I found the superb Musée des Années Trente (Museum of the 1930s), the site of my solitary communion with vintage furniture. It was one of several museums I had more or less to myself during my trek. Another was the Musée de l'Histoire de l'Immigration, in a monumental Art Deco palais at the edge of the Bois de Vincennes, where I caught an exhibition of Eugène Atget's photographs of the Roma encampments that were fixtures of Paris's perimeter up until World War I.

That evening I made my way to the other side of the city for a concert at the Philharmonie de Paris, which opened in 2015 and, like the Fondation Vuitton, is seen as a symbol of an outer-Paris renaissance. Designed by Jean Nouvel, it cuts a striking silhouette: a wedge-like, vaguely biomorphic rejection of symmetry that's approached via a wide uphill esplanade paved with tiles in the same bird shape as those cladding the building itself. The whole setup creates a convivial feeling of pilgrimage as throngs of well-heeled, perfumed Parisians stroll en masse from the tram station to the entrance.

If central Paris were a face, my route on days 5 and 6 would look like a frilly ruff collar, swooping back and forth across the city's southern boundary. Interesting things seemed to present themselves with uncanny frequency.

In the suburb of Montrouge, I visited La Boutique du Futur, a shop selling corkscrews made from cow bone and baby spoons shaped like airplanes. In Gentilly, I discovered an enormous but impeccably curated wine-and-spirits shop, Caves Fillot, in a former winery that still had the bewitching musty smell of aging barrels. Just inside the Périph near the river, I chanced upon a burgeoning arts corridor anchored by a handful of spartan-looking galleries devoted largely to graffiti.

Photographs by
Joann Pai

On the last day of my trip I decided to take the Métro back to the eastern suburb of Montreuil, which I'd heard described, for better or worse, as the Brooklyn of Paris. As I popped out of the Métro, I saw a small public park heaving with young families, many of them clustered around a makeshift bar that had been strung with holiday lights and furnished with what looked like lawn furniture.

A few blocks beyond that was La Marbrerie, the marble factory–turned–music venue. The cumbia band was in full swing, and a few dozen people, ranging in age from 20 to 60, were dancing with the kind of joyful abandon I associate with weddings.

I splurged on a cab back to my hotel. As the driver eased onto the Périph, flowing smoothly at this late hour, I reflected that after I'd crossed over and under it so many times on my walk, it no longer felt like much of a barrier at all.

WHAT TO READ AND WATCH

A Walk through Paris, by Éric Hazan. Armed with a long familiarity with the city and knowledge of its literature and history, Hazan meanders from Ivry-sur-Seine to Saint-Denis.

Paris Walking Guide: 20 Charming Strolls. A collection of walks designed and described by various authors and published by Parigramme.

A Year in Paris: Season by Season in the City of Light, by John Baxter. As described by Liesl Schillinger in *The New York Times*, this book "strings together the beautiful beads of the French everyday."

Creating Feeling with Frank Gehry, a short film by the Nowness video channel. Gehry speaks about the creative process, revealing that it was by drawing fish shapes that he arrived at his unique style.

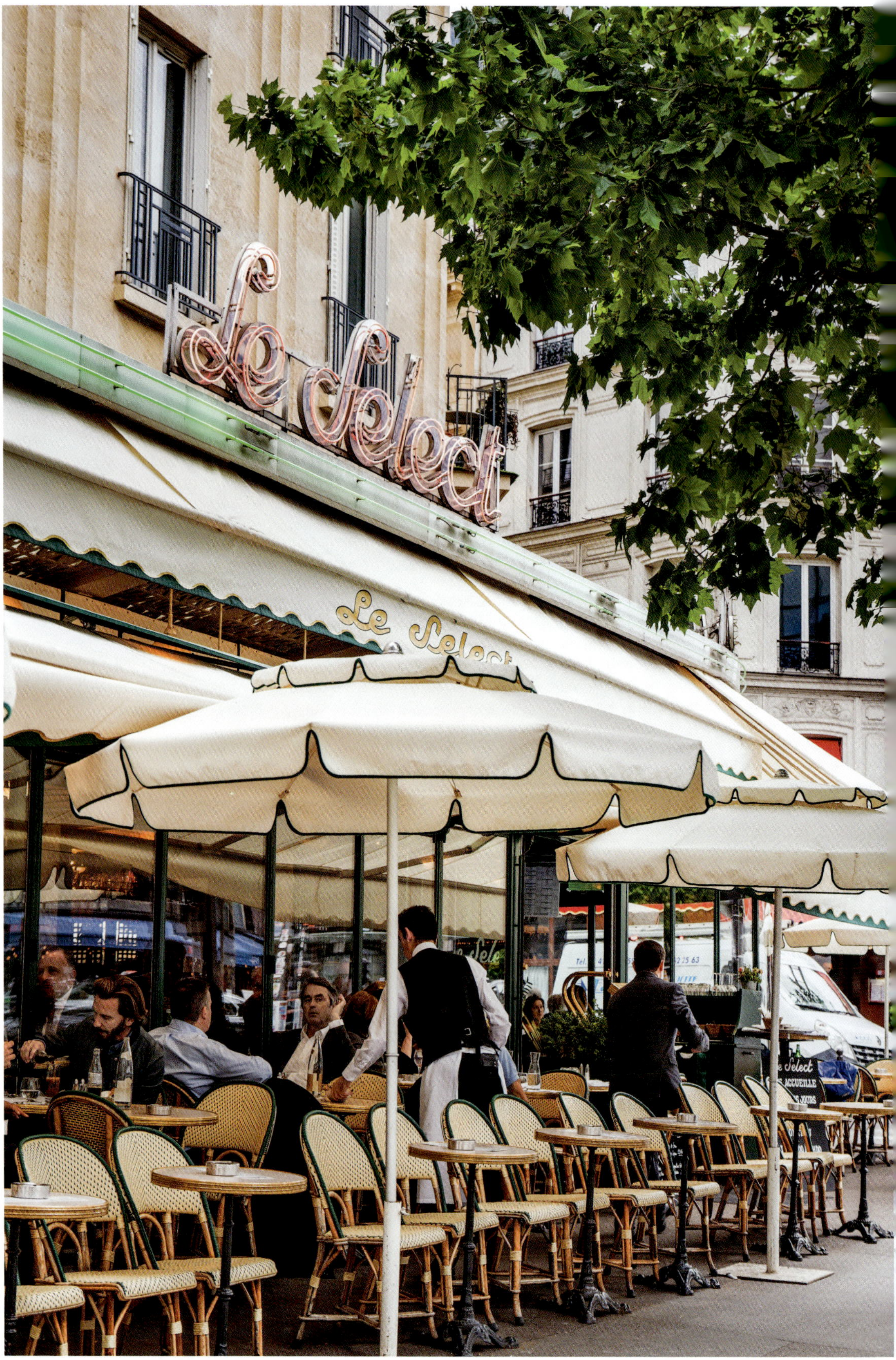
Le Select

WHERE JACKIE KENNEDY GOT HER PARISIAN POLISH

As a college girl in France, Jacqueline Bouvier embraced culture and sophistication. — BY ANN MAH

In August 1949, a 20-year-old Jacqueline Bouvier arrived in France and began a year that would change her life. Before her marriages to Jack Kennedy and Aristotle Onassis, before the glamour and the tragedy, before she lived in the White House or worked at a publishing house, she was a college student boarding a ship to spend her junior year abroad in Paris.

With her French name and heritage (one-eighth French from her father's side), she was already predisposed to admiring France. But the academic year of 1949 to 1950 cemented her passion, allowing her to absorb the country's language and culture. From the genteel 16th Arrondissement where she lived with a host family to the narrow streets of the Latin Quarter where she attended university classes, Jacqueline's time in battered postwar Paris would inspire an unabashed intellectual flowering that enriched the rest of her life.

"Paris was the perfect incubator for her myriad talents. Her style, her razor-sharp wit, her ways of imagining, were honed there," said Alice Kaplan, the author of *Dreaming in French: The Paris Years of Jacqueline Bouvier Kennedy, Susan Sontag, and Angela Davis*, which takes a thorough look at Jacqueline's transformative Paris experience. "Whether she was turning to Proust and Saint-Simon as a guide to the hornet's nest of Washington politics, or shaping a symbolic wardrobe as first lady, France was always her compass."

Much has changed since 1949, but the essential Paris that gave Jacqueline what she called "the high point in my life, my happiest and most carefree year" is still there to discover. Intrigued by the powerful role the city played in her life, I set out to retrace her steps.

Previous Le Select, a student hangout when Jacqueline Bouvier, later Jacqueline Kennedy, lived and studied nearby.

Left The Westin Paris-Vendôme, once the Hotel Continental. Jacqueline and Lee Bouvier stayed there in 1951.

Opposite Jacqueline Bouvier, third from left, with other students in Smith College's study-abroad program.

Her sojourn began on the *De Grasse*, a liner sailing from New York to Le Havre, as one of 35 young women taking part in the Smith College Junior Year in Paris. Because her college, Vassar, lacked a study-abroad program, she had applied to Smith's. It was the oldest American study-abroad program in Paris —begun in 1925, paused during World War II, and resumed in 1947. Smith required its participants to pledge that they would speak only French at all times.

Jacqueline first sharpened her language skills at a six-week immersion course in Grenoble. "I have an absolute mania now about learning to speak French perfectly," she wrote in a letter to her stepbrother, Yusha Auchincloss. Once she was in Paris, her coursework focused mainly on art history and literature. Her classes took her to the Sorbonne, the École du Louvre, the prestigious Institut d'Études Politiques (known as Sciences Po), and the Parisian center of American study abroad, Reid Hall.

In the heart of Montparnasse, Reid Hall has welcomed American students since the 1920s. Today it is part of the Columbia Global Centers, an ambitious educational network in nine cities around the globe; it also houses the study abroad programs of more than a dozen American and British colleges and universities. I found Smith's offices up a lopsided wooden staircase, in a warren of narrow rooms and worn terra-cotta tile floors hinting at the building's origins as an 18th-century porcelain factory.

"A lot has changed, but some things haven't," Marie-Madeleine Charlier, the associate director of Smith in Paris, told me in her office. Students still live with host families, take the language pledge, and lounge in Reid Hall's spacious courtyard on sunny days; they still discuss politics, architecture, and theater in small seminars. There remains, as well, one eternal similarity: "Every student goes through an identity change," said Mehammed Mack, the program's faculty director.

Reflecting on her academic year in Paris, Jacqueline Bouvier wrote in 1951, "I learned not to be ashamed of a real hunger for knowledge, something I had always tried to hide."

In 1949 World War II still cast a shadow over France. Heat and hot water were scarce; baths were limited to one a week. Everyone, including Jacqueline, had a ration card for coffee and sugar. Postwar housing shortages meant most Smith students lived in a spartan dormitory at Reid Hall, but Jacqueline's mother, Janet Auchincloss, used her social connections to secure more comfortable lodging for her daughter.

A discreet plaque on an exterior wall of 78 Avenue Mozart, in the slightly stuffy 16th Arrondissement, boasts of Jacqueline's residence there that year. A majestic seven-story building, it is adorned with glazed bricks of sea-foam green and embellished with Art Nouveau flourishes. Inside, she shared a rambling bourgeois apartment with seven other people.

Her host mother, the aristocratic Comtesse Guyot de Renty, had suffered greatly during the war. Unmasked as members of the Resistance, she and her husband had been deported to Germany in 1944. The Comte de Renty died in a slave labor camp, and his wife spent the duration of the war at the Ravensbrück concentration camp. After the war, the Comtesse de Renty found herself in reduced circumstances, and "being from a bourgeois family, she decided to take in students," said Claude du Granrut, one of her daughters, who lived with Jacqueline that year. (The household also included du Granrut's sister, her sister's young son, and two other Smith students.) "The apartment was large and pleasant," she told me as we sipped tiny cups of coffee in her sunny living room. "But there was only one bathroom. And no heat! It didn't work. Jacqueline put on gloves to study. I remember her always being covered up."

Jacqueline and Claude forged a lifelong friendship that year—both born in 1929, both university students on the Left Bank. "She was part of our family," du Granrut said. "My mother was very fond of her, and she loved to go with my mother because my mother couldn't speak a word of English."

The Comtesse de Renty took Jacqueline to museums, in particular the Musée des Arts Décoratifs in a wing of the Louvre building on the Rue de Rivoli. Here, they viewed collections of Sèvres porcelain and French furniture and discussed the characteristics of each era—lessons in the history of French design and decorative arts that must have proved useful years later, when, as first lady, Jacqueline Kennedy redecorated the White House. "When I visited the White House, I saw every room had its own style," du Granrut said. "Some pieces were purchased, some were borrowed, but she had the flair of combining them to create a small collection."

Above In letters home, Jacqueline wrote of "being swanky" at the Ritz Hotel. Its bar is still posh seven decades later.

Opposite A room at the Château de Courances, a country estate where Jacqueline often spent weekends.

The Musée des Arts Décoratifs is a labyrinth of rooms displaying objets d'art from several centuries. I saw a gallery there devoted to the Empire period of Napoléon Bonaparte and later learned that Jacqueline decorated the Red Room at the White House with elements of this same classic French style. She spoke eloquently about it in her 1962 television special, *A Tour of the White House with Mrs. John F. Kennedy*.

"Although Jacqueline enjoyed being in a French home," du Granrut said, nevertheless "she left on the weekends." Her destination was often the Château de Courances, the grand country estate of the aristocratic de Ganay family, about 40 miles from Paris. Jacqueline had met Paul de Ganay through society connections of her stepfamily (her stepfather, Hugh Auchincloss, was a Washington financier), and she enjoyed horseback riding on the chateau grounds. "She rode very, very well. She loved it," du Granrut said.

Today, the Château de Courances and its manicured 185-acre park are open several months of the year, limited to weekends and holidays. Its stables were destroyed by a fire in 1978. But horseback riding in Paris seemed a quintessential Jackie experience, and so I contacted a company called Horse in the City for a morning ride in the Bois de Boulogne. The park has long been a popular spot for equestrians, and according to at least one of her biographies, Jacqueline rode there, too.

My guide, Baptiste Auclair, met me in the park with a picnic of coffee and croissants. With him were two horses tucked into a trailer. We rode them along wooded trails, passing artificial lakes and streams, the sun casting dappled shadows through the trees.

When she wasn't studying, Jacqueline wrote of behaving "like the maid on her day out, putting on a fur coat and going to the middle of town and being swanky, at the Ritz." The Ritz has been renovated,

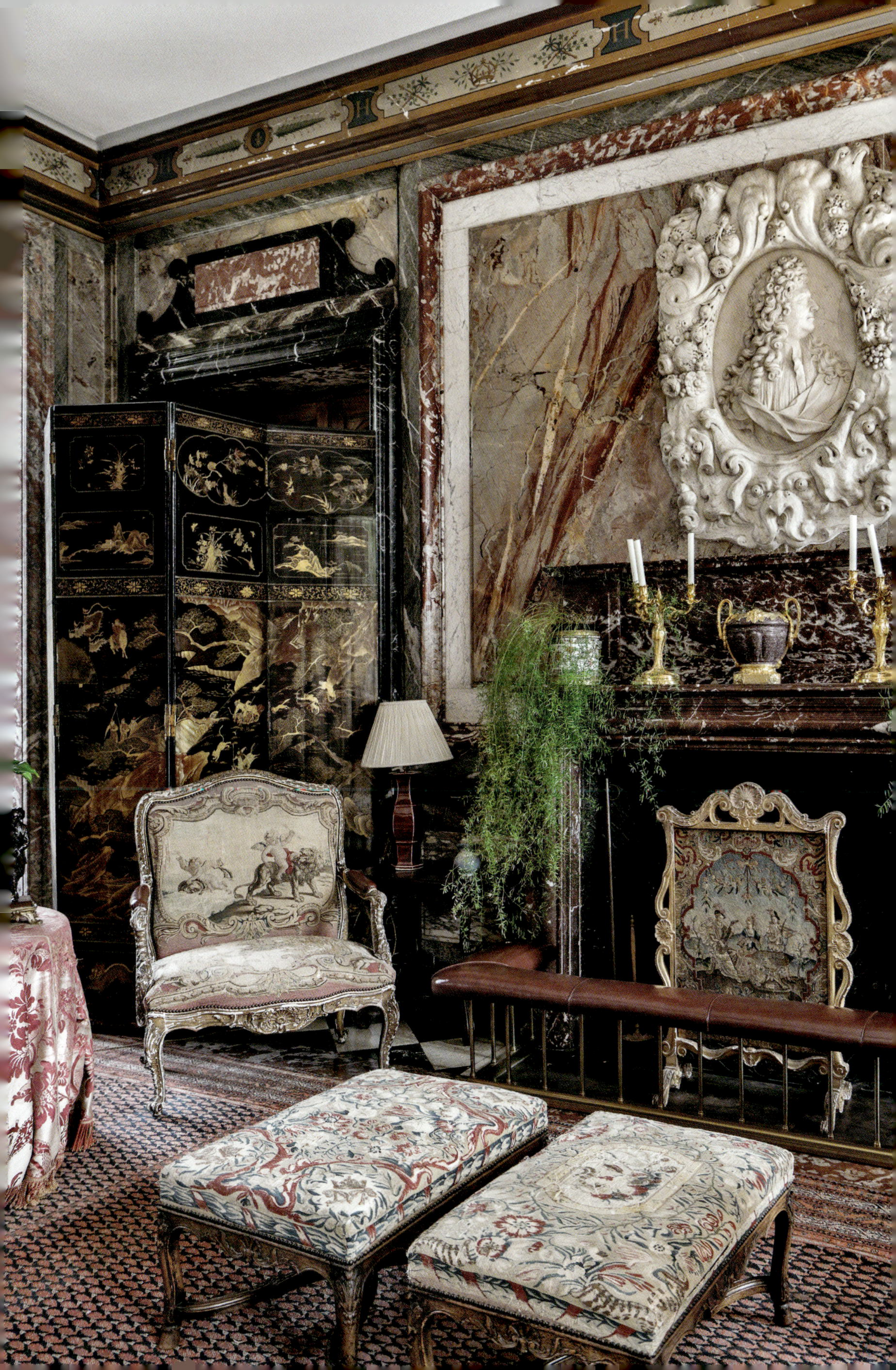

Above The elegant facade of the Château de Courances. Jacqueline rode horses on the grounds of the estate.

Opposite The building where Jacqueline stayed. Her hostess, an impoverished countess, helped her get to know Paris.

but its Ritz Bar, resplendent with Art Deco trimmings, still feels swanky indeed.

A few blocks away is the former Hôtel Continental, now the Westin Paris-Vendôme, where Jacqueline stayed briefly in 1951 while touring Europe with her sister, Lee. The Bouvier sisters recorded their high-spirited adventures in a tongue-in-cheek illustrated scrapbook that was eventually published in 1974 under the title *One Special Summer*.

Jacqueline's next trip to Paris — the state visit of June 1961 when she was 33 and John F. Kennedy was five months into his term as president — was a public declaration of her Francophilia. French newspapers celebrated her style and her keen interest in French culture. "She prefers the 'intellectual' films of our avant-garde directors," wrote the weekly *Paris Match*. With her French fluency and French-influenced manners, she also smoothed Kennedy's tense moments with Charles de Gaulle. Recognizing the importance of the impression his wife was making, Kennedy wryly declared himself, in a famous comment, "the man who accompanied Jacqueline Kennedy to Paris."

The three-day visit swept through grand spaces at the Hôtel de Ville, Versailles, and the Élysée Palace. But Jacqueline remembered old friends like the de Rentys, the de Ganays, and Jeanne Saleil (the former Smith in Paris director) and invited them to events.

Paris continued to call to Jacqueline after her 1968 marriage to the Greek shipping magnate Aristotle Onassis. He owned an imposing apartment there and had his own preferred table at Maxim's. At that point, however, her desire for privacy had grown intense, and from then on we can only guess at her French life from bread-crumb clues, such as the books she edited at Viking and Doubleday after Onassis's death in 1975. The final one, *Paris After the Liberation*, by Antony Beevor and Artemis Cooper, included the period of her student days.

Photographs by Joann Pai

On my final day, I wondered how Jacqueline would spend a free evening in Paris today. I settled on a public lecture at Reid Hall, in French, as the type of event she would have enjoyed. The hall was packed as three writers discussed social class and mobility, cultural identity, sexuality, and the influence of family. Afterward, as I strolled home, the remnants of a super moon glowing against the sky, the cafes along the Boulevard du Montparnasse overflowed onto the sidewalk, their patrons filling the mild night with their chatter.

I thought back to something Claude du Granrut had told me: "We showed Jacqueline things no one else could have shown her. Above all, we showed her the French way of life, the intellectual life, the artistic life, the charm of France."

WHAT TO READ

Dreaming in French: The Paris Years of Jacqueline Bouvier Kennedy, Susan Sontag, and Angela Davis, by Alice Kaplan. Includes a thorough look at Jacqueline's transformative Paris experience.

Mrs. Kennedy: The Missing History of the Kennedy Years, by Barbara Leaming. Makes the case that Jacqueline Kennedy's social skills and sophistication played an important role in her husband's presidency.

Paris in the Fifties, by Stanley Karnow. A remembrance of Paris in the era when Jacqueline Bouvier experienced it, by a Pulitzer Prize–winning American author who was a student there in the late 1940s.

One Special Summer, by Jacqueline and Lee Bouvier. The sisters' scrapbook from a European trip, featuring their impressions and drawings, transformed into a book.

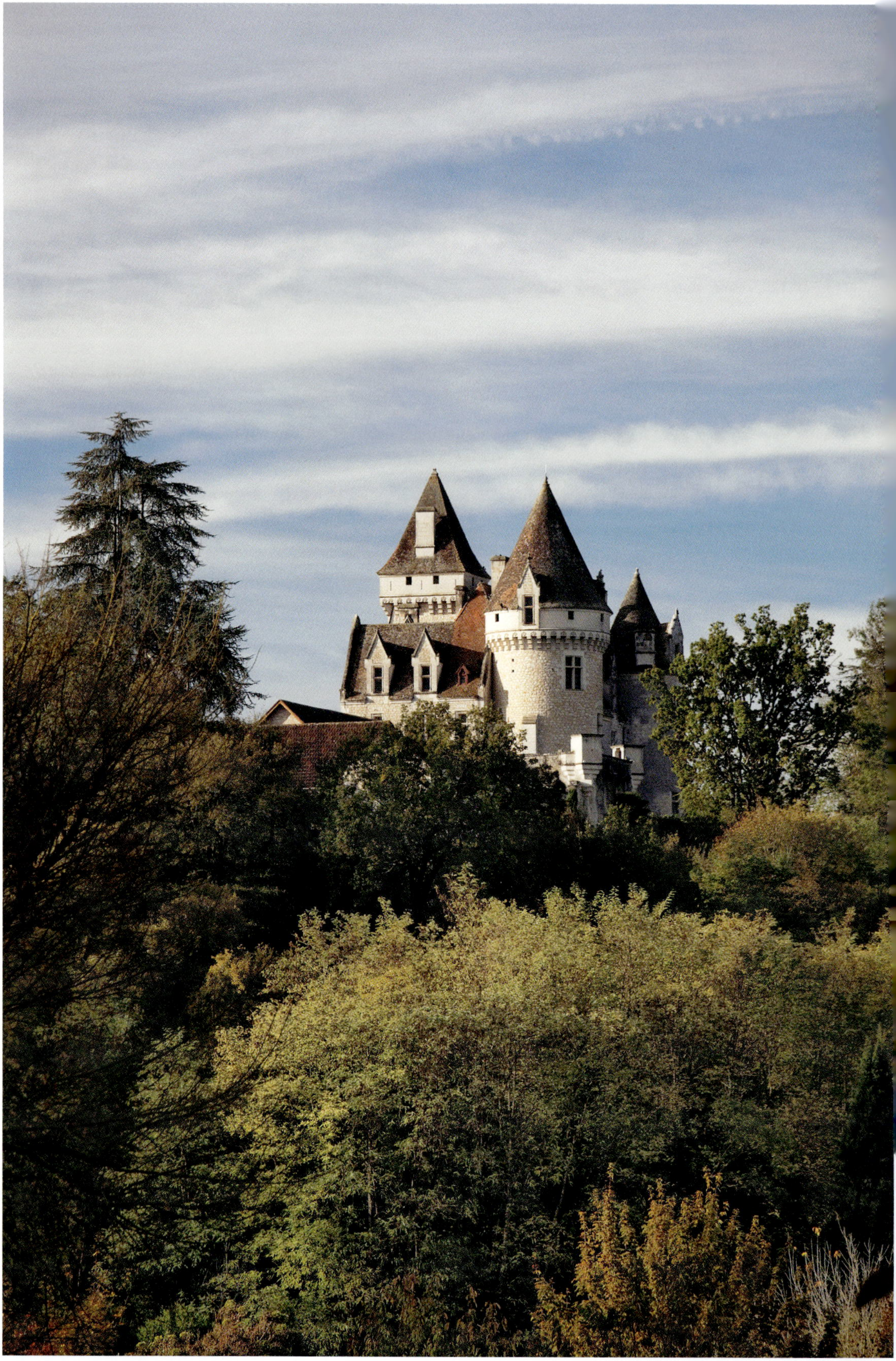

FRANCE   PARIS & PÉRIGORD

WHEN FRANCE BELONGED TO JOSEPHINE BAKER

She was a superstar, and her story lives on in Les Milandes, the chateau she loved and lost, as much as in Paris. — BY SLOANE CROSLEY

The first time I saw Josephine Baker up close was at an Alexander Calder exhibition at the Tate Modern in London. There, at the entrance, was a wire sculpture of her. I could see why it was one of the very first wire sculptures that Calder made: The subject demanded a new medium. With all due respect to Beyoncé, Josephine Baker had the most famous physique in showbiz history — a body so often compared to a spring that it's only natural an artist would try to capture her in that form, complete with spiraling breasts.

Four months later, I was in the Périgord region of France and decided to pay a visit to the Château des Milandes, a breathtaking Renaissance castle overlooking the Dordogne River. This, it turns out, is where Josephine Baker, who was born in St. Louis in 1906, lived during much of the second half of her life. She married and raised children there. "I have two loves," sang the queen of the Jazz Age in "J'ai Deux Amours," her most enduring tune, "my country and Paris." If she had recorded a late-in-life remake, she might have added a third love to the list: Milandes.

Here, I thought, I could learn more about Baker's passionate relationship with France — and France's fascination with her.

The chateau is up a twisting, idyllic road bordered by ivy-covered trees and stone walls. Walking in the front door, I was greeted by the sound of radio interviews with Baker and an exhibition of her stage costumes. There were over a dozen gowns, bustiers, and jumpsuits, most involving crystals, all in size remove-a-rib. I was not prepared for such a display.

Because most French chateaux are privately owned (including this one, currently inhabited by Angélique

Previous The Château des Milandes, where Josephine Baker raised her "Rainbow Tribe" of children.

Left Baker and friends in 1927, in the era when she was the star of the nightclub scene of Paris.

Opposite An Art Deco–era bas-relief of a dancer at the Folies-Bergère. France fell in love with Baker and vice versa.

de Saint-Exupéry, whose husband is a relative of the author of *The Little Prince*), most are limited in access. But here visitors could wander through a labyrinth of children's bedrooms furnished with gramophones and trunks; Art Deco bathrooms; a huge kitchen; and a vaulted gun room (not the official name of the room, but there was a rifle on a tripod pointed at my head as I entered). There were also cases of military medals and a commendation letter from Charles de Gaulle for Baker's efforts during World War II.

Baker was a spy for her adopted country. As an international celebrity who knew how to charm powerful people, she was able to continue to travel and perform during the Nazi occupation of France. She smuggled documents across the border to neutral countries, tucking them beneath gowns like the ones on the first floor of the chateau. She also hid weapons for the French Resistance.

The crown jewel of the tour was Baker's famous banana belt, which she wore — along with nothing else — in the Danse Sauvage at the Folies-Bergère in 1926. Baker did more for the sexualization of bananas than the collective sex-ed class demonstrations of the last century. The bananas are gold, not yellow — something impossible to tell in the black-and-white footage filmed in her era. As I admired the belt, a British tourist next to me turned to her husband and said, "She wasn't actually naked all that much, it's just what everybody chooses to remember."

"Everybody" included me. It's exactly what I saw when I looked at the Calder piece, and it's probably what Calder saw when he looked at Josephine Baker: an outline. But it's worth noting that there is so much more to Baker, and to Baker's France, than meets the eye. In addition to being a performer and a spy, she was the last speaker before the Rev. Dr. Martin Luther King Jr. at the 1963 March on Washington.

Slightly less celebrated is the fact that, in her 40s, she began adopting children from different countries. There were 12 in all, and they would come to be known as the Rainbow Tribe. For Baker, they were the living embodiment of a Utopian multiracial ideal. When they became an attraction for tourists, she fully embraced the gawking. Then, after World War II, Baker firmly settled at Milandes. She employed half the town. Her brother married the postwoman. Unlike her hectic nights of performing, her days in the Périgord were peaceful. Or as peaceful as anyone's days can be with 12 small children, multiple monkeys, and a pet cheetah.

Once I started listening for Josephine Baker, I heard her everywhere. Josette Garrigue, the elderly owner of a nearby farm, nodded and smiled when I told her I had been to the chateau. "I remember her well," she said, "Back then, this place was only little roads, just a romantic spot where she could drive around in her old cars. It's tragic what happened to her."

What happened was bankruptcy. Baker, who once claimed to be the richest woman in the world, fell into insurmountable debt despite the help of high-profile friends like Grace Kelly and Brigitte Bardot. In 1968 she was forced to give the chateau over to creditors. After the bananas, the second most famous image of Baker is of her sitting in the rain, locked out of her home by the new owner. The local loyalty to her is unwavering to this day; in an email, Angélique de Saint-Exupéry referred to the owner who bought the chateau from Baker as "a bad guy."

"I don't want to speak about him!" she wrote. "Josephine sold because she was without money, and a lot of people exploited the situation."

Michel Salon, a retired waiter who served everyone from Serge Gainsbourg to the king of Belgium, had his own Josephine story. "The first time I saw her was a Sunday," he recalled. "She was cleaning dishes in the castle cafe. A little girl was watching her, and Josephine called to her, picked her up, and hugged her. She loved children but couldn't have any of her own. The girl's mother yelled at her husband for not bringing a camera.

"Oh, she was so famous. But she was an artist and she didn't know how to manage money. She employed people who billed her for projects she didn't order. I know one waiter who would steal money from the cafe while Josephine was in Paris. Can you imagine someone doing something like that to her in Paris?"

I could not. Then again, I imagined Baker's life as a young woman in Paris was light on the dishwashing in general—but who knew? So after seeing this place so important in the latter half of her life, I decided to head back toward the beginning.

Julia Browne, who runs Walk the Spirit Tours: Black Paris and Beyond, sent me to David Burke, an American author and film producer whose documentary *Bonjour Paris*, produced with his wife, Joanne, is about the experiences of African Americans in Paris. I met David outside the boutique Hotel Joséphine, right at the Baker epicenter of Montmartre and Pigalle.

"It's funny," he said, "Josephine wasn't really a jazz person, and she was a dreadful singer at first, but she was involved with the whole Jazz Age community. She's the most famous person in the whole group, the most famous of any American to ever live in France."

I raise my eyebrows. Really?

Burke mostly gives Lost Generation tours: Hemingway, Stein, Fitzgerald, so his answer had authority: "Really."

We set out on the Rue Fontaine, which leads to the Moulin Rouge. Burke described the area in its heyday as being "like 52nd Street back in the bebop days." The street was dotted with jazz clubs, none of which still exist. It took a bit of an imaginative leap to picture the scene; our conversation took place between a nail salon and a pizzeria. The one structure still standing was the former Le Grand Duc, where Langston Hughes was employed as a busboy and where Ada Smith, a.k.a. Bricktop, who later took Baker under her wing, first performed.

Six Degrees of Josephine Baker would be too easy a game to play in France. Or in America, for that matter. Baker was a star even before she arrived in Paris (starring in *Shuffle Along*, one of the first all-black musicals). But Paris made her a megastar.

"People just went wild for her," Burke said. "There was a need for something fresh, and Josephine brought this combination of Africa, jazz, humor, and America in her presentation. And she was personable. Everyone loved her."

Well, not everyone. I broached the subject of *The Hungry Heart*, a scathing portrait of Baker I had read on the train up to Paris. It was written (with a

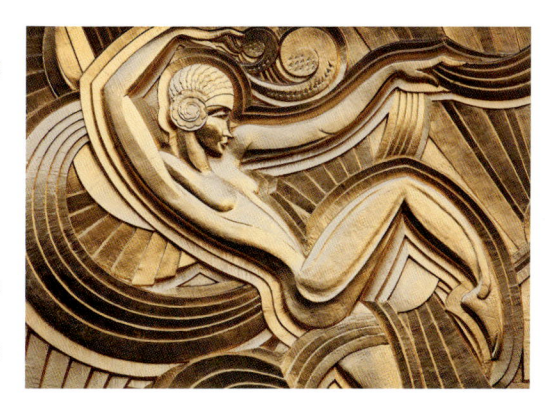

Above The Moulin Rouge, now primarily a tourist attraction, was one of a cluster of Paris nightclubs in Baker's heyday.

Opposite Baker's Château des Milandes. Inside, tourists see costumes, mementoes, and military decorations.

co-writer) by Jean-Claude Baker, her unofficial 13th son, who met Josephine when he was already a young man. Burke said he found the book "unreliable and worrisome." I can see why. In it, Baker is an oversexed fabulist who, "like a black Chaplin," stepped on anyone "to get where she wanted to get," answered the door naked for George Balanchine, and referred to Marlene Dietrich as "that German cow." Burke recommended I read *Josephine Baker in Art and Life* by Bennetta Jules-Rosette instead.

We turned onto the Rue de Clichy. The stained-glass arch of the Casino de Paris—Baker's third music-hall home, where she performed with feathered wings—rose up in the distance.

"Josephine almost never played an American," Burke said. "She was always playing a woman of color from somewhere else. So she would play a Vietnamese girl who was in love with a French planter in occupied Vietnam."

"That's quite the colonial fantasy," I said. "'Thank you for occupying us, how can we serve you?'"

"And it was Josephine," Burke said, "so it's everyone's fantasies at once."

Next, we made our way over to the Avenue Montaigne off the Champs-Élysées, a Céline- and Fendi-flanked stretch that was familiar to Baker. One side effect of immense fame is a fluency in fashion: Josephine was beloved by designers like Balmain and Dior. Were she alive now, she surely would have had her own line of perfume. Instead, she had the lucrative Baker Fix, a hair pomade inspired by her own shellacked curls.

But the area also symbolizes the end and the beginning of Baker's Parisian life. At one end of the street is the lovely Théâtre des Champs-Élysées. It was here, in October 1925, that Baker performed in *La Revue Nègre*, her first performance in Paris. And a short walk away is L'Église de la Madeleine, the

Photographs by Andy Haslam

site of her funeral procession in April 1975; she was given full French military honors and drew over 20,000 mourners. Brian Scott Bagley, a cabaret singer and choreographer who has devoted much of his professional life to paying homage to Josephine Baker on stage in Paris, told me he believes Baker's charisma was so stupendous that it still "latches on" to performers like him. He, too, has his preferred Baker narratives (he's partial to *Remembering Josephine Baker* by Stephen Papich). "But it doesn't matter what you read," he said. "What matters is embracing Paris the way she embraced it."

Like Paris itself, Baker is at once idolized and familiar — once you fall in love with her, you want to both share that love and keep it for yourself. This is evidenced by the fact that not a single person with whom I spoke referred to her by her last name, as they did Hemingway, Fitzgerald, Stein, and Porter. Everyone feels as if Josephine was theirs.

> **WHAT TO READ AND WATCH**
>
> ***Josephine Baker in Art and Life: The Icon and the Image***, by Bennetta Jules-Rosette. A well-researched biography.
>
> ***Josephine Baker: The Hungry Heart***, by Jean-Claude Baker, the close friend Baker referred to as a son. "I loved her, hated her, and wanted desperately to understand her," he wrote.
>
> ***Remembering Josephine Baker***, by Stephen Papich, a Baker friend and choreographer. Ishmael Reed, in a review for *The New York Times*, called this "a memorable, entertaining, and moving book."
>
> ***The Josephine Baker Collection***. A DVD set of three of Baker's movies: *ZouZou*, *Princess Tam Tam*, and *Siren of the Tropics*, including dance scenes.
>
> ***Josephine Baker: The First Black Superstar***, directed by Suzanne Phillips. A well-crafted 2006 documentary for the BBC.

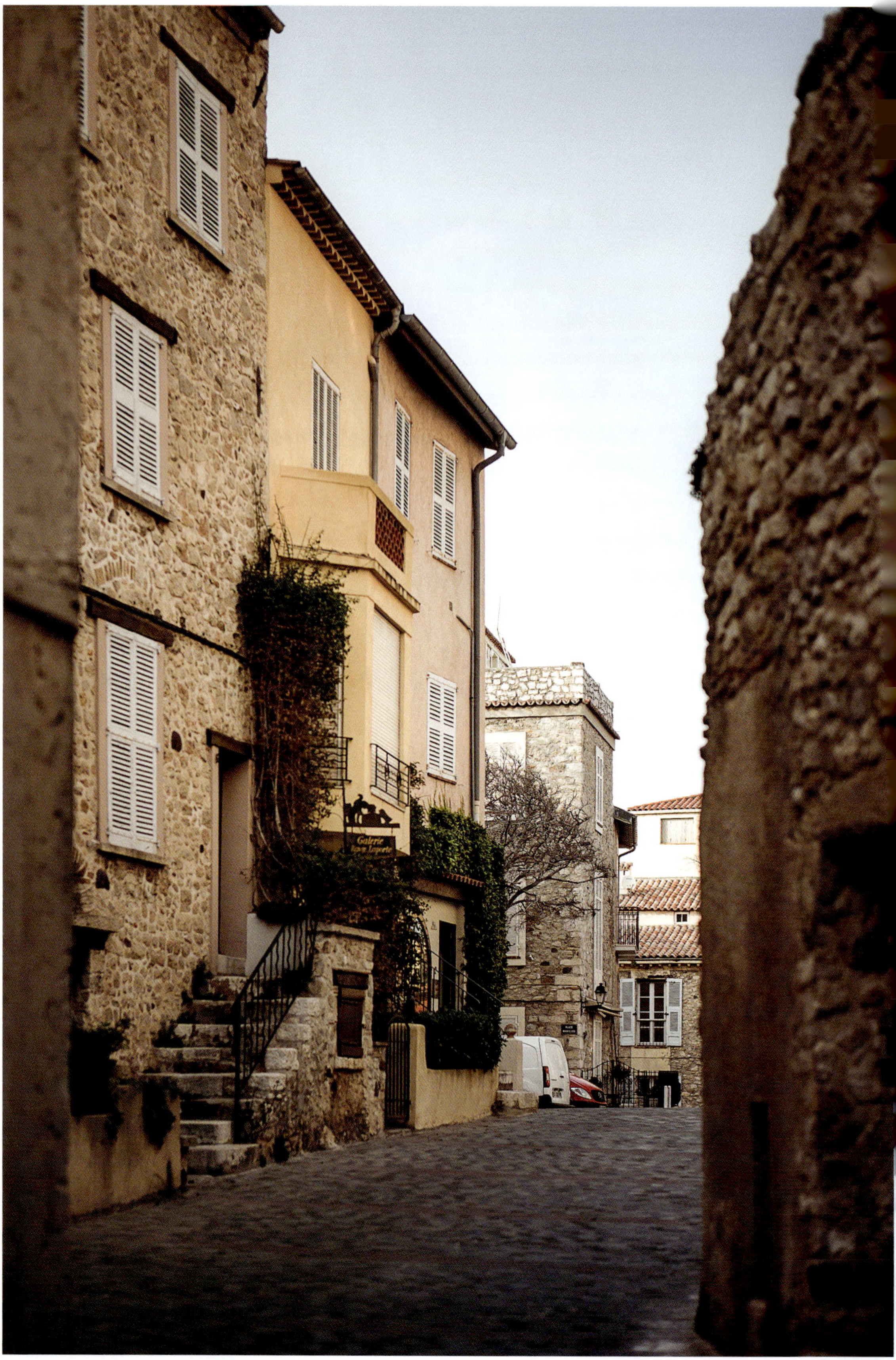
Galerie

ON PICASSO'S TRAIL, ANTIBES TO AVIGNON

In southern France, an aging Pablo Picasso thrived in the sunshine and painted on the walls.
— BY ANDREW FERREN

One of the most familiar photographs of Pablo Picasso is Robert Capa's famous image of him in the sand on the French Riviera shore, a barefoot old man holding a big beach umbrella over the head of a beautiful young woman. It's a small vignette in the long and complicated life of a monumental artist. But southern France is Picasso country, the place where he spent most of the last three decades of his life. And Antibes, where he and his lover, Françoise Gilot, were that day, is the place to pick up his trail on the Riviera and in Provence.

The essential first stop is the enchanting Musée Picasso, to see lyrical Picasso works permanently on display and savor the story of how they got there.

Picasso's Antibes period is characterized by an almost palpable sense of joy owing to the presence of Gilot, a new love 40 years younger than he, as well as the end of World War II. He had spent the war years in Paris, living with his earlier lover Dora Maar, painting in his studio, being harassed by the Gestapo, and finally meeting Gilot, an art student. In the summer of 1946, Picasso and Gilot were staying in a villa near the Château Grimaldi, a provincial antiquities museum to which its enterprising curator, Romuald Dor de la Souchère, had hopes of adding a collection of modern painting. During a chance meeting on the beach one day, he approached Picasso about donating a painting, and though Picasso at first demurred, in the end this conversation led to Antibes getting a museum full of Picassos.

Dor de la Souchère later recounted the scene in a short text called "Chance." Picasso, after rather

PROVENCE-ALPES-CÔTE D'AZUR   FRANCE

Previous A street in Antibes. A chance meeting on the beach led to the creation of the town's Picasso Museum.

Left Vallauris, a few miles from Antibes, has its own Picasso Museum, where exhibits include this sculpture.

Opposite Picasso in Vallauris in 1953, with ceramic figures he made in clay. With him is Suzanne Ramié of the Madoura pottery.

weakly promising to look for a drawing of Antibes to give to the museum, complained that he had never been given large walls on which to paint.

"Walls? You want walls? I can give you some walls," Dor de la Souchère responded, and offered Picasso a room in the chateau to use as a studio. Picasso accepted and, according to Gilot, announced: "While I'm here I'm not just going to paint some pictures. I am going to decorate your museum for you."

In an astonishing burst of activity, he began painting frescoes and then quickly switched to painting just about everything else in reach. One day it seemed that one of the museum's many 19th-century military portraits was missing, until it was discovered that Picasso had painted over it with a work known as *The Sea Urchin Eater*.

Picasso's at-hand art supplies during those early days of postwar reconstruction included panels of fiber cement and Ripolin—basically drywall and house paint—as well as plywood, and he used them all to create pastoral scenes like *La Joie de Vivre*, in which a curvy female nude clearly modeled on Gilot dances joyously in an idyllic Mediterranean landscape amid flute-playing fauns and dancing goats. The painting, the unofficial icon of his Antibes period, is among the most beloved treasures of the museum's collection, which also includes portraits of striped-shirted fishermen and dreamily reclining nudes.

Both the artist and the museum curator acknowledged that if they had set out to create a Picasso museum, it might never have happened. In the end, the sheer quantity and scale of the works Picasso painted in that brief period determined that some sort of legacy would remain at the chateau. He could not take the large works with him when the cold drove him from the drafty chateau in November.

This was also the era of Picasso's "femme-fleur" —images of a woman (again, Françoise Gilot) transformed into a flower—that seem almost childlike representations of fertility. Indeed, in the fall of 1946, she was already pregnant with the first of their two children, but as she recounted in her 1964 memoir *Life with Picasso*, their day-to-day existence was not all flowers and joie de vivre. Picasso is famous for taking over his women's lives, leaving them devastated when he moved on, but in 1953 it was Françoise who left him, the only one of his many lovers to do so. (Later in life, she was married for 25 years to Jonas Salk, the inventor of the first polio vaccine.)

Not far from the museum, Picasso often sketched at the beach at La Garoupe, a cove on the Cap d'Antibes. Today, beyond the usual swimming and sunbathing, the beach offers travelers a lovely promenade winding along the sea. In the Old Town of Antibes, there are charming cafes, restaurants, and crêperies to try out, and a bustling morning produce and flower market changes in the afternoon to a place where artisans sell handicrafts.

A few miles northwest of Antibes is Vallauris, where Picasso and Gilot moved in 1948 and raised their two young children, Claude and Paloma, together until 1953, and where Picasso explored the medium of ceramics. Georges and Suzanne Ramié, owners of the Madoura factory, a producer of the region's traditional platters, pitchers, and other pottery, were as clever as Dor de la Souchère had been at the Château Grimaldi. By offering Picasso a place to work, they in turn created a good business for themselves. He wanted to create large, independent sculptures in clay, but when many of these did not survive firing in the kiln, he set about decorating and sometimes tweaking the traditional vessels and forms that the factory had been producing for years. These playful works — wine jugs molded into curvy women and oval platters painted

Above Dominating the scene at a Vallauris market is *Man with Sheep*, a sculpture Picasso donated to the town.

Opposite Antibes and the Mediterranean. With his new lover, Françoise Gilot, Picasso came here after World War II.

to look like bullrings—delighted Picasso, and he allowed the Ramiés to replicate some of them in limited editions.

Vallauris has its own Musée Picasso, in the chateau on the main square where the bronze cast of the sculpture *Man with Sheep* has stood since Picasso donated it to the town in 1949. The museum exhibits some of his ceramics, but its biggest draw is the *War and Peace* memorial that Picasso painted from 1952 to 1957 to decorate the building's small Romanesque chapel. Considered his last work of overtly political art, it juxtaposes menacing images of war and idyllic scenes of shepherds and rural life.

From 1959 to 1961, Picasso and his new companion, Jacqueline Roque, whom he married in 1961, lived near Aix-en-Provence, the delightful Baroque city that is perhaps best known as the home of Paul Cézanne. Cézanne's art was an important influence on Picasso early in his career. After he saw a Cézanne retrospective in 1906, "Cézanne's influence gradually flooded everything," Picasso said. His personal collection (which was broken up and dispersed after his death) included paintings by Cézanne.

In 1958 Picasso bought a home near Aix, the Château de Vauvenargues. It was situated at the foot of Mont Sainte-Victoire, the mountain that Cézanne had returned to again and again in his own paintings, and it was here that Picasso and Jacqueline, with her daughter from a previous marriage, settled for several years. Interestingly, though he was literally in Cézanne's backyard, it was the work of another French master, Manet's *Le Déjeuner sur l'Herbe*, that inspired much of Picasso's work at Vauvenargues.

The Château de Vauvenargues is visible at a distance but not open for tours, although Picasso and Jacqueline are both buried there.

From Aix, the other Provençal towns on a traveler's Picasso itinerary are within easy distance. Arles, with

Photographs by
Ed Alcock

its bullring and colorful atmosphere that reminded Picasso of his native Spain, is worth a visit. The last stop is Avignon, which Picasso first visited in 1912 with his fellow painter Georges Braque. Though Picasso's pivotal masterpiece *Les Demoiselles d'Avignon* was actually painted in Paris five years before he ever visited the town, it was in this former city of popes that the high priest of 20th-century art began his enduring love affair with the south of France.

WHAT TO READ AND WATCH

Life with Picasso, by Françoise Gilot. A memoir by the woman who was Picasso's muse in his first years in southern France. Candid and critical.

A Life of Picasso, by John Richardson. An authoritative multivolume biography written by a close friend.

Picasso, by Gertrude Stein. A one-of-a-kind personal view of the young Picasso and the influences that shaped him during his critical years in Paris.

Surviving Picasso, directed by James Ivory. Anthony Hopkins plays Picasso "with superb swagger," Janet Maslin wrote in a *New York Times* review.

Picasso: Love, Sex and Art, directed by Hugues Nancy. A BBC documentary that does justice to Picasso's artistic genius while also documenting his personal life.

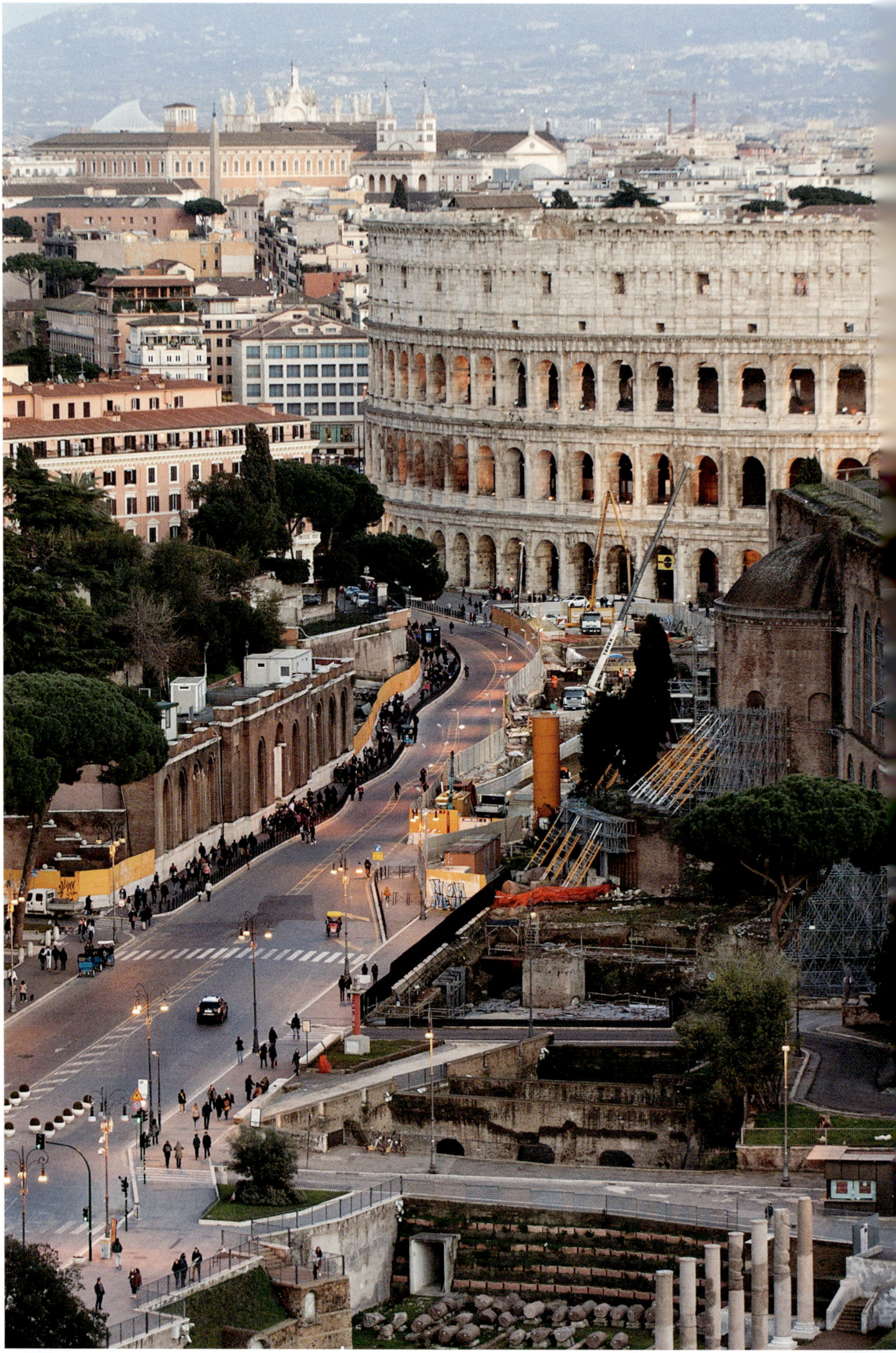

ROME IN THE FOOTSTEPS OF FLAVIUS JOSEPHUS

Two thousand years ago, a keen observer chronicled a plunderer's parade. The route is still easy to follow.
— BY DAVID LASKIN

Even without a book or a guide, even after two millenniums of crumbling, the image of the seven-branched candelabrum—the Jewish menorah—is unmistakable on the inner wall of the Arch of Titus in the Roman Forum. Stand at the base of the single-passage arch and look up, and the scene in bas-relief ripples to life with almost cartoon clarity: Straining porters, trudging along what is plainly the route of a Roman triumph, bear aloft the golden menorah and other sacred loot plundered from the Temple in Jerusalem in A.D. 70. The opposite side of the arch depicts the victory lap of the chief plunderer, Emperor Titus, who as an ambitious young general crushed the Jews' revolt, leveled their Temple, and brought enough booty and slaves back to Rome to finance an epic construction program that included the Colosseum.

I've gazed on the Arch of Titus many times, marveling at its muscular grace, recoiling from its brazen braggadocio. But it wasn't until I returned to Rome with Flavius Josephus as my guide that I fully grasped the significance of this monument in Jewish and Roman history.

"The luckiest traitor ever," in the words of the historian Mary Beard, Flavius Josephus was a first-century Jewish general who threw in his lot with the Roman legions that destroyed his homeland. When Titus and his father, Vespasian, returned to Rome after the Judean war to inaugurate the Flavian dynasty—successor to the Julio-Claudian dynasty that Augustus founded and Nero destroyed—Josephus went with them. "The Jew of Rome," as the German writer Lion Feuchtwanger called him in an eponymous historical novel, spent the rest of his days living in luxury in Flavian Rome and writing the history of his times.

Turncoat? Asylum seeker? Pragmatic visionary? Historians have long debated Josephus's motives and

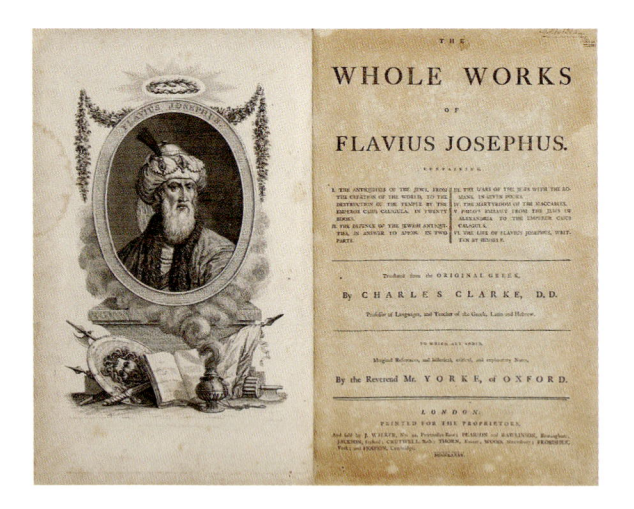

Previous The Colosseum, the most visible relic of ancient Rome, was financed with treasure looted from Judea.

Left An unlikely chronicler of Roman triumph over his ancestral land, Flavius Josephus nevertheless left the best record.

Opposite above The Arch of Titus still clearly tells the 2,000-year-old story of an emperor's victory celebration.

Opposite below A panel on the arch shows the procession into Rome bringing religious treasures taken from Jerusalem.

character. What's indisputable is that most of what is known about the violent encounter between Rome and Judea during this period comes out of his work. What's astonishing is that, with a sharp eye and a bit of research, you can still walk in Josephus's footsteps in contemporary Rome. Where but in the Eternal City is it possible to map a 2,000-year-old eyewitness account onto an intact urban fabric?

The morning light was silvery, but traffic was already roaring along Via di San Gregorio as I waited by the gate of the Palatine Hill for Mirco Modolo, the archaeologist-archivist who had agreed to take me on a walking tour of Flavian Rome. Today this street is a rather featureless channel running between the Colosseum and the Circus Maximus. But Mirco, whose youth and reserve belied a tenacious erudition, reminded me that we were standing on the likely processional route chiseled into the marble of the Arch of Titus and inked even more indelibly on the pages of Josephus's book *The Jewish War*.

"At the break of dawn," Josephus writes, "Vespasian and Titus issued forth, crowned with laurel and clad in the traditional purple robes, and proceeded to the Octavian walks" — the Portico d'Ottavia, now a soaring ruin at the edge of the Jewish ghetto. From the Portico d'Ottavia to the top of the Capitoline Hill, where all proper Roman triumphal processions culminated, is — and was — a 10-minute stroll. But it is clear from Josephus's account that the imperial entourage took the long way around, circling counterclockwise around the outer precipices of the Palatine before entering the Forum on the side now dominated by the Colosseum.

Mirco and I hiked halfway up the Palatine to a terraced ledge overlooking the Forum. "See those tourists following the lady with the flag?" he asked. "They're walking on the Via Sacra, the main axis through the Forum that the Flavian procession traversed before ascending the Capitol."

I tried to mentally erase the T-shirts and selfie sticks and resurrect the fallen columns. Vespasian and Titus, riding chariots, would have been two dabs of purple surging up the ramparts of the Capitoline through a sea of white togas. In their train, thousands of Jewish slaves shuffled with bowed heads while the heaps of plundered gold and silver bobbed above them, winking in the sun. "Last of all the spoils," writes Josephus, "was carried a copy of the Jewish Law" — the Torah.

Josephus reveals exactly where these spoils ended up. Vespasian had a new temple — the Templum Pacis (Temple of Peace) — built adjacent to the Forum where "he laid up the vessels of gold from the temple of the Jews, on which he prided himself; but their Law and the purple hangings of the sanctuary he ordered to be deposited and kept in the palace." The *palace*, in ancient Rome, meant the Palatine (the word palace derives from the hill's name) and so, as the autumn sunlight brightened from silver to gold, I mounted the imperial summit.

After the buzzing, marble-strewn congestion of the Forum, the Palatine is like a country stroll. The huge squares of weedy grass and clumps of umbrella pines outlined in brick stubs could almost be farm fields, but in fact most of the stubs are remains of a colossal royal residence, the Domus Flavia, inaugurated by Vespasian and completed by his wicked, wildly ambitious second son, Domitian. Josephus, whose life spanned all three Flavian emperors, would have come to the Domus Flavia to pay homage to his patrons and perhaps murmur a prayer before the sacred scroll they had cached here.

I lingered on the Palatine for half an hour, trying to conjure the nerve center of an empire from its ruins. Somewhere buried under the dandelions and broken shards stood an inlaid niche or marble alcove where the stolen Torah was caged like a captive king.

Josephus's footsteps lie closer to the surface in the Templum Pacis. I'd never heard of this monument, though I must have passed its ruins a score of times on the wide, glaring Via dei Fori Imperiali (Street of the Imperial Fora) that Mussolini carved out as his own triumphal route between the Colosseum and Piazza Venezia. On my second morning in Rome, Josephus's text in hand, I stood by the railing near the Forum ticket booth and peered down at the ongoing excavations of the temple's sanctuary, arcades, fountains, and gardens. Josephus notes that the Templum Pacis, built "very speedily in a style surpassing all human conception," housed not only the spoils of Jerusalem, but "ancient masterpieces of painting and sculpture...objects for the sight of which men had once wandered over the whole world."

These masterpieces have long since vanished, but a wall of the temple still stands at the entrance of the sixth-century Basilica of Saints Cosmas and Damiano, now a Franciscan convent. One of the resident brothers, who humbly insisted on anonymity, showed me around. "The Templum Pacis was not only a shrine but a kind of cultural center," he said. "We're standing on the site of the temple's library, where the Forma Urbis, an immense marble map of the city, was displayed." He pointed out a rusty bent spike that once fixed marble veneer to the rough-hewn stone. "Go ahead and touch—it's been here since the first century A.D."

I was itching to get down to the crypt, which covers part of the footprint of the Templum Pacis, but first we ducked into the basilica and took a moment to savor its principal artistic treasure: a shimmering sixth-century apse mosaic of Christ surfing roseate clouds flanked by saints. Perhaps I've read too many

Above The Temple of Romulus, with its original bronze doors now weathered to green, survives from the fourth century.

Opposite The Portico d'Ottavia is now a soaring ruin at the edge of what was once the Jewish ghetto in Rome.

thrillers, but as I gazed up at this solemnly joyous creation, I imagined a plumb line dropping from the tiles of Christ's outstretched hand and coming to rest, magically, on the exact spot where the menorah had been stashed—fanciful, but not impossible.

The sacred loot has disappeared without a trace, but a shelf of thrillers could be spun from the theories, myths, sightings, and urban legends about where it supposedly ended up: hidden in a cave, glittering on the altar of the Basilica of St. John Lateran, carted off to Constantinople, tossed in the Tiber, squirreled away in a sub-subbasement of the Vatican. Alessandro Viscogliosi, a professor of the history of architecture at the University of Rome whom I met toward the end of my stay, has a more plausible, though mundane, explanation: When the Templum Pacis burned in A.D. 191, the gold and silver vessels melted and were subsequently salvaged and recast, probably as coins.

"No one really knows what happened to the stuff," said Steven Fine, a professor of Jewish history at Yeshiva University in New York and the director of the Arch of Titus Project. "There's a common desire to establish continuity through things, and certainly the visual environment of Rome fosters this."

Copies of Josephus's books likely burned in the fire as well, but the texts survived, thanks in large part to Christian scholars who embraced him for his early, impartial (but much disputed) mentions of the historical Jesus—the so-called Testimonium Flavianum—in *Jewish Antiquities*. His fellow Jews, on the other hand, have until recently written Josephus off as a traitor and a Roman sycophant.

Still, 19 centuries after his death around A.D. 100, Josephus remains one of the most famous Jews of Rome—best-selling author, confidant of emperors, member of a religious community that was already well established when he arrived in A.D. 71. It's still

Photographs by Susan Wright

going strong today, with families tracing their lineage "da Cesare," from the time of Caesar.

I reflected on Josephus's life and legacy as I made a final trek to the Palatine at the end of my stay. The southwest edge of the hill commands an unforgettable view over the Circus Maximus to the skyline beyond, and in the luminous October haze I picked out the distinctive squared-off metallic dome of the Tempio Maggiore—the main Jewish synagogue—and beyond it, the majestic drum of St. Peter's. Roman, Jewish, Christian: Josephus's footsteps lead us through the time and place where these three spheres aligned most exuberantly, most surprisingly.

WHAT TO READ AND WATCH

The Jewish War, by Josephus, Oxford World's Classics edition. A 21st-century translation of Flavius Josephus's first-century account.

The Jew of Rome, by Lion Feuchtwanger. Volume 2 of a trilogy of historical novels based on the life of Josephus.

Last Man Standing, hosted by Simcha Jacobovici. *The Naked Archaeologist*, Season 1, Episode 13. Summoning archaeological evidence to prove or disprove Josephus's descriptions of ancient events.

The Roman Triumph, by Mary Beard. Ancient Rome's victory processions as seen by a historian and prolific writer on Roman history, also the author of *SPQR*.

The Silver Pigs, by Lindsey Davis. Book 1 in the *Marcus Didius Falco* series about a wisecracking ancient Roman detective. In Chapter LVI, he and his fractious extended family watch the Flavian Procession.

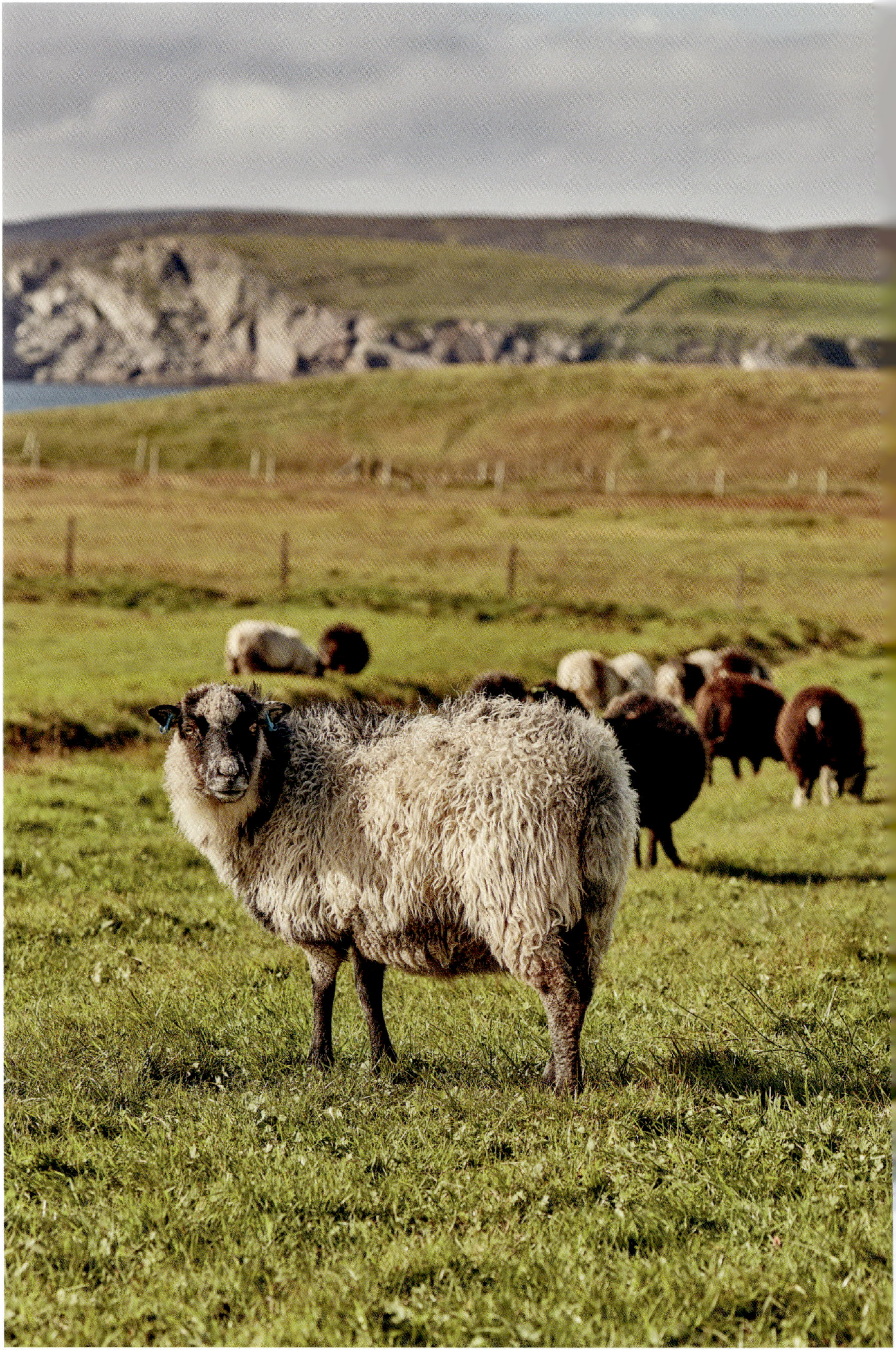

WHERE THERE ARE SHEEP, THERE MUST BE WOOL

The Shetland Islands have more going on than knitting, but at knitting they excel. — BY NELLIE HERMANN

A few days into my trip to Shetland, the Scottish subarctic archipelago across the sea from Norway, I found myself on the top of a cliff face, peering through the fog at a huge rock in the northern Atlantic Ocean. The rock was topped with a spike of white: the Muckle Flugga lighthouse, built in 1854, a mind-boggling feat since the rock's cliff face juts straight up out of the roiling sea. In the early days of the lighthouse, a guide was saying, a man had to be hoisted by ropes around his arms to safely cross the gap between his boat and the landing area on the rock.

At this most northerly point in Scotland, I felt a profound sense that I was very far from home.

I was on the tiny island of Unst, the most northern and rocky of the Shetlands. It has a population of about 600. I was with a tour of mostly women, from all over the world, all of us attendees of Shetland Wool Week, a knitting and textile festival hailed through the world's knitting grapevine as the mecca of all knitting and textile festivals.

To get to this spot, our bus had driven us up the length of "mainland" Shetland, the largest of the 16 populated islands, then crossed on a ferry to the smaller island of Yell, then driven up a snaking road to Yell's tip and to a second ferry ride (this one on more of a raft than a boat, with the bus exposed on all sides) to Unst.

Now we stood at the top of the cliffs of Hermaness, home to some of the largest colonies of nesting seabirds in the United Kingdom. We squinted through the fog, our knitted scarves whipping in the wind, trying to keep our feet on the ground and our knitted hats (many of them made for Wool Week, which sends a new hat pattern to participants every year) on our heads as the howling gusts of wind pulled at us.

SHETLAND ISLANDS   SCOTLAND

Previous The native sheep are bred to grow a soft, lightweight fiber that makes Shetland wool unique.

Left Shetland was a clandestine link to Nazi-occupied Norway during World War II. These boats at a local pier were loaded with mines.

Opposite Color and texture at a gathering of knitters during Wool Week.

Before I left New York, the only thing I really knew about Shetland was that it is the birthplace of Fair Isle knitting (Fair Isle being the most remote of the islands), a technique of colorwork recognizable in traditional sweaters. What I found was a place with a complex history, difficult to get to but well worth the journey.

In Shetland, knitting is a tradition that goes back centuries and is embedded in the place's rich history. Sheep here outnumber people by 20 to 1, and inclement weather on the islands has encouraged the local sheep to grow a softer and lighter-weight fiber that makes Shetland wool unique.

For much of the 20th century the textile industry was an important element of Shetland's local economy; women farmers, before production was moved to factories, knitted the yokes of sweaters to be sent abroad while they walked to and from the fields. Today knitters in Shetland are unambiguously celebrated for their vision and skill; frequent signs on the road advertise local designers whose homes double as shops.

The growing resurgence of interest in knitting around the world — likely linked to the easy communication of our digital age — has made knitting festivals worldwide increasingly popular (tickets for classes at knitting festivals in Edinburgh or Iceland, for example, have sold out within hours). In as small and remote a place as Shetland, however, the festival is actually helping to bring textiles back into view as a player in the economy.

There are about 100 islands in Shetland, though most are uninhabited. To get to mainland Shetland from the Scottish mainland, one takes an overnight ferry or a small plane from Aberdeen. I took the ferry, a very memorable roller-coaster experience on the heaving sea, and landed in Lerwick, the islands' central port and biggest city, with a population of about 7,500, and the hub of the festival.

The writer Ann Cleeves set a series of popular murder mysteries on Shetland, and they were the basis of an excellent BBC series, *Shetland*, that the islanders are understandably quite proud of. It's easy to see why this is a good spot for a crime novel. Driving around the tiny islands is an experience in moodiness; you snake down one-way roads through pockets of brightly painted houses and grazing sheep, the seething ocean on one side or the other of you — or sometimes both, the North Sea on one and the North Atlantic on the other. Often when you curve around a bend in the road the view before you is breathtaking, and if you are driving a car you have to be careful not to drive right off the road. Cliffs drop precipitously just feet from the pavement; inlets have choppy waves and, in summer, killer whales who pick off sleepy seals; enormous rocks jut up from the ocean just off the coast; and everywhere, roofs and boats and houses are painted cheerful colors that burst against the overcast sky.

I had watched the BBC series, but even such a well-crafted show is no substitute for being there. It's impossible to experience the Shetland wind through a television. I was there for a full week, and there was only one night when I didn't hear the loud howl of wind all night long. At one point, someone asked a local farmer whether the wind was normal, whether it kept up all year long. "Wind?" he said incredulously. "This is nothing! It's been calm ever since you came!"

The wind is a large part of life on the islands. As winter approaches, everything that might blow away is removed from yards: wheelbarrows, lawn mowers, wooden benches. When a keeper still lived at the Eshaness Lighthouse on the northwest of the main island, our guide told us, he used to chain his car to the cliff to make sure it didn't blow away. The wind is also the reason we were given for the diminutive stature of Shetland ponies.

In the winter, there is a month of near-perpetual darkness, and in the summer, a month of continuous sunlight; the wind, I was told, is constant no matter the time of year, though at certain times it is known to gust harder, stronger, or more or less predictably.

The people of Shetland, though, really could not be nicer — one is tempted to think their isolation and hardiness have formed them for kindness. At the bed-and-breakfast where we stayed, Virdafjell, the owner, Dorothy Stove, greeted us with a plastic bin of clean house slippers to choose from, and every morning put out a breakfast spread fit for 10 hungry men (though my friend and I were the only people there): scones, assorted bread, eggs, yogurt, fruit, at least 10 different kinds of cereal, and even decorative butter slices.

Considering the size of Shetland, Wool Week is surprisingly vast and diverse. The program is eight full days and features myriad classes and exhibitions, tours, gatherings, teas, and lectures on nearly all of the islands; on a random day, I counted 54 different offerings.

Community halls in tiny towns all over the islands host Wool Weekers every day of the festival, local people serving lunch or tea and exhibiting local crafts. A day tour of the main island, for example, included a stop at Ollaberry Hall, an exhibition space on the west shore, where a table more than eight feet long boasted plate after plate of handmade cakes and cookies ("homebakes"), and local women served us all tea. This spread accompanied an exhibit of lace haps, or shawls — most of them made by local schoolchildren — knitted with cobweb-thin yarn, so thin the whole shawl could pass through a wedding ring. My fellow bus-riders and I, once all the shawls had been exclaimed over, sat and happily ate the homebakes while working on whatever knitting project we had brought with us. There is a lot of knitting being done, as one might imagine, during Shetland Wool Week.

Shetland offers more than textiles. There are ancient archaeological sites scattered all over the islands, which sit atop a network of tectonic plates.

Above There are about 100 islands in Shetland, though most are uninhabited. This is a view of Bressay.

Below Sheep sport their wool coats at a farm on Bressay Island in the Shetlands.

Opposite A rainbow over the Shetland Islands. In this subarctic archipelago, wool is a tool of defense against the weather.

Some visitors go caving and kayaking. Others come to see the enormous diversity of nesting seabirds; puffins, which nest here in summer, are a popular draw. Two of the nights we were there, there were sightings of the northern lights, ethereal streaks of color across the night sky.

In the winter, a tremendous fire festival dating back to the 1880s celebrates Shetland's Viking history all over the islands with costumes and a torch procession resulting in the burning of a full-size replica Viking long ship. Nearly 1,000 torch-bearing islanders show up in Lerwick alone.

There's history, too. Scalloway, once the islands' capital, has an ancient castle and in World War II was the base of the Shetland Bus, a clandestine special operations group that carried resistance fighters, materials, and refugees to and from German-occupied Norway.

Despite all of this, the main action at the time of my visit was Wool Week, which takes place in the fall. Every local person who has anything to do with textiles or wool seemed to be featured in some way. Even Hazel Tindall, the world's fastest knitter (325 stitches every four minutes, I was told), taught a few classes. I visited Uradale Farm, which is trying

*Photographs by
Andy Haslam*

to bring back more of the traditional Shetland sheep, which are black or brown (or "moorit"). White sheep get preference in the marketplace because their wool is easier to dye.

Nearly every person who shared with us the good news about a resurgence of interest in the knitting industry was also quick to share the difficulties their line of work still faces. The general demand is still for inexpensive, mass-produced white wool, and the market for handmade goods is still small and imperiled as fewer people buy knitted clothing. But standing on the shores of Shetland during Wool Week, a knitter can't help but feel optimistic, and a person can't help but feel swept away.

WHAT TO READ AND WATCH

Ann Cleeves' Shetland, by Ann Cleeves. A companion to the writer's popular novels, capturing the essence of Shetland through its people, its past, its festivals, and its changing seasons.

The Shetland Guide Book, by Charles Tait. A touring guide to the islands, with hundreds of photographs.

In the Footsteps of Sheep: Tales of a Journey through Scotland, Walking, Spinning, and Knitting Socks, by Debbie Zawinski. Scenery, the islanders, and a sock pattern for each breed of sheep along the way.

The Knitting Brigades of World War I: Volunteers for Victory in America and Abroad, by Holly Korda. The story of a volunteer knitting project that produced millions of pounds of socks, sweaters, hats, and bandages for Allied soldiers.

Shetland, a BBC television series. Based on the crime novels of Ann Cleeves.

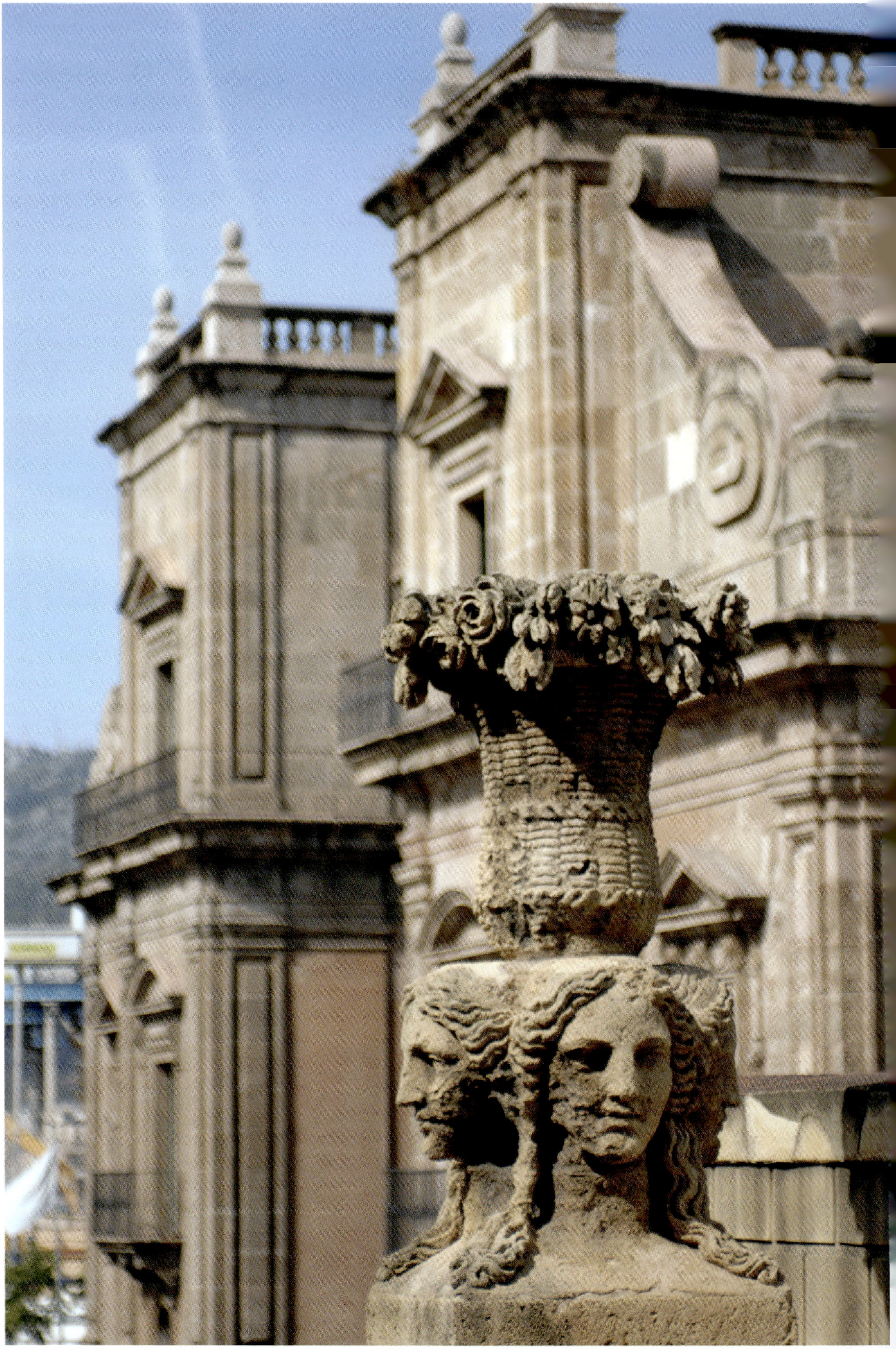

SICILY, THROUGH THE EYES OF THE LEOPARD

A classic Italian novel, written by a Sicilian prince, captured the beauty and sadness in arid landscapes and decaying palaces. — BY ADAM BEGLEY

Ask a roomful of readers about Lampedusa's *The Leopard* (*Il Gattopardo* in Italian), and more often than not you'll find a few who will put hand to heart and say it's their favorite book, and a few others who will simply shrug — never heard of it — or ask if it has anything to do with the Luchino Visconti movie starring Burt Lancaster (yes, it does). I suppose it's a coincidence that a roomful of travelers will poll in a similar fashion if you ask them about Sicily, the marvelous, maddening island disparaged and adored in *The Leopard*: it's either a favorite place, or they haven't even thought of going there.

Is the coincidence significant? I believe that if you love the novel (or the movie), you should start planning your trip right away, not because you'll find Lampedusa's Sicily waiting for you when you touch down (you won't, believe me), but because the bitter, resigned romantic nostalgia that pervades *The Leopard* is also the sensibility that savors the decaying grandeur of an island burdened with layer upon layer of tragic history — and blessed also with startling beauty, much of it perpetually waning.

The test comes when you're a little lost, nervously peering down a deserted back street in Palermo that's crooked and gloomy, with litter strewn on the dusty pavement and a narrow slice of blue sky overhead. Right in front of you is the smudged and crumbling facade of a derelict Baroque palazzo, unheralded, or perhaps marked with only a tiny plaque bearing a forgotten name and a date (late 17th century, usually, or early 18th). The sight of this noble structure is dizzying, even if the ornate balconies are wrapped

Previous The massive Porta Felice city gate in Palermo. The city is the essential start to a *Leopard*-based tour of Sicily.

Left Giuseppe Tomasi di Lampedusa was a Sicilian prince. His novel, *The Leopard*, tells a story of a crumbling aristocracy.

Opposite A familiar sight for both Lampedusa and his fictional prince: the countryside between Palermo and Santa Margherita di Belice.

in netting to keep chunks of masonry from raining down and there's a scraggly shrub sprouting on the rooftop. You dream of what it once was and what it might be again, but mostly you like it just as it is, a glorious residence ravished by time and neglect, and probably still inhabited. Just imagine its fabulously tattered apartments, still clinging to the memory of vanished splendor! (Sicily does this, it inspires wildly impractical reveries.)

Giuseppe Tomasi di Lampedusa (1896–1957) was an aristocrat—a prince, no less. He inherited a palace in Palermo, and had it not been demolished by an Allied bomb on April 5, 1943, the Palazzo Lampedusa would probably be scrubbed clean today, assiduously restored in honor of an author whose only novel, published posthumously in 1958, is one of Italy's best-loved books. *The Leopard* is about the decline of a noble Sicilian family. The patriarch, proud Fabrizio, prince of Salina (based on Lampedusa's great-grandfather, Prince Giulio), is acutely aware of this decline and seems almost to embrace it. Set partly in Palermo and partly deep in the island interior, the story plays out in the early 1860s, during the tumultuous years of Garibaldi's Risorgimento, when Sicily was annexed to a united Italy. The novel could fuel a seminar's worth of meditations on political and social transformation.

(The famous line, which becomes a mantra of sorts for Don Fabrizio, is this: "If we want things to stay as they are, things will have to change.") But though it has sparked heated debates about Sicilian history, most readers respond to the book's shimmering beauty, and to the towering figure of the prince himself.

Wise and perplexed, stern and indulgent, loyal and essentially solitary, even in the midst of his crowded household, Don Fabrizio is the indispensable companion for traveling around Sicily. He's one of those unforgettable literary characters who seem more real than people you've actually met. The trait that defines the prince is his dignity, which stems in part from his clear-eyed sense of himself; he claims to be "without illusions"—he lacks, he says, "the faculty of self-deception." He surveys himself, and Sicily, with unflinching honesty.

It is not in fact possible to maintain an unruffled dignity as a tourist in Sicily, not unless you're willing to spend a small fortune and steer clear of all but the most manicured resorts. The rest of us are likely to encounter haphazard service, accommodation that somehow just misses the mark, pungent urban odors, and the horrors of Mafia-financed postwar construction. The island's dependable delights—brash summer sunshine; seafood fresh off the boat and simply, sometimes exquisitely prepared; excellent, inexpensive wine; churches galore, in every shape and size; and the best Greek ruins anywhere—fit comfortably in any travel budget.

To see Sicily honestly, the way the prince of Salina would have you see it, you must start with the chaos of Palermo (or "the sloth of Palermo," as he would put it)—the lawless traffic, the grime, the noise, the hint of menace. Don't be put off: It's a beautiful city, crammed with architectural and artistic monuments from every century, squeezed between dramatic mountains and the Tyrrhenian Sea.

When Luchino Visconti wanted to film the magnificent ball at the end of *The Leopard*, he chose the Baroque Palazzo Valguarnera-Gangi in the heart of Palermo. Behind the monumental, almost sullen facade is the glittering ballroom where Burt Lancaster, magnificent as the prince, waltzed with the radiant Claudia Cardinale while her fiancé, an impossibly young Alain Delon, looked on indulgently.

The Palazzo Valguarnera-Gangi can be toured in private group visits that must be arranged ahead of time, usually through a tour company. But if you're on your own, you can still get a good idea of how the 19th-century Palermitan aristocracy lived by visiting the Palazzo Mirto, just off the Piazza Marina. If you stop a moment and stand before the gates, you'll see around you all the charm and frustration of Palermo, from the crest of the Princes of Mirto, a bold double-headed eagle carved in honey-colored stone above the massive doors, to weeds growing out of cracks. (Were it the Prince of Salina's crest, you would see the leopard, il gattopardo, rampant.) To the right stretches a typical balcony-lined, stone-paved Palermo street, brightly festooned with laundry, with a refreshing clump of trees at the far end. Behind you, in the Piazza Marina, a shambolic Sunday flea market offers every unwanted knickknack and oddment you ever yearned to throw away, plus, of course, a few priceless treasures.

Inside the Palazzo Mirto—bequeathed to the state in 1982 by the family's last heir—is a succession of sumptuously decorated rooms, at once lovely and ever so faintly ridiculous, like the grand ballroom Lampedusa describes with such a tender eye in *The Leopard*:

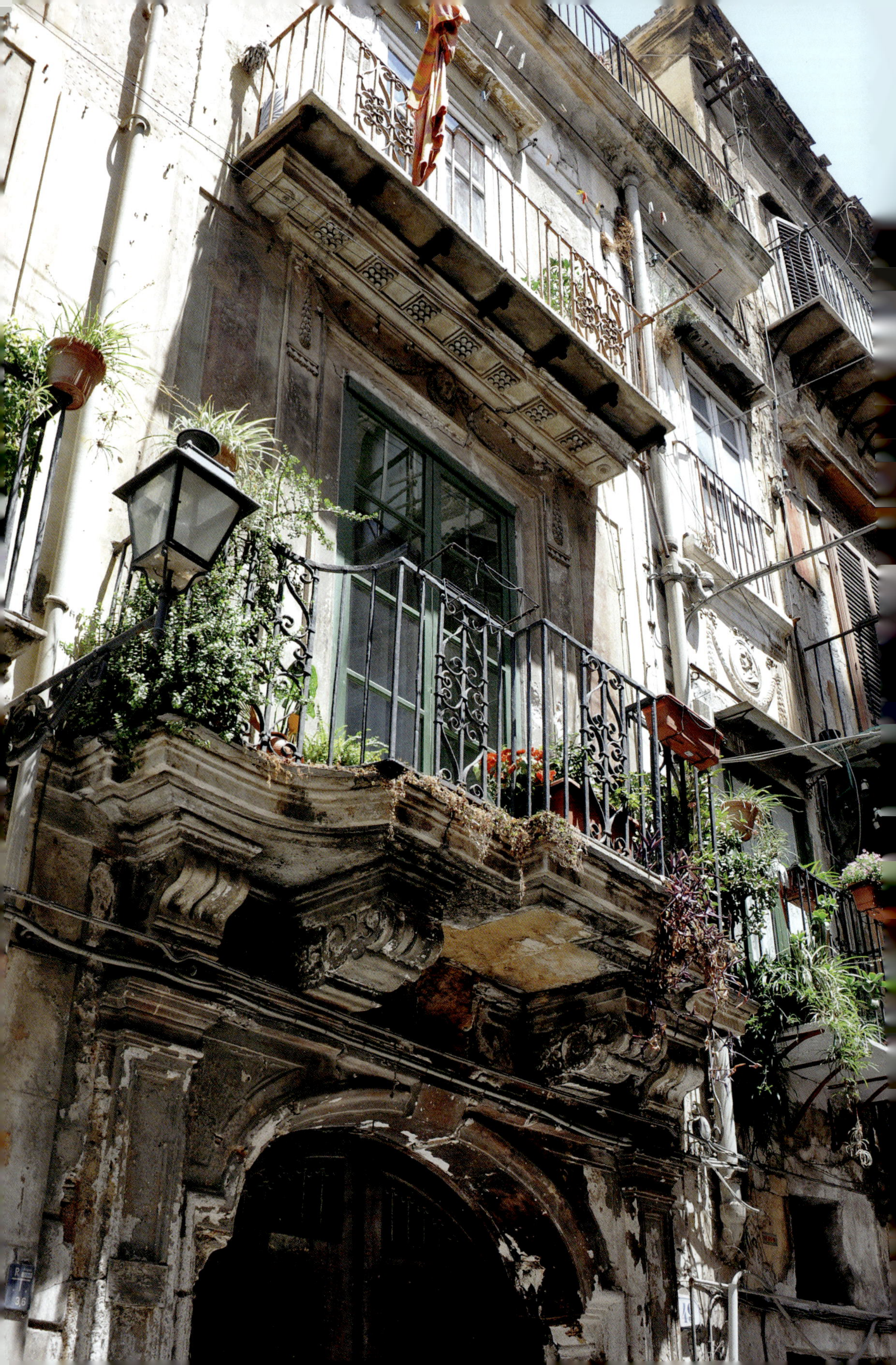

Opposite Balconies, flowers, and aged stonework overlook Palermo's Piazza Marina.

Right Bright graffiti glows in the Sicilian sun near a Palermo marketplace.

"The ballroom was all golden; smoothed on cornices, stippled on door-frames, damascened pale, almost silvery, over darker gold on door panels and on the shutters which covered and annulled the windows, conferring on the room the look of some superb jewel-case shut off from an unworthy world. It was not the flashy gilding which decorators slap on nowadays, but a faded gold, pale as the hair of certain Nordic children, determinedly hiding its value under a muted use of precious material intended to let beauty be seen and cost forgotten. Here and there on the panels were knots of rococo flowers in a color so faint as to seem just an ephemeral pink reflected from the chandeliers."

It's easy to imagine that even a century and a half ago, the apartments of the Palazzo Mirto reeked of the "slightly shabby grandeur" Lampedusa ascribes to the prince of Salina's household, and to Sicilian aristocracy in general, circa 1860. On my visit I saw the rooms preserved, but dusty and dilapidated at the edges, as though the effort of caring for so much decorative fabulousness was too much for our modern age. I watched one museum guide helpfully point out to an Italian tourist the sepia photo of a whiskered gentleman: "il ultimo principe"—the last prince.

The palace that features most prominently in *The Leopard* is not in Palermo but 45 miles or so southwest, in a town Lampedusa calls Donnafugata. He based the town on Santa Margherita di Belice, where as a boy he spent his idyllic summer holidays in the Palazzo Filangeri-Cutò, a splendid 18th-century building that belonged to his mother's family. The palazzo, a self-contained compound with three courtyards, seemed to him "a kind of Vatican," and he remembered the garden as "a paradise of parched scents."

In the first decade of the 20th century, when Lampedusa was a child, the journey from Palermo to Santa Margherita took 12 hours, half of it by train, the other half by horse-drawn carriage. In *The Leopard*, when the prince and his family make the trip in late August 1860, it's an arduous three-day expedition in a convoy of five carriages over dismal roads. (The prince travels in his top hat, of course.) "They had passed through crazed looking villages washed in palest blue; crossed dry beds of torrents over fantastic bridges; skirted sheer precipices which no sage and broom could temper. Never a tree, never a drop of water; just sun and dust."

Now an outing to Santa Margherita takes no more than an hour. The roads are good, nearly empty, and the views spectacular: a daunting, jagged landscape,

Above *The Leopard* brought fame to Santa Margherita. A museum there contains parts of the Lampedusa palazzo.

Opposite Guiding sheep through ruins from a 1968 earthquake in Santa Margherita. The town was rebuilt close by.

desiccated and profoundly lonely. When the prince looks out at what he considers "the real Sicily"—the landscape around Donnafugata—he sees it "aridly undulating to the horizon in hillock after hillock, comfortless and irrational, with no lines that the mind could grasp, conceived apparently in a delirious moment of creation; a sea suddenly petrified at the instant when a change of wind had flung the waves into a frenzy."

Lampedusa's description is exaggerated for effect—poetic license—but it's accurate in ways the author would have been horrified to discover. In 1968, a decade after his death, that petrified sea convulsed again: Santa Margherita was flattened by an earthquake. A new Santa Margherita was built next to the ruins.

The palazzo remained partly standing, and it has been righted and restored, after a fashion, as part of the officially designated Literary Park of Gattopardo. The grounds have been replanted, and inside, along with offices of the municipality, is a small museum devoted to Lampedusa, with manuscripts and various editions of *The Leopard*, family portraits, and photographs of Santa Margherita before the cataclysm.

It is while walking through the streets of Donnafugata early in the morning, taking note of its squalid poverty, that the prince, depressed, comes to a sour conclusion: "All this shouldn't last; but it will, always; the human 'always' of course, a century, two centuries…and after that it will be different, but worse. We were the Leopards and Lions; those who'll take our place will be little jackals, hyenas; and the whole lot of us, Leopards, jackals, and sheep, we'll all go on thinking ourselves the salt of the earth."

You might think that standing in the dazzling late-morning sun, gazing at what's left of the Palazzo Filangeri-Cutò, would be a dispiriting experience. The "human 'always'" has proved more fragile than

Photographs by
Chris Warde-Jones

even the pessimistic prince dared imagine. But Santa Margherita, assisted by what Lampedusa calls "the languid meandering stream of Sicilian pragmatism," is clearly on the mend, a hill town refreshed by a cooling breeze even in the brutal summer months, where the view from almost any street is of crisp blue sky. And beyond that, as the cherished novelist assures us, "the immemorial silence of pastoral Sicily."

WHAT TO READ AND WATCH

The Leopard (Il Gattopardo), by Giuseppe Tomasi di Lampedusa. A classic masterpiece.

The Leopard, directed by Luchino Visconti. This 1963 film shows its age but remains one of the greatest Italian movies. Burt Lancaster is perfect as the proud, clear-eyed prince, though his Italian dialogue is dubbed.

The Last Leopard, by David Gilmour. An excellent biography of Lampedusa.

The Kingdom of Sicily 1130–1860, by Louis Mendola. The long history of Sicily by a famed Italian scholar, readable and thorough.

Rick Steves Sicily, by Rick Steves, Sarah Murdoch, and Alfio Di Mauro. A good guidebook devoted solely to Sicily.

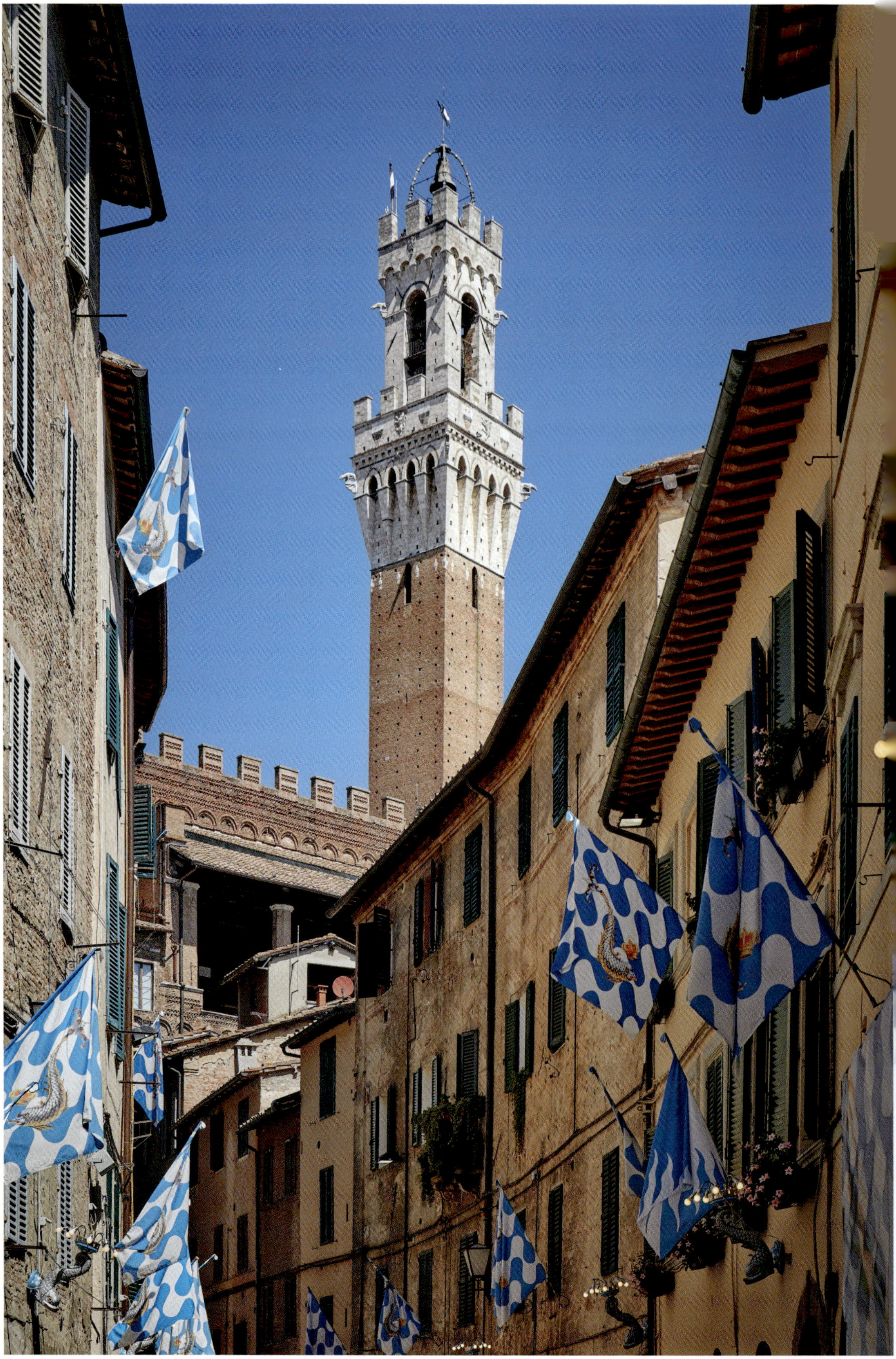

THE PALIO DI SIENA: A SURVIVOR'S TALE

It's all crowds and chaotic thrills at a thunderous, lawless, medieval-style horse race. — BY DWIGHT GARNER

When Hunter S. Thompson took the English artist Ralph Steadman to the Kentucky Derby in 1970, he tried to prepare him for the chaos into which they were descending. "Just pretend you're visiting a huge outdoor loony bin," Thompson said. He added, because he was rarely out of character, "If the inmates get out of control we'll soak them down with Mace."

"Huge outdoor loony bin" is not the most precise description of the Palio di Siena, the thunderous, lawless, bareback medieval-style horse race held twice each summer in front of tens of thousands of spectators on a track of packed clay laid down in the downtown heart of Siena, in Tuscany. But it will do for the moment.

This is a race in which jockeys — they ride for various *contrade*, or neighborhoods — feel free to bribe one another, out in the open, before the contest begins. Betrayal is common. Guile is prized. There are no rules but one: A rider may not interfere with the reins of another horse.

Jockeys whip their horses, and each other, with crops made from cured distended bulls' penises. If a jockey is thwacked off his mount, his riderless horse can still win on its own, like Garfunkel arriving without Simon.

The jockey who finishes second is held in more contempt than the one who comes in last. After the race, the victors celebrate by sucking on pacifiers or drinking cheap wine from baby bottles to symbolize rebirth. Siena comes to resemble a playpen in which many of the toddlers have hairy legs and five o'clock shadows.

A few years ago, when the Contrada Pantera (the Panther) was beaten by its long-established enemy, the Contrada dell'Aquila (the Eagle), a loudspeaker

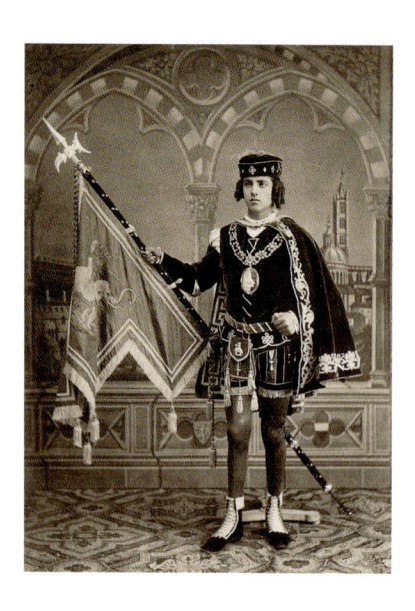

Previous Flags of Onda (Wave), one of the competing Siena neighborhoods known as *contrade*. Onda's symbol is a dolphin.

Left Decked out to represent the Torre (Tower) contrada in 1903. The Palio horse race dates back to the 13th century.

Opposite An evening view of Siena. Two towers dominate the skyline: the Torre del Mangia, left, and the Duomo.

mounted on the Eagle's church tower reportedly boomed out a motto mocking the Panther 24 hours a day for more than a month, the way the United States military blasted heavy metal songs in the direction of Manuel Noriega's quarters in 1989 to drive him insane.

I know these things — they barely scratch the surface of this festival's part-circus, part-theater ambience — because my English friend, Valentina Rice, has been attending the Palio each summer since she was a child. She tells good stories. I finally witnessed the Palio spectacle for myself when she invited me along.

On a blistering August afternoon, 93 degrees in the shade, we were not in the shade. We were standing in the center of Siena's main square, the Piazza del Campo, waiting amid a boiling sea of spectators for the race to begin. We'd been there for hours, having staked out a plum spot on high ground. I'd forgotten my cap. In the strong sunshine, one side of my potato head, I fear, had gone from pink to a gruesome tomato-and-bacon sort of hue.

It's possible to purchase bleacher seats for the Palio, but they are expensive — as much as several hundred dollars — and look a bit rickety. If you have the right connections, or several thousand dollars to spend, you can view the race from a variety of windows and balconies that ring the piazza and function like opera boxes.

In Valentina's family the tradition is to be in the center of the piazza, in the scrum. This is free. It's also a bit of an endurance test.

One woman fainted. There was a good deal of jostling for position. Men and women who'd had hard weekdays were not going to put up with being pushed around on this particular weekend, especially by tourists. A man near me had stripped down to tiny red briefs in the heat and was pouring ice water down his grizzled chest.

Behind me groups of men broke into ribald ballads that honor their contrade. Many women attend the Palio and take part in various aspects, but it is as strenuously male and macho as Nascar or professional wrestling. Yet the scene is mostly peaceful and upbeat.

As the sun moved lower on the horizon, a solemn and highly choreographed two-hour pageant, the Corteo Storico, began. More than 600 people in historical costume, many on horseback, began moving slowly around the piazza. Many of the faces were nearly medieval in their El Greco thinness. There were skilled flag tossers, severe-looking military-style drummers, oxen-pulled chariots, floats of ancient design.

The pageant and the race are an eyeful. They feature in the opening chase scene of the James Bond movie *Quantum of Solace*. At least a few viewers of that film hoped that Daniel Craig would go all Indiana Jones on a bad guy with a cured bull's penis, but this sadly was not to be.

Watching this pageant, I realized my cheeks were wet. The parade and the sea of packed-in spectators and the old city center combined to produce a tableau so stirring it brought my heart up under my ears. I'd always found it hard not to tear up when participating in ritual, from weddings and funeral processions to the singing of anthems and old songs. There is more ritual at the Palio that can be easily comprehended.

The race, which occurs twice a year, on July 2 and August 16, dates back to the 13th century, and most likely began as Roman military training. The races were on buffalos at first, and then on donkeys. The word *palio* itself means banner in Italian, and that's all that the winning contrada receives. This banner bears the image of the Virgin Mary, in whose honor these wild races are held.

Siena has 17 fiercely rivalrous contrade. These tend to be named after animals: snails, porcupines, she-wolves. Each contrada has its own museum, church, public square, fountain, traditions, and banner. Once there were more than three times as many contrade. One of the most moving portions of the pre-race procession is watching the banners of past contrade wind by, ghosts of earlier contests.

There may be 17 contrade, but there is room in each race for only 10 horses. A form of musical chairs must occur, and the seven contrade that cannot fit in one race are included in the next. The contrade are allowed to choose their jockeys but not their horses, all of which are mixed breed and chosen in part for their ability to resist being easily spooked among the crowds and chaos. These are arranged marriages: Each contrada meets its horse for the first time just four days before the race. The contrade pay their jockeys handsomely to ride for them, yet these jockeys are hired guns and fundamentally unfaithful. Everyone is a potential double agent.

There's no official betting at the Palio, but allegiances are purchased for tens of thousands of

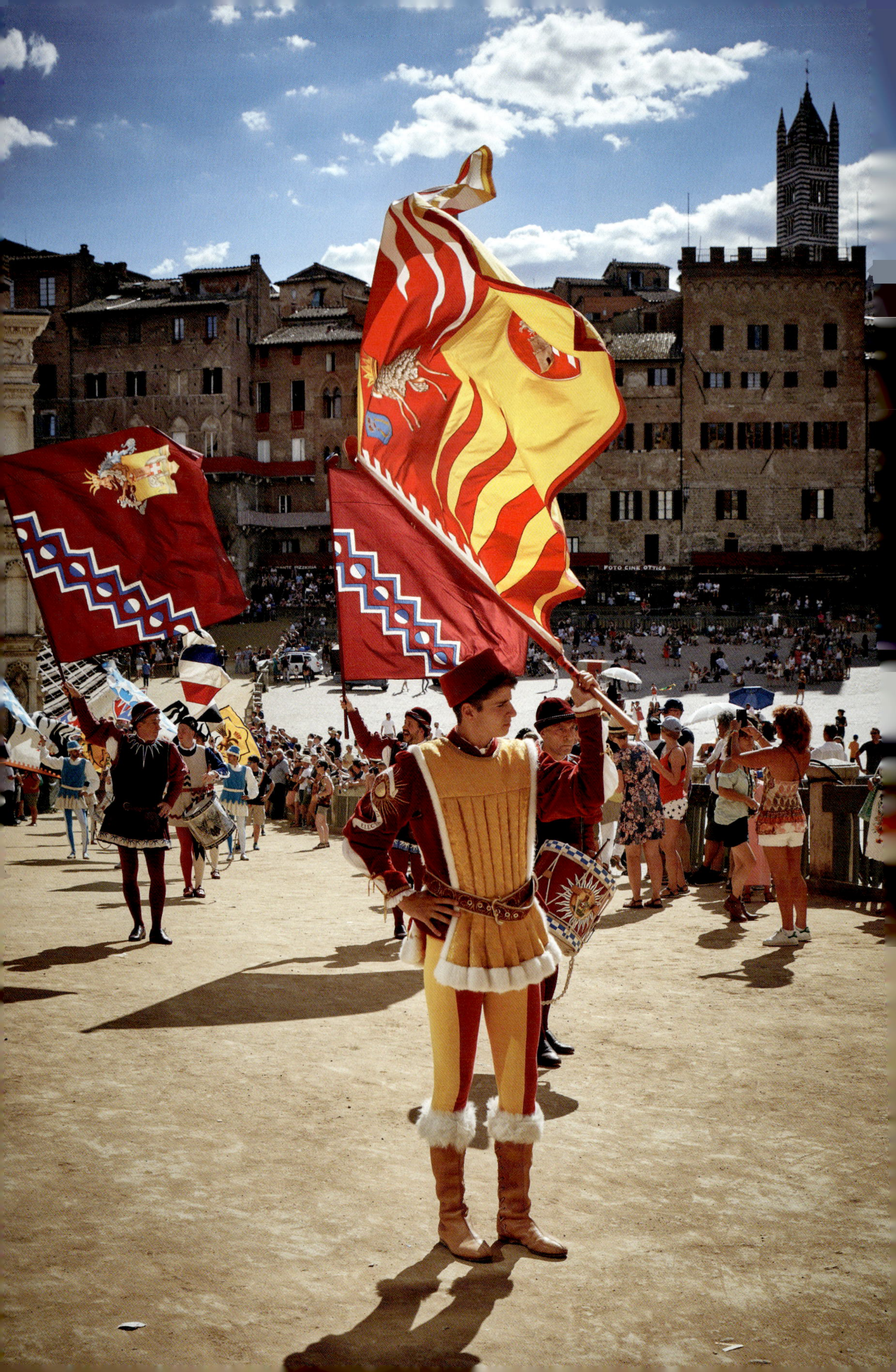
FOTO CINE OTTICA

Opposite The pageantry of the Palio lasts far longer than the race. Hundreds participate, wearing historical costumes.

Above The Palio race has few rules and plenty of skullduggery. Betrayal is common. Guile is prized.

dollars. Secret negotiations abound. Did your contrada's jockey miss his opportunity to peak ahead at that turn, or was he paid to fall back? There's no knowing.

This sort of existential criminality, in nearly any other country, would lead to madness among horse people and spectators. Yet in Siena, no one wishes to change a thing about the Palio.

There's been a good deal of commentary over the years about how the race illustrates the Italian soul. The Italians admire people, it's often said, who make good via the wily bending of rules and conventions. Witness Silvio Berlusconi, the former prime minister, who has confidently brushed off sex and corruption scandals. Benito Mussolini is said to have adored the Palio.

Sometimes more than guile and payoffs are used to secure a Palio victory. In past years, horses have reportedly been drugged and jockeys kidnapped. Writing in *Condé Nast Traveler*, Steve King reported a bit of Palio skullduggery that involved inflaming a stallion's lust: "By the time the race began the poor beast didn't stand a chance—indeed, could hardly stand at all and barely managed to stagger his knock-kneed way around the course."

During the race, jockeys take their lives into their hands. The race involves three clockwise laps around a third-of-a-mile track, and there are tight turns. There have been dozens of serious injuries; videos of spills are all over YouTube. Horses are more vulnerable. More than 50 have died in these races since 1970; animal rights protesters have staged repeated protests. In response, Palio administrators have increased the padding on some turns and instituted other safety controls. Critics say these measures are not enough.

The parade ended and a booming cannon-like shot scattered every bird within two miles. The crowd grew quiet as the horses and their riders entered the

Above Each contrada has its own museum, church, public square, fountain, and traditions.

Opposite The door of the Duomo. After the race, crowds pour in to watch the winner get the first-place banner.

piazza. Nine of the 10 racers took up their assigned positions at the starting rope. The tenth rider would determine when the race started: It would begin when he made a go for it.

While this was happening, the riders conversed, swapped taunts, and offered bribes. Impatient horses jostled and reared off the crowded line and were ridden back. The tenth horse made multiple exploratory false starts. This to-ing and fro-ing took more than 10 minutes.

And then they were off. The race was a clattering blur, whipping around us. It took less than 90 seconds but seemed even shorter. Several riders fell from their horses, but none were seriously injured.

The winner was La Contrada dell'Onda (the Wave), its colors aquamarine. Its jockey, Carlo Sanna, known as Brigante, was an instant hero, hoisted upon shoulders. He and his horse were whisked off to receive the winning banner and be blessed at the Siena Cathedral, the Duomo. This event was not hard to find. Hundreds, if not thousands, of people poured through the streets to make their way there, as the carabinieri kept close watch.

Out came the pacifiers and baby bottles. The winners wept with happiness. Meals commenced at huge tables set up in the streets. The festivities ran all night, which frankly they'd done for the four days leading up to the race, sometimes keeping us awake in our hotel.

That night we ate pizza margherita, one of Valentina's Palio-night traditions, at an outdoor table at one of the restaurants that line the piazza. (Tables are hard to come by on Palio night. To watch Valentina secure one in the front row is to witness charm, fortitude, and kung fu Italian-language skills in action.) We sat, caught our breaths, drank rehydrating beer over post-Instagram photographs. What else is vacation for?

**Photographs by
Andy Haslam**

The pizza was delicious — not so delicious that I'll forget to remind you that August is also the time to find plentiful and inexpensive white truffles in Siena. Some restaurants have entire wings of their menus devoted to their glory. Dishes come buried beneath them, the way the poutine in Montreal comes covered with cheese curds. Again, I wanted to cry.

I'd heard that truffle dogs could be rented for an afternoon in Siena. I asked my hotel's concierge about this. He told me yes, they're 600 euros. I said, "That's a lot of euros." He replied: "Do you know what a truffle dog's time is worth?"

This outdoor loony bin is one I will happily be committed to.

WHAT TO READ AND WATCH

Palio, directed by Cosima Spender, a native of Siena. A highly recommended 2015 documentary about the Palio di Siena.

Palio, by John Hunt. The companion book to the documentary. Photography, film stills, and archival images.

Strolling around Siena, by Irene Reid. A guidebook to Siena based on four self-guided walks. Walk No. 1 covers the Piazza del Campo.

The Scribe of Siena, by Melodie Winawer. In this time-travel novel, a neurosurgeon goes to Siena to settle her brother's estate and winds up being transported back to the year 1347, just in time for the Plague.

Four Days in the Summer, directed by Jonathan Darby. A 1989 documentary about the Palio, with emphasis on the pageantry and the emotion of the crowd.

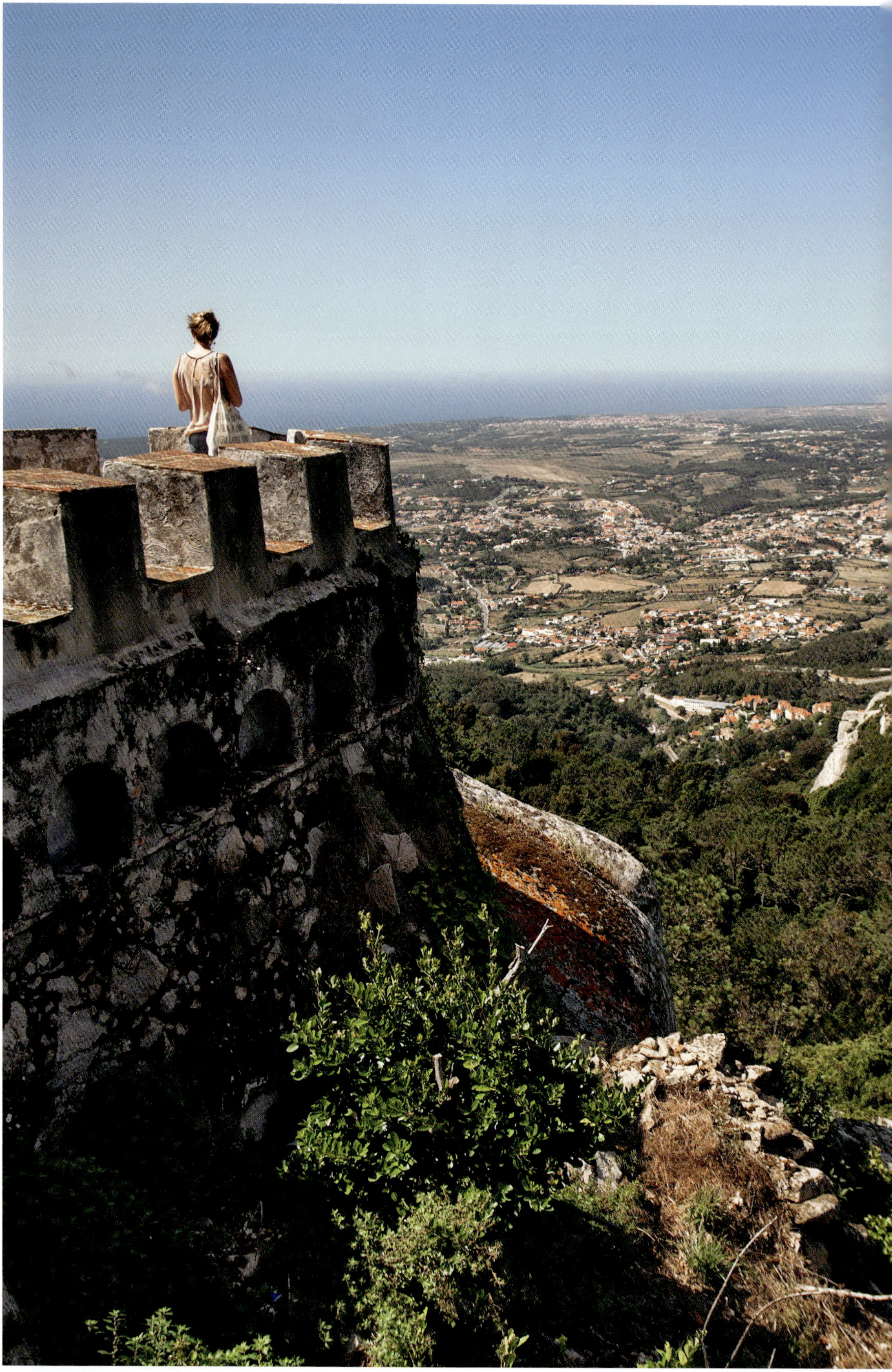

CASTLES, PALACES, AND SINTRA'S GREEN EMBRACE

Byron called it an Eden, and Sintra, where Portuguese kings liked to summer, still inhabits a verdant world.
— BY ELISA MALA

From Lisbon, 53 minutes is all it takes to travel back several centuries. That was the length of my train ride to Sintra, a town that for centuries was the preferred hideaway for the Portuguese royal family. Staring out the window as the train grew close, I marveled at the swirls of color whooshing past: Gray apartment complexes turned into quaint pastel houses until even those were replaced by messy rows of stubby trees.

By the time I stepped out of the train at the Sintra station, all traces of Lisbon and its suburbs had disappeared. What greeted me were hallmarks of quaintness: a smattering of restaurants and mom-and-pop shops, pleasantly sleepy streets, and a street clock as old-fashioned as they come. In the distance were the steep slopes and explosion of greenery depicted in local postcards.

Moorish rulers built a castle on a rocky Sintra peak in the eighth century, and as early as the 14th century, Portuguese kings were abandoning Lisbon in the summer and moving their courts to Sintra, 20 miles away, to get out of the heat. A heartbeat away from the political and economic center of the capital, Sintra's lush slopes provided the aristocracy with a quiet, breezy escape.

But it wasn't until Ferdinand II arrived in the mid-1800s and built an elaborate vacation home that the entire region acquired most of the features that now give it Unesco World Heritage status: sprawling estates that showcase a millennium's worth of architectural influences. The Portuguese monarchy was overthrown in 1910, and much of Sintra is now owned by the national government and open to the public.

The mere sight of Sintra's green landscape is enough to explain why Lord Byron described it as a "glorious Eden." Verdant forests extend in every direction. Greenery envelops every surface, from

Previous The view of the Sintra landscape from the Palace of Pena, a retreat built by Portuguese royalty.

Left Start a tour of Sintra at its oldest building, a forbidding castle originally built by Arab rulers in the eighth century.

Opposite A statue of Hermes at the Quinta da Regaleira, a luxurious Sintra estate.

moss-covered rocks to sinewy vines that wrap around trees. Thick roots of felled trees point skyward, and wispy sprouts break through minuscule crevices in stone walls. There's a feeling of being embraced in a mystical sort of world.

I deposited my bags at my hotel and set out to explore the area on foot. A serene sunset walk took me past a half-dozen ornate statues and sculptures, all part of a public art project reminiscent of a vast private garden. (The artwork changes every year.) As darkness fell, the surrounding castles glowed, illuminated by colored spotlights.

At a bar in the center of town, I ordered the local specialty, *queijada de Sintra*, a sweet pastry with a cheesecake-like filling, and a *ginjinha*, a tipple of cherry liqueur in an edible chocolate shot glass. Given Sintra's layout, a good starting point for serious touring is the eighth-century Moorish castle, and the next morning, that's where I decided to begin. A holdover from Arab rule, it's the oldest structure in the area, a military fortress meant to turn away invaders: austere and uniformly gray, with walls of granite and limestone. A 15-minute walk on a flat, scenic path leads to the main gate. Once inside, a quarter-mile loop is formed by walkways atop the castle's inner walls. "No matter where you start,"

a park ranger said of the simple path around the perimeter, "you can't get lost."

The knights of old earned their stripes by remaining watchful — ducking beneath low entryways and tiptoeing up the tiny steps while ascending turrets. At the castle's strategic vantage points, it's easy to imagine them proudly guarding the kingdom, looking intently out over agricultural land stretching off into the distance.

Looming over the castle on a nearby promontory, surrounded by forest, was my next stop, the Pena Palace. In a lighthearted contrast to the no-nonsense Moorish castle, the palace has an unmistakable whimsy. It is also much younger. This was the royal vacation home built by Ferdinand II, who had it constructed on the ruins of an old monastery. It is a hodgepodge of cheerful colors (canary yellow, bright salmon, lavender) and towers (narrow and cylindrical, widely rectangular), generating an understated *Alice in Wonderland* vibe that architecture aficionados would attribute to 19th-century Romanticism.

If the Moorish castle invited purposeful forward marches, Pena Palace encouraged aimless wandering. Three gathering spots were especially popular with tourists taking selfies: a mythically significant but comically hideous gargoyle hovering above a

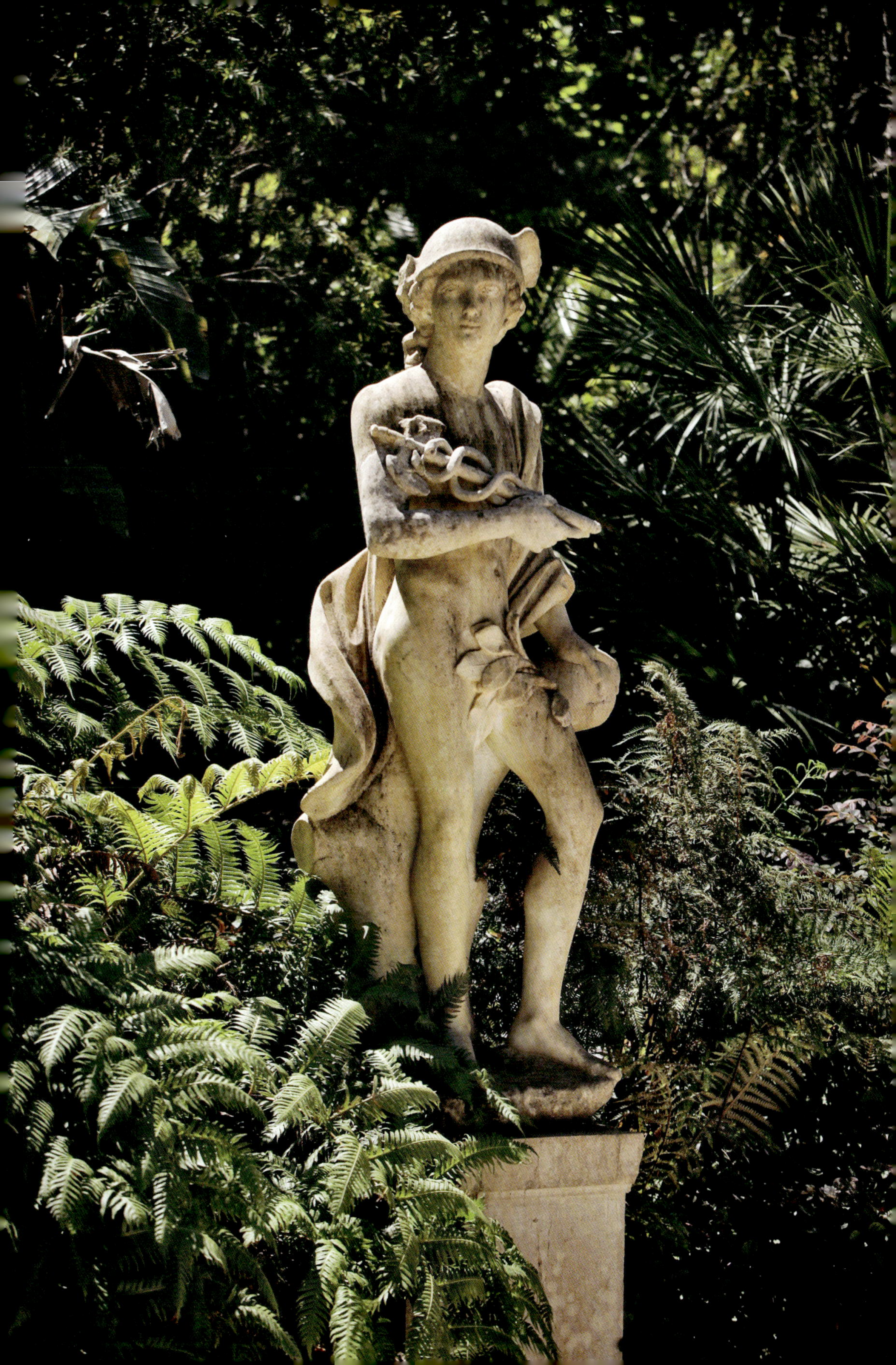

Above The town of Sintra lies in the center of a landscape long favored as a cool summer getaway.

Opposite Built to look ancient, the Quinta da Regaleira was actually established by 19th-century trading barons.

main entry, breathtaking mountain views seen through pointed arches, and the stained-glass windows of the chapel.

Back in the center of town, I edged my way into another royal edifice, Sintra National Palace, just before the last entry at 6:30 p.m. Its white exterior belied rooms furnished with period pieces and ceilings covered in festive tiles, the most striking of which featured wall-to-wall *azulejos*, classic glazed white tiles with blue paint that are aligned to depict historical scenes. But what struck me was what I couldn't see: visitors. Between beautiful June weather drawing everyone else outdoors and the late hour, I pretty much had the place to myself. Wandering around in solitude, with only the docents for company, provided the most authentically royal experience I had that day.

There is more to see in Sintra: the bubblegum-hued Monserrate Castle, with its exotic gardens; the lemon-yellow Queluz Castle; the Convent of the Capuchos, with cork-lined cells; the Cabo da Roca lighthouse a few miles out of town, at the westernmost point of continental Europe. I could have ridden around town in a horse-drawn carriage. I could even have chosen to be whisked away in a charmingly kitschy tram to Praia das Macas, a resort town with steep cliffs overlooking the white sand beaches along Portugal's western coast.

But I had only one more day, and I chose to spend it in the wonderland of architecture and nature at Quinta da Regaleira, a walled park and estate established by 19th-century trading barons. Quintas were country estates, many of them established by the noble families that followed the royal family out of town. The name *quinta* comes from their status: in theory, a fifth of the land belonged to the king. There are several quintas around Sintra, some of them now converted to hotels. But this one is exceptional.

Photographs by
João Pedro Marnoto

Although smaller than the Moorish castle and Pena Palace, the Quinta da Regaleira is luxurious. It has several structures—five-story Romantic palace, Roman Catholic chapel, and multistory gazebo—dotted across nearly 10 acres.

For families, the showstopper is the initiatic well, a massive, cylindrical upside-down tower that plummets deep into the ground, with a spiral staircase embedded in its walls. Children-turned-spelunkers investigated the scene with flashlights attached to their heads, more a novelty than necessity.

The parkland was lush and inviting, with footpaths and fountains. Regardless of the direction I wandered, it yielded surprises: stunning waterfalls, serene grottoes, a maze of tunnels. This was the destination that every Sintra resident and visitor I had spoken to said could not be missed, and I was happy to agree.

WHAT TO READ AND WATCH

A Concise History of Portugal, by David Birmingham. A survey of the country and its people, from its early days to the present.

Journey to Portugal: In Pursuit of Portugal's History and Culture, by José Saramago. A personal exploration of the country, published in 2002, from the Portuguese novelist who won the 1998 Nobel Prize for Literature.

The website **sintra-portugal.com** is a fount of practical information and capsule histories of the city's tourist sites.

Frankie, directed by Ira Sachs. Released in 2019, a contemplative film about one day in a family vacation in Sintra. Isabelle Huppert plays the title character.

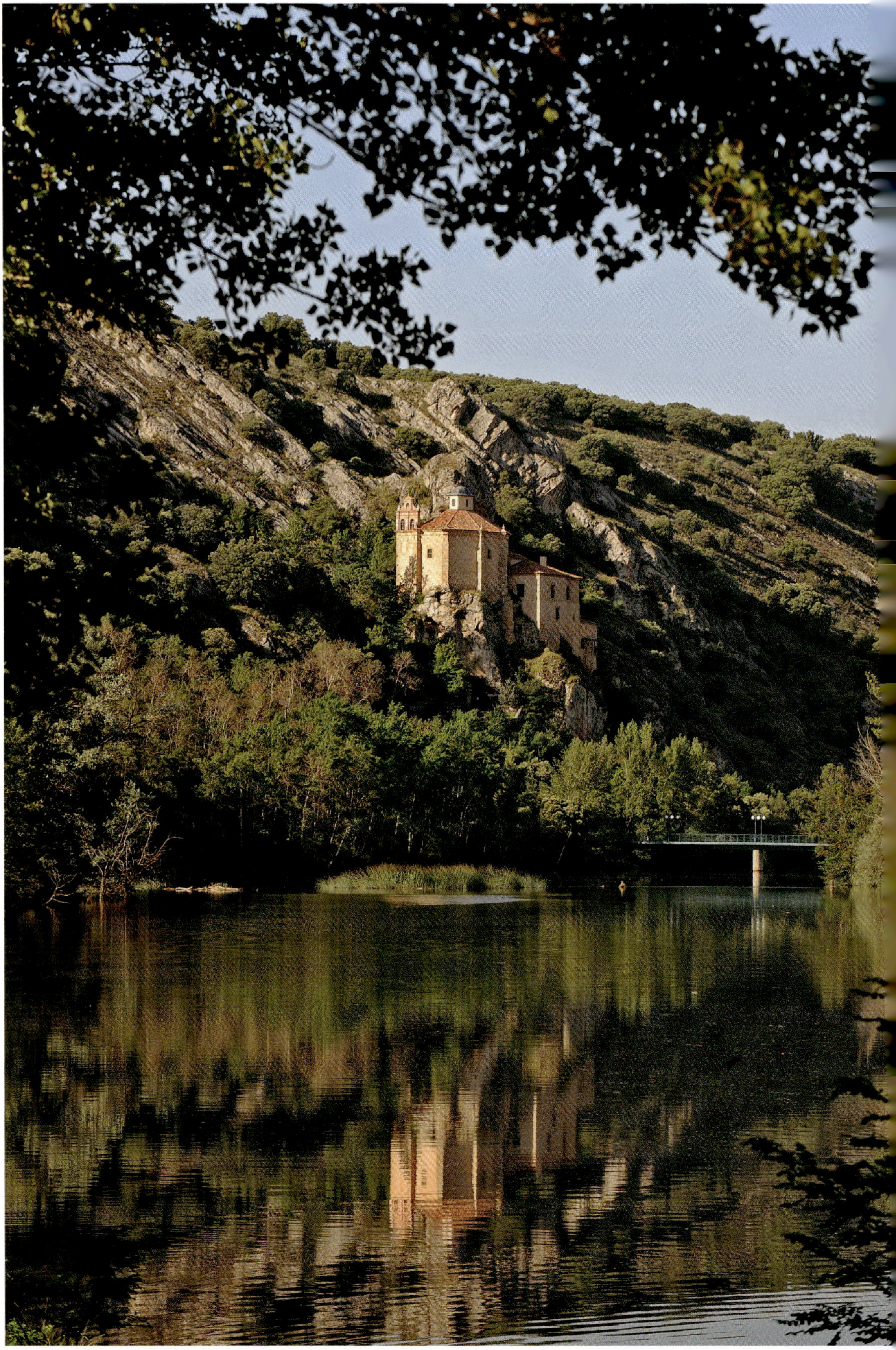

A POET'S REALM OF MYTH AND REALITY

To Antonio Machado, Spain's beloved lyric poet, the rugged Duero River province of Soria was where "the rocks seem to dream." — BY JOHN MOTYKA

Stone-strewn, steep gray hills studded with bristly shrubs loom to the left of the white road along the Duero River in Soria, an old city in the heart of Spain. Two storks cavort in a stiff wind above as the road winds uphill toward the hermitage of Soria's patron saint, San Saturio, a sacred site since the sixth century.

If this scene from reality is also a timeless poetic idyll, it's because the Duero, as it flows past Soria in Spain's Castilla y León region, is as much a part of literature as it is of the landscape. The city, the windswept expanse of the surrounding *meseta*, Spain's high central plateau, and the nearby mountains were both home and a kind of mythical dreamtime realm for Antonio Machado, one of the great lyric poets of the 20th century.

Soria — "Soria fría, Soria pura" ("Cold Soria, pure Soria"), as Machado described it in one of his poems — is much changed since he left the city in 1912 after the death of his child bride, Leonor. Yet, off the international tourist map and largely left behind by Spain's sprawling development, the city of Soria and the province of the same name, of which it is the capital, retain a powerful sense of place.

Only 147 miles from Madrid, Soria is a world apart. The air is clear and the climate chilly. Its ascetic grandeur remains: "somber oaks, harsh stony wastelands, bald peaks" and fields "where the rocks seem to dream," in Machado's vision. Though he lived in the city only five years, Machado wove the impressions from his walks through the Sorian countryside with the theme of time and the tragic story of Leonor, who died when she had barely reached adulthood, to create poems of elemental vision that capture the soul of Spain.

Previous Only 147 miles from Madrid, Soria is a world apart. The air is clear, the climate chilly, the land stony and harsh.

Left A likeness of the poet Antonio Machado on a Spanish postage stamp. He arrived in Soria and fell in love.

Opposite The San Juan de Duero monastery, a place where, Machado wrote, "the Duero flows limpid, tamely, mute."

In the contemporary city of Soria, with a population of about 40,000, I began my search for Machado at the lively Plaza Ramón Benito Aceña, which is ringed by two- and three-story stone buildings that house shops, bars, and banks. A sign fashioned from light bulbs suspended above the Calle El Collado, which emerges from the plaza, evoked Machado with a single word: *caminante*, or wayfarer. "Wayfarer, your footsteps are the road, and nothing more. Wayfarer, there is no road, the road is made by walking," he wrote in widely anthologized verse.

I wove through the morning bustle to the narrow, cobblestoned Calle Aduana Vieja, where stanzas from Machado's poems were displayed on plaques on the walls of two buildings. My destination was the Antonio Machado Institute, the secondary school (then called the General and Technical Institute of Soria) where Machado taught.

He arrived in town by train in 1907, hired to teach French. His classroom in the school, a stone structure that dates from 1585, holds student desks and a bulky wooden instructor's desk on a raised platform. Ángel Sebastián, the headmaster, told me enthusiastically that Machado's poems, already published in many European languages, had recently been translated into Chinese.

Machado was at first disenchanted with Soria, then a rough-hewn rural town of 7,000. Born in Seville and raised in Madrid, he had by this time already published a book of poetry. But before long, Soria worked its spell on him.

*I found my homeland where the Duero flows
between gray cliffs
and phantoms of old black oaks,
up there in Castile mystic and warlike,
Castile the genteel, humble and brave
Castile of arrogance and power.*

He took a room near the school and fell in love with Leonor Izquierdo, his landlord's 13-year-old daughter. They married in 1909, when she was 15 (not a shocking marriage age in that time and place) and he was nearly 34. He often accompanied her to Mass at the church of Santo Domingo, which today attracts admirers of Romanesque architecture.

I started downhill to the east of the city on one of Machado's favorite walks where, he wrote, "the Duero flows limpid, tamely, mute." At the foot of the hill a small stone bridge crosses the river, and on the other side the aptly named Camino del Monte de las Ánimas (Mount of the Spirits Way) runs parallel to the river for about 100 yards to the ruined medieval monastery of San Juan de Duero.

Once a 12th-century church, San Juan was refashioned into a monastic complex by the Hospitallers, a group founded during the First Crusade. The shell of the cloister, with spans of arches done in different styles and evidence of Islamic influence, is unique in Spain.

A short distance away, a path leads to the small white road to the hermitage of San Saturio, a stone structure built in the 18th century over a grotto where the saint retreated from the world to pray. Plaques outside bear Machado's likeness and a stanza from "Fields of Soria" that fondly recognizes the local people "of the high Numantian plain."

I hired a taxi to visit Numantia, a hilltop site with a prehistoric pedigree and some scant, evocative Roman ruins five miles north of Soria near the tiny village of Garray. Archaeologists say the hill was inhabited as early as the third millennium B.C. Numantia is best known for the heroic defense put up by Celtiberian people against Roman forces. Their efforts were futile: Numantia fell to the Roman general Scipio, the victor of Carthage, in 133 B.C. Ancient historians referred to the rugged terrain, lashed by the north wind. I walked around the only original features to survive, bases of Roman columns.

Machado's work began to reflect the influence of his trips to the countryside outside of Soria. Laguna Negra, a lake 30 miles north of the city, is nestled in the Picos de Urbión, a mountain range that is the setting of *The Land of Alvargonzález*, his dark morality tale about three brothers and their father.

He went to the lake in September 1910 with friends to see if he could reach the source of the Duero. (The river is 557 miles long and flows through renowned wine country in Portugal, where it is called the Douro; but it begins in Soria.) They made the trip through extensive pine forests. Today, a provincial road crosses the Revinuesa River, the line of the southernmost advance of glaciers in the last ice age, three and a half miles south of the lake. As I walked past huge boulders to a cold stream descending from jagged peaks, it was easy to see how Machado could set a pared-down patricidal tale on this place "where vultures nest."

Above Gormaz Castle was a Muslim fortress that fell to Christians in 1059 and came under the leadership of El Cid.

Opposite Numantia, where indigenous people were conquered by the Roman general Scipio in 133 B.C.

Two castles in the south-central part of the province of Soria are illustrative of Machado's description of Castile in *Alvargonzález* as "parched, fine and warlike." The ruins of one, a 15th-century structure with 13th-century walls, loom above the town of Berlanga de Duero. I followed Calle Nuestra Señora de las Torres through porchlike galleries to the sleepy main plaza, where the towering castle comes into view.

Gormaz, about six miles away, was once one of the largest castles in Europe. Situated on a hilltop with breathtaking views to the horizon and the Duero on both sides, it was a Muslim fortress that fell to Christians in 1059 and came under the leadership of El Cid. This mighty structure, a symbol of the gore and the glory of Castile, controlled the routes of travel to the north.

In 1910, Machado received a fellowship to study in Paris, where Leonor fell ill, apparently with tuberculosis. They returned to Soria, but she died in 1912; she was just 18. She is buried behind the church of Our Lady of Espino in Soria.

Machado, distraught, sought a transfer from Soria and went on to teach in several cities. He never remarried. John Dos Passos, who knew him years later, described him as "a lonely widower" who "gave the impression of being helpless in life's contests and struggles."

Machado's last book, *Poems of the War*, which included a poem honoring the poet Federico García Lorca after he was murdered by Francisco Franco's forces, foreshadowed the role the Spanish Civil War was to play in bringing his own life to a dramatic close.

Machado supported the Republican side. Traveling with his mother, in her late 80s, and other family members, he stayed one step ahead of Franco's troops as they were hounded from Valencia to Barcelona to the French border in 1939. He and his mother were soaked in a rainstorm while traveling by truck on

Photographs by Denis Doyle

the last leg of the journey and died of respiratory infections within three days of each other in Collioure, France, now a sister city of Soria.

Soria was still a theme in *Poems of War*. But Machado had perhaps recalled it best in a poem written a few years earlier, in about 1930:

> *You ask me why my heart flies from the coast*
> *back to Castile, to towering raw terrains,*
> *why, near the sea, in fertile fields, I most*
> *long to be back on the high and barren plains.*

The next stanza, beginning with these words, seems to give the answer:

> *No one chooses his love.*

WHAT TO READ AND WATCH

Border of a Dream: Selected Poems of Antonio Machado, translated by Willis Barnstone. A comprehensive collection of the poet's work with an introduction that has been called the best short guide to Machado in English.

Antonio Machado: Selected Poems, translated by Alan S. Trueblood. Poems in the original Spanish with their English translations on facing pages. Includes annotation and a biographical introduction.

A River in Spain: Discovering the Duero Valley in Old Castile, by Robert N. White. Covers Castilla y León's architecture, history, and geography thoroughly and sometimes eloquently.

La Vida de Antonio Machado en Soria. A three-minute Spanish-language video with scenes of Soria and photos of Machado's child bride, Leonor. Viewable on YouTube.

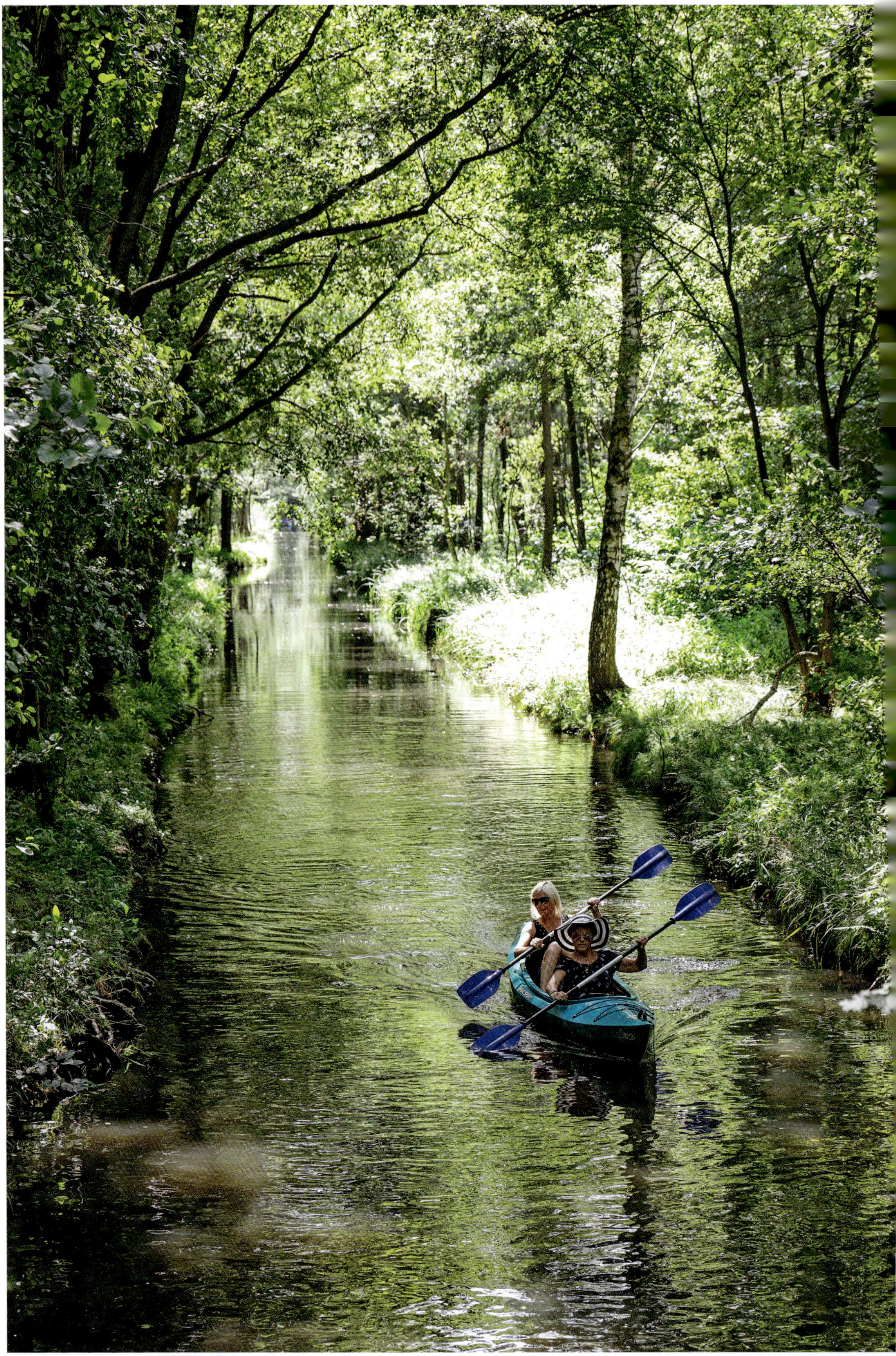

GERMANY　　　　　　　　　　　　　　　　　　　　　　　　　　　　　　THE SPREEWALD

BY KAYAK, A TRIP INTO A STRANGE WATERY LAND

Just an hour from Berlin, the Spreewald is a world apart, a maze of waterways and the refuge of an ancient people, the Sorbs. — BY SAMI EMORY

From its source in southeastern Germany near the Czech border, the Spree River flows steadily to the northwest until it reaches Berlin, slices the city in two, and then joins the Havel, a tributary of the Elbe. For Berliners, the Spree is an urban river where tour boats motor past the Reichstag and summer sunbathers bask on artificial beaches. But midway back upstream, toward its source, the river flows through the Spreewald, or Spree Forest, a maze of woodland, meadows, and 800 miles of crisscrossing waterways that is now recognized as a Unesco biosphere reserve.

For more than a thousand years, this pocket of confusing countryside, where traditionally people got around solely in boats and only the locals could easily find their way, has also sheltered an enduring Slavic minority, the Sorbs.

Only an hour from Berlin, the Spreewald is a 185-square-mile landscape where the river divides itself into hundreds of narrow waterways, drawing a labyrinthine map across the sand and scree flattened near the end of the last ice age, before eventually resolving itself again into a single stream. Historically, the Spreewald provided the isolation that allowed the Sorbs to maintain their culture and language. Today Sorbic is still spoken, but the Spreewald has become a welcoming destination for visitors who want to enjoy its natural beauty and glimpse what remains of Sorbic culture.

On a warm spring morning, my partner and I boarded a double-decker regional train that follows the Spree southeast from Berlin's Alexanderplatz station through the concrete and clubs of East Berlin

Previous Kayakers on one of the many small waterways between Lübbenau and Lehde.

Left In 1895, when the German writer Theodor Fontane visited, the Sorb people were still isolated enough to live in the old ways.

Opposite Ferrying tourists in a *Kahn*, a flat-bottomed boat propelled with a pole. Kahns are multipurpose transport here.

and into the open fields of Brandenburg, a state in what used to be East Germany. The train glided past lonely farmhouses and stumbling calves unconcerned by their proximity to a major metropolis.

We got off in Lübbenau, the Spreewald's largest town. For most visitors, Lübbenau serves a primarily utilitarian purpose: a place to rent kayaks and bikes or to book accommodations and tours before setting out to explore. It's also a place to stock up on Spreewald gherkins, pickles so prized that they enjoy the same kind of European Union product protection granted to Champagne and Parmigiano-Reggiano.

The locals here will be happy to tell you, too, about their connection to Theodor Fontane, Germany's greatest 19th-century realist novelist and its most famous domestic traveler from that time. It was Fontane who first put the Spreewald on the tourist map, extolling it for the unspoiled character and natural beauty that to a surprising extent have survived into the 21st century.

Lübbenau itself is subdued, slow-paced, and, like all German holiday villages worth their salt, features a castle. (Lübbenau's is more Austen than Grimm.) Downtown, tourists strolled cobblestone streets or sat at cafes, nursing ice creams or pilsners or both. The more ambitious visitors passed us on our way to the kayak rental shop, wafting a trail of mosquito repellent in their wake.

After stepping unsteadily into our royal-blue two-seater kayak, we pushed off from the dock. In just a few minutes on the river, we had drifted away from civilization, and Lübbenau's mild pleasures were replaced by more complicated ones. A few leggy spiders made themselves comfortable near my knees in the shade of the kayak's thick plastic hull. Crickets whirred under baroque summer clouds, and frogs drowned out the distant roar of planes headed to Berlin's Schönefeld Airport.

The Spreewald is home to about 5,000 species of plants and animals—kingfishers, otters, ospreys, river mussels, storks, butterflies, eagles. Its moorland is dotted with birch, alder, pine, willow, and linden trees, between which rest hivelike stacks of hay, called *Schober*, which make for an iconically Spreewaldian image.

After a soporific Berlin winter, each sign of wildlife brought a particular thrill. We saw hawks, a bevy of swans, and a nutria, a semiaquatic rodent easily mistaken for a beaver, that was splitting green algae with a determined stroke. We spotted dragonflies, fish, and a snake slithering on the river's milky surface.

Behind us, a kayak blasting techno music from a handheld speaker was gaining. We escaped into a tributary marked with a wooden sign indicating that it led to Leipe. After a few steady strokes, the thumping bass faded and bird calls once again drowned out all indications of urbanity. Twenty minutes later, we were in Leipe.

Snug inside the Spreewald's network of waterways are the villages of Lehde and Leipe, with fewer than 300 residents between them. Though both towns are partly accessible by car, many of the houses in Lehde and Leipe are completely cut off from the mainland (save for footbridges) and rest on *Kaupen*, little sand islands. Leipe offers peaceful waterside accommodation and a cafe known for its *Hefeplinzen*, blintzes brushed with cinnamon sugar and butter. They are soft and yeasty, and we ate them with cappuccinos topped high with whipped cream. After spiking our blood sugar, we folded our legs back into the boat and turned our plastic vessel toward Lehde.

Fontane, in his *Travels through the Mark of Brandenburg*, described Lehde in 1859 as "a pocket-size lagoon city. Venice, as it might have looked 1,500 years ago." Now visitors who reach it by boat or from Lübbenau via a short stretch of the 161-mile-long Gurkenradweg (literally: pickle bike path) stop there for a pint of the local Babben beer, a meal at the popular restaurant Kaupen No. 6, or a stroll through the Freilandmuseum Lehde, an open-air local history museum.

Much of the lore, culture, and traditions of the Spreewald come from the Sorbs and the Wends: descendants of Slavic tribes who have been in the region since around A.D. 800. Some 60,000 Sorbs and Wends live in Lusatia, a region encompassing sections of both Germany and Poland, and comprise one of Germany's few recognized minorities. In modern times, Sorbic customs and languages have faded. Still, Sorbic culture permeates the area, and more recently the Sorbian language has been reintroduced into local school curriculums. Today, many of the Spreewald's signs are bilingual, in German and Sorbian. Visitors may see people wearing Sorbian dress, donned for the benefit of tourists. Once, in a lucky moment, my partner and I looked up from our glasses of Babben to see a Sorbic wedding party on its way to a ceremony in one of the museum's historic buildings.

On our way to Lehde, we had paddled for more than 20 minutes before we consulted the laminated map the kayak rental company had provided and realized we were lost. Ten minutes after leaving Leipe, we had taken a fork in the river, and since then we hadn't seen another soul. We were now floating down a watery avenue framed by vines dripping white flowers into the river. A stork flew overhead.

In Spreewald, a kayak seems to impart a sense of delusion to its navigators. Despite our situation, I felt, at the boat's bow, supremely confident in our navigational abilities. Nothing (and nobody) stood between us and those 800 miles of water—nothing except hunger and German engineering. In the early 1900s, after several centuries of human habitation in the area, an extensive water management system was built in Spreewald. Today, water levels and flow are maintained through an assemblage of weirs, fish passages, dams, and locks.

Like the gondolier for Venice, the figure that stands as symbol for Spreewald is the *Kahn* captain. A *Kahn* is a punt made, historically, of wood and

Above Kayakers on the main waterways find restaurants with kayak parking lots to serve them.

Opposite A traditional Spreewald house in the Freilandmuseum Lehde, a local history museum.

propelled through the water with a pole tipped with metal teeth. The profession is a traditional one that often runs through the generations. "It's a family matter for most people," explained Steffen Franke, the head of a professional cooperative for Kahn captains. "So the father naturally likes the son to follow in his footsteps."

Steffen Bülow, a Lehde local and Kahn captain, learned how to punt when he was six years old. It was how he would visit his grandmother's house, and how his family reached their asparagus crop, more than half a mile from their home, to tend to and harvest it. "We had to, even in the summertime, reach the field using the punt at least once, maybe twice a day," he told me. Though now it was not his full-time job, as it was his father's, he still took the boat out on weekends and holidays. In the towns' harbors, tourists hire Kahns and their captains for excursions that often feature a round of schnapps.

But Kahn boats are not just a way to ferry tourists around; they are even now also a vital means of transport. Mail is delivered by Kahn. Police patrol by Kahn. Firefighters respond to emergencies by Kahn. Manure, hay, and tractors are transported by Kahn.

Every year Sebastian Kilka, a fifth-generation farmer and one of Lehde's last, punts his cattle to and from the pasture. The operation, he said, is generally a smooth one, though animal instincts do sometimes kick in at inopportune moments. "I had problems this year," he said with a laugh, "because my big bull said, 'I don't want to go boating anymore.'" It took the encouragement of six or seven men before the bull complied.

Eventually, my partner and I found our way to Wotschofska, a hotel and restaurant on an island of the same name. Its menu, like most in local restaurants, is a variation on a theme: blood sausage (*Grützwurst*); potatoes served with the yogurt-like

Photographs by Andreas Meichsner

dairy product called Quark and dribbled with linseed oil; and, in late spring and early summer, white asparagus engorged with saltwater and blanketed in hollandaise sauce.

We sat on folding beach chairs in the sun to watch the traffic of Kahns and kayaks. Everyone, even those with small children, appeared to be in a genuinely good mood. Many of them, like ourselves, were probably destined for a late-afternoon train back to the city, away from this waterlogged fairy-tale world where restaurants have kayak parking lots and mail is delivered by boat. When our drinks ran dry, we stretched our sore shoulders and slid into our kayak and back out into the water.

WHAT TO READ AND WATCH

Slav Outposts in Central European History: The Wends, Sorbs, and Kashubs, by Gerald Stone. Who are the Sorbs? A British scholar traces their history and culture, now alive only in "tiny enclaves."

Effi Briest (Oxford World's Classics), by Theodor Fontane, translated by Mike Mitchell. One of several Fontane novels available in English. Often compared to *Anna Karenina*, it tells the story of a wife trapped in a loveless marriage.

This German Town Is Crazy for Gherkins, a German National Tourist Board video. Brief, amusing, and with good Spreewald views.

Good Bye, Lenin!, directed by Wolfgang Becker. Spreewald's gherkins play a cameo role. Communist-indoctrinated mother believes the Berlin Wall has not fallen. Funny and revealing about East Germany's reabsorption into the reunited Germany.

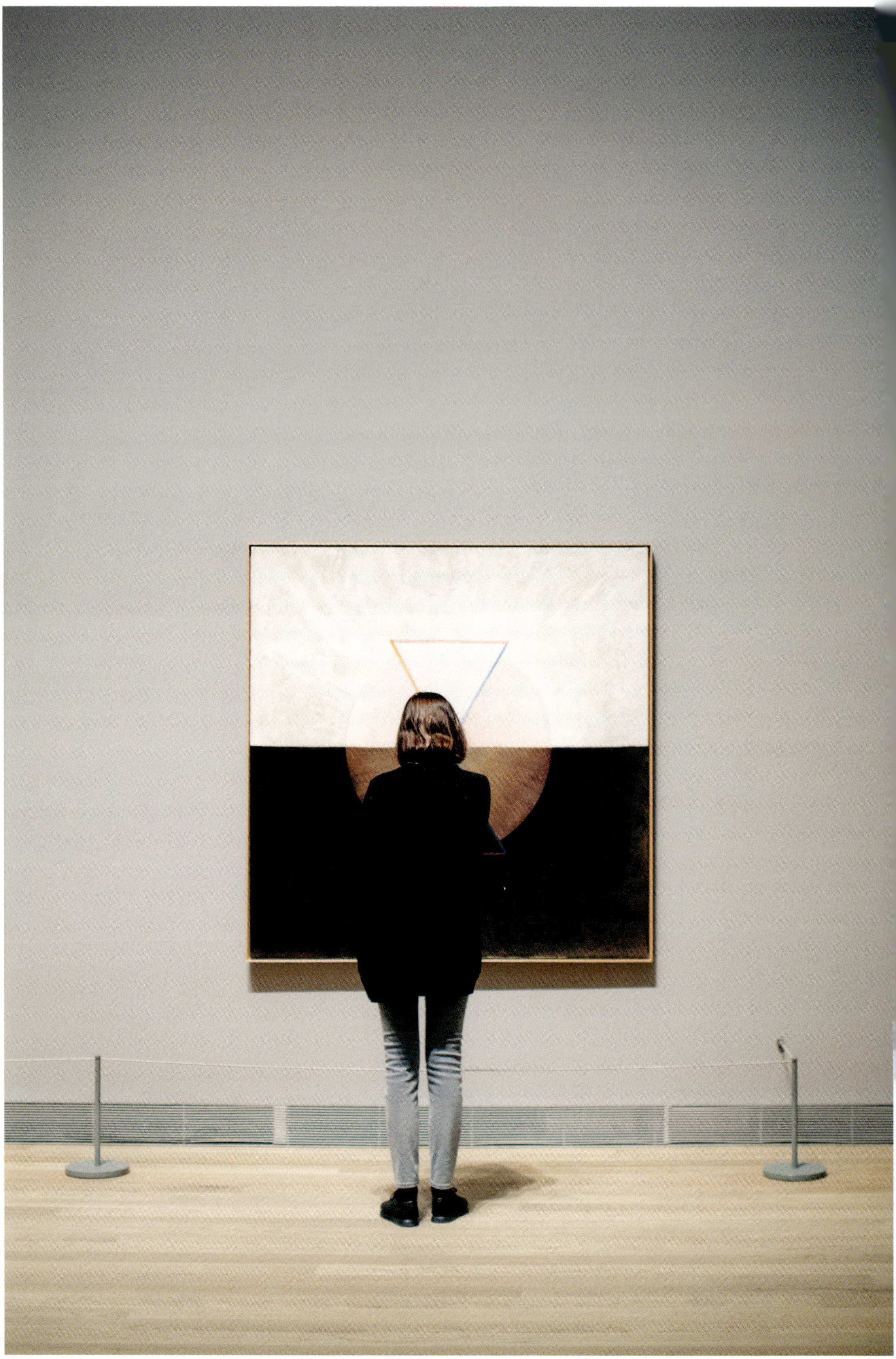

FOR HILMA AF KLINT, ART WAS A MISSION

Startlingly innovative, informed by a "spiritual guide," her bold abstract paintings predated Kandinsky's. And then her work went into hiding. — BY ANDREW FERREN

It seemed a daunting challenge to follow in the footsteps of a secretive artist who destroyed all her correspondence more than a decade before her death in 1944. Someone who, between 1906 and 1915, had created an astonishing cache of nearly 200 novel paintings — bold abstract compositions as large as 10 by 8 feet — mostly in a small, shared studio in the heart of a major European city, with virtually no record of anyone having seen or discussed the work.

But if the artist is Hilma af Klint and the city is Stockholm, I was ready to take on some sleuthing.

Now celebrated as a pioneering abstract painter working years before the modernist male titans Wassily Kandinsky, Kazimir Malevich, and others supposedly "invented" the concept of abstract painting, af Klint was virtually unknown anywhere until a few of her works were included in the 1986 exhibition "The Spiritual in Art" at the Los Angeles County Museum of Art. After that, interest grew slowly but steadily. Swedish galleries took notice and began showing her paintings. A few traveling exhibitions appeared in Europe, although more often af Klint's canvases were part of larger shows focusing on spirituality or other themes. The Moderna Museet in Stockholm held a large solo af Klint exhibition in 2013 and later opened a Hilma af Klint room. Another exhibition attracted attention in the Serpentine Galleries in London in 2016.

And then, in 2019, came a milestone on the other side of the Atlantic. A six-month exhibition, "Hilma af Klint: Paintings for the Future," at the Guggenheim Museum in New York set attendance records (600,000 visitors) and attracted wide publicity in art circles and the international press. American art critics,

STOCKHOLM & ADELSO

SWEDEN

Previous Contemplating an af Klint at the Moderna Museet in Stockholm. The artist's style resists classification.

Left The Moderna Museet. Tours of af Klint works prompted some viewers to tears.

Opposite Hilma af Klint in 1885. Her conflation of art and spiritualism was not out of step in her time.

with little previous knowledge of the artist, were effusive about the originality and power of her work, the public was clearly fascinated, and art lovers everywhere took notice.

On my visit to Sweden, my search was for Hilma af Klint herself, and I discovered with the help of museum curators, biographers, and af Klint family descendants that it is possible to move around Stockholm, one of Europe's most evocative cities, and connect with her life—almost from cradle to grave—and its artistic context.

It helps that Stockholm was untouched by the destruction of 20th-century wars and still looks rather 19th century, with ornate, low-rise buildings, and both tall ships and vintage-looking ferries darting to and fro on bustling waterways.

To the extent af Klint was known to art historians before the 1980s, it was as a portraitist, illustrator, and painter of descriptive botanical studies. As far as was known, she had shown the abstract works—lush, flowing fields of color punctuated by looping floral and biomorphic forms, as well as letters, shapes, often indecipherable words, and symbols that float across the paintings' surfaces—to only a handful of people. Perhaps because of their reactions, she came to fear the world was not ready to understand her nonfigurative work and instructed her heir not to show the abstract paintings until 20 years after her death.

That heir was her nephew, Erik af Klint, a naval man who knew nothing about art and happily complied with his aunt's hibernation clause. In the late 1960s, when the crates were finally opened, the paintings astonished. So did the 26,000 pages of the artist's accompanying notes, many detailing the paintings' creation starting in 1906, led by a spiritual guide named Amaliel who contacted her during séances and not only "commissioned" the paintings but, at least at the outset, had, she claimed, directed her hand as she painted.

"The pictures were painted directly through me, without any preliminary drawings and with great force," af Klint wrote in one of her journals of the 193 mostly abstract works known as *The Paintings for the Temple*, meditations on human life and relationships in the most elemental terms. "I had no idea what the paintings were supposed to depict, nevertheless I worked swiftly and surely without changing a single brushstroke."

She went on to paint many more abstract series, totaling nearly 1,300 works, as well as a few portrait commissions and other naturalistic works, many of whose whereabouts today are unknown. In addition to painting, af Klint spent the last decades of her life pursuing her spiritual journey. Her search for a home for the paintings led as far as Dornach, Switzerland, where she had hoped Rudolf Steiner, the idealist and mystical philosopher, might want them for his new spiritual center. At one point she even planned to build "the temple" she referenced in the *Paintings for the Temple* series on an island off southern Sweden. When no solution was found, she asked her nephew to give the world time to catch up.

Though a lack of financial resources would be a constant feature of her long life, Hilma af Klint was born in a palace, a perfect spot to pick up her trail. Completed in 1795, Karlberg Palace, where her father taught naval studies, remains a military academy and is closed to the public. But there are fantastic views of its commanding, buttoned-down neoclassical facade from across the water on Kungsholms Strand, as well as a lovely public park behind it.

Af Klint was born in 1862 into a family with a long naval history. Besides admirals and officers, there were also cartographers who mapped the Baltic Sea and whose knowledge of those waters at least once gave Sweden an advantage over Russia. Because of this long history of service, the family was ennobled in 1805, which accounts for the "af" in Hilma af Klint.

I was lucky to spend several hours visiting sites in and around Stockholm with several af Klint family descendants, including Hilma's great-nephew Johan af Klint, Erik's son, who was five when she died. While Erik af Klint had been close to his aunt, he knew nothing of her work or spiritual ideas, which Johan says included theosophy, Rosicrucianism, hermeticism, and an esoteric strain of Christianity. "It was a very male-dominated society, and she was strong-willed and sort of knocked into this square family," he said.

In the late 1960s, Erik af Klint attempted to donate Hilma's entire body of abstract paintings to Stockholm's Moderna Museet, but was rebuffed. By 1972, he had created a foundation to administer and preserve the collection.

I asked Julia Voss, a biographer of Hilma af Klint, where I might follow in af Klint's footsteps. Of all places, she directed me to Stockholm's 13th-century cathedral to view two centuries-old works of art that she is convinced af Klint absorbed from a young age. The first is a massive sculpture of St. George and the Dragon, a story that became a theme in one of her series. The other is a painting depicting the parhelion, a rare atmospheric optical effect of multiple halos appearing in the sky over Stockholm in 1535. Halos, rings, and other luminous effects are a hallmark of *The Paintings for the Temple*.

Visits to other museums further enhance a sense of af Klint's world—especially the artistic environment. The National Museum provides the city's most international display of late 19th-century art, with Swedish and Scandinavian artists like Anders Zorn, Bruno Liljefors, and Julia Beck shown alongside French and other European artists. Among the Swedes there is a notable amount of work by female artists.

In 1882 af Klint enrolled in the Royal Academy of Fine Arts. Although the academy had been opened to women, it was usually expected that they would copy masterpieces or paint charming domestic scenes rather than aspire to become great artists.

A visit to the academy today, with its elegant entry and halls lined with plaster casts of classical

STOCKHOLM & ADELSO — SWEDEN

Opposite *Group IV, No. 7,* an af Klint work from 1907.

Right Displayed in a grouping, in a space large enough to project their power, af Klint's works invite contemplation and awe.

sculptures contrasting with the bohemian spirit of students and professors buzzing about, feels much as it might have in af Klint's day. The environment was so collegial I stayed for a lunch of lentil curry and a glass of rosé in the cafe.

In 1887, af Klint graduated from the academy with honors and was awarded use of a shared studio at Hamngatan 5 that she maintained until 1909 and where she painted the first 100 or so *Paintings for the Temple*—including *The Ten Largest*, mesmerizingly powerful works that measure almost 10 by 8 feet—between 1906 and 1908. The building was leveled to create modern Stockholm's major shopping district, but at the time, this area was the center of cultural life.

It's known that Hilma participated in séances as a teenager and dedicated even more time and energy communicating with the spiritual realm after her sister died when Hilma was 18. She joined a circle of female artists known as the Edelweiss Society who held séances, and by 1896, she participated in weekly séances with four other women. They called themselves The Five. After prayers and Bible readings, the séance would begin, and the women would collaboratively record their experiences in journals and in automatic drawings that include motifs later explored in af Klint's *Paintings for the Temple*.

These women were hardly alone during that era in searching for existential answers and universal truths from a higher realm. In Europe the tenets of Buddhism, theosophy, and anthroposophy were in vogue, and many other artists of the period—including Kandinsky and Malevich—explored a spiritual basis for their art. But perhaps because we have spent a century studying their work, while we are now seeing af Klint's paintings almost completely unfiltered, she can have a surprising effect.

Iris Muller Westermann, who curated the 2013 af Klint exhibition at the Moderna Museet, remembered leading tours "with very pulled-together bourgeois types who appeared completely in control of everything until they suddenly burst into tears. Neither happy nor sad, it was as if spending time with Hilma's paintings spurred something inside them that needed an outlet."

It's believed most of The Five's meetings took place at Mathilda Nilsson's house at Kammakargatan 6. Most of the attendees (eventually more than five) lived in Ostermalm, central Stockholm's fashionable new eastern district that was developed at the turn of the 20th century. From about 1898 to 1918, Hilma lived with her mother at Brahegatan 52. Anna Cassel, another member of The Five and a lifelong friend

Above The Swedish Academy of Fine Arts. Women art students in af Klint's day were confined to painting domestic subjects.

Opposite The Maritime Museum in Stockholm.

of af Klint, lived at Engelbrektsgatan 31. Pilgrims will still find the ambience of the streets much as Hilma likely did — with charming cafes, taverns, and shops on street level, and tidy rows of apartment windows above.

Erik af Klint and his family lived at Karlavagen 56, where his son Johan recalls his great-aunt's paintings were stored rolled up in boxes in an unheated attic for more than 20 years. Miraculously, they emerged in almost impeccable condition.

Aristocrats were expected to be landowners, so the af Klint family acquired property on the island of Adelso in Lake Malaren. If Stockholm surprises visitors for seeming to have more water than land, Lake Malaren, which stretches west of the capital, is the opposite — a body of water so dense with islands, peninsulas, and outcroppings that it can appear more like a network of rivers. Approaching Adelso by car in early summer is like flipping through one of Hilma's sketchbooks, with rapidly alternating glimpses of water and forest, thickets and clearings, deer and other wildlife, not to mention the exuberant wildflowers whose colors and forms she celebrated in her work.

Today one can see from the road the modest but pretty wooden house at Hanmora, as the estate is still called, though it is no longer in her family's possession. It was here that Hilma spent childhood summers and in her early adulthood taught Sunday school at the quaint church, which can be visited. She returned to Adelso and the neighboring island of Munso throughout her life.

Back in central Stockholm, tucked behind the Nordic Museum, is the Naval Cemetery where Hilma is buried alongside her parents. In general, Swedish cemeteries are pretty restrained affairs, but the granite block marked "Kommendor Viktor af Klint Familjegrav," beneath which Hilma lies, is among

*Photographs by
Erika Gerdemark*

the most humble, a fitting finish for an artist who hid her life's work rather than let it be misunderstood.

"It's not likely she'll be hidden away again," said her great-great-niece, Ulrika af Klint.

As Hilma herself wrote: "The experiments I have conducted…that were to awaken humanity when they were cast upon the world were pioneering endeavors. Though they travel through much dirt, they will yet retain their purity."

WHAT TO READ AND WATCH

Beyond the Visible — Hilma af Klint, directed by Halina Dyrschka. An eye-opening documentary on af Klint and her work. "Bristles with the excitement of discovery and also with the impatience that recognition has taken so long." — A. O. Scott in *The New York Times*.

Hilma af Klint: Paintings for the Future, edited by Tracey Bashkoff. Essays by art experts and historians explore the artist's work and motivations.

Hilma af Klint: Seeing Is Believing, edited by Daniel Birnbaum. Reproduces the last abstract images series made by af Klint in the 1920s, with essays based on lectures given at the Serpentine Galleries in London.

Hilma af Klint: Visionary, by Kurt Almqvist, Louise Belfrage, and others. Based on a seminar held at the Guggenheim Museum in New York at the opening of its first af Klint exhibition.

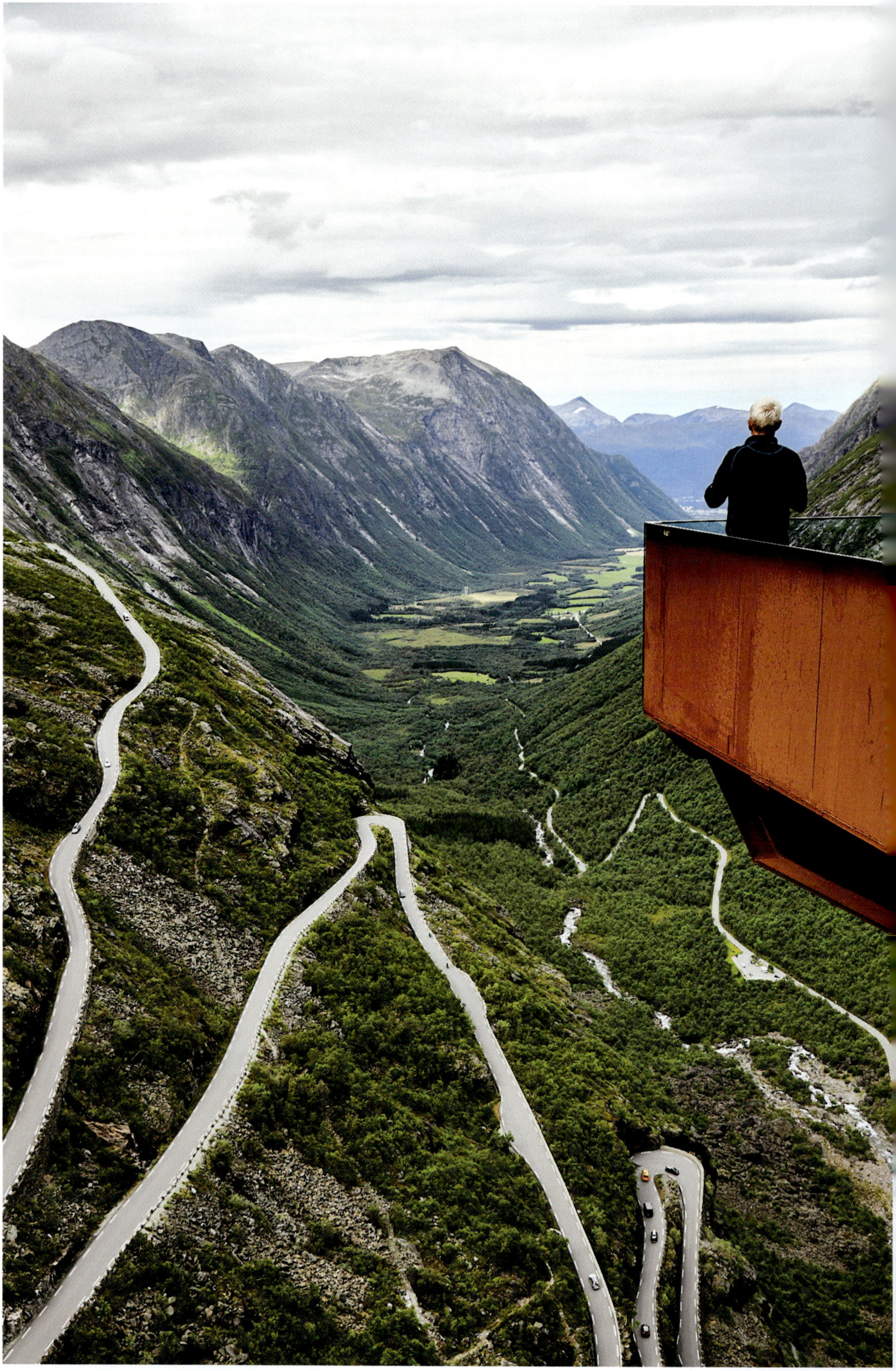

NATURE + ART = NORWAY

In a country already gifted with beauty, the National Tourist Routes add bold architectural elements for a synergy of landscape and design. — BY ONDINE COHANE

On a remote road in central Norway, 11 switchbacks cut into a sheer mountainside in a region that is basically impassable from early November to May. On a map, this spectacular example of highway engineering looks like a chaotic configuration of squiggles and loops. On the ground, it is a forbidding series of sharp bends, and driving it feels like playing an advanced-level video game.

This is the Trollstigen, or the troll's path, once part of a trade route that crisscrossed through the country. It's now part of Norway's National Tourist Routes, designated scenic highways that wind and climb to vistas of peaks, fjords, and surprising new installations of art and architecture.

On the autumn day when I drove the Trollstigen, my little white rental car shuddered up the narrow passes. A driver here has to be attentive, but I struggled to focus on the road ahead of me. The beauty of my surroundings was breathtaking. Trees were brilliant gold, russet-red, and pumpkin-orange. Dramatic sculptural mountain peaks stretched up into a lonely, foreboding sky. A silvery waterfall cascaded from the top of one of the adjacent cliffs, and a dramatic sunset deepened and changed hues every second, with puffy clouds reflecting the last pink and fire-red rays.

I heard about the National Tourist Routes from a friend in New York who is passionate about architecture, especially in Nordic countries. The Routes have been a decades-long project, beginning in the late 1990s, to transform 18 highways into cultural destinations by marrying their natural beauty to adventurous new architectural features: rest stops, scenic walkways and overlooks, picnic areas, new bridges — all designed to both complement the landscape and draw the eye with their own artistic appeal.

TROLLSTIGEN TO KRISTIANSUND NORWAY

Previous The view from the Trollstigen platform, an installation designed by Reiulf Ramstad Architects.

Left A three-headed troll guards a highway stop for ice cream and camping.

Opposite A gracefully curving walkway complements the landscape and the view of the arched Storseisundet Bridge.

Parking my car at the viewing point of Trollstigen toward the top of the peak, I found myself at a place that seemed more architectural wonder than highway stop. A suspended pathway from the parking lot led to a modernist-style cafe with floor-to-ceiling windows and crossed a tranquil pool that seemed almost Zen Buddhist in inspiration. From there, a staircase cut through the steep mountainside to a rust-colored steel viewing platform.

The vantage point hangs over the valley and road that I had just maneuvered, an installation all its own, and a new destination that seemed only to amplify the aesthetic pleasure of one of Norway's most famous mountain ranges, the Romsdal Alps, and one of its most photographed roads.

In fact, the combination here — of new architecture to augment already spectacular natural surroundings, alongside a beloved country roadway — is only one example of the many such projects I had the pleasure of discovering on my trip. At this point I was on the Geiranger-Trollstigen route, Route 63, which also goes through Geiranger, at the head of the famous Geiranger Fjord. Fjordsetet, an installation at the Flydalsjuvet lookout, is literally a seat, thronelike in its height and commanding view over the fjord.

In recent decades, Norway has become a hotbed for young and midcareer architects, and it's no wonder, given the remarkable support of architecture and architects in one of the wealthiest countries in the world.

After a nationwide competition for both the roads to be chosen and the new structures proposed, Norway drew its plan in the 1990s for the Tourist Routes (sometimes called the Norwegian Scenic Routes). Each stop would have a new pavilion, observation deck, bridge, restaurant, hotel, or other structure, all to be conceived by young emerging architects, and predominantly Norwegian ones. Alongside would be installations by artists of note (like the French-American artist Louise Bourgeois's evocative memorial for women and men burned as witches in the 1600s). The timeline was 30 years, but the project moved fast.

The goal was to develop the tourist economy and increase traffic in the more remote, and geographically diverse, areas of Norway. The official assessment is that it has worked. "The Norwegian Scenic Routes have been a game changer for the tourism industry in Norway and the Fjord Norway region," Kristian B. Jorgensen, chief executive of Fjord Norway, the official tourism board of the fjords, told me when I contacted him.

Yet when I first heard about the National Tourist Routes project, it seemed implausible to me that something so vast and inventive had not received more international attention than it has. Now I was glad to see for myself.

The primordial mountain range I found at Trollstigen could not have looked more different from the wind-whipped seaside landscape where I started my journey near the Kristiansund Airport on the Norwegian Sea about 300 miles north of Oslo. There I drove out onto a trippy highway known as the Atlanterhavsvegen, or Atlantic Road, another amazing engineering feat. It twisted and turned over the coastal islands like the tracks of a roller coaster — looping high over bridges between the small islands that sit close to the mainland, only to descend again to hug the coastline alongside the brooding, steel-gray, furious waves of the ocean.

Here Ghilardi and Hellsten, young architects from Oslo, had constructed their installation, called Eldhusoya. An elevated walkway leads around one of the picturesque islands and provides a 360-degree view of the adjacent bridge, the seascape, and neighboring islets alongside, in order to bring them organically into one frame of vision.

"Richard Serra was one of our inspirations," Franco Ghilardi said. "Nature, landscape design, architecture become very site-specific. And we concentrated on local materials like the stainless steel they use on Norwegian oil rigs because we knew they would wear well over time even in extreme weather."

Because the walkway is both elevated and prefabricated, the impact on the natural setting is minimal, meeting one of the other goals for all the installations.

"We were actually encouraged to be more daring and courageous when we submitted our design," Ghilardi said. "Usually the client tries to cut the budget and tone down the scope of our projects, so this was quite a radical thing for us."

Daring and courageous. I thought about his words often as I drove for five days, sometimes for as long as eight hours at a stretch. I was becoming a more daring driver as I tackled more of the Norwegian roads, but I was alone on this trip, and I was not used to being without a passenger in a country where I didn't speak a word of the language. Sometimes an

Above A cabin at the Juvet Landscape Hotel, an inviting stop in Valldal.

Opposite Another installation by Reiulf Ramstad Architects is at the top of the winding Trollstigen highway.

hour passed without another car coming into view, even on major highways.

After a couple of days though, the peace and diversity of the countryside became meditational, a panorama that seemed dreamlike through my windscreen. Traditional country cottages built into mounds of earth with grass-topped roofs and green weathered doors looked as if they were out of *The Hobbit*. Dark thick forest alternated with bucolic sun-dappled farmland and bare, desolate mountains overlooking quaint lakeside towns. One late afternoon as I drove into a village, the sun appeared to drop like a fireball into a fjord.

Spectacular modern installations appeared on remote corners in the most far-fetched of places, so unexpected that they sometimes seemed like figments of my imagination.

Above Trollstigen, another project conceived along these routes is the Juvet Landscape Hotel, designed by the architects Jensen and Skodvin, and the creepy, if certainly appropriate aesthetically, setting for the 2015 film *Ex Machina*.

From the exterior, the compound, in a nature reserve called Reinheimen, looks almost like a hippie campsite with its low-slung, wood-encased cabins on stilts. But as I was shown into my room, the rustic vision was completely turned on its head. The natural wood or in some instances stone that covers the rear of the structures hides glass walls and raw cement cubes facing front, with views onto the gentle valley, and onto the surrounding peaks and meandering river that cut through the landscape.

The perspective created the effect that I was both inside and outside the hotel, part of the natural surroundings, both the voyeur and the inhabitant.

After a dip in the outdoor hot tub, I joined other travelers and guests in a candlelit communal dining room, an intimate warm environment where locally

*Photographs by
David B. Torch*

hunted venison was served alongside foraged mountain vegetables that were like strange fairy-tale versions of carrots and beets with curly tendrils and odd shapes. A roaring fire and candles were our only light.

When I look back now, my Norwegian road trip seems like one of the most surreal and meaningful of any journeys I have taken, even after many years of absorbing trips. The pristine beauty, the sense of drama, the network of beautiful art and architecture — the memory turns in my head like a film trailer, so cinematic and surprising that I still almost can't believe it was real.

WHAT TO READ AND WATCH

National Tourist Routes in Norway, Multilingual Edition, by Jan Andresen and Arne Hjeltnes. Photos, essays, and drawings for all 18 scenic drives, with emphasis on architectural and artistic viewpoints.

Nasjonaleturistveger.no, a website with a good overview of the Norwegian Scenic Routes. Maps and photos are included.

The Geirangerfjord: A Guide to One of Norway's Most Beautiful Fjords, by Paul Imanuelsen. Travel advice, places to visit, and scenic photographs.

Ex Machina, directed by Alex Garland. A futuristic fantasy movie filmed partly in the high-design Juvet Landscape Hotel, along the Geiranger-Trollstigen Tourist Route.

The Wave, directed by Roar Uthaug. A Norwegian disaster movie that features gorgeous scenes of Geirangerfjord and surrounding mountains — until the landslide and tsunami.

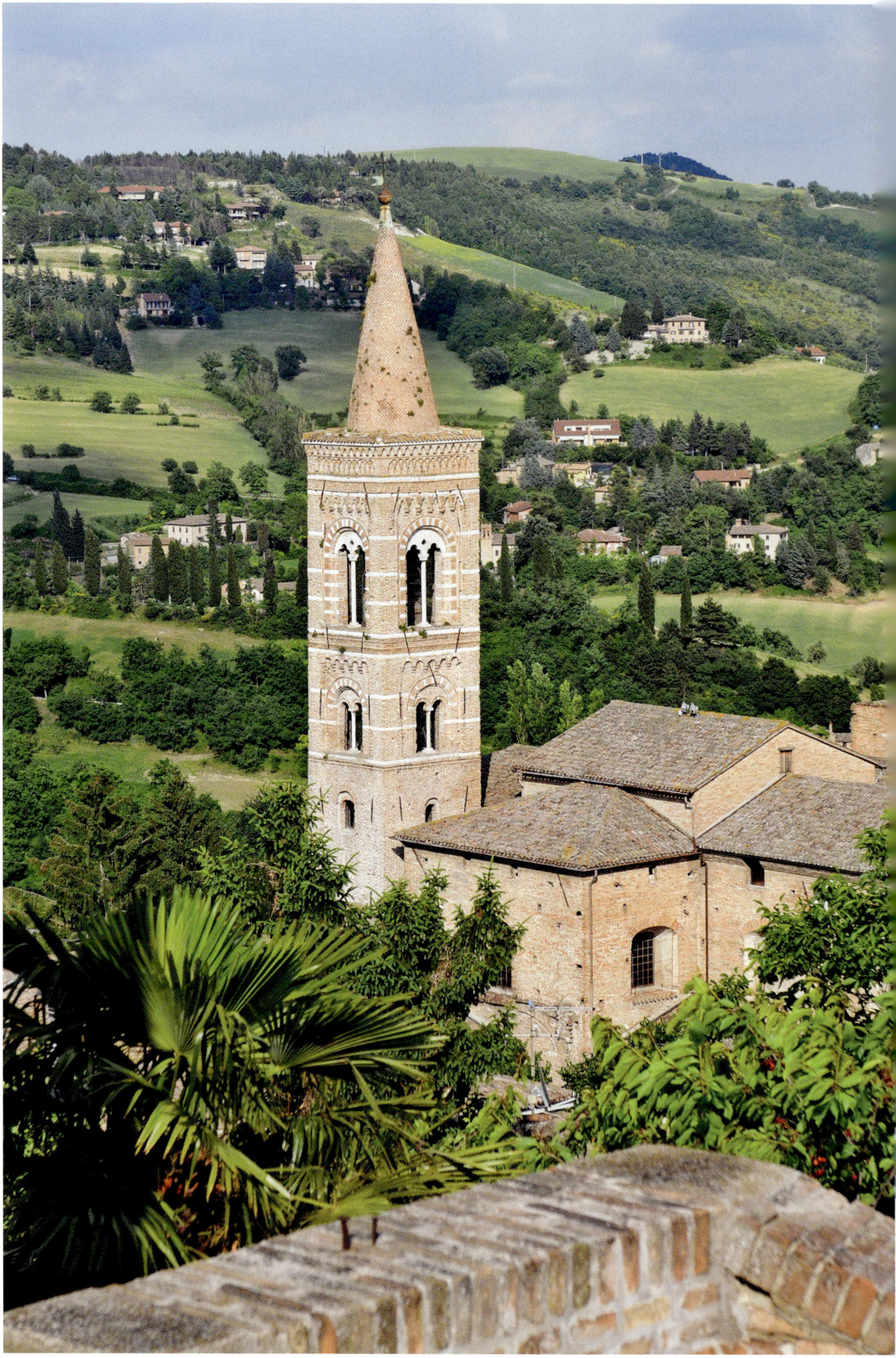

ITALY　　　　　　　　　　　　　　　　　　　　　　　　　　URBINO

THE PEARL OF
THE RENAISSANCE

Urbino had its moment in the 16th century, at the palace where a worldly duchess set the standard for social success. — BY DAVID LASKIN

In March of 1507, in a lofty high-windowed room in a palace in the Marche region northeast of Rome, the High Renaissance reached its pinnacle. For four successive nights, a company of poets, artists, scholars, and nobles, assembled on the occasion of a papal visit, gathered around a table in Urbino's magnificent Ducal Palace to chat about love, law, morals, manners, beauty, sex, seemliness, art, hats, cosmetics, tennis, and whatever else most pressed the minds of Renaissance men and women.

These were the conversations that the diplomat Baldassare Castiglione recreated (and no doubt embellished) soon afterward in *The Book of the Courtier*, a kind of manual on how to be cool at court that for centuries afterward was required reading throughout Europe for all who aspired to a life of power and polish.

"Here, then, gentle discussions and innocent pleasantries were heard," Castiglione wrote, describing the delightful ambience fostered by Elisabetta Gonzaga, the cultured 36-year-old duchess who presided over those days of fabled gatherings. "And on everyone's face a jocund gaiety could be seen depicted, so much so that the house could be called the very abode of joyfulness. Nor do I believe that the sweetness that is had from a beloved company was ever savored in any other place as it once was there."

At a stroke of the quill, Castiglione made the windy little hill town of Urbino a byword for refinement, elegant nonchalance (*sprezzatura* was his word for it), and the perfect marriage of money and art. It didn't hurt Urbino's reputation that Raphael, already a rising star and much in demand at noble courts, had been born right up the street from the Ducal Palace

URBINO   ITALY

Opposite The church of San Francesco in Urbino, a city of Renaissance nobles and the birthplace of Raphael.

Left Baldassare Castiglione. His *The Book of the Courtier* served as a how-to manual for Renaissance social climbers.

Opposite Windy hill country of Urbino. In the power struggles of Italy, Urbino lost its dukedom to Lorenzo de' Medici.

in 1483 and had learned to paint in Urbino. Florence was always far larger, Venice more extravagant, Rome more august, but for a few decades at the end of the 15th century and the start of the 16th, Urbino was truly the ideal city of the Renaissance.

Half a millennium later, what struck my wife and me as we drove toward Urbino was its rugged remoteness. We approached the city on tortuous two-lane roads that skimmed the margins of grain fields pitched like ski slopes. When the town came into view, it looked like something a Cubist craftsman had assembled out of an infinite supply of buff-colored bricks — city walls, looming palace with dainty dunce-capped twin towers, black-domed cathedral, hive of houses — all of it roofed in terra-cotta and fitted together like an intricate tan puzzle.

We parked outside the city wall and headed for the Ducal Palace, striding through narrow streets lined with cafes and loud with students enrolled at Urbino's ancient university. We found the oddly unimposing entry portal at the rear of the palace. Inside, we darted through rooms devoted to an archaeological museum and finally emerged in the miraculous interior courtyard called the Cortile d'Onore, or Court of Honor.

After the gorgeous chaos of the surrounding countryside and the crabbed medieval cityscape, the cortile is like a single crystalline equation emerging from a chalkboard of squiggles. White Corinthian columns joined by arches define a rectangle of noble proportions. Latin text inscribed in the stone proclaims the "justice, clemency and liberalism" of the palace's builder, Duke Federico da Montefeltro, Duchess Elisabetta's father-in-law, who had passed on the palace to her sickly husband, Guidobaldo. Tall, dark windows centered above the arches draw the eye upward and the mind inward to muse on the ideal beauty of the place. Here, distilled in stone, brick, and geometry, is the quintessence of the Italian Renaissance.

The ladies and gentlemen who strolled through this courtyard 500 years ago would have been richly but soberly dressed, preferably in black — "more pleasing in clothing than any other color," Castiglione declared. "For my part," intoned one of the fashion connoisseurs he wrote of, "I should prefer [courtiers' dress] not to be extreme in any way, as the French are sometimes in being over-ample, and the Germans in being over-scanty." The duchess's aristocratic guests would have been graced with beautiful teeth ("very attractive in a woman") but the good sense not to "laugh without cause solely to display" them.

Adept alike at the gentle pursuits of music and dancing and the serious business of war and hunting, the duchess's guests over those four rarefied nights were masters of what Castiglione called a "cool disinvoltura," or ease. It made them "seem in words, in laughter, in posture not to care," he wrote, and caused "all who are watching them to believe that they are almost incapable of making a mistake."

Even if they behaved only half as elegantly as Castiglione made out, it must have been quite a party. Certainly the setting was incomparable. Castiglione boasted (modestly) that Urbino's Ducal Palace was "thought by many the most beautiful to be found anywhere in all Italy," with "countless ancient statues of marble and bronze, rare paintings and musical instruments of every sort," and a vast library.

Duke Federico, who lived from 1422 to 1482, was a fabulously successful *condottiere* — in essence a Renaissance mercenary — so feared that he was paid not to fight. He amassed a great fortune and lavished it on the finest artists and architects of the day, creating the setting for the duchess's parties in 1507. Sadly, the Montefeltro family lost control of Urbino only a few years later, and in time the bulk of the palace's treasures and all of its books were carried off to Rome and Florence. (Elisabetta, a widow by then, was expelled and went north to Ferrara; Lorenzo de' Medici became the new duke of Urbino as well as the ruler of Florence.)

Today, the visitor to the palace will find that carved door lintels, ceiling medallions, fireplace mantels, a couple of chests, and Federico's huge painted box of a bed are pretty much all that remain of the original décor.

The one glorious exception is the small private study in the duke's suite — the Studiolo — a masterpiece of trompe l'oeil intarsia (inlaid wood) so ingenious and exact you're tempted to pluck an apple from the basket of fruit perched by a window. A similar intarsia studiolo taken from Federico's palace in Gubbio is in the Metropolitan Museum of Art in New York.

The other rooms around the Court of Honor have been whitewashed and repurposed as a museum of medieval and Renaissance art. The collection's masterpieces — Raphael's *La Muta*, an incomparable portrait of a melancholy beauty, and Piero della Francesca's humble, dusky *Madonna of Senigallia* and surreal, puzzling *Flagellation of Christ* — are ghostly reminders of how dazzling this court once was. The duchess's suite, including the Room of the Vigils, where Castiglione's book is set, has been used for special exhibitions — one some years ago was an international show of Raphael's work.

William Butler Yeats, in a poem touching on the long-ago conversations in this setting, conjured up a room "where the Duchess and her people talked / The stately midnight through until they stood / In their great window looking at the dawn."

La Casa Natale di Raffaello, a 10-minute walk from the Ducal Palace, is the house where Raphael was born and raised. It's worth a visit even though it has only one original work attributed (by some) to him — a touching little fresco of the Madonna and child painted most likely in boyhood. Raphael's father, Giovanni Santi, was an esteemed painter in Federico's court, and his house exemplifies the considerable style and comfort in which even moderately successful families lived under the duke.

At the top of Via Raffaello, a short stroll along the city wall leads to a gate in the side of a massive bastion. Up the stairs are the ramparts of Fort Albornoz

Above Urbino was the setting for Elisabetta Gonzaga's elegant and refined gatherings of thinkers, artists, and nobles.

Opposite The Ducal Palace lost most of its treasures when Florence took over Urbino in the early 1500s.

and a splendid panorama of town, Ducal Palace, and surrounding countryside.

If you've got a car, really the only way to tour the region, you'll want to make long, leisurely loops through the satellite towns and supremely beautiful countryside that Federico controlled. We started with Urbania, 10 miles from Urbino on a literally breathtaking road of hairpin turns and drop-dead views. The town's majolica industry has resurged in recent years, and a handful of shops in the historic center offered intricately painted ceramics at fairly reasonable prices.

The Barco Ducale, the duke's stately domed hunting lodge, stood outside of town. The original building is gone, but an 18th-century monastery stands in its place, in a lush green field outside town. Back in the day, the surrounding country was walled for miles and planted with greensward and oak groves where poets and humanists idled away the drowsy summers. Today the building is under restoration.

Another stretch of divinely unspoiled country separates Urbania from Acqualagna, 11 miles to the southeast, and here we picked up a highway to Gubbio, Duke Federico's birthplace, 22 miles farther south and just over the line in Umbria. Gubbio's Ducal Palace feels more like a fortress than Urbino's, and few of its decorative touches remain, but its views of rooftops and hills are fantastic.

Gubbio itself, to my mind, is more appealing than Urbino — quainter, quieter, catering more to tourists than to students, and chockablock with tempting ceramics shops. With more time and money, it would have been fun to play courtier at the Hotel Relais Ducale, the former guest quarters of the Ducal Palace, now a luxury hotel.

But we ate like royalty at Cà Andreana, a charming old farmhouse turned country inn where we stayed, just outside of Urbino. These days, a different kind of Renaissance is unfolding amid the "fertile and

*Photographs by
Chris Warde-Jones*

bountiful countryside" that Castiglione celebrated in his book. Chefs, bakers, cheesemakers, meat curers, fruit and vegetable growers, truffle purveyors, wine and olive oil producers are the artists working most creatively today in the old demesne of the Montefeltros.

Were he to return from Renaissance heaven, Castiglione would surely judge our manners coarse, our conversation lacking in wit, and our clothes unspeakable — but I suspect that even he would be impressed by the fare we dined on in a cozy, humble inn a stone's throw from the city he immortalized.

WHAT TO READ AND WATCH

The Book of the Courtier, by Baldassare Castiglione, translated by Charles S. Singleton. A manual for functionaries, guests, and hangers-on in the palaces of the Italian Renaissance, told as a series of conversations. First published in 1528.

Urbino: The Story of a Renaissance City, by June Osborne. Covers the city's art, architecture, and history, and includes detail on *The Book of the Courtier*.

The Marches, published by the Touring Club of Italy. An indispensable guide for anyone traveling the area by car.

Italian Renaissance Courts: Art, Pleasure and Power (Renaissance Art), by Alison Cole. Examines the role played by art and architecture in the competition of the city-states of Naples, Urbino, Ferrara, Mantua, and Milan.

The Borgias. Showtime television series inspired by Renaissance history.

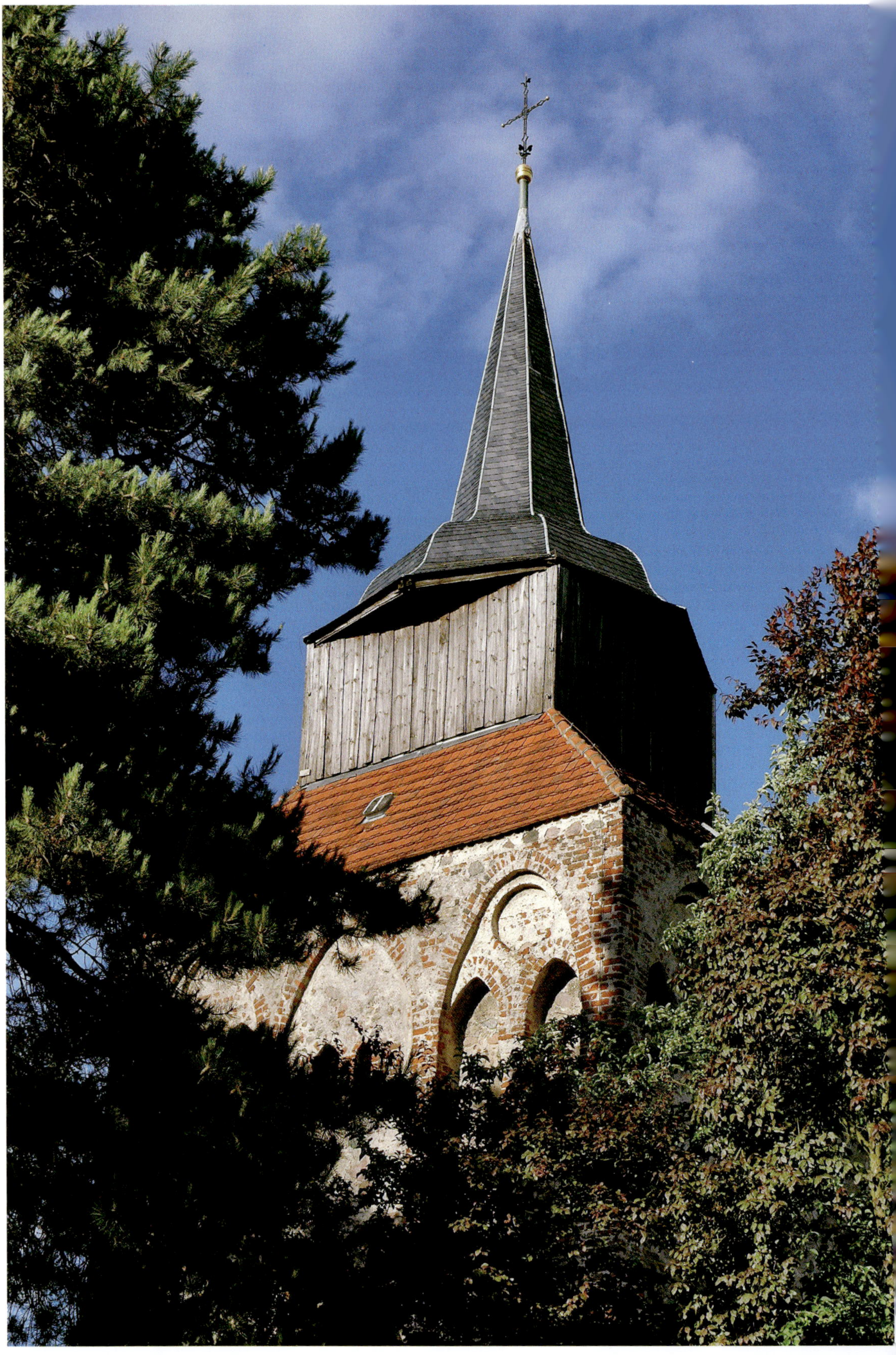

ROARING ROCKETS AND SINGING SAND

The Nazi birthplace of modern rocket science, now a sea-splashed resort, inspires contemplation of war and peace. — BY GISELA WILLIAMS AND RICHARD BERNSTEIN

These days, the claw-shaped island in the Baltic Sea called Usedom is a family-oriented vacation resort, crowded especially on holiday weekends by middle-class Germans playing in the sea, rejuvenating in spa treatments, or riding rented bicycles through the fragrant pine forests. The sun warms the water in the long summer days, and the sand is so fine it "sings" — when the conditions are just right, rubbing the sugar-white grains sets off a small chorus of little squeaks, like music from a tiny orchestra of invisible violins.

Just two and a half hours from Berlin, Usedom has become a weekend destination of choice for many stylish Berliners and expatriates. They are repeating a pattern of the late 19th century, when the island was called "Berlin's bathtub." Two German emperors, Friedrich III and Wilhelm II, were frequent visitors, and wealthy Berliners built palatial villas in fashionable styles from French Renaissance to Art Nouveau. Aristocratic merrymakers would visit for six weeks in the summer, strolling like peacocks along the promenade, sometimes changing costumes two or three times a day.

But between its golden age before World War I and its current era as an egalitarian beach resort, Usedom went through different, much darker times. In the East German communist republic, its pleasures were reserved for well-connected apparatchiks. And before that, during the Third Reich, it was important not as a place of pleasure, but as an incubator of a monumental weapon of war.

In the 1930s, Hitler ordered the construction of a secret military laboratory and weapons factory on Usedom's northern coast, in the tiny fishing village of

Previous A church on Usedom. The island's serene ambience was jolted when it was taken over for Nazi rocket research.

Left After the Nazi surrender, the Russian military set about blowing up what remained of the Peenemünde rocket sites.

Opposite Usedom's bucolic charms, like this view of an old windmill, long predated the era of Nazi rocketry.

Peenemünde. Wernher von Braun, 23 years old in 1935, was the technical director at the site and saw it as a perfect place for developing a secret weapon, remote and little known, with plenty of space for testing rockets. Its crowning achievement was the V-2, which terrorized London in the final fall and winter of World War II while also laying the foundation for modern rocket science and space travel. Peenemünde's role in the Nazi war effort ended when it was bombed by Allied planes, but its technological significance remained influential for decades afterward.

A visit to Usedom today can explore both sides of its story: its historical roles in both the pursuit of innocent pleasure and the worst human impulses to violence.

Barely adrift on the Baltic Sea, where Germany meets Poland, Usedom stretches about 30 miles in length. Since 1945, its far eastern end has actually been part of Poland, where it is called Uznam, but its history as a resort is German. Its connection to Berlin is as legendary as that of Brighton to London, or the Hamptons to New York City. The best way to get a feel of it is to rent a bike and ride along the five-mile-long promenade that connects Usedom's three imperial spa villages: Heringsdorf, Ahlbeck, and Bansin. On one side, the route passes Wilhelminian villas; on the other, happy Germans sunning themselves on wicker beach chairs, known as *Strandkörbe*. Vacationers walk their dogs and build elaborate sandcastles in the singing sand.

Between the villages are small pine forests and the occasional beach shack that serves smoked fish, usually herring and pike perch, with a cold shot of *Kümmel*, a regional schnapps made with caraway seeds. It's a popular way to achieve a Usedom buzz.

During the cold war, privileged East Germans descended on Usedom's beaches for some rare R & R and to get naked: In the 1950s the *Freikörperkultur* or FKK (Free Body Culture) movement, flourished on the island's squeaky beaches.

Today there are still FKK beaches on Usedom, but the nudists are outnumbered by health-conscious visitors who flock year-round to the island's medical and wellness spas. Centers like the Puria Spa at the Strandidyll Heringsdorf operate inside luxury resorts. Others, like the OstseeTherme, are like stand-alone hospitals, complete with thermal water pools and treatments designed to relieve allergies, respiratory ailments, and skin problems.

So entrenched is the spa culture that even a brisk seaside walk on Usedom is considered to have health benefits, which some call a "wind cosmetic."

Usedom's beaches have also made it a film location. In 2009, Roman Polanski chose it as a stand-in for Martha's Vineyard in his film *The Ghost Writer*, a political thriller based on a Robert Harris novel and starring Pierce Brosnan, Ewan McGregor, and Kim Cattrall. Pockets of Peenemünde were reimagined with the cedar-shingled houses and picturesque sandy dunes identified with the Vineyard.

Travelers also find traditional Baltic cooking, updated for modern diners, in Usedom's restaurants. Most dishes are recognizable, but one pioneering local chef was known to serve up herring pralines, a surprisingly delicious combination of smoked herring and dark chocolate.

None of this was in evidence in the Nazi years, when some 18,000 German technicians and scientists toiled feverishly in Peenemünde with war, not sunbathing, on their minds. Among their products were the V-1 buzz bomb, essentially a cruise missile, and the V-2, the forerunner of the rockets that put astronauts on the moon, but also of the ballistic missiles that Russians and Americans aimed at each other during the cold war. In World War II, the V-rockets were used to bomb civilian targets, especially London.

Both the V-1 and the V-2 are on display at the Peenemünde Historical Technical Museum, in a huge industrial shed that once housed the power plant for the weapons complex. In the postwar decades when Usedom was part of East Germany, this was a restricted military area. After the reunification of Germany, local people in Peenemünde organized a first version of the museum, using the vastness of the power station to assemble exhibits on the work that took place there. Six thousand people came in the first month, and over time the museum was expanded and improved.

The museum does just what most 21st-century visitors would want it to do. It presents a largely technological story while making it clear that the technology was pursued on behalf of an evil regime that "craved world domination," as one explanatory sign put it. Part of the museum shows how different conditions were for the two halves of the Peenemünde population—the soldiers and engineers lived very well; the thousands of enslaved laborers who did the manual work lived badly. Many were from the very countries where the weapons were intended to wreak havoc. Other prisoners, inmates of the Dora-Nordhausen camp in the Harz Mountains near the Thuringian town of Nordhausen, produced the V-2 rockets that Peenemünde had developed.

With wartime debris and scenes of destruction, the museum invites contemplation of the suffering the rockets caused, and, by implication, the danger of advanced technology when it is ill-used.

But there is much else in its displays, including a reminder that the scientists who first dreamed of creating rockets in Germany wanted to devise a faster means of travel and to open up space for exploration, which, paradoxically, they did. The museum displays a group portrait of 118 German scientists who once worked at Peenemünde, including Wernher von Braun. But in a sign of the quick strategic shifts that occurred once the war was over, the picture was taken at the United States Army rocket research center in Huntsville, Alabama, where all 118 were recruited to work after the war.

The V-2s that struck London from bases in the Netherlands climbed to an altitude of 50 miles, which put them at the very edge of space, and reached their target, more than 100 miles away, in just under five minutes. Numerous technological innovations were required, from new heat-resistant metals to guidance systems. Londoners found the V-2s particularly frightening because they flew faster than the speed of sound, so that people were struck before they could hear the missile coming.

About 4,000 V-2 rockets, bearing 2,000 pounds of high explosive each and steered by their preset guidance systems, were launched against Britain and the

Above Wicker beach chairs at dusk along a Usedom beach. Once an exclusive resort, it is now egalitarian.

Opposite The promenade pier at Ahlbeck, a symbol of Usedom since 1898.

Low Countries in 1944 and 1945, causing thousands of deaths.

In 1943, British aerial surveillance discovered what was going on in Peenemünde, and the Allies tried to put a stop to it. Over 24 hours, 600 British bombers raked the area. Sadly, the heaviest cost of the raid was paid by some 500 slave laborers killed in their barracks.

What the bombs didn't accomplish, the Allies did after the war, following a Potsdam Agreement mandate that the site be demolished as part of Germany's weapons-building capacity. But that was not until most of the technology had been carried off by Red Army units and most of the important scientists had been taken to the United States.

Von Braun and others later spearheaded the American space flight program, and some ultimately proved an embarrassment. In 1984, Arthur Rudolph, manager of the Saturn 5 rocket program, left the United States and surrendered his citizenship rather than face Justice Department charges that he had been party to atrocities committed against slave laborers at Peenemünde and Nordhausen. Von Braun, the program genius, who died in 1977, also came under attack. He defended his work as driven by the dream of space flight.

The effects of the war still linger for Usedom. Millions of tons of unexploded ammunition lie in the Baltic Sea, where they were dropped in air raids. And in 2013, *Der Spiegel* reported a particular danger for the beachcombers who pick up amber that washes up on Baltic beaches. About 40 percent of the British bombs intended for Peenemünde actually landed in the sea, and some were incendiaries that eventually leaked white phosphorous. When lumps of the phosphorous wash inland, they look like amber. It's dangerous to pick them up. "Phosphorus is highly toxic," *Der Spiegel* reported, "and merely touching it can

Photographs by
Mark Simon

cause organ damage." Fortunately, incidents of this are relatively rare. But on Usedom, you still have to be careful what you collect.

Usedom remembers how it got this legacy, but it long ago reclaimed its historical role as a resort, and now it lives in the present. Its annual Musikfestival in September and October brings classical performers from around the Baltic region; orchestral concerts take place in the old Peenemünde power station. The island also marks Oktoberfest and organizes other events to gather in the merrymakers. Past festivals have celebrated street performers, electronic music, and creative cocktails.

Overwhelmingly, it is the Usedom of sunshine and singing sand that prevails.

WHAT TO READ AND WATCH

The Rocket and the Reich: Peenemünde and the Coming of the Ballistic Missile Era, by Michael J. Neufeld. History by a writer affiliated with the National Air and Space Museum in Washington, D.C.

Peenemünde to Canaveral, by Dieter K. Huzel, with an introduction by Wernher von Braun. The autobiography of one of the scientists who worked at Peenemünde and, later on, American rocket programs.

The Peenemünde Raid: The Night of 17–18 August 1943, by Martin Middlebrook. Draws on first-person accounts of the bombing of Peenemünde.

Doodlebug Summer, directed by Peter Williams. A British television series documenting the era of Nazi rocket weapons from the English point of view.

V-2, by Robert Harris. The prominent British novelist sets a story at Peenemünde, with a rocket scientist as protagonist.

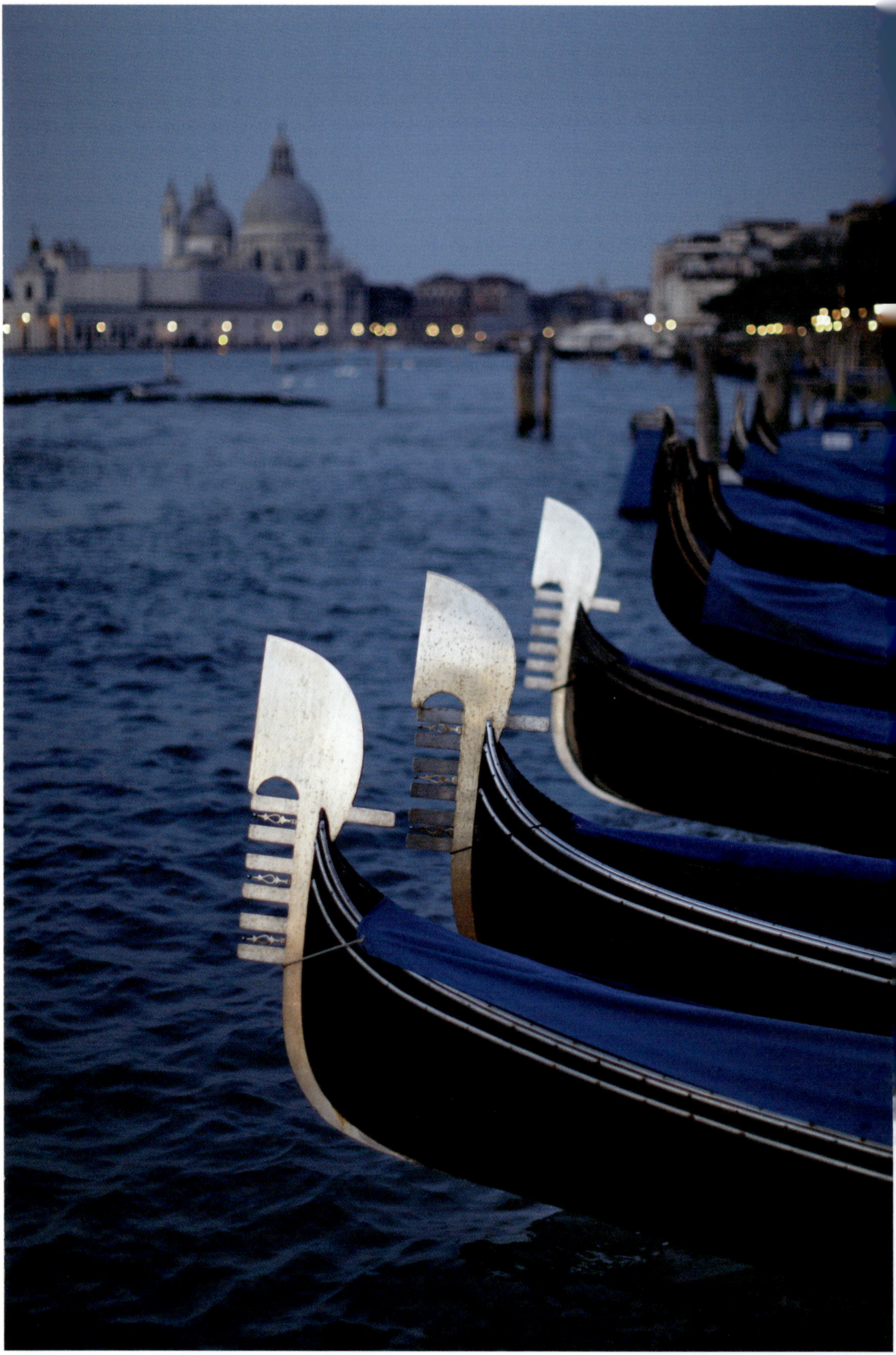

VENICE IN WINTER

Share the allure of a quiet season with Joseph Brodsky, who wrote, "I would never come here in summer, not even at gunpoint." — BY RACHEL DONADIO

I hadn't been back to Venice in years when I found myself there briefly on a writing assignment. It was November; the city's scattered trees had begun to turn brown. The light, as always, was beyond compare, and there was a watery chill in the air. I loved it immediately.

Or rather, I remembered how much I loved it. Italy can do strange things to your perspective. Memories of a place become more real than the place itself. I had lived for years with the Venice of my recollections — traveling there at 19, drinking peach iced tea in the July heat, discovering the paintings of Giorgione. Now I was older, and so was Venice.

My appetite was whetted, and on a freezing January weekend I returned, armed with sweaters, boots, and a well-worn copy of *Watermark*, Joseph Brodsky's marvelous prose poem about Venice in winter. It is an emotional guidebook more than a practical one, but, I would argue, just as reliable. In Venice, maps fail. As everyone knows, to be in that floating city is to be forever lost and disoriented, as if in a labyrinth.

On that November foray, I had listened to a group of American college students talking as they wandered around near the Rialto Bridge. "I don't mind if we're, like, lost all day," one told his friends. "Dude," another replied, "I don't think we have a choice."

Goethe could not have put it better. Venice, as he famously wrote, can be compared only to itself. So many wonderful writers have captured Venice, from Goethe to Henry James to Evelyn Waugh, that it is all the more remarkable that in 1992 Brodsky, in *Watermark*, managed to create a truly original piece of writing about this cliché-worn city.

Previous In the winter dawn, gondolas are tucked in for the night near Piazza San Marco.

Left Let the summer crowds have July. In winter the city slows down and reveals its soul to a visitor equipped with sweaters, boots, and a book.

Opposite Flooding, the *acqua alta*, at Saint Mark's Basilica in 1933. Even those wet times have their charms.

In summer Venice is torrid and overwhelmed by millions of tourists. That season was not for Brodsky. "I would never come here in summer, not even at gunpoint," he wrote in *Watermark*. Instead, he longed for cold. In a series of rented apartments over a series of Januaries toward the end of his too-short life, he came, froze, and wrote. (Brodsky, who won the Nobel Prize for Literature in 1987, was born in Russia, died in New York at age 55, and is buried in San Michele, Venice's wonderful cemetery island.)

"In winter you wake up in this city, especially on Sundays, to the chiming of its innumerable bells, as though behind your gauze curtains a gigantic china teaset were vibrating on a silver tray in the pearl-gray sky," Brodsky wrote. "You fling the window open and the room is instantly flooded with this outer, peal-laden haze, which is part damp oxygen, part coffee and prayers."

I read that passage at breakfast, over cappuccinos with dollops of foam that looked like pointed doges' hats, before venturing into the city. The first stop on my loose itinerary was the Palazzo Ducale, home to the doges who ruled Venice for centuries. I had never actually been inside — in summer, the lines stretch well around it, and I am an impatient tourist. But that January morning, once I left my cozy pensione and ventured into the damp air, I had no trouble joining a tour, complete with a viewing of the cell where Casanova, the infamous lover and libertine, was jailed on charges including blasphemy and Freemasonry. His daring escape was aided, it appears, by guards who hated his inquisitors as much as he did.

High up in the palazzo, the doges' offices were small wooden boxes, surprisingly modest but pleasantly warm. But in the public room where the Council of Ten, which governed Venice for five centuries until nearly 1800, convened in judgment, it was so cold that I could see my breath.

The palazzo was a glorious den of secrets, the setting for any number of intrigues. In one room, the secret service kept its cabinets of traceless poisons. In another, the door to the staircase leading to the hidden prison was disguised as a file cabinet. (In Italy, bureaucracy is always the ultimate means of deception.) In the torture chamber, where the prisoners met their inquisitors, darkness was also part of the torture, the tour guide explained. In this city of resplendent light, how could it not be?

On sunny days, the winter light is brilliant and clear; but on gray days, it diffuses, and land and water merge. In *Watermark*, Brodsky explains to some of his own skeptical inquisitors in New York why he is drawn to Venice in winter. "I thought of telling them about *acqua alta*"—the high waters that flood the city when it rains in winter—"about the various shades of gray in the window as one sits at breakfast in one's hotel, enveloped by silence and the mealy morning pall of newlyweds' faces; about pigeons accentuating every curve and cornice of the local Baroque in their dormant affinity for architecture…about a brave sparrow perching on the bobbing blade of a gondola against the backdrop of a sirocco-roiled damp infinity."

Distorted by light and water, time thickens in Venice. So does sound. What I love best about the city is its glorious quiet, and its strange pace, as if you were living in slow motion. In Venice, hurrying will get you nowhere fast—or perhaps get you lost faster. Then again, it's best to walk briskly in winter, since the city is so damp, the air off the canals so bone-chillingly cold that you have to keep moving to stay warm.

I traipsed down innumerable alleys, stopping sometimes for coffee, past pockets of gondoliers who bounced on their feet against the cold, checking their text messages as they half-heartedly called out for tourists looking for winter rides. The locals were layered in fur coats and hats. I bought myself a pair of maroon and fuchsia leather gloves in a tiny shop that I may never be able to find again.

Inside St. Mark's Basilica, with its splendid gold mosaics and cow-eyed Four Evangelists, the winter light was dusky. I had missed the one hour each morning when it was illuminated and found myself in its "obscure aquarium dimness, the movie-palace dark" that Anthony Hecht describes in his poem "The Venetian Vespers."

On winter nights, the lights of every trattoria beckon, little pockets of warmth against the damp. Once inside, my glasses were forever fogged. More than their southern counterparts, Venetians drink. I took to sipping prosecco at lunch, not a warming drink, but one that paired well with strips of fried polenta and crispy fried fish or with *sarde in saor*, sardines marinated with onion and sugary vinegar. In the weeks before Carnival, 40 days before Easter, when the city becomes a winter zoo, the pastry shops sell *frittelle*—fantastic fried dough baked with raisins and stuffed with ricotta or zabaglione—a meal in itself, and a memorable one.

Above Snow deadens everyday sounds and whitens the air over Venice's liquid highways.

Below The boat traffic is thinner in winter but keeps moving whatever the season.

Opposite Saint Mark's Basilica may be chilly, but its grandeur is undiminished.

My love of Venice began in Boston, where, as an impressionable 12-year-old, I first saw the Isabella Stewart Gardner Museum, a Venetian palazzo built smack in the middle of New England by Gardner and her husband to house their art collection. That visit also instilled my love of house museums, the idiosyncratic collections built up by individuals. Venice is full of such places, from the storied Palazzo Grimani, designed in the Roman style and once home to a celebrated 16th-century archaeological collection, to the Museo Fortuny, a crumbling pile filled with opulent textiles from the Fortuny textile dynasty.

But that winter weekend, with its flat gray skies and thin clouds, it was time to revisit the Peggy Guggenheim collection, which may well be the best 20th-century house museum in the world. Inside the unassuming, low-slung box, I ogled the silver bedpost designed by Alexander Calder, with its happy underwater scene, and contemplated Jackson Pollock's *Enchanted Forest*, an action painting thrumming at a velocity far greater than that of anything else in Venice.

But even here, in this best of collections, the art still somehow felt secondary to the water. Out the mottled glass windows, the canals flowed jade green.

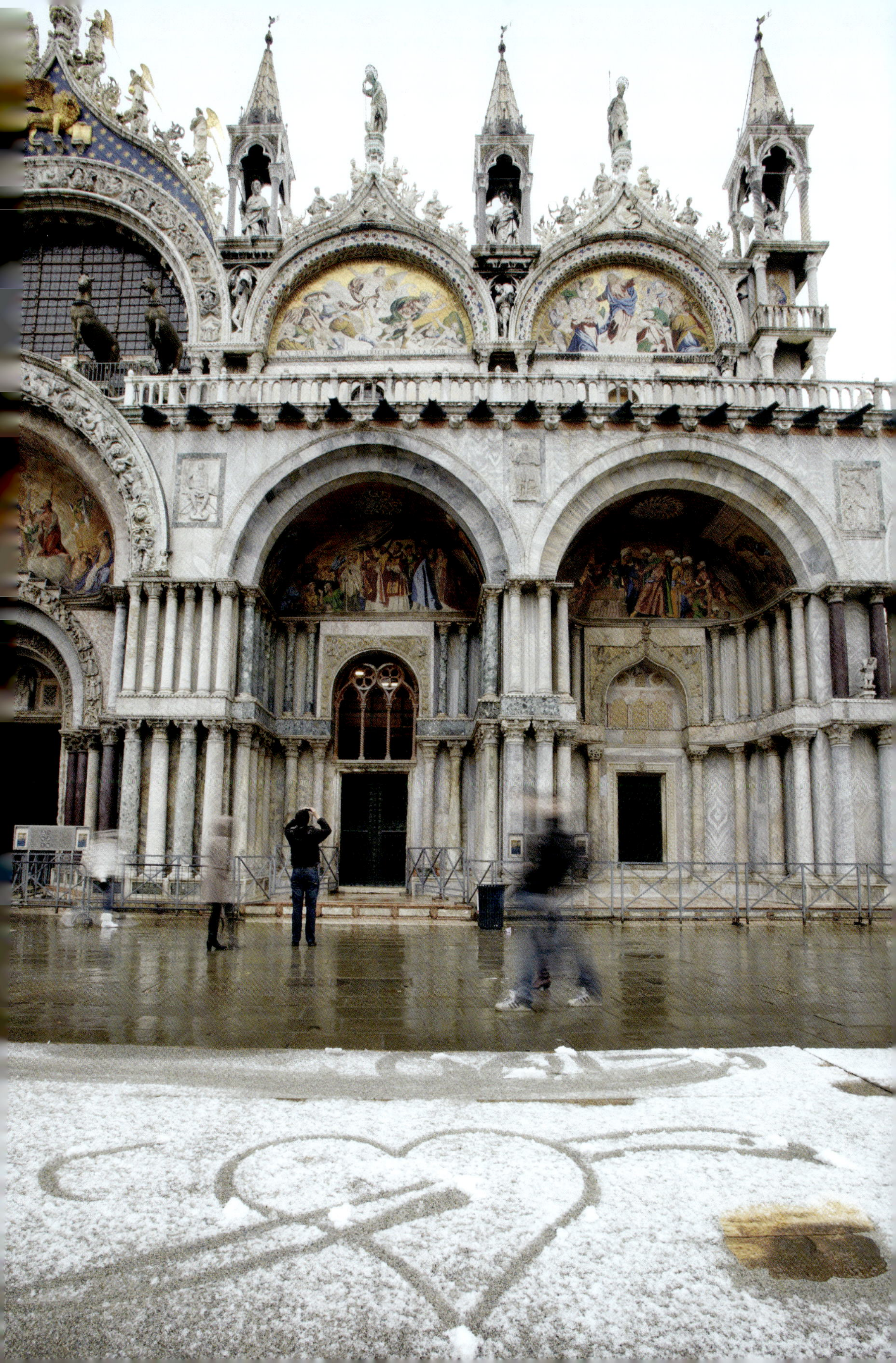

Above Sweepers take a break in the predawn hours in Piazza San Marco.

Opposite Joseph Brodsky described the winter air of Venice as "part damp oxygen, part coffee and prayers."

Boats bobbed on their moorings. I thought of one of my favorite lines from the Italian poet Eugenio Montale: "In the future opening ahead / the mornings are moored like boats."

In the gift shop at the Querini Stampalia Foundation, where water rushes through the ground-floor spaces and the upstairs rooms are filled with art by Giovanni Bellini and Pietro Longhi, I found a copy of Casanova's *My Escape from Venice Prison*. A typical chapter heading: "The Escape, I Nearly Lose My Life on the Roof; I Get Out of the Ducal Palace, Take a Boat, and Reach the Mainland; Danger to Which I Am Exposed by Father Balbi; My Scheme for Ridding Myself of Him."

Late one night in Piazza San Marco, I came upon six women holding an impromptu party. They had brought their food in Tupperware, and as they popped open a bottle of prosecco, they sang "Happy Birthday" in German, their out-of-key voices ringing into the clear night air. At midnight, the bells boomed and echoed across the vast marble expanse of the piazza.

In winter, by day, even the pigeons in the square seem subdued. In a haunting passage in Evelyn Waugh's *Brideshead Revisited*, the narrator likens pigeons to memories. "These memories, which are my life — for we possess nothing certainly except the past — were always with me," he begins. "Like the pigeons of St. Mark's, they were everywhere, under my feet, singly, in pairs, in little honey-voiced congregations, nodding, strutting, winking, rolling the tender feathers of their necks, perching sometimes, if I stood still, on my shoulder or pecking a broken biscuit from between my lips; until, suddenly, the noon gun boomed and in a moment, with a flutter and sweep of wings, the pavement was bare and the whole sky above dark with a tumult of fowl."

I had first read those lines at an early age, and they had shaped me somehow, so that when I first

*Photographs by
Dave Yoder*

visited Venice at 19 — staying in a horrible hostel on the Giudecca run by surly nuns — I felt as if I already knew those pigeons. They were already my memories, too, even if I had only just met them.

On that first visit to Venice and on every single one since, one thing has been the same: I didn't really want to leave. As I headed back to the train station at the end of my Brodsky weekend, carrying my little suitcase, a wet snow began to fall. It landed on the trees in the semi-hidden courtyard gardens and melted into the canals. En route, I took a few wrong turns, but I didn't mind at all. "Anzi," as the Italians say, au contraire. I thought that this might just be true happiness: being semi-lost in Venice on a cold and snowy day.

WHAT TO READ AND WATCH

Watermark, by Joseph Brodsky. The Nobel Prize–winning poet's prose poem to Venice.

Venice: A New History, by Thomas F. Madden. Storytelling and scholarship in a narrative history of the city.

Blue Guide Literary Companion to Venice. An anthology of writing on Venice from authors including Lord Byron, Casanova, Dickens, Goethe, Henry James, Thomas Mann, and Mark Twain.

Death at La Fenice, by Donna Leon. A book in the engaging Commissario Guido Brunetti series featuring an erudite Venice cop who solves crimes among the canals and stone bridges.

Wings of the Dove, directed by Iain Softley. A 1997 adaptation of the Henry James novel. It's not winter, but the Venice in this film is atmospheric and tourist-free, with glimpses of life in a palazzo.

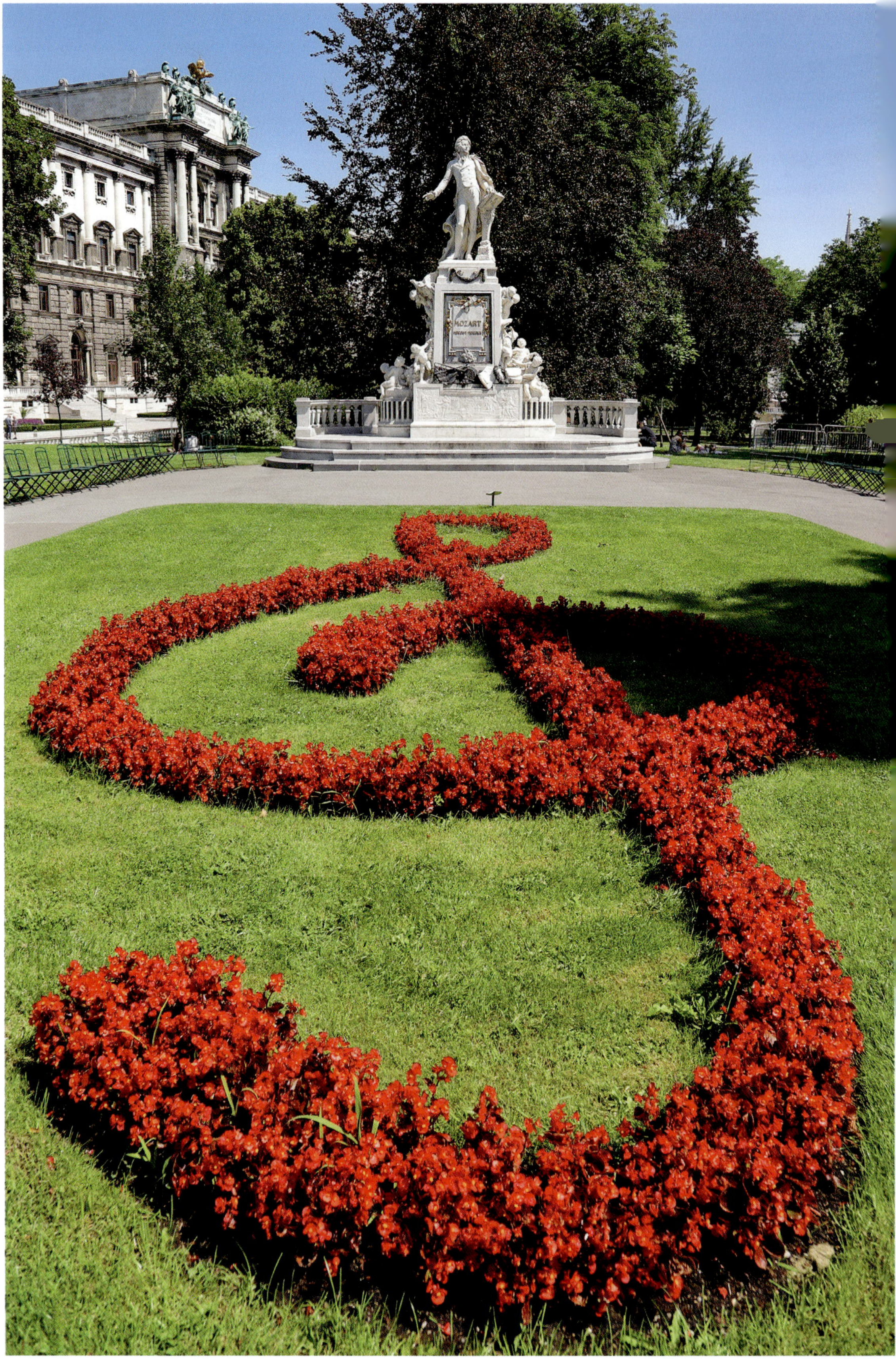
MOZART

STALKING THE MEMORY OF MOZART IN VIENNA

Kitschy souvenirs and musical fluff trade on his fame, but to feel the great composer's presence, a disciple has to go deeper. — BY LISA SCHWARZBAUM

Leopold Mozart would have admired the marketing skills of the persistent young men in ratty wigs and fraying red waistcoats prowling the Stephansplatz, Vienna's central square. Just as the elder Mozart aggressively promoted the talents of his son Wolfgang Amadeus, these costumed hawkers were on a similar promotional mission: Their assignment was to drum up customers for the steady output of ingratiatingly light, short-attention-span classical performances programmed around town especially for tourists drawn to one of the most famous cities in Western music history.

A visitor couldn't go terribly wrong listening to these barkers in their cartoon costumes mimicking the great composer, whose image also graces the boxes of foil-wrapped, chocolate-and-marzipan *Mozartkugeln* sold around town. After all, a bite-size portion of *Eine Kleine Nachtmusik* is better than no "Little Night Music" at all. But I waved off all enterprising impostors, with their handbills and hustles. I was in Vienna looking for remnants of the real man.

Inevitably, while I was at it, I walked in the footsteps of plenty of other giants of the classical repertory who made Vienna their home over the last three centuries. Celebrated resident musicians have included Ludwig van Beethoven, Johannes Brahms, Anton Bruckner, Franz Schubert, Antonio Vivaldi, Franz Liszt, Gustav Mahler, Arnold Schoenberg, Hugo Wolf, and a passel of Strausses, among them Johann senior and junior, and the unrelated Richard.

The little pension in which I set up Mozart-stalking headquarters was on an unprepossessing side street equidistant from the Vienna State Opera and the Stadtpark. In one direction stood the imposing opera

VIENNA   AUSTRIA

Previous A monument to Mozart in the Burggarten park. Vienna venerates its deep connections to classical music.

Left Mozart's grave is unmarked, but it is thought to be in St. Marx Cemetery, where this monument carries a message of hope.

Opposite Mozart introduces appreciative Viennese to the music of *Don Giovanni* in this 19th-century engraving.

house (rebuilt and restored after wartime destruction in 1945), where Mahler conducted from 1897 to 1907 and introduced the radical notion of dimming the theater lights during performances. (A quick detour on a street behind the building leads to a plaque noting where Vivaldi once lived.) In the other direction lay the stately Stadtpark, with its sculpted monuments to Bruckner, Schubert, Franz Lehar, and Johann Strauss Jr. That last, an ornate masterwork of selfie bait called the Johann Strauss Golden Statue, features the waltz king poised with fiddle and bow as if to strike up "The Blue Danube" waltz.

Mozart probably set some kind of record for changes of Viennese address. Born in 1756 in Salzburg, 160 miles to the west, he moved to Vienna in 1781, when he was 25. And in the next 10 years, until his death in 1791, Wolfgang (along with his wife, Constanze, and the two of his six children who lived past infancy) occupied some dozen apartments, all of them within the city's inner District 1. Sometimes the tenancy lasted a matter of weeks or months.

There are plaques, but no extant homes, to show for Mozart's first two addresses, at Singerstrasse 7 and Milchgasse 1 beside St. Peter's Church. There is no plaque at all at Graben 17. And to find any commemorative notification of Mozart's last address, on Rauhensteingasse 8, I had to head to the rear of the Steffl department store, which occupies the footprint of the apartment building, demolished in 1847, in which Mozart and his family were living when he died.

On the other hand, one very solid edifice where the great man once walked continues to do big business. After two years as husband and wife, Wolfgang and Constanze moved in 1784 to fine digs at Domgasse 5, and they lived there for three years. (That was a record of stability for the couple; pity the missus, forever packing the family knickknacks and supervising 18th-century moving vans.)

Music poured out of Mozart in that happy, prosperous time — concertos, chamber works, *The Marriage of Figaro*. And drink flowed, too, for guests including Haydn. Johann Nepomuk Hummel moved in for a time as Mozart's student. Beethoven, still in his teens, intended to pop in for lessons, too, and set out from Bonn, Germany, to do so, but had to turn around and head home when his mother became ill.

Today the building is renamed Mozarthaus Vienna. Managed by the city's Wien Museum, it has been substantially renovated and spiffed up to emulate a model of modern exhibition showmanship: a relatively small nub of historical authenticity padded out with slick, somewhat Disneyfied interpretive displays and audiovisual installations. Above all, the gift shop looms large, hawking Mozart pencils, key chains, perfumes, playing cards, paper napkins, thimbles, miniature busts, chocolates, golf balls, and snap-on cases for cell phones.

Leopold Mozart would have been so impressed. But all those gaudy golf balls left me feeling vaguely bested by souvenirs. I walked back toward Stephansplatz, the setting of the Gothic St. Stephen's Cathedral (the Stephansdom) and a central point in the city since well before Mozart's day.

Steps from the cathedral is Café Frauenhuber, said to be Vienna's oldest coffeehouse. Mozart loved the place (although in his day it was at a different address), and reportedly made his last public performance there. An even shorter walk from the cathedral, in the other direction, is Griechenbeisl, a restaurant serving carnivores since 1447, including Mozart, Beethoven, and Schubert, and Mark Twain, too.

But it was inside the Stephansdom, a magnificent symbol of all Vienna, and not over lunch that I found relief from my consternation over the gift-shop frivolity. Indeed, I contemplated life and death. After all, Wolfgang Amadeus and Constanze were married in the Stephansdom, in 1782. Two of their children were christened there. And an unspectacular requiem Mass (with none of Mozart's music) was celebrated there after Mozart's death. A plaque commemorates the event.

Haydn, once a Stephansdom choirboy, was married in the church (in 1760), as was Johann Strauss Jr. At the other end of life's procession, the names of Vivaldi, Antonio Salieri, and Schubert appear in the cathedral's death register.

Clearly, it was time for me to visit the final resting place of the man whose music Albert Einstein described as "so pure that it seemed to have been ever-present in the universe, waiting to be discovered by the master." But where exactly was he resting? I took a tram ride away from the city bustle to the divinely quiet St. Marx Cemetery, where Mozart's coffin was transported by coach. In contrast to legend and a scene in the Oscar-winning 1984 movie *Amadeus*, the body was not interred as that of a nameless pauper.

Above Mozart-themed souvenirs are all over Vienna, even in the Christmas market. Look for the *Mozartkugel* confections.

Opposite The Burgtheater today. In the 18th century, when Mozart operas premiered there, it was located at a site nearby.

Rather, adhering to a decree by the efficiency- and sanitation-minded Emperor Joseph II, his burial, like all others, took place in a communal, unmarked grave.

Unfortunately, without marking, Mozart's resting place could not be found by the time his widow went looking for it years after his death (ill from grief, she hadn't attended his funeral). In the intervening years, the bones in his contingent of dead souls had probably been dug up and reinterred to make room for the more recently deceased. Not until 1855 was an approximation of the grave site selected in a grassy stretch of those communal graves, and a memorial built.

The cemetery stayed open for new business only another 19 years, closing in 1874. No wonder it is such a satisfyingly moody, atmospherically disheveled sanctuary, thick with vegetation and mournful with pockets of disrepair. Lilacs bloom there in springtime, but late November was a nicely raw time to walk among the Biedermeier-period headstones.

And it was easy to find the romantically lachrymose memorial so often photographed today; just enter the main gate and follow the signs to Mozartgrab (Mozart grave), where a grieving angel rests a right elbow, heavy with sorrow, on the base of an artfully broken marble column, and flowers are enhanced by offerings from reverent visitors.

Then again, this particular statuary has been around only since 1950, while the stone artwork installed in 1855 was moved to one last, and lasting, Viennese site of Mozartean contemplation. And so off I went by tram again, to the city's central cemetery, the Zentralfriedhof. It is central, that is, to the history of the city: One of the largest burial sites in the world, it is, in fact, on the outskirts of town. Yet the founders were canny.

To draw visitors, Zentralfriedhof plans always included a selection of "honorary" graves (*Ehrengräber*). And chief among the honored are the city's

Photographs by Franz Neumayr

musical greats, which is why the graves of Brahms and Schoenberg receive such regular foot traffic. And why the remains of Beethoven and Schubert were moved there in 1888, now flanking Mozart in a place of honor.

A stiff wind picked up as I stood in front of the three. Bits of Mozart's own transcendent Requiem played in my head. Far from the concert carnies of Stephansplatz and the kitschy key chains of Mozarthaus Vienna, I was refreshed, sated. As I took the No. 71 tram back toward my pension, I experienced the fervor Schubert felt when he wrote in his 1816 diary, "O Mozart, immortal Mozart, how many, how infinitely many inspiring suggestions of a finer, better life you have left in our souls!"

WHAT TO READ AND WATCH

Mozart: The Man Revealed, by John Suchet. An enjoyable and well-written biography of Mozart, digestible for readers who are not music scholars.

1791: Mozart's Last Year, by H.C. Robbins. A well-known musicologist and editor of Mozart's collected works looks at the composer's last months, separating fact from myth.

Mozart's Women: His Family, His Friends, His Music, by Jane Glover. Glover, a conductor and Mozart scholar, brings to life the women who shared Mozart's world, supporting and inspiring his work.

"A Genius Finds Inspiration in the Music of Another," by Arthur I. Miller, *The New York Times*, January 31, 2006. Albert Einstein, besides upending the world of physics, played the violin and was fascinated with Mozart.

Amadeus, directed by Milos Forman. The classic 1984 film, adapted from Peter Shaffer's play.

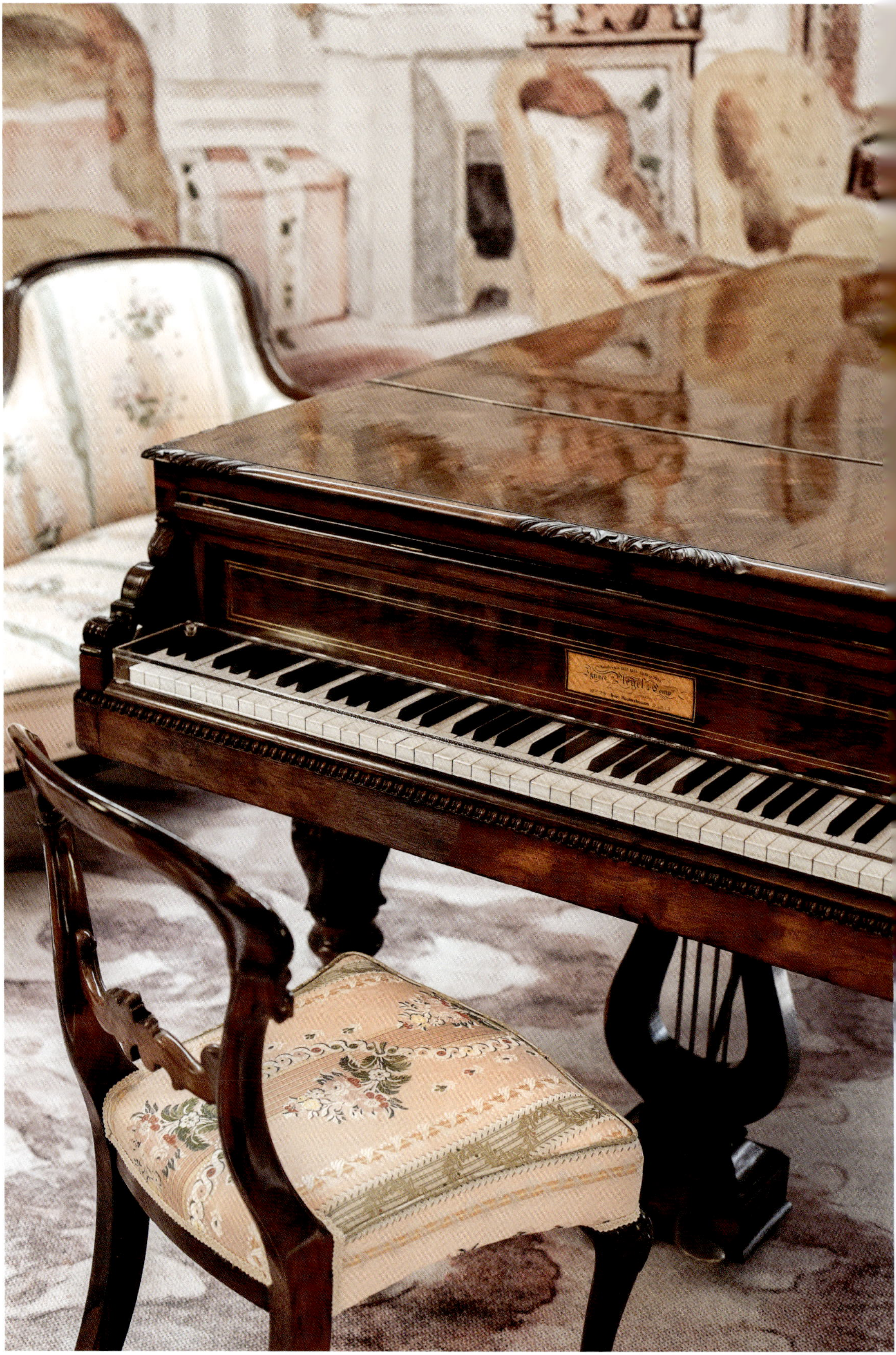

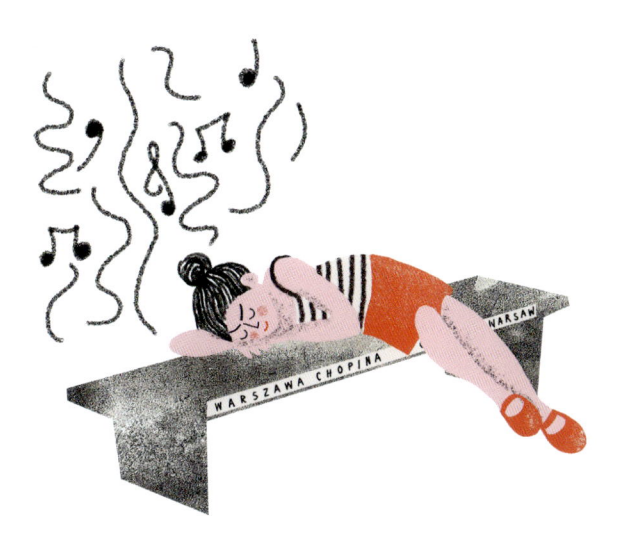

WARSAW'S LOVE AFFAIR WITH CHOPIN

The composer spent much of his life in France, but he was a patriot, and his heart, literally, is in Poland.
— BY LUCAS PETERSON

When I was growing up and taking weekly piano lessons, I loved playing Chopin. His melodic lines soared above a sea of dreamy romanticism. While culturally adopted by the French, Frédéric (Fryderyk, in his native language) Chopin was, of course, Polish, born outside Warsaw in 1810 to a Polish mother and a father who had emigrated from France, reared in the city from the age of 6. The November Uprising, however, forced him from his homeland at a young age, and he was never able to return before his death at 39.

Chopin is Poland's superstar composer, and in Warsaw, the national pride in him runs deep. There are events, concerts, monuments, museums, even entire schools named for Chopin. My personal love for the composer's music brought me to his hometown, eager to learn about his life. But with the help of some local connections, I gained much more from my visit — a deeper understanding and appreciation of a city that was historically one of Eastern Europe's most cosmopolitan capitals, yet repeatedly disrupted by invasions and wars.

"Don't make a picture of that, please," said Malgorzata, my kind and generous Polish host with whom I stayed (she is the mother of a friend). I obeyed, tilting my camera down from the Palace of Culture and Science, an impressive ornate structure in the center of the city that's also the tallest building in Poland. She laughed and said she was just joking, but there was a kernel of truth in her jest. The building, she explained, was Russian, not Polish — an important distinction. "A gift from Stalin," she said dryly.

Warsaw, like many places in Eastern Europe, has a painful and many-faceted relationship with neighboring powers. Russia's influence (and its "gifts") are evident in much of the prosaic, blocky architecture found throughout the city. The Old Town, with its

Previous Chopin's last piano, treasured and proudly displayed in the Fryderyk Chopin Museum in Warsaw.

Left The Dutch artist Ary Scheffer painted this portrait of Chopin in 1847.

Opposite Ruined in World War II, the Old Town was painstakingly restored and now looks much as it did in Chopin's day.

beautiful muted colors, is old in name only — a faithful reconstruction of the original that was almost destroyed by the Nazis during World War II. Like many an intrepid tourist, I made the 150-step climb up to the top of the St. Anne's Church bell tower for its great views of the Old Town.

Malgosia (a nickname for Malgorzata) and I walked toward the Warsaw Philharmonic to attend an evening concert. The concert hall was originally built between 1900 and 1901 and was reconstructed in the 1950s. I suggested we take an Uber, which I found to be safe and reliable in Warsaw; she said she preferred her tried-and-true (and much cheaper) public transportation. We compromised, taking the bus and Metro there and an Uber back. She jokingly chided me with a "tsk" as I pulled up the app on my phone. I felt downright profligate.

The concert program, which included an Alexandre Tansman piano concerto and a Pawel Klecki orchestral piece, was excellent and featured great musicianship from the pianist Jonathan Plowright. During the intermission, we walked across the parquet floor of a high-ceilinged reception hall, stopping to admire busts of Chopin and Ignacy Jan Paderewski, a prominent composer and politician. Paderewski, who fought for Polish independence from Germany in the early 20th century, was an even more important Polish figure than Chopin, Malgosia said, "emotionally and politically."

Music is in the streets in Warsaw's center, and I heard plenty of it during my downtown perambulations. Public benches were doing double duty as boombox and furniture around the city — in locations like Krasinski Square, or Saski Palace, the Chopin family's former residence — playing snippets of some of Chopin's famous nocturnes and polonaises.

Sometimes a more direct approach is used to lure music lovers. "Chopin Concert Today at 6 p.m." read a large banner hung on a building on Swietokrzyska Street. It was the House of Music, a venue for concerts and recitals, and I purchased a ticket to the evening's performance, solo piano. The environment was perfect for an intimate recital — a parlor-like setting with tables where patrons could sip tea or coffee. Probably this was how the music was originally heard.

The pianist, María Márquez Torres, burst through the door a few minutes after start time, threw off her coat, and took her place at the piano. Her hasty entrance translated to a somewhat sloppy performance of a polonaise and a ballade. She settled in, though, with a crowd-pleasing rendition of Albéniz's "Suite Española." Different artists rotate through the House

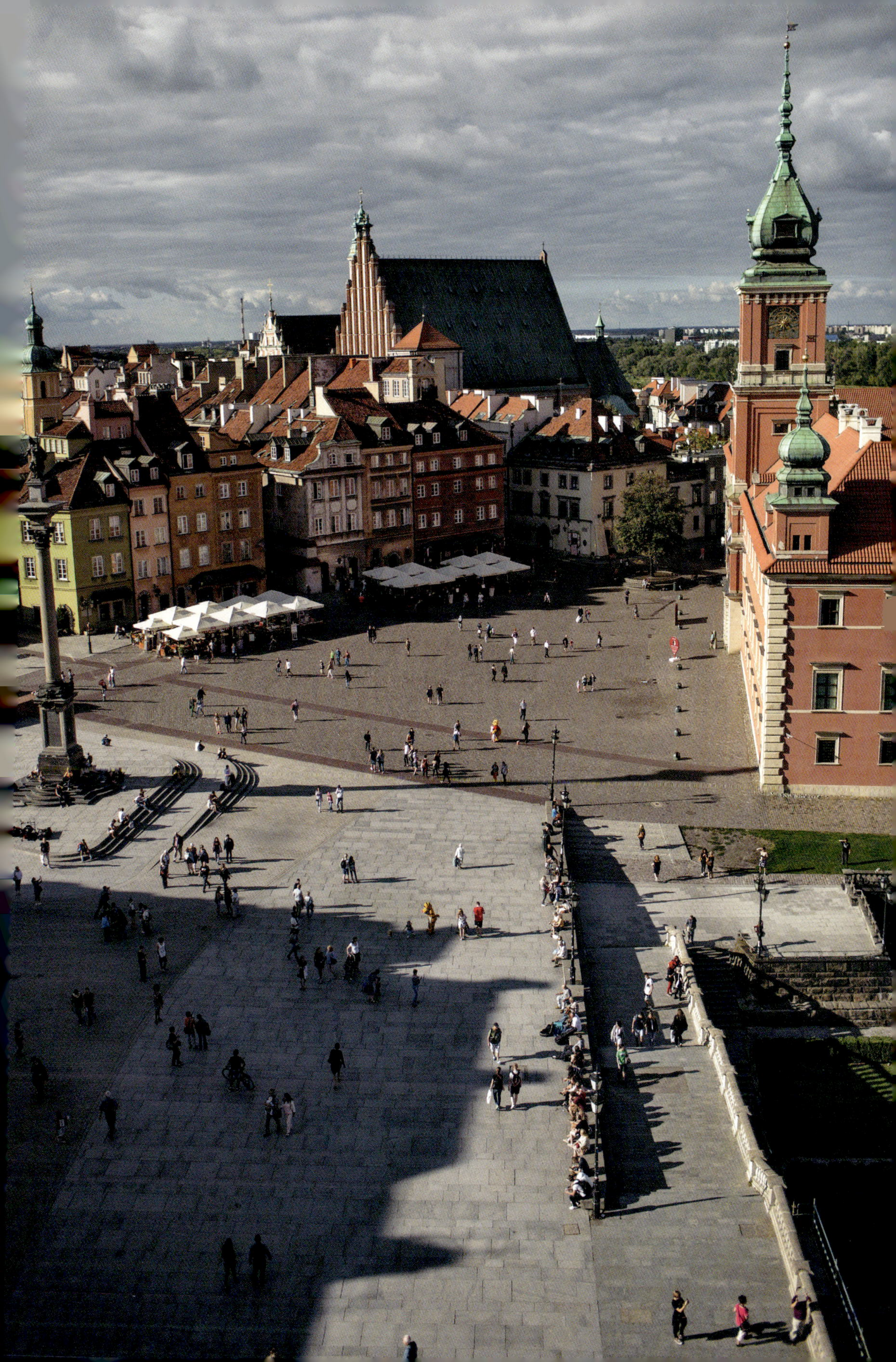

Above A pedestrian street in the old city. On some blocks, benches play Chopin's music when a button is pressed.

Opposite Chopin pilgrims take day trips to his birthplace in Zelazowa Wola, west of Warsaw.

of Music, and the schedule changes frequently — my experience was fun, although not up to the level of the Philharmonic concert.

The Fryderyk Chopin Museum, a quick walk from the House of Music, is a must for anyone with even a passing interest in Chopin. There are old manuscripts, concert posters, personal effects, and interactive exhibits (for example, something called *Twister Muzyczny*—musical Twister) that take you through nearly every stage of the composer's brief life. One of the highlights for me was getting to see his last piano. Built sometime in the 1840s by Ignace Pleyel, the beautiful 82-key specimen seemed to radiate the energy and sadness that characterized much of Chopin's music.

There's an entire room dedicated to the women in Chopin's life (he was a popular fellow, apparently). The details of his relationships with Maria Wodzinska, the opera singer Jenny Lind, Jane Stirling, and, of course, George Sand are all represented. What I found particularly fascinating, though, was the exhibit that focused on Chopin's love of opera. The young composer was obsessed with Italian opera, particularly the work of Rossini, and would attend performances at the National Theater whenever he had a chance. While he never wrote an opera, Chopin's adoration makes perfect sense — the concept of bel canto is readily reflected in the melodies of his works.

After leaving the museum, I went across the way and walked around the Fryderyk Chopin University of Music, where I could hear students practicing their instruments, singing, or accompanying one another.

Getting to know Chopin doesn't mean being bound by the city limits. An easy day trip from Warsaw is to his birthplace, Zelazowa Wola, a 35-minute train ride from central Warsaw followed by a short bus ride. The museum is limited — it's essentially just a small

Photographs by Adam Lach

house—but there is a beautiful surrounding park where concerts are held on summer weekends.

The most moving monument to Chopin's life, however, is free. When Chopin, who was chronically ill throughout most of his adult life, died, apparently of tuberculosis, his body was buried in Paris's famous Père Lachaise cemetery (today's fans have been known to leave cough drops on his grave). His heart, however, belonged to Poland—literally. Chopin made a request to his sister, Ludwika, that she return his heart to Poland to be buried. She agreed, secreting it out of France.

When I visited the Church of the Holy Cross, across from Warsaw University, I approached a white pillar with a simple inscription: "Tu Spoczywa Serce Fryderyka Chopina." Here rests the heart of Frédéric Chopin—a sad, but deeply poetic denouement for a man who was truly one of the great poets of the keyboard.

WHAT TO READ AND WATCH

Fryderyk Chopin: A Life and Times, by Alan Walker. Described in a *New York Times* review as "a magisterial portrait."

Chopin: Desire for Love, directed by Jerzy Antczak. Film centered on the relationship between Chopin and George Sand.

In Search of Chopin, written and directed by Phil Grabsky. An absorbing portrait of Chopin, accompanied by his music.

Impromptu, directed by James Lapine. A young Hugh Grant takes his turn playing Chopin.

Chopin Picture Album, a two-and-a-half-minute video available on YouTube. As several dozen images of Chopin flash by, his Étude Op. 10, No. 9 sounds in the background, played by Paul Barton.

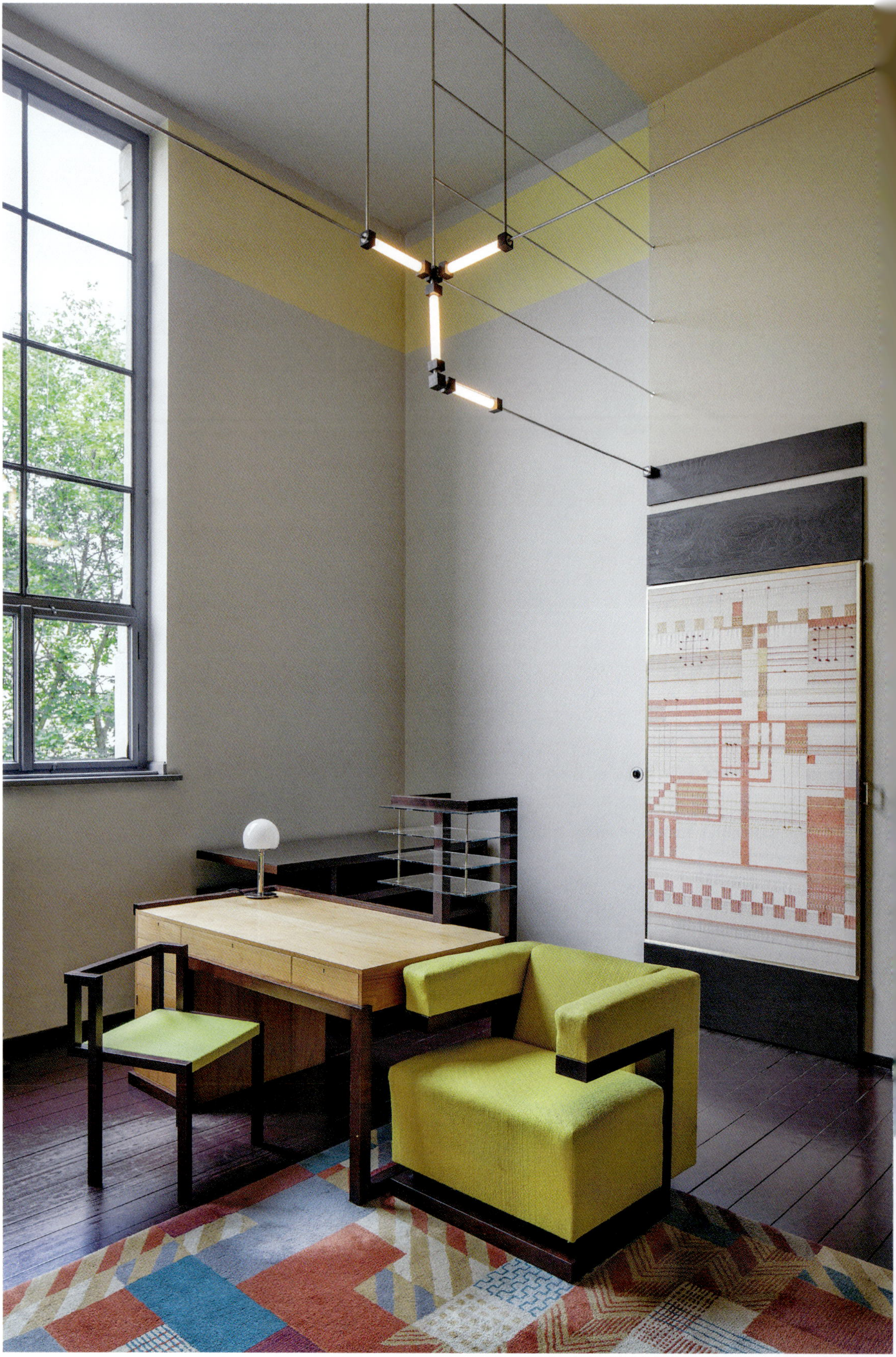

GERMANY　　　　　　　　　　　　　　　　　　　　　　　　WEIMAR & DESSAU

ON THE BAUHAUS TRAIL

In three German cities, over 14 years, artists and architects redefined design for the modern world.
— BY CHARLY WILDER

Weimar, a leafy picture-book tourist town about 50 miles southwest of Leipzig, has an outsized cultural significance in Germany. The hometown of Goethe and Schiller, and the first seat of the short-lived democracy between the world wars, it is increasingly conscious of its importance for another cultural milestone: It was the birthplace of the Bauhaus.

It was here that Walter Gropius, a handsome 36-year-old architect decorated for valor in World War I, was asked to head a new school formed from the merger of the Weimar state schools of applied and fine arts. When he opened the Bauhaus in 1919, he recruited master teachers and called for artists and craftsmen to create the "building of the future." For the next 14 years, the Bauhaus pursued a global vision, one so wildly influential that it's difficult today to find some corner of design, architecture, or the arts that doesn't bear its traces. The tubular chair, the glass-and-steel office tower, the clean uniformity of contemporary graphic design — so much of what we associate with the word *modernism* — has roots in this small German art school.

Now the Bauhaus is experiencing something of a revival, with interest in its unique contributions growing around the world, especially among young artists. Yet when I followed the Bauhaus trail by train, traveling among Germany's major Bauhaus sites, I encountered a historical oddity: Despite its global import, the Bauhaus is not widely revered in its country of origin.

This has something to do with the fact that Bauhaus is also the name, somewhat confusingly, of Germany's largest home improvement chain. But there's a bigger reason, which can be glimpsed through the window of a Deutsche Bahn train hurtling through the outskirts of nearly any German city. The proliferation of

Previous Walter Gropius's office at the original location of the Bauhaus in Weimar.

Left The Bauhaus Building, designed by Gropius, rises over Dessau like a futuristic message from the past.

Opposite Masters of the Bauhaus: Lyonel Feininger, Wassily Kandinsky, Oskar Schlemmer, Georg Muche, and Paul Klee.

cheap, boxlike concrete-slab high-rises that spread like bacteria throughout Germany's bombed-out cities after World War II is seen by many as a Bauhaus legacy, for better or worse.

The Bauhaus combined the fine arts, crafts, and design under one roof with the aim of creating a Gesamtkunstwerk, or total work of art. Although it moved twice, to Dessau and then Berlin, it began in Weimar, and its development paralleled that of the Weimar Republic, rising from the rubble of the First World War, flourishing amid the political, economic, and cultural chaos of the interwar years, and ending with the rise of Hitler. Bauhaus teachers included some of the most important artists of the modern era —notably Wassily Kandinsky and Paul Klee—many of whom fled Germany after the school's closure, leading them to pollinate Bauhaus ideas throughout the world.

The small but striking Bauhaus Museum Weimar, in a building designed by the architect Heike Hanada, has about 1,000 items on permanent display, including 168 objects donated to Weimar by Gropius when the school left the city in 1925. There are also examples of Bauhaus design like Marcel Breuer's tubular steel and leather chairs and a variety of household objects and toys.

From there it's about a 20-minute walk to the Bauhaus campus, which occupied a suite of Art Nouveau buildings and is now the home of Bauhaus University, an arts academy. Current and former students lead Bauhaus Walks through the studios where the Bauhaus students attended workshops categorized by craft—woodworking, painting, weaving, and such.

Visitors can also see reconstructions of fantastic wall murals (the originals were destroyed by a Nazi-appointed administration) with Oskar Schlemmer's stylized human figures, a clear influence on Fritz Lang's 1927 film *Metropolis*. Tours visit Gropius's faithfully reconstructed office, which was a showpiece for the first official Bauhaus exhibition in 1923. Like an antigravity Rubik's Cube, the entire room is defined by a square-within-a-square concept, from the seemingly floating arms of the rectangular wood-and-canvas armchair to a lighting system made of tubular bulbs affixed to aluminum rods by wooden linking cubes.

The early Bauhaus was "more than a school," as Tom Wolfe wrote in his 1981 book *From Bauhaus to Our House*. "It was a commune, a spiritual movement, a radical approach to art in all its forms, a philosophical center comparable to the Garden of Epicurus."

With their long hair and androgynous clothing, Bauhaus students lived together, worked together, and held wild, legendary parties built around themes (Lantern Festival, Kite Festival) that in later years became increasingly high-concept (Metal Festival; Beard, Nose, and Heart Party).

Life at the Bauhaus was in many ways a precursor to the bohemianism that took hold in America's liberal arts colleges half a century later. The student body was international and diverse, with women making up about half. Though this gender balance was outwardly encouraged, Gropius internally asked that all women be funneled into the weaving workshop, with pottery and bookbinding as alternatives. Nevertheless, several women made names for themselves, including the metalworker Marianne Brandt, whose slick, otherworldly teapots became icons of industrial design.

The school's early Expressionist direction was shaped by the eccentric Swiss painter Johannes Itten, who taught the Bauhaus's famous required course on the fundamentals of color, form, and material. A self-styled mystic who shaved his head and dressed in robes, Itten was the school's resident mad priest. His studio was in the Tempelherrenhaus, a mock-Gothic tower partly designed by Goethe that was damaged in World War II. Its ruins today look out on the spot where Itten required his first-year students to do yoga, chanting, and breathing exercises.

When Nazis joined the Thuringian regional parliament in 1924, the Bauhaus knew it was time to ship out. In 1925 it moved to the rising factory town of Dessau, and work began on its new, radically modern headquarters. Today the Bauhaus Building rises over Dessau like a futuristic message from the past. With its suspended glass facades, exposed steel gridding, and asymmetrical layout, the three-wing complex feels both modern and familiar. But when it was finished in 1926, it was downright alien.

Dessau opened a new Bauhaus museum in 2019, a low-lying glass structure designed by the Barcelona architecture firm González Hinz Zabala. But the Bauhaus Building is still at the heart of Dessau's Bauhaus experience. Like a transparent cube levitating over the town, it was the crystalline culmination of the Bauhaus's global vision. Now it houses a research and teaching institution dedicated to furthering

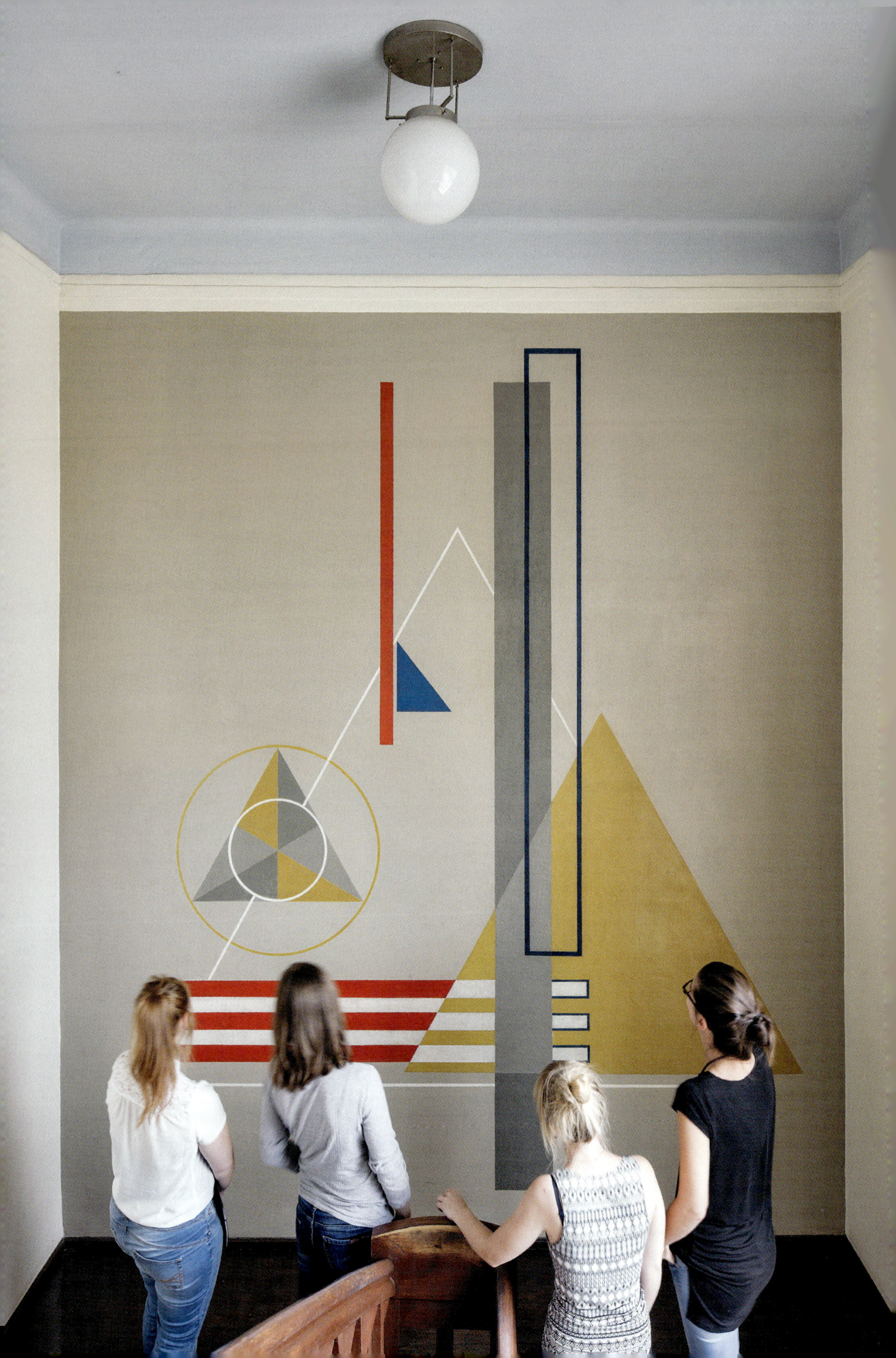

Opposite A Herbert Bayer design on a wall in the Bauhaus building in Weimar.

Right Gropius's office in Dessau. The Bauhaus group moved there in 1925 to escape Nazi influence in Weimar.

Bauhaus ideas. Guided tours explore the building and the nearby Masters' Houses, a suite of partly reconstructed residences where Gropius, Klee, Moholy-Nagy, Albers, and the other Bauhaus masters lived.

It's impossible to experience the prismatic, cinematic effect of the Bauhaus Building without moving through and around it. The building looks out at itself, glass-and-steel grids that layer into lattice, creating ever-new angles and futuristic vistas. Glass curtain walls extend to transparent corners. Large panels of steel-framed glass windows open with the pull of a chain. It's not hard to trace a thread between the building and the layered transparencies and light play in the work of the Hungarian artist Laszlo Moholy-Nagy, who joined the Bauhaus in 1923 at age 28, replacing Itten, and quickly became Gropius's most influential colleague.

For visitors who want an immersive experience, the Bauhaus Dessau Foundation offers overnight stays in the Studio Building, which once housed junior masters and promising students. Historical authenticity extends to the communal bathroom on each hall, but for the Bauhaus pilgrim, there's no better way to spend the night.

Lying in a studio room, looking out huge paneled windows over the pitched red roofs of Dessau, I wondered what it must have been like for students inside this futuristic laboratory while, outside, a poverty-stricken Germany churned with reactionary chaos. What seems spartan today felt to many Bauhaus students, according to their written recollections, like paradise: a room and three meals a day, served in the Studio Building's first-floor canteen, which today offers hearty, no-frills German fare.

The canteen connects to the auditorium, where Oskar Schlemmer, as head of the Bauhaus theater workshops, put on his phenomenal avant-garde stage productions, including his masterpiece, the *Triadic Ballet*, first performed in 1922. Dancers in Schlemmer's rigid, voluminous, geometric costumes became living sculptures moving mathematically, like marionettes, over fields of color—a plastic metaphysical vision that would haunt the performance art of Robert Wilson, David Bowie, Lady Gaga, and others.

Over time, the emphasis at the Bauhaus shifted more and more toward architecture, especially residential buildings for the working class. Under the motto "Licht, Luft und Sonne" (light, air and sun), designing the living space of the future became the highest purpose of the Bauhaus and the German modernist architectural movement known as *Neues Bauen*.

Above Gropius designed this students' building in Dessau. Bauhaus architecture was adventurous, its influence lasting.

Opposite The Fagus Factory near Hanover, designed in part by Gropius, is a Unesco World Heritage Site.

The construction of low-cost prefab housing became increasingly important to Gropius, who resigned from the Bauhaus in 1928 to devote himself to it. His successor, Hannes Meyer, a radical functionalist, reorganized the school, yet his staunch Communist affiliations led to the rise of a large Communist cell within the school.

The press attacked, and Meyer resigned in 1930, heading to Moscow with a "red Bauhaus brigade." His pragmatic replacement, Ludwig Mies van der Rohe, transformed the Bauhaus in its latter years into a full-fledged school of architecture.

When the Nazis took control of the Dessau City Council, the Bauhaus was forced to move yet again. In 1932, Mies set up the school in an abandoned factory in Berlin, financing it with his own money. But 10 months later the Gestapo shut the Bauhaus down for good.

Though the Bauhaus existed in Berlin for less than a year, the city is filled with remnants of the movement —from the Bauhaus-Archiv, housed in a building that was one of Gropius's last designs, to the Museum Berggruen's collection of around 60 Paul Klee paintings and the Kandinskys of the Mies-designed Neue Nationalgalerie. Berlin's most substantial Bauhaus building is the ADGB Trade Union School in the suburb of Bernau, a zigzagging functionalist complex of brick, steel, and glass surrounded by pine forests that was built in 1930 by Hannes Meyer.

Bauhaus-related tours in Berlin visit places like the Mies van der Rohe House, his last architectural project in Germany before he fled the Nazis, and Erich Hamann Bittere Schokoladen, a confectionery housed in a 1928 factory complex designed by the Bauhaus's mad priest himself, Johannes Itten. After the Bauhaus's closure, the Nazis continued to persecute its former members, accusing them of "cultural Bolshevism." Some died in the camps, but many escaped to western Europe and the United States.

*Photographs by
Andreas Meichsner*

Gropius and Breuer were hired by the Harvard Graduate School of Design, where they reshaped the curriculum. Moholy-Nagy founded Chicago's New Bauhaus, which evolved into the Chicago Institute of Design. Mies also settled in Chicago, where he became a celebrated architect. And Josef and Anni Albers set up an art school in the hills of North Carolina called Black Mountain College, a tremendous incubator of the American avant-garde that helped launch the careers of John Cage, Merce Cunningham, Buckminster Fuller, Robert Rauschenberg, and Cy Twombly, among others. In 1938, the Museum of Modern Art cemented the influence of the Bauhaus with a major exhibition.

The great irony of Nazi persecution of the Bauhaus is that driving it out of Germany only served to spread its ideas.

WHAT TO READ AND WATCH

Bauhaus, by Magdalena Droste, published by TASCHEN. An exhaustive survey of the Bauhaus through photographs of its designs and biographies of its key personalities.

From Bauhaus to Our House, by Tom Wolfe. A readable, though disapproving, critique tracing the aesthetics of 20th-century architecture back to the Bauhaus.

The Bauhaus Group: Six Masters of Modernism, by Nicholas Fox Weber. Focuses on six Bauhaus principals: Walter Gropius, Ludwig Mies van der Rohe, Paul Klee, Wassily Kandinsky, and Josef and Anni Albers.

Gropius: The Man Who Built the Bauhaus, by Fiona MacCarthy. A humanistic view of Walter Gropius and the difficult times he lived through.

Metropolis, directed by Fritz Lang. This landmark 1927 silent movie feature features startling visuals heavily influenced by Bauhaus design.

- Agadir to the Sahara Desert 518
- Osun-Osogbo 564
- Cape Coast & Elmina 526

AFRICA & THE MIDDLE EAST

- **Nazareth** 550
- **Jerusalem to Jericho** 538
- **Nile River** 556
- **Maji Moto** 544
- **Dar es Salaam** 532

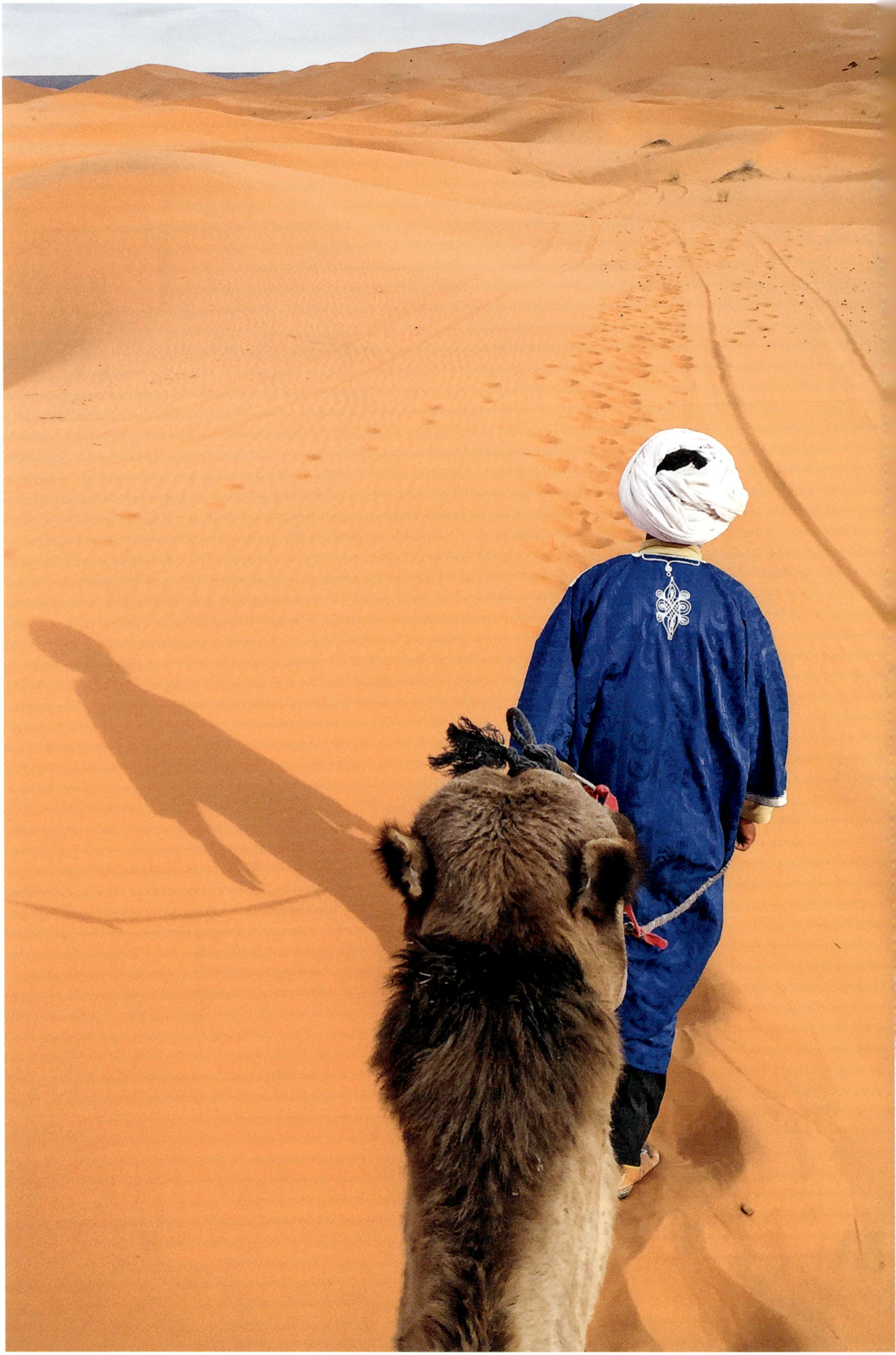

THE SHELTERING SKY OF NORTH AFRICA

Inspired by the travels of American expatriates in Paul Bowles's best-known novel, a journey in Morocco leads into the mystery of the Sahara. — BY SETH SHERWOOD

My head was wrapped in a long blue *chech*, the sun protection worn by Moroccan desert nomads. Nearby, camels snorted and moaned while handlers outfitted them with saddles. Behind me loomed a long two-story dune and an ocean of sand, undulating toward the vanishing point. Several days into a trip in Morocco, I was about to venture into the Sahara.

"Water?" asked Mohamed, the young manager of my hotel, pointing at the tote bag containing my provisions: an orange, a toothbrush and, yes, a bottle of water. The supplies suddenly struck me as recklessly meager. I awaited parting counsel about sun protection, desert navigation, survival tactics, and worst-case scenarios, but Mohamed just smiled. A spring breeze had picked up, conjuring a paranoid thought.

"There's no risk of sandstorms?" I asked. "They start in summer, right?"

"No, they start around now," he said with a grin. Then he walked back into the hotel, leaving me with a teenage guide.

I tried to laugh off the remark. After all, this was only the world's largest desert, a relentless world of sun and scorching sand some 3.5 million square miles in size, where you might stagger directionless for days or weeks in lethal heat without glimpsing any human or animal life, save perhaps a scorpion. What was the worst that could happen?

The Saharan winds first blew through my life when I read *The Sheltering Sky*, Paul Bowles's existential 1940s novel of the unraveling lives of three Americans traveling in the North African desert.

From the first words I was enthralled and unnerved: "He awoke, opened his eyes. The room meant very little to him; he was too deeply immersed in the

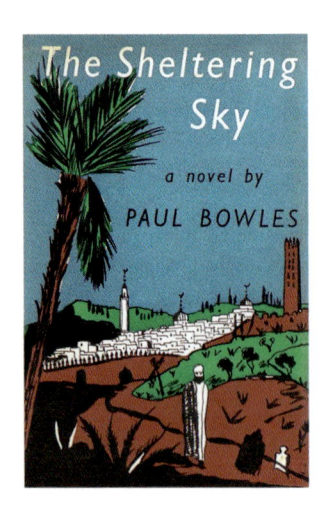

Previous Leading a camel at the Ksar Bicha hotel in Merzouga, Morocco. The hotel takes guests to a camp in the Sahara Desert.

Left A first edition of *The Sheltering Sky*, Paul Bowles's 1949 novel about three naïve Americans in Morocco.

Opposite Paul Bowles's Volkswagen at a stop on a Moroccan mountain road in 1959.

non-being from which he had just come." Elegiac sentences carried me along paths as wondrous as those trod by the novel's nomads, who voyage ever deeper into the indifferent desert. "She was struck by the silence of the place," Bowles writes of Kit Moresby, who is traveling with her husband, Port. "She could have thought there was not a living being within a thousand miles. The famous silence of the Sahara."

The famous silence of the Sahara. The phrase echoed. I ended up writing my master's thesis on the strange fiction of Bowles's wife, Jane, a model for Kit. (Jane and Paul Bowles were based for decades in the Moroccan port city of Tangier until their deaths in 1973 and 1999.) In the succeeding years, I nurtured the same dream as the sheltered mountain girls whose tale forms the thematic filament of *The Sheltering Sky*: to visit the desert, to climb the highest dune, to drink tea in the Sahara. Now the moment had arrived.

I was near the end of a seven-day journey from Atlantic shores to Saharan dunes, inspired by the travels of Port, Kit, and their friend Tunner. My trip took me into a kaleidoscope of centuries-old souks, dusty colonial-era outposts, livestock markets, luxury restaurants, and settings used for Hollywood films.

On the first day, I landed in Marrakesh and then took a bus to Agadir, a coastal getaway favored by Europeans. Knowing I would soon be far inland, I indulged in fresh seafood, cocktails, and the beach. On the boardwalk, the Moroccan middle classes—mustachioed men, shrieking children, women in colorful caftans—strolled among the familiar characters and rituals that unite the world's beaches: the guy twisting balloon hats, the line for ice cream, the teenage boys showing off for local girls.

Come nightfall, I went to the city's marina, a complex of white Spanish-Moorish buildings, and slurped foie gras–topped oysters while listening to two strolling guitarists strumming an Andalusian adaptation of Dave Brubeck's "Take Five." A lively group of Moroccan women with slim leather jackets applauded between drags on cigarettes and sips of cocktails. The whole scene paired perfectly with Domaine de Sahari, a Moroccan vin gris, a light rosé.

The next morning, I set out in the first of several buses, from the CTM and Supratours lines, that I rode on my trip. They took me across the sparse mountain and canyon landscapes of the Berbers, the fair-skinned inhabitants of North Africa who predate the seventh-century Arab invaders and still make up most of southern Morocco's population. The Moresbys and Tunner also traveled on buses, but as Bowles describes their experience—and as it appears in

Bernardo Bertolucci's 1990 film version of *The Sheltering Sky* — it was far less comfortable than mine.

Two hours later I was in Taroudant. I found a maze of narrow lanes lined with low, worn buildings. Veiled women and men in djellabas drifted past rows of halal butchers, bicycle repair stalls, and machine shops. A cacophony of noises resounded: buzzing cheap scooters, honking taxis, clip-clopping horse carts, radios blasting Moroccan pop.

So this was La Petite Marrakesh, as Moroccans have nicknamed Taroudant. Both cities retain time-worn crenellated ramparts, labyrinthine souks, and lively central squares populated with folk healers and snake charmers, but the similarities appeared to end there. Taroudant felt pleasantly devoid of the luxury sheen and global brands that crowd Marrakesh. No Club Med or casinos greeted me here.

Nor did many travelers. I glimpsed few in the outdoor Sunday market beyond Taroudant's walls, accessible through a keyhole-shaped gateway called Bab El-Khemis. The market was a dusty field filled with piles of mismatched shoes, cheap kitchenware, children's clothes, sundry produce, and electronic parts along with fresh-squeezed orange juice (five dirhams a glass). A woman proudly swung a new scythe, almost harvesting a few customers in the process.

A salesman saw me eyeing his goat and grinned. "Miyya dirham!" he bellowed in Arabic. ("A hundred dirhams!") Essential advice: always haggle.

I found a different marketplace in Place el Alouine, the central square where buskers strum long-necked lotars and healers promote their wares. I observed a man swinging a cobra and shrieking in Arabic to amazed onlookers. Across the square, a Berber band strummed and fiddled strange instruments, conjuring cosmic rhythms. Between them, an African man in a skullcap sat on a blanket covered with the vacant skulls, blackened bones, and bowling-ball-size eggs of dead ostriches. "It's medicine for the stomach," he said of the eggs. Then he handed me a plastic bottle whose label was written in French. For "Frigidité sexuelle," it read. "Remède de Testicules."

I politely declined, saving my bargaining skills for the covered lanes of stalls that form Taroudant's souks. My proving ground was Chez Brahim, filled with colorful boxes and bowls made from *tadelakt*, a lime plaster polished with black olive-oil soap for a smooth finish, and silver jewelry inlaid with red coral, turquoise, malachite, jade, and other stones.

"We find these among the mountain people, who wear them for their wedding day and then sell them to us when they need money," said Brahim, the owner, who humored my haggling attempts with the amused countenance of a father watching a child eat his first ice cream cone.

"It used to be the Jews who made them, and the artisans who make them now are following the Jewish tradition," he said, explaining that the city once had a thriving Jewish minority. "They're gone, but we still have the synagogue and the cemetery, with stones written in Hebrew."

He showed me the adjacent Mellah, the old Jewish quarter. No trace of the neighborhood's original character or inhabitants remained. Inside a doorway marked "Riad Argane," I found two middle-aged Berber women sitting on stools and turning grindstones. A young Moroccan man explained in excellent English that the women were crushing nuts from argan trees into an extract that would become oil. In fact, he said, Taroudant province supplies nearly half of Morocco's argan oil, used for cooking and skin care. The women were part of a nationwide antipoverty program employing widows and divorcées.

"It's changed many women's lives by giving them financial autonomy," said Mohamed Zeroual, who expressed surprise at meeting an American in Taroudant. "Americans normally stick to the big cities, Marrakesh, Fez, Tangier." He mused over that last word. "Have you ever read the American writer Paul Bowles?" he asked.

"I am here because of *The Sheltering Sky*," I answered, amazed. "I'm headed to Merzouga to see the desert."

"Ah," he said with a nod before slipping into French. "Merzouga, c'est bien."

Beyond Taroudant the landscape became a world of stone, sand, and scrub with the jagged summits of the Atlas Mountains in the distance. Geological curiosities—huge spilled guts, oversized sand-drip sculptures—rushed past the bus windows. A switchback

Opposite Fruit stands at the bus station in Taroudant, a city known as Little Marrakesh.

Right Argan nuts at different stages, with Berber women's tools for processing them into argan oil.

climbed high ridges and descended into a valley dotted with one-street towns. Then the barren plains resumed.

Suddenly, four hours after leaving Taroudant, the bus was coasting along urban streets lined with shiny new cars, ocher buildings, wrought-iron lampposts, and functioning fountains. Built by the French colonists in the 1920s as a garrison town, the city of Ouarzazate radiated an orderly European feel. Only its sprawling old fortress, a Babel-like jumble of towers and battlements called Kasbah Taourirt, broke the modern aura.

Along Boulevard Mohammed V, the main drag, tour companies trumpeted day trips to valleys, gorges, oases, mountains, fortresses, perched villages, and desert expanses. The town also caters to a more rarefied flock: international film directors. Thanks to their dramatic landscapes, the regions around Ouarzazate have starred in dozens of movies, including *Lawrence of Arabia*, *The Man Who Would Be King*, and *Alexander*.

At Chez Dimitri, the city's oldest restaurant (it opened in 1928), photos of former clients like Ben Kingsley, Gérard Depardieu, Orson Welles, and John Malkovich peered out from the walls. I asked about Malkovich, who played Port Moresby in Bertolucci's film. The restaurant's owner, Pierre Katrakazos—he inherited the restaurant from his father, the namesake Dimitri—said that Malkovich had visited during the shooting.

So had Bowles himself. Bowles had a cameo in the film—as an observant narrator who speaks in the novel's words. "A small man with white hair, accompanied by his driver in an old Ford Mustang," Katrakazos said. "He spoke an excellent French with a few words of English mixed in, like a typical American." Bowles had wanted to chat with Dimitri, whom he had befriended while passing through decades earlier. Told that Dimitri had died, he uttered an English expletive and left.

Local bus No. 1 took me a few miles out of town to Atlas Studios, the place where much of the cinematic magic happens. Led by our guide, Aziz, my tour group walked past a fake fighter jet from the 1980s comedy-adventure film *The Jewel of the Nile*; a Tibetan pagoda-like building from Martin Scorsese's biopic of the Dalai Lama, *Kundun*; and an ersatz ancient village that had figured in *Gladiator*. A fake castle set theatrically before real mountains was used for *Kingdom of Heaven* and then again in *Game of Thrones*.

"This is a legendary location," Aziz told us. He explained that one of its greatest advantages is its

Above In the Dadès Valley, a roadside view of undulating red rock, fortresses, and settlements.

natural light: "It's crisp and clear and golden." Then he turned serious. "The only big enemy here is a potential sandstorm," he said. "You never know. It can happen over a period of an hour. Nobody can predict it."

With those unsettling words in mind, I rode for eight hours the next day in a nearly empty bus toward my final destination, Merzouga. By the time I arrived, night had fallen.

"Monsieur Sherwood?"

Two men in long robes explained that my hotel had sent them. In a subcompact car we rattled down unpaved streets until we reached Ksar Bicha, a sand-colored fortress-like complex. The manager, Mohamed, welcomed me, led me to a second-floor balcony, and pointed into the night. "Tomorrow, when the sun comes up, you will see the dunes," he said. "They are right next to us, just beyond the wall."

Indeed they were. I woke at dawn to the snorts and shouts of camels and their handlers just outside the hotel grounds. Beyond them there was only sand. This was the day when Mohamed tied the chech around my head and helped me and another guest mount our camels to venture into the desert. Then he vanished. A teenage boy named Said, dressed in a blue robe, led our two-camel train into the dunes.

Like boats, we buffeted up and down the waves of sand to the rhythm of the camels' thudding feet. In rudimentary Arabic, I asked Said my camel's name. He told me that camels don't have names. "I will give him one now!" he declared. "What about Bob Marley?" And so, after a few hours, Bob Marley carried me into the hotel's desert camp, a rectangular arrangement of boxy tents made from carpets and blankets. Behind them soared a reddish dune. I dismounted, threw my pack in a tent, and ran up the dune, slipping and stumbling in the powder.

Staggering upward, I reached a flat landing after 30 excruciating minutes. I had conquered only half

*Photographs by
Malú Alvarez*

the dune but felt a rush of satisfaction as I panted. Above, the summit's silhouette cut a shadow against the low-slanting sun. Before me, a panorama of golden desert spread in all directions. No threat of sandstorm was visible on the horizon, only a long plateau of rock: Algeria.

"The desert landscape is always at its best in the half-light of dawn or dusk," Bowles wrote. When I slid back down to camp, jagged stars blazed overhead, as if in a van Gogh painting. An employee in a djellaba approached with a silvery pot. After a week crossing Morocco, my two-decade dream was realized: tea in the Sahara.

WHAT TO READ AND WATCH

The Sheltering Sky, by Paul Bowles. The story of three naïve and overconfident Americans traveling in North Africa soon after the end of World War II.

The Sheltering Sky, Bernardo Bertolucci's 1990 film adaptation of the novel, starring John Malkovich and Debra Winger.

Morocco, a photographic view by Barry Brukoff. With accompanying text by Paul Bowles written decades after *The Sheltering Sky*.

The Sahara: A Cultural History, by Eamonn Gearon. A readable in-depth look at the Sahara Desert by a seasoned North Africa adventurer and academic specialist.

A Little Original Sin: The Life and Work of Jane Bowles, by Millicent Dillon. A biography of Paul Bowles's wife, Jane, who was praised as a writer in her own right by Tennessee Williams and John Ashbery.

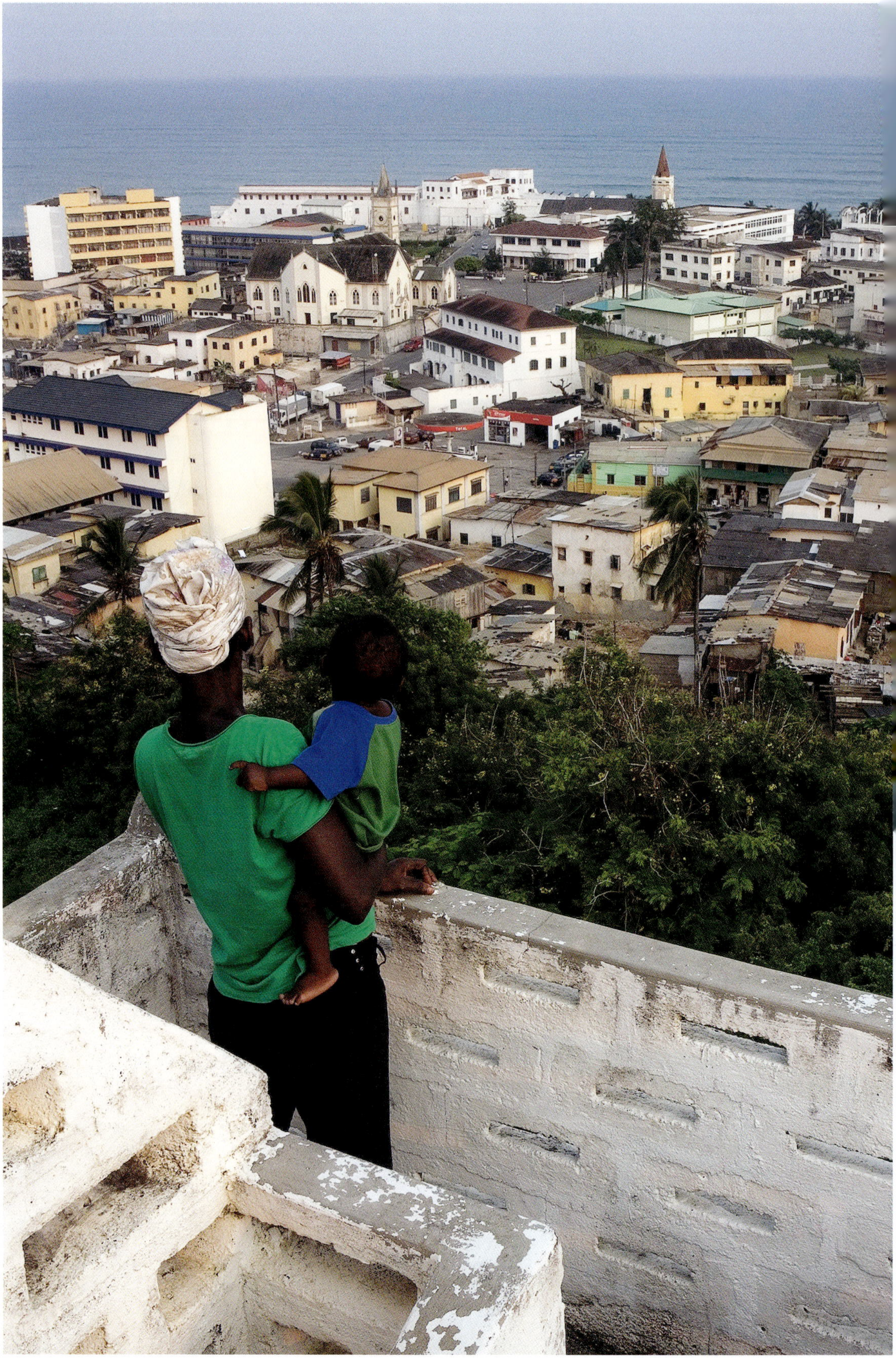

THE TWO FACES OF GHANA

Victims of the slave trade are remembered, but Ghanaians know how to live joyfully in the present.
— BY LABAN CARRICK HILL

At midday, the heat was so palpable that it had its own color, a pulsing, iridescent yellow. I paused at a tiny market stall and bought half a peeled, sliced pineapple — sweet and juicy, not like the tart pineapples in the markets at home in Vermont. Then I stopped a young woman carrying a tray of hard-boiled eggs on her head. She took the tray down, knelt, and, with a plastic bag over her hand, peeled and salted the egg for me. To complete my meal, I bought a tiny sachet of filtered water from a small boy carrying a bucket of them on his head.

I was in the Kotokuraba Market in Cape Coast, a city in the West African nation of Ghana, on a Wednesday morning. The market rocked with music, from hip-hop, pulsing from loudspeakers, to tribal drumming. Honking taxis fought pedestrians for space. The stalls seemed to sell just about anything — machetes and huge cast-iron cooking pots, pirated DVDs and homemade slingshots. A blacksmith worked a piece of iron over an open-air hearth; I picked up one of his earlier creations: a *gangkogui*, which is an elongated cowbell, the kind used as percussive accompaniment in drumming ceremonies. Its forged and hammered metal had been wrought into elegant, almost arabesque, curves.

At every turn I was met with a friendly "Akwaaba!" which means "welcome." Small children shouted, "How are you, Obruni?" In Fante, the local language, *obruni* is the word for "white person." In one of the market aisles, a woman dressed in a colorful batik dress with an infant tied to her back offered mortars and pestles for making fufu, an African staple of pounded cassava and unripe plantain. The mortar was a deep wooden bowl about two feet in diameter,

Previous Cape Coast encapsulates Ghana's spirit and historical sorrow.

Left Cape Coast Castle, where enslavers held kidnapped Africans before shipping them to the New World.

Opposite above A holding cell where captives were kept at St. George's Castle in Elmina.

Opposite below The beach at Cape Coast. Modern Ghana offers beach resorts and ecotourism.

the pestle a tree trunk five feet tall, requiring two hands to maneuver. When I stopped and inquired about the prices, the woman laughed and teased, "Obruni, you make fufu?"

Ghana has been known to many people in the West primarily for its tragic role as a major shipping point for enslaved Africans who were taken away to the Americas. But today's Ghana, which has a population of about 30 million, is one of the few African nations with a history of smooth transitions of power in free elections. And as an English-speaking country with abundant natural gifts and an appealing culture, it now draws international tourists who not only want to explore the slave trade's dark past, but also desire a joyous African experience.

The Ghanaian city best known to foreigners is Accra, the capital, a densely populated and often cacophonous city of two and a half million people on the Gulf of Guinea. But a compelling and memorable trip can be found in Cape Coast and the region nearby — an area of stunning sunsets and sunrises, 400-year-old fishing traditions, and the best preserved of the historic forts that spawned so many tears. And everywhere, the friendliness that Ghanaians take pride in.

I was in Ghana organizing a creative writing program at the University of Cape Coast and working on the Ghana Poetry Project, which was created to support contemporary African literature through readings, workshops, and other activities. The more I explored, the more I was seduced by Ghana's bright colors, spicy foods, and intense rhythms. This is a country in love with music and dance — a preoccupation that shows not only on special occasions like the Fetu Afehye, a festival that draws foreign visitors in September, but every day.

Though I could spend hours shopping, my goal as I walked through the market that morning lay beyond the shops and stalls. I was on my way to the Cape Coast Castle, the last stop in Africa for countless, perhaps millions of people taken away as slaves, a number we can never really know.

As I left the market behind, the traffic and crowds died off, and the closer I came to the castle, the more somber the mood felt. Ahead of me, visitors clustered close together and slowed their steps almost to a shuffle. Even the young men who had gathered at the castle gate to solicit donations for fictitious youth soccer teams spoke in hushed tones. I realized that I had just walked the same path through town that the captives took, force-marched and traded to the British for guns, liquor, and other goods, and then funneled into ships.

The castle, an imposing stone fortress of ramps, stairs, parapets, and holding pens, is a Unesco World Heritage Site and draws not only a steady stream of tour groups but also many visitors, including large numbers of African Americans, traveling on their own. The castle boggles the mind with the businesslike efficiency of its neatly laid out spaces: the dark caverns of the men's and women's dungeons located deep within; the bright, airy residence halls on the upper floors for the administrators and paid workers; the high ramparts lined with enough cannons to repel an armada. Kidnapped Africans were held for months at a time in the most hellish conditions. Many died in dungeons so crowded that they could not lie down.

Those who survived left through the Door of No Return—a small wooden door built into a stone archway that led to waiting ships. I paused there, overcome by emotion. It was difficult, almost terrifying, to step through this door despite the fact that no enslaved person has been forced through it for two centuries.

In the women's dungeon, a windowless hole, a small bouquet of flowers lay on the floor below the single bare bulb now lighting the space. The utter emptiness and silence seemed to intensify the overwhelming feeling of loss. Visitors filed in but did not linger. Afterward, out in the courtyard, conversation ceased as all seemed lost in their private grief.

A small market tucked just inside the castle entrance provided a transition before going back out into the larger world—low-key shopping as decompression. A dozen vendors offered Ghanaian crafts and bargains. I was glad to return to my car for a quiet ride along the coast, retreating to the Coconut Grove Beach Resort just outside the town of Elmina, about six miles west of Cape Coast.

The Coconut Grove is one of Ghana's premier resorts (although to a traveler from a more affluent country, the prices seemed unbeatable). At the beachside restaurant I ordered grilled local tilapia with a fresh pepper, tomato, and ginger relish, and *banku* (boiled corn dough). I watched the sunset on the gulf, surrounded by diners relaxing after a busy day on the golf course or around town. Out on the water, brightly painted dugout canoes cut through the waves on their way out to fish as they have done for centuries. I could just make out the hand-carved message on one of the hulls, "Nyame Yie," or "God Is Good," cresting over a wave.

As I walked along the beach the next morning, another guest galloped along nearby on one of the hotel's horses. Its hooves kicked up sand at the surf's edge, scattering white egrets to the wind. I knew I had found a kind of paradise.

Ghana doesn't flinch from its past, but it is creating a new future with forays into ecotourism—tours to remote villages and dense rain forests, as well as the more prominent of its national parks. Maya Angelou, who lived several years in Ghana, described it as a place "improving the quality of man's humanity to man."

Elmina is a small town with a long history: Founded in 1471 as a Portuguese gold trading port, it was taken over by the Dutch in the 1630s. It, too, has a horrifyingly efficient slave castle—St. George's Castle, which is twice the size of the one in Cape Coast and stands like a giant immobile obstruction on the shore—the oldest colonial building still standing in

Above Traditional Ghanaian fishing boats, with colorful flags, on the shore near Cape Coast Castle.

Opposite Tourists on the roof of St. George's Castle. The slave castles were models of ruthless efficiency.

sub-Saharan Africa. The imposing moat around the land side looked like something out of a movie, and the Dutch Reformed chapel directly over the women's dungeons suggested a kind of brutal indifference to the captives that was still manifest as I stood in the church. Included with the price of admission were an excellent guided tour and a very good museum focusing on the history of the Akan and Fante people who originally settled this region.

The oldest building in the village itself, the Bridge House, was built in the 17th century for the Ghanaian mistress of the castle's Dutch commander and survives as an affordable guesthouse and restaurant offering fresh seafood prepared in a spicy Ghanaian style.

Elmina also offers more to see, with its colonial architecture and its elaborate concrete shrines called *posubans*. Many were originally used as storage houses by local militias called *asafo* companies—now civic organizations—and survive as shrines to the companies. The one dedicated to Asafo Company Five is two stories tall, with several life-size carved statues on the first floor and a sculpture of a ship with three sailors on the second.

About an hour's drive north of the Coconut Grove, I sampled Ghanaian ecotourism at Kakum National Park. A canopy walkway, 1,150 feet long and swaying 131 feet above the forest floor, was suspended among seven trees and broken up by a number of viewing platforms. It was a breathtaking experience. More than 200 species of birds have been sighted in this forest; I glimpsed an amazing yellow-casqued hornbill. Numerous monkeys seemed to fly as well, swinging in the trees.

There's another kind of exhilaration in Ghanaian music and dancing. Back at Cape Coast, as the sun set, I sat at a nightclub's table under a thatch canopy. The bar filled up with Westerners, Rastafarians, and Ghanaians. Local beer and shots of Mandingo, a

Photographs by Olivier Asselin

red, syrupy aperitif, flowed freely. As darkness fell, a performance of drumming and dancing began, with athletic young men dressed in brightly patterned chief pants and young women wrapped in handmade batik fabrics. It evolved quickly into audience participation. No invitation was necessary. Diners just pushed back their chairs and joined in.

Ghana is like that. Traditional boundaries of performer and audience are often ignored, even on the most formal of occasions. Eventually, the DJ spun the rhythms of hiplife, an African fusion of highlife and hip-hop with lyrics sung in Akan tribal languages. The crowd clapped and laughed and spun as though time had stopped and this moment would never end.

The heat, along with any worries, vanished into the clear, star-filled night.

WHAT TO READ AND WATCH

The Ghana Reader: History, Culture, Politics, edited by Kwasi Konadu and Clifford C. Campbell. Five hundred years of history, from the Asante kingdom to modern democracy.

The Ghana Cookbook, by Fran Osseo-Asare and Barbara Baëta. Recipes for cooking in the Ghanaian tradition, emphasizing fresh, seasonal, and local ingredients.

Homegoing, by Yaa Gyasi. Through the story of a fictional Ghanaian family divided by the slave trade, this novel contemplates the consequences of human trafficking on both sides of the Atlantic.

Fonko: Contemporary Africa through Its Urban Music, Season 1, Episode 5: *Ghana*, directed by Lamin Daniel Jadama, Lars Lovén, and Gören Olsson. Ghana revealed through its music and the ideas the music embodies.

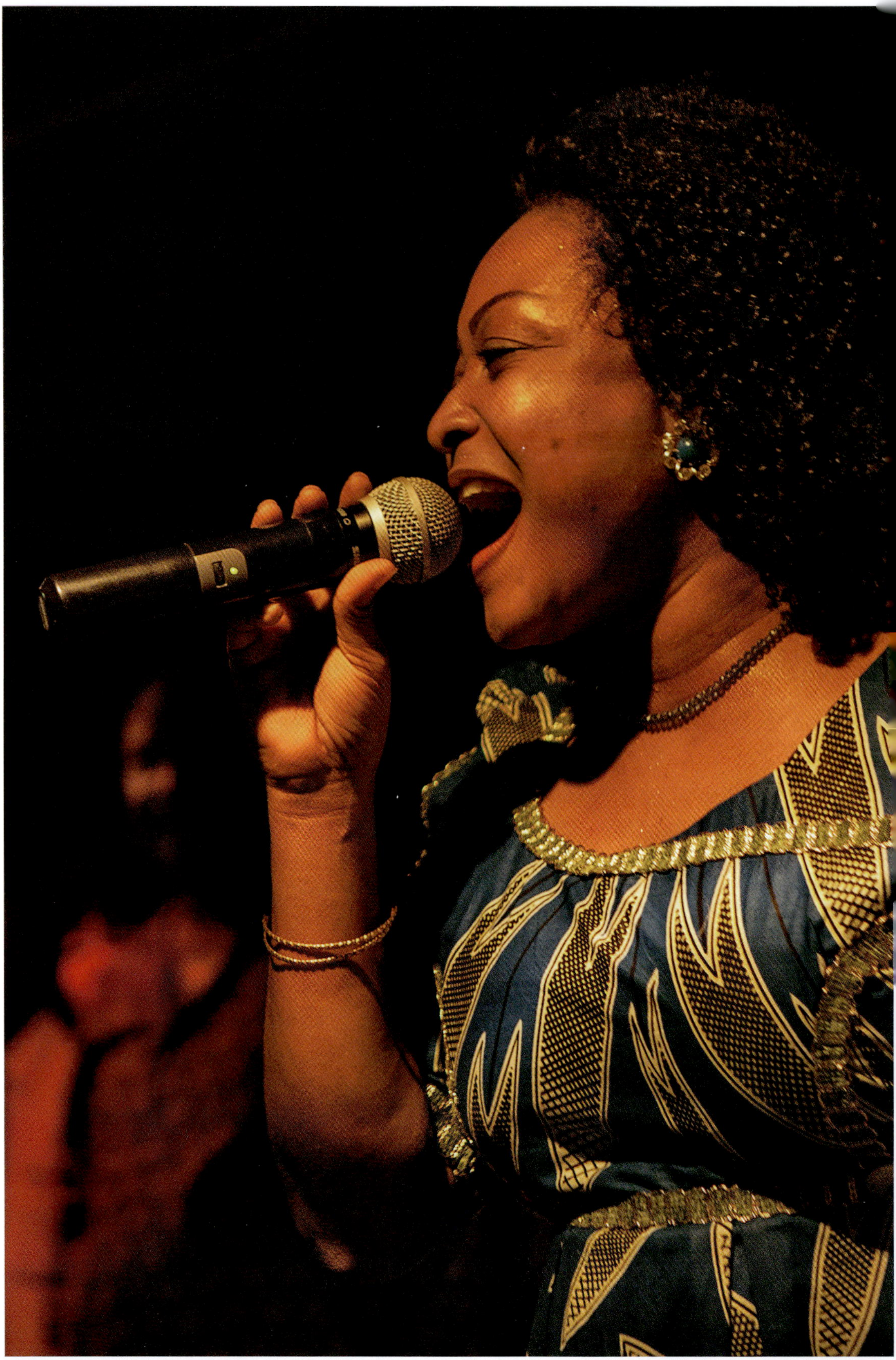

WHERE TANZANIA TAPS ITS FEET

To catch the vibe of a dynamic music town, drop in at a few night spots in Dar es Salaam. — BY RACHEL B. DOYLE

The concrete lot next to the Hotel Travertine in downtown Dar es Salaam was full of swaying women in elaborate floor-length gowns trimmed with sequins. Spotlights reflected off bottles of Kilimanjaro beer, and the scent of shisha smoke hung in the air.

It was 11 on a Sunday night in Tanzania's largest city, and members of Jahazi Modern Taarab, a popular local group, were performing a spirited song about love gone wrong, featuring a pattern of male-to-female call and response. Young men, chewing khat leaves and tapping their feet to the music, sat in white plastic chairs next to older women in neon-colored headscarves. For certain songs, the crowd rushed to the dance floor en masse.

This was a regular Sunday gig for the band, typical in Dar es Salaam. Many bands in this laid-back city on the Indian Ocean play at the same venues every weekend and perform in as many as four other clubs during the week — all part of a boisterous and exciting music scene that rivals that of any in East Africa.

Dar's soundscape is a riot of genres, from the music on offer that evening, called modern *taarab*, which mixes a traditional Swahili sung-poetry style with electronic and Arab-influenced rhythms, to *mchiriku*, the raw, urban sound that Jagwa Music plays, which is generally found at neighborhood block parties. You can also dance to classic rumba or *bongo flava*, the local brand of hip-hop, on soft white sand at any number of palm-laden beach clubs while a pink sun sets over the ocean.

At the open-air venue Mango Garden, diners enjoyed a tasty chicken pilau dish while dancers in matching outfits stomped to the catchy Congolese-style rhythms of African Stars Band, whose songs blare from radios across the city. Amid the greenery

Previous A vocalist with Kilimanjaro Band. Dar es Salaam has a vibrant, wide-ranging music scene.

Left Greeting friends at a celebration near Dar es Salaam.

Opposite Album cover for the compilation *Zanzibara Volume 5: Hot In Dar (The Sound of Tanzania 1978–1983)*. Vijana Jazz Orchestra reached its peak of popularity in the 1980s.

at the outdoor Triniti Bar, a young crowd mixed hip-hop and soul with poetry slams. At Selander Bridge Club, fans danced in formation to Kilimanjaro Band's hypnotic grooves under a massive thatched roof.

The scene bleeds into the streets as well. Wander behind a downtown high rise and you may find locals feasting on roasted goat in a nondescript courtyard that will turn into a bustling music scene later that night. Follow the tinny strains of taarab on a transistor radio to discover members of the city's South Asian community playing cards and eating Indian street snacks like *pani puri* on tables set up on the sidewalk.

Leo Mkanyia, a Dar musician, attributed this diversity to the country itself. "We have 125 tribes, and all of them have different tunes, different melodies, different music, and even different traditional musical instruments," he said.

I met Leo at Kibo Bar at the Serena Hotel, where he was performing for guests as the leader of a five-piece band. He shared the stage with his father, Henry, who performed for 15 years in the city's legendary Mlimani Park Orchestra, but now was playing guitar alongside his son in a group that mixed Tanzanian drumming with blues melodies and *dansi*, an indigenous dance music. Leo called this style "Swahili blues."

He told me about a visit to Nairobi, where he met Kenyan musicians. "They were all praising Dar, like 'I wish I could be in Dar,'" he said, adding that such envy is a source of pride here. "People here are proud of their music. They love their music, and support it."

One Sunday, Leo and I watched a group called Super Maya Baikoko perform a combination of traditional *ngoma* drumming and risqué dancing that originated in the Digo villages of the country's northeast coast and is a favored genre in Dar. The venue was an open courtyard where the only decorations were a large six-point star hung behind the eight-person band, and posters for Safari Lager taped up on electric-blue walls.

The lineup consisted of two percussionists beating makeshift drums made out of plastic drainage pipes, a duo wielding shakers made from tin cans, a male singer, and three barefoot female dancers. The drumming began slowly, with the dancers languidly moving their hips and the singer repeating a phrase in Swahili that Leo translated as "dance mama dance."

Soon the drumming and rattling grew more feverish and the dancers began gyrating; one slid to the floor and began undulating her entire body. In a distinctively raspy voice, the singer had segued from "dance mama dance" to a riff on police corruption to a "story about a woman who had an abortion and whose husband threw her away," Leo explained.

"You need to be very good to sing like that, with nothing giving you a melody," he added, admiringly. "No keyboard, nothing. You have to grow up with this music."

Local beats didn't always dominate in Dar. In colonial times, interest in Tanzanian musicians among the country's British rulers was generally limited to finding a few of them to play foxtrots for ballroom dances. Meanwhile, performances of traditional drumming and dancing encouraged resistance against the colonizers.

In 1961, when Tanganyika, now the Tanzanian mainland, gained independence, a revival of indigenous cultural practices was high on the agenda of Julius Nyerere, the country's first president. The government sent engineers to Tanzanian villages to find ngoma groups to record for broadcast. Later it took control of the sole radio station. Music venues, some of which were nationalized, began hiring house bands to play several times a week. The government also

Above The Swahili Blues Band mixes traditional music with blues melodies and classic *dansi*, the indigenous dance music.

Below Dancers perform to the catchy Congolese-style rhythms of the African Stars Band.

Opposite Jagwa Music at a naming celebration for a newborn baby in a poor suburb of Dar es Salaam.

encouraged public institutions to have what were known as "entertainment units."

In the 1970s Kilimanjaro Band began performing dansi, which combines traditional drumming and a relaxed backbeat, with Congolese-inspired guitar and horn sections. John Kitime, a guitarist for the group, remembered this time well. "There were a number of police bands, a number of army bands, Immigration had a band," he said. "These bands were just playing ordinary popular music."

With government agencies paying salaries, pensions, health care, and transportation for many groups — in essence, removing almost everything about being a musician that isn't fun — the cultural flowering in Tanzania was immense. But while government sponsorship certainly encouraged the local music scene, there were many independent music groups active during that era, too.

"Some of the classic bands from the '70s are still playing around Dar," said David Tinning of the Tanzanian Heritage Project, a project to digitize rare music recordings. "They have these huge events. They are titans, giants in their scene."

Mlimani Park Orchestra, the dansi group that Leo's father performed in, was perennially beloved;

Photographs by Nichole Sobecki

people here compare them in terms of popularity with the Beatles and in longevity with the Rolling Stones. "Their music, everybody knows it, and loves it," Leo said.

I found confirmation of that one night in a beat-up taxi whisking me from a buzzing nightclub to my guesthouse. I asked the driver if he was a fan of Mlimani Park Orchestra.

"It'd be strange if I said no," he answered.

The warm breeze from the Indian Ocean blew through an open window as we sped along the coastal road, past Maasai men in their red-checked *shukas*, past stylish women in high heels heading home from the clubs.

The taxi driver smiled. "It's just the melody," he said.

WHAT TO READ AND WATCH

Live from Dar es Salaam: Popular Music and Tanzania's Music Economy, by Alex Perullo. Performers and entrepreneurs search for opportunity in a vibrant but complex music scene.

Hip Hop Africa: New African Music in a Globalizing World, edited by Eric Charry. Essays on the popular music scene in modern Africa and its deep connection to traditional cultures.

Tanzania, Culture Smart! The Essential Guide to Customs & Culture, by Quintin Winks. Information for Western visitors on interacting with the people of Tanzania: what to expect and how to proceed.

Béla Fleck: Throw Down Your Heart, directed by Sascha Paladino. A Grammy-winning American banjo player travels in Africa, where the banjo originated, and finds it in several countries, including Tanzania.

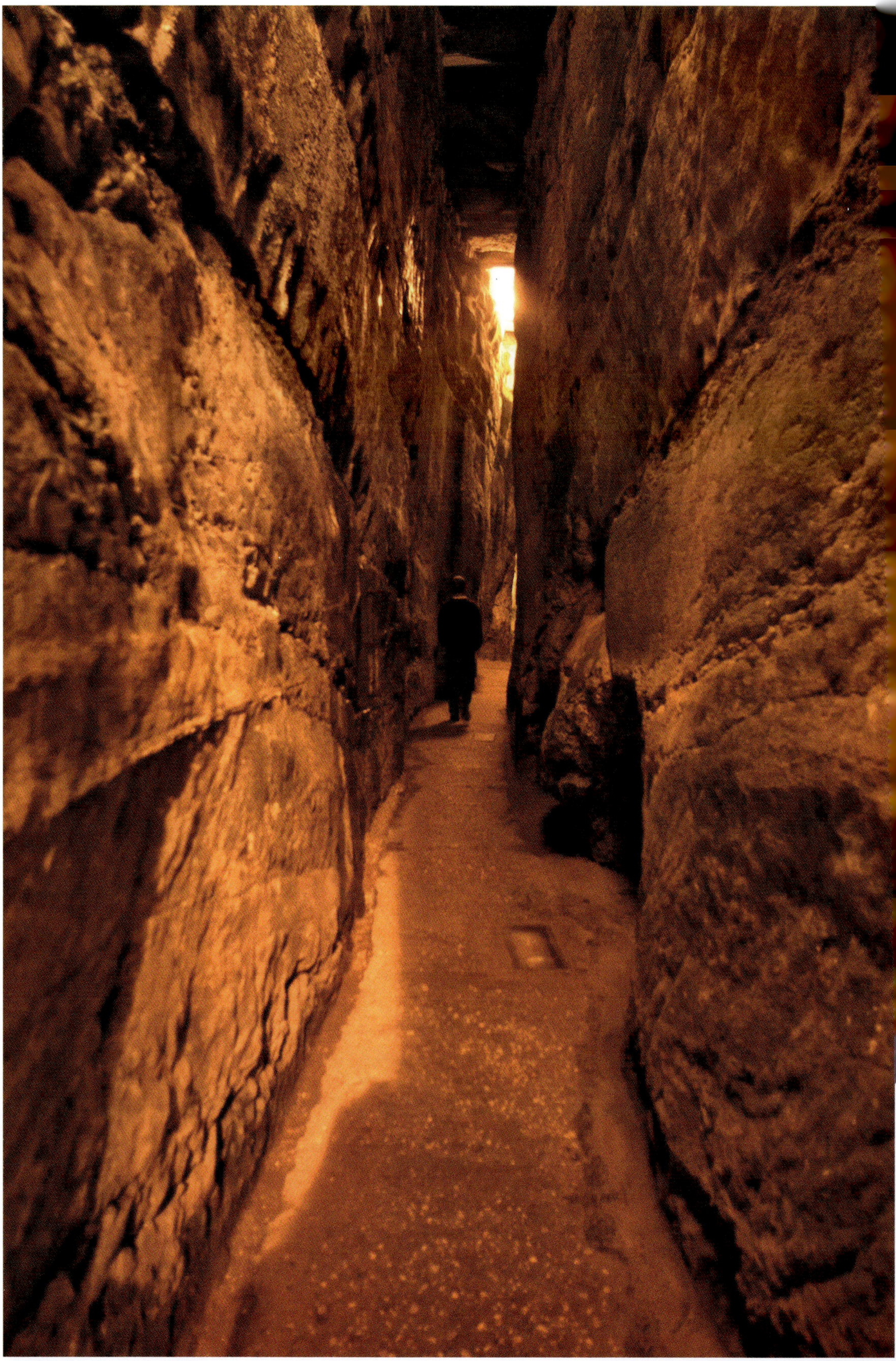

HEROD THE ARCHITECT

The reviled king who died in 4 B.C. ruled Judea with an iron fist, but he was also one of the world's great builders. — BY DAVID LASKIN

I traveled to Israel to search for Herod the Great and I found him, or at least his ghost, at his tomb at Herodium. Halfway up an artificial mountain that the king had conjured from the desert for his final resting place, I stood gazing at what was left of the royal mausoleum: a couple of courses of limestone blocks as exquisitely faceted as jewels. Below, the arcing rows of a Roman theater descended in diminishing semicircles to the disc of the stage. Everything around me, even the contours of the earth itself, had been altered at the decree of this ancient ruler. Time has toppled the columns and blurred the carvings, but the majesty and hubris of this place remain intact.

Herod's Temple in Jerusalem may be more transcendent, and his mesa-top retreat at Masada more spectacular, but Herodium (about 10 miles south of Jerusalem in the occupied West Bank) was where I channeled the spirit of the man. I was also channeling the spirit of a monster. From 37 to 4 B.C., Herod the Great (not to be confused with a slew of lesser heirs and successors who shared his name) ruled Judea with a bloody iron fist. Though the Gospel writer Matthew's account of Herod slaughtering the innocents of Bethlehem is probably apocryphal, the king did murder a wife, a mother-in-law, and three sons, along with untold numbers of enemies and rivals.

Yet he was one of the world's great builders — an instinctive architectural genius who planned, sited, sourced, and landscaped magnificent structures of classical antiquity. Epic was his preferred scale. No project was too ambitious or daring, whether it was throwing up a city from scratch or replacing Judaism's holiest site from the ground up. Judea rejoiced when Herod died, but I found myself breathless with admiration after a week spent tracking his footsteps.

Previous The Western Wall Tunnels, excavations beside the remaining wall of Herod's Great Temple in Jerusalem.

Left Herod the Great. Little is left of his landmarks, but the remainders are revealing.

Opposite Ruins of Herod's palace at Caesarea, a city near modern Tel Aviv that he built from 25 to 13 B.C.

"Herod was a vicious murderer, but he was also very sensuous, very attuned to nature," said David Mevorah, a curator for the Israel Museum in Jerusalem. "The desert was where he went for peace and serenity."

And to be buried. Josephus Flavius, the Roman Jewish historian who is the prime source on Herod, wrote that upon the king's death in 4 B.C., his body was placed on a gem-encrusted solid gold bier and conveyed with due pomp from Jericho to Herodium for interment, but for centuries the location of the tomb remained a mystery. Its discovery in 2007 by the Israeli architect and archaeologist Ehud Netzer after a career-long search created an international sensation.

Herodium National Park makes the most of this dramatic story. A path ascends from the visitors' center to the ruins of the palace-fortress. From the circular courtyard recessed into the summit, a narrow staircase descends into a maze of tunnels and cisterns. When you reemerge into the glare of daylight, you're standing on a ledge between the theater and the site of the mausoleum. Here, Professor Netzer fell to his death in an accident in 2010.

The bookends of Herod's life were Herodium and Jericho. Herodium was where the king chose to be buried; his winter palace at Jericho, part desert spa, part seasonal headquarters, was where he lived most pleasurably. When the end came—and, according to Josephus, it was a protracted and hideously painful end—Jericho was where he went to die.

Netzer called the Jericho winter palace, which he excavated from 1973 to 1987, "perhaps the most refined building" in the king's oeuvre. I arrived by car with a guide from Israel, a problematic approach, since Jericho is now under control of the Palestinian National Authority. Most tourists come from Jerusalem by bus and taxi. My guide, Shmuel, a naturalized Israeli, assured me that he had clearance to guide in Jericho, but it took some tense dickering to persuade the armed Palestinian soldiers at the check-point to wave us through.

The archaeological site is situated at that forlorn fringe between impoverished city and desiccated farmland. It could have been the outskirts of Las Vegas or Albuquerque. But I was learning to see the ancient splendor beneath the modern degradation. Walls of beautifully preserved opus reticulatum—a Roman building technique in which pyramidal bricks are set like diamonds to form a rippling mosaic-like pattern—crisscrossed the desert floor. Stone circles traced the outlines of long-drained pools and fountains. Wadi Qelt, the streambed that cuts through the site, was bone dry, but when Herod held court here in winter, it would have brought the music of flowing water into the courtyards and sunken gardens.

If a bit of historical background is useful to appreciate Herodium and the Jericho winter palace, Herod's city of Caesarea is something different. Not so much an archaeological site as an antique theme park, Caesarea combines glorious ruins and tasteful modern amenities. You can, if you choose, leave the guidebook behind and just soak it up.

Herod's creation of ancient Caesarea was a feat of Roman-era engineering and construction—a deep water port (between modern-day Tel Aviv and Haifa) surrounded by a bustling, cultured, polyglot city that he willed into existence in 12 years from 25 to 13 B.C. Modern Caesarea is a miracle of Israeli verve, nerve, and ingenuity. Herod's seaside city, uncovered in a series of continuing excavations and preserved as Caesarea National Park, has been commandeered as the backdrop for a gorgeous Mediterranean playground with restaurants, bars, and galleries sprinkled through the ruins and a modern concert venue superimposed on the 4,000-seat Roman theater.

On the bright, breezy Saturday afternoon when I visited, Israeli families were out in droves to stroll by the sea, scuba-dive in the ancient harbor, and eat and drink in the harborside restaurants and bars.

According to Josephus, Caesarea was the site of a temple that Herod dedicated to his friend and boss, the Roman Emperor Augustus Caesar. All that remains of that temple today is the podium, a featureless platform that I missed altogether. But there was no missing Herod's Caesarea palace. Characteristically, he chose the city's most dramatic real estate for his abode. Not content with waterfront, he suspended his palace over the sea on a semi-submerged reef. A few of the columns have been partly reconstructed, and to my mind all the luxury and beauty of the classical Mediterranean shimmers around those tawny limestone shafts rising against a perfect turquoise sea.

An essential stop for the Herod tourist is Masada. Although it is best known as the fortress site where the last Jews rebelling against Roman rule were defeated and committed mass suicide in A.D. 70, that was decades after Herod's time. He fortified Masada, on an isolated rock plateau, and built another of his

Above Herodium, where Herod was buried, is now an Israeli national park.

Opposite Ancient walls at Caesarea. Herod constructed an artificial harbor and built his city around it.

architectural wonders on its heights, a breathtaking palace perched over the Dead Sea. Archaeologists have uncovered walls, storage areas, outlines of a bathhouse and swimming pools, and even what appears to have been a pleasure garden. At Masada National Park, some visitors take a cable car to the top while others walk up, an experience more in tune with Herod's time. Both the palace and the rebels' last stand make for a dramatic story, and despite its remoteness, this is one of the most visited tourist areas in Israel. I had been there before, and on this trip I wanted to see something a little more off the beaten track. I got my wish and then some at Omrit, hidden away in the Golan foothills near the Syrian border.

It took about four hours to drive there from Jerusalem, and even Shmuel had trouble finding the site in a web of back-country dirt roads. But Omrit was worth the effort. Once Shmuel killed the engine of his well-worn Toyota, no filtering out of the modern was required. Omrit reminded me of the rugged, chromatically muted uplands where the Ancestral Puebloans built their stone cities in the American Southwest. Column, capital, mountain, sky: Omrit was like a haiku distilled from Herod's ancient epic.

We had the temple steps, wall-painting fragments, and carved plinths and pediments completely to ourselves. Omrit, to me, felt like a coded message from the ancient world, a place where beings at once so like us and so wildly different hid their secrets in the rock. I was grateful that silence and slow time had left so much to the imagination here.

On my last morning, I went to the site of Herod's most famous construction, the Great Temple in Jerusalem. "He who has not seen Herod's building has not seen a handsome building the days of his life," the Talmud intones of the Temple. Tragically, all that remains standing is a single prayer-encrusted retaining wall—the so-called Western or Wailing

*Photographs by
Rina Castelnuovo*

Wall that holds up one flank of the Temple Mount. I had signed up for a tunnel tour, an hourlong guided visit to the excavations beside the wall, and as my group descended from the glare of contemporary Jerusalem to the twilight of the buried city, all of Herod's contradictions converged in my mind. His Jewish subjects reviled him as a mongrel pseudo-Jew (his father was a convert, his mother an Arab), and yet every pebble of the temple he erected is still revered two millenniums after its destruction by Rome. His crimes against humanity were legion, and yet during his 33-year reign, Judea enjoyed an unparalleled stretch of stability, prosperity, and building.

The tour guide pointed to a block of dressed limestone the size of a tour bus and the weight of nine tanks. "We still don't know how Herod moved these stones here," he told us. "Herod was a very complex individual. He was very mentally ill, but when it came to building, 'Wow' was what he wanted."

WHAT TO READ AND WATCH

Architecture of Herod, the Great Builder, by Ehud Netzer. Architectural and archaeological survey by the leader of the team that discovered Herod's tomb.

Herod the Great: Statesman, Visionary, Tyrant, by Norman Gelb. A readable account of the life and historical impact of Herod by a popular history writer.

The True Herod, by Geza Vermes. Makes the case for Herod as a consummate diplomat and visionary, though a brutal one.

The Real King Herod, directed by Ian Denyer. A British television documentary with scenes played by actors and commentary provided by scholars.

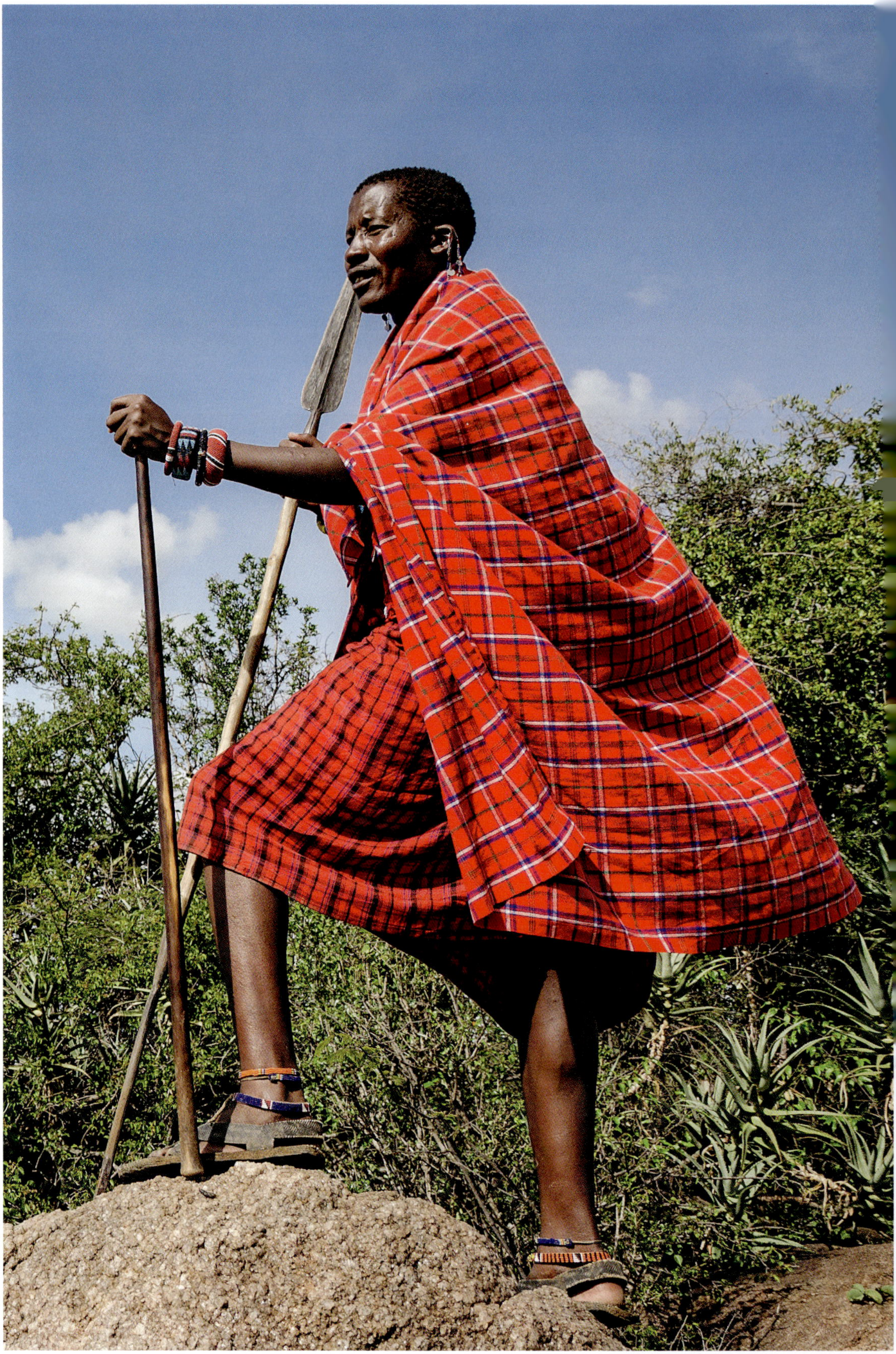

TEN DAYS WITH THE MAASAI

A gracious host, a ritual scream, and a sheep in the taxi.
— BY MICHAEL BENANAV

In the market town of Narok, 90 miles west of Nairobi, I was buying a Kenyan SIM card for my cell phone when I heard someone behind me calling my name. He was wearing a bright red *shuka*, the traditional shawl of the Maasai people. Colorful beaded jewelry circled his neck, hung from his ears, and ringed his wrists. At his waist, a short steel sword was sheathed in red leather. His feet were clad in sandals made from old tires.

"Salaton?" I asked.

"Yes! Welcome!" he said, adding, "I'll wait for you outside."

A Maasai chief, Salaton Ole Ntutu had come to take me to his village, Maji Moto, where he runs the Maji Moto Maasai Cultural Camp. There, visitors stay in his tribal community, learning about the ways of the Maasai and getting a feel for the landscape they live within. Though I had read good things about the camp on travel websites, I wasn't really sure where the experience would fall on the spectrum between "farcically touristy" and "viscerally authentic" (which aren't official review categories, but perhaps should be). Before we even left Narok, I had my first indicator, as Salaton loaded a brown-and-white ewe, which he had just bought at the market, into the taxi with us; liking the sheep's looks, he had decided to add it to his flock.

The paved road turned to dirt, then became a muddy track as we cut across the Loita Plains. Herds of Thomson's gazelles, wildebeests, and zebras casually grazed on the lush carpet of grass that had sprouted during unusually heavy December rains.

Reaching Maji Moto, I realized it was not a village in the classic sense of the word. Though there was a "town center" with a few basic dry-goods shops, a

MAJI MOTO   KENYA

Previous Salaton Ole Ntutu, a Maasai chief, at the Maji Moto Maasai Cultural Camp west of Nairobi.

Left Maasai warriors in Kenya during the 1940s. Even today, many traditions are preserved.

Opposite above Sinti Nasi, a cook at Maji Moto, heads back from the market in a taxi. A sheep is in the back seat.

Opposite below A mother cheetah with one of her cubs at Masai Mara National Reserve.

butcher, a grain mill, and a tin shack of a pub serving warm Tusker (Kenya's most popular beer), most Maasai in the area didn't live near it. Each family dwells in a *manyatta*—a small compound of stick-and-mud huts, with wooden pens for herds of cattle, sheep, and goats, and no next-door neighbors. Maji Moto's manyattas are spread out over miles of undeveloped semiarid rangelands at the foot of the Loita Hills and are home to some 3,000 people.

Salaton's camp was basically a manyatta of its own. My guest hut was simple but clean, with a comfortable bed, a mosquito net, and solar-powered light. Meals like stewed goat meat, fried potatoes, pasta, carrot salad, and *ugali* (similar to polenta) were freshly cooked over charcoal or propane by a charming warrior named Sinti, who was as good with a spatula as a spear (and the ritual scarring on his leg, earned when he helped kill a lion, was proof of his skill with the latter). Showers were gravity-fed from tanks filled with water hauled up from the nearby hot spring that gives Maji Moto—"hot water" in Swahili—its name.

Soon after I arrived, Salaton, who spoke fluent English despite never having attended school, told me that a circumcision ceremony would be held the next day at a manyatta about a mile away. Did I want to go? "Sure," I said, as long as the family holding the ceremony didn't mind. I imagined it would bear little resemblance to any Jewish bris that I'd attended, especially since the boys being circumcised would be teenagers.

The next morning we headed out just before dawn. While we walked, the searing orange sun slipped up over the distant horizon. Salaton pointed out animal tracks in the dirt: first a giraffe, then a cheetah, then, a bit later, a lion.

We were a little late, reaching the manyatta just as a boy was being carried into a hut on a cowhide blanket, having just passed into a new stage of his life.

I can't say I had too many regrets about missing the surgical portion of the morning, and there was plenty still to see. A few cows were held down and each was shot in the jugular with a blunt arrow. The blood that spurted from their necks was caught in calabashes, then served to the newly circumcised like an all-natural protein drink, to help them regain their strength. The cows' wounds were stanched and the animals survived, seemingly no worse for the wear. Meanwhile, some family members' faces were being dabbed with white butter and red ocher, and fires were ritually started by rubbing sticks together.

Before long, I learned that a girl from the manyatta was also due to be circumcised, a common practice among the Maasai. I had a few moments of intense ethical reckoning before Salaton assured me that he had persuaded this family to join his campaign to end female genital mutilation in Maji Moto. Inside the hut, he said, the girl would receive a ritual nick on her thigh while screaming loudly enough for people outside to hear.

"The screaming is the important part," Salaton explained, when we talked about it later, adding, "We are not changing our culture, we are ending a harmful practice." A substantial portion of the money that his Cultural Camp earned, he told me, helped finance a boarding school in Maji Moto for Maasai girls from around Kenya who had been rescued from the knife and needed to leave their villages to ensure their safety.

About an hour after the girl's ceremony commenced, a couple of sheep were slaughtered, skinned, and roasted. I was given a few ribs and shown how to crack them so the meat peeled off in one solid strip. Then I was invited into a dimly lit hut with a smoky cooking fire smoldering in the center and offered multiple cups of Maasai moonshine, made from fermented honey. It was sharp on the tongue and, fortunately, less potent than it tasted.

By early afternoon, a siesta-like lull had settled over the manyatta, so Salaton and I headed back to the camp, where I was happy for the chance to lie down in my little hut and drowsily digest everything I'd seen, and consumed, that morning.

I stayed in and around Maji Moto for 10 days. Before three travelers from California arrived, the only other guests were two Kenyans who were collaborating with Salaton on a regional conservation project. Through our conversations about land rights issues, wildlife migrations, livestock grazing patterns, and cultural traditions, I began to piece together an increasingly nuanced picture of the context into which I had landed.

And day by day, I saw more of the world of the Maasai of Maji Moto. There was the bustling weekly livestock market in the nearby town of Ewaso Nero where Maasai herders filled a dusty corral half as large as a football field with sheep, goats, and cows, selling them mostly to meat merchants from Nairobi. I bathed in the Maji Moto hot springs with the locals and was led on guided hikes into the easily climbed Loita Hills, where it seemed as if everything that grew had some medicinal, nutritional, or spiritual significance. The leaves of the sage-like compa bushes, for instance, are rubbed under the armpits like deodorant; twigs from the leafy olkisikongu tree are used as natural toothbrushes; and the sacred oreteti trees, under which the Maasai pray to their god, Enkai, are said to have the power to dispel bad energy and instill peace.

A couple of hundred yards behind the Cultural Camp was the "widows' village." In Maasai communities, women often outlive their husbands and are forbidden from remarrying. Some of these widows, and their children, are left destitute, with no livestock (the traditionally favored currency of the Maasai). Urged by his mother to address this problem, Salaton built a manyatta where poor widows live together like a family, earning money by working at the camp and selling beautifully beaded jewelry to tourists;

Above Traditional singing and dancing, performed for visitors at Maji Moto Maasai Cultural Camp.

Opposite A guest hut at the cultural camp. Travelers come for a glimpse of the world of the Maasai.

the camp also pays for their and their children's medical expenses.

I got to know the Maasai who were working and volunteering at Salaton's camp, especially those who spoke English. There was Rose, a teenage seamstress with a hair-trigger smile, who was teaching the widows how to sew when she wasn't working with tourists; Joyce, a college graduate in her early 20s recently hired to help Salaton with the business side of the camp; and Meeri, who was in her last year of high school after fleeing her village a few years earlier to escape a marriage her parents were arranging. "I'd heard that the leader here helped girls like me," she said, and described her three-day walk alone across the bush, sleeping in the branches of trees at night.

We compared differences between Maasai and American marriages. When I explained that we don't have dowries, don't practice polygamy, and get to choose our spouses, they liked the way all of that sounded. But they didn't immediately embrace the idea that a wife might be older than her husband. "That would never happen here," Joyce said, laughing at the thought.

Since Maji Moto is only about 35 miles from Masai Mara National Reserve, Salaton arranged for a two-day / one-night Land Cruiser safari for me with a Maasai driver. It was a bonanza of wildlife. Seeing these animals truly move, not pace or sleep in a zoo enclosure, was a revelation. Once, we stopped to watch a cheetah with three cubs slinking through the grass in front of a family of elephants, as a warthog pranced off in the opposite direction, a hyena lurked to the south, and groups of impalas grazed to the north. It was like a live version of the opening scene of *The Lion King*. I put down my camera. It was simply too magnificent, too moving, to want to experience through a viewfinder.

Photographs by Michael Benanav

Before I left Maji Moto, I asked Salaton how he became chief. He said that Maasai medicine men have a vision and see which young boy in the community is meant to be a future tribal leader. Then that boy must consume what he called "dangerous plants"; if he survives, he will be made chief. "And if he doesn't survive?" I asked. "Then the elders were wrong," he said.

"Oh…" I said, torn between conflicting impulses to judge and to understand with an open mind. After 10 days in Maasai country, it was a feeling that had become quite familiar.

WHAT TO READ AND WATCH

Maasai, by Tepilit Ole Saitoti, with photos by Carol Beckwith. A coffee-table book by a Maasai man who moved abroad and then returned. Cultural insights and many photos.

Among the Maasai: A Memoir, by Juliet Cutler. The author's observations over 20 years, beginning in 1999, as a teacher at a school for Maasai girls.

Maasai: The Last Dance of the Warriors, directed by Kire Godal. A documentary following young men graduating to full adulthood — from warrior to elder — in elaborate ceremonies.

Men of Salt: Crossing the Sahara on the Caravan of White Gold, by Michael Benanav. In the same spirit that motivated his visit to the Maasai, the author of this article joined salt traders traveling on camels.

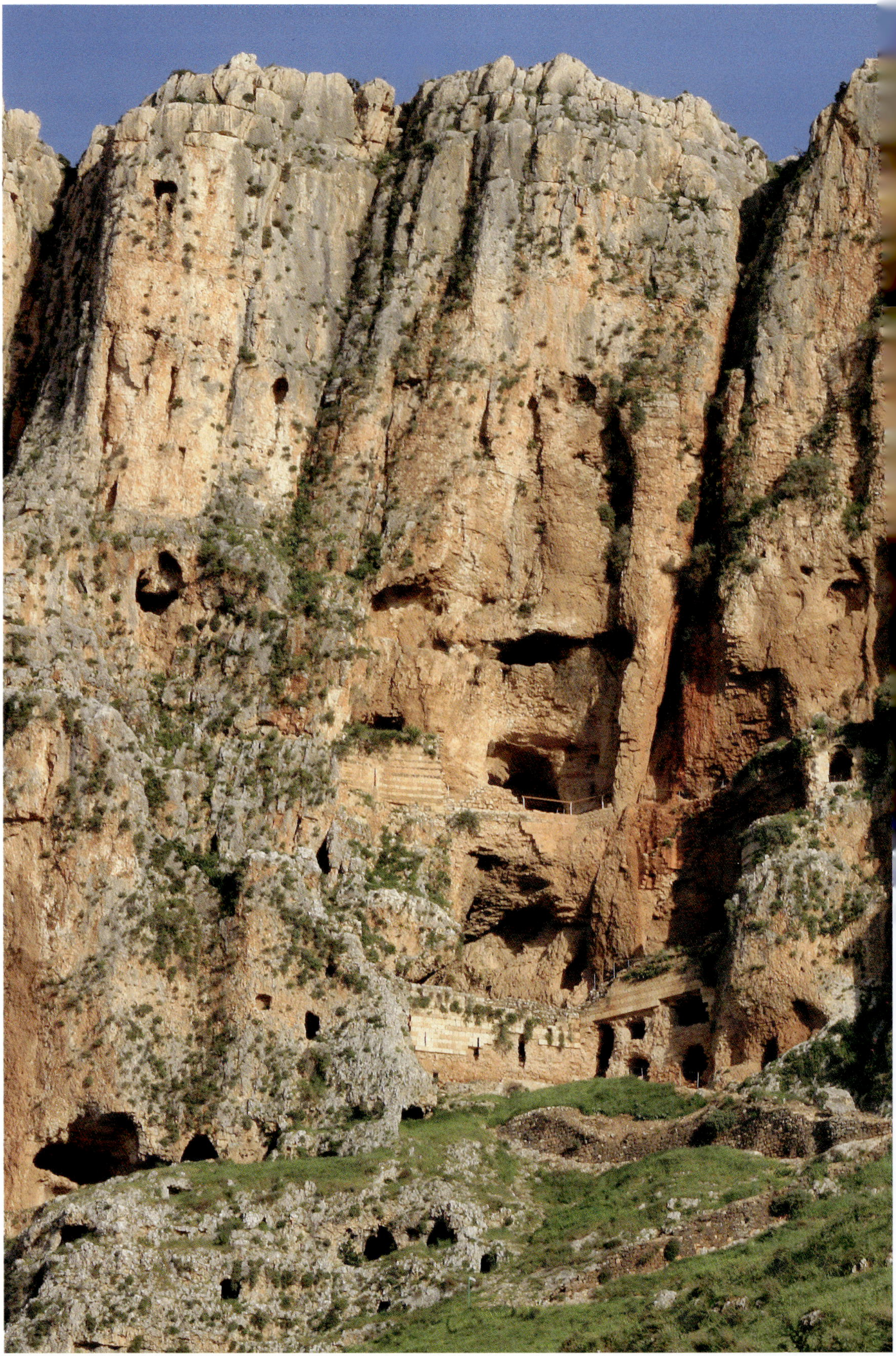

ISRAEL — NAZARETH

THE JESUS TRAIL

Exploring biblical back country in Galilee, hikers cover ground familiar from the Gospels. — BY BRAD WETZLER

Around the corner from Nazareth's Old City market, in the shadow of 200-year-old Ottoman mansions, there was a cobblestone street so narrow I could almost touch the houses on either side. An arrow pointing up some stairs was painted on one rough wall, along with the words "Jesus Trail." It was the de facto trailhead for a 40-mile hike through the Galilee region of Israel in the footsteps, more or less, of Jesus of Galilee.

The Jesus Trail was the brainchild of two hiking enthusiasts, Maoz Inon, an Israeli who owned the Fauzi Azar Inn in Nazareth, and David Landis, a guidebook writer from Pennsylvania. The pair met in 2005 while hiking in Israel and came up with the idea of creating a path linking key historical sites related to the life of Jesus. Some of those sights — including the Mount of Beatitudes, the traditional site of the Sermon on the Mount — were already popular on commercial bus tours. But others, like the Roman road where Paul is believed to have been blinded by a brilliant light, leading to his conversion to Christianity, were not accessible from nearby highways.

Landis returned to Israel in 2007 and, with the permission of local governments and the help of Google Earth and a GPS, he and Inon figured out what they hoped would be the most "beautiful, logical, and feasible" way to connect the dots through a mosaic of public land and parks. In 2008, the Society for the Protection of Nature in Israel blazed the trail, which officially opened the next year.

Curious about the route, I rode a bus north from Jerusalem on a day in February, and for the next four days hiked through a biblical landscape, staying at small inns along the way.

Previous The Arbel Cliffs along the Jesus Trail. Caves and cliff dwellings provided refuge in ancient conflicts.

Left Jesus and apostles on the Sea of Galilee in a woodcut by Michael Wolgemut, a teacher of Albrecht Dürer.

Opposite "Nobody knows exactly where Jesus walked," said an Israeli tourism official. "You have to use your imagination."

Though the official start is at the Church of the Annunciation in Nazareth, I began my hike at Inon's inn, which had become the trail's information hub. Accompanied by two other hikers, I followed the arrow up the stairs just outside the inn and found more, steeper stairs, hundreds of them. I sighed. But when I finally reached the top, the reward was a panoramic view of Galilee, a hilly quilt of pastures and olive farms.

I had always pictured this territory as arid, but the land was lush and green after the winter rains. Soon we were walking through a valley filled with wildflowers, headed toward Capernaum, the village that marks the end of the trail and the place where Jesus is believed to have done much of his teaching. As I walked, the familiar stories flooded my mind. Healing the sick, raising the dead, turning water into wine. This definitely wasn't going to be an ordinary hike.

Which was exactly what its creators had in mind. While most Christian tourists spend their time in Jerusalem and on bus tours, some yearn to see Jesus's backcountry. Two travelers I encountered on the path, Keith and Kathy Springer from Illinois, hiked the trail on days off from their stint as volunteers at Nazareth Village, a living history museum. "I couldn't think of anything more exciting than following in the footsteps of Jesus," Kathy said.

But Christian pilgrims weren't the only people Landis and Inon had in mind. In routing the path through Jewish and Arab villages that the tour buses bypassed, they figured that some of the money from Christian tourism—which accounts for a large chunk of Israel's tourist industry—would be funneled into the hands of local businesses.

At Mile 5 on the first day, we arrived at Zippori National Park, which is scattered with Jewish and Roman ruins. Suddenly, we heard somebody shouting. Scanning a muddy field, we spotted a man, the leader of a tour group whose minivan was stuck.

"I think his van's bogged down," said Andrew, one of my fellow hikers. Indeed, the black minivan was stuck in six inches of mud. His customers—elderly tourists from Haifa—stood at a distance. We waded into the mud and pushed. After a few tries, with our shoes sinking and shins mud-spattered, the minivan zoomed out of the mud. The tourists applauded.

In this place, I couldn't help but think that excessive pride is sinful, so I tried not to be too pleased with myself. Anyway, it was lunchtime.

After picnicking on pita bread and apples next to the Crusader Church, we explored the park's ruins.

Some biblical experts believe Zippori is the village where Mary grew up. Now the site includes a Roman-era villa with tiled floors that depict Isaac being bound by Abraham, scenes from the life of the Greek god Dionysus, and the woman known as the "Mona Lisa of the Galilee," whose mosaic eyes seem to stare at you no matter where you stand.

We followed the trail through a pine forest into the Arab village of Mashhad, where we were welcomed by a growling dog, a crowing rooster, and the muezzin's call to prayer. We walked past mosques and a traditional grave site of Jonah, the Old Testament prophet (another traditional site for Jonah's grave is in Iraq), then crossed a grassy valley to the village of Cana, where Jesus's first miracle, turning water into wine, is believed to have taken place. With a busload of Filipino pilgrims, we toured the Franciscan Wedding Church, a 19th-century castlelike structure built atop Byzantine ruins.

Tired from 10 miles of walking, we trudged down the main street, which has no shortage of curio shops selling small bottles of "miracle" wine and mineral water, and up a narrow lane to the Cana Wedding Guesthouse. There we drank coffee on the balcony, ate flatbreads, hummus, and lamb, and slept very well.

Not much happens in Israel without controversy, and the Jesus Trail is no exception. In 2011, in a move that annoyed Inon, the Israeli Ministry of Tourism opened its own version of the Jesus Trail, a 37-mile path called the Gospel Trail that goes through forest areas, bypassing Cana and most of the historical sites.

"Why didn't they just invest in our trail instead of spending millions of dollars on a new version?" asked Inon, who joined us during the second half of our hike. He said he thought he knew the reason: to avoid areas that have safety issues. Translation: to avoid Arab villages in favor of Jewish areas.

But Haim Gutin, an Israeli tourism commissioner, told me that that was not the reason. "The Gospel Trail was part of an overall plan that we developed over many years to market Israel to evangelical Christians," he said. "Besides, nobody knows exactly where Jesus walked. You have to use your imagination."

I hiked part of the Gospel Trail, but I wanted to visit sites that it bypassed. So I stuck with the Jesus Trail.

Above In the area of Arbel, ruins of a synagogue built of rock in the fourth century B.C.

Below At prayer near the Sea of Galilee. Many on the trail find deep meaning in experiencing the places mentioned in the Bible.

Opposite The trail is routed through villages and farms, with many places to stop along the way.

Day 2 began at 9 a.m. beneath a blue sky. We walked along a dirt road with views into the Tur'an Valley, a gentle dip teeming with wildflowers and olive trees. The road follows the stony remains of a Roman road through an oak forest, ending at a Holocaust memorial set up by residents of the nearby Kibbutz Lavi, which also operates a tourist hotel.

The next morning, we continued on to the Horns of Hattin, a double-peaked volcanic formation that resembles bull horns, where we caught our first glimpse of the Sea of Galilee. Long after Jesus's days on earth, Muslim forces defeated Frankish Crusaders at the Battle of Hattin in 1187.

We made our way to Nebi Shueib, a Druze shrine and the tomb of Jethro, father-in-law of Moses. At the end of the day we found ourselves at Moshav Arbel Guesthouse on a small farm, where our hosts — a jovial older couple — were waiting with a meal of lamb, veal, homemade sherry, and chocolate.

On our last day, our feet and knees were sore — we had covered 30 miles at this point — but some of the best sights awaited. At the 1,200-foot Arbel Cliffs, we had an unobstructed view of the Sea of Galilee; from there we hiked down a rocky slope aided by metal handholds, then down near caves and cliff dwellings

*Photographs by
Rina Castelnuovo*

where, according to the historian Josephus, Jewish rebels hid from Herod the Great. In a valley dotted with carob trees we headed toward Magdala, the traditional home of Mary Magdalene.

We met the bus tours again at the Church of the Beatitudes, a small church next to a stand selling sodas and candy. At a dirt overlook where Jesus supposedly performed the miracle of turning a few fish and loaves of bread into a feast, an American preacher was leading his flock of 40 in the singing of "Onward, Christian Soldiers."

Another half mile and we could smell the end of the trail, literally: a fish restaurant called Peter's. Even though Capernaum, which marked the trail's end, was close, we chose to rest our feet and drink an Israeli Goldstar beer.

WHAT TO READ AND WATCH

Walking the Jesus Trail: Nazareth to the Sea of Galilee, by Anna Dintaman and David Landis. Detailed information and maps for hikers who want to cover the trail from end to end.

Jesus Trail and Jerusalem, by Jacob Saar. Matches the trail's locations to the Biblical stories that cite them. Includes references to a website with GPS links.

The Sage from Galilee: Rediscovering Jesus' Genius, by David Flusser and Steven Notley. A solidly academic portrait of the historical Jesus.

The Naked Archaeologist, Season 1, Episode 9: *Jesus: The Early Years*. In Nazareth, two Bethlehems, and other locations, the archaeologist Simcha Jacobovici pursues clues to Jesus's life before his ministry.

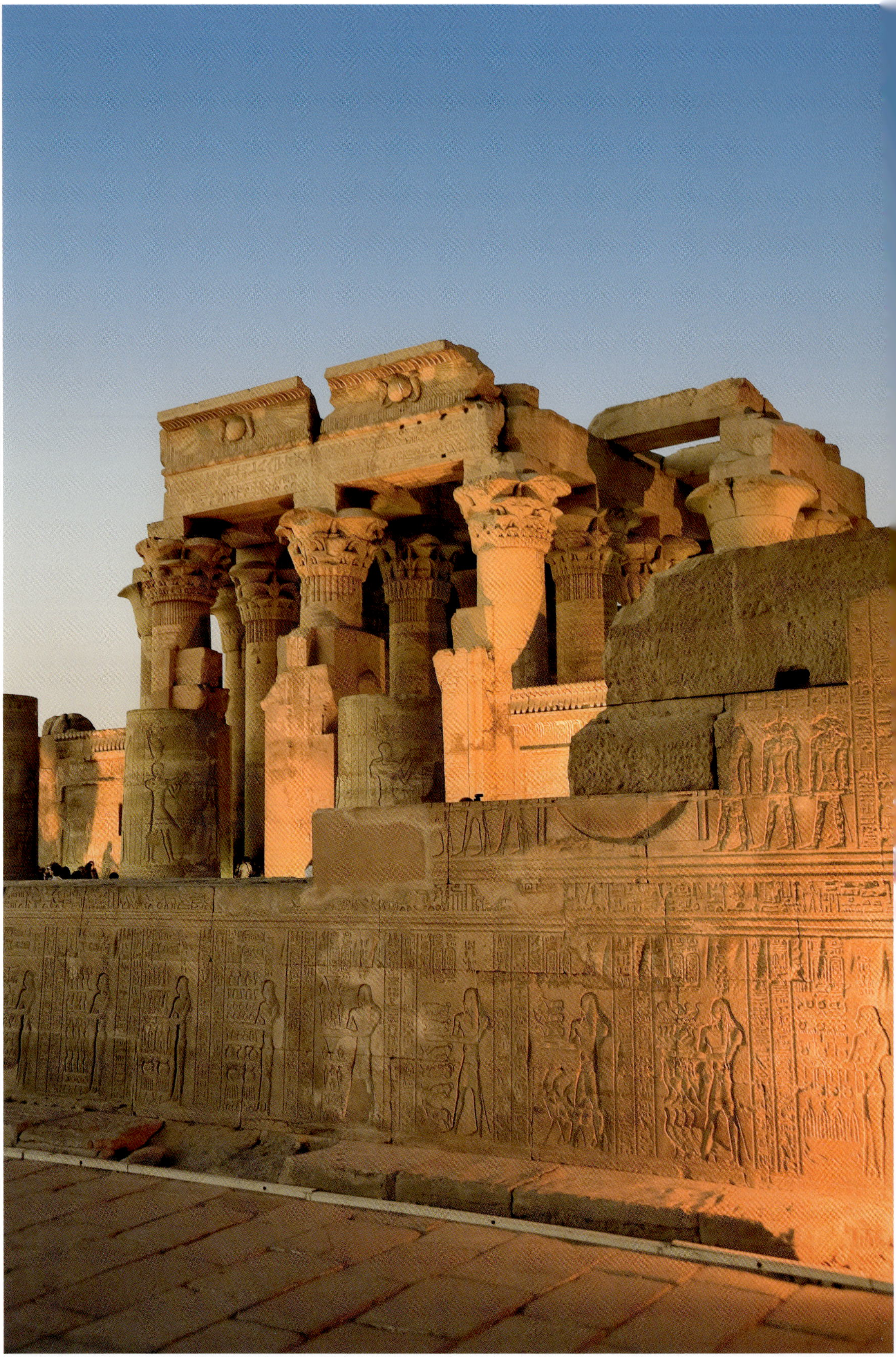

AN EXPEDITION ON THE NILE

Women explorers in the 1800s wrote vivid accounts of Egypt. Can a kindred spirit replicate their adventures today? — BY MICHELLE GREEN

Huddled on a chaise on the upper deck of the *Orient*, the *dahabiya* that I had chosen for a cruise down the Nile, I sipped hibiscus tea to ward off the chill. Late in February, it was just 52 degrees in Aswan, where I had boarded this boat, a traditional Nile craft with sails. But the scenery slipping past was everything the guidebooks had promised: tall sandbanks, curved palms, and the mutable, gray-green river, the spine of Egypt and the throughline in its history.

I'd been obsessed with Egypt since childhood, but it took a cadre of female adventurers to get me there. *Reading Women Travelers on the Nile*, a 2016 anthology edited by Deborah Manley, I'd found kindred spirits in the women who chronicled their expeditions to Egypt in the 19th century. Spurred on by them, I'd planned my trip.

From Cairo, I had already been to Giza to see the Pyramids and the Sphinx. Now I was cruising downriver — north, in the direction of the river's flow — from Aswan, 438 miles by air south of Cairo, to Esna, our gateway city to Luxor. Beside my chair were collections of letters and memoirs written by intrepid female journalists, intellectuals, and novelists. Relentlessly entertaining, the women's stories reflected the Egyptomania that flourished in Europe after Napoleon invaded North Africa in 1798. The country had become a focal point for artists, architects, and newly minted photographers — and a fresh challenge for affluent adventurers.

Their dispatches captured Egypt's exotica — vessels "laden with elephant's teeth, ostrich feathers, gold dust, and parrots," in the words of Wolfradine von Minutoli, whose travelogue was published in 1826. And they shared the thrill of discovery: Harriet Martineau, a groundbreaking British journalist, feminist, and social theorist, described the pyramids

Previous The temple at Kom Ombo, a stop on Nile cruises, honors Horus, the falcon god, and Sobek, the crocodile god.

Left A *felucca*, a traditional riverboat, on the Nile at Aswan.

Opposite European women in the 1800s found a kind of freedom as they traveled in Egypt, far from domestic life.

edging into view from the bow of a boat. "I felt I had never seen anything so new as those clear and vivid masses, with their sharp blue shadows," she wrote in her 1848 memoir, *Eastern Life, Present and Past*. The moment never left her. "I cannot think of it without emotion," she wrote.

Their lyricism was tempered by adventure: *In A Thousand Miles Up the Nile*, Amelia Edwards, one of the century's most accomplished journalists, described a startling discovery near Abu Simbel. After a friend noticed an odd cleft in the ground, she and her fellow travelers conscripted their crew to help tunnel into the sand. "Heedless of possible sunstroke, unconscious of fatigue," she wrote, the party toiled "as for bare life." With the help of more than 100 laborers supplied by the local sheikh, they eventually descended into a chapel ornamented with dazzling friezes and bas reliefs.

Though some later took the Victorians to task for exoticizing the East, these travelers were a daring lot: They faced down heat, dust, floods, and (occasionally) mutinous crews to commune with Egypt's past. Liberated from domestic life, they could venture out as men did.

Wolfradine von Minutoli wrote of camping out under the stars by the pyramids. Florence Nightingale, then 29 and struggling to gain independence from her parents, recalled crawling into tombs illuminated by smoking torches. Nightingale, among others, was struck by the otherworldliness of it all. Moved by the fragmented splendor of Karnak, the sacred complex in Luxor, she wrote to her family, "You feel like spirits revisiting your former world, strange and fallen to ruins."

Taken with their sense of adventure, I wanted to know whether the Nile journey had retained its mystique. Would I feel the presence of these women along the way? And could modern Egypt rival the country that they encountered?

Dozens of double-masted dahabiyas and river cruisers now ply the Nile, but I was drawn to the low-key *Orient*, a charming wooden sailboat. It has a capacity of 10 people, but I was joined by only four. On the upper deck, I could lounge on oversize cushions and watch storks skim the river. In the salon, a low sofa and carved armchairs were perfect for dipping into vintage *National Geographic* magazines. My cabin was compact, with twin brass beds and floral wallpaper.

Before 1870, when the entrepreneur Thomas Cook introduced steamers (and déclassé package tours), a cruise on the world's longest river lasted two or three months and typically extended from Cairo to Nubia and back. After renting a vessel, travelers were obliged to have it submerged to kill vermin. The boats were then painted, decorated, and stocked with enough goods to see a pharaoh through eternity. M. L. M. Carey, a correspondent in *Women Travelers on the Nile*, recommended packing "a few common dresses for the river," along with veils, gloves, and umbrellas to guard against the sun.

With my fellow passengers and our guide, I spent the first afternoon at a temple near the town of Kom Ombo. Reggae music drifted from a cafe, and shrieks rose from a neighborhood playground. Dedicated to Horus, the falcon god, and Sobek, the crocodile god, the temple has a separate entrance, court, and sanctuary for each. Hypostyle halls, spaces in which massive columns support a roof, were paved with stunning reliefs: Here was a Ptolemaic king receiving a sword; there, a second being crowned. Sobek, a mutable figure who was both aggressor and protector, was worshipped, in part, to appease the crocodiles that swarmed the Nile. Next to the temple, 40 mummified specimens—from hulking monsters to teacup versions—are enshrined in a dim museum, along with their croc-shaped coffins.

As we were leaving, folks in shorts and sun hats kept coming, fanning out until the complex became a multilingual hive.

Back on the *Orient* that night, we learned that our generator would stop at 10 p.m. The darkness was nearly complete, but silence never set in: Creaks, thumps, and splashes resounded through the night.

In the morning, we headed north to the sandstone quarry and cult center of Gebel Silsila. With their rock faces still scored with tool marks, the cliffs have an odd immediacy—as if armies of stonecutters could reappear at any moment. The compelling part of the site is a cluster of rock-cut chapels and shrines.

Dedicated to Nile gods and commissioned by wealthy citizens, they are set above a shore lined with bulrushes. Eroded but evocative, some retain images of patrons and traces of paintings.

We traveled downriver to Egypt's best-preserved temple, at Edfu. Tourism has made its mark in this agricultural town: Cruise boats lined the quay, and the drivers of the horse-drawn carriages known as calèches stampeded all comers. Begun in 237 B.C. and dedicated to Horus, the temple was partially obscured by silt when Harriet Martineau visited in 1846. "Mud hovels are stuck all over the roofs," she wrote, and "the temple chambers can be reached only by going down a hole like the entrance to a coal-cellar, and crawling about like crocodiles."

Excavated in 1859 by the French Egyptologist Auguste Mariette, the temple is an ode to power: A 118-foot pylon — a grand gateway — leads to a courtyard where worshippers once heaped offerings, and a statue of Horus guards hypostyle halls whose yellow sandstone columns look richly gilded. Feeling infinitesimal, I focused on details: a carving of a royal bee, an image of the goddess Hathor, a painting of the sky goddess Nut.

Later I thought of something Martineau had written: "Egypt is not the country to go to for the recreation of travel. One's powers of observation sink under the perpetual exercise of thought." Even a casual voyager, she wrote, "comes back an antique, a citizen of the world of six thousand years ago."

Our dinner that night was festive: When someone asked for music, our purser returned with the entire crew. Retrieving drums from an inlaid cabinet, they launched into 20 exuberant minutes of song.

For our final outing, we docked at the town of Esna. Built during the reign of Ptolemy V and dedicated to a river god, Esna's temple was conscripted by the Romans and then abandoned. Only its portico had been excavated when Nightingale visited. In a letter to her family, she said, "I never saw anything so Stygian."

Now partly reclaimed, the temple is 30 feet below street level. Beyond the portico is a hypostyle hall whose columns are inscribed with sacred texts and

Opposite While their boat awaits nearby, travelers from a Nile cruise dine alfresco on the riverbank.

Above Friezes tell ancient stories on the walls of the temple at Kom Ombo.

hymns. Still traced with color, they blossom into floral capitals. On the walls are images of Roman emperors presenting offerings to Egyptian gods.

After a celebratory breakfast the next day — crepes, strawberry juice, Turkish coffee — our cruise ended, but our trip had not. A driver from the dahabiya company was waiting to take us to Luxor, about an hour away. Near the town is Karnak, one of the world's largest sacred monuments, and across the Nile is the Valley of the Kings.

Founded chiefly by Amenhotep III and originally dedicated to Amon-Re, the complex at Karnak was modified and enlarged by rulers including Ramses II. In the 19th century its pylons, halls, and courts were still mired in detritus: Nightingale was unsettled by the temple's "dim unearthly colonnades" when she visited on New Year's Eve in 1849. "No one could trust themselves with their imagination alone there," she wrote. With enormous shadows looming, said Nightingale, "you feel as terror stricken to be there as if you had awakened the angel of the Last Day."

Though it is now busy with tourists, Karnak is still haunting. An avenue of ram-headed sphinxes leads to an imposing first pylon; beyond, 138 pillars soar into empty space. Wandering without a guide, I lingered over details: the play of light on a broken column; the base of a shattered statue that had left its feet behind.

On the way to the Valley of the Kings, I thought about the desecration described by Victorian travelers. Jewelry, cartouches, and body parts were all on the market, and Amelia Edwards, author of *1,000 Miles Up the Nile*, was among those who were offered a mummy. After casually expressing an interest in an ancient papyrus, wrote Edwards, she and a companion had been "beguiled into one den after another" and "shown all the stolen goods in Thebes."

Sheltered by limestone cliffs and set off by a limitless sky, the Valley of the Kings has been brought to

Above For an updated Nile cruise, one choice is the *Orient*, a traditional double-masted *dahabiya*.

Below A view to the shore. In Egypt, Florence Nightingale wrote, "You feel like spirits revisiting your former world."

Opposite A passenger's choice: dip into her books or gaze out the cabin window at the flowing Nile.

order: Vendors now sell their wares in a visitors' center, and tourists can hop an electric train to the burial grounds.

One of the most spectacular tombs in the royal warren belonged to Seti I; it was known to Victorians as "Belzoni's tomb." The entrance was breached in 1817 by the Italian adventurer Giovanni Belzoni, who removed the sarcophagus of Seti I and sold it to a collector. In 1846, Martineau visited the chamber that had held the sarcophagus and reported, "We enjoyed seeing the whole lighted up by a fire of straw." With its brilliant paintings set off by the flames, she said, "it was like nothing on the earth."

It still is: The deepest and longest tomb in the necropolis, the resting place of Seti I is adorned with astonishing reliefs. Scenes from texts including the Book of the Dead lead from one spectacular enclave to another. When I visited, there were no crowds, and the silence was profound.

The pharaoh who eluded the Victorians, of course, was Tutankhamun. Cloaked in obscurity for 3,000 years, his tomb was unsealed by Howard Carter at a time when the valley was believed to hold no more surprises. Though most of Tutankhamun's treasures make up the marquee display for the new Grand

*Photographs by
Maria Mavropoulou*

Egyptian Museum in Giza, his outer sarcophagus is still in the burial chamber we were visiting. Stripped of its bandages, his corpse now lay in a glass box— a desiccated figure blanketed in linen. Only his blackened head and feet were exposed, but he looked exquisitely vulnerable.

Surrounding the remains of the boy king are murals depicting him as a divinity; he enters the afterlife in the company of Anubis and Osiris and Nut. Set against a gold background, the images temper the pathos of his remains. In the end, the tomb lost for so long is a reminder that in Egypt, the past continues to evolve. Perspectives can shift; voices can change. And something astonishing may be just around the corner.

WHAT TO READ

***Women Travelers on the Nile: An Anthology of Travel Writing through the Centuries**, by Deborah Manley. Observations in Egypt by women from the 1700s to the modern era.*

***Letters from Egypt: A Journey on the Nile, 1849–1850**, by Florence Nightingale. Before she was a nurse in Crimea, Florence Nightingale took a trip to Egypt. These are her letters home.*

***Down the Nile: Alone in a Fisherman's Skiff**, by Rosemary Mahoney. A 21st-century real-life adventure story.*

***A World beneath the Sands: The Golden Age of Egyptology**, by Toby Wilkinson. An account of the European pillage of Egyptian artifacts in the years when theft was the flip side of thrilling discovery. "This is a riveting, sometimes appalling story."* — Rosemary Mahoney in *The New York Times*.

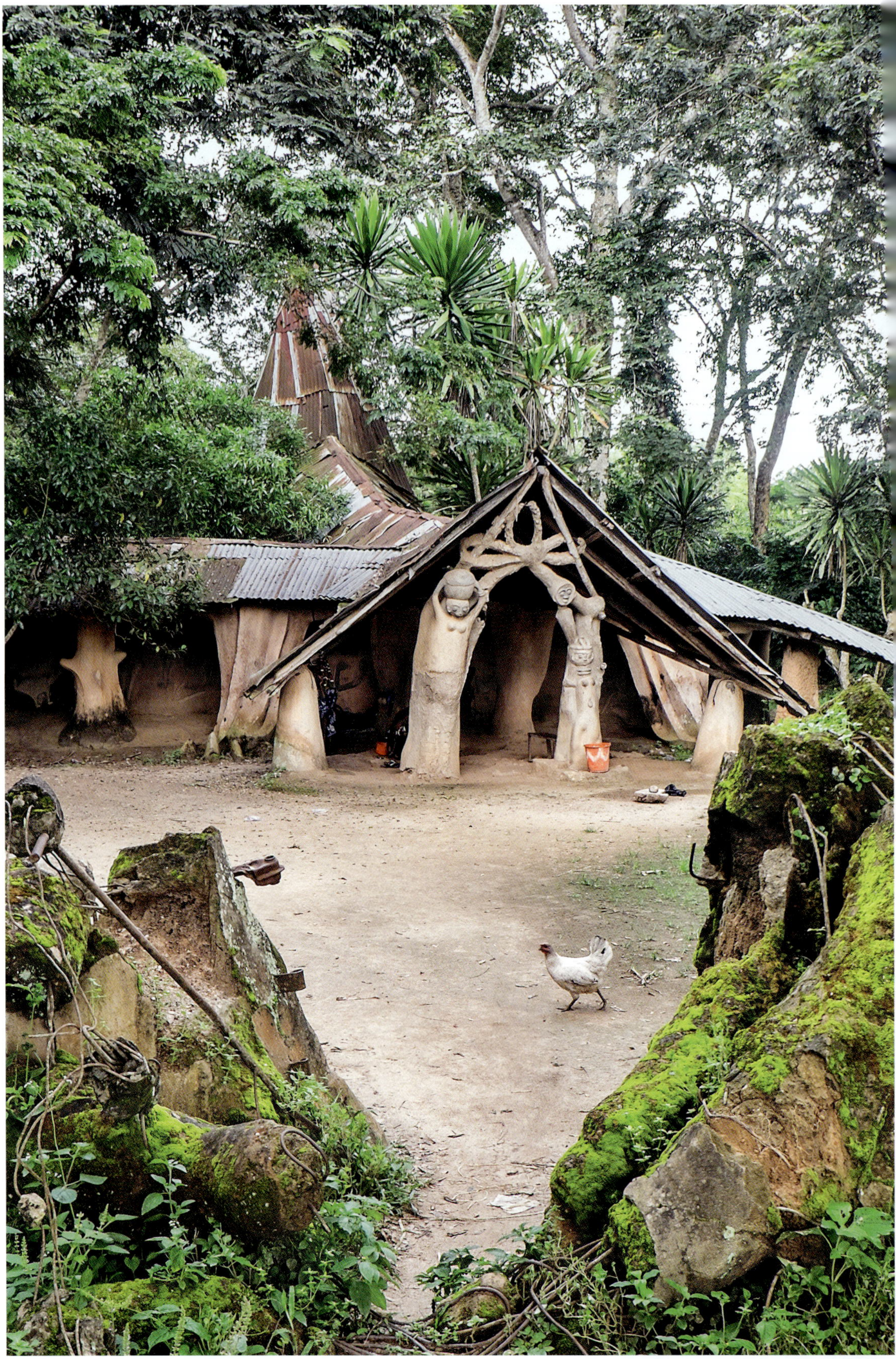

CEREMONY IN A SACRED GROVE

A goddess of the Nigerian forest retains her power, woven into the tapestry of a people's history and identity. — BY FEMKE VAN ZEIJL

The ritual drummers preceded her as she strode down the broad steps toward the Osun shrine, carefully balancing on her head a calabash filled with kola nuts, palm oil, and other offerings to the Yoruba gods. She was not used to walking barefoot, so the sticks and stones on the forest floor sometimes hurt her feet, yet she continued on her course with a trancelike resolve.

It was all part of an initiation ceremony of the traditional Ifa religion of the Yoruba, the largest ethnic group in southwest Nigeria, and the main reason she had traveled to the Osun-Osogbo Sacred Grove in Nigeria. At home in Brooklyn people know her as AnnMarie Sealey. Here in Osogbo they call her Ifaseye Orisabunmi Adeegbe.

Sealey is one of many visitors from abroad with an ancestral connection to Africa who come to the Sacred Grove, the high priestess Adedoyin Talabi Faniyi said, standing next to Sealey and a few other devotees on the bank of the Osun River. There, a statue of the goddess Osun was spreading her arms as if to welcome visitors to the 185 acres of dense forest dedicated to her. Osun, one of many Ifa deities, is the Yoruba goddess of fertility.

"People come here looking for their roots," Faniyi said. As a high priestess of Osun, she guided Sealey through her initiation process.

In the past, most Yoruba settlements had sanctuaries like the Osun-Osogbo Sacred Grove in the forests near them, but now there is no other place like it left in the cultural region of Yorubaland. Located in the primary high forest just outside the city of Osogbo in southwest Nigeria, it is a Unesco World Heritage Site.

OSUN-OSOGBO   NIGERIA

Previous A traditional sculptural building, not yet restored, at the Osun-Osogbo Sacred Grove, a Unesco World Heritage Site.

Left Sculptures in traditional style. The Sacred Grove is a preserved forest with shrines to gods and goddesses.

Opposite A restored structure. The religion of the Sacred Grove is Ifa, a traditional faith of the Yoruba people.

Osun-Osogbo contains over 40 shrines and is visited by Osun worshippers, traditional healers who gather the medicinal plants that grow there, and tourists from all over the world. Hunting, fishing, and farming are prohibited in the area, and on a walk through the woods visitors might glimpse a sitatunga antelope or encounter troops of white-throated monkeys (categorized as vulnerable by the International Union for Conservation of Nature) playing in the trees or begging for the bananas they are accustomed to getting from passersby.

The thatch roof of the temple of Osun is held up by carved pillars resembling totem poles, and the walls are painted with geometric patterns. This is where it all started, the high priestess explained as she removed her slippers to enter the shrine. Archaeological excavations show that people first moved to the grove about 400 years ago, and according to local oral history settled at this site near the river.

Little did they know that they were treading on sacred ground. One day, the story goes, one of the early settlers was cutting down a tree when a voice came from the river, instructing him to move away. "It was the voice of Osun, who turned out to live in this river," Faniyi said, pointing to the calmly flowing water. The settlers left the site for higher ground, establishing what would become the city of Osogbo, and dedicated the forest to the goddess. Every August, thousands come to the city for the Osun Festival and to celebrate the special pact between the Osogbo people and the Yoruba goddess.

But Osun is not the only deity worshipped in the Sacred Grove. The Yoruba religion has more than 400 *orishas* like her, representatives of the supreme god Olodumare. Strolling through the forest, visitors come across a big-eyed statue of Obatala, the orisha of creation, and a two-story-high figure of Iya Mapo, the orisha of women's crafts like pottery and dyeing, extending six arms toward heaven.

The magic starts on the asphalt leading into the forest. The sculpted faces and figurines poking out of the roadside fences seem to be announcing the enchanted world that lies behind them. One of the walls even has a keyhole-shaped entrance, which might make some feel like Alice in Wonderland.

The scene is watched over by ancient kapok, abachi, and black afara trees. Footpaths covered with crackling leaves lead past silent houses dedicated to the gods, their interiors molded like a large animal's intestines. In a small glade a sculpted two-headed snake sticks out of the ground, and elsewhere statuettes of round-bellied men gather at giant tree roots.

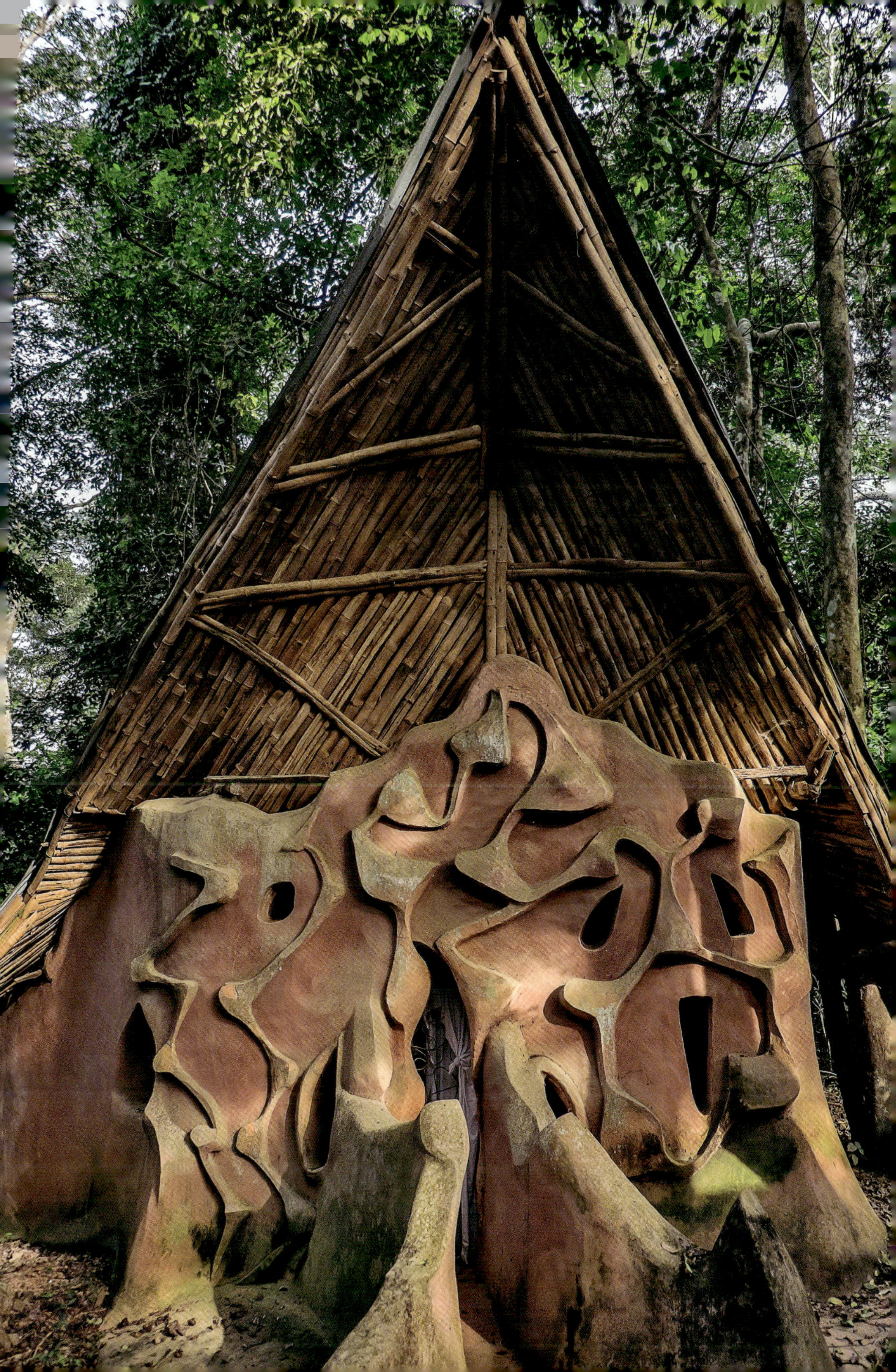

Above The high priestess Adedoyin Talabi Faniyi. "People come here looking for their roots," she said.

Opposite The grove attracts descendants of the African diaspora, many from Brazil and the United States.

These are the works of artists of the New Sacred Art movement who started embellishing the grove in the mid-1950s. They built the stylized houses for the gods, erected the statues, and sculpted the temple doors. Adebisi Akanji, one of the sculptors, said he was inspired by the termite mounds in this region, where he was born and raised, to become an artist, and built his first statues of wet mud. He moved on to sculpting with concrete, a technique he used with Susanne Wenger, an Austrian artist who moved to Nigeria in 1950, got deeply involved in Yoruba culture and religion, and lived and worked in Osogbo until her death in 2009.

When Wenger came to Osogbo, the Sacred Grove was on its way to disappearing. Termites had eroded the shrines, the roof of the Osun temple had caved in, more and more of the woodland was being cultivated as farmland, and the city of Osogbo was expanding toward the grove. With the local craftsmen and artists she befriended, she made the restoration her life's work. Money to keep the work advancing comes from donations and the Nigerian government.

Some of the grove's most devoted visitors come from abroad, mostly from the United States, Brazil, and Cuba. Many are people of the African diaspora, searching for more information about who they are, and for emotional connection to their roots.

Sealey, the initiate from Brooklyn, had never traced her forefathers, but she said she imagined they might have come from Nigeria. Born in Trinidad, she grew up in a Baptist family but began searching outside her religion for guidance. When her sister-in-law introduced her to an orisha ceremony, she felt a strong connection and learned more about Ifa online. She first traveled to Yorubaland in 2009 to be introduced to the religion and then frequently returned.

"Here I have found my life's path," Sealey said when she returned from the river, where she had

Photographs by Adolphus Opara

completed her initiation by making an offering to Osun—the content of which only the devotee and the priestesses knew. The sound of the brass bells the priestesses rang to invoke the goddess's spiritual energy had faded away. Clad in a simple piece of white cloth and without her usual makeup, Sealey fit right in with the other believers under the ako tree next to the Osun temple.

Her initiation over, she would return in three days to her job at a New York investment firm, a world away. But the spirit of the grove would remain with her, she said. "It is the only place in the world I feel really at peace."

WHAT TO READ AND WATCH

Sacred Journeys, Season 1, Episode 6: *Osun-Osogbo*. A PBS documentary of the annual Osun-Osogbo festival, which attracts thousands from around the world and where joy goes hand in hand with reverence.

Osun Osogbo: Sacred Places and Sacred People, by Afolabi Kayode. The text and photos explore the basic questions: Who is this Yoruba river goddess, and where does she get her cultural power?

Priestess of Osun: My Nigerian Initiation, directed by Rainer Doost and Valeria Watson-Doost. This documentary follows an African American woman's journey to find and experience her indigenous culture.

A History of the Yoruba People, by Stephen Adebanji Akintoye. Traces the journeys of the Yoruba people, both in Africa and scattered in diaspora, back to the early Yoruba kingdoms and cities.

Dunhuang 596

● Amritsar 572

● Chandigarh 590

Ubon to
Khong Chiam 660 ●
Mekong River 618 ●
● Bangkok 578
Cambodia
584

● Tamil Nadu 648

● Kerala 604

Singapore
636

ASIA &
OCEANIA

Kyoto 610

Tokyo & Osaka 654

Naoshima 624

Shanghai 630

Sydney 642

Yogyakarta 666

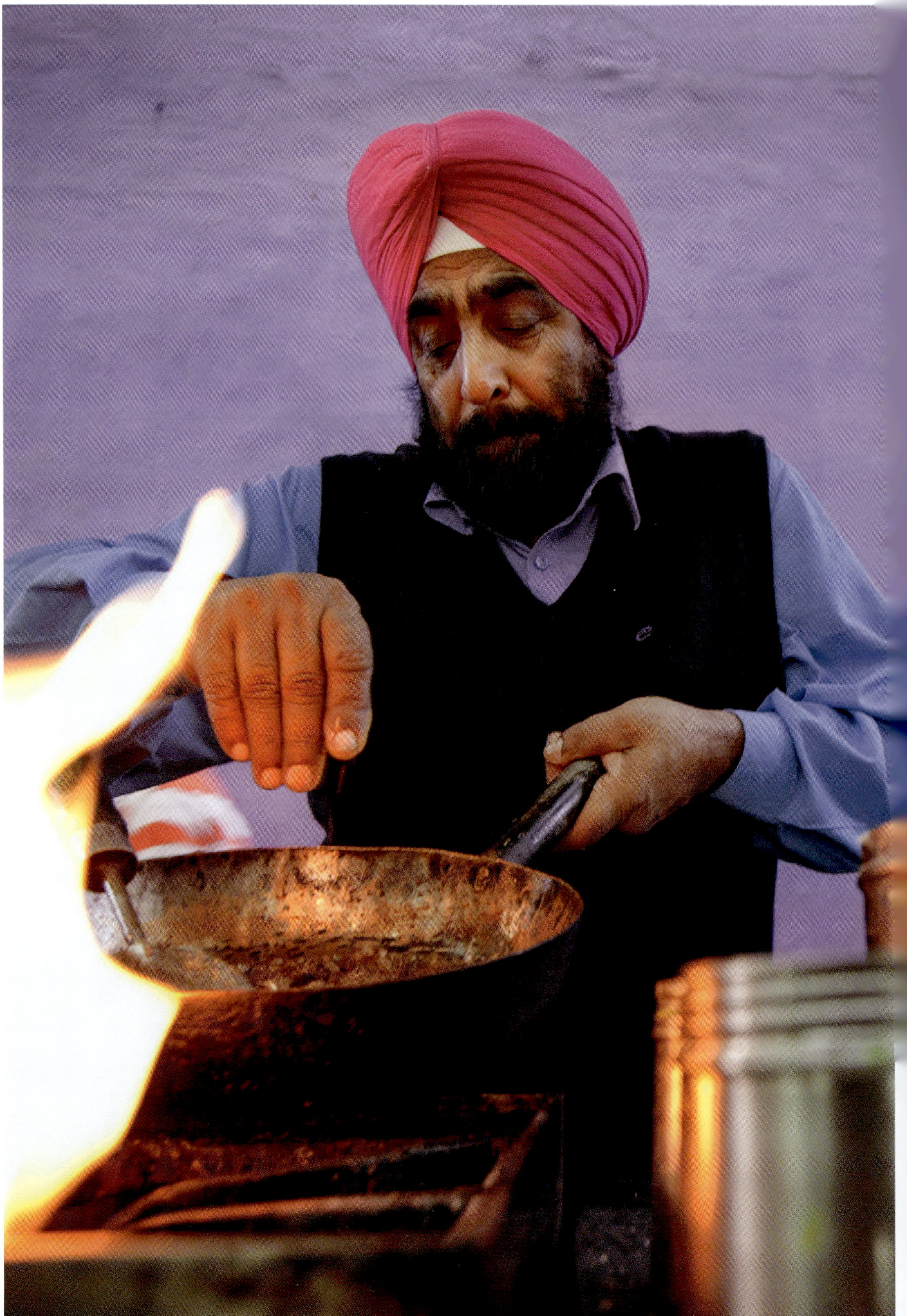

A CULINARY PILGRIMAGE TO PUNJAB

Multitudes go to Amritsar to pray at the Golden Temple. Another crowd worships the comfort food.
— BY SHIVANI VORA

Within five minutes of our ordering three deluxe *thalis* at the large and bustling Bharawan da Dhaba in Amritsar, India, a waiter brought us round steel trays filled with them — our three-dollar lunch. Each tray held a half-dozen dishes, including spicy chickpeas with a hint of pomegranate powder; the black lentils known as daal; and the Punjabi comfort food equivalent of macaroni and cheese: creamy mustard greens with *kadhi*, a yellow chickpea-flour-and-yogurt curry swimming with fried onion fritters. *Lachedar parantha*, whole wheat butter-layered bread, fresh from the tandoor clay oven, accompanied the thalis.

These were the same dishes that Bharawan, a casual restaurant known as a *dhaba*, first served when it opened in 1912 as a covered tent restaurant, and they are what keep the crowds coming back more than a century later.

Amritsar, in the state of Punjab in northern India, is a city for pilgrimages. There are those who come to visit the Golden Temple, the Sikh house of worship built in the 16th century, and then there are the presumably less pious who make the trip for the dhabas — divey-looking joints famous for quick, inexpensive, and remarkably tasty Punjabi cuisine.

My mother-in-law, my sister, and I had come to pay homage to the dhabas, and over the course of three days, we ate our way through the most notable ones in town. As a Punjabi growing up in New Delhi, I heard constant stories from my family about the dhaba feasts to be had in Amritsar, and now I was experiencing them myself.

Although each dhaba has its own specialties, there are similarities. Most have been around for a

Previous Cooking at Surjit Food Plaza, a *dhaba* in Amritsar. Dhabas are traditional casual restaurants.

Left Fried fish, tandoori chicken, and mutton tikka at Surjit Food Plaza.

Opposite Food trolleys were fixtures at train stations, serving an early 20th-century version of fast food.

half century or more and are family-run — actually, make that male-run, often with two or three generations of fathers and sons working together. And they have cultish followings because the dishes are authentic, using so much ghee (clarified butter) that even the most traditional French cook would blush.

My primary concern about my ambitious tour was whether my stomach would hold up, given the American standards of hygiene I had become accustomed to in 25 years of living in the United States. But Rashmi Uday Singh, the Mumbai-based food writer who is a judge on the Indian series *The Foodie Show* and who filmed an episode about Amritsar dhabas, eased my fears. "The thing about dhabas is that they usually have no fridges and buy only enough ingredients every morning that they will use in a day, so everything is very fresh," she said.

Nostalgia led me to our first stop, the nearly half-century-old Kundan, for its legendary *chole poori* breakfast. Located near the railway station, the small and square, strictly vegetarian spot had plastic chairs and tables and dim lighting, but we weren't there for the ambience. This morning meal of poori — round, deep-fried puffy bread — with spicy chickpeas was a beloved weekend tradition at my grandmother's New Delhi house when I was a child.

A cook standing outside over a large black vat of bubbling oil flattened the dough for our pooris and fried them to a golden finish. Each of our stainless-steel trays held four pooris, a generous bowl of chickpeas, another one of cooling yogurt, and a side of spicy mango pickle. Our intention was to try just a bit, to save room for the abundance of eating ahead of us that day, but a few bites of the crispy and chewy bread cradling the tangy and spicy chickpeas weren't enough. Before long, nearly everything on our platters was gone.

The next objective in our culinary quest was the favorite Punjabi dish, the spicy black lentils called *daal makhani*. Around the world, they are a top order in Indian restaurants. We headed to Kesar da Dhaba, which we reached by walking through a series of narrow streets in the city center. Rickshaws and bicycles were the only vehicles around.

The owner, Ajay Kumar, was chopping cauliflower in the open kitchen. Behind him were more than a dozen men furiously mincing large bunches of vegetables and cilantro. Kumar's great-grandfather, Lala Kesar Mul, started Kesar, a vegetarian restaurant, in 1916. Back then, daal makhani was the prized dish, and it's still the reason for the place's popularity; on an average day Kesar serves 700 customers. "We go through 220 pounds of daal a day, and it's sold out by the evening," Kumar said.

Making a batch in the massive steel cauldron is a nine-hour endeavor that begins at 4 a.m., when one of the cooks washes and boils lentils until they are soft. Adding salt and red chile powder is next, and a mixture that includes onion, ghee, turmeric, and the pungent sweet spice asafetida goes in just before serving. The word *makhani* means "with butter" in Hindi, and the hot and thick brown daal isn't complete until it's scooped into shallow steel bowls and topped with at least half a stick, which gradually melts in and makes for the creamiest rendition we had ever tasted.

By the evening, my sister and I were hankering for a meat fix. That took us to Pal, another half-century-old restaurant, for the goat leg curry, a dish we were both trying for the first time. The rickety benches and five green tables with cracks running through them were an unglamorous setting, but as we took in the aroma of the curry simmering in a round cast-iron pot in the tiny open kitchen, we forgot about our surroundings.

Jasbir Singh, one of Pal's owners, said the secret to the curry's deep flavor is roasting and grinding the spices, such as garam masala, cumin, coriander, and red pepper, every day. The chewy and rich goat legs in the soupy gravy beg for naan to scoop it all up, but instead of giving us the standard plain variety, Singh presented us with a version filled with minced mutton. "We are not a place for those who don't eat meat," he said.

Because most dhabas are vegetarian, Pal stands out, but rarer still are the ones that sell fish. Singara, fried catfish, was a household staple for us in Delhi, and I was happy to find it at two of the most respected dhabas in town, independently owned by members of the same family. Makhan Fish & Chicken Corner was a stand near the railway station opened by a father and two sons half a century ago. At the time, fish was

Above Pooris, deep-fried puffy bread, are breakfast stars in Amritsar. They pair well with spicy chickpeas.

Below Daal makhani at Kesar da Dhaba. "We go through 220 pounds of daal a day," the owner said.

Opposite The older generation at Kesar da Dhaba. Most dhabas are family operations many decades old.

unheard-of in Amritsar, but they sold fried singara fillets crusted in chickpea flour, caraway seeds, and red chile powder.

The brothers eventually split. One kept the Makhan name and opened a two-story dhaba where the original recipe is still the reason to dine. The first floor is a place for men to bring in alcohol to enjoy with their heaping platters, while families and women with children are relegated to the second floor, an alcohol-free zone.

The other branch of the family owns Surjit Food Plaza, which, with its glass tables, clean white walls, and wooden chairs, was the most upscale of the dhabas that we visited. Although the same crisp fish is on the menu, the place also had more adventurous dishes, like incredibly tender spinach-coated fish kebabs. My mother-in-law declared that Surjit's homemade paneer, an Indian cheese, was the softest she had ever tried — even softer than hers.

Part of the charm of dhabas is that they function much as they did when they first opened, although they can be savvy about modern marketing. A handful, including Surjit, Kesar, and Bharawan, have Facebook pages or websites. Bharawan's owner, Subash Vij, opened an outpost in a mall food court.

Photographs by
Kuni Takahashi

"Even in such an old and successful business, change is the law of nature," he said.

He sat with us while we ate our thalis, and after he saw that we needed more bread, an oversize leavened flatbread called a *kulcha* appeared, tempting us with its gentle steam and glistening ghee.

We eyed one another. Who would have the first bite? Without any discussion, all three of us tore off pieces at once.

WHAT TO READ AND WATCH

The Dhabas of Amritsar: A Cookery Book with a Difference, by Yashbir Sharma. Recipes from the owners and cooks of Amritsar's most famous dhabas.

Around the World in 80 Plates: The Gourmet's Guide to Vegetarian Cuisine, by Rashmi Uday Singh. Meatless recipes from the celebrity Indian food writer and author of 36 books.

Tasting India: Heirloom Family Recipes, by Christine Manfield. A well-known Australian chef explores India through its food, landscapes, and traditions.

Bride and Prejudice, directed by Gurinder Chadha. Bollywood meets Jane Austen in this unusual take on *Pride and Prejudice* featuring an Amritsar family hoping to marry off its daughters.

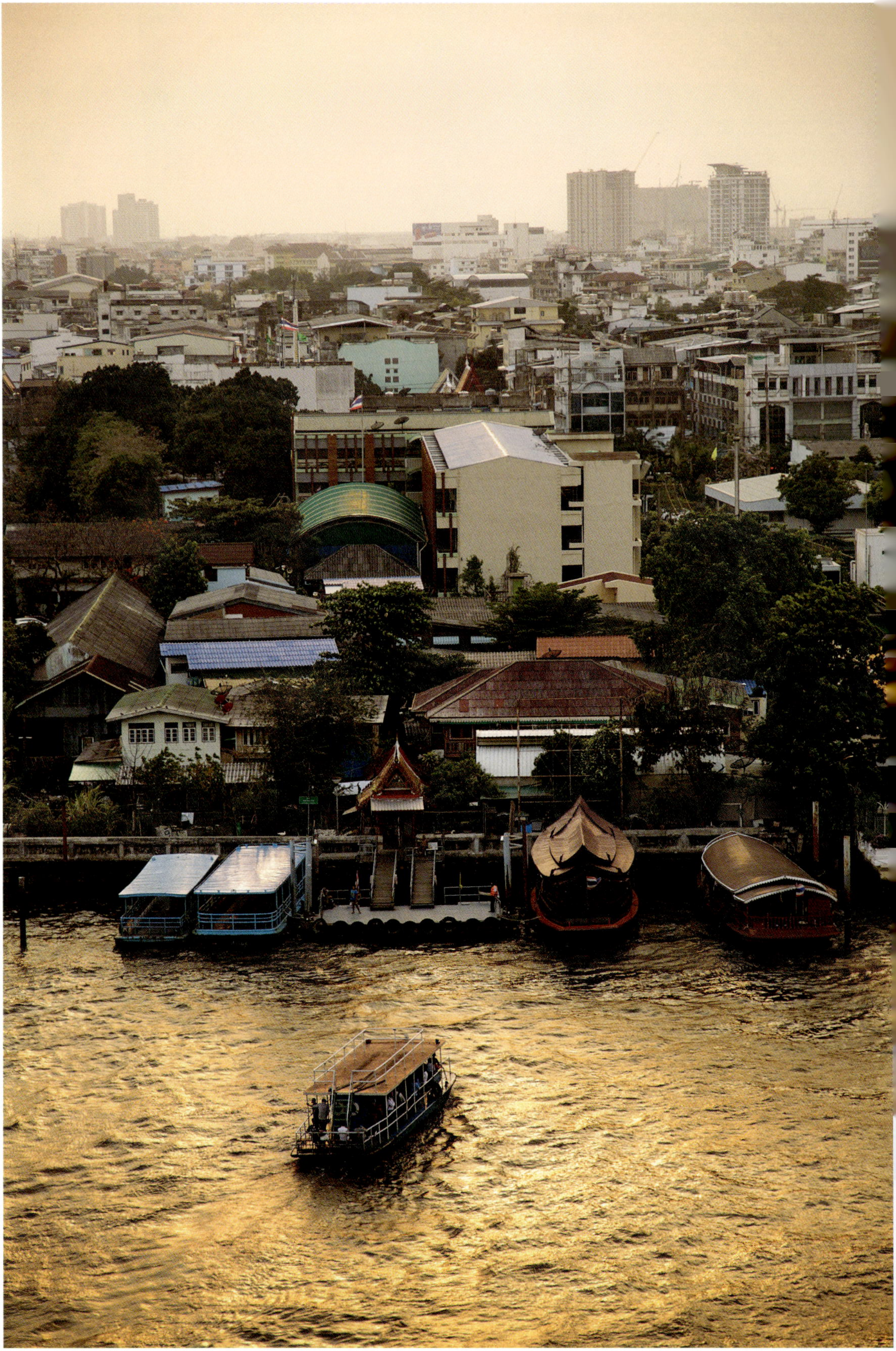

BANGKOK'S RIVER OF KINGS

On the rediscovered Chao Phraya, old Thailand stays put while a new bohemian chic moves in.
— BY TONY PERROTTET

When Somerset Maugham staggered from the Bangkok train station one steaming day in 1923, he knew exactly where to head: the Chao Phraya—the River of Kings—whose fresh breezes and open skies were even then a relief from the intensity of the Thai capital. Feeling the onset of malaria, Maugham checked into the Oriental Hotel, where verandas overlooked the busy waterfront. As his temperature climbed to 105 degrees, soaked in sweat and addled by hallucinations, he overheard the Oriental's owner telling his doctor that it would be bad for business if he should die on the premises.

Maugham's verdict on Bangkok would make a brutal online review today. In his travel memoir *The Gentleman in the Parlor* he reviled the city's "dense traffic," its "ceaseless din," its "insipid" cuisine and "sordid" houses. The Thai, he declared petulantly, were "not a comely race."

But once he recovered, Maugham experienced a rush of euphoria at the waterside setting. He watched the parade of barges, sampans, and tramp steamers pass by with "a thrill of emotion," and conceded that the *wats*, the gilded and glittering temple complexes rising along the river, made him "laugh out loud with delight to think that anything so fantastic could exist on this somber earth."

I had a taste of Maugham's extreme reactions as I sat in Bangkok's nefarious traffic trying to get to the river on the first morning of a trip there, although I was addled by nothing more dangerous than jet lag from the epic 21-hour flight from New York.

Laden with literary reference, the Oriental—now the Mandarin Oriental, although nobody calls it that—is still the obvious introduction to the Chao Phraya, which has in recent years returned to its status as an escape from the city's urban chaos. The

Previous The Chao Phraya River as seen from the venerable Mandarin Oriental, Bangkok, which opened as the Oriental Hotel in 1876.

Left The Oriental in earlier years. Its famous guests included Somerset Maugham, Joseph Conrad, and Noël Coward.

Below A Bangkok street from the passenger seat of a tuk-tuk, the ubiquitous three-wheeled taxi of Thailand.

Opposite A long-tail boat, a distinctive Southeast Asian watercraft, speeds along the Chao Phraya.

colonial-era edifice where Maugham stayed is now called the Author's Wing. Although overshadowed by a 1970s addition, its exterior looks much as it did when it opened in 1887 and astonished the city with its luxurious imported carpets, Parisian wallpaper, and electrified chandeliers. And the setting has not lost its soothing effect.

I pulled up a chair feet away from the "liver-colored water swirling by," as another famous guest, Noël Coward, put it. A parade of ferries, barges, and steamboats battled the surging currents, while islands of vegetation floated past, washed downriver from the jungles of the northern provinces. It was a step back into a leisurely past, worlds away from the explosive neon energy of the central city.

It's no secret that, despite bouts of political disorder, Bangkok has emerged as the unofficial capital of Southeast Asia. Everyone from Swedish aid workers to Vietnamese IT specialists prefers living there and commuting around the region to being based in less dynamic cities.

The most alluring consequence for travelers has been the revival of the Chao Phraya, which was once the heart and soul of Bangkok. It was by its shores that the sumptuous royal district was built in the 18th century and, although Thailand is one of the few Asian countries never to be colonized, where European powers erected their legations and warehouses in the 19th.

It was along the river that Bangkok's first road was built (an elephant track that became known as the New Road) and where a raucous Chinatown sprang up. The river was then so alluring that Bangkok was affectionately called "the Venice of the East," a serene warren of canals, floating markets, and stilt houses.

But after World War II, the focus of Bangkok moved north and east. The river districts fell into decay, their waters polluted. Travelers mostly stayed away, visiting the waterfront only in day trips to the famous wats. It was well into the new millennium before the river was rediscovered by bohemian Thais and intrepid expats, creating a mix of decay and contemporary chic evoking an Eastern New Orleans.

"The Chao Phraya is a lifeline of history, culture, and spirituality," said David Robinson, director of Bangkok River Partners, founded in 2013 to help coordinate the revival. "It's changing but keeping its traditions. There are roast duck and congee shops there that are 100 years old." The novelist Lawrence Osborne, who moved to Bangkok from New York, agreed: "The modern city was thrown up over the last 40 years in gimcrack style. It looks like it might collapse any moment. You don't feel that at all by the river—there's a real sense of continuity."

The parallels to Western cities' adventures in urban renewal are not lost on Thai preservationists. Bangkok River Partners invited Joshua David, the co-founder of the High Line linear park in New York, to speak at a conference. He became fascinated by the Chao Phraya. "The river allows you to experience Bangkok in a completely different way," said David. "An amazing variety of watercraft is still used by local communities and will take you to places you would never imagine existed."

To me, the river also made Bangkok seem manageable. Over years of travel in Asia, I had somehow failed to venture outside the city's airport, in part because I was daunted by the prospect of navigating a megalopolis of over 8.5 million people that can seem like an alternate set from *Blade Runner*. But the idea of exploring by water made Bangkok more human in scale. I decided to spend my time entirely on the river to reimagine its golden age.

My inspiration would be less the jaundiced Maugham than Jozef Konrad Korzeniowski, a Polish sailor soon to be renowned as the author Joseph Conrad, who found himself in 1888 frequenting the Oriental Hotel saloon for a little over two weeks, chatting with the barflies, as was his wont, "of wrecks, of short rations, and of heroism."

Conrad had taken over command of an Australian ship, the *Otago*, but was stuck in Bangkok waiting for his crew to recover from tropical illnesses—an experience that is reworked in his novel *Lord Jim* and the shorter works *The Shadow-Line*, *Falk*, and *The Secret Sharer*. Although he had his life savings of 32 pounds stolen by his Chinese steward (who thoughtfully brushed and folded his clothes before disappearing), Conrad still felt fondly toward Bangkok, and never forgot its "gorgeous and dilapidated" temples, or the city's "vertical sunlight, tremendous, overpowering, almost palpable, which seemed to enter one's breast with the breath of one's nostrils and soak into one's limbs through every pore of one's skin."

As Conrad would surely agree, if the river traffic was hypnotic to watch, it was more satisfying to join. The variety of watercraft churning between the bobbing jetties was bewildering, ranging from high-speed long-tail boats to private vessels and public ferries. I found the ferries definitely the most exotic, if not always the most comfortable. In peak hours, crowds squeezed into the sweltering below-decks like sardines, with yellow-robed monks and dapper businessmen alike jostling for elbow room while harangued by boat workers with megaphones, who bellowed, "Go down! Go down! Go down!"

There were no continuous walkways along the river, so I made surgical strikes from the piers on foot, ducking in and out of laneways to the lapping waves. All along the right bank stood poetic ruins. The splendid 1887 offices of the East Asiatic Company appeared vacant, although the building is preserved and has been used as an event space and as a venue in the Bangkok Biennale. Catholic cathedrals and European embassies staggered on in crumbling glory, while the iron pins used to moor steamers in Conrad's day have quietly rusted.

One crooked lane led to the river temple where albino elephants were cremated, another to the sacred slab upon which Thai royals could be executed. (It

Above Wat Arun at night. Somerset Maugham said the fantastic sight of the wats made him "laugh out loud with delight."

Below Pork collar at Never Ending Summer. Chao Phraya eateries and food shops range from new to a century old.

Opposite Modern Bangkok exists side by side with the old world of the Chao Phraya.

was forbidden for royal blood to be spilled, so a bag was placed over the victim's head and he was cudgeled to death — a considerate gesture.)

And yet, around every corner, ventures of startling modernity were sprouting: boutique hotels, restaurants, and bars, often housed in small antique buildings, alongside a pioneering art gallery called Speedy Grandma or a bespoke furniture store like P. Tendercool. A Creative District has even been designated on both sides of the river to promote local talent.

The marquee site was the Jam Factory, a renovated warehouse complex set around a grassy courtyard with a high-end restaurant, all designed to appeal to natives first, tourists second. "Our real ambition is to get Bangkokians back to the river," said Robinson of River Partners. "Travelers will follow. People want authenticity."

To get a sense of the potential for the grandiose historic structures, I headed a few minutes away to Sathorn Road on the back of a motorbike-taxi. A century ago, this was the Fifth Avenue of Bangkok, lined with the palatial mansions of Thai sea merchants. Now a lonely vestige from 1896, the House on Sathorn, is dwarfed on three sides by glassy skyscrapers.

Photographs by Lauryn Ishak

Originally the residence of a rice baron, it survived the demolition blitz that has ravaged Bangkok since the 1960s because it housed the Russian Embassy. After a multimillion-dollar renovation, the building reopened in 2015 as a glamorous restaurant and event space and quickly became a symbol of a new spirit of preservation.

By 2025 or so, Robinson predicted, the Chao Phraya will be transformed but still recognizable. "Our vision is of a cleaner river, with more walkable areas, enriched with creative industries and renovated warehouses and clusters of art galleries you can visit without sitting all day in a taxi," he said. "But at the same time, all the old roast duck shops and congee stores will still be there. They'll just be 10 years older."

Even Somerset Maugham would have to approve.

WHAT TO READ

The Gentleman in the Parlour, by Somerset Maugham. A witty, Anglocentric memoir of Maugham's travels in Southeast Asia in 1922 and 1923.

Bangkokriver.com, the website of the Bangkok River Partners. An excellent resource for finding out the latest on the ever-changing waterfront.

Very Bangkok: In the City of the Senses, by Philip Cornwel-Smith. A veteran travel writer in Thailand explores the city in depth, emphasizing cultural and historical context.

Bangkok Wakes to Rain, by Pitchaya Sudbanthad. A novel that powerfully evokes a sense of modern Bangkok and the experience of living there.

Bangkok Days, by Lawrence Osborne. An eyes-wide-open exploration of Bangkok by a prominent British novelist who moved there after living and working in cities around the world.

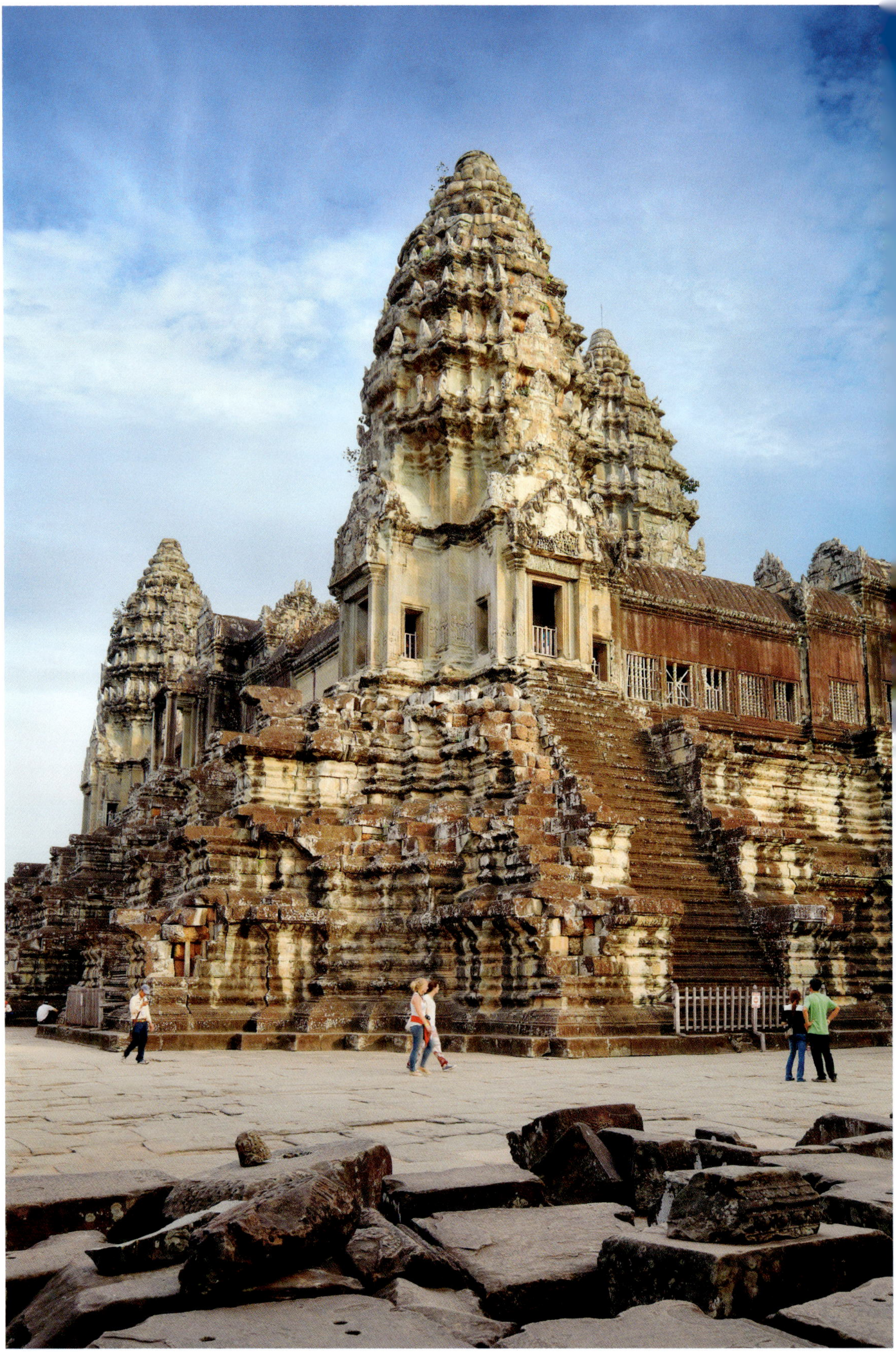

IN CAMBODIA WITH A CANTANKEROUS GUIDE

Henri Mouhot, the explorer of Angkor Wat, could be irritable, but he's still the man to follow to the mystifying, mesmerizing temples. — BY KAREN J. COATES

I tiptoed across the wood planks of a wobbly orange boat heading from the riverside town of Kampot to the Gulf of Thailand. I burned my bare feet on the shiny outdoor tiles surrounding a Buddhist stupa at Udong, the old capital of Cambodia. At the 11th-century ruins of Phnom Banan, I spelunked through deep, damp caverns steeped in legends of magic and superstition. All the way, I followed a Frenchman named Henri. Over two decades and more than 20 trips, he has led me through the heart of Cambodia.

If only we had met—or even lived in the same century. Henri Mouhot, an explorer and naturalist, was born in 1826 in eastern France. He had a passion for learning and travel, beginning with Russia, where he spent time as a young man. But his name is most associated with the Angkor ruins, which he made famous in Europe after first encountering them in 1860.

As a diarist, Mouhot, pronounced moo-HOE, could be cantankerous ("the present state of Cambodia is deplorable and its future menacing") and condescending ("this miserable people"). But he also revered nature and loved exploring. "I have never been more happy," he wrote, and "In truth, this life is happiness to me." Between 1858 and 1861 he traveled in Cambodia, Siam (now Thailand); Annam (now central Vietnam); and Laos, where he is buried. His diaries endure as some of the most prescient, insightful literature on the region.

Our odyssey together began in 1998, the year I spent in Phnom Penh, Cambodia's capital, working at a newspaper. I first read Mouhot for background and quickly found parallels to the country I was experiencing. The diaries contain a black-and-white

CAMBODIA

Previous Today's Angkor Wat would still be recognizable to Henri Mouhot, who explored it in 1860.

Left A drawing of Angkor Wat as it was 150 years ago, based on a sketch by Mouhot.

Opposite A pancake cart at Angkor Archaeological Park, where tourists find plenty of food choices.

drawing based on one of his sketches of a thatch hut on wooden stilts with a longboat on shore. The image could have been sketched today. And that cantankerous comment? Sadly, it could easily have applied to more recent phases of the country's history.

The touristy scene at Angkor Wat is another story. Yet even when I approached it on the back of a motorcycle, amid hundreds of other visitors, I still felt the same awe he described from another age: "At first view, one is filled with profound admiration, and cannot but ask what has become of this powerful race, so civilised, so enlightened, the authors of these gigantic works?"

One memorable trip took me south, to Kampot. When Mouhot visited, this was Cambodia's bustling port town. "Six or seven ships loading at one time," he wrote. "Chinese and European vessels may be constantly seen going up and down the stream."

Today, the main port has moved west to Sihanoukville; gone are Kampot's ships. Gone, too, is the public debauchery Mouhot depicted: "Almost every vice seemed prevalent at Komput — pride, insolence, cheating, cowardice, servility, excessive idleness." It now boasts a reputation of beauty and calm and is a favorite among both locals and tourists who like a slower pace of life.

Mouhot arrived 150 years too early to stay at the lovely Mea Culpa, where, in rooms that seem impossibly inexpensive, French doors open onto a patio with river views. He didn't clutch a cup of coffee while watching the daily parade of fishing boats heading to sea, as I did. And he didn't spend a morning with a boatman named Math Ly.

Math Ly and I set out on his flame-colored longboat at 7:30 a.m. The river was mostly empty, fishermen having already gone to sea. Only a long line of skiffs sat tethered to shore. As we headed south, rows of metal shacks gave way to mangroves in a faint, salty breeze. The river widened, and the horizon opened to distant islands dotting the gulf. Water and sky were both the hazy teal of sand-etched sea glass.

Mouhot spent time in this then-cacophonous town, where traders sold all manner of goods: "The dealers in fish and vegetables, and the Chinese restaurateurs, dispute the street with pigs, hungry dogs, and children of all ages." The Kampot market today still feels clamorous and claustrophobic — a maze of low-ceilinged stalls seemingly selling everything: mangoes, rice, cabbage, watermelon, pickles, shrimp, fermented fish, flowering chives, laundry soaps, toothbrushes. But though there are children, dogs are scarce, and any pigs you encounter will be of the fried variety.

The king, in Kampot at the time of Mouhot's visit, advised him to escape the clamor: "Go to Udong; go about." Udong, or Oudong, as it is also spelled, was then the capital, about 100 miles north, beyond modern-day Phnom Penh. "An eight-days' journey travelling with oxen or buffaloes," Mouhot wrote. "With elephants you can accomplish it in half the time."

My journey out of Kampot, by air-conditioned bus, took me first to Phnom Penh, less than four hours on a paved highway — no elephants. It sits at the confluence of the Mekong and Tonle Sap rivers and was known to Mouhot as "the Great Bazaar."

Now a city of 2.2 million people, Phnom Penh is the seat of modern-day power. Though travelers aren't accorded the royal audience Mouhot had, Cambodia does still have a king, Norodom Sihamoni, and tourists can glimpse the high life with a visit to the Royal Palace. In contrast to the city around it, the compound has well-tamed gardens and an open-air gallery painted with Buddhist and Hindu legends depicting tigers, monkeys, sailors, warriors, and intricate tales of honor and loss. The king's quarters are roped off, but visitors can peek inside the Throne Hall and the Temple of the Emerald Buddha, with its floor of solid silver tiles.

From Phnom Penh, it's an hour's drive to Udong through congestion and then a green belt of rice farms. Mouhot wrote of cottages with fruit gardens and country houses for the aristocracy "who come here in the evening for the sake of breathing a purer air than they can find in the city." Phnom Penh was just a market town then, and "the city" was Udong, a spirited place of mandarins, chiefs, and noisy courts of justice.

"How do you like my city?" a second king asked Mouhot. (Cambodia had a first and second king at the time.)

"Sire, it is splendid, and presents an appearance such as I have never seen elsewhere."

Little of that remains. The royals left in 1866 when the king chose Phnom Penh as a new capital. Udong suffered through decades of subsequent war, though today the remnants are slowly being rebuilt. Pilgrims now brave constant heat to climb steps to a series of hilltop temples and shrines.

As I entered the complex, children clung to my legs, attempting to sell me bracelets or cool me with handheld fans. Elderly and disabled beggars lined the steps, each with a plate onto which visitors dropped money.

At a giant golden Buddha with ruby lips and a golden sash, children occupied the entryway, guarding visitors' shoes for tips. This temple, once in shambles, has a new roof. A child monk sat amid burning incense, taking offerings and dispensing blessings. I stood by an open window, soaking in a welcome breeze, and gazing upon the paddies below. A few incongruous factories are scattered among the fields, but mostly it's a green landscape that stretches to the broad waters of the Tonle Sap River, the artery of Cambodia.

I rented a wooden cruise boat and burbled up the river, hoping for a picturesque sunset. But this time the sky only dimmed in a thickening haze, not the dazzling reds and pinks that often cascade across the river as the sun falls.

Mouhot found his light at Angkor Wat (Ongcor), "the most beautiful and best preserved of all the remains," in Siem Reap. It is still the world's largest religious structure, encompassing 401 acres — so commanding that a traveler forgets what Mouhot called "all the fatigues of the journey."

Angkor is a bit more boisterous now, with millions of visitors each year. And it has lost some of its Indiana Jones appeal. The multitudes have prompted the construction of wooden steps, railings, danger signs, and a litany of rules. I headed to the back of the temple, where a guide was leading foreigners to their first glimpse of the site. He'd chosen a divergent but dramatic approach. The tourists' view was blocked by trees until they came around the corner and sighed collectively. "Oh, wow, look at that!" one man shouted.

Above The main temple of Angkor Wat. When Mouhot first saw it, elephants were the best transport for getting there.

Opposite A produce market in the riverside town of Kampot.

Late in the day, I sought solitude. Most crowds flock to the top of Phnom Bakheng, an ancient hilltop temple, for a sunset view over Angkor Wat, but I headed instead to Ta Prohm, the overgrown temple famous for the tenacious trees that smother its stone. It was nearly closing time, and almost no one was there. There is no sunset to be viewed in these tree-wrapped grounds, as twilight is heard more than seen. The light fades, and the ruins erupt in a riot of birdsong—mynas, parrots, and a hornbill with swooshing wings.

The Angkorian ruins extend far beyond Siem Reap. In the 12th century, under King Suryavarman II, the Khmer empire reached its apex, stretching into modern-day Myanmar, Laos, and Thailand. A few sites endure, in various states of dilapidation and looting, between Siem Reap and the Thai border.

Phnom Banan, a mountaintop temple, is about 13 miles from the city of Battambang, a pleasant jaunt through the countryside. It's a near-vertical climb up laterite steps to the ruins above undulating hills. In Mouhot's day, the temple still had eight towers connected by galleries of "fine workmanship, and great taste and skill in construction." Now only portions of towers remain.

What I wanted most to see was down the steps, at the mountain's base. A sandy path led to a "magic cave," as tourists call it today, a deep cavern of stalactites in the limestone rock. "The water dropping from these is considered sacred," Mouhot wrote, able to impart "knowledge of the past, present, and future." The cave is cool and dark, the soothing yin to the scorching yang outside. A guide named Phuoc Ran took me to an inner room where a Buddha statue sat amid candles.

Phuoc Ran was born in Saigon but fled to the Thai border during wartime. He told me he knows about New Mexico, where I live, because the American

Photographs by
Jerry Redfern

soldiers he met during the war watched movies full of Southwestern cowboys.

Mouhot, Phuoc Ran, me—we keep treading ground here because we keep finding stories to tell. That's how we learn about past, present, and future.

Mouhot understood the capacity for travel to enhance insight; he devoted his life to these gifts. Before he died—brutally, from malaria—in Laos at 35, he wrote to his sister-in-law about his passions. "Seeing so much that is beautiful, grand, and new," he wrote. "From these I draw my contentment."

WHAT TO READ

Travels in the Central Parts of Indo-China (Siam), Cambodia, and Laos During the Years 1858, 1859, and 1860, by Henri Mouhot. Based on Mouhot's notes and sketches and published by his brother after his death.

Cambodia Now: Life in the Wake of War, by Karen J. Coates. She is also the author of *Eternal Harvest: The Legacy of American Bombs in Laos*.

This Way More Better: Stories and Photos from Asia's Back Roads, by Karen J. Coates, with photos by Jerry Redfern. Essays and vignettes from Cambodia by the husband-and-wife team who wrote and photographed this article.

Angkor and the Khmer Civilization, by Michael D. Coe. An informative work by a professor of anthropology at Yale.

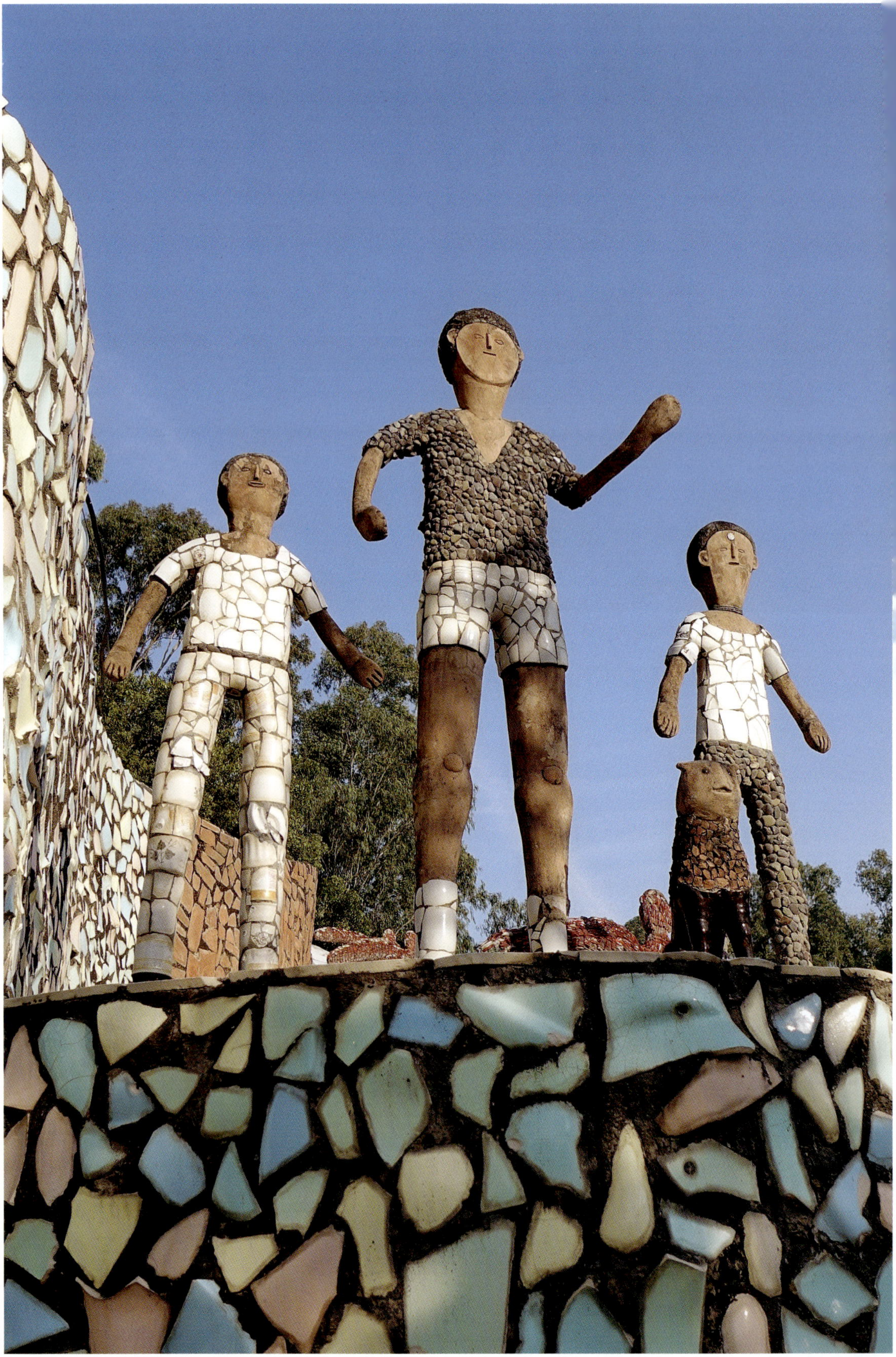

CHANDIGARH, WHERE OUTSIDER ART MEETS LE CORBUSIER

An architectural monument coexists with ruins of the villages it displaced, now transformed into phantasmagoric sculpture. — BY JADA YUAN

A tiny figure in flowing blue fabric ran in front of me, giggling; then another, then another, then perhaps a hundred more. They filed through what looked like a handcrafted version of a canyon from the moon: a narrow passageway of pockmarked concrete embedded with rocks, stretching two stories into the air.

There they were again, taking selfies next to a man-made waterfall tumbling from some kind of shrine on a hill. And then, quick as panthers, they were behind me, waving from a bridge festooned with clay vines: "Hello! Hello! Where are you from?"

When I had arrived by rickshaw at Nek Chand's Rock Garden, I had been prepared to gorge on a 40-acre extravaganza of outsider art, and I was not disappointed. Think Antoni Gaudí's similarly sized Park Güell in Barcelona, but homespun, distinctly Indian, and made entirely of industrial waste and found rocks by the self-taught artist Nek Chand Saini. Every turn of a corner brings new mosaics, waterfalls, sculptures of imaginary animals, pillars hung with swings. What I had not anticipated was the sheer joy of sharing that playground with uniformed children on school trips, families, honeymooning brides in elaborate pink saris, the occasional stray dog, and workers asleep on walls.

This life-affirming scene was playing out in Chandigarh, India, the dual-capital city of the states of Punjab and Haryana, recognized in architectural circles worldwide as a city designed by the pioneering architect Le Courbusier. The sprawling Chand garden arose independently in one of the planned green spaces and has become one of India's biggest tourist sites.

Previous In Nek Chand's Rock Garden, every turn of a corner reveals a sculpture of shards, stones, and debris.

Left Le Corbusier, the architect of Chandigarh, at the site of its construction in 1951.

Opposite Entryway to the High Court. For all of Chandigarh, Le Corbusier combined function and aesthetics.

That so much space has been given over to the organic expression of one artist's vision in Chandigarh, of all places, seems far-fetched. This is independent India's first planned city, designed by the pathbreaking Le Corbusier, the Swiss-French architect whose real name was Charles-Édouard Jeanneret, and built with the help of his cousin Pierre Jeanneret and a team of international and Indian architects. Here you'll find monumental concrete Brutalist buildings with striking, colorful interiors amid one of the only urban-grid layouts in India.

Le Corbusier divided the city into numbered sectors meant to be self-sufficient neighborhoods, each with its own health center, schools, shops, and green space. Between them run wide boulevards lined with trees. He and his team designed public buildings and housing complexes, and his cousin Pierre designed furniture for them that collectors now buy for prices as high as $12,000 for a teak chair. (Pierre stayed on for many years as chief architect of the city and became a locally beloved figure; his house is now a museum, and although he died in Switzerland, his will specified that his ashes be scattered in Chandigarh's Sukhna Lake.)

"It's the best city in India," said Suri Kumar, an Air Force officer I'd met on the subway in New Delhi. "The cleanest, the most organized, the best."

Chandigarh exists only because of the painful Partition on religious lines that created Pakistan, following independence from British rule in 1947. Punjab was one of the states that was cleaved in two, with its prosperous western side, including the capital city of Lahore, given to Muslim Pakistan. Indian Punjab needed a new capital, not just to govern the state, but also to house nearly a million Hindu and Sikh refugees.

As I learned from talking with Rajnish Wattas, the former principal of the Chandigarh College of Architecture, Prime Minister Jawaharlal Nehru was determined to make a new capital city that would be the pride of modern India, with no references to a past of palaces and fortresses. The planning had begun with the American architect Albert Mayer and his partner, Matthew Nowicki, but halted when Nowicki died in a plane crash. Nehru's selection committee then convinced Le Corbusier to come onboard, using some of the first team's sketches of the city layout.

Le Corbusier, it turned out, had long dreamed of building a new city. He'd even come up with a plan for modernizing Paris with vertical towers. (Fortunately, that one never came to fruition.) "If Chandigarh was lucky to get Corbusier," Wattas said, "then Corbusier, too, was very lucky to get Chandigarh because this was his biggest realization."

The jewel of that realization is the Capitol Complex, which has received Unesco World Heritage recognition as part of the architect's "outstanding contribution to the Modern movement."

After registering for one of three free daily tours, I stood on a vast concrete plaza. On one end was the High Court, where lawyers in black cloaks with white neckbands paced beneath huge pillars painted in bright yellow, green, and red. On the other end was the Legislative Assembly, where the governing bodies for Punjab and Haryana meet twice a year and the interior is decorated with cloud-shaped panels that contain cotton for sound absorption. In the middle was the city's symbol, seen on signs everywhere: an open hand made of iron and mounted on a pole that moves with the direction of the wind. It is meant to symbolize nonviolence and peace. "According to Corbusier," the tour guide said, "an open hand cannot hold a weapon."

All that planning, though, couldn't quite account for the activity that would inevitably move in. Walking along those wide boulevards, a friend and I rarely found a sidewalk, but we did see roadside barbershops and portable Hindu temples and playgrounds with trash cans in the shape of strawberries. In a nature preserve next to the vast, artificial Sukhna Lake, we came upon two monkeys vigorously mating. In a roundabout thick with traffic, I once looked out the window of an Uber car and saw a horse cart go by.

After hearing Chandigarh's story from Kumar, my acquaintance on the train, I'd been surprised to arrive at the Chandigarh station on the superfast Shatabdi Express and see the same scene I'd left behind three and a half hours earlier in New Delhi. Dozens of people were asleep in the station lobby, waiting for their trains; I had to hoist my bags over

Above The Legislative Assembly, with its reflective pool, in Chandigarh's Capitol Complex.

Opposite Stones are repurposed into a fanciful gateway at the Rock Garden.

them and step gingerly to reach the door. Rather than using the stairs, families jumped down onto the tracks to cross from platform to platform.

Chandigarh, after all, was once countryside. Some 58 villages stood where the city now does, and only 16 are still intact. Along with the slums that formed later, they make up an impoverished periphery to a city whose per capita income, car ownership, and real estate prices are among the highest in India. The city's population is more than double the half million it was built to hold. "No one ever thought to prepare for rickshaws and pavement hawkers, the fringe people," Wattas, the expert from the architectural college, told me.

The rock garden, too, wouldn't exist without the Partition. Nek Chand's family was living on the side of the divide that became Pakistan in 1947. They fled to New Delhi for safety, and he moved to Chandigarh when it was still under construction and became a road inspector for the public works department. He began collecting debris from some of the 40 villages that were demolished to make way for the new city, carrying it on his bike to a secret spot in a forest.

Chand's debris haven was in a Corbusier-designated urban wilderness near the Capitol Complex where building was illegal, and for 18 years he went there at night to craft sculptures out of discarded electrical sockets, broken tiles, and the like, along with rocks he collected from the river.

"He wanted to depict the stories about gods and goddesses, kings and fairies," said Wattas. "And it grew, but it was in a forest area and he was afraid that there would be an official reprimand." Yet he couldn't stop. His secret project ballooned to 12 acres of courtyards and twisting passages. The 2,500 sculptures he made, Wattas said, look like the kind of tribal figures you'd find in village homes. Having lost his own village, Chand wanted to create a magical,

Photographs by
Jada Yuan

indestructible one out of the wreckage of other villages. All of the doorways are designed so you have to bend down, in a gesture of respect, as you do while entering a temple.

When the authorities did find the site in 1975, some city officials wanted to tear it down while others thought it should be preserved. As they argued, people began making treks into the forest to see this act of passionate art. Eventually the government not only relented and preserved the site, but also gave Chand an official title, a salary so that he could continue his artistic work full time, and a crew of 50 to help him expand it.

I went to the Rock Garden twice, for multiple hours, to soak in the spirit of Nek Chand's creativity. It is an oasis of spontaneity and deliberate chaos in the midst of a city built on laws and structure. And even then, I felt that I had barely scratched the surface, that I would have to return.

WHAT TO READ

Chandigarh Revealed: Le Corbusier's City Today, by Shaun Fynn and Maristella Casciato. How Chandigarh lives within its carefully designed master plan.

Chandigarh Redux: Le Corbusier, Pierre Jeanneret, Jane B. Drew, E. Maxwell Fry, by Martin Feiersinger and Werner Feiersinger. A 21st-century view of Chandigarh in more than 300 photographs.

Le Corbusier, by Jean-Louis Cohen and Peter Gössel. A succinct look at Le Corbusier's work and its impact. Part of TASCHEN's Basic Architecture series.

Nek Chand's Outsider Art: The Rock Garden of Chandigarh, by Lucienne Piery, John Maizels, and Philippe Lespinasse. Includes a site map.

"A City That Sat on Its Treasures, but Didn't See Them," *The New York Times*, March 19, 2008. A report on local amazement at the skyrocketing value of furniture designed for Chandigarh by Pierre Jeanneret.

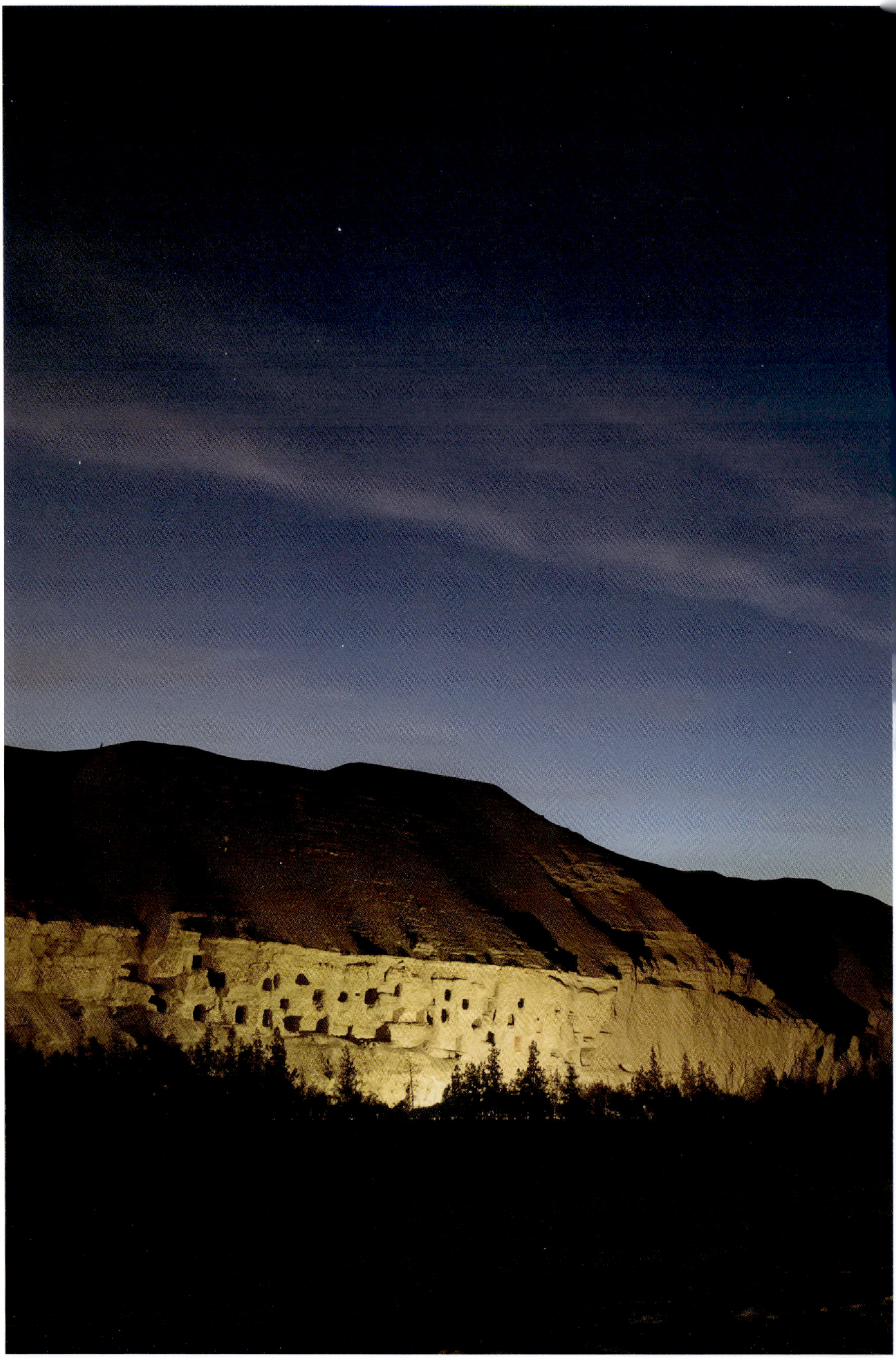

THE ANCIENT ART OF DUNHUANG

Hewn from rock and filled with Buddhist paintings and sculpture, caves at a Silk Road oasis transport awestruck visitors back 1,700 years. — BY JANE PERLEZ

The first inkling that we were getting close came toward the end of our flight from Beijing into northwestern China when snow-blanketed mountains suddenly appeared above the beige miasma of the desert floor. Morning sunlight sparkled off the grand Kunlun range that borders the northern edge of the Tibetan plateau and the southern rim of the Gobi Desert, a welcoming note on our journey to a distant world of Buddhist art painted and carved in grottoes centuries ago.

We were a group of seven — an American gallerist in Beijing, a Thai publisher of art books, a Singaporean businessman, among others — connected by our interests in Chinese art and history. Our intrepid leader, Mimi Gardner Gates, a specialist in Chinese art and the former director of the Seattle Art Museum, is dedicated to the preservation of what we had come to see: the Dunhuang caves where delicate, brightly hued wall paintings and carvings depict religious and social life from the fourth to the 14th centuries, during the height of Buddhist culture in China.

The city of Dunhuang, a hodgepodge of cheap stores and a mediocre night market, was once a thriving oasis on the Silk Road, beckoning caravans of pilgrims and merchants from Central Asia and India. As we arrived at the modern airport, it was hard not to think about more recent intruders: European and American scholars who visited the caves in the early 20th century, fell in love with what they found, and snatched priceless sculptures, manuscripts, and frescoes for museums in London, Paris, and Cambridge, Massachusetts.

Theirs had been arduous treks compared with ours. The Harvard art historian and archaeologist

DUNHUANG   CHINA

Previous Nighttime illumination casts an eerie glow on a section of the Mogao Caves in Dunhuang.

Left Photography in the caves in 1956. The art in the caves had its long heyday from the fourth century to the 14th.

Opposite A reclining 50-foot Buddha surrounded by his disciples, created in the Tang Dynasty.

Langdon Warner endured more than three months on an ox-drawn cart as he headed back to Beijing from Dunhuang in 1924 with a three-and-a-half-foot bodhisattva wrapped in his underwear for his patrons in Cambridge. In contrast, our journey was a comfortable three-hour flight from Beijing on Air China.

And while some of these early scholars — it is tempting to call them scoundrels — spent months in Dunhuang, recovering from their journeys, dodging diphtheria and other diseases, we spent four days in a pleasant hotel on the edge of the dunes. Over breakfasts of dumplings and Chinese porridge on the roof deck, we watched the sun rise and the sky change from flamingo pink to lapis blue. At sunset, we drank local wine pressed from new vineyards coaxed out of the sandy soil.

And, of course, our gear was far less elaborate than that of our predecessors. In a display near the caves that is devoted to the travesties of the Western scholars, a photo of Warner depicts him in knee-high boots, his hat at a rakish angle and a shovel in his right hand, ready to dig for antiquities. We, on the other hand, wore running shoes for the easy trek along the outdoor passageways that connect the caves, and carried little more than cell phones and cameras. (Taking photos, however, is banned in the caves to keep visitors moving swiftly, since the carbon dioxide in our breath damages the wall art. Camera flashes don't help either.)

When Warner and others like him arrived, they found 1,000 years of art that told the story of China's imperial dynasties and their long relationship with Buddhism, which seeped into China from India in the first century. In A.D. 366, according to legend, a monk named Yuezun arrived in Dunhuang and had a vision of a thousand Buddhas. He was so overwhelmed that he chiseled a cave for meditation in a vast sandstone cliff about 15 miles from the city center at a place now known as the Mogao Caves. Master artists and their apprentices began painting images of Buddha and his life story in murals that stretched across cave walls, and, in some cases, onto the ceilings.

The monk sparked a trend; over the years, about 1,000 caves were carved out of the mile-long escarpment as shrines or living quarters for monks, or the equivalent of private art museums where rich families could show off their wealth. By 1400, the exuberant show of art and religion faded as maritime routes supplanted the Silk Road.

When the caves were abandoned, the sweeping desert sands took over, ruining some, damaging others, but preserving many. Today 735 caves remain, and nearly 500 are decorated.

These days, streams of Chinese tourists arrive in great numbers—thousands per day. The biggest challenge for the Dunhuang Academy of China, the institution that manages the site, is crowd control, as we learned at the visitors' center, a building designed by the Chinese architect Cui Kai to blend into the desert dunes.

With a theater that gives a 360-degree digital representation of one of the caves, the center is an important tool in the battle to keep the Dunhuang caves intact. Tourists who are not on a private tour like ours are required to go there first, and watch the digital show, a substitute for lengthy tours that are no longer allowed for most visitors.

Most of these tourists are limited to a quick visit in the caves themselves. We, however, had almost unfettered access. We were there under the auspices of Mimi's Dunhuang Foundation, which has raised significant funds for their maintenance. (She married Bill Gates Sr., father of the Microsoft entrepreneur, but her commitment to Chinese art far predated that connection.) The foundation arranges regular cave tours on a limited basis.

On our first morning, a shuttle bus dropped us in a grove of aromatic pines, and soon we were at the foot of the rock face that inspired the monk Yuezun nearly 1,700 years ago. Looking up, we could see a honeycomb of dark holes where the caves pierced the rock. Much of the rock is now buttressed with concrete, a utilitarian reinforcement devised in the 1960s when China was short of cash and architects.

The most splendid cave art was produced during the height of the early Tang dynasty, from roughly A.D. 618 to 718, a period when the statues and mural paintings were the most sumptuous. In one tableau, which is rendered in greens, browns, and beige, a wide-girthed, beautifully dressed Chinese emperor listens closely to a debate on Buddhist doctrine. The artists, who usually painted with rabbit-hair brushes, achieved their rich colors by grinding and mixing mineral and organic pigments—red ocher, cinnabar, lapis lazuli—much as painters do today, according to Susan Whitfield, the director of the International Dunhuang Project at the British Library.

After the Tang, there was a 70-year interlude of Tibetan rule, followed by a long line of local clans

Above A 10th-century painting. Art in the caves is said to have begun when a monk had a vision of a thousand Buddhas.

Opposite An unrestored section of the rock face. For hundreds of years the caves were abandoned.

who commissioned life-size portraits of themselves. The Cao family, for example, loved their women and had them painted on the cave walls with rouged cheeks, layers of splendid necklaces, and voluminous gowns. Some of the caves used as chapels featured floor-to-ceiling paintings in lapis blue and earth reds that depict the life of the Buddha.

In several caves, scenes show daily village life: figures bathing, wheat being winnowed, preparations for a wedding ceremony. Some caves are as large as a small ballroom, with high coffered ceilings covered with fields of patterns that give the illusion of draped fabric in a desert tent. Others feature deep niches with life-size sculptures of Buddha and his disciples. Much of the painting is devoted to Buddha, but it was also easy to imagine from the mortal figures in the murals that during its heyday Dunhuang was alive with traders dealing in silk, furs, ceramics, gold, and ivory.

The size of some of the sculptures is startling. A 75-foot-tall Buddha stands bolt upright, carved from the rock face and covered in plaster, protected from the elements by the facade of the Nine-Story Temple. In a nearby cave, a 50-foot-long Buddha statue from the Tang dynasty lies on its side, tranquil in death, surrounded by paintings of anguished disciples.

On our second day, we drove two hours in a minibus on a paved road to Yulin, another rock face punctuated with caves. The desert and the distant snow-encrusted mountains along the route were a reminder of the terrain. We clambered with a young Chinese guide, Wang Yan, to Cave No. 3 at Yulin, a space measuring about 20 by 20 feet. Here the 10th-century artists painted with ink and brush in rich blues and greens the color of malachite. Landscapes with graceful waterfalls and willowy trees surrounded scores of Buddha's followers dressed in robes, their hair tightly knotted on top of their heads. One follower sailed

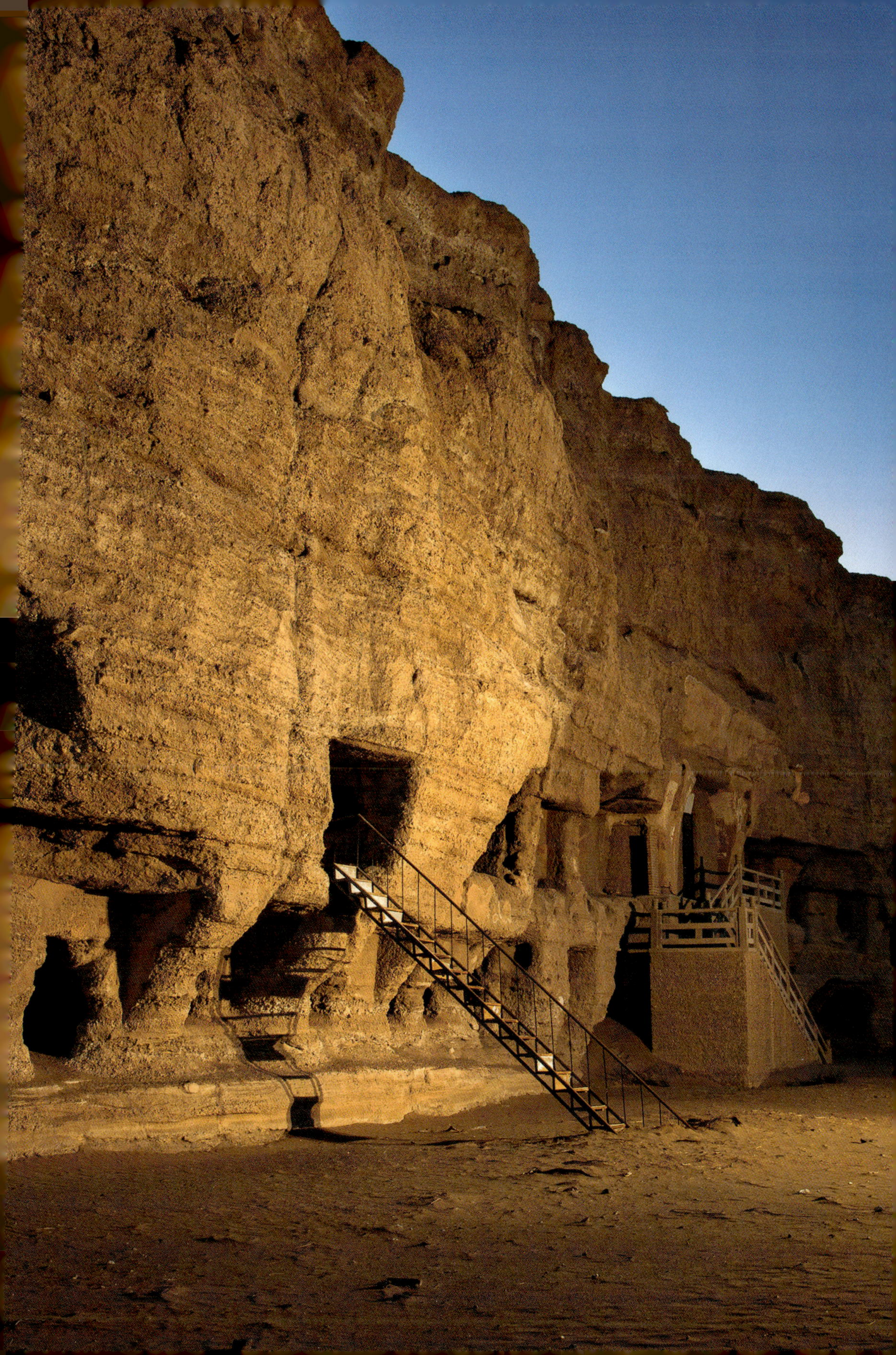

Above A walkway at the Yulin Caves. While monks lived in some caves, others were used as shrines or even private art galleries.

Below Stupas housing relics of long-dead monks dot the landscape around Dunhuang.

Opposite Built to blend in, the visitors center in Dunhuang imitates undulating desert dunes.

through the landscape on the back of an elephant whose feet were planted on lotus leaves. We had to wonder who the artists were, but they were almost always anonymous, and many were paid only with food.

At Yulin, we ate a delicious farm-cooked lunch at a no-name rustic restaurant set beside the Yulin River, a fast-flowing narrow stream. The menu came from the fields: elm-tree seeds coated in flour and steamed, stir-fried green beans, steamed pumpkin slices, and soup with freshly made noodles and veal.

Back at the Mogao Caves, another local guide, Liu Qin, an art historian at the Dunhuang Academy, was eager to show us the spot where Warner ripped out the statue. In Cave No. 328, he showed us a Buddha set on a low platform surrounded by a half-dozen attendants. On the far left at an easy-to-reach height, one attendant is missing, a gap that destroys the symmetry of the tableau. A slightly raised gray plaster disc marks the place where Warner and his men removed the bodhisattva.

Liu was also anxious to take us to the place where Aurel Stein, a British historian, and Paul Pelliot, a French scholar, took thousands of books and manuscripts. Inside the entrance to Cave No. 17, he pointed to a small, nearly empty room where Stein found

Photographs by
Adam Dean

7,000 manuscripts, including one of the world's oldest printed books, the Diamond Sutra, produced in A.D. 868. It is now at the British Library. Stein paid a local monk £130 for his booty. A little later, Pelliot took another substantial haul of scrolls for the Musée Guimet in Paris, and paid even less.

The days when unscrupulous collectors could walk away with the ancient art are long past. Today the biggest threat to the caves is tourism. To reduce demand and to ensure preservation, the Dunhuang administrators are digitizing all of the cave art. Eventually, visiting the caves by virtual reality may become a globally accessible experience.

Meanwhile, we knew we were fortunate to tour as we did. As Mimi Gates was careful to tell us, we were seeing original art in situ, an experience of dazzling authenticity.

WHAT TO READ AND WATCH

The China Collectors: America's Century-Long Hunt for Asian Art Treasures, by Karl E. Meyer and Shareen Blair Brysac. An account of America's fascination with Chinese art, including a highly readable chapter on Langdon Warner.

Cave Temples of Mogao at Dunhuang: Art and History on the Silk Road, by Roderick and Susan Whitfield and Neville Agnew. A more scholarly account of Dunhuang.

Porcelain Stories: From China to Europe, by Julie Emerson, Jennifer Chen, Mimi Gardner Gates. Porcelain, once a rare Chinese luxury, became a passion of European collectors.

The Silk Road, Season 1, Episode 13, directed by Xavier Lefebvre, an Arte France television documentary. Dunhuang is explored in geographic and historical context, with views of the modern city and the caves.

PAI DOSA
PAIDOSA
36 PAI BROTHERS FAST FOOD
Varieties of Dosas

A SOFT, SPICY LANDING IN INDIA

In easygoing, inclusive Kerala, foodies find a paradise in the Cardamom Hills. — BY KIM SEVERSON

The skinny 80-year-old Indian yogi was doing his best to suggest ways I might adjust my ample 55-year-old American body into a passable downward dog. I admired his ambition. I'm an enthusiastic but generally bad practitioner of yoga. But here in the darkened yoga hut at Spice Village, a botanically focused resort on 14 organic acres in the middle of the Cardamom Hills of Kerala, on India's southwestern coast, I thought I had found a kindred soul on the mat next to me. Her downward dog wasn't looking so good, either. We smiled at each other in that awkward, supportive way tourists sometimes do.

After class, we chatted. She was a 37-year-old mom from Mumbai and had come to Kerala because she needed a break. She and her husband, both born and raised in India, had left their young son with relatives for the weekend and headed south to this land of coconuts and clear air—the way a tired Manhattanite might take to the Hudson Valley or a Londoner to Brighton.

I ran into more than one city-bound Indian tourist like her as I roamed through the spice plantations, tea estates, and beaches in this slice of Southwest India. Younger Indians, flush with disposable income and a newfound appreciation of organic food, holistic living, and the cultural riches within their own borders, have discovered Kerala.

"There has been a revival in local, regional things," said Shelton Pinheiro, an executive at Stark Communications, a tourism and marketing agency, "especially among people who have traveled abroad and come home to discover what they have here is just as special."

We were talking over lime sodas and spicy chunks of chicken, curry leaves, and shallots fried crisp in

Previous Kerala, with little chaos and congestion, is seen by some as "the soft landing for India." This shop is in Kochi.

Left A roadside scene in the Cardamom Hills. Getting there can be a challenge.

Opposite above In the hands of Asha Gomez, a chef and cooking teacher, fish get a spice rub before being grilled.

Opposite below Nutmeg at the source. The seed inside is nutmeg; the red coating is mace.

coconut oil at the Marari Beach Resort near the Malabar coastal village of Mararikulam, where city dwellers come to get Ayurvedic treatments and swim in the Arabian Sea.

Asha Gomez, a chef and cooking teacher I first met in Atlanta, was at the table, too, taking a break from the intense late-spring South Indian sun. The author of a well-received cookbook called *My Two Souths: Blending the Flavors of India Into a Southern Kitchen*, she had been pestering me to travel to Kerala almost from the day I met her several years before. "Kim," she would say, grabbing my hands, "you must come discover why we call it God's own country."

Asha grew up in Thiruvananthapuram, Kerala's capital city on the Arabian Sea, about a four-hour drive farther south. Many of the white beaches along the Kerala coast are rustic and inviting. A pleasant morning can be spent watching traditional wooden fishing boats come and go. Asha swears that the sand is softer and the water is bluer as you get closer to India's tip.

In the United States, she made a career out of blending the foods of her native part of the Indian South and the American South. The two styles of cooking work together beautifully. The hot, vinegary sauce in a dish of pork vindaloo is not far from the one that moistens a whole-hog barbecue sandwich in Eastern North Carolina. The black pepper that grows everywhere in Kerala helps tame the innate sweetness in a Southern-style carrot cake. And for both American southerners and Indian southerners, eating fried chicken is deeply woven into the cultural fabric.

Western travelers interested in tea or drawn to the vast nature preserves that hold tigers and elephants have long made their way to Kerala, starting and ending their trips in Kochi, a city of about 600,000 that is easier to navigate and less tradition-bound than New Delhi, Mumbai, or Bangalore. Now many travelers come for the subtropical beaches on the Kerala coast or to tour in comfortably furnished wooden houseboats through a series of river communities called the backwater.

Even outside the city, Kerala is more distinctly laid-back than most of the other 36 states and union territories in India. It's the most religiously diverse part of India — half Hindu, but with plenty of Muslims and Christians. Both life expectancy and the literacy rate among its 33 million residents are the country's highest.

"Most of my friends say Kerala is the soft landing for India because then you are used to India and ready for all of its glorious chaos in other places," Pinheiro said.

The Portuguese, who landed here in the 15th century and took up the spice trade, introduced Latin Catholicism; their influence shows up in many Latin-sounding surnames. They also brought with them a love of pork and the chilies that would come to define a lot of Kerala's food. Kerala's cooking is light and infused with chili and coconut; its dishes are built largely around rice and fish.

For any serious cook who comes to Kerala, the high point has to be the Cardamom Hills, which are laced by vast tea estates and spice gardens. To get there from Kochi, Asha and I spent nearly five hours in a van grinding its way up the steep hills of the Western Ghats mountain range, stopping only for plates of vegetable curry and glasses of fresh pineapple juice. The road narrowed as we worked our way past wildlife sanctuaries and forests of sandalwood. The oppressive humidity of the city lifted. Tea estates cascaded down the steep valleys, their tight, trimmed shrubs looking as manicured as a formal English garden.

Manoj Vasudevan, a photographer who teaches tourism in Kerala and who has been exploring the mountains here for decades, acted as our guide. That included informing us about the finer points of mountain driving in India, which requires faith, acceptance, and a good horn.

The strips of pavement hugging the mountainside were often wide enough to hold only one vehicle, but sometimes three would try to navigate a stretch at once. Horns were essential to blast our gentle warnings on blind curves. Inevitable bottlenecks that brought traffic to a stop were solved when a driver or a passenger would hop out and calmly direct cars and buses to back up or edge around each other. Everyone would then head on without a harsh word or even a friendly wave. "We practice a kind of practical politeness," he explained.

Many of the sprawling tea estates we passed are owned by Tata Global Beverages, which maintains 51 estates in India and Sri Lanka. We stopped for lunch at the Briar Tea Bungalow, a rambling, low-slung Colonial-style building northwest of Munnar that the British, in their days of dominance in India, built on a mountaintop surrounded by 2,500 acres of tea plants. We waded out into hip-high tea bushes and hiked to where women armed with small hedge clippers spend the day trimming the very tips from the tea bushes. A day's work brings in a little over $6, more if they can beat their daily quotas.

Soon, we were back on the road and headed for the heart of spice country. We began to see small spice gardens, some offering tours for a couple of hundred rupees. Some declared themselves to be organic and had small shops selling packets of vibrant ground turmeric, nutmeg, and green cardamom pods for prices that would make cooks on the other side of the world fall to their knees.

Then there's black pepper. From the time of the Roman Empire, people have been coming to Kerala for black pepper. Wars have been fought over it. The plants that produce the fruit are everywhere. Their thin green vines wrap around jackfruit, mango, and coconut trees that grow with such abandon they don't seem to need a bit of human effort to thrive.

Cardamom is a big moneymaker here, but black pepper remains the coin of the realm. Even though

Above Tea leaf harvesters processing the bounty in Munnar.

Opposite Spice shops rule on a street in Thekkady, high in the Cardamom Hills.

Indian pepper growers are fighting off cheaper production in countries like Vietnam, there are still plenty of wealthy owners who oversee vast plots of pepper plants. But in every village and small town, you can find someone who grows a little pepper and sells a few kilos when a bill comes due or there's a wedding to fund.

Asha and I found our way to a small organic spice garden in Thekkady where Thomas Puttampurakkal, a retired Kerala police officer in his 80s, tended to pepper vines that twisted around jackfruit and nutmeg trees growing in what seemed to be an agricultural system with no real pattern or structure. He used only elephant dung for fertilizer.

Pepper, he explained, is all about terroir. The best grows naturally here in the high elevations, the green berries protected by the shade until they ripen. The green pepper berries become black pepper after they spend four or five days in the sun. Those same green berries can also produce white pepper, whose pungency is softened by a long soak in water before they are dried and their husks removed.

Asha and I wandered through Puttampurakkal's spice garden like kids in a toy store. We rubbed curry leaves between our fingers and dug up turmeric roots. We searched around the bottom of willowy cardamom stalks 12 feet tall, looking for green buds. We sucked the custardy pulp off the seeds inside cacao pods, smelled clove buds, and peeled a bit of bark from a cinnamon tree.

We found a nutmeg tree and pulled down a round piece of fruit the size of my palm. Someone had a knife, so we sliced it open to reveal a glossy dark gem covered in a lacy red coat. The seed is nutmeg, the red covering mace.

In the little shop, I bought bags of the small, local black Malabar peppercorns locals call tribal pepper and then turned to the fat, fragrant peppercorns

Photographs by
Evan Sung

called Tellicherry, named after a famed growing region in Northern Kerala. I bit into one. It tasted like citrus and flowers. In a split-second, heat overtook the flavor, like hot perfume in my mouth.

Asha wandered in, her hands filled with nutmeg. "You have no idea how excited I am," she said. Puttampurakkal was laughing, probably at us. It was hard to tell, and it didn't matter. I had made it to the Cardamom hills.

Asha was right. It was God's own country. Or, at least, a cook's.

WHAT TO READ AND WATCH

My Two Souths: Blending the Flavors of India into a Southern Kitchen, by Asha Gomez and Martha Hall Foose. A well-received cookbook by a chef and cooking teacher.

The Spice Companion: A Guide to the World of Spices, by Lior Lev Sercarz. A guide to spices by the owner of La Boîte, a New York spice shop, who custom-blends spices for chefs.

Where the Rain Is Born: Writings About Kerala, edited by Anita Nair. An anthology in which a diverse selection of Indian authors, including Arundhati Roy, write about their perceptions of Kerala.

The God of Small Things, by Arundhati Roy. A widely praised modern classic, winner of the Booker Prize in 1997, set in Kerala.

Anthony Bourdain: No Reservations, Season 6, Episode 13: *Kerala*. The late globe-trotting foodie explores Kerala food and culture.

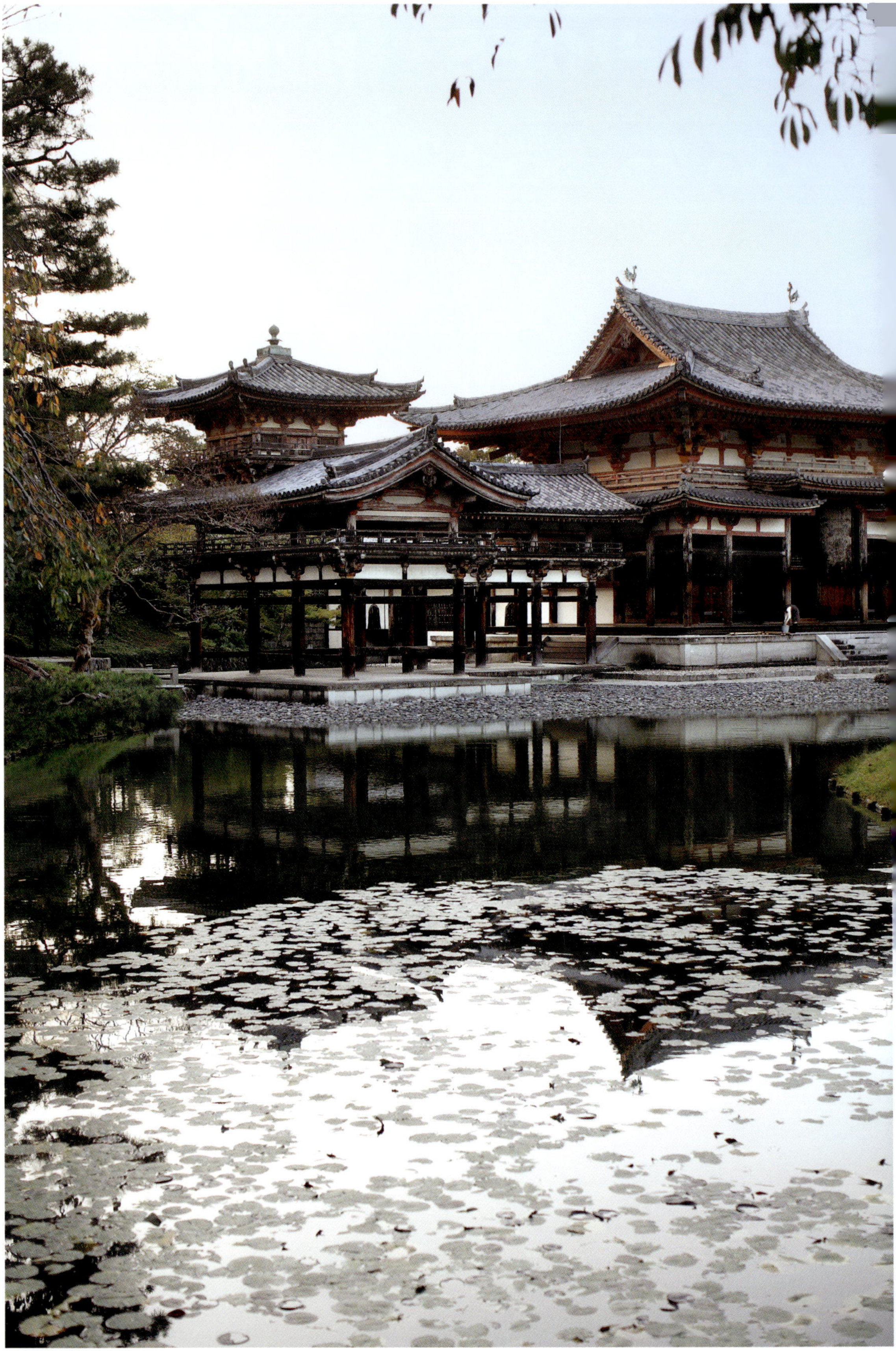

KYOTO'S FAVORITE STORY

Japan's most traditional city continues its thousand-year love affair with The Tale of Genji, sometimes considered the world's first novel. — BY MICHELLE GREEN

On a glaring, color-drenched day in Kyoto, I walked unsteadily out of a tatami room where I had spent the morning being costumed, painted, and bewigged. Two chic dressers minded the train flowing behind my heavy robes. Hiking up my red silk trouser skirts as I minced forward, I squinted without my glasses — a modern touch that would have betrayed the fact that I was only pretending to be a noblewoman straight from *The Tale of Genji*.

Considered by some to be the world's first novel, *The Tale of Genji* (*Genji Monogatari* in Japanese) evokes particular pride in Kyoto, Japan's ancient capital, a city known for its shrines, temples, and blazing autumn hills. The city celebrates this thousand-year-old tale by Murasaki Shikibu (Lady Murasaki, as she is called), an episodic story of love and loss among the imperial set. Dressing up like its characters is only one of the activities offered to *Genji*'s modern fans.

Lady Murasaki's ancestral home was on Teramachi Street, and she served as a lady-in-waiting at the imperial court. She set much of the amorous action involving her decadent hero, the Shining Prince, in the mansions and palaces of Heian-kyo, as Kyoto once was called.

For two hours (and well over $200), I indulged in the local custom of swanning about in traditional costume — in this case, the *juni-hitoe*, or "12 layers of robes," fashionable in the Heian era. My outing included a leisurely boat ride with friends on the Katsura River. As a boatman poled through the water, I pretended to be an aristocrat admiring "red leaves, beautiful in the autumn wind," in the words of Lady Murasaki.

But that idyll was eclipsed when we stepped into a parking lot full of buses. An ant trail of tourists bound for the river halted and redirected itself, bemused by

Previous A temple in Uji, outside of Kyoto. Uji is also home to the Tale of Genji Museum.

Left Traditional art based on *The Tale of Genji*. Lady Murasaki captivated the imperial court with her stories.

Opposite The world of *Genji* returns in this purification ceremony at the Jonan-gu Shrine in Kyoto.

the sight of a foreigner with a pale-moon face, cherry-blossom lips, and a raven wig. There were shouts of laughter. "Beautiful!" exclaimed a tweedy man, stepping into my path with his camera.

At a time when fiction — in the form of fables — was dismissed as brain-candy for females, Lady Murasaki produced an epic whose psychological resonance was unprecedented. And she crafted her tales in Japanese, whose written form was still being developed. Genji was "a pyrotechnical display of literary creativity," in the words of the anthropologist Liza Dalby, who imagined the writer's life in her book *The Tale of Murasaki*.

At the Museum of Kyoto, visitors inspect illustrated scrolls and painted screens depicting Genji's exploits, and then walk out with refrigerator magnets bearing images of the Shining Prince.

Few people today digest the original epic, which is written in archaic Japanese and runs more than 1,000 pages in English. Eager to reach the masses, publishers offer racy mangas and abridged renditions in modern Japanese that can be "quite crude and even obscene," said Donald Keene, a professor emeritus of Japanese literature at Columbia.

An unusually popular translation into contemporary Japanese, published in the 1990s, was by Jakucho Setouchi, an elderly Buddhist nun who was already a famous author renowned for her racy novels (while simultaneously serving as the head of a Kyoto temple). Other modern translations tended to be in a formal Japanese that few people today can easily understand, so Setouchi decided to produce a more readable *Genji*. Her version was a bestseller, and she became a television star on the national lecture circuit.

"When a man and a woman are in love, the situation hasn't changed in the last thousand years," Setouchi told the *New York Times* writer Nick Kristof in 1999, explaining the popular success of her Genji. "There's jealousy. There's agony. Even a modern career woman can feel those same pains of love."

While *The Tale of Genji* spans three generations, the best-known sections focus on its title character, a son of the emperor. Genji's mother, one of the emperor's lesser consorts, dies when he is a young boy. He has no chance of succeeding his father, but he's a lethal charmer. Lady Murasaki describes him at 17: "Over soft, layered white gowns he had only a dress cloak, unlaced at the neck…lying there in the lamplight, against a pillar, he looked so beautiful that one could have wished him a woman."

To modern readers, the book's enormous, emotive cast can seem overwrought: Addicted to "the rare amour fraught with difficulty and heartache," the married hero impregnates his stepmother, falls in love with a child whom he raises to be his wife, and retreats into exile after he's discovered in mid-tryst with the daughter of a political enemy. Supporting characters fall victim to amnesia and die of heartbreak; they exchange poems and dampen brocade sleeves with bitter tears.

Though a fragmented diary and her poetry survive, details about the author, whose stories captivated the Heian court, have faded. She belonged to a minor branch of the powerful Fujiwara clan, but her given name (like those of other women) was omitted from genealogies. Her nickname, Murasaki, is the name of one of Genji's loves. Shikibu comes from an office held by her father, a regional governor and Chinese scholar.

Look around, and her spirit materializes around Kyoto and beyond. Ishiyama-dera temple, for example, is built atop a massive rock on Mount Garan, a half-hour train journey from the city. Begun in the middle of the eighth century, the temple complex, a shrine to the goddess Kannon, is known for its wild beauty; in a mossy forest punctuated by the neon maroons of Japanese maples and the brassy golds of gingkoes, the open-sided main hall, or *hondo*, feels like a whimsical treehouse.

But Ishiyama-dera is also, in a sense, a shrine to Lady Murasaki. According to tradition, *The Tale of Genji* was conceived on a single night there in August 1004, as the author contemplated the moon.

On a steel-gray November day, I found the sacred hall of the temple suffused with the sedate buzz of the temple circuit in high season. Pleasant-looking women in eerily well-coordinated autumn colors padded about in their stocking feet, murmuring to one another. Older couples trailed crisp-looking guides holding pennants.

A visitor stood apart: a solemn young woman whose floor-length mane fell over the blue-green mantle of a multilayered juni-hitoe. A companion followed her with a camera as she tugged a heavy rope to ring a sonorous bell and tossed coins into a wooden box. Gliding past a counter where others were choosing cell phone charms, she paused on the veranda before

Above The Shimogamo Shrine was important in Lady Murasaki's day and would have been known to her.

Opposite Ishiyama-dera temple. In 1004, legend says, Lady Murasaki's tale came to her here as she contemplated the moon.

a pair of narrow rooms (with a moon view) where, as the story goes, the author had her epiphany.

In the front alcove, isolated as if on stage, a life-size Murasaki doll knelt behind a writing desk with her violet and green robes spilling around her; nearby was a screen used for privacy. Far behind her was a figure representing her daughter, Katako, staring past her mother's shoulder with the look of an only child too proud to acknowledge that she's lonely.

The real Lady Murasaki was hardly a cloistered figure. At a time when mastering Chinese was considered unwomanly, she devoured the work of Chinese writers. Unlike the aristocratic women who became her readers, she cultivated a traveler's perspective; before she married a wealthy courtier, she almost certainly accompanied her widowed father to a posting in Echizen province, northwest of Kyoto.

She was also able to eavesdrop on life at court. Her husband's observations may have helped fuel her vivid stories, according to Dalby. In 1006, the regent Fujiwara Michinaga invited Lady Murasaki (by then widowed) to become Empress Shoshi's companion and tutor — apparently because early sections of *Genji*, which is believed to have been completed around 1008, had found a delighted audience in her household.

In her diary, Lady Murasaki reveals that her privileged neighbors were given to jealousy, drunkenness, and ennui. She felt estranged from vapid figures, including a lady-in-waiting who spread "malicious, unfounded rumors" about her.

"I cannot be bothered to discuss matters in front of those women who continually carp and are so full of themselves: it would only cause trouble," she writes. "So all they see of me is a facade. There are times when I am forced to sit with them, and on such occasions I simply ignore their petty criticisms, not because I am particularly shy but because I consider it pointless. As a result, they now look upon me as a dullard."

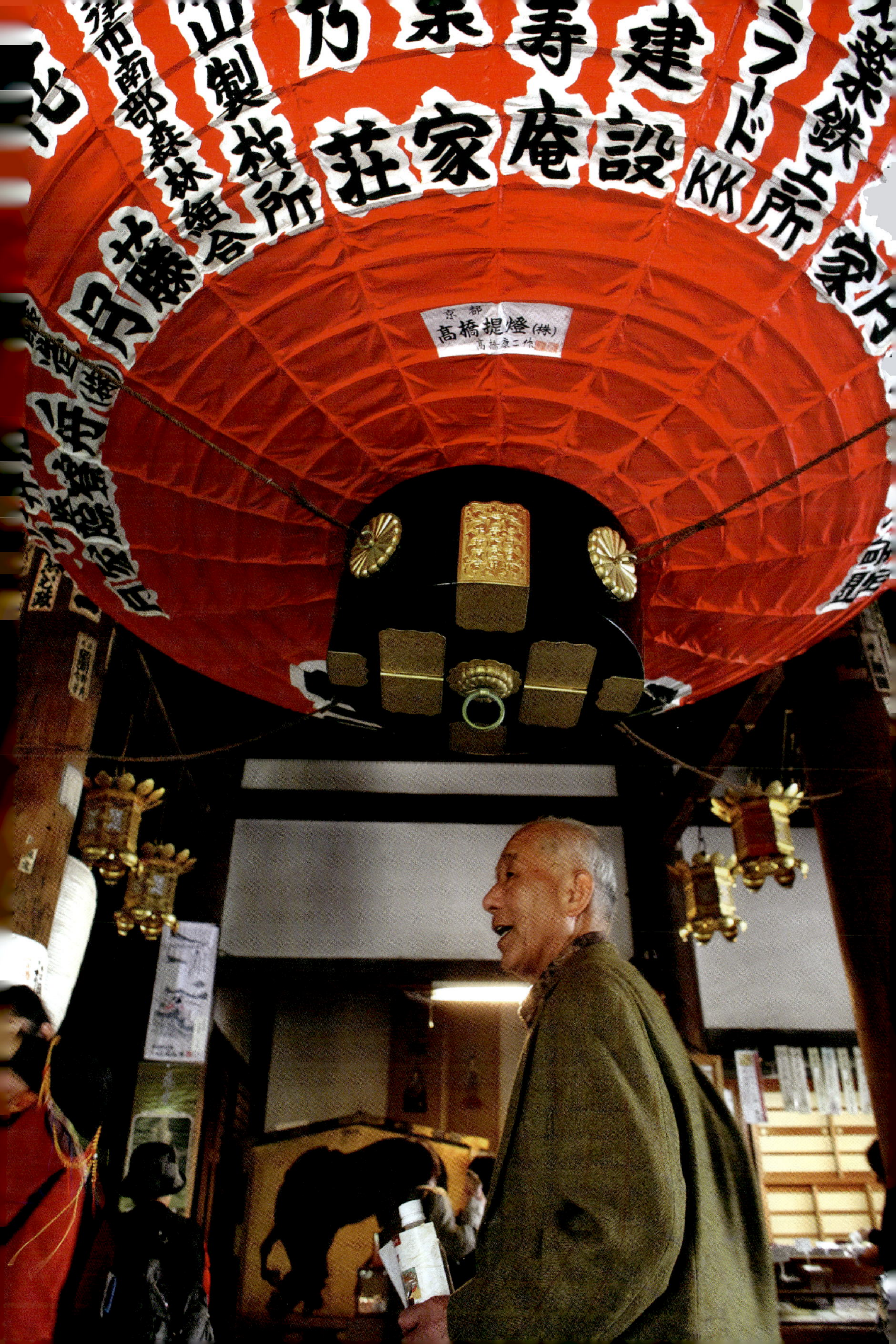
京都
高橋提燈(株)
高橋康二作

Above Love, courtly manners, and all things romantic figure heavily in *The Tale of Genji*. This statue is in Uji.

Opposite Rozan-ji temple stands on property that belonged to Lady Murasaki's father.

The woman who held her tongue, of course, had the last word.

I went on another pilgrimage popular with Murasaki fans, to Uji (about 20 minutes by train from Kyoto), where the Tale of Genji Museum channels the sensuality of Lady Murasaki's work. A rugged but romantic retreat for Heian-era aristocrats, Uji is set in hilly and fertile terrain; Japan's most highly prized green tea is grown there.

On an ancient bridge across the Uji River, weekend visitors savoring soft-serve green-tea ice cream leaned against the railings to watch cormorants wading in the shallows. Nearby, at a monument to Lady Murasaki, *Genji* fans took photos of each other posing with her statue.

Uji's centerpiece is its museum, an artfully landscaped glass structure that evokes Genji's world with ceremonial costumes, an ox-drawn carriage, and a scale-model version of his mansion. A display of exotica used to concoct incense was a reminder that the Shining Prince could be identified by his alluring scent alone.

Fragrant coils of incense were burning in the gift shop, which was selling hard candies bearing Genji's likeness. Next door, there was a happy ruckus as well-dressed visitors crowded around computers where they could insert photos of their faces onto images of Lady Murasaki's characters.

The atmosphere was more serene—and the author's spirit closer—at the site of her ancestral home in Kyoto, where tradition has it that at least part of *Genji* was written. Just east of the Imperial Palace Park, the site is occupied today by Rozan-ji temple, a brooding, tile-roofed structure in a leafy neighborhood. Only one tile from the home remains. When I visited Rozan-ji on a drizzly afternoon, the property was flooded by a tour group. While they gazed at the black and gold altar room, I slid along the ancient,

Photographs by
Ko Sasaki

satiny floor in my socks. An enormous obsidian crow from the throng in the park shrieked comically and landed on the garden wall.

I sat on the porch by the Zen garden. Unlike other places touched by Lady Murasaki's legacy, it seems timeless: white gravel defines the simple curves of moss islands punctuated by the occasional tree or rock. Stare at the design for long minutes, and it turns into a puzzle — one that may look the same in a thousand years.

WHAT TO READ

The Tale of Genji, translated by Arthur Waley. Of four well-known English versions, Waley's is favored by many readers for its entertaining style. Others prefer Edward Seidensticker, Royall Tyler, or Dennis Washburn, all competent and accessible.

The Tale of Genji: A Visual Companion, by Melissa McCormick. Reproductions of paintings and calligraphy from the Genji Album (1510) in the Harvard Art Museums, with McCormick's essays illuminating the images and the story.

The Tale of Murasaki, by Liza Dalby. A novel imagining the life of Murasaki Shikibu, the court lady who wrote The Tale of Genji, using the author's diaries and hints from the Genji stories.

World of the Shining Prince: Court Life in Ancient Japan, by Ivan Morris. An introduction to Lady Murasaki's world: complex, ritualistic, and intricately mannered.

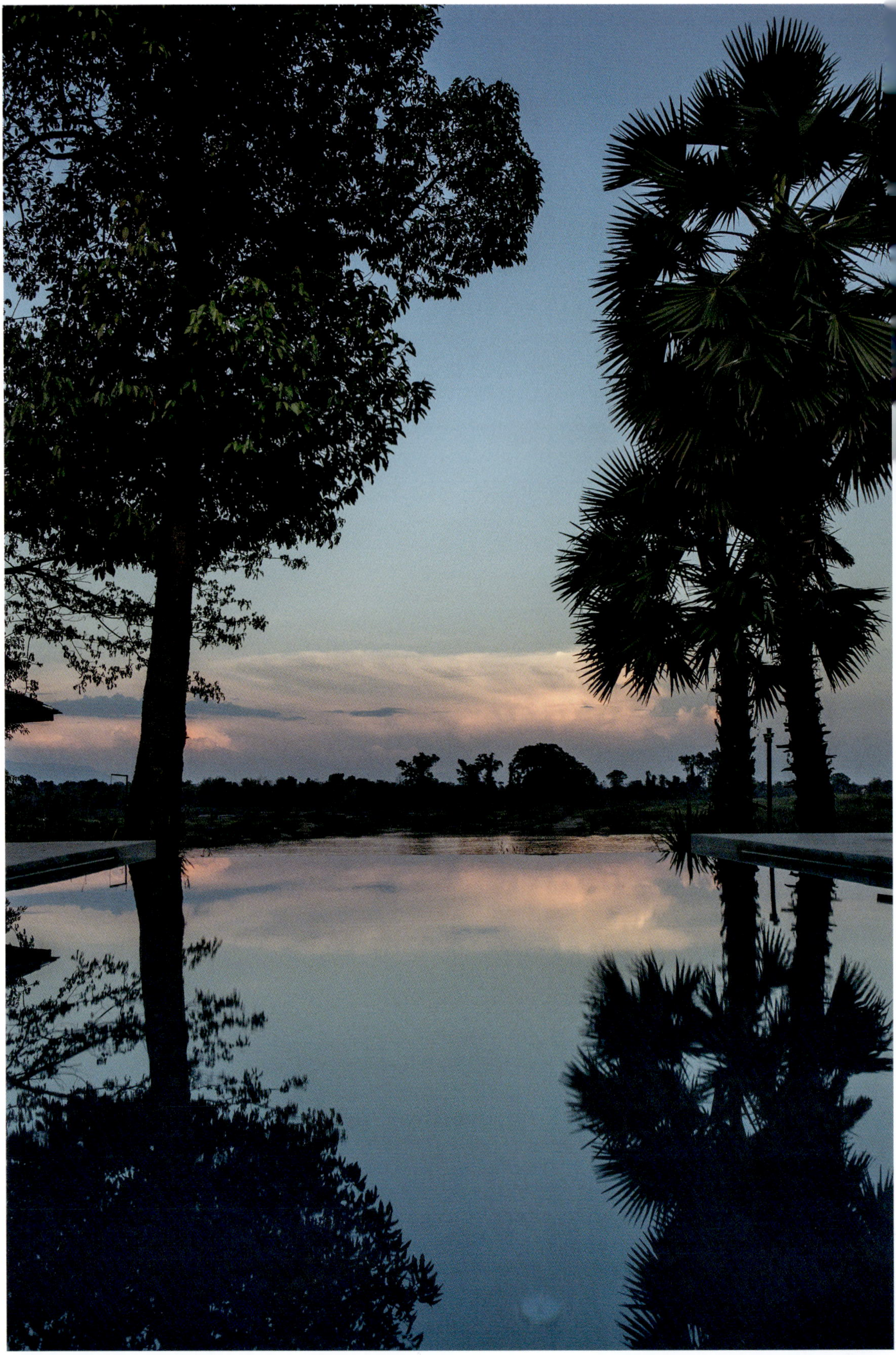

ALONG THE MEKONG IN LAOS

Where an ancient Khmer temple looks down on a timeless landscape, the people march to the beat of the present. — BY EDWARD WONG

Deep in the folds of the hill, up steep stone stairs flanked with frangipani trees, stood the inner sanctum of the ancient Khmer temple of Vat Phou. We faced the mountain ridge, our backs to the waters of the Mekong River, looking for the chamber. From this angle, it was hidden. But other parts of the temple had begun revealing themselves to us. Down here, along the rutted stone path leading to the stairs, we watched as a construction crane lifted a block onto the wall of one of the outer chambers.

To our right, a few carvers chipped away at other blocks with small tools. Through their hands flowed the tales of Hindu mythology, the millenniums-old narratives of gods in love and war that had originated on the Indian subcontinent and traveled to distant Java and to Khmer temples across Cambodia and Laos. Now that transmission of stories and beliefs and ideas was continuing here, like the flow of the Mekong, in the shadow of one of the most beautiful of those temples.

Built more than 1,000 years ago at the high point of an axis stretching from a range of mountains down to the Mekong, Vat Phou is one of the most sacred temples of the vanished Khmer kingdoms. The Khmer ruled a wide swath of Southeast Asia from the ninth to the 15th centuries, and their dedication to art and architecture is best embodied in the famous temples of Angkor Wat in Cambodia. Lesser known and distinct from Angkor in its intimacy is Vat Phou, sometimes written in English as Wat Phu.

To see the temple and this stretch of the Mekong, my wife, Tini, and I, with our three-year-old daughter, based ourselves for three nights at a riverside hotel outside the town of Champasak. Tini and I were both

Previous One of two riverside pools at the River Resort in Champasak in Laos.

Left Children cool off by jumping into the Mekong in Ban Nakasang.

Opposite Traditional boats at Don Daeng island in the middle of the Mekong.

journalists who had been working in China. We had a special attachment to Southeast Asia because Tini is Vietnamese American.

Laos is the land of the Mekong, with palm trees lining the riverbanks, freshwater dolphins swimming between islets, and fishermen casting nets over the side of skiffs. The pace of life is slower, much slower, than in Beijing, where we had come from. But it would have been wrong to think of the region as timeless. The restoration of Vat Phou that we witnessed belied notions of ancient ruins lost in eternal mists. And it was there, near the entrance to the temple complex, that we discovered we were not the only escapees from the rush of development in China. As we set foot that morning on the eastern end of the pathway leading up to the inner sanctum, we met a Chinese couple from Shanghai who were in the middle of a monthlong trip through Laos with their six-year-old daughter.

Our daughter, Aria, instantly began following the older girl around. We told the family we were fleeing the notorious Beijing pollution. "The situation is very bad in Shanghai, too," the father said.

We had begun our trip with a flight from Beijing to Chiang Mai in Thailand; the area of Laos we wanted to explore is at a point where Thailand, Cambodia, and Laos all come together. We crossed into Laos near the Laotian town of Pakse. There, on a sleepy street (towns in Laos only have sleepy streets), we had lunch at Dok Mai, a restaurant run by an Italian, Corrado. He told us he had tried living and working in India, but that had been tough. "Pakse chose me," he said.

Our hotel, the River Resort, was about a half hour away, built along the Mekong. After a hotel driver took us there, we found ourselves in the middle of nowhere, but that was the point. The resort consisted of two-story luxury buildings and had riverside swimming pools. In our room, we could wake up in bed gazing across the waters to the sunrise. At sunset, a golden light bathed the river and trees and stones. We would have enjoyed spending an entire day just on the riverbank, but Khmer civilization beckoned us. In the mountains looming to our west, hidden by jungle, lay Vat Phou.

A hotel employee, Taiy, told me of the importance of rituals at the temple and said there is a big festival once a year. "I've been to Vat Phou four times," he said. "My family goes once a year. Because I have to work, I usually don't go. I don't have much time, so I would only be able to go at night."

We arrived in Vat Phou after a 15-minute taxi ride and walked up stone steps to the inner sanctum. Along the main walkway, we passed a seven-headed naga statue draped with yellow garlands. A bell rang somewhere. Inside the inner temple, a family made offerings to a statue of the Buddha. Sweet smoke from incense sticks drifted through the temple. On our walk, Aria had picked up a white frangipani flower, and now she placed it on a wooden table, atop dried candle wax. It was her offering.

Around the sanctum were lintels carved with ornate scenes from Hindu mythology. One showed the god Indra atop a three-headed elephant. Another depicted deities taking part in the churning of the Ocean of Milk, an image that I had also seen a decade earlier at Angkor. Then there was the scene of Krishna tearing his uncle Kamsa in half.

Outside, more worshippers were arriving. We walked along the slope of the mountain behind the temple. On the site were a sacred spring, a cave shrine, and the ruins of a small library. At a cistern, Laotians anointed themselves with water that flowed from mountain springs.

Atop the hill, staring down the axis and toward the Mekong to the east, I could see frangipani flowers below, bursts of white on the brown landscape.

The next morning, we arranged with our hotel to take a boat over to the island of Don Daeng, in the middle of the Mekong. We had brought bicycles with us, and I strapped Aria to my back with a baby sling. A herd of water buffalo wandered languidly down the sandy beach to drink at the river.

We biked along dirt paths to villages. There were five main ones on the island, with a total population of 3,000. Locals walked from one to another or sat on the rear of trundling tractors. Outside their homes, women fried up rice cakes in pans.

At lunchtime, we stopped at La Folie, a French-run colonial-style lodge. While our hotel was all modernist glass and concrete, La Folie had polished wooden panels on the floors and walls. It overlooked the river and faced the spine of mountains to the west. We could see Vat Phou in the hills.

Top, a smiling young man from Pakse, was working in the dining room. He had just started there one month earlier. When he found out I was from the United States, he asked about the Ultra Music Festival in Miami — had I heard of it? Had I been there? I shook my head.

Above Fresh produce in living color at a market in Pakse.

Opposite Buddha and his entourage come in many sizes. At Vat Chomphet, the range is extra large to small.

"I really want to go," he said. "My favorite DJs from around the world go there." He said that was his goal, to be a DJ, and that there were two bars in Pakse where DJs played. Timeless Asia, indeed.

That evening, we took a sunset boat ride on the Mekong with a Dutch couple. Over canapés and bottles of Beerlao, we spoke with Kanh, a 25-year-old hotel worker accompanying us. He had begun working at River Resort three months earlier. He was from Pakse, he said, the son of a Vietnamese mother and a father who was Laotian and Chinese. While his mother had been born here, her parents were from Hue, the old imperial capital in central Vietnam. They had fled the fall of South Vietnam to Communist forces in 1975, only to eventually settle in another Communist country.

"He's the original mixed Southeast Asian," Tini said with a laugh. Her ancestors, too, were from Hue, and she and her family had also fled Vietnam in 1975. They ended up deep in the American South. So went the vagaries of history.

The next morning, we took a ferry across the river, then a bus to a river port to the south, where we hopped on a wooden boat crammed with backpackers for a ride to what is known as the Four Thousand Islands area, or Si Phan Don, on the border with Cambodia. This stretch of the Mekong was filled with small islets and rocks. Waterfalls abounded. It was here that French colonists were unable to navigate ships up the Mekong to southwest China without building a small railroad across Don Khon and Don Det.

We stayed for a couple of nights on the northern side of Don Khon, renting a riverside room at Sengahloune Villa, a more rustic place than the River Resort. In the daytime we biked around the island and then watched the sunset from the old French railroad bridge next to our hotel.

Photographs by
Justin Mott

One afternoon we hired a small boat off the southern tip of Don Khon, near the old railway tracks, to see the area's famous freshwater dolphins. As we strained from our boat to catch a glimpse of the dolphins, we saw a group of monks in saffron robes sitting in a skiff. They had come over from Cambodia. Their boat flew the Cambodian flag, with an image of the main temple at Angkor Wat.

They sat there with umbrellas to shield themselves from the sun and pointed whenever the head or back of a dolphin poked above the water for a few seconds. The river flowed onward, passing around their boat and continuing for hundreds of miles to the ocean far away.

WHAT TO READ AND WATCH

The River's Tale: A Year on the Mekong, by Edward Gargan. A trip on the entire 3,000 miles of the river, exploring from many angles. "Far more than a picturesque personal travel diary." — *The New York Times*.

Last Days of the Mighty Mekong, by Brian Eyler. Discusses the future of the river, now threatened by far-reaching change from Chinese dam projects.

Ancient Luang Prabang & Laos, by Denise Heywood. An illustrated guide emphasizing cultural elements. Includes Vat Phou.

Vat Phou and Associated Ancient Settlements. A three-minute Unesco video with limited views of the temple.

Asia from Above, Season 1, Episode 4: *Laos*, directed by Rohan Fernando and Christian Schidlowski. An informative documentary that gives a feel for the country and its people.

LIVE AND DIE
DIE AND DIE
SHIT AND DIE
PISS AND DIE
EAT AND DIE
SLEEP AND DIE
LOVE AND DIE
HATE AND DIE
FUCK AND DIE
SPEAK AND DIE
LIE AND DIE
HEAR AND DIE
CRY AND DIE
KISS AND DIE
RAGE AND DIE
LAUGH AND DIE
DIE AND LIVE
SHIT AND LIVE
PISS AND LIVE
EAT AND LIVE
SLEEP AND LIVE
LOVE AND LIVE
HATE AND LIVE
SPEAK AND LIVE
LIE AND LIVE
HEAR AND LIVE
KISS AND LIVE
RAGE AND LIVE
LAUGH AND LIVE
TOUCH AND LIVE
SING AND DIE
SCREAM AND DIE
YOUNG AND DIE
OLD AND DIE
CUT AND DIE
RUN AND DIE
STAY AND DIE
PLAY AND DIE
KILL AND DIE
SUCK AND DIE
COME AND DIE
GO AND DIE
KNOW AND DIE
TELL AND DIE
SMELL AND DIE
FALL AND DIE
RISE AND DIE
SING AND LIVE
SCREAM AND LIVE
YOUNG AND LIVE
OLD AND LIVE
CUT AND LIVE
RUN AND LIVE
STAY AND LIVE
PLAY AND LIVE
SUCK AND LIVE
COME AND LIVE
GO AND LIVE
KNOW AND LIVE
TELL AND LIVE
SMELL AND LIVE
FALL AND LIVE

ON NAOSHIMA, THE ART IS EVERYWHERE

Stunning architecture and artworks are so integrated into the landscape of a tiny Japanese island that the visitor becomes a part of it all. — BY INGRID K. WILLIAMS

On a chilly night on the small island of Naoshima in the Seto Inland Sea of southern Japan, I found myself alone in a dark concrete gallery at the Benesse House Museum, a 10-room hotel set inside a contemporary art museum. Unable to sleep, I had left my room to visit the deserted museum galleries — guests of the hotel are permitted to wander after closing time. Before long, I was transfixed by Bruce Nauman's installation *100 Live and Die*, a neon billboard of flashing phrases. "CRY AND LIVE," it read in large, glowing letters. "THINK AND DIE." "SMILE AND LIVE."

I moved on past a whitewashed alphabet by Jasper Johns and the blue hues of a David Hockney swimming pool. No guard hovered over Cy Twombly's scribbles; no tour group blocked Jackson Pollock's splatters. This was the essential appeal of the Benesse's unusual hotel-within-a-museum setup: an exhilarating intimacy with art. Finally, I shuffled out of the gallery and crawled into bed.

That accessibility to art is not uncommon on Naoshima, where a cultural convergence has been percolating since the late 1980s as museums, art installations, cutting-edge architecture, and nature blend in astoundingly novel ways. The result is a sleepy island that has become a destination for globe-trotting art pilgrims who reach it by a 20-minute ferry from Uno, a city west of Osaka.

The emergence of modern art and architecture in this unlikely place can be credited to corporate donations from Benesse Corporation, a Japanese company that specializes in test-prep and language schools. The company's longtime leader, a native of nearby Okayama, is the billionaire art lover Soichiro Fukutake, whose support has fueled the

Previous The Benesse House Museum. On Naoshima island, art, architecture, and nature blend in novel ways.

Left Both public bath and art installation, *I Love Yu* plays with words in its title, using the character for "hot water," which is pronounced "you."

Opposite Monet in Naoshima, displayed under natural light in an underground room at the Chichu Art Museum.

transformation of Naoshima and a number of nearby fishing islands with aging populations.

Naoshima, about three square miles in size, supports a population of about 3,000. Local residents have opened a few traditional guesthouses and restaurants, but it is the art that brings visitors. The Pritzker Prize–winning Japanese architect Tadao Ando designed several structures on Naoshima, including museums. One of the more recent examples is wholly dedicated to works by Lee Ufan, a Korean artist. Like Ando's other buildings, it is a modern concrete creation.

Before my nighttime visit to the Benesse galleries, my husband and I had explored the other impressive buildings affiliated with the hotel. A six-seat monorail took us up the wooded hill behind the museum to another of Ando's sleek structures, a six-room hilltop annex called the Oval. The spare space is anchored by a dramatic black oval pool and blends seamlessly into the natural surroundings, with tumbling waterfalls and a grassy rooftop lawn with panoramic views.

The next day, a rainy one, we hopped on a minibus to Honmura, on the eastern side of the island, where in an innovative effort called the Art House Project, artists have transformed abandoned houses (left behind by the Seto Islands' population decline) into stand-alone projects woven into the fabric of a traditional neighborhood.

One contribution that did involve the creation of a new structure is Minamidera, designed by Ando to house a work by the American artist James Turrell. Entitled *Backside of the Moon*, it's an interactive, mind-bending experience for the viewer. (A full explanation would spoil the exhibit's surprise.)

The artists' messages weren't always easy to decipher. At *Haisha*, the artist Shinro Ohtake had installed a hodgepodge of neon-light pieces and a two-story simulacrum of the Statue of Liberty. At the secluded *Go'o Shrine*, Hiroshi Sugimoto's work was more straightforward: a glass staircase descending from an above-ground shrine to a subterranean cave.

The island's big-ticket draw is Ando's Chichu Art Museum. Chichu means "in the ground," and indeed, the museum, built into a hilltop, is entirely underground, though it doesn't feel that way to the visitor, thanks to a series of open courtyards and strategic skylights.

On the lowest level of the museum is an installation by the American sculptor Walter De Maria. On the floor above, a set of three progressive works by Turrell culminates with *Open Sky*, where viewers recline on

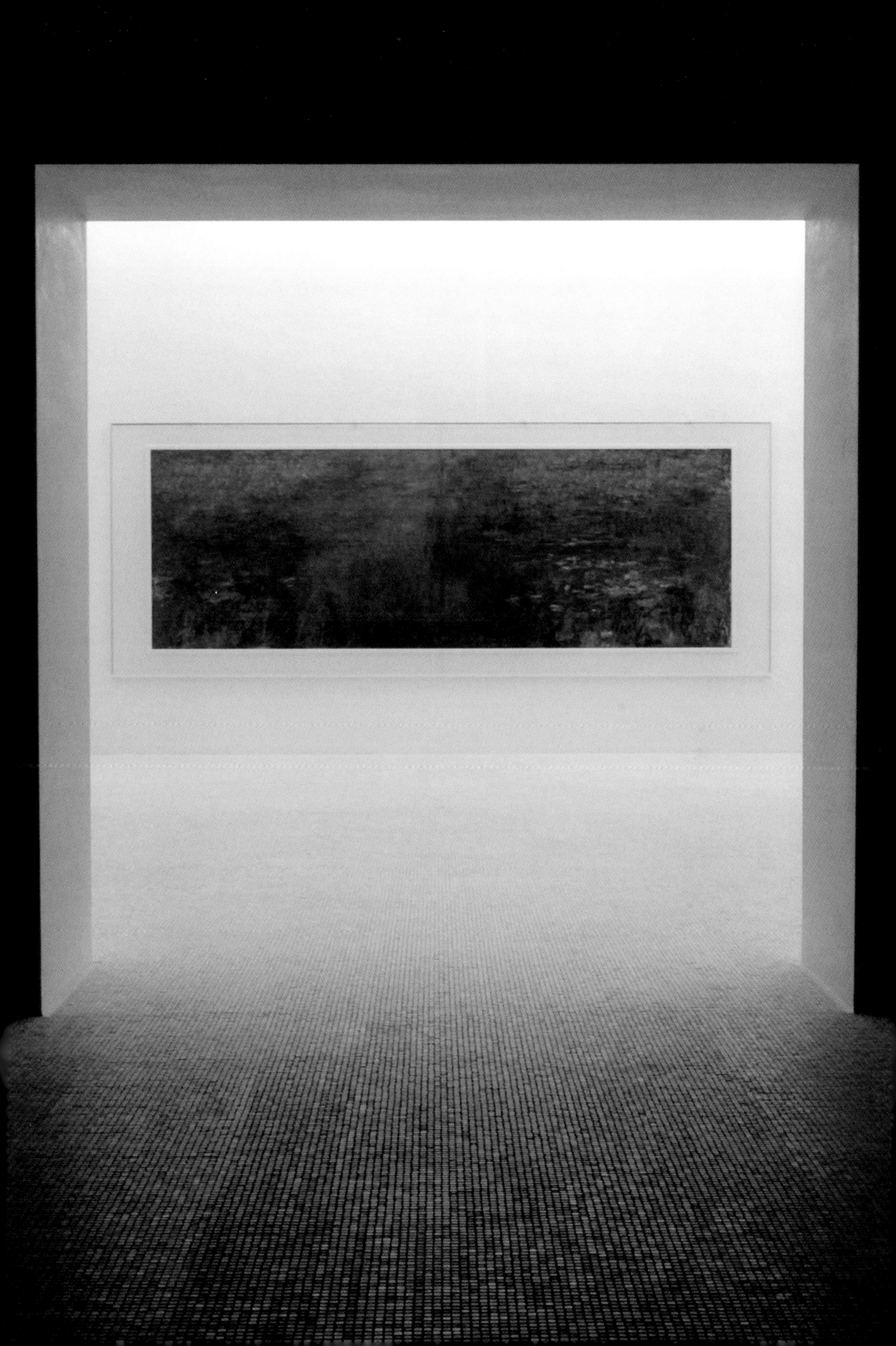

Above An alfresco display of Hiroshi Sugimoto prints at the Benesse House Museum.

Below A pool at the *I Love Yu* public bathhouse.

Opposite The Oval, a Tadao Ando structure, is anchored by a black pool and a grassy rooftop lawn.

stone benches to watch the evolving sky framed by the open ceiling; during our visit, raindrops pattered onto the floor.

But the central piece at Chichu is familiar: one of Claude Monet's famous large-scale water-lily paintings. The room that houses it features an inlaid floor of die-sized cubes of white Carrara marble and rounded walls that shimmer with natural light from above. Outside the museum is a garden modeled on Monet's own in Giverny.

After the rain stopped, my husband and I set out to explore works strewn about Naoshima in outdoor installations, creating a sort of art lover's scavenger hunt. On a densely wooded hill, spindly silver tines twirled above the treetops. At the end of a pier, a jumbo-size, polka-dotted yellow pumpkin squatted above the sea. Beside a road, a band of 88 Buddha statues made from industrial slag blurred the line between waste and art.

We spent our last evening on the island immersed — literally, as it turned out — in an Ohtake-designed artwork that is also a Japanese-style public bathhouse, the Naoshima bathhouse *I Love Yu*. (A bilingual word play, the name uses the character for "hot water," which is pronounced "you.") Although many visitors

Photographs by Kosuke Okahara

simply snap photos of the bathhouse's fantastically eclectic facade, fully experiencing it demands active engagement.

Once stripped of my notebook, camera, and every last stitch of clothing, I soaked in the warm water, absorbed in the piece of art that surrounded me. As happens often on Naoshima, the divisions between art and life simply dissolved.

WHAT TO READ AND WATCH

Ando: Complete Works 1975–Today, by Philip Jodidio, published by TASCHEN. A weighty and exhaustive compilation of works by Tadao Ando. TASCHEN also publishes the smaller and much less expensive *Ando*, part of its Basic Architecture series.

Naoshima (Dream on the Tongue), directed by Claire Laborey, produced by Films de Force Majeure. A journey across the island, examining the art and its impact on traditional life.

The Pursuit of Art: Travels, Encounters and Revelations, by Martin Gayford. An art critic recounts his travels around the world to see artworks and his meetings with artists from Henri Cartier-Bresson to Marina Abramovic.

The Inland Sea, by Donald Richie. First published in 1971, Richie's travel memoir brings the Seto Islands to life as they were in the 1960s. The metaphorical "inland" is his parallel psychological journey.

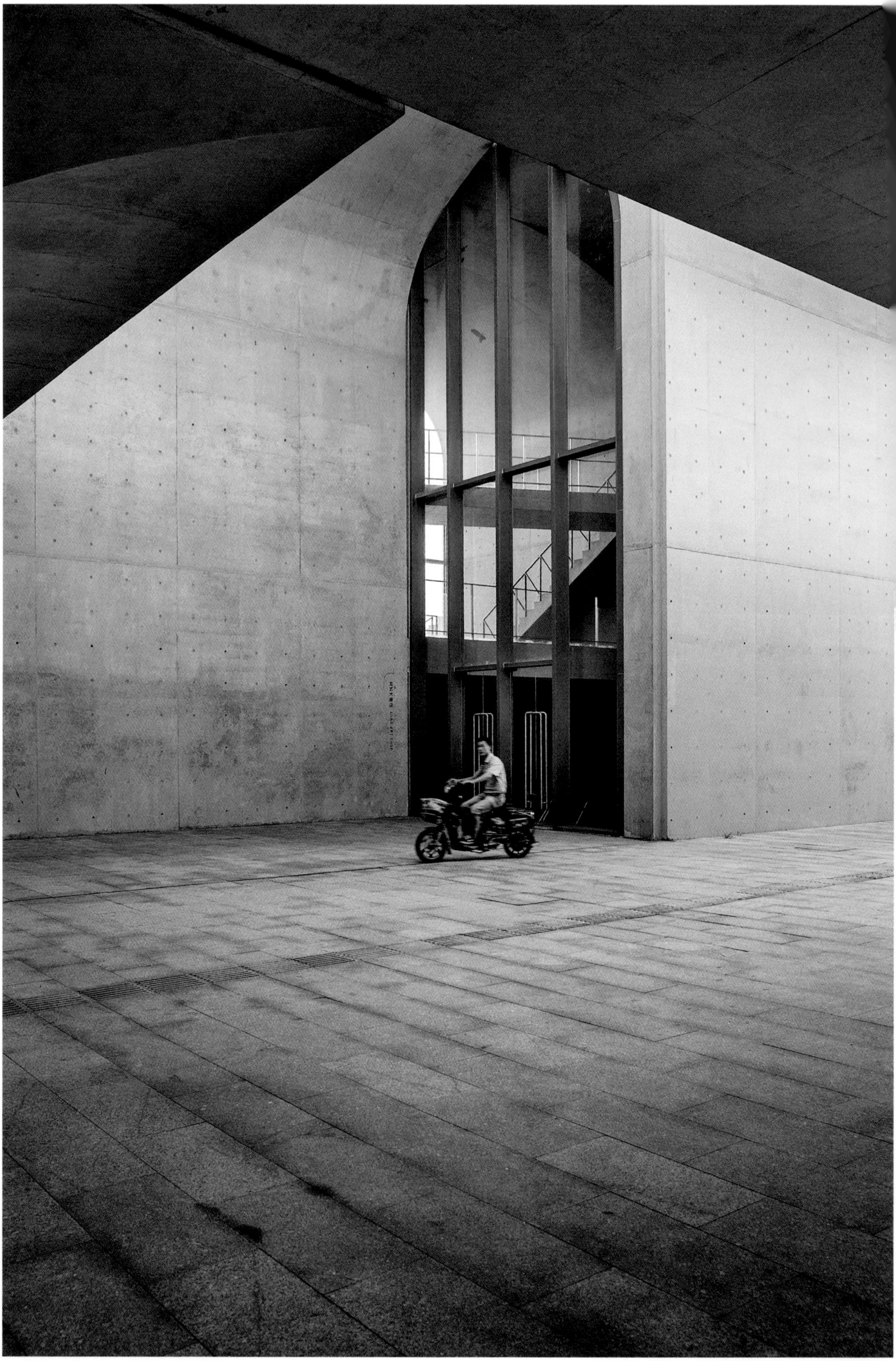

SHANGHAI'S RIVERFRONT ART PROJECT

Museums, galleries, art fairs, and parks sprawl over the West Bund, a Chinese Museum Mile.
— BY JUSTIN BERGMAN

In Shanghai, the historic Bund, a stretch of former banks and trading houses along the Huangpu River, grabs much of the spotlight. Built a century ago in a kaleidoscope of architectural styles, it's a monument to the grandeur of another era. It can also be downright suffocating on weekends, with tourists jostling for selfie positions.

For congestion-weary residents, another part of the riverfront, now known as the West Bund, has become a far more appealing place to spend the weekend. Here, a once-forlorn industrial area known for aircraft manufacturing has been transformed into a lush green corridor where Shanghainese come to ride bikes and skateboards, scale outdoor rock-climbing walls, and, a rarity in this city, enjoy picnics on the grassy riverbank.

They also come, along with increasing numbers of international visitors, to look at art. In a carefully crafted counterpoint to the parkland, museums and galleries have colonized the West Bund, elements in the city's plan to turn it into a world-class arts and culture hub — Shanghai's answer to Museum Mile in New York or South Bank in London.

On one end of the West Bund waterfront, two massive industrial buildings have been repurposed and transformed into the Yuz Museum, focusing on contemporary works, and the West Bund Art Center, site of an annual art fair that draws exhibitors from galleries around the world. On the other end is the Long Museum West Bund, which exhibits a mix of classical antiquities and modern Chinese art. Clustered nearby are smaller private galleries.

Previous The Long Museum West Bund, which incorporates a former coal-unloading bridge.

Left A repurposed airplane hangar accommodates oversized art installations at West Bund Art & Design.

Opposite The Bund waterfront in 1920, when foreign traders and bankers reigned supreme.

Shanghai's ambition is to transform itself from a flashy commercial center known mostly for its spectacular skyline and luxury shopping into a cultural heavyweight superior to its local rivals Beijing and Hong Kong and perhaps someday in the same league as the major art centers in the West. The world's image of the city may not quite have made this transition, but Shanghai has become an increasingly interesting destination for art-loving travelers.

The city has gone on a museum building spree, and not just in the West Bund. The result is a plethora of gorgeous state-of-the-art institutions. One example is the Shanghai Natural History Museum, designed by the American architects Perkins & Will to resemble the spiral shape of a nautilus shell. Another, higher-profile entry is the Power Station of Art, a Tate Modern–inspired, state-run contemporary art museum in a former power plant that has hosted the Shanghai Biennale and a show of the Chinese artist Cai Guo-Qiang's gunpowder drawings and installation works.

Across the river from the West Bund in Pudong, the massive Jean Nouvel–designed Museum of Art Pudong, with more than 100,000 square feet of exhibition space in a minimalist white-granite-clad structure, opened in 2021 with a show of over 100 works from the Tate. Nearby, two former pavilions from the 2010 World Expo have been repurposed as museums. The oversize (even by Chinese standards) glossy-red former China Pavilion is the home of the China Art Museum, and the old French Pavilion is now the Shanghai 21st Century Minsheng Art Museum.

It's a far cry from the early 2000s, when a group of artists took over the abandoned warehouses of a former textile mill on Moganshan Road to establish an arts colony. "There weren't many art museums in Shanghai. Nobody came to Shanghai for art," said Lorenz Helbling, the Swiss founder of ShanghART, one of China's oldest and most-respected galleries, which moved to Moganshan Road in the early 2000s. "This was for a long time the only place… but it's a small place, and this is a big city."

This could perhaps explain Shanghai's desire to establish a more outsize arts district at West Bund, a costly and logistically complex endeavor that only the government could pull off. "Usually an art zone is started spontaneously by artists themselves," said Zhou Tiehai, a well-known Chinese artist who was brought on to spearhead a new annual art fair in the cultural corridor. "But West Bund is totally from the government."

Indeed, the project might never have gotten off the ground if the local government in Shanghai's Xuhui district hadn't persuaded Zhou and several major collectors to take a chance on it. The 1.5-mile stretch of waterfront that it now occupies had been neglected since the closing of factories and an airport years ago.

When Zhou was first approached by the state-owned West Bund Development Group to organize an art fair in a 92,000-square-foot abandoned airplane factory, however, he didn't blanch at the enormousness of the building — or at the task of cleaning it up.

"I turned down a lot of art fairs, but once I saw this building, I knew I could make something special out of it," said Zhou, who gained fame in China for his *Joe Camel* portraits — in which the cartoon camel used in cigarette advertising appears in many guises, including as European royalty and the Mona Lisa. Zhou also got attention for not actually picking up a paintbrush himself; he delegates the actual art work to his staff.

The building had potential but desperately needed refurbishing and a paint job. To bring in more light, two walls were torn down and replaced with glass. The back of the building was lopped off to build a road to the nearest metro station, and a second-floor exhibition space was added. This kind of renovation could take years in most other cities, not to mention the time needed to organize a major art fair. "It only took us eight months," Zhou said matter-of-factly, just in time for the inaugural West Bund Art & Design fair in September 2014. In the next seven years, the fair grew from a couple of dozen exhibitors to 120.

Local leaders also persuaded the Chinese-Indonesian tycoon Budi Tek to move in. A former poultry magnate, Tek had spent a considerable chunk of his fortune collecting Chinese art over the last decade and was looking to build his own museum in China, preferably in Shanghai, his wife's hometown. "When I first committed to this place, there was no West Bund," Tek said. It was still, he added, "a vision." Soon after, he found a former airplane hangar and hired the Japanese architect Sou Fujimoto to renovate it.

Tek's Yuz Museum opened in May 2014 with a statement piece in its striking, glass-covered atrium: a live olive tree planted in a giant block of dried

Above A display at West Bund Art & Design.

Opposite Part of the Long Museum is an old coal unloading bridge left over from an industrial past.

earth, a work by the Italian artist Maurizio Cattelan. Inside were more innovative installations, many owned by Tek, that could fit only inside a hangar, such as Xu Bing's *Tobacco Project*, an assemblage of more than 600,000 cigarettes resembling a tiger-skin rug; and *Freedom* by Sun Yuan and Peng Yu, a giant metal tank with a high-pressure hose inside that comes to life every hour, spraying the portholes with frightening jolts of water to the squeals of camera-snapping crowds.

Few museums in China open with such a bang. Yuz has maintained its momentum with exhibitions of works by the likes of Alberto Giacometti, Picasso, and Andy Warhol.

"I call myself a start-up museum," Tek said. "To make a statement to the world that we are a serious museum, we want to do very exciting programs…. Museums are not for ants, birds — they're for people to come, as many people as you can."

This philosophy is shared by the collectors Wang Wei and her husband, Liu Yiqian, a taxi driver–turned–billionaire financier, who made names for themselves with art purchases like $36 million for a Ming dynasty porcelain cup and $45 million for a 600-year-old embroidered silk tapestry. After building a sizable collection, Liu and his wife began looking for space to build museums in Shanghai to exhibit their purchases. The Xuhui district government provided a plum spot on the West Bund riverfront, and it's now transformed into the Long Museum West Bund. The site was a wharf where coal was unloaded from barges throughout much of the 20th century. A 1950s-era concrete bridge that was used to transport coal to train hoppers was preserved, and the Shanghai architecture firm Atelier Deshaus constructed a new museum around it with a similarly stark concrete design.

As the West Bund took off, more galleries joined Yuz and Long on the waterfront. One is the Shanghai

Photographs by Qilai Shen

Center of Photography (SCoP), a project of the Hong Kong–born, Pulitzer Prize–winning photojournalist Liu Heung Shing. Next to the West Bund Art Center, ShanghART opened a gallery designed to resemble stacked shipping containers.

Helbling, the ShanghART founder, said launching a new space is a risk, but when he looks out at the barges floating by on the tree-lined river, he knows that on the West Bund a risk was worth taking.

"It's quite a unique place," he said. "You can actually walk, you can get out. You can go for the weekend, stay half a day, a day there. It's not full of buildings. I think it could give Shanghai a different identity."

WHAT TO READ AND WATCH

Brand New Art from China, by Barbara Pollack. An art critic attempts to explain the dynamic, often puzzling, and sometimes multimillion-dollar art of the Chinese millennial generation.

Seven Days in the Art World, by Sarah Thornton. "A field guide to the nomadic tribes of the contemporary art world...poised to endure as a work of sociology." — Mia Fineman in *The New York Times*.

Shanghai Free Taxi: Journeys with the Hustlers and Rebels of the New China, by Frank Langfitt. A National Public Radio correspondent's account of getting to know people in Shanghai by offering rides in exchange for conversation.

Sky Ladder: The Art of Cai Guo-Qiang, directed by Kevin Macdonald. A Netflix documentary on a contemporary artist known for spectacular pyrotechnics, featuring his project *Sky Ladder*.

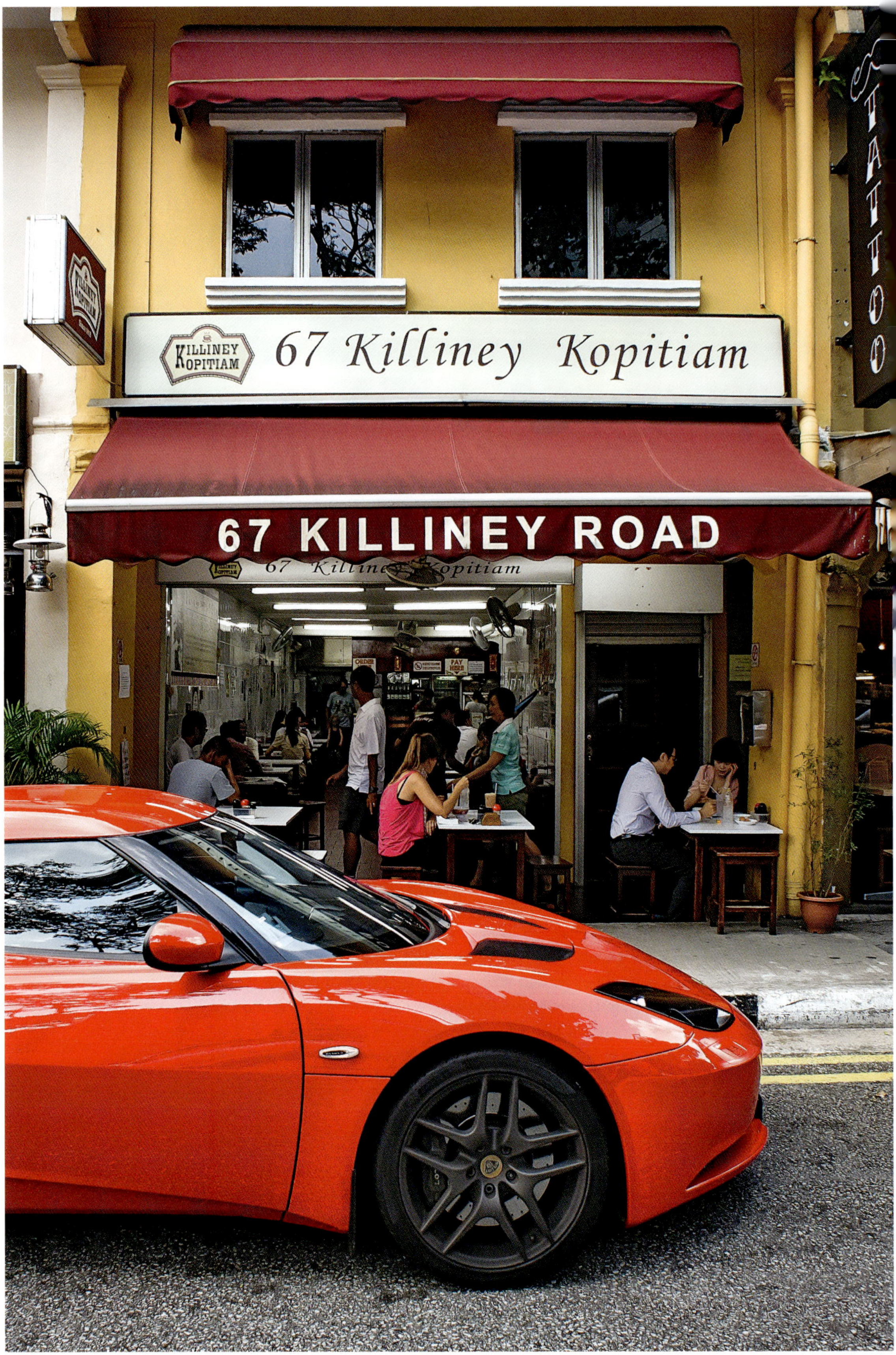

67 Killiney Kopitiam
67 KILLINEY ROAD
TATTOO

BREAKFAST IN SINGAPORE, WITH BUTTER IN THE COFFEE

The customers are unpretentious and the menu is time-tested in the humble restaurants called kopitiams.
— BY CHERYL LU-LIEN TAN

Wading through the plume of smoke from a thicket of men puffing away outside, my father and I made our way to the only available table in sight. At just after 9 a.m., the morning crowd at Heap Seng Leong *kopitiam*—a coffee shop, in Singaporean vernacular—was steadily thickening. The thin veneer on our wood table was chipped; my plastic chair stuck to the back of my legs. And the scrawny man who materialized as soon as we sat down grunted with impatience when we paused to think before ordering.

And yet, when our coffees, saucers of watery soft-boiled eggs, and crisp slices of toast slathered with thick yellow butter and *kaya*, an eggy coconut jam, showed up soon afterward, I recognized the moment for what it was: a perfect kopitiam experience in Singapore.

There are many ways to explore Singapore—through its casinos, its busy nightclubs, its botanical gardens. As a teenager there, I became well acquainted with its Burger Kings and malls. But the most authentic view of the city is always at a kopitiam: one of the old-school coffee shops that dot almost every neighborhood in the country, serving up cheap breakfasts, uniquely Singaporean coffee, and, later in the day, cold beer and simple meals.

"In Western countries, they have pubs; in Singapore, we have kopitiams," said Leslie Tay, a doctor and writer who created one of Singapore's most popular food blogs, *I Eat I Shoot I Post*. "The kopitiam is the center of life for many Singapore neighborhoods. You can sit at the kopitiam and watch the old men sitting around for hours, drinking beer and talking, playing a game of checkers."

The word *kopitiam* itself reflects the polyglot culture of Singapore—*kopi* is the Malay word for

SINGAPORE

Previous Kopitiams are coffee shops of a uniquely Singaporean variety. Killiney dates back to 1919.

Left Serving coffee at Heap Seng Leong. Casual attire is accepted.

Opposite Tong Ah Eating House began in 1939 with a special brew: three kinds of coffee beans, sugar, and butter.

coffee, while *tiam* is the Hokkien (or Fukienese) word for shop. Kopitiams are usually open-air affairs, some resembling mini food courts, packed with a handful of food stalls, on the first floor of the ubiquitous government-built apartment complexes that span whole blocks. While Singapore coffee culture today also thrives in hawker centers — essentially, sprawling outdoor food courts — and in a growing number of spiffy, sometimes air-conditioned, modern kopitiams, the setting at such places tends to be colder, the eating and drinking perfunctory.

They hardly resemble the kopitiams that first proliferated when Singapore was a British colony. In the early 1900s, Chinese men who had been hired to cook in expat homes began leaving and opening coffee shops to offer cheap meals to a growing working class. These Chinese cooks introduced the British habit of drinking coffee to Singaporeans, along with staples like toast and eggs for breakfast.

The coffee they served up was unlike any found in Western coffee shops. Because the cooks could often afford only cheap beans, they enhanced their aroma by wok-frying them with butter (or lard) and sugar. The resulting basic kopi is a cup of thick coffee, strained through a cloth sock several inches long and packed with teaspoons of sugar and sweet condensed milk.

Variations on the standard have spawned a mind-boggling vernacular. A kopi C substitutes lighter evaporated milk (the C stands for "Carnation") for the condensed milk. Because *kosong* means zero in Malay, a kopi kosong has no sugar. Kopi O is the real zero: black coffee. Kopi O poh is diluted black coffee with sugar. Kopi peng is a basic kopi on ice. And yuan yang, a surprising combo for most Westerners, is half coffee and half tea, with the usual condensed milk and sugar.

Though ordering coffee can be a complicated affair, the food choices are often simple at kopitiams. At a place called Heap Seng Leong, I ate a runny egg spiked with white pepper and squirts of sweet, dark soy sauce while I scanned the gallery of older men lining one wall. One was fast asleep, his head so far down on his chest his large belly almost cradled it. Outside, the kopitiam *ah cheks* (Hokkien for uncles) were embroiled in a heated conversation I could barely make out — except for the word *kar chng* (backside) at one point.

At a small counter next to the abacus, which served as the cash register, a man wearing striped pajama bottoms and a thin white sleeveless T-shirt made an endless stream of kopis. Whenever anyone ordered kaya toast, rhythmic scraping noises would soon fill the air — a server removing the burned bits with the lid of a metal can.

The contrasting flavors and textures in these breakfasts is always heavenly: The zing of white pepper counters the salty sweetness of soy sauce; the warm goo of soft eggs and the thick kopi offset the crispness of toast.

I found a more inviting setting at Chin Mee Chin Confectionery on East Coast Road, the slender artery that slices through Singapore's sleepy Eastern shore. Housed in a prewar shophouse, it had the trappings of kopitiams of yore: slender wooden chairs and tables outfitted with pristine white marble tops. Its cups were traditional kopitiam cups, squat, small, and very thick all around, specially designed to preserve the heat of the contents. Unlike many kopitiams, which rely on kaya from a can, Chin Mee Chin made its own kaya, which had a slightly more eggy aroma and was denser than most. It also served kaya on hot rolls baked at the shop.

The success of kopitiams has led to a "McDonaldization" of two of Singapore's oldest: Ya Kun and Killiney Kopitiam, both of which date back to the early 20th century and have morphed into chains with dozens of locations across the country. I'd been to many of Killiney's gleaming new outlets but had never been to the first, which opened in 1919 in an old shophouse at 67 Killiney Road, near the shopping district. When my father and I went there, we found a more extensive breakfast menu than is typical at kopitiams. I ordered *roti prata*, an Indian bread, with chicken curry that turned out to be delicious.

That experience brought to mind an old kopitiam in this city's Chinatown that I had heard was as beloved for its dinners as for its kopi and kaya toast. So as soon as we could eat again, my father and I trekked to Tong Ah Eating House at 35 Keong Saik Road, an open-air kopitiam in a triangular building. "We are four generations," said Tang Chew Fue, the owner, explaining that his great-grandfather founded the kopitiam in 1939 with a secret recipe that involved roasting three kinds of coffee beans with sugar and butter.

We ordered a sampling of dishes for dinner: braised tofu topped with a scrumptious mound of minced pork sautéed with salty pickled radishes; claypot-cooked chicken coated in a gingery, garlicky

Above Leslie Tay, a food blogger, says it all: "In Western countries, they have pubs; in Singapore, we have kopitiams."

Below *Butter kopi*, the epitome for some. Another choice is *yuan yang*, half coffee and half tea.

Opposite Grandmother and grandson having the traditional egg, toast, and coffee at Chin Mee Chin Confectionery.

glaze; a large omelet packed with juicy oysters; and a platter of noodles featuring tender beef. Each dish was more delicious than the last. There was still a kopi quest ahead. Although butter has its place in much of Singapore's traditional coffee, there is a holy grail, the cup known simply as butter kopi. "It's basically coffee with butter in it," Willin Low, chef of Singapore's Wild Rocket fusion restaurant, had said with great reverence when I asked him about it. "Years ago, butter was expensive, so butter coffee became a symbol of wealth."

I had been met mostly with quizzical looks when I asked for butter kopi. But at Hua Bee Restaurant, a dusty little kopitiam that's been around since the 1940s, the kopi uncle was unfazed. All he said was "Twenty cents extra," before disappearing and returning with a thick square of butter on a toothpick, which he then popped into my coffee.

I watched, transfixed, as the edges of the yellow square got fuzzy and then dissolved. Within a minute, just a glistening film on my kopi remained. Giving it a stir, I took a sip; it was a little greasy and had a very faint salty element to it.

When I asked the kopi uncle about butter coffee, he shrugged it off, saying, "Not anything special,

Photographs by
Edwin Koo

lah." And perhaps he was right—flavorwise, there wasn't anything distinctive that might make the extra 20 cents worthwhile.

But when you took into account the steamed slices of kaya-topped bread, a phalanx of ah cheks sitting nearby and sipping their kopi, the sounds of a sleepy morning slowly rousing around me, I realized the kopi uncle was wrong. There was, indeed, something special here.

WHAT TO READ AND WATCH

A Tiger in the Kitchen: A Memoir of Food and Family, by Cheryl Lu-Lien Tan. The author, also writer of this article, returns to Singapore after years away to learn the family recipes and reconnect with the city.

The Food of Singapore: Simple Street Food Recipes from the Lion City, by Djoko Wibisono and David Wong. Authentic recipes from a city famous for its street food.

Aunty Lee's Delights: A Singaporean Mystery, by Ovidia Yu. The first novel in a series about a tirelessly inquisitive Singapore restaurant owner and occasional sleuth.

Crazy Rich Asians, directed by Jon M. Chu. Singapore is the setting for this romantic comedy about an Asian American woman meeting her boyfriend's wealthy family.

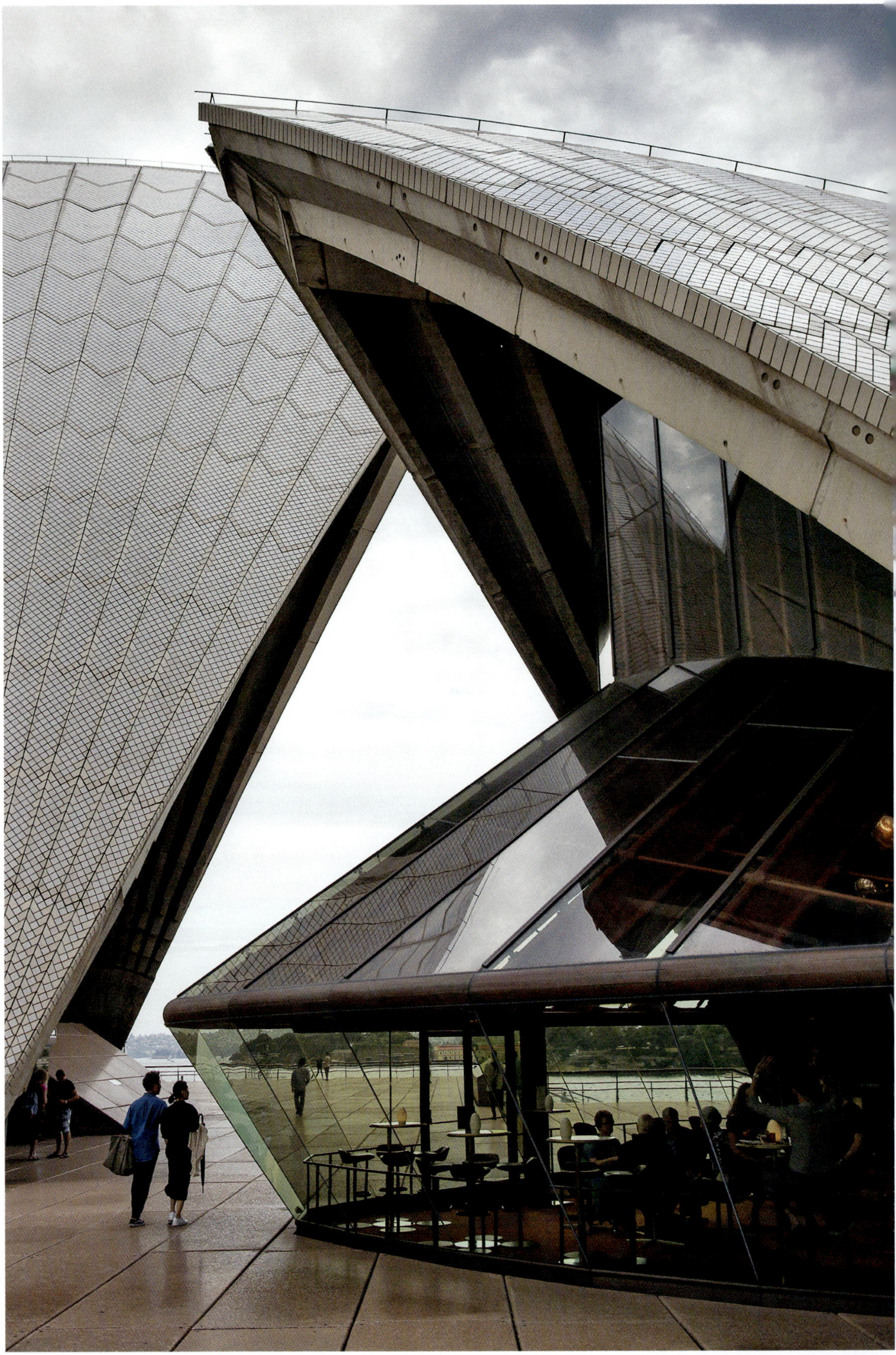

AUSTRALIA   SYDNEY

THE SYDNEY THAT GOES TO THE OPERA

The beaches are still great, but so are the festivals, the literary life, the "arts precincts," and the arias in that iconic Opera House. — BY TONY PERROTTET

The Australian writer and art critic Robert Hughes once complained that in the eyes of many non-Australians (he specified Americans) *Crocodile Dundee* was regarded as a work of social realism. A rhetorical exaggeration, of course, but he had a point. As an Australian living abroad, I've long been puzzled at the dominance of charming clichés about the country as a sun-dappled frontier. Advertising campaigns still promote the "ocker" image — that's Australian for redneck — depicting beer-swilling, happy-go-lucky folk barbecuing steak at the beach.

I protest to friends in vain that Australia has a lot more to offer than rampant hedonism and cuddly koalas. Its cities are wildly cosmopolitan, I argue, and even, dare I say, sophisticated. Its museums are packed, its cultural life raucous, and endless film and arts festivals clutter the social calendar.

The gulf between image and reality is most extreme in Sydney, my hometown, which is renowned for its Rio-like natural beauty. It's also known for the Sydney Opera House, an instantly recognizable piece of architecture — though few Americans seem to consider that opera is actually performed there.

Sydney exports planeloads of stars to Hollywood — even though, because of their talent for accents, many aren't recognized as Aussies. For me, the final straw came when I had to spend half an hour convincing a New York–based magazine editor that Cate Blanchett, who has been decorated as a Companion of the Order of Australia, is not, in fact, British. I began to feel the need to update my own view of the city, if only to gather ammunition for dinner parties.

And so, as Australia was basking in the glory of an antipodean summer, I escaped the frozen sidewalks

Previous The Sydney Opera House, iconic as viewed from a distance, welcomes music lovers at ground level.

Left An exhibition at Roslyn Oxley9 Gallery in Paddington.

Opposite A skateboarder on the Goods Line, a public walkway on an old railroad bed.

of New York to emerge Down Under, blinking like a startled marsupial in the shimmering light. Heroically, on this visit I resisted the siren call of Sydney Harbor and the beaches. Instead, I stalked the creative populace of the city, who exist in a parallel dimension to the classic tourist trail. And I was reminded of just how original and imaginative Sydney's inner life could be.

Checking in at the QT, a psychedelic "art hotel" that exists a long way from the glitzy high-rise lodgings that pack in tourists, I found décor that evoked a Jean Cocteau dream sequence set in a high-class bordello. The lobby featured found art and dressmaker's mannequins painted as nudes. The bellhop, sporting a crimson wig and black beret, escorted me into a nearly pitch-black elevator showing a digital video of cascading points of light. It was fitted with sensors to select music depending on the number of passengers: techno for crowds, romantic pop for couples. (Traveling solo, unfortunately, I kept getting Elvis Presley's "Are You Lonesome Tonight?")

The QT was the ideal base to explore the "inner city," which comprises a number of bohemian neighborhoods surrounding the central business district. These once seedy areas were originally crowded with tenement-style housing, the kind with one whole family per crowded room. Today they are prized for their Victorian flourishes, like the elegant iron lace decorating their balconies. The once mean streets are dotted with chic cafes, cocktail bars, and bespoke tailoring shops, along with retro gems like the Golden Age Cinema ("Founded MMXIII"), a movie house in the Paramount Pictures building.

As a sentimental gesture, I hopped a cab to Edward Street, where I used to live as a student in a gritty neighborhood called Chippendale. It was a mild shock. The streets were now quiet and leafy, and my old flophouse terrace was freshly painted and overflowing with flowers. Even more shocking to me, Chippendale had been established as a nonprofit "Creative Precinct" with art and history walking tours. A foldout map directed me to galleries with names like Pompom and Kaleidoscope, as well as White Rabbit, a former factory housing a cutting-edge museum of Chinese contemporary art, complete with soothing teahouse. Nearby, a reception was in full swing at the NG Art Gallery in a former Gothic Revival church.

Leaving "Chippo," as it's called by some, I bounced around the established galleries in the Paddington and Woollahra areas, but realized I was only scratching the surface. A tour leader named Jenny Garber reminded me that Sydney's Biennale dates back to 1973. "Only Venice and São Paulo are older," she said.

The most evocative art site was tucked away in Surry Hills, back near the busy business center: the studio of Brett Whiteley, whose voluptuous use of light and color redefined modern Australian painting. The studio was exactly as Whiteley left it at the time of his heroin overdose in 1992—an affecting array of paint brushes, LP records, seashells, and a half-finished canvas with his signature curves. Whiteley was also Sydney's bad boy celebrity, and intimate snapshots of him with Bob Dylan were displayed alongside scraps of graffiti on his philosophy and art.

Whiteley's famous Sydney Harbor paintings sent me racing down to the Rocks, in the very tourist zone I'd planned to avoid, for a stop at the Museum of Contemporary Art. After wandering its galleries —the most memorable were devoted to modern Aboriginal art—I retired to the rooftop patio of the museum cafe for panoramic views and a glass of crisp Tasmanian sparkling wine.

I was in the wrong season for another art extravaganza, Sculpture by the Sea, a springtime event in which a hike along the crashing seashore is adorned with enormous artworks, while cafes and restaurants await at both ends.

Strolling around the promenade of Circular Quay, another popular tourist spot, I averted my eyes from the green-and-yellow harbor ferries departing for white-sand beaches to read the plaques of the Sydney Writers Walk underfoot. Bronze discs offer quotes from local wordsmiths both obscure to outsiders (the colonial poet Henry Lawson) and recognized (Patrick White, Nobel Prize laureate of 1973). The Writers Walk even quotes the cranky Australian poet A. D. Hope, who disparaged the country as a land "Where second hand Europeans pullulate / Timidly on the edge of alien shores.")

Some surveys have found that Australians read more books per capita than anyone else in the English-speaking world, and Sydney loves its literary readings in venues like Ariel Bookstore in Paddington and Gleebooks in Glebe, which are often packed to the rafters. The pace comes to a frenzy in May with the Sydney Writers' Festival, which organizes hundreds of events throughout the city. Readings and panels have been held in stunning settings like the Sydney Wharf, a revamped harborfront pier that includes stylish auditoriums, and Cockatoo Island, a historic convict site set amid the monolithic stone ruins of a shipyard. During the festival, poems by the likes of Rainer Maria Rilke and Judith Wright, a local, have even been plastered on the sides of garbage trucks.

It's no surprise that some readings have been held at the Bondi Surf Pavilion, another beloved venue, which offers not just a theater and art gallery, but also changing rooms and showers. A good deal of the talent at the readings would come from North Bondi, home to many in Sydney's film, fashion, and music community.

I decided to track down one peripatetic member of that community, the poet and screenwriter Luke Davies, author of the classic 1997 Sydney novel *Candy* about two heroin addicts in love. (Later, he wrote the Academy Award–winning screenplay for *Lion* and co-wrote, with Paul Greengrass, the screenplay for *News of the World*.) I wandered past North Bondi's hole-in-the-wall surfer cafes and quirky restaurants to

Above The beach is an expected urban amenity in Sydney.

Opposite A view of the Rocks district from Sydney Harbour Bridge. The Opera House glows on the horizon.

his apartment, where we sat on the veranda chatting about film projects. Then, with towels over our shoulders, we ambled down to North Head, a sandstone bluff at Bondi's entrance marked in places with Aboriginal carvings, then plunged from a rocky ledge straight into the churning ocean. "There is some good fortune involved with being a writer in Sydney," Davies said as we bobbed in the swell, which seemed to loom over the entire sandy arc of Bondi. "The natural beauty here is so in-your-face, you can get lost in it. You enter a trancelike state, which is perfect for creative tasks."

I was starting to accept that every art experience in Sydney is somehow enhanced by nature. The stroll to the Art Gallery of New South Wales passed eucalyptus groves alive with native birds. *La Bohème* at the Opera House was preceded by cocktails on a balcony in the velvety summer dusk. A play at the Sydney Theatre Company was followed by an oyster supper at the End of the Wharf, where you can casually watch the watercraft parading below.

"I think the physical beauty of Sydney is an important element for a sense of possibility in the arts," the director Neil Armfield, who worked with such young unknowns as Cate Blanchett, Hugo Weaving, and Geoffrey Rush, told me later. "When you grow up here, you have a sense of being surrounded by something miraculous. It alters the framework inside of you somehow."

On my last night in Sydney, I managed to experience the perfect marriage of art and nature at the Open Air Cinema. For two months every year, stadium seating is erected in the Royal Botanic Gardens, close by the lapping waters of Sydney Harbor and facing the floodlit Opera House. My every sense was catered to. I ate tempura-battered fish and chips from the cafe, sipped fine wine from the bar, and took a seat beneath the ancient trees in which fruit bats

*Photographs by
Andrew Quilty*

were frolicking. As darkness fell, an enormous cinema screen majestically rose from water level, accompanied by triumphal music.

Almost any film would seem magical under these conditions, but I was there for *Tracks*, an adaptation of Robyn Davidson's novel about crossing the Outback deserts with a team of camels. The whole event seemed like a conceptual artwork about the essential strangeness of Australia's environment.

I ran into Davies there, and we spoke again. "Thanks to technology, the world is a smaller place," he told me, "but Australia is still uniquely isolated, so our concept of the world is already different. We see ourselves more as outsiders, and in the arts, that feeling becomes metaphorical."

As we chatted, a trio of bats let out a prehistoric shriek from the branches above, then flew low over the dark water.

WHAT TO READ AND WATCH

The Fatal Shore, by Robert Hughes. An acclaimed, informative, and highly readable history of Australia from its beginnings as an English convict colony, with Sydney's story an integral part.

The House: The Dramatic Story of the Sydney Opera House and the People Who Made It, by Helen Pitt. A real-life saga of vision, creative conflicts, financial roadblocks, and defection of the original architect.

Shell, by Kristina Olsson. The story of the Opera House told through a historical novel. A sculptor working on the project in 1965 meets a woman actively opposed to the Vietnam War, and their complicated lives intersect.

Whiteley, directed by James Bogle. A documentary film about the artist pioneering Brett Whiteley.

Australia's Impressionists, by Christopher Riopelle, Tim Bonyhady, and others. An illustrated survey of a past generation's avant-garde.

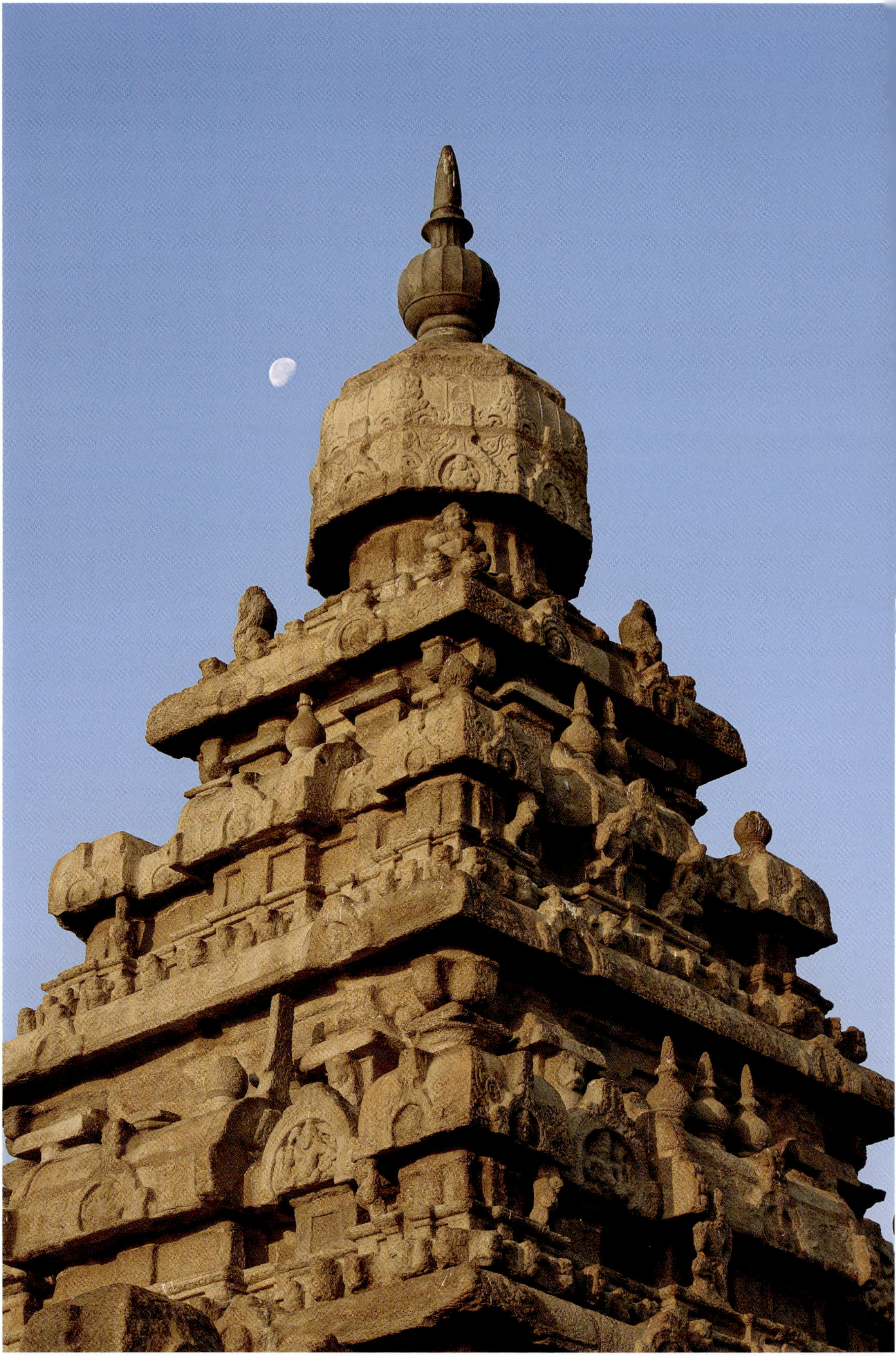

THE GODS OF TAMIL NADU

At ancient stone temples in India's South, the deities live so vividly in the present that they even meet for sex.
— BY EDWARD WONG

The god was ready for his night of conjugal bliss. The priests of the temple, muscular, shirtless men with white sarongs wrapped around their thighs, bore his palanquin on their shoulders. As they marched slowly along a stone corridor, drumbeats echoed and candles flickered. In an inner sanctum the fish-eyed goddess Meenakshi awaited the embrace of the god in the palanquin — her husband, Sundareshwarar, an incarnation of that most priapic of Indian gods, Shiva.

Worshippers surged forward in mass delirium, snapping photos with their cell phones, bowing to the palanquin, and chanting hymns. They stretched out their hands to touch the carriage. Priests ordered them back.

This union of Meenakshi and Sundareshwarar is a nightly ritual in Madurai, a city in the southern Indian state of Tamil Nadu, drawing feverish crowds of Hindu devotees. In much of India, the gods are not creatures of distant myth to be worshipped as abstractions. They exist in our world, in our time, and are fully integrated into the daily lives of Hindu believers. They move simultaneously through the world of the divine and the world that we inhabit, and are subject to all the emotions and experiences that we humans are all too familiar with — including carnal desire.

Few things in India express the continuous presence of the gods better than the ancient, massive temple complexes of Tamil Nadu. Walk through any city there and what catches your eye first are the soaring temple entrances known as *gopuras*, sacred skyscrapers decorated with phantasmagorias of Hindu statues of multi-armed, bug-eyed gods, mythical

Previous Some residents see Tamil Nadu and its temples as a repository of a pure ancient culture.

Left Making tea in front of a cafe in Mahabalipuram.

Opposite Tamil Nadu stone sculptors work in shops along roadways. Hindu deities are the usual subjects.

beasts, and chiseled warriors. Thousands of such statues adorn the largest gopuras, like the ones rising from the Meenakshi-Sundareshwarar temple in Madurai, one of the holiest pilgrimage sites in India.

"Here, we have a proverb: 'Where there is a temple, people can live,'" said Ram Kumar, a tourist guide I had hired in Madurai. "The temple is the center of a person's living space."

Though Kerala, the state just to the west, draws larger tourist crowds, Tamil Nadu is an increasingly popular destination. Although it is one of India's most developed states, it also has beaches and lush farmland, and its cuisine is among the most flavorful—and hottest—in India.

But it is the temple circuit that is the main draw, as it has been for centuries. Indeed, many of Tamil Nadu's residents see the state as a repository of "pure" Hindu culture. In many ways, it is a country within a country, proudly preserving its ancient Dravidian culture, most noticeably in the widespread use of the Tamil language.

I had been to India several times, but never to the south, so I had little idea of what to expect when I flew with my friend Tini into Chennai, the capital of Tamil Nadu. We were met by a driver from a hotel in Mahabalipuram, a beach town 36 miles south. He whisked us into an Ambassador, a grand 1950s-style sedan ubiquitous throughout India, and off we went. Flying through insane traffic, we veered past cows, motor rickshaws, and overcrowded buses.

Then we pulled into Mahabalipuram. I could see the ocean when we cruised into town, and the air smelled of salt as we drove through quiet lanes to our seaside hotel. The beach here is not of the golden-sand-and-swaying-palms kind found in Goa or Kerala, but it is a pretty stretch for walking along and unwinding from sightseeing. (Think fishing skiffs and seafood restaurants.)

It is the town's stone architecture, some of the oldest in India, that makes Mahabalipuram a good first stop on the temple crawl. Biking between the temples seemed the most relaxed way of taking in the sights.

We began by cycling to the Five Rathas, a set of seventh-century mini-temples on the southern edge of town. We found the place crowded with Indian tourists. Juice vendors stood next to carts piled high with green coconuts. The site seemed designed to be a big outdoor showroom exhibiting the skills of the town's ancient architects. Incredibly, the five temples were carved from a single large slab of granite, models in the Dravida style.

Pedaling north from there, I heard the chiseling of stone coming from roadside workshops — a sound I would hear throughout the day — reminding me that Mahabalipuram is still the stone-sculpting capital of India, just as it was in ancient times. Likenesses of major Hindu gods like Shiva, Vishnu, and Ganesh roll out of these workshops and into homes and offices around the country.

I stopped in at a few of the workshops, where men sat on the floor chiseling. They were creating statues of Hindu gods and of Buddha in various poses: Buddha reclining, Buddha meditating beneath the bodhi tree, Buddha's head. At one workshop, I held up a statuette of Ganesh, the elephant-headed god. He was typing on a laptop.

"Computer companies like to buy these," the manager said.

This was India: the modern alongside the classically ancient.

By the crashing waves of the Bay of Bengal sits Mahabalipuram's most important architectural site, the Shore Temple. My guidebook said the Shore Temple was built in the early eighth century, during the Pallava dynasty, and is considered the earliest stone temple in southern India. Its two towers were modest compared with some of the gopuras I would later see, but the style — a layered, wedding-cake look — had enormous influence on the development of later temples both in both India and Southeast Asia. The corncob towers of the beautiful Angkor complex in Cambodia, built by the Hindu Khmer rulers, are one example.

Perhaps the most beautiful piece of art in Mahabalipuram, an open-air bas relief known as Arjuna's Penance, lies in the heart of town. Its dozens of figures from Hindu mythology are carved from the surface of an enormous granite boulder.

The central scenes depict a well-known tale from the Mahabharata — that of the revered warrior Arjuna turning ascetic and going into the forest to seek the aid of Shiva in a coming battle. Tourists were kept far from the rock by a rail, but monkeys clambered all over it, just like the forest creatures in the mythological scene.

Traveling on south from Mahabalipuram, Tini and I hopped on a bus to Pondicherry, the former French colonial town. Pondicherry is a good stop for dining and some new boutique hotels, but it does not have much in the way of grand temples. We hired a car there to reach the temple of Gangaikondacholapuram, a few hours' drive southwest. This temple's detailed statues and friezes, from the Chola dynasty, are as remarkable as its elongated name. What astounded me were the demon-protector statues flanking each doorway, towering over me, snarling at me with fanged teeth, telling me in a not-too-subtle way that I didn't belong there.

The drive to the temple had taken us deep into the Tamil Nadu countryside, past the electric-green rice fields of the Cauvery Delta. Storms broke out as we were leaving the temple, but I didn't mind. It all seemed part of the landscape, these rains that would bring a harvest for the farmers making a living the same way their ancestors had thousands of years ago.

Eager for a roof over our heads, we told our driver to head for Thanjavur, where I hoped to see the finest surviving works of the Chola dynasty. The Cholas ruled a large swath of southern India for hundreds of years before falling out of power in the 13th century.

The downpour was ceaseless, continuing through the night and the next day. I spent my first morning in Thanjavur looking at marvelous bronze statues in the Royal Palace compound. I saw one motif that has been replicated endlessly: a famous bronze depiction of Nataraja, lord of the dance, standing in a ring of fire with strands of the cosmos swirling from his head.

The next morning, with the rain lessening, I went to the Brihadishwara Temple, the most jaw-dropping architectural achievement of the Cholas. Its impressive scale was apparent as soon as I walked past the temple's pet elephant in the outer courtyard and

Above The traffic varies in Madurai, but the road leads straight to a temple tower.

Opposite A temple and its lotus pond west of Madurai.

toward the interior. The *vimana*, the tower above the inner sanctum, rises 216 feet into the air and is topped with an 81-ton block of granite holding a 25-ton octagonal cupola, all intricately carved. One theory says that the builders used a 3.5-mile-long elevated plank to roll the ball to the top.

As I peered at the thousands of statues decorating the tower, pilgrims streamed into the compound, many going into the inner sanctum to be blessed by the priests and to gaze on the 10-foot-tall black lingam. In appearance, a lingam is essentially a big phallus. It is the most common representation of Shiva—the destroyer, the transformer, the god who embodies both life and the negation of life—at temples across India.

Male pilgrims draped in orange robes shuffled past us to stand in front of the lingam. Many were Shaivites, easily recognized by three white lines drawn on their foreheads. I saw them everywhere in Tamil Nadu.

Our final stop was Madurai, the city where we watched the procession carrying the male god Sundareshwarar to spend a night with his consort, Meenakshi. Madurai is one of the most ancient cities in India, so it is only fitting that this temple complex, which some call the most magnificent on the subcontinent, stands at the center of its teeming bazaars. It is actually two temples joined, one dedicated to Meenakshi and the other to Sundareshwarar. In a departure from the pattern at many Indian temples, Meenakshi, the female god, is the dominant one here.

A massive, brightly painted gopura rises above each of the four entrances to the temple, the 12 towers visible for miles around. The tallest, above the south entrance, is more than 150 feet tall.

"This temple is a special one," my guide, Ram Kumar, said. "You feel it as soon as you walk in."

At least 15,000 visitors come each day. That afternoon, pilgrims kept pouring in. Ram said many

Photographs by
James Estrin

had temporarily left behind their material lives — jobs as software engineers, rickshaw drivers, whatever — to spend weeks walking to these temples barefoot and in robes. As I stood by the bathing tank in the courtyard outside the Meenakshi shrine, I watched pilgrims dunking their heads or entire bodies into the water, a scene repeated as part of religious practice at rivers, lakes, and pools all across India.

That night, when I went to see the ceremony that would bring about the union of the husband-and-wife gods, the pilgrims were there as well, bearing witness to the holy coupling.

They believed the gods had given them life. But it was clear to me that they were breathing life into the gods.

WHAT TO READ

***Meeting God: Elements of Hindu Devotion**, by Stephen P. Huyler. A comprehensive view of Hindu rituals, processions, and other practices in India, told in stories and photographs.

***American Veda: From Emerson and the Beatles to Yoga and Meditation, How Indian Spirituality Changed the West**, by Philip Goldberg. A historical look at the rise of Indian philosophy and religion in popular culture over the past century.

***The Sensuous and the Sacred: Chola Bronzes from South India**, by Vidya Dehejia. A look at an art form with deep connections to Tamil Nadu from a professor of art at Columbia University.

***Novels and stories of R. K. Narayan**, a Tamil Nadu writer whose work was championed by prominent American and English writers. His fictional town of Malgudi is thought to be based on the Tamil Nadu city of Coimbatore.

adidas
JR東日本
明治
ブルガリア
ヨーグルト
NITTAN
JINRO
GIANTS
RYOBI
RYOBI
ONAMI
OIZUMI
フコク生命
コニカミノルタ
Canon
CASIO

WATCH THE FASTBALL AND PASS THE BENTO BOX

Where better than a ballpark to see Japan's easy mix of Western culture and its own unique personality?
— BY INGRID K. WILLIAMS

Hanami, or cherry-blossom viewing, is jokingly referred to as the most popular spectator sport in Japan. In truth, the title belongs to baseball. But "spectator" is a misnomer, because attending a baseball game in Japan involves active, enthusiastic participation.

On a Sunday afternoon in April, I was crammed into a seat in the upper deck of the Tokyo Dome to watch the biggest rivalry in Japanese baseball. The Yomiuri Giants were set to battle the visiting Hanshin Tigers, whose devoted fans made up nearly half of the crowd of about 44,000 in the jam-packed stadium.

As soon as the game began, so did the coordinated cheering. Led by cheer captains in the outfield bleachers, the batting team's fans chanted, sang, and rhythmically banged plastic bats for every pitch to every batter. Their deafening, synchronized roar dominated the dome. Each hit ignited a burst of still louder cheers and frantic towel waving.

"It's a manifestation of perfectionism," said Robert Whiting, the author of several books on Japanese culture and baseball. "If you are going to be a fan, then you have to go all the way."

Yet the fans of the team in the field maintained a respectful hush, interrupted only by an exuberant wave of applause after each out. Questionable calls were never booed. No jeers rang out when an error was made. These fans radiated only love for their teams.

Love and an endless reserve of energy. After 12 innings of play — and 4 hours, 36 minutes of sustained cheering — the score was still tied, 6–6. And that's when everyone packed up their paraphernalia and quietly shuffled out of the stadium. Game over.

Previous Baseball, an integral part of Japanese life, was introduced to Japan in 1872 and went professional in the 1920s.

Left A Waseda University baseball team in 1916.

Below In the Tokyo Dome, the seats closest to the baseball field may come with helmets and gloves.

Opposite Fans raise a flag overhead for the Yomiuri Giants.

The lack of resolution was unnerving. But in Japan, ties are not uncommon because games are called after 12 innings — win, lose, or draw. The game I attended was only the Giants' ninth of the season, but already their second tie.

Otherwise, the rules for the 12 teams in Nippon Professional Baseball, Japan's equivalent of Major League Baseball, are largely the same as those in the American version. As in the United States, there are two major leagues in Japan, with one, the Pacific League, allowing the designated hitter, and the other, the Central League, eschewing it. The regular season runs from early April to October, followed by playoffs that culminate in a championship series, called the Nippon Series, in early November.

Even visitors who aren't particularly interested in the game itself will find that attending a baseball game in Japan provides an illuminating peek into Japanese culture and an opportunity to taste some culinary curiosities. Concession stands around the stadium offer a dizzying variety of food options — many of which are completely unidentifiable to untrained foreign eyes.

One recognizable item is the ubiquitous bento box. Stacked neatly beside photographs of their contents, the boxes can contain pretty much anything — sushi, tofu, grilled eel, rice balls with egg, pickled vegetables. Fried mashed-potato balls are a pleasant substitute for French fries, but the more daring will opt for *takoyaki*, small dough balls filled with octopus. Hot dogs are also for sale, though it's much more fun to battle a bowl of slippery soba noodles with chopsticks. And if the Baskin-Robbins ice cream stand is familiar, some of its perplexingly named flavors — like the refreshing Popping Shower (it's minty) — are not.

To round out the gustatory experience, try sipping some sake or whiskey. You can bring your own, though you'll have to pour it into plastic cups at the gate.

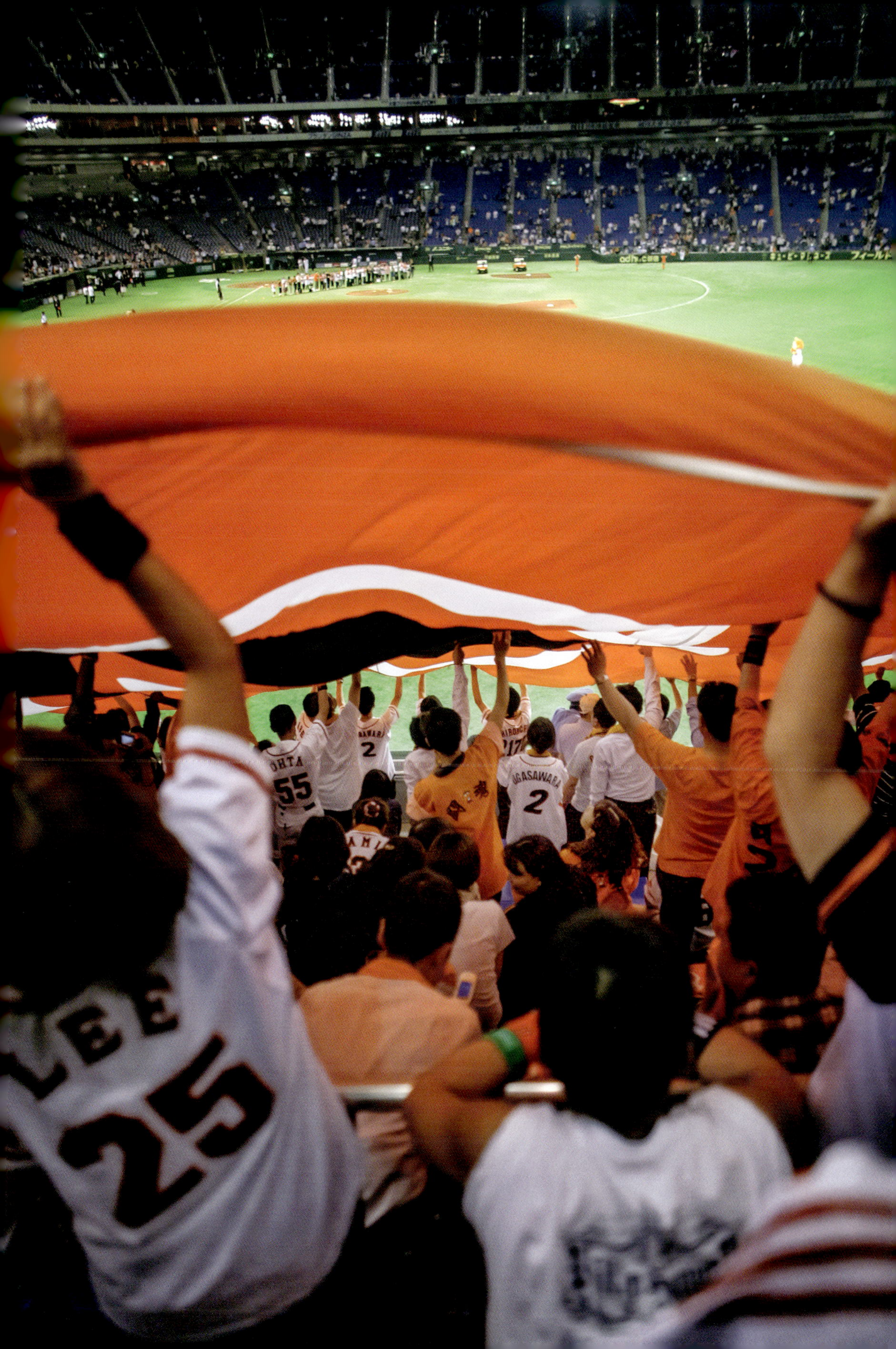
OHTA
55
OGASAWARA
2
LEE
25

Above The Giabbits, mascots of the Yomiuri Giants, cheering at a home game.

Opposite A cheerleader pumping up fans at the Tokyo Dome.

The long lines that are common at concession stands in American ballparks were blissfully absent at the game I was watching. Perhaps that is because Japan has beer girls. Running up and down the aisles with pony kegs strapped to their backs, the smiling young girls were easy to spot in their colorful uniforms and matching caps (not to mention their shorts with hemlines as short as sartorially possible).

For the benefit of beer girls and fans alike, shrill whistles warned of every incoming foul ball, after which officials rushed to the impact site to check for injuries. The seats closest to the field even came with protective helmets and gloves.

Furthering the calculated effort to accommodate all and irritate none, glassed-in smoking lounges featured televisions showing the game. And for entertainment during some of the lulls between innings, Giants cheerleaders in white gloves and orange leg warmers flipped and danced on the field.

A few days after the tie in Tokyo, I caught a Tigers home game against the Chunichi Dragons at Hanshin Koshien Stadium, the country's oldest, having opened in 1924. Situated just outside Osaka, Koshien was packed with the home team's fans, which made their seventh-inning tradition a spectacular event. After gleefully blowing up jumbo baseball-bat-shaped balloons — a seventh-inning stretch of the lungs, not legs — the crowd released the colorful balloons in unison to awesome effect.

The former Yomiuri Giants pitcher Hideki Okajima, who also played for the Boston Red Sox, described Koshien Stadium as a "party house" when I contacted him by email (with the help of a translator). He added that while playing for the rival Giants, he "almost feared visiting Koshien because of the fans there. When Tigers hitters are at the plate, fans don't stop singing, beating drums, and waving the flags."

Photographs by
Yana Paskova

And the game I attended was no different. Living up to their raucous reputation, the fans created a heady, carnival-like atmosphere.

Two innings later, when the Tigers clinched a 4–3 victory, the crowd offered a second, equally dazzling balloon display. As the players celebrated in the middle of the dark brown, all-dirt infield, fans cheered and balloons rocketed around the stands like confetti fireworks. On this night, there was plenty of joy in Mudville.

WHAT TO READ AND WATCH

You Gotta Have Wa, by Robert Whiting. An enjoyable read for Americans seeking to understand not only Japanese baseball culture, but the broader cultural differences between the two countries. Full of wonderful stories.

Slugging It Out in Japan: An American Major Leaguer in the Tokyo Outfield, by Warren Cromartie with Robert Whiting. Written by a player who left the Montreal Expos to spend six turbulent seasons with the Tokyo Giants.

Taking In a Game: A History of Baseball in Asia, by Joseph A. Reaves. Covers everything from baseball in Qing Dynasty China to the 2000 Sydney Olympics bronze-medal match between Japan and Korea.

Mr. Baseball, directed by Fred Schepisi. Tom Selleck stars in this 1992 comedy about an American baseball player trying his luck on a Japanese team.

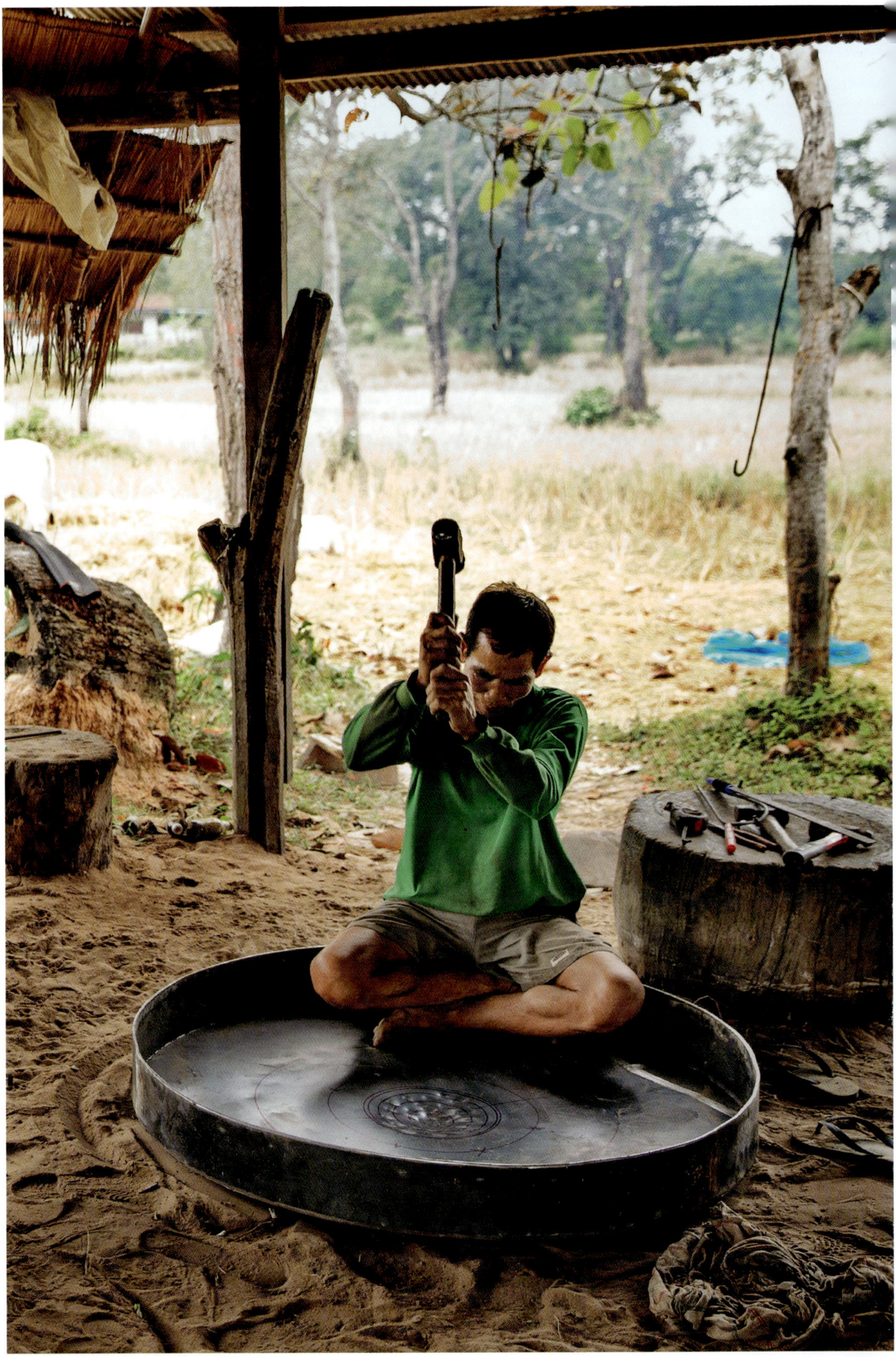

A RESOUNDING DAY ON THE GONG HIGHWAY

In a corner of Thailand near Laos, workshops shape and pound metal, keeping thousands of temples sonorously supplied. — BY JODY JAFFE AND JOHN MUNCIE

It was a noisy day at the gong factory. Between the bangers, the bongers, the grinders, and the polishers, there wasn't a square inch of silence to be found. The hardware symphony was punctuated by the putt-putt of passing motorbikes. Amid the mayhem, a gong tuner searched for the right sound.

Facing a nearly finished gong hanging from a tree limb, the tuner struck it dead center with a mallet and listened. Then he took a ball-peen hammer and whacked the upper right corner twice. He switched back to the mallet, struck the gong, and listened again. Not satisfied, he kept repeating the process, whacking different parts of the gong with the hammer.

"He's stopping the dissonance," explained Warong Boonaree, known as Yodh, about the alternating banging and bonging. "He wants to make just one sound project out."

This is the soundtrack along Thailand's "gong highway," a 21-mile stretch of road in the easternmost corner of the country. It starts 30 miles outside the area's largest city, Ubon Ratchathani (called Ubon locally), and ends in Khong Chiam, a fishing village on the cliffs above the Mekong River that overlook Laos. Boonaree, an optical shop owner by trade, a horticulturist by training, and a musician by passion, was our guide and translator on this trip. He was providing us with an essential service in this isolated region of Thailand, where there are few foreign visitors.

"Normally tourists come to Ubon and go straight to Laos," Boonaree said. "You just go to the border of Laos and you will see foreigners. But not here."

As the road trip began, Boonaree obligingly changed the car stereo CD from '80s disco to *molam*,

Previous The gong industry is centered on the village of Sai Mun. A "banger" there refining a gong's shape.

Left How to strike a gong: Who better to demonstrate than this Buddhist monk?

Opposite A formidable gong at a temple, photographed circa 1920.

traditional Lao songs accompanied by traditional Thai instruments. Boonaree plays three of these instruments, and promised a brief concert at the end of the day.

Skirting Ubon, the drive proceeded through the town of Phibun Mangsahan—past a crowded street market selling everything from athletic shoes to knobs of ginger to motor scooter tailpipes—then crossed the Mun River and on to Route 2222, a flat, two-lane road edged by scrub brush, rectangular rice paddies, swaths of adolescent rubber trees, a few modest houses, and, by our unofficial count, 18 gong stores.

Gongs are serious business here. Families have been making them for generations, and, according to the Tourist Authority of Thailand, the area supplies gongs to most of the country's more than 30,000 Buddhist temples.

"Gongs are everyday alarm clocks for the monks," Boonaree said. "They get up at 4:30 in the morning. First a little bit of meditation, then a little bit of a walk to get fed."

The gong industry is centered on the village of Sai Mun. Some 50 local family-owned operations make gongs—about 7,000 a year—as well as bells and drums. But on this morning, the gong business seemed to have fallen silent.

After passing the third closed gong store, Boonaree looked perplexed. "Might be Sport Day," he said, explaining that villages set aside one day a year for the residents' athletic activities. But then he struck up a conversation with a local woman. Her family made gongs, and he quickly arranged a tour of the gong-and-bell factory run by her niece, Pranatda Rungruang.

The Rungruang operation was about a mile north of the gong highway and about two miles from the family home. "We wouldn't make them there," Rungruang said. "It's too loud."

Her family had been making gongs and bells for a century. They employed 20 people and made about five gongs a day. They sold their gongs and bells to stores on the gong highway.

The Rungruang gong factory consisted of three open-air, dirt-floor buildings, ranging in size from about 20 by 20 feet to 40 by 60 feet. At the largest building, where the bells were cast and the gongs were cut and welded, Rungruang grabbed a hammer and joined two others smashing clay chunks, the first step in making bell molds.

Nearby, one of the gong makers, a man in camo pants and plastic sandals, knelt on a stack of sheet metal, snipping out a three-foot circle with something that looked like a giant tobacco cutter. Once the edges are smooth, the circle goes to the welder to attach the sides. Then a design is drawn on the back in blue marker to show the bangers where to pound out the center hump and surrounding eight "nipples" characteristic of Thai gongs.

The banging building was a couple of hundred yards away down a dirt lane. There a barefoot banger pressed the face of a gong into sandy soil and hammered out the nipples and center hump. Next to him, his young daughter did an imitation of her father, pounding away at an imaginary gong.

Once a gong was hammered, it would be taken to the paint shop, another hundred yards away, for a shiny coat of black enamel.

Bells were being made at the factory, too. The bell-making operation looked like something from the Bronze Age, with workers dipping long-handled ladles into vats of curry-colored wax bubbling atop open-air fires. Nearby, crucibles of molten metal with carrying arms jutting out pushed up against piles of rasps, scraps of sheet metal, stacks of buckets, and a small tower of tires. This was a place where you wanted to step carefully.

Everything was done by hand, from smashing the clay to carving intricate decorations. To make their ornate four-foot bells, we were told, the Rungruang family used the same "lost wax" technique that has been used by metallurgists for 5,000 years. They made molds from the clay, covered them with wax, then more clay, then a gridwork of metal rods for reinforcement. Molten metal was poured between the layers, and the wax melted away, leaving the metal to set into a bell shape. The whole process took 35 days.

Back on the gong highway, it seemed that Sport Day might have ended because, east of Sai Mun, the gong stores were open. They featured gongs of all sizes, from three inches—souvenir size—to six feet in diameter. Gongs can be made up to 20 feet wide, one gong shop owner told Boonaree, but anything larger than three feet is for decoration, not sound. Prices ranged from about $25 for the souvenir-size gong to about $1,800 for a temple gong with an ornate rosewood stand.

Some stores on the gong highway made the gongs on site. At one, gongs were arranged in tidy rows, big ones in the back, little ones on shelves in the front.

Everything was in the traditional black and bronze colors except for a row of two-foot-tall jaunty yellow bells with red trim. "A gift from your country and others," Boonaree said. They were recycled military shell casings.

The gong highway ends at the riverside village of Khong Chiam, the easternmost point of Isan. Made up of 19 northeast provinces, Isan covers one third of Thailand yet is off the well-traveled Chiang Mai–Bangkok–Phuket path. "It's pretty rare to meet travelers who aren't Thai," said Tim Bewer, of Isan Explorer, a "slow tour" company with the motto "Showing You the Other Thailand."

"Mostly the people who come here are people who have already been to Thailand before and are looking for something different and/or some place not corrupted by tourism, and Isan is both," he said.

Twelve miles north of Khong Chiam is Pha Taem National Park, known for its massive mushroom-

Above The Mekong from a restaurant in Khong Chiam, where the gong highway ends.

Opposite Tuning a gong. Dozens of small family-owned workshops make up the gong highway.

shaped boulders, panoramic views of the Mekong, open canopy woodlands, and prehistoric rock paintings. A two-mile loop trail cuts along the cliff face with scores of rust-colored paintings — handprints, elephants, catfish, rice farming — estimated to be 3,000 years old.

Leaving the past behind, Boonaree took us to Araya, his favorite floating restaurant in Khong Chiam. Isan cuisine mixes Lao, Vietnamese, and central Thai elements to produce what he considers Thailand's finest food, and it was hard to disagree after feasting on fried catfish with mint, fish *larb*, and green papaya salad. Isan is known for its fiery spices, and the meal was bracingly hot, but it turned out that Boonaree had asked the kitchen to keep it mild. "This," he said, motioning to our plates, "is for kids."

The Isan menu also incorporates beetles, silkworms, and other insects. Before we sat down to lunch, a vendor had sold a variety of leaf-wrapped packages to a family at the table next to us. Inside were clumps of gray and black. "Ants," Boonaree said. "Workers, queens, and eggs."

A drive back to Ubon through the Isan countryside offered a series of vivid scenes of Thailand. Wooden fishing boats trailed nets in Lake Sirindhorn; sliced cassava root dried on tarps and flat rocks; bags of rice and rice farmers rode on the beds of tractors that look like alien lawn mowers. A woman walked down the road with an eight-foot pole over her shoulder, a basket attached at one end. She harvested tree-dwelling ants.

"You want to see?" Boonaree asked, and pulled off the road. Pointing to a clump of leaves that seemed to have been glued together at the edges, he banged it with a stick, and a frenzy of red ants charged out. An Isan meal yet to be cooked.

Ubon itself is a city of more than 100,000, with two universities, a gracious downtown park anchored by

Photographs by
Adam Ferguson

a massive and massively ornate "candle" sculpture that commemorates the Thai king's birthday and, since this is Thailand, an impressive selection of gong-laden temples, including Thung Si Muang, famous for its wooden library on stilts that sits in the middle of a lily pond to prevent termite invasions.

The day ended with a concert, as Boonaree had promised. He played the *khaen*, a bamboo wind instrument with multiple pipes like a mini organ. The sound was melodic, unexpected, and timeless: a lyrical coda to a day spent on the gong highway.

WHAT TO READ AND WATCH

Gongs Get Going at Top Dealer, an Associated Press video featuring an American entrepreneur of gong sales. Glimpses of shining golden-colored gongs and sounds of their ringing tones.

Thailand's Traditional Molam Music Finds New Groove, a *Wall Street Journal* video. This revival of traditional Thai music, mixed in with Western sounds, includes various traditional instruments, although no gongs.

What's What in a Wat: Thai Buddhist Temples, Their Purpose and Design, by Carol Stratton. A guidebook to the objects, shapes, patterns, and symbolic elements in Thai temples.

A Man in Saffron Robes: A Rainy Season as a Buddhist Monk at a Hilltop Temple in Northern Thailand, by Maitree Limpichart, translated by Stephen Landau. A well-known Thai author's experiences of Buddhism.

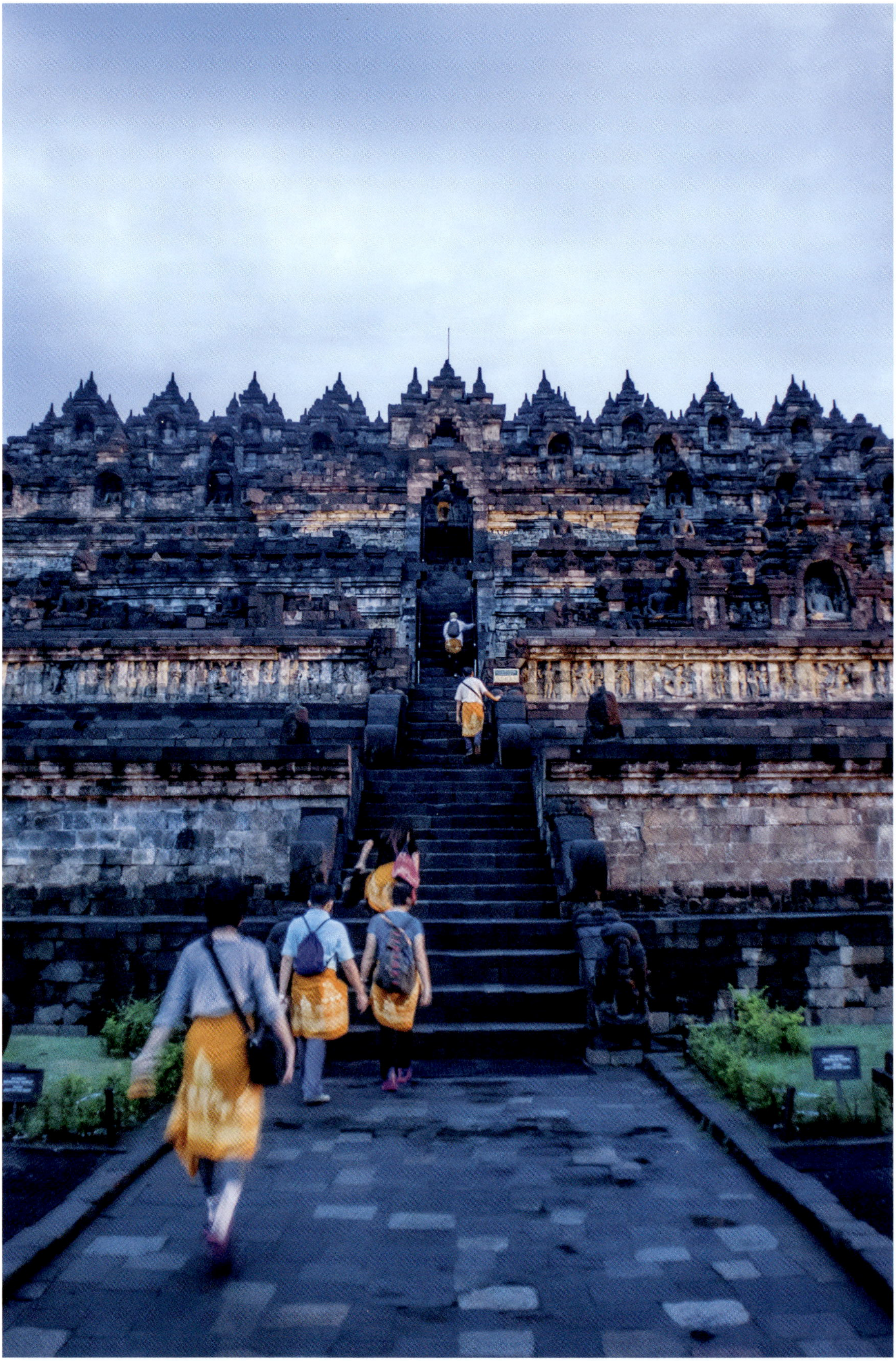

INDONESIA'S CAPITAL OF ART

Yogyakarta has it all: shadow puppetry, gamelan orchestras, Javanese dance, rappers, DJs, Basel-worthy art, and even a sultan. — BY DONALD FRAZIER

After the tropical thunder rolls across south Java comes the rain, and each drop has a character. Some sweep across the bamboo roof in high-pitched volleys, and some plop into the puddles one by one, luminous, like silver. Others hit the dried banana leaves with a solid, resonant thunk.

In early Java, they heard music in these sounds and rhythms. They refined it over the centuries into a complex, ethereal form of auditory theater that needs as many as 10 instruments at once, so expansive in tones and harmonies that it cannot fit into any Western style of notation. It is called gamelan, and you hear it all over this ancient capital, from the airport public address system to the marbled palace of the local sultan.

All of Java's courtly arts, including shadow puppetry and classical dance, first flourished in Yogyakarta. They made this small city the heartland of traditional Javanese culture, protected during colonization, wartime, occupation, revolution, and years of authoritarian rule.

Little known in the West but familiar throughout Southeast Asia, the city known simply as Yogja (pronounce the "Y" as "J") has been a royal center of art and power since the eighth century, even after Dutch colonials made Jakarta the capital. With several major universities, it has always attracted an artsy, intellectual crowd. As an ancient city — still ruled by a sultan — it has long nurtured the presentations that, for Javanese, give symbolic form to everything from official ritual to the routines of daily life.

Performance throbs from this city's heart. On the expansive grounds of the Kraton, the Sultan's palace at the center of the old city, dance troupes and

Previous The ninth-century complex at Borobudur, near Yogyakarta, is the world's largest Buddhist temple.

Left Javanese dance captured in 1895 by Kassian Cephas, a court photographer of the Yogyakarta Sultanate.

Opposite Gamelan musicians at the Yogyakarta Sultan Palace.

gamelan ensembles perform on a grand covered pavilion. To signal religions at peace, it is lavishly decorated with symbols of the three traditions that inform life here: Hinduism, Buddhism, and, the largest, Islam. In its shadow, children play with stick puppets representing Sita and Rama, iconic lovers of Hindu myth, as the call to prayer issues from loudspeakers.

The traditional arts endure and are fascinating to see as they have long been performed, but a new generation of artists has sprung from these rich but formalized traditions. All over the city, choreographers, musicians, filmmakers, puppeteers — even DJs and rappers — burst the boundaries of these styles and their conventions. Galleries thrive, too, with painters, sculptors, and cartoonists whose works have made contemporary art from Indonesia a sensation at events like Art Basel in Hong Kong.

The good news: There's always something happening on the cutting edge of culture. An art gallery will host a visiting performance artist; a new dance troupe will be reenacting an ancient myth as interpreted, perhaps, at the Edinburgh Fringe. Only a few events require tickets, and reservations are nearly unheard of. You just show up.

Even private homes readily welcome strangers to gamelan concerts that are less like performances and more like happenings. Restaurants, coffee houses, and a few hotels offer themselves as art centers, ready to host the next filmmaker or an impromptu act by an electronica DJ working with hundreds of gamelan tracks. Rappers set up on the plaza across from the Kraton, sometimes calling attention to social and political issues like the plight of marginalized peoples of the East Indies. Festivals pop up like jungle flowers that bloom and fade overnight.

The bad news — or perhaps it's an exciting opportunity — is that little of this is announced or scheduled in a way that fits into a world of prearranged vacations or advance-purchase airfares. Web-based information is sketchy. You could always call, but don't count on anyone answering. Official sources like the city's tourism group and most hotels know mainly about traditional attractions like the museums and temples. Word of mouth, through new acquaintances and friends, is how you come to see the city's hidden cultural life.

So you show up at the right places, find the right people (this town has coffee and pastry shops like Boston has Irish bars), and leave plenty of messages. You spot the few other travelers at recitals and galleries and become comrades at a glance, comparing hand-scrawled notes as travelers did a hundred years ago. You get invitations to gamelan evenings, or hear of a gallery opening as if it were a rave, show up, and meet an artist who last week was lionized in Paris.

I once got a cryptic text message telling me to be at a crossroads outside of town. That was the only hint something special might be going on up a dusty farm road, past pens of chickens, goats, and a few munching water buffalo. But at its end, a large postindustrial studio was throbbing with activity. Dancers, stagehands, musicians carrying heavy brass gongs, computer technicians with clipboards, all in a swirl; and at its center, the intent, black-clad choreographer Martinus Miroto.

Miroto, who died in 2021, well after my visit, was born and raised in Yogyakarta, where dance class is required in high school. He toured the world and won praise from acclaimed choreographers like Pina Bausch. Rather than remaining in Berlin or Los Angeles where he studied, he started the Miroto Dance Company, building an arts campus around his high-roofed studio clad in aged coconut trunks.

For traditional dance, one of Java's most vivid full-scale productions is just a few miles north of town. The Ramayana Ballet, a spectacular staging of the South Asian epic *The Ramayana*, takes place every night of the year — with firelight, extravagant costumes, a full gamelan orchestra, and grandeur — in the shadow of the nearby ninth-century Prambanan, the largest Hindu temple in Indonesia. (The region's other World Heritage Site, the ninth-century monument at Borobudur, is the largest Buddhist temple in the world and an easy day trip.)

Rather than waiting for that random text message about a lower-profile event, a good place to start any search may be the Padepokan Seni Bagong Kussudiardja, a clutch of stages, verandas, studios, and classrooms on a red dirt jungle lane. Founded by a leading local painter and choreographer as a retreat for artistic meditation and experiment, it has become Yogja's all-purpose center for rehearsals, jam sessions, and impromptu performances. Almost all of this is open to visitors, but little of it is scheduled.

For the more traditional arts, drop by the Yogyakarta Cultural Office, the Dinas Kebudayaan, in the university district. The staff is a fount of advice and news on all of the classical forms. The

Above Kampung Code, an award-winning architecturally designed village on a former dump in Yogyakarta.

Opposite Prambanan, a ninth-century Hindu temple, is the place to see the Ramayana Ballet.

office has the timetable of performances at the palace, and information may be available about informal gamelan gatherings throughout the city.

This is also a place to learn about the different styles of *wayang*, the distinctive Javanese puppetry. Populated by a world of demons, monsters, princes, and clowns, wayang is as alive today in Jogja as it has ever been. Be warned that the wayang on the Sosona Hinggil pavilion, to the south of the Kraton, is an all-night affair with a cast of hundreds of leather puppets—so if you go, take along a pillow.

One puppet act in Yogja, however, is far from traditional. The Papermoon Puppet Theater has become a staple of the global arts festival circuit, with enigmatic modernist puppets that tell stories from myth to the birth of modern Indonesia. In one production, a simple tale of long-lost love plays out against a backdrop of the mass killings that took up to a million lives in 1965 and 1966—such a traumatic subject that it is seldom discussed, even in textbooks. Words are few for these puppets with moon-shaped faces who, like mimes, express everything in evocative, poignant gestures.

Between tours scattered throughout the year, you can visit the puppets, and the people who use and make them, at their studio and performance space near the Chinese cemetery south of the city center.

The theatrical spirit runs so strong in Yogyakarta that it has energized the figurative arts as well. Local painters like Agung Kurniawan, the duo known as Indieguerillas, and the puppet maker and cartoonist Eko Nugroho offer an emphatic, whimsical, yet brutal approach that can deliver scabrous commentary on politics and pop culture. As contemporary art of Southeast Asia attracts more attention all over the world, these locals have gained global reputations.

With the Indonesian national dance institute based here, there are events almost every weekend, ranging from formal productions to pop-up events.

Photographs by
Justin Mott

Western-style celebrity doesn't seem to be anyone's goal. That was clear at an event at the Dusun Jogya Village Inn, a homegrown resort that feels as if it's deep in the jungle though it's just a few minutes out of the city. Billed as an opening for 11 female artists, it had a documentary film, a hip-hop troupe with two rappers, a lightweight gamelan ensemble, an immersive performance-art work, and a dance performance with stark modern choreography, but in traditional Javanese costume.

"In Indonesia we have a concept for this, an event where anyone joins in, and everyone here is at home," Amron-Paul Yuwono, a theater director and actor, said. "We call it the village, the *kampung*, but it really means the community."

WHAT TO READ AND WATCH

Indonesia, Etc.: Exploring the Improbable Nation, by Elizabeth Pisani. Part travelogue, part history, a wide-ranging exploration of a complicated country.

Music in Central Java: Experiencing Music, Expressing Culture, by Benjamin Brinner. Gamelan music and its origins in depth.

Sound Tracker - Gamelan (Indonesia). An eight-minute YouTube video, with four million views, that presents the sights and sounds of gamelan.

The Wayang Puppet Theatre. A brief video from Unesco, explaining this unusual art form.

A Brief History of Indonesia: Sultans, Spices, and Tsunamis: The Incredible Story of Southeast Asia's Largest Nation, by Tim Hannigan. Historical background written in an approachable style.

BIOGRAPHIES

WRITER BIOGRAPHIES

Mark Adams (pages 28–35) is the author of *Tip of the Iceberg*, *Turn Right at Machu Picchu*, *Meet Me in Atlantis*, and *Mr. America*. His articles have appeared in *The New York Times*, *Men's Journal*, and *Rolling Stone*.

Laurie Lico Albanese (pages 182–187) wrote *Stolen Beauty*, a novel about the creation of Gustav Klimt's iconic portrait of Adele Bloch-Bauer, which was stolen by the Nazis. She is the author of *Hester* and *Lynelle by the Sea*.

Liz Alderman (pages 238–243) is the Paris-based chief European business correspondent for *The New York Times*. She likes to write about extraordinary places that inspire her in the countries she covers.

Gustave Axelson (pages 118–125) has contributed several articles to the Travel section of *The New York Times*. He is the editorial director at the Cornell Lab of Ornithology and the editor of *Living Bird* magazine.

Adam Begley (pages 268–273, 428–435) is the author of *Updike*, *The Great Nadar, The Man Behind the Camera*, and *Houdini: The Elusive American*. He lives in Cambridgeshire, England.

Michael Benanav (pages 544–549) is a writer and photographer whose work has appeared in *The New York Times*, *Geographical*, and other publications. He is the author of *Men of Salt*, *The Luck of the Jews*, and *Himalaya Bound*. He is also the founder of the nonprofit Traditional Cultures Project.

Justin Bergman (pages 630–635) reported on China and Southeast Asia for seven years as the Shanghai correspondent for *Monocle* and is a contributor to *The New York Times* and other publications. He is now an editor at *The Conversation*, a nonprofit media outlet based in Melbourne.

Richard Bernstein (pages 482–487) is a former reporter, foreign correspondent, and culture critic for *Time* and *The New York Times*. He is the author of *China 1945: Mao's Revolution* and *America's Fateful Choice*.

Célestine Bohlen (pages 280–285) is a former correspondent for *The New York Times* who was based in Moscow, Budapest, and Rome. She now teaches journalism at Sciences Po, the Paris Institute of Political Studies.

Thad Carhart (pages 274–279), an American writer living in Paris, is the author of *Finding Fontainebleau*, *The Piano Shop on the Left Bank*, and *Across the Endless River*, a historical novel about Jean-Baptiste Charbonneau, the son of Sacagawea.

Doreen Carvajal (pages 164–169), a former staff writer for *The New York Times*, is the author of a memoir, *The Forgetting River: A Modern Tale of Survival, Identity, and the Inquisition*.

Karen J. Coates (pages 584–589) is the author of *Cambodia Now: Life in the Wake of War* and co-producer of the documentary film *Eternal Harvest*, based on her book *Eternal Harvest: The Legacy of American Bombs in Laos*.

Ondine Cohane (pages 470–475), who is based in Italy, writes frequently for the *New York Times* Travel section, is a contributing editor at *Condé Nast Traveler*, and is co-author of *Always Italy*, published by *National Geographic*.

Colleen Creamer (pages 286–293), a magazine writer and reporter, has had articles published in *The New York Times*, *Salon*, and other publications.

Sloane Crosley (pages 404–409) is the author of three books of essays; the novel *The Clasp*, set in the United States and France; and the memoir *Grief Is for People*.

Gregory Dicum (pages 74–79) has written for *The New York Times*, *The Economist*, *Harper's*, and numerous other publications. He is the author of *Window Seat: Reading the Landscape from the Air* and *The Coffee Book*.

Rachel Donadio (pages 488–495) is a Paris-based writer and journalist, a contributing writer for *The Atlantic* and a former *New York Times* foreign correspondent and Rome bureau chief.

John L. Dorman (pages 20–27), a senior politics reporter at *Business Insider*, has been a contributor to the Travel section of *The New York Times*, where he formerly was a senior news assistant.

Rachel B. Doyle (pages 532–537), a writer and editor based in Brooklyn, has reported on culture from more than 20 countries. Her work has appeared in *The New York Times*, *National Geographic Traveler*, *The Guardian*, and other publications.

Jeremy Egner (pages 338–345) is the *New York Times* television editor, overseeing coverage of the medium and the people who make it. He joined *The Times* in 2008.

Sami Emory (pages 456–461) is a freelance writer who lives in Berlin.

Andrew Ferren (pages 36–41, 188–193, 294–299, 322–329, 410–415, 462–469), a freelance writer based in Spain, writes frequently about cultural travel for *The New York Times*. His work has also appeared in *The Wall Street Journal*, *Travel + Leisure*, *Architectural Digest*, *El País*, and other publications.

Donald Frazier (pages 666–671) has written about East Asia for *The New York Times*, *The Washington Post*, a number of glossy Hong Kong–based magazines, and *Forbes Asia*.

Dwight Garner (pages 436–443) is a book critic for *The New York Times*.

BIOGRAPHIES

Anand Giridharadas (pages 104–109), a journalist and political commentator, is the author of *Winners Take All: The Elite Charade of Changing the World*, *The True American: Murder and Mercy in Texas*, and *India Calling: An Intimate Portrait of a Nation's Remaking*.

Elaine Glusac (pages 50–55, 218–223) writes frequently for *The New York Times* and has also written for *Afar*, *Condé Nast Traveler*, *Departures*, and *National Geographic Traveler*. She is the coauthor of *Top 10 Chicago* and has contributed to Fodor's, Knopf, and *National Geographic* guidebooks.

Eli Gottlieb (pages 152–157) is the author of several novels, including *Best Boy*. He is a winner of the Rome Prize and the McKitterick Prize from the British Society of Authors.

Michelle Green (pages 556–563, 610–617) is the author of *The Dream at the End of the World: Paul Bowles and the Literary Renegades in Tangier*. Her work has appeared in *The Wall Street Journal*, *The Washington Post*, *The New York Review of Books*, and other publications.

Nellie Hermann (pages 422–427) is the author of the novels *The Season of Migration* and *The Cure for Grief*.

Laban Carrick Hill (pages 526–531), author of several books and co-founder of the Writers Project of Ghana, was based in Vermont. He died in 2021.

Stephen Hiltner (pages 360–365) is an editor on the *New York Times* Travel desk and a contributor to the weekly "World Through a Lens" column.

Jody Jaffe (pages 660–665) is the author of the Nattie Gold newspaper/horse show mystery series. As a feature writer for *The Charlotte Observer*, she was on the team that won a Pulitzer Prize for its coverage of the televangelist Jim Bakker.

Ian Johnson (pages 256–261) is a Pulitzer Prize–winning writer focusing on society, religion, and history. He writes frequently for *The New York Times* and is the author of *The Souls of China*, *A Mosque in Munich*, and other books.

Martha S. Jones (pages 384–389), the Society of Black Alumni Presidential Professor and professor of history at the Johns Hopkins University, is the author of *Vanguard: How Black Women Broke Barriers, Won the Vote, and Insisted on Equality for All*.

Russ Juskalian (pages 346–351), a writer and photographer based in Munich, concentrates on science, culture, and adventure. His work has appeared in *The New York Times*, *Smithsonian Magazine*, *Discover*, and other publications.

David Laskin (pages 300–307, 416–421, 476–481, 538–543) is the author of the novel *What Sammy Knew* as well as nonfiction titles including *The Family: A Journey into the Heart of the 20th Century*, *The Long Way Home*, and *The Children's Blizzard*.

Alexander Lobrano (pages 352–359) is the author of *Hungry for Paris* and *My Place at the Table: A Recipe for a Delicious Life in Paris*. He has written about food and travel for *The New York Times*, *The Wall Street Journal*, *The Guardian*, and many other publications.

Sam Lubell's (pages 132–137) books about architecture include *Never Built New York* and *Never Built Los Angeles*, *London 2000+* and *Paris 2000+*, and East and West versions of *Mid-Century Modern Architecture Travel Guide*.

Suzanne MacNeille (pages 88–95) is a longtime travel editor and writer for *The New York Times*.

Ann Mah (pages 314–321, 396–403), is the author of *Jacqueline in Paris: A Novel* and *The Lost Vintage*. She lives in Paris.

Elisa Mala (pages 444–449) has reported from 27 countries for *The New York Times*, *The Wall Street Journal*, *The Associated Press*, and other news outlets, covering subjects ranging from terrorism to fashion.

David McAninch (pages 390–395) is the author of *Duck Season: Eating, Drinking and Other Misadventures in Gascony, France's Last Best Place*.

Freda Moon (pages 14–19), a San Francisco–based journalist, is a frequent contributor to *The New York Times*. Her work has also appeared in periodicals including *Sunset*, *National Geographic Traveler*, and *Afar* and in books including *Best American Travel Writing*.

John Motyka (pages 450–455), a freelance writer based in New Jersey, has been a longtime librarian at *The New York Times*.

John Muncie (pages 660–665) is a former editor and writer for newspapers including *The San Diego Union-Tribune*, *The Los Angeles Times*, and *The Baltimore Sun*. He and Jody Jaffe have coauthored two novels.

Tim Neville (pages 126–131), a correspondent for *Outside* magazine, has written for *The New York Times* since 2004, often about adventure travel and outdoor sports. His work has appeared in the anthologies *The Best American Travel Writing*, *The Best American Sports Writing*, and *Best Food Writing*.

John O'Connor (pages 96–101), from Kalamazoo, Michigan, has had work published in *The New York Times*, *The Oxford American*, *Saveur*, *The Financial Times*, *The Boston Globe*, and the anthologies *The Best American Food Writing 2018* and *The Best Creative Nonfiction Vol. 1*.

Danielle Pergament (pages 176–181) frequently writes travel articles for *The New York Times*. Her work has also appeared in *GQ*, *Condé Nast Traveler*, *National Geographic Traveler*, *Travel + Leisure*, and *New York* magazine.

BIOGRAPHIES

Jane Perlez (pages 596–603), a longtime foreign correspondent for *The New York Times*, is a former chief of its Beijing bureau. She was a lead member of the group of reporters who won the Pulitzer Prize for international reporting in 2009.

Tony Perrottet (pages 42–49, 378–383, 578–583, 642–647) has written for *The New York Times*, *Smithsonian Magazine*, *WSJ Magazine*, and other publications. He is the author of several books, including *¡Cuba Libre! Che, Fidel and the Improbable Revolution That Changed World History*, and has spoken on the History Channel on topics from the Crusades to disco.

Lucas Peterson (pages 502–507) is a former columnist and video producer for *The Los Angeles Times*. He wrote the *New York Times* Frugal Traveler column for nearly three years and hosted and produced more than 100 episodes of the food series "Dining on a Dime" for *Eater*.

Francine Prose (pages 138–143) is the author of more than 20 works of fiction and nonfiction, among them the novel *Blue Angel*, a National Book Award nominee, and the guide *Reading Like a Writer*, a *New York Times* bestseller. Her most recent novel is *The Vixen*.

Larry Rohter (pages 144–149) was the *New York Times* bureau chief in Rio de Janeiro from 1998 to 2008. He is the author of three books about Brazil, including a biography of the explorer, scientist, and statesman Cândido Rondon.

Justin Sablich (pages 56–61, 308–313), who is based in London, is a writer and editor with a focus on travel. He has been a digital editor and strategist at *The New York Times* covering travel, among other topics.

Christopher F. Schuetze (pages 230–237) is a staff reporter at the *New York Times* Berlin bureau, where he covers news, politics, and society. Previously he was based in the Netherlands, where he covered everything from war crimes tribunals to tulip sales.

Lisa Schwarzbaum (pages 194–199, 496–501), a former longtime film critic at *Entertainment Weekly*, is now a freelance journalist.

Kim Severson (pages 62–67, 604–609) covers food culture for *The New York Times*. She is the author of *Spoon Fed: How Eight Cooks Saved My Life* and *The New Alaska Cookbook* and coauthor with Julia Moskin of *Cook Fight: 2 Cooks, 12 Challenges, 125 Recipes, an Epic Battle for Kitchen Dominance*.

Christopher Shaw (pages 250–255) lives in Vermont and the Adirondacks, canoeing and writing about place and consciousness. His most recent books are *The Power Line: A Novel* and *The Crazy Wisdom: Memoir of a Friendship*.

Seth Sherwood (pages 262–267, 518–525) is a travel writer based in Paris. He writes frequently for *The New York Times* about Europe, North Africa, and the Middle East.

Russell Shorto (pages 158–163) is senior scholar at the New Netherland Institute and a contributing writer at *The New York Times Magazine*. He is the author of *Amsterdam*, *The Island at the Center of the World*, *Revolution Song*, and several other books.

Henry Shukman (pages 80–87, 366–371, 372–377) is a prize-winning poet and novelist originally from Britain. He is also a Zen master who has taught meditation at Google and the Harvard Business School.

Nina Siegal (pages 230–237, 244–249), who is based in Amsterdam, specializes in writing about Dutch old masters, as well as modern and contemporary art and culture. Her second novel, *The Anatomy Lesson*, told the story of Rembrandt's first group portrait masterpiece.

Ron Stodghill (pages 110–117), a professor of journalism at the University of Missouri, has worked at *The New York Times*, *Time*, *Business Week*, and *Savoy*, where he was editor-in-chief. He is the author of *Where Everybody Looks Like Me* and *Redbone: Money, Malice and Murder in Atlanta*.

Oliver Strand (pages 68–73) lives in New York and writes about food, travel, design, and coffee. His work has appeared in *The New York Times*, *Vogue*, *Bon Appétit*, and *Gourmet*.

Cheryl Lu-Lien Tan (pages 636–641) is the author of the novel *Sarong Party Girls* and the memoir *A Tiger in the Kitchen*, and the editor of the fiction anthology *Singapore Noir*.

Ratha Tep (pages 212–217), based in Dublin, is a frequent contributor to *The New York Times*. Her work has also appeared in *The Wall Street Journal*, *Food & Wine*, *Travel + Leisure*, and several other publications.

Amy M. Thomas (pages 200–205), a Brooklyn-based food and travel writer, is the author three books and, in addition to writing about Belgian chocolate, has covered Connecticut's coast, Paris's Left Bank, and Grenada's spices for *The New York Times*.

Shivani Vora (pages 206–211, 572–577), a travel and lifestyle writer, is a regular contributor to *The New York Times* and has also written for publications including *The Wall Street Journal*, *National Geographic Traveler*, *Condé Nast Traveler*, and *Departures*.

Brad Wetzler (pages 550–555), a former senior editor at *Outside* magazine, has written for *The New York Times Magazine*, *GQ*, *Wired*, *Travel + Leisure*, and other publications. He is the author of a memoir, *Into the Soul of the World: My Journey to Healing*.

Charly Wilder (pages 508–515), who is based in Berlin and Mexico City, writes frequently about culture and travel for *The New York Times*.

BIOGRAPHIES

Sarah Wildman (pages 330–337), a staff editor and writer for the *New York Times* Opinion section, is the author of *Paper Love: Searching for the Girl My Grandfather Left Behind*.

Gisela Williams (pages 482–487) writes about culture, art, and design for *T: The New York Times Style Magazine*, *Elle Decor*, and *Departures* and contributes on various topics to *Surface* and *The Financial Times*.

Ingrid K. Williams (pages 624–629, 654–659) writes about travel, food, art, fashion, and culture for *The New York Times* and other publications. A New Jersey native, she currently splits her time between Stockholm and a small beach town in northwestern Italy.

Jason Wilson (pages 170–175, 224–229) is the author of *The Cider Revival: Dispatches from the Orchard*, *Boozehound*, and *Godforsaken Grapes*. He has been the series editor for *Best American Travel Writing* since 2000 and has written for *The Washington Post*, *The New York Times*, *The New Yorker*, and other publications.

Edward Wong (pages 618–623, 648–653), a diplomatic and international correspondent for *The New York Times*, reported from Iraq and China for 13 of his more than 22 years at *The Times* and was chief of the Beijing bureau. He received a Livingston Award for his Iraq War coverage and was on a team of Pulitzer Prize finalists.

Jada Yuan (pages 590–595) is a writer for the Style section of *The Washington Post*, with a focus on national politics. She spent 2018 circumnavigating the globe as the 52 Places Traveler for *The New York Times* and before that was a longtime culture writer for *New York* magazine.

Femke van Zeijl (pages 564–569) is a Dutch journalist and writer based in Lagos, Nigeria. Her fourth book, published in Dutch, is *Do-It-Yourself Society: About Life in Lagos*.

PHOTOGRAPHER BIOGRAPHIES

Jenn Ackerman (pages 96–101), a Minneapolis-based photographer, specializes in reportage, travel, and portraiture. Her work has appeared in publications including *National Geographic*, *Vanity Fair*, *People*, *Rolling Stone*, *The New York Times*, *The Wall Street Journal*, and *Travel + Leisure*. ackermangruber.com

Ed Alcock (pages 250–255, 410–415), a British photographer living in Paris, is a longtime contributor to *The New York Times*. His work has been exhibited in museums and festivals internationally, and his portraiture appears regularly in *Télérama*, *Libération*, *M Le Magazine du Monde*, *The Guardian*, and *El País Semanal*. He is a member of Agence MYOP. edalcock.com

Lalo de Almeida (pages 144–149) is a longtime photographer for the newspaper *Folha de São Paulo* and a contributor to *The New York Times*. His documentary projects have covered traditional populations in Brazil, and his photo essay *Pantanal Ablaze* won first place in the Environment category at the World Press Photo competition of 2021. lalodealmeida.com.br

Malú Alvarez (pages 518–525), born in Mexico City, lives and works in Austin, Texas. Her work has appeared in *The New York Times*, *The New Yorker*, and *Travel + Leisure* and has been featured in gallery exhibitions. malualvarez.com

Olivier Asselin (pages 526–531) grew up in Quebec and has worked for media and development organizations in over 25 countries in Africa, Asia, and Latin America. He is director of the documentary *The Permaculture Orchard: Beyond Organic* and the creator of possiblemedia.org, which promotes sustainability initiatives. olivierasselin.com

Michael Benanav (pages 544–549), michaelbenanav.com. See writer biographies.

Robert Caplin (pages 104–109) specializes in documentary, travel, celebrities, and portraiture. He has been a regular contributor to *The New York Times* and *The Los Angeles Times*, and his work has been published in *National Geographic*, *Sports Illustrated*, *Time*, and *Newsweek*. robertcaplin.com

Rina Castelnuovo (pages 538–543, 550–555) is an Israeli photojournalist and a longtime photographer for *The New York Times* Jerusalem bureau. She has been covering wars and peace, Israelis and Palestinians, for over three decades, and her work has been featured in international exhibitions. She is the director of the documentary film *Muhi: Generally Temporary*.

Matías Costa (pages 176–181) is a photographer and journalist interested in memory and identity issues. He has received professional awards, including two World Press Photo awards, and has published the books *Zonians*, *Photobolsillo*, and *The Family Project*. He is represented by Panos Pictures. matiascosta.com

Alex Crétey Systermans (pages 352–359), based in London and Paris, photographs for media and commercial clients. His work has appeared in *The New York Times*, *The Financial Times*, *Monocle*, *Afar*, *Travel + Leisure*, *National Geographic*, *The Fader*, and other publications. systermans.com

Adam Dean (pages 596–603), a photo editor on the International desk of *The New York Times*, was formerly a freelance photographer based in Bangkok. In 2018 he won a George Polk Award for Photography for his work on the Rohingya crisis with Tomas Munita. adamdean.net

Denis Doyle (pages 450–455), based in Madrid, focuses his photography primarily on corporate events, portraiture, sports, and breaking news. denisdoylephotos.com

Rodolphe Escher (pages 206–211), a France-based photojournalist, is represented by Divergences Images.

BIOGRAPHIES

James Estrin (pages 648–653) is a *New York Times* staff photographer and writer and a founder of *Lens*, the *Times* photography blog. He was part of a team that won a Pulitzer Prize for a series of articles entitled "How Race Is Lived in America." jamesestrin.photoshelter.com

Adam Ferguson (pages 660–665) is an Australian freelance photographer based in New York. His commissioned work has appeared in *New York*, *Time*, *Vanity Fair*, *The New York Times*, *The New Yorker*, *Wired*, *National Geographic*, and other publications. adamfergusonstudio.com

Jock Fistick (pages 200–205) is based in Florida. His photographs have appeared in *The New York Times*, *USA Today*, *The Times of London*, *The Guardian*, *Die Zeit*, and other publications. His many commercial clients have included Procter & Gamble, Hewlett-Packard, and the European Commission. archive.fistick.com

Erika Gerdemark (pages 462–469) is based in Stockholm but works internationally, primarily with portraits, travel, and weddings. Her clients have included Microsoft, *Svenska Dagbladet*, *The New York Times*, Bloomberg, the Swedish Royal Family, and others. gerdemark.com

Yannick Grandmont (pages 68–73) is a Montreal-based street photographer and cinematographer with special interest in the offbeat art scene, stop-motion animation, and cycling adventures.

Djamila Grossman (pages 256–261) is based in Berlin and Zurich. She shoots editorial and commercial work internationally. Her many clients have included *Stern*, *Der Spiegel*, *The International New York Times*, and *Condé Nast Traveler*. djamilagrossman.com

Brett Gundlock (pages 138–143), based in Toronto and Mexico City, is a freelance photographer dividing his time between personal projects and assignments. His work has appeared in *The New York Times*, *The Washington Post*, *Le Monde*, and *Time*. Commercially, he has been commissioned by Canada Goose, the Bill & Melinda Gates Foundation, and Kids in Need of Defense. brettgundlock.com

Andy Haslam (pages 212–217, 274–279, 286–293, 308–313, 404–409, 422–427, 436–443) is a travel, lifestyle, and architectural photographer based in the United Kingdom. He is a frequent contributor to the *New York Times* Travel section. andyhaslamphotography.com

Todd Heisler (pages 110–117) has been a staff photographer at *The New York Times* since 2006. He has received a Pulitzer Prize in feature photography and an Emmy for national news and documentary. He lives in Brooklyn. toddheisler.com

Jason Henry (pages 74–79), based in San Francisco, has contributed photos to *The New York Times* since 2009. His projects on the Haitian island of Île-à-Vache and in his home state of Florida look at the increasing impacts of invasive species. jasonhenryphoto.tumblr.com

Stephen Hiltner (pages 360–365), sahiltner.com. *See writer biographies.*

Lauryn Ishak (pages 578–583) is a commercial and editorial photographer based in Singapore and working primarily in Asia. She is fluent in English, German, and Indonesian. Her clients have included *Afar*, *Condé Nast Traveler*, *Die Zeit*, *Monocle*, *The New York Times*, *Outside*, *Travel + Leisure*, and *The Wall Street Journal*. laurynishak.com

Tom Jamieson's (pages 314–321) work has covered migration across Europe, Cornish trawlermen, and conflict in Ukraine. His editorial clients have included *The New York Times*, *Vogue*, *Monocle*, *The Telegraph Magazine*, *GQ*, *CNN*, *Time*, and *National Geographic*. He is based in London. tom-jamieson.com

Ann Johansson (pages 36–41) is working on a long-term project visually connecting climate-change causes, effects, impacts, and solutions globally. The images are used in exhibitions, public art installations, and speaking engagements with the goal of making climate change relatable on a personal level. annjohansson.com

Russ Juskalian (pages 346–351), russjuskalian.com. *See writer biographies.*

Edwin Koo (pages 636–641) is a native of Singapore. His personal work focuses on themes of identity and home. His work has been published in *GEO*, *The International Herald Tribune*, and *The New York Times* and has been exhibited in Europe and Asia. He grew up in a time when Singapore had more *kopitiams* than Starbucks. edwinkoo.com

Adam Lach (pages 502–507), based in Warsaw, is cofounder of Napo Images. He has photographed for *The New York Times*, *Le Monde*, *L'Espresso*, *Die Zeit*, *GEO*, *Newsweek*, *Svenska Dagbladet*, and other publications. His photo essays have been shown in international exhibitions. lachadam.com

Robert Leon (pages 88–95), a longtime documentary and travel photographer based in Vancouver, Canada, died in 2022. His work was published by *National Geographic*, *National Geographic Traveler*, *GEO*, *American Express Departures*, *Fodor's*, *The Lonely Planet*, and *The New York Times*.

Javier Luengo (pages 164–169), a Spanish freelance photographer, has had work published in several magazines and newspapers. javierluengoimages.com

João Pedro Marnoto (pages 444–449), based in Porto, Portugal, has been a professional photographer for two decades. His projects reflect on issues of identity and the human condition within an environmental and sociological perspective.

Maria Mavropoulou (pages 238–243, 556–563) lives and works in Athens. Her work has been presented in numerous exhibitions in Greece and abroad and published in multiple magazines. mariamavropoulou.com

BIOGRAPHIES

Andreas Meichsner (pages 194–199, 456–461, 508–515), based in Berlin, is known for documentary and architectural photography. His work has appeared in *The New York Times*, *Harper's*, and many other publications. He has published two books dealing with the need for security and structure in Western society. andreasmeichsner.de

Alexandre Meneghini (pages 132–137), born in Brazil, has been based since 2014 in Havana, where he photographs for Reuters and coordinates its Cuban photo coverage. Much of his earlier career was with the Associated Press, on assignments ranging from politics and sports to armed conflicts. alexandremeneghini.com

Christopher Miller (pages 28–35), a freelance photographer based in Juneau, Alaska, focuses on commercial fishing, backcountry skiing and snowboarding, and photojournalism. His work has appeared in publications including *The New York Times*, *The Anchorage Daily News*, *Alaska Magazine*, and *People*. csmphotos.com

Kevin Miyazaki (pages 14–19, 20–27), based in Milwaukee and represented by Redux Pictures, shoots regularly in Chicago and the Midwest and also in Hawaii, where he has deep family roots. His clients include the Food Network, Southwest Airlines, HGTV, *Architectural Digest*, AARP, and *Smithsonian Magazine*. kevinmiyazaki.com

Moris Moreno (pages 50–55), who maintains photography studios in Miami and Seattle, concentrates especially on architecture and design. For commercial clients, he views professional photographs as an essential part of building and marketing a brand. morismoreno.com

Justin Mott (pages 618–623, 666–671) is an editorial, travel, and commercial photographer who is based in Vietnam and travels throughout Southeast Asia on assignments. His clients have included *Time*, *Forbes*, the BBC, CNN, *The Wall Street Journal*, *The Guardian*, *Condé Nast Traveler*, the European Union, and the United Nations. justinmott.com

Franz Neumayr (pages 496–501), a freelance photographer for magazines and newspapers since 1986, is based in Salzburg, Austria. He has covered political and cultural events all over the world and also produces travel photography. neumayr.cc

Ilvy Njiokiktjien (pages 158–163, 230–237, 244–249) is based in the Netherlands. As a documentary photographer, she covers current affairs and social issues; one project was a 12-year documentation of the born frees, the first generation born after apartheid ended in South Africa. ilvynjiokiktjien.com

Kosuke Okahara (pages 624–629) specializes in an intimate documentary style. He has received awards including a W. Eugene Smith Fellowship, *Photo District News*' 30, and a Getty Images grant, and his photos have been exhibited in museums and international photo festivals. He is represented by Polka Galerie in Paris. kosukeokahara.com

Adolphus Opara's (pages 564–569) work, often inspired by people's daily effort to exist amid obstacles, has appeared in exhibitions and galleries from Lagos to London and Malaysia to Vienna. His media clients have included *The Guardian*, *African Magazine*, *Time Out Nigeria*, *New African Magazine*, *The New York Times*, and *The Economist*. adolphusopara.com

Robert Ormerod (pages 338–345), based in Edinburgh, shoots photographs for news outlets, magazines, non-governmental organizations, and businesses. His client list includes *The Guardian*, *The New York Times*, *National Geographic*, *Le Monde*, *Monocle*, Greenpeace, and Save the Children. robertormerod.co.uk

Joann Pai (pages 390–395, 396–403), a food and travel photographer in Paris, is originally from Vancouver, Canada. She has traveled around the world on assignment for clients including *The New York Times*, *Saveur*, and *Condé Nast Traveler*. sliceofpai.com

Emilio Parra Doiztua (pages 322–329) is a Madrid-based freelance photographer specializing in architecture and interiors. His work has taken him to nations around the world. epdoiztua.com

Yana Paskova (pages 654–659) is a Bulgaria-born, Chicago-bred, Brooklyn-based photojournalist, writer, and educator. Her clients have included *National Geographic*, *The Washington Post*, *The New York Times*, *The Wall Street Journal*, and NPR. She has received grants through Leica Camera, the Getty, the National Geographic Society, and the Pulitzer Center. yanapaskova.com

Jonathan Player (pages 366–371), based in London and Hungerford, England, has spent much of his career freelancing for *The New York Times* in Britain, Ireland, and continental Europe. His work has also been published in *The Telegraph*, *The Guardian*, *The Independent*, *The Wall Street Journal*, and *Life*.

Josef Polleross (pages 182–187) has lived and worked as a photojournalist in cities including New York, Cairo, and Bangkok. Now based in Vienna, he concentrates on artistic photography. His triptychs have been featured in numerous exhibitions in Austria and abroad, and he has produced photo books. polleross.com

Andrew Quilty (pages 642–647) is a photographer currently living in Sydney. He covered Afghanistan's violent conflicts from 2013 to 2021, while based in Kabul. He has won a Polk Award, Picture of the Year International awards, a World Press Photo award, and the Gold Walkley, the highest prize in Australian journalism. andrewquilty.com

James Rajotte (pages 152–157), a photographer originally from Pennsylvania, is now based in Spain. jamesrajottephotographs.com

Jerry Redfern (pages 584–589), a veteran photojournalist, is the director of the documentary film *Eternal Harvest*.

BIOGRAPHIES

He also reports on the oil and gas industry in New Mexico. jerryredfern.com

Piotr Redlinski (pages 294–299) is an architect by education and a photojournalist by vocation. He is based in New York and contributes regularly to *The New York Times*. He has also been a still photographer on feature film productions. redlinski.net

Federico Rios Escobar (pages 118–125, 126–131) is a Colombian documentary photographer focusing on social issues in Latin America. His work is regularly featured in international media. His books include *The Path of the Condor* and *Fiestas de San Pacho, Quibdo*. federicorios.net

Daniel Rodrigues (pages 170–175) was born in France but grew up in Portugal and is based there, in Porto. He has been a contributor to *The New York Times* since 2015 and is a winner of a World Press Photo award. danielrodriguesphoto.com

Ko Sasaki (pages 610–617) is a Japanese portrait photographer whose subjects are often global figures in politics, business, and the arts, but who most likes photographing people in ordinary life. His journalistic clients have included *The New York Times*, *The Wall Street Journal*, *Afar*, *Wired*, and *Forbes*. kosasaki.photoshelter.com

Cédrine Scheidig (pages 384–389) a French-Caribbean photographer and videographer, works in Paris. She is a graduate of the École Nationale Supérieure de la Photographie d'Arles and 2021 winner of the Dior Prize for Photography and Visual Arts for Young Talents. cedrinescheidig.studio

Rick Scibelli Jr. (pages 80–87), a longtime photojournalist based in the southwestern United States, also has a degree in geology. His clients have included *The New York Times*, *USA Today*, *The Los Angeles Times*, *Der Spiegel*, *The Wall Street Journal*, and other news outlets. rickscibelli.com

Lourdes Segade's (pages 188–193, 330–337) work has been published in *The New York Times*, *The Chicago Tribune*, CNN Photos, *Magazine La Vanguardia*, and other outlets, and has been shown in festivals and exhibitions. She was a founding member of EVE Photographers.

Susan Seubert (pages 42–49), a recipient of a Life Magazine Alfred Eisenstaedt Award, is a commercial and editorial photographer based in Portland, Oregon, and Maui, Hawaii. She travels the world shooting for clients including newspapers, travel magazines, Norwegian Cruise Lines, and Lindblad Expeditions. sseubert.com

Qilai Shen (pages 630–635) is a Shanghai-based editorial, corporate, and portrait photographer and a graduate of Davidson College in North Carolina. Since returning to China, he has worked for publications including *Time*, *Newsweek*, *Forbes*, *Stern*, and *The New York Times* and for multinational corporations. qilai.photoshelter.com

Mark Simon (pages 482–487), a photographer, filmmaker, and lecturer, is based in Berlin. He has worked on assignment around the world for clients including *National Geographic*, *Geo-Saison*, *Smithsonian Magazine*, *Stern*, *Time*, *Newsweek*, *Der Spiegel*, *Granta*, *The New York Times*, and others.

Nichole Sobecki (pages 532–537) is a photographer based in Nairobi and represented by the photo agency VII. She has completed assignments in Africa, the Middle East, and Asia for *National Geographic*, *The Washington Post*, *The New York Times*, *The Guardian*, and *Le Monde*, and her work has been exhibited internationally. nicholesobecki.com

Linus Sundahl-Djerf (pages 262–267) is a Swedish photojournalist based in Stockholm. His work has appeared in *Svenska Dagbladet*, *Aftenposten*, *The New York Times*, *Dagens Naeringsliv*, *Die Zeit*, *The Guardian*, and other publications. linusdjerf.com

Evan Sung (pages 604–609) is a food, lifestyle, and travel photographer based in Brooklyn. He is a frequent contributor to *The New York Times*, and his work has also appeared in *Vogue*, *GQ*, *Bon Appétit*, *Food & Wine*, *Gourmet*, *Art Culinaire*, and other publications. He has provided photographs for more than 40 cookbooks. evansung.com

Thor Swift (pages 74–79) is the lead photographer at Lawrence Berkeley National Laboratory, where he photographs researchers working on solving fundamental questions and finding scientific solutions to pressing needs. He has also worked as an independent photographer for a variety of editorial and corporate clients.

Kuni Takahashi (pages 572–577) has covered major news events across Africa, the Middle East, and Asia since 1992. A native of Japan, he spent six years in India before moving to Vancouver, Canada. He has published five photo books in Japan. kunitakahashi.com

Andrew Testa (pages 378–383) spent six years in Kosovo covering the Balkans, Eastern Europe, Central Asia, and the Middle East for publications including *The New York Times* and *Newsweek*. He later worked in New York and now lives in London. He has won three World Press Photo awards and was twice named photojournalist of the year by Amnesty International. andrewtesta.co.uk

David B. Torch (pages 470–475), based in Brooklyn and Oslo, has contributed frequently to *The New York Times*. His photographs have also appeared in *The New Yorker*, *Spin*, *Rolling Stone*, *The Fader*, and other publications. davidbtorch.com

Clara Tuma (pages 218–223) is a photographer based in Zurich and Provence and concentrating on travel, food, and interiors. Her photos have appeared in a variety of magazines and newspapers in several countries. claratuma.com

Danielle Villasana's (pages 280–285) documentary work focuses on human rights, gender, displacement, and health

BIOGRAPHIES & CREDITS

with an emphasis on Latin America. She's a Magnum Foundation awardee, National Geographic Explorer, Women Photograph grantee, and an International Women's Media Foundation fellow. daniellevillasana.com

Chris Warde-Jones (pages 268–273, 372–377, 428–435, 476–481) was born in Rome and has spent most of his life there. In a photojournalism career of more than 30 years, he has traveled the world for *The New York Times* and other publications. He is also a videographer for the Associated Press and Canadian Broadcasting. warde-jones.com

William Widmer (pages 62–67), a narrative photographer based in Louisville, Kentucky, covers news and feature stories throughout the southern United States, often exploring human ecology, environmental justice, and the changing landscape of the Gulf Coast. His client list includes many nationally circulated American publications. widmerphoto.com

Robert Wright (pages 56–61), originally from Ajax, Ontario, lives in Brooklyn and has shot photos for *Budget Travel*, *Departures*, *Elle*, *Elle Decor*, *Details*, *Fortune*, *House & Garden*, *People*, *The New York Times*, *Time*, *W Magazine*, and other publications. robertwrightphoto.com

Susan Wright (pages 300–307, 416–421) is based in Florence and has traveled widely in Italy, Eastern Europe, and the Mediterranean creating images for international magazines, newspapers, and books. An extensive collection of her images has been curated into an online stock library at her website. susanwrightphoto.com

Andrea Wyner (pages 224–229) grew up in Los Angeles and now divides her time between New York, California, and Italy. She is fluent in Italian. Her work has appeared in *Afar*, *Condé Nast Traveler*, *Departures*, *Dwell*, *Martha Stewart Living*, *The New York Times*, *Travel + Leisure*, and other publications. andreawyner.com

Dave Yoder (pages 488–495), now based in Milan, was born in Goshen, Indiana, but grew up at the foot of Mt. Kilimanjaro in Tanzania. A regular contributor to *National Geographic Traveler*, *The New York Times*, and other publications, he is especially interested in human interest projects. daveyoder.com

Jada Yuan (pages 590–595), *see writer biographies.*

CREDITS

All images and text in this volume are © *The New York Times* unless otherwise noted. Any omissions for copy or credit are unintentional, and appropriate credit will be given in future editions if such copyright holders contact the publisher.

akg-images: 499, 511; Apic/Getty Images: 316; Archives Yves Debraine: 220; The Art Institute of Chicago: 333; Bettmann/Getty Images: 399; Biblioteca-Pinacoteca Ambrosiana, Milan: 303; Boyer/Getty Images: 289; Burton Holmes Historical Collection: 406; *Civitates orbis terrarum* by Georg Braun and Franz Hogenberg: Historisches Museum, Frankfurt: 246/247; CPA Media – Pictures from History/GRANGER: 663; Danita Delimont Creative/Alamy Stock Photo: 404; Danvis Collection/Alamy Stock Photo: 283; Dunhuang Academy, Northwestern University: 598; Ernest Hemingway Collection. John F. Kennedy Presidential Library and Museum, Boston: 98; Estate of Harold Stein: 46; Fine Art Images/Bridgeman Images: 466; The Francis Frith Collection: 374; J. Paul Getty Trust. Used with permission. Julius Shulman Photography Archive, Research Library at the Getty Research Institute: 39; Jas Hennessy & Co/Jacques Goguet: 208; Heritage Auctions, HA.com: 30 above, 65, 82 above, 209, 311; Honolulu Museum of Art: 47; IMAGNO/Austrian Archives, Vienna: 184; Keystone-France/Getty Images: 491; Koninklijk Museum voor Schone Kunsten, Antwerp: 355; Libraries Digital Collections. University of Miami. Library. Cuban Heritage Collection: 167; Library of Congress: 161, 325, 656 above; Library of Congress, Prints and Photographs Division, Fine Prints: Japanese, Pre-1915: 612; Library of Congress, Music Division: 227; Look and Learn/Bridgeman Images: 277; Look and Learn/Elgar Collection/Bridgeman Images: 265; Jack Manning/The New York Times: 113; Alexandre Marchi/Getty Images: 378; Stefano Politi Markovina/Alamy Stock Photo: 188; Mitsuo Masuoka: 624; McCord Stewart Museum: 70; The Metropolitan Museum of Art. Fletcher Fund, 1919: 348; The Metropolitan Museum of Art. Purchase, George Delacorte Fund Gift, in memory of George T. Delacorte Jr., Ronald S. Lauder, Mr. and Mrs. Richard L. Chilton Jr., and Mr. and Mrs. Frederick W. Beinecke Gifts, 2016: 302; Sammlung Museum des Landkreises Oberspreewald-Lausitz: 458; PA Images/Alamy Stock Foto: 362; Pictures from History/Bridgeman Images: 586; PjrXX/Alamy Stock Foto: 452; Pump Park Vintage Photography/Alamy Stock Photo: 546; Foto Edward Quinn, © edwardquinn.com: 413; REDA&CO/Getty Images: 556; Alan Riding/The New York Times: 107; Henry Ries/The New York Times: 484; Rijksmuseum, Amsterdam: 234, 559; Pere Sanz/Alamy Stock Photo: 191; Science & Society Picture Library/Getty Images: 575; Science History Images/Alamy Stock Foto: 253, 465; Image reproduced courtesy of Shetland Museum and Archive: 424; Talland House, Leslie Stephen photograph album, Mortimer Rare Book Collection, MRBC MS 00005, Smith College Special Collections, Northampton, Massachusetts: 214; Collection of the Vancouver Art Gallery, Emily Carr Trust: 91; Verlag Galerie Welz, Salzburg: 185; Robert Walker/The New York Times: 59; Barrie Wentzell: 310.

© F.L.C./VG Bild-Kunst, Bonn 2024 for the works of Le Corbusier
© Successió Miró/VG Bild-Kunst, Bonn 2024 for the works of Joan Miró
© Succession Picasso/VG Bild-Kunst, Bonn 2024 for the works of Pablo Picasso
© VG Bild-Kunst, Bonn 2024 for the works of Herbert Bayer, Walter Gropius, Bruce Nauman, and Wilhelm Wagenfeld

We would like to thank everyone at *The New York Times* and at TASCHEN who contributed to the creation of this book.

Special recognition must go to Alexi Alario, Nazire Ergün, Jonna Frappier, and Sarah Southard, the dedicated editors behind the scenes at TASCHEN; to photo editor Cecilia Bohan; and to illustrator Joanna Grochocka.

Great thanks must go to all of the writers and photographers whose work appears in the book, both *Times* staffers and freelancers, and to the many *Times* editors who brought these articles to life in the pages of the newspaper and at nytimes.com.

Guiding the transformation of newspaper material to book form at TASCHEN were Anna-Tina Kessler and Thomas Grell. Florence Stickney copy-edited the manuscript; Anna Skinner and Thea Miklowski proofread the book. Translators for the German and French editions included Juliette Blanchot, Petra Frese, Lisa Heilig, Kirsten Lehmann, Ulrike Lowis, Alice Pétillot, and Carolin Polter.

Sincere acknowledgment must go to Benedikt Taschen, whose longtime readership and interest led to the partnership of our two companies that produced this book.

— Barbara Ireland and Trish Daly

Copyright © 2024 *The New York Times*.
All Rights Reserved.

Editor Barbara Ireland
Project management Trish Daly
Photo editor Cecilia Bohan
Illustrations Joanna Grochocka/marlenaagency.com
Editorial coordination Alexi Alario, Nazire Ergün, Jonna Frappier
Design and layout Anna-Tina Kessler
Production Thomas Grell

EACH AND EVERY TASCHEN BOOK PLANTS A SEED!
TASCHEN is a carbon neutral publisher. Each year, we offset our annual carbon emissions with carbon credits at the Instituto Terra, a reforestation program in Minas Gerais, Brazil, founded by Lélia and Sebastião Salgado. To find out more about this ecological partnership, please check: www.taschen.com/zerocarbon
Inspiration: unlimited. Carbon footprint: zero.

© 2024 TASCHEN GmbH
Hohenzollernring 53, D–50672 Köln
www.taschen.com

ISBN 978-3-8365-7173-9
Printed in Bosnia-Herzegovina

USA & CANADA

- Vancouver Island
- Chicago
- New York City
- Miami
- Oaxaca
- Managua
- Cartagena

LATIN AMERICA & THE CARIBBEAN

- Salvador da Bahia

- Kristiansund
- Oxford
- Fontainebleau
- Barcelona
- Sahara Desert
- Osun-Osogbo